The State of Nature: Histories of an Idea

History of European Political and Constitutional Thought

VOLUME 6

The titles published in this series are listed at *brill.com/hepct*

The State of Nature

Histories of an Idea

Edited by

Mark Somos and Anne Peters

BRILL

LEIDEN | BOSTON

Cover illustration: Detail from Hieronymus Bosch, *The Garden of Earthly Delights*, c. 1490–1510. Museo del Prado. Public domain.

The Library of Congress Cataloging-in-Publication Data is available online at https://catalog.loc.gov
LC record available at https://lccn.loc.gov/2021044694

Typeface for the Latin, Greek, and Cyrillic scripts: "Brill". See and download: brill.com/brill-typeface.

ISSN 2589-5966
ISBN 978-90-04-39517-6 (hardback)
ISBN 978-90-04-49962-1 (e-book)

This book is printed on acid-free paper and produced in a sustainable manner.

Contents

Illustrations

Figures

Map

Notes on Contributors

Daniel S. Allemann
is a Senior Research and Teaching Fellow in the Department of History at the University of Lucerne, Switzerland. He holds a Ph.D. from the University of Cambridge. He is the co-editor of *Conceptions of Space in Intellectual History* (Routledge, 2020) and specializes in the history of early modern political ideas in a global context. His current book project focuses on visions of slavery and empire in the wider Iberian world.

Pamela Edwards
is the author of *The Statesman's Science: History, Nature and Law in the Political Thought of Samuel Taylor Coleridge*. As well as having contributed chapters to *The Cambridge History of Philosophy in the Nineteenth Century, Blackwell's Companion to eighteenth-century British Political Thought*, and *The Oxford Handbook of Coleridge*, she has written extensively on the Atlantic Enlightenment. She has formerly held a joint appointment in History and Political Science at Yale University, and been a visiting scholar at St Katherine's College Oxford.

Ioannis D. Evrigenis
is Professor of Political Science and Director of the International Relations Program at Tufts University. He is the author of *Fear of Enemies and Collective Action* and *Images of Anarchy: The Rhetoric and Science in Hobbes's State of Nature*, co-editor of Johann Gottfried Herder's *Another Philosophy of History & Selected Political Writings*, as well as the author of a number of articles on the concept of the state of nature in the history of political thought.

Mary C. Fuller
is Professor of Literature and MacVicar Faculty Fellow at MIT, where she has served as department head and Associate Chair of the Institute faculty. Her research focuses on early modern English geography and exploration, and the related histories of practices, narratives, and material texts as these extend across space and time. She is currently completing a book about Richard Hakluyt's *Principal Navigations of the English Nation* (1600), and editing materials on the Northwest Passage for the projected Oxford edition of Hakluyt's compilation. Her publications include *Voyages in Print: English Travel to America 1576–1624* (Cambridge, 1995) and *Remembering the Early Modern Voyage* (Palgrave, 2008) as well as numerous articles and book chapters.

David Singh Grewal
is a Professor of Law at the U.C. Berkeley School of Law, and a member of its Jurisprudence and Social Policy Program. He was a Professor at Yale Law School before moving to Berkeley and a Junior Fellow of the Harvard Society of Fellows before that. His first book, *Network Power: The Social Dynamics of Globalization*, was published by Yale University Press in 2008. His second book, *The Invention of the Economy*, is forthcoming from Harvard University Press. He holds B.A. (Economics) and Ph.D. (Political Science) degrees from Harvard University and a J.D. from Yale Law School.

Francesca Iurlaro
is an Alexander von Humboldt Postdoctoral Fellow at the Max Planck Institute for Comparative Public Law and International Law (Heidelberg). She holds a Ph.D. in Law from the European University Institute (Florence, 2018). Her book *The Invention of Custom: Natural Law and the Law of Nations, ca. 1550–1750* is forthcoming with Oxford University Press.

Edward J. Kolla
is the author of *Sovereignty, International Law, and the French Revolution* (Cambridge, 2017). He teaches history at Georgetown University's campus in Qatar and is currently writing a book on the history of passports.

László Kontler
is Professor of History at Central European University (Budapest/Vienna). His research and publications focus on intellectual history, the history of political thought, translation and reception, and the production and circulation of scientific knowledge in early modern Europe, mainly the Enlightenment. His books include *Translations, Histories, Enlightenments: William Robertson in Germany, 1760–1795* (Palgrave, 2014) and (with Per Pippin Aspaas) *Maximilian Hell (1720–1792) and the Ends of Jesuit Science in Enlightenment Europe* (Brill, 2020).

Grant S. McCall
is an Associate Professor of Anthropology at Tulane University and the Executive Director of the Center for Human-Environmental Research, a New Orleans-based nonprofit research institute aimed at exploring and improving human responses to environmental change. McCall received his Ph.D. in Anthropology from the University of Iowa. He is also the author of *Before Modern Humans: New Perspectives on the African Stone Age*, *Prehistoric Myths in Modern Political Philosophy* (with Karl Widerquist), *the Prehistory*

of Private Property (with Karl Widerquist), and *Strategies for Quantitative Research: Archaeology by Numbers*.

Anne Peters
is Director at the Max Planck Institute for Comparative Public Law and International Law Heidelberg (Germany), and a professor at the universities of Heidelberg, Freie Universität Berlin, Basel (Switzerland), and L. Bates Lea Global Law Professor at the Law School of the University of Michigan. She is a member of the Permanent Court of Arbitration, and an associate member of the Institut de Droit International. She was a member (substitute) of the European Commission for Democracy through Law (Venice Commission) in respect of Germany (2011-2015) and a legal expert for the Independent International Fact-Finding Mission on the Conflict in Georgia (2009). She is currently President of the German Society of International Law (DGIR). She was the President of the European Society of International Law (2010-2012) and has served on the governance board of various learned societies, such as the German Association of Constitutional Law (VDStRL) and the Society of International Constitutional Law (I CON-S).

Among her books (authored, co-authored, or (co-)edited) are: *Animals in International Law* (Brill, 2021); *Remedies against Immunity?* (Springer, 2021); *Völkerrecht* (Schulthess, 5th ed. 2020); *Due Diligence in the International Legal Order* (Oxford University Press, 2020); *Max Planck Trialogues on the Law of Peace and War* (co-ed. with C. Marxsen): *Self-Defence against Non-State Actors* (vol. 1, Cambridge University Press, 2019), *Law Applicable to Armed Conflict* (vol. 2, 2020), *Reparation for Victims of Armed Conflicts* (vol. 3, 2020); *The Legal Framework of the OSCE* (Cambridge University Press, 2019); *Global Constitutionalism from European and East Asian Perspectives* (Cambridge University Press, 2018); *Beyond Human Rights* (Cambridge University Press, 2016); *The Freedom of Peaceful Assembly* (Nomos, 2016); and *Immunities in the Age of Global Constitutionalism* (Brill, 2015)

Emile Simpson
holds a Ph.D. in the history of international law from King's College London. He was formerly a Junior Fellow at the Harvard University Society of Fellows. He is currently a barrister practising in London. His academic research is focused on the history of legal and political thought, and in particular, the history of international legal order. He is the author of *War From the Ground Up: Twenty-First-Century Combat as Politics* (Oxford University Press, 2012) and various articles.

Mark Somos
holds the Deutsche Forschungsgemeinschaft's Heisenberg position at the Max Planck Institute for Comparative Public Law and International Law. He studied history, political science and law at Cambridge, Harvard, Sussex and Leiden, and taught law and political science at Harvard, Yale, Tufts and Sussex universities. He is the author of *Secularisation and the Leiden Circle* (Leiden: Brill, 2011), *American States of Nature: The Origins of Independence, 1761–1775* (Oxford: Oxford University Press, 2019) and over 50 scholarly papers; co-author, with Dániel Margócsy and Stephen Joffe, of *The Fabrica of Andreas Vesalius* (Leiden: Brill, 2018); and co-edited *Trust and Happiness in the History of European Political Thought* (Leiden: Brill, 2017) with László Kontler. Mark is co-editor-in-chief of *Grotiana* and edits the book series, *History of European Political and Constitutional Thought.*

Tom Sparks
is a Senior Research Fellow at the Max Planck Institute for Comparative Public Law and International Law, Heidelberg. His research interests include international environmental law, statehood and sovereignty, international adjudication, and legal theory. He completed his doctoral thesis at the University of Durham in 2018.

Benjamin Straumann
is ERC Professor of History at the University of Zurich and Research Professor of Classics at New York University. He is also Alberico Gentili Senior Fellow at New York University School of Law. Benjamin is the author of *Roman Law in the State of Nature: The Classical Foundations of Hugo Grotius's Natural Law* (Cambridge: Cambridge University Press, 2015), and of *Crisis and Constitutionalism: Roman Political Thought from the Fall of the Republic to the Age of Revolution* (Oxford: Oxford University Press, 2016).

Karl Widerquist
is a Professor of Philosophy at Georgetown University-Qatar. He specializes in distributive justice – the ethics of who has what. He holds two doctorates – one in Political Theory from Oxford University (2006) and one in Economics from the City University of New York (1996). He published eight books including, *A Critical Analysis of Basic Income Experiments for Researchers, Policymakers, and Citizens* (Palgrave Macmillan, 2013), *Prehistoric Myths in Modern Political Philosophy* (coauthored by Grant S. McCall, Edinburgh University Press, 2017) and author of *Independence, Propertylessness, and Basic Income: A Theory of Freedom as the Power to Say No* (Palgrave Macmillan, 2013). He was one of

the founding editors of the journal, *Basic Income Studies*. He has published more than twenty scholarly articles in journals such as *Raisons Politiques, Political Studies*; *the Eastern Economic Journal*; *Politics and Society*; and *Politics, Philosophy, and Economics*. His book, *The Prehistory of Private Property* (coauthored by Grant S. McCall, Edinburgh University Press) was published in 2021.

Sarah Winter
is Professor of English and Comparative Literary and Cultural Studies at the University of Connecticut, Storrs, USA and Co-Director of the Research Program on Humanitarianism at the UConn Human Rights Institute. An interdisciplinary scholar of British literature of the long nineteenth century, human rights, and the history of law and the modern disciplines, she has published most recently a co-edited collection, *From Political Economy to Economics through Nineteenth-Century Literature: Reclaiming the Social* (Palgrave Studies in Literature, Culture and Economics, 2019). Her current book project focuses on habeas corpus, empire, and human rights narratives.

Simone Zurbuchen
is Professor of Modern and Contemporary Philosophy at the University of Lausanne. She has published widely on the history of early modern moral and political philosophy, with a focus on Samuel Pufendorf and the reception of his work in the eighteenth century. Among her areas of expertise is also early modern theories of the law of nations. She was the director of the SNF research project, 'Natural law in Switzerland and beyond: sociability, natural equality, social inequality' (2014–2018), and she is the editor of *The Law of Nations and Natural Law 1625–1800* (Leiden & Boston, Brill, 2019).

Introduction

Mark Somos and Anne Peters

Magna superstes, the "great survivor", is a hypothetical organism that evolved a survival mechanism it can use to switch between reproducing its DNA, in good times, and repairing its DNA in adverse conditions. David Sinclair, Professor of Genetics at Harvard, postulated its existence not as a mere thought experiment.

> Like Adam and Eve, we don't know if *M. superstes* ever existed. But my research over the past twenty-five years suggests that every living thing we see around us today is a product of this great survivor, or a primitive organism very much like it. The fossil record in our genes goes a long way to proving that every living thing that shares this planet with us still carries this ancient genetic survival circuit, in more or less the same basic form. It is there in every plant. It is there in every fungus. It is there in every animal. It is there in us.[1]

Positing the existence of *M. superstes* has enabled teams of geneticists to look for and discover empirically confirmed biochemical mechanisms and longevity genes, including sirtuins and mTOR.

M. superstes may or may not have existed, but today it is certainly fictitious insofar that it was invented without a corresponding fact verified in reality. It may turn out that the mechanisms ascribed to the Great Survivor evolved not in a single organism but arose from a collection of entities and sequence of events. Yet this would not change the reality and utility of medical facts gained by postulating *M. superstes*. It is not fictitious like Frankenstein or Cinderella: *M. superstes* is effective fiction, a tale with real-life effects, including therapeutic and pharmaceutical protocols already in use. What are other examples of effective fiction? Is language one? Money? Most laws?

One could argue that "effective fiction" is an effective fiction, since no fiction is likely to be wholly ineffective. Presumably we learned something from the stories of Frankenstein and Cinderella. Perhaps they had salutary real-world effects, given for instance the use of Frankenstein metaphors in legislative and public debates about artificial intelligence. But there is no causal link between

1 David A. Sinclair, with Matthew D. LaPlante, *Lifespan: Why We Age – and Why We Don't Have To* (Thorsons, 2019), 7.

 | DOI:10.1163/9789004499621_002

Frankenstein and artificial intelligence the way there is between *M. superstes* and the discovery of sirtuins, or William Gibson's *Neuromancer* and its thousands of readers who went on to develop Gibson's fiction into the real-world facts of virtual reality hardware and software.

This book grew from a long fascination with the state of nature as an historically vibrant effective fiction. The phrase, "state of nature", has been used over the last centuries to denote the uncultivated condition of lands and animals, nudity, innocence, hell, the postlapsarian, pre-historic or pre-industrial conditions of humankind, and other unrelated or tangentially related things. The essays in this book touch on many of these meanings, but they were selected for their focus on uses of the state of nature that connect specifically to the idea of law, for which it has long served as an effective fiction.

In other words, the book presents case studies in which the state of nature is effective legal fiction. A legal fiction has been defined as "a legal assumption that something is true which is, or may be, false – being an assumption of an innocent and beneficial character, made to advance the interests of justice."[2] Legal fictions are created to argue specific points. They support arguments by clarifying a situation, for instance by reducing that situation to its essentials in order to bring additional clarity. Applied to problems such as inter-state war or anti-social behaviour, the effective legal fiction that is the state of nature brings into focus states' or individuals' proclivities to violence or cooperation by relegating other variables into the background.

Within the history of legal thought, the 'state of nature' has sustained multiple semantic ranges, such as humans' pre-political condition, inter-state relations, and a repository of pre- and supra-legal civic rights, such as the right to resistance, the right to property, the right to constitute and leave polities, and the freedom of religion, speech, and opinion, which may be reactivated or reprioritised when the positivised law fails. Some writers imagined states of nature that were idyllic and irrecoverable, or a condition of justice and equality that we can and ought to restore. Others saw it as a violent place that humankind escaped and must stay away from; or a condition that applied to inter-state relations, but remained unacceptable within the State.

The importance of the state of nature fiction in the history of legal thought is evident from the primary sources. Its influence extends from ancient accounts of divine law in and after the Golden Age and Paradise, through medieval and early modern natural law discourses, to current paradigms of constitutionalism

2 Anderson, *Dictionary of Law*, cited in Sidney T. Miller, "The Reasons for Some Legal Fictions," *Michigan Law Review* 8 (1910), 623–36, at 623.

and international ethics. Thomas Hobbes, John Locke, and Jean-Jacques Rousseau are most readily associated with the concept and its attendant ambiguities.[3] And in one form or another, a complex version of the state of nature has also been important for Hesiod, Plato, Aristotle, Cicero, Lucretius, Thomas Aquinas, William Ockham, Samuel Pufendorf, Montesquieu, Emer de Vattel, Immanuel Kant, Carl Schmitt, John Rawls and many others.[4]

Alongside the predominant role of the state of nature as legal fiction, writers have often been (intentionally) ambigious about the historic reality of a state of nature. Did such a state ever exist? Does it continue to exist? Some writers proposed that it did, among peoples at an early stage of social development.[5] Others saw the state of nature everywhere, as a permanent background to established polities or ever-present threats of anarchy. A few, including Jean-Jacques Rousseau and William Blackstone, argued that it does not matter whether the state of nature has ever existed: as a useful legal fiction it must be considered in thinking about liberties, rights and obligations.[6]

Constitutional models that relied on the idea of a social contract – whether an original, historical, or proposed new explicit contract, or a tacit one re-enacted daily – drew both their overall shape and specific provisions from the

3 Thomas Hobbes, *Elementorum Philosophiae: sectio tertia: de cive* (Paris, 1642); *Elementa Philosophica de cive* (Amsterdam: Elzevier, 1647); *Leviathan* ... (London: Andrew Crooke, 1651). John Locke, *Essay Concerning the True Original, Extent, and End of Civil Government* (London: Awnsham Churchill, 1689). Jean-Jacques Rousseau, *Discours sur l'origine et les fondements de l'inégalité parmi les hommes* (Amsterdam: Marc Michel Rey, 1755); *Du contract social* ... (Amsterdam: Marc Michel Rey, 1762).

4 Hesiod, *Works and Days* [ca. 700 BCE] in Hesiod, Vol. I, trans. and ed. Glenn W. Most (Cambridge MA: Harvard University Press, 2007). Plato, *The Republic* [ca. 375 BCE], trans. and ed. Desmond Lee (London: Penguin, 1987). Aristotle, *Politics* [ca. 350 BCE], trans. and ed. Carnes Lord (2nd ed., London: University of Chicago Press, 2013). Thomas Aquinas, *Commentary on Aristotle's* Politics [ca. 1270], trans. and ed. Richard J. Regan (Indianapolis: Hackett Publishing, 2007). William Ockham, *Opus nonaginta dierum* [ca. 1332], in *A Translation of William of Ockham's* Work of Ninety Days, trans. John Kilcullen and John Scott (Lewiston NY: Edwin Mellen Press, 2001). Samuel Pufendorf, *De officio hominis et civis juxta legem naturalem libri duo* (Lund, 1673), trans. Andrew Tooke (1691) as *The Whole Duty of Man According to the Law of Nature,* eds. Ian Hunter and David Saunders (Indianapolis IN: Liberty Fund, 2003). Montesquieu, *De l'esprit des loix* (Geneva, 1748), eds. Anne M. Cohler, Basia Carolyn Miller and Harold Samuel Stone (Cambridge: Cambridge University Press, 1989). Emer de Vattel, *Le droit des gens* (Leiden, 1758), eds. Richard Whatmore and Béla Kapossy as *The Law of Nations* ... (Indianapolis IN: Liberty Fund, 2008). John Rawls, *A Theory of Justice* (Cambridge MA: Harvard University Press, 1971; rev. ed. 1999).

5 R.L. Meek, *Social Science and the Ignoble Savage* (Cambridge: Cambridge University Press, 1976).

6 Rousseau, *Du contrat social.* William Blackstone, *Commentaries on the Laws of England* (Oxford: Clarendon Press, 1765–69), I.1.119–21.

version of the state of nature that their authors endorsed. Descriptions of savages, noble or otherwise, situated them in a state of nature. Stadial theories of progress, and attempts to justify slavery and the occupation of uncultivated lands, often involved a state of nature theory. Arguments about humanity's relationship with the natural environment, about similarities and difference between humans and animals, or about human stewardship over nature and animals, have invoked the state of nature.[7]

Yet these uses are unfairly relegated to legal theory and history alone. After all, state of nature writers, including those mentioned above, put forward their formulation of the state of nature as effective fiction in order to have profound real-life impact. Locke's comparison between the state of nature and America, lawfully seizable to those who cultivate it, or Schmitt's development of the state of nature tradition into the state of exception, are well-known examples. By thinking of them as historical, rather than effective or applied uses, we lose sight of past creativity and future potential. This is particularly problematic because the state of nature remains an effective fiction in daily legal practice, routinely invoked in forensic arguments and court decisions about States' rights and obligations, parental rights and gay marriage, reasonable search and seizure, and other legal themes with real-life effects. However, today's judicial uses are hardly as informed or creative as former uses by Pufendorf, Kant, Rawls and others.[8] Can we creatively revisit sovereignty, property, solidarity or humanity's relation to the environment by recovering past arguments that used the state of nature fiction to ingenious effect?

In short, this collection seeks to address not one, but two problems: the fragmented historiography of the state of nature as effective legal fiction, and the loss of creative problem-solving potential in current uses due to a neglect of past ingenuity. The essays are arranged in chronological order, while the themes arc across the whole book. The relationship between nature and humanity, between the State and the individual, and between justice and reality is examined through the fictive device of the state of nature in each and every chapter. The abstracts eloquently and economically state the thesis of each chapter, but to capture this collection's proposed solutions to the two problems of fragmented historiography and recent loss of creative imagination, the reader is gently encouraged to read the essays together.

7 See, e.g. Annabel Brett, "Rights of and over Animals in the *ius naturae et gentium* (Sixteenth and Seventeenth Centuries)", in Anne Peters (ed.), *Global Animal Law* (Heidelberg: Springer, 2020), pp. 17–24.

8 Somos, *American States of Nature*, Appendix 2.

We are grateful to the Max Planck Institute for Comparative Public Law and International Law for providing a supportive institutional setting for this project, and for the opportunity to gather all participants to discuss their chapters and the volume as a whole at the authors' workshop in the Harnack House of the Max Planck Society in Berlin in 2019. We thank the Alexander von Humboldt Foundation and the Deutsche Forschungsgemeinschaft for financial support.

As we finish this introduction in April 2021, the June 2019 workshop in Berlin seems a vivid yet distant memory. It would be impossible to gather the authors now, with the world's population exposed to the risk and reality of the coronavirus. States are imposing travel restrictions, curfews, bans on public gatherings and other measures that vary from state to state, yet are supposed to be based on the best available scientific evidence, which changes almost every day. The state of nature is a useful fiction during this emergency, and probably events will help us test the competing state of nature theories described in this volume: those based on the vision of humans as 'by nature' essentially benevolent and sociable, who need only solve collective action problems, against those who regard law as a key part of civilisation's answer to 'natural' selfishness and short-sighted egocentrism. The one thing we are sure of is our gratitude to the authors, the publisher, the reviewers and you, dear readers, for a timely conversation.

CHAPTER 1

Thucydides, Hobbes, and the Melian Dialogue

Benjamin Straumann

Abstract

Thucydides and Hobbes are often interpreted as 'realists'. States vis-à-vis each other remain in the state of nature and are conceptualized in analogy with individuals in the state of nature. States are therefore seen as engaging in the kind of self-interested behavior that makes cooperation elusive. In this chapter I argue that Thucydides's Melian Dialogue might have shown Hobbes that the analogy between individuals and states does not really go all the way. For Hobbes, states are the artificial structures within which individuals may satisfy their subjective desires; once the Melian commonwealth could no longer guarantee its citizens' safety, it would have been rational for the Melians to surrender, rather than risk an overwhelmingly probable catastrophe. States and individuals are also distinct in that the former may develop better knowledge of the laws of nature than individuals ever could. This fissure in the individual-state analogy is the lesson Hobbes drew from the Melian Dialogue, as can be seen in his analysis of sovereignty by acquisition in the *Leviathan*. Thucydides was important because his history, Hobbes thought, was true and could therefore provide useful examples of reason and its defects in action; the Melians might thus in addition have provided an illustration for what Hobbes believed was wrong with the Foole's reasoning. Accordingly, Thucydides can be seen to have provided a foundation for Hobbes's argument for peace and individual self-preservation.

Keywords

Thucydides – Thomas Hobbes – state of nature – Melian Dialogue – domestic analogy – natural law – Foole – practical rationality – international law – political order

 | DOI:10.1163/9789004499621_003

1 Gladiators in the State of Nature

Thucydides (ca. 460-ca. 400 BC) was of great importance to Hobbes (1588–1679).* Hobbes's translation of Thucydides, published in 1629, was Hobbes's first publication (at least under his own name), and there can be little doubt that Thucydides's outlook and general sensitivity impressed Hobbes and had a shaping influence even on his mature political philosophy as formulated in the *Leviathan*.[1] It is quite difficult, however, to point to specific instances or arguments that show Thucydides's formative influence. One of the obvious places to look has been Hobbes's account of the state of nature. The descriptions Thucydides gives of primitive Greece, of the effects of the plague early in the Peloponnesian war and, most strikingly, of the civil war (*stasis*) at Corcyra betray obvious parallels with Hobbes's conception of the state of nature.[2] It has often been noticed, too, that the three 'principal causes for quarrel' Hobbes finds in human nature – competition, diffidence, glory – correspond very closely indeed to the motives the Athenian ambassadors at Sparta claim according to Thucydides to have forced them to expand their empire: 'chiefly for fear, next for honour, and lastly for profit'.[3]

Thucydides describes the condition of primitive Greece as one of great insecurity, lack of walled settlements and lack of commerce. Departing from prevailing Greek myths which postulated the priority of agriculture[4] he speculates that ancient man was a hunter and gatherer and that those who lived near the sea or on islands eventually turned to piracy, which was then seen

---

* I would like to thank Mark Somos and Anne Peters for inviting me to Berlin, and Tilmann Altwicker, Charles Beitz, Hun Chung, Ioannis Evrigenis, David Grewal, Francesca Iurlaro, László Kontler, Phillip Mitsis, Neville Morley, Johan Olsthoorn, Peter Schröder and Mark Somos as well as audiences in Princeton and Zurich for criticism, discussion and valuable suggestions.

1 Hobbes's Thucydides must have already been published slightly earlier than the date it indicates, in 1628. See K. Hoekstra, 'Hobbes's Thucydides', in A. P. Martinich and K. Hoekstra (eds.), *The Oxford Handbook of Hobbes* (Oxford: Oxford University Press, 2016), ch. 24, p. 552, n. 15.

2 See R. Schlatter, 'Thomas Hobbes and Thucydides', *Journal of the History of Ideas*, 6:3 (1945), pp. 350–362; Clifford W. Brown, Jr., 'Thucydides, Hobbes, and the Derivation of Anarchy', *History of Political Thought*, 8:1 (1987), pp. 33–62; C. Orwin, 'Stasis and Plague: Thucydides on the Dissolution of Society', *Journal of Politics*, 50:4 (1988), pp. 831–847; G. Slomp, 'Hobbes, Thucydides and the Three Greatest Things', *History of Political Thought*, 11:4 (1990), pp. 565–586.

3 Thuc. 1.75.3; David Grene (ed.), *Thucydides, The Peloponnesian War: The Complete Hobbes Translation*, with notes and a new introduction (Chicago: University of Chicago Press, 1989), p. 44 (all following references to Thucydides in English are to this edition).

4 Burkert, *Homo necans*, p. 22.

as a potentially glorious, if not legitimate, activity. Thucydides reckons that it was not until king Minos that attempts were made to free the seas of piracy. Because 'it was uncertain when another should invade them and carry all away, especially not having the defence of walls', Thucydides writes in his armchair investigation of the primitive condition of prehistoric Greece, 'traffic was not, nor mutual intercourse ..., neither by sear or land, and every man so husbanded the ground as but barely to live upon it without any stock of riches and planted nothing'. The uncertainty, the lack of safety and protection, makes civilization impossible: 'they were of no ability at all, either for greatness of cities or other provision'.[5] Such a view of a primitive natural condition carries obvious affinities with broad Hobbesian themes[6] and was often adduced by early modern political writers to justify imperial conquest,[7] leading to a tradition of interpreting both Thucydides and his translator as advocates of a Machiavellian power politics favoring expansionary polities, war and conquest.[8]

Yet Hobbes cannot easily be assimilated with this so-called 'realist' tradition of international politics. While we usually assume Hobbes's context to be that of the English Civil War, Kinch Hoekstra has drawn attention to the fact that Hobbes produced his translation of Thucydides in the 1620s during the debate over whether or not England should go to war with Spain. Once Hobbes had finished his translation, he might have deemed it inopportune to publish it, given his own preference for non-intervention on the Continent and the increasing support for warlike policies both in Parliament and at court.

5 Thuc. 1.2.

6 Quoting Hobbes's translation of Thucydides's account of primitive Greece could amount to 'surreptitiously waving a Hobbist flag', as Noel Malcolm points out: 'Hobbes and the Royal Society', in id., *Aspects of Hobbes* (Oxford: Oxford University Press, 2002), pp. 317–335, p. 328. Cf. Matthew Wren, *Monarchy Asserted*, 2nd ed. (London: F. Bowman, 1660), pp. 34–36. For the very close parallels between Hobbes's state of nature for individuals (*Leviathan*, ch. 13) and Thucydides's account of early primitive Greece (Thuc. 1.2), see G. Klosko and D. Rice, 'Thucydides and Hobbes's State of Nature', *History of Political Thought*, 6:3 (1985), pp. 405–409.

7 See K. Hoekstra, 'Thucydides and the Bellicose Beginnings of Modern Political Theory', in K. Harloe and N. Morley (eds.), *Thucydides and the Modern World* (Cambridge: Cambridge University Press, 2012), pp. 25–54, p. 28.

8 For that tradition, see the references in T. Christov, *Before Anarchy: Hobbes and His Critics in Modern International Thought* (Cambridge: Cambridge University Press, 2015), ch. 4 (Christov himself argues convincingly *against* a 'realist' Hobbes); and N. Malcolm, 'Hobbes's Theory of International Relations', in id., *Aspects of Hobbes* (Oxford: Oxford University Press, 2002), pp. 432–456, esp. pp. 432–435. For a very sensible treatment of Hobbes's use of Thucydides's account of primitive Greece, see C. Warren, 'Hobbes's Thucydides and the Colonial Law of Nations', *The Seventeenth Century*, 24:2 (2009), pp. 260–286, pp. 271–275. Warren's article also contains an excellent analysis of the colonial context of Hobbes's translation.

By 1627, support for war was much diminished and with Charles's support for peace, publication of the translation may well have seemed more congenial. The reason why he had not felt comfortable with publication earlier, Hoekstra suggests, should be sought in Hobbes's interpretation of Thucydides's work as lending support to his own anti-war outlook.[9]

Hoekstra believes that with his translation, by way of Thucydides's description of Athens's Sicilian expedition and the resulting calamities, Hobbes sought to present his audience 'with a stark existential warning against a naval expedition against a powerful enemy', putting before his readers the 'case of Athens' error and downfall and advis[ing] them to listen to the counsel of fear'.[10] Hobbes decided not to publish his translation, however, when he realized that his own didactic purposes might be frustrated by his potential audience's misinterpretation of Thucydides, Hoekstra argues, quoting the reason Hobbes himself gave for withholding his translation from publication at first. In his preface to the readers, Hobbes wrote that 'his desire to communicate' the translation 'ceased', for the following reason:

> I saw that, for the greatest part, men came to the reading of history with an affection much like that of the people in Rome: who came to the spectacle of the gladiators with more delight to behold their blood, than their skill in fencing. For they be far more in number, that love to read of great armies, bloody battles, and many thousands slain at once, than that mind the art by which the affairs both of armies and cities be conducted to their ends.[11]

This shows, Hoekstra suggests, that Hobbes feared that his audience would fail to understand the didactic purpose he and Thucydides had in mind, preferring accounts of 'bloody battles, and many thousands slain at once' to reading about skill and 'the art by which the affairs both of armies and cities be conducted to their ends'.

This is a possible explanation of Hobbes's initial hesitation, right after finishing his translation, to publish it. But there is another interesting aspect to

9 Hoekstra, 'Hobbes's Thucydides'. Hoekstra points out (p. 561) that Thucydides's description of the plague would also have strongly resonated with English readers, as London had just been devastated by the plague in 1625–26. For the political context of the late 1620s, see also Luca Iori, *Thucydides Anglicus. Gli* Eight Bookes *di Thomas Hobbes e la ricezione inglese delle* Storie *di Tucidide (1450–1642)* (Roma: Edizioni di Storia e Letteratura, 2015), ch. 8.

10 Ibid., p. 559.

11 Thucydides, *Peloponnesian War*, p. xxiii.

Hobbes's reasoning and his choice of words here, one that may afford us an opportunity to bridge the gap between the *Eight Books of the Peloponnesian War* (1629) and *Leviathan* (1651). We should not make too much of this, but it is striking and at the very least suggestive that Hobbes, both in his preface to his readers in the Thucydides translation and in *Leviathan*, uses Roman gladiators to illustrate something that is of key importance to him. In the preface to the translation, Hobbes draws an analogy between his readers and the audience at Roman gladiator games. Both will split into the many who delight in gory detail and the cheaper aspects of entertainment and the discerning few, who will pay attention to the underlying didactic goals, to the 'skill in fencing' and 'the art' by which political affairs are 'conducted to their ends'. Hobbes motivates his eventual decision, in 1628, to publish the Thucydides translation after all, by resolving to 'content himself with the few and better sort of readers'.[12]

In *Leviathan*, gladiators make a well-known and very visible appearance in Hobbes's account of the state of nature, where Hobbes uses gladiators to illustrate the international state of nature, which in turn is supposed to illustrate aspects of the original state of nature between individuals:

> But though there had never been any time, wherein particular men were in a condition of warre one against another; yet in all times, Kings, and Persons of Soveraigne authority, because of their Independency, are in continuall jealousies, and in the state and posture of Gladiators; having their weapons pointing, and their eyes fixed on one another; that is, their Forts, Garrisons, and Guns upon the Frontiers of their Kingdomes; and continuall Spyes upon their neighbours; which is a posture of War.[13]

This passage has served as a key exhibit for those seeking to impute a 'realist' outlook to Hobbes, but if we connect it to his early use of the gladiator analogy in the Thucydides translation, it will gently point in another direction. Gladiators, if they do not exhibit the necessary skill and art, will descend into 'bloody battles', with 'many thousands slain at once', and this is of course what the less discerning part of the audience would like them to do. However, there is a standard of skill, and gladiators who do exhibit this kind of skill will be

12 Ibid.

13 Hobbes, *Leviathan*, ed. by N. Malcolm, vol. 2 (Oxford: Clarendon Press, 2012), ch. 13, p. 196. For the gladiator analogy in *De cive*, see I. D. Evrigenis, *Images of Anarchy: The Rhetoric and Science in Hobbes's State of Nature* (Cambridge: Cambridge University Press, 2014), pp. 121f.; cf. also pp. 148–150 for the *Leviathan* passage.

better at preserving themselves and, in keeping with the suggested analogy, their commonwealths. If they do that, they will appeal to those who appreciate this kind of skill, those already well versed in Thucydides's and Hobbes's underlying didactic purposes – the 'better sort of readers' who have been, to change into Hobbes's later idiom, 'diligently, and truly taught'[14] the principles he expounded in his mature political philosophy.

It bears mentioning that for Hobbes this 'better sort' of readers need not exclude the 'Common people'. Not only are they 'of capacity enough to be made to understand' the true principles of political philosophy according to Hobbes, but, 'unlesse they be tainted with dependence on the Potent', are 'like clean paper, fit to receive' Hobbes's doctrines.[15] This anti-elitist slant of Hobbes's educational program might in fact be connected with Hobbes's reading of the Melian Dialogue, as we shall see. For now, let us focus on the fact that for Hobbes, in keeping with Renaissance scholarship such as Justus Lipsius's, gladiators could be appreciated not only for the gorier aspects of their trade, but also, more rationally, for their know-how and skill.[16]

Gladiators who betray such skill will behave differently if they are taken to represent commonwealths rather than individuals in the state of nature. Hobbes makes this basic asymmetry between individuals and sovereign persons very clear when he continues the passage quoted above as follows:

> But because they uphold thereby, the Industry of their Subjects; there does not follow from it, that misery, which accompanies the Liberty of particular men.[17]

---

14 *Leviathan*, ch. 30, p. 522.

15 *Leviathan*, ch. 30, p. 524. There is a view that the early Hobbes was more elitist than the Hobbes of *Leviathan*; but note Hobbes's translation of *hoi polloi* at Thuc. 5.103, which he renders neutrally as 'many men', rather than 'common crowd' or 'the vulgar' or something along those lines. In 'On the Life and History of Thucydides', Hobbes asks the wise to write 'in words understood by all men', implicitly holding out the possibility that the many could be properly educated 'in the characters of men's humours and manners', and their application 'to affairs of consequence', such as seditions. Thucydides, *Peloponnesian War*, p. 584. For a decreasingly elitist Hobbes, see D. Johnston, *The Rhetoric of Leviathan: Thomas Hobbes and the Politics of Cultural Transformation* (Princeton: Princeton University Press, 1986), p. 76. For an argument that Hobbes meant to be accessible to different audiences, see Evrigenis, *Images of Anarchy*.

16 Justus Lipsius, *Saturnalium Sermonum libri duo, qui de gladiatoribus: Lipsius' Saturnaliengespräche, eine textkritische Ausgabe mit Übersetzung, Einführung und Anmerkungen*, ed. Andrea Steenbeek (Leiden: Brill, 2011).

17 *Leviathan*, ch. 13, p. 196.

In the present chapter I would like to draw on the intuition that Hobbes, in his translation of Thucydides, sought to give us illustrations of sovereign states behaving more or less skillfully, maintaining the 'posture of Gladiators' in ways that are more or less conducive to upholding 'the Industry of their Subjects' and keeping misery at bay. I should like to argue that Hobbes, with his translation, not only sought to expose to his contemporaries 'the folly of the Athenians' and their misguided naval ambitions as revealed in the disaster of the Sicilian expedition,[18] but that Thucydides might have raised questions that opened Hobbes's eyes with regard to certain ideas that were to occupy central positions in the edifice of his mature political philosophy. These ideas are: the objective nature of the real good (preservation) and the real bad (death) for people;[19] the rationality of certain means chosen for safety and self-preservation; the idea that fear needs to have a rational foundation for it to be prudent; and the limits of the analogy between individuals and states. An important reason for Thucydides's educational value lies, for Hobbes, in Thucydides's account being *true* – because it is true, the *Peloponnesian War* helps to identify, e.g., what is and what is not a skillful way to achieve self-preservation, where 'skillful' implies acting according to reason and the laws of nature.

As I said above, whenever commentators have tried to show Thucydides's influence on Hobbes's concept of the state of nature, they have traditionally focused on famous passages from Thucydides on primitive Greek life, or the plague, or the stasis at Corcyra. In what follows, by contrast, I will focus on the Melian Dialogue instead, which I believe should help to elucidate the relationship between Thucydides and Hobbes in a particularly salient way.

2 Hobbes's Translation of the Melian Dialogue

Thucydides's Melian Dialogue is oftentimes read as a typical example of 'realist' power politics. In the fifth book of the *Peloponnesian War*, Thucydides describes how in 416 BCE 38 Athenian ships and over 3000 soldiers sail to the

18 As Hoekstra argues convincingly. See 'Hobbes's Thucydides', esp. pp. 558–560: Hobbes attempted (p. 560) to 'to use history to extinguish the flame of misguided ambition'.

19 For a persuasive argument that Hobbes is not a subjectivist with regard to either reason or value, see A. Abizadeh, *Hobbes and the Two Faces of Ethics* (Cambridge: Cambridge University Press, 2018), ch. 3; and for a convincing argument that Hobbes held a substantive, normative view of the real good (*bonum verum*), see ibid., ch. 4. I see far more continuity, however, between Hobbes's laws of nature and his account of contractual agreement and the respective obligations produced by either than Abizadeh does (see n. 60 below).

southern Aegean island of Melos, a Spartan colony, which had sought to maintain neutrality in the war and had entered into war only after the Athenians had started to ravage their open lands. It is the goal of the Athenians to integrate Melos into the Delian League, like all the other Aegean islands, while the Melians would prefer to maintain neutrality. 'Now', Hobbes's Thucydides writes, 'the Athenian commanders … being encamped upon their [the Melians'] land with these forces, before they would hurt the same sent ambassadors to deal with them first by way of conference'. Melos is an oligarchy and the Melians refuse to bring the Athenian envoys before the people, insisting to have them speak to their magistrates and the ruling few instead. Let us see how Thucydides, in Hobbes's rendering, has the Athenian envoys react to these Melian constraints:

> Since we may not speak to the multitude, for fear lest when they hear our persuasive and unanswerable arguments [*epagôgà kaì anélenkta*] all at once in a continued oration, they should chance to be seduced [*apatáô*] (for we know that this is the scope of your bringing us to audience before the few), make surer yet that point, you that sit here; answer you also to every particular, not in a set speech, but presently interrupting us whensoever anything shall be said by us which shall seem unto you to be otherwise. And first answer us whether you like this motion or not?[20]

First, we should pay attention to the way Hobbes translates the Athenians' own characterization of their arguments here. He writes 'persuasive and unanswerable', but one might do more justice to Thucydides by translating 'attractive and unchallenged'. Hobbes slides from the allure, or temptation of the Athenian arguments to a much stronger claim; he in fact makes sure that the Athenian envoys portray their reasoning as *irrefutable*. The translation does not do violence to the Greek, however: Hobbes merely exploits an ambiguity inherent in Thucydides's Greek, where the potential for irrefutability is certainly also present and where there is a spectrum from a factual 'not having been refuted' to 'impossible to refute'.[21] Furthermore, Hobbes chooses to render as seduction something one might as well render as deception or cheating.[22] Not only

20 Thuc. 5.85. For a lucid analysis of the tendentious way Hobbes introduces the motivation of fear into his translation, see L. Iori, 'Thomas Hobbes Traduttore di Tucidide: Gli *Eight Bookes of the Peloponnesian Warre* e le prime tracce di un pensiero Hobbesiano sulla paura', *Quaderni di Storia*, 75 (2012), pp. 149–193, at 170f.

21 See LSJ, s.v. '*anélenktos, on*'.

22 See LSJ, s.v. '*apatáô*'.

does this suggest that Hobbes thought that the Athenian envoys' arguments deserved being characterized as very strong, at least in their own eyes, and – something Thucydides is also keen to show – as irrefutable even in the more taxing context of a dispute in dialogue form. It may also betray the anti-elitist intuition, on Hobbes's part, that the many – the Melian people – would have let themselves convince more easily by the arguments put forward by the Athenian envoys than their oligarchic betters.[23]

Second, in view of the role the Melian Dialogue has played in the argument of those eager to enlist both Thucydides and Hobbes to the 'realist' cause, we should pause to note the weight that argument, as well as the modalities in which it is conducted, assumes here. It is prima facie rather odd to be told to that Hobbes, with his translation and elsewhere, gives expression to a Machiavellian 'inexorable logic of aggression' and territorial expansion – presumably neither Thucydides nor Hobbes would have required seven Oxford pages of closely argued debate to do so.[24] The realist interpretation is the result, as one recent commentator has aptly remarked, of a 'misreading of Hobbes' that 'has arisen from a misreading of Hobbes's Thucydides'.[25] In particular, it is assumed by realist interpreters that the Athenians in the Melian Dialogue are giving voice to a stance of sophistic and proto-Machiavellian power politics and that this stance is tantamount to Hobbes's own. While I agree that Hobbes must have felt a strong affinity for the Athenian view as rendered in his translation, I do not think that it is tenable or fruitful to characterize the Athenian arguments as expressing mere power politics – especially not when one considers these arguments in light of Hobbes's translation and overall political philosophy. Rather, or so I will argue, Hobbes must have considered the Athenian arguments as a persuasive expression of a much subtler point. In order to appreciate the subtlety, we would do well to keep in mind that the relevant audience for the Athenian arguments are the Melian few as well as latter-day Melians prone to resort to similar claims as those made by the Melians in Thucydides's history. But of course, given the inability of the

23 See n. 15 on Hobbes's elitism. There is a hint here of a connection between internal Melian order (oligarchy) and external behavior – almost amounting to a (proto-Kantian) constitutional requirement for international peace, which would be in line with the Athenian people coming eventually to the rescue of the Mytilenean people (Thuc. 3.37–49).

24 For this Machiavellian interpretation of Hobbes and his use of the Melian Dialogue, see D. Wootton, 'Thomas Hobbes's Machiavellian Moments', in D. R. Kelley and D. H. Sacks, *The Historical Imagination in Early Modern Britain* (Cambridge: Cambridge University Press, 1997), pp. 210–242, p. 232.

25 See Hoekstra, 'Hobbes's Thucydides', p. 565, n. 77.

Athenians to convince the Melians, Hobbes must have been keenly aware of the didactic work ahead of him.[26]

The Melians share the suspicion of many modern interpreters that what the Athenians are up to is not really argument: 'The equity of a leisurely debate is not to be found fault withal; but this preparation of war ... seemeth not to agree with the same'. The Melians see that the Athenians have come as judges, and suspect that even if they were 'superior in argument', the result would be war.[27] The Athenians reply by defining what they see as the real object of the debate: 'how to save your city from destruction'. On this the Melians now explicitly agree: 'this consultation being held only upon the point of our safety, we are content, if you think good, to go on with the course you have propounded'.[28]

At this point, the Athenians proceed to discuss the normative criteria applicable to the debate, making it clear that they do not think that criteria of justice are relevant in this case. Strikingly, they assume that this is something the Melians would acknowledge:

> But out of those things which we both of us do really think, let us go through with that which is feasible, both you and we knowing that in human disputation justice is then only agreed on when the necessity is equal; whereas they that have odds of power exact as much as they can, and the weak yield to such conditions as they can get.[29]

This is often taken to express a sophistic view of power politics. But, as has been noticed before, the Athenians here do not advance the sophistic claim that might is right (or should be right). They say, instead, that considerations of justice are excluded in certain contexts.[30] Importantly, the Melians do not disagree, but, grudgingly admitting that the Athenians indeed have a point, seek to point to the general *usefulness*, or profit, of having norms that allow one to 'plead reason and equity ... though somewhat without the strict compass of justice'.[31]

---

26 One might add that the interpretation of commentators such as Wootton lends weight to Thucydidean pessimism, rather than Hobbesian optimism.

27 Thuc. 5.86.

28 Thuc. 5.87f.

29 Thuc. 5.89.

30 For the relation of this passage and 5.105.2 to sophist ideas, see S. Hornblower, *A Commentary on Thucydides*, vol. III (Oxford: Oxford University Press, 2008), pp. 223f., 234, 244 (and see the literature referenced there).

31 Thuc. 5.90.

We need to be sensitive to Hobbes's choice of words here. Entirely in keeping with his later thought, Hobbes in his translation draws a distinction between 'strict justice', which he – consistent with the Athenians – must believe not to be applicable to the situation at hand, on the one hand, and 'reason and equity', on the other. This is, again, a reasonable translation of the Greek, but it does impose a distinction where there is none in Thucydides's text. The Melians in effect argue that invoking the reasonable and just (*tà eikóta kaì díkaia*) should help one's cause, even if the claim 'falls short of exactness' (*kaí ti kaì entòs toû akriboûs peísanta*). Hobbes replaces this with pleading reason and equity, which is 'without the strict compass of justice'. Hobbes's Melians, that is, are made to agree even more with the Athenians at this point in the debate, but we should not overemphasize the distance between the translation and the Greek. One might even say that Hobbes, imposing his terminological discipline, brings out more clearly the fact that the Melians do agree with the Athenians on both the subject matter of the debate – the safety of Melos – and the applicable criteria – practical reason and usefulness, maybe even a kind of equity, but certainly not strict justice. We should note how this prefigures Hobbes's explicit definition of justice as performance of covenants in *Leviathan* and the distinction between justice and natural law.[32]

The Athenians reply by pointing out that if saving the city of the Melians really is the goal, then there is a bargain to be had for both the Melians and the Athenians. The Athenian seek to enlarge their own dominion but offer to save Melos: 'we would have dominion over you without oppressing you [*apónôs mèn humôn árxai*], and preserve you to the profit of us both'. The Melians wonder, '[b]ut how can it be profitable for us to serve [*douleûsai*] ...?' The Athenian answer: 'Because you, by obeying [*hupakoûsai*], shall save yourselves from extremity; and we, not destroying you, shall reap profit by you'.[33] The Athenians believe that this is an offer the Melians cannot refuse. The Athenian offer could easily be described as a way out for the Melians, an outcome that both Athenians and Melians would find it individually rational to adhere by.[34] Here, again, it is important to note how Hobbes imposes terminology that makes his

32 *Leviathan*, ch. 15, p. 220. For the distinction between 'human justice' and natural justice, see Hobbes, *A Dialogue between a Philosopher and a Student of the Common Laws of England*, in W. Molesworth (ed.), *The English Works of Thomas Hobbes*, vol. 6 (London: John Bohn, 1840), p. 29. One may acknowledge the distinction without positing entirely independent realms of contractual obligation on the one hand and natural law on the other. For stark independence, see A. Abizadeh, *Hobbes and the Two Faces of Ethics*.

33 Thuc. 5.92f.

34 This outcome can be described as a game-theoretic equilibrium. We could conceptualize this as a sequential game, where the Melians have to move first and either accept or decline the Athenian offer. Acceptance would lead to the Athenians' preferred and

Melian Dialogue consistent with his later political philosophy, in a way that will help us decipher the way Hobbes must have read the dialogue. This is necessarily speculative, but it seems as if Thucydides made Hobbes recognize certain problems that came to occupy the very centre of Hobbes's mature political philosophy. Hobbes's Athenians seek dominion over the Melians 'without oppressing' them, but the adverb *apónôs* could also be understood to mean that the Athenians will rule with a light touch, not causing too much trouble to themselves. Hobbes goes on to translate *douleûsai* as 'to serve', while there is of course clearly something to be said for translating 'to be your slaves'.[35]

3 Melos and Hobbes's Commonwealth by Acquisition

Hobbes's choice here is revealing, I think, pointing to the conceptual context in which he situated the Melian Dialogue, namely that of 'commonwealth by acquisition', as he would call it in *Leviathan*. There we encounter this view of '[d]ominion acquired by Conquest, or Victory in war': conquest gives the right of dominion over the vanquished 'when the Vanquished, to avoyd the present stroke of death, covenanteth either in expresse words, or by other sufficient signes of the Will, that so long as his life, and the liberty of his body is allowed him, the Victor shall have the use thereof, at his pleasure'. It is not victory itself, therefore, that creates political obligation, but the fact that the conquered, in exchange for 'his life in security' and 'corporall liberty', promises obedience. The relationship between the vanquished and the sovereign is no different, henceforth, from that of the subject and the sovereign in cases of sovereignty by institution. The relationship is one of at least a minimum of trust. The vanquished, Hobbes writes, after promising obedience and being trusted with corporal liberty, is a 'servant'. The contrast is with those who do not submit to the victor and cannot be trusted; these are 'commonly called Slaves', and have 'no

to the Melians' second-ranked outcome given that the Athenians prefer most (A) where they both cooperate (i.e. the Melians accept the Athenian offer), followed by (B) the outcome where the Melians accept and the Athenians renege on their promise, followed by (C) where neither cooperates (i.e. what actually happened: the Melians decline and the Athenians kill and enslave them), and they least prefer (D) where they uphold their offer even though the Melians opt for war. The Melians *should* order D > A > C > B and choose A in light of Athenian preferences. But the Melians might expect unreasonably high payoffs when they choose rejection of the Athenian offer – they harbor irrational hopes, as we shall see, which leads to different expected payoffs and different ordering that makes declining the offer seem attractive.

35 See LSJ, s.v. '*douleúô*'. Cf. Hornblower, *Commentary*, p. 236.

obligation at all; but may break their bonds, or the prison; and kill, or carry away captive', the victor 'justly', if they can.[36]

The distinction that carries the argumentative weight is that between subjects or servants with a minimum of liberty, on the one hand, and slaves, on the other, and it is not farfetched to think that the Melian Dialogue helped Hobbes develop his account of political obligation.[37] The Melians are offered the option, by the Athenians, to submit to them, without being made slaves – to become subjects 'by acquisition', in other words.[38] Hobbes believes that the Athenian argument against the Melians is convincing because it goes to the very purpose of the state – safety, life, corporal liberty – which the Melian oligarchs can no longer guarantee for the Melians. As Hobbes would formulate it in the *Leviathan*, the obligation of the subject is derived either from explicit consent, 'or else from the End of the Institution of Soveraignty; namely, the Peace of the Subjects within themselves, and their Defence against a common Enemy'.[39]

This shows, I believe, that for Hobbes, the Melian Dialogue illustrated perfectly the fact that in the state of nature, the analogy between individuals and commonwealths does not go all the way, that there is instead a basic asymmetry

---

36 *Leviathan*, ch. 20, p. 312. Sovereignty by institution of course does not feature a contractual relationship between the people and the sovereign, but, in the case of sovereignty by acquisition, once the sovereign discharges his contractual obligation by not killing the vanquished, the vanquished do no longer have any contractual claim against the sovereign; henceforth, therefore, the relationship between subjects and sovereign is exactly the same as in sovereignty by institution. Cf. also Emile Simpson's contribution to this volume on the status of slaves and servants in Grotius.

37 Hobbes alludes to Greek armies taking enemies alive, or giving quarter, as a preliminary stage of obligation following victory, but it is not until the 'Victor hath trusted him with his corporall liberty' that the life of the vanquished is 'in security' and obligation arises. *Leviathan*, ch. 20, p. 312. Hobbes says that the Greeks called this *Zôgría*; for the related verb *zôgréô*, see Thuc. 7.23.4.

38 Cf. Kinch Hoekstra's characterization of the way in which Hobbes can be taken to be a consent theorist: '[W]here Hobbes has been taken to be outlining a contract by which citizens authorize a government, he is, strictly speaking, describing the supposition of a covenant given the necessity of it'. Hoekstra, 'The *de facto* Turn in Hobbes's Political Philosophy', in T. Sorell and L. Foisneau (eds.), Leviathan *After 350 Years* (Oxford: Oxford University Press, 2004), pp. 33–73, at 69.

39 *Leviathan*, ch. 21, p. 336. It goes beyond the scope of this chapter, but Hobbes's account of commonwealth by acquisition suggests that it is really the *purpose* of the state on which the statics of Hobbes's architecture of political obligation ultimately depend (even in the case of sovereignty by institution), rather than contractual agreement itself. For a similar view, see R. Harrison, *Hobbes, Locke, and Confusion's Masterpiece* (Cambridge: Cambridge University Press, 2003), ch. 4, esp. pp. 128f.

opening up.[40] States are the frameworks within which individuals may satisfy their subjective desires, but once the Melian oligarchy could no longer warrant the very purpose of their commonwealth and 'the Industry of their Subjects' could therefore no longer be upheld,[41] it would have been rational for the Melians to give up their independence and accept the Athenian conditions. The Melian oligarchs, it must have seemed to Hobbes, were not very skillful gladiators. The Melian stance was owed to – falsely, in Hobbes's view – equating the following two outcomes: collapse of their state, and death and slavery for the Melian population. But extinction of the state is not tantamount to death and slavery of the population, the equation rests on a fallacy of composition. Compounded by irrational hopes concerning the rejection of the Athenian offer and the ensuing war, this would explain the Melian decision.

The basic lack of rationality, in Hobbes's eyes, could be traced to this fissure between individuals and sovereigns in the state of nature. For the Melians, or at least for the Melian ruling elite, surrendering their sovereign independence seemed tantamount to being enslaved or killed – loss of independence, that is, is as bad as the loss of individual liberty and lives. But this, Hobbes must think, is a mistake. And even apart from revealing an erroneous analogy between individual and state in the state of nature, the Melian decision to fight instead of accepting the Athenian offer must to Hobbes have shown other hallmarks of irrationality, such as exaggerated pride and irrational hopes for the future.

4 Reliance on "Absurd Means of Safety"

Let us look at the Melian outlook more closely. As we have already noted, the Melian argument is not really an argument from justice – at least not from within 'the strict compass of justice'. It is, rather, portrayed as an argument from superstition and hope. The Melians believe that 'if we yield presently, all our hope is lost; whereas if we hold out, we have yet a hope to keep ourselves

40 My interpretation supports Hoekstra's conclusion that for Hobbes, Thucydides provided a 'starting point' for his own argument for 'peace and the preservation of the people'. Hoekstra, 'Hobbes's Thucydides', p. 569. Cf. also id., 'Hobbes on the Natural Condition of Mankind', in P. Springborg (ed.), *The Cambridge Companion to Hobbes's* Leviathan (Cambridge: Cambridge University Press, 2007), pp. 109–127, esp. p. 118. For an excellent analysis of the asymmetry, see Malcolm, 'Hobbes's Theory', esp. p. 448. For an argument that Hobbes's solution to domestic strife also offers a solution to international conflict which is consistent with the view defended here, see D. S. Grewal, 'The Domestic Analogy Revisited: Hobbes on International Order', *The Yale Law Journal*, 125 (2016), pp. 618–680.

41 *Leviathan*, ch. 13, p. 196.

up'. The Athenian reply is sarcastic: 'Hope', the Athenians say, is 'the comfort of danger', a 'thing by nature prodigal'. To those who rely on it, hope 'at once by failing maketh itself known; and known, leaveth no place for future caution'. The Athenians urge the Melians to 'presently save themselves by human means', rather than relying on, first, 'apparent hopes', and then, once these 'fail them, betake themselves to blind ones, as divination, oracles, and other such things which with hopes destroy men'.[42] The Melians counter that they will have the gods on their side, and 'for power, what is wanting in us will be supplied by our league with the Lacedaemonians'. This invocation of Spartan help is not based on actual Spartan obligations under an alliance, but simply on a hope that the Spartans, given their kinship with the Melians, would help. The Athenian dismiss both claims and are especially amused by the hope for Spartan help – 'we bless your innocent minds, but affect not your folly'. The Melians, according to the Athenians, rely on 'now absurd means of safety'.[43] The Athenians sum up their view of Melian irrationality:

> But we observe that, whereas you said you would consult of your safety, you have not yet in all this discourse said anything which a man relying on could hope to be preserved by; the strongest arguments you use are but future hopes; and your present power is too short to defend you against the forces already arranged against you.[44]

These irrational hopes are connected with a desire for glory and the passion for honor. The Athenians suspect that an inflated sense of pride might have a detrimental effect on the Melians: 'For many, when they have foreseen into what dangers they were entering, have nevertheless been so overcome by that forcible word dishonour that that which is but called dishonour hath caused them to fall willingly into immedicable calamities, and so to draw upon themselves really, by their own madness, a greater dishonour than could have befallen them by fortune'. The choice, the Athenians say, is one between 'war or safety',

42 Thuc. 5.102f.

43 Thuc. 5.104f. What Philip Pettit calls Hobbes's 'commonwealth of ordered words' also seems indebted to Thucydides. Cf. Thuc. 3.82.4 for the use of *alogistos* and the idea that it is the arbitrary change of the meaning of terms which is symptomatic of the collapse of order. But, *pace* Pettit, Hobbes may not so much fall away from a Thucydidean world where our 'beastly natures' pose the problem, as he returns to Thucydides and his formulation of the problem as one where in civil war, 'the received value of names' is changed arbitrarily, causing therewith arbitrary domination. Pettit, *Made with Words* (Princeton: Princeton University Press, 2008), p. 99; ch. 8.

44 Thuc. 5.111.

and their 'so reasonable conditions' will merely result in the Melians 'enjoying [their] own under tribute'.[45]

The desire for glory, or honor, is one of the passions which for Hobbes tend to exacerbate violent conflict in the state of nature (and we have already noted the close correspondence of Hobbes's passion for glory with one of the Thucydidean motives for Athenian expansion).[46] The desire for glory easily tilts into vainglory and rises to levels where we are 'feigning or supposing of abilities in our selves, which we know are not', abilities and powers only 'supposed' by us, 'for delight in the consequences of it'.[47] This makes for a particular kind of shortsightedness and a tendency, in Jean Hampton's words, 'to underestimate our opponent's powers and overestimate our own. Thus emboldened, we are more likely to think it reasonable to wage war with our opponent. … We tend to overestimate the probability of our winning a conflict and underestimate the probability of being beaten by our opponent'.[48] Pride and an exaggerated sense of honor thus conspire to create irrational hopes in the Melians.[49]

When the Melians finally decide not to yield and to hold on to their neutrality, the Athenian envoys, before departing, give a description of what they believe is the chief problem with the Melian outlook:

45 Ibid.

46 There is of course scholarly disagreement whether for Hobbes it is reason or the passions that chiefly cause conflict in the state of nature. For a lucid discussion of the two accounts, see J. Hampton, *Hobbes and the Social Contract Tradition* (Cambridge: Cambridge University Press, 1986), ch. 2, arguing in favor of shortsightedness as the most plausible cause of conflict. *Pace* Hampton, I do not believe that the rationality and passions accounts are inconsistent. The passions account need not necessarily (p. 68) 'have us think reason actually counsels cooperation', it may simply *compound* the problem posed by the rationality account by compounding the trust problem in the state of nature. For a convincing argument that *uncertainty* plays a crucial role in creating conflict in Hobbes's state of nature, see H. Chung, 'Hobbes's State of Nature: A Modern Bayesian Game-Theoretic Analysis', *Journal of the American Philosophical Association*, 1:3 (2015), pp. 485–508.

47 *Leviathan*, ch. 6, p. 88.

48 Hampton, *Hobbes*, p. 87. For Hobbes's view of shortsightedness, and what could remedy it, see *Leviathan*, ch. 18, p. 282: 'For all men are by nature provided of notable multiplying glasses, (that is their Passions and Selfe-love,) through which, every little payment appeareth a great grievance; but are destitute of those prospective glasses, (namely Morall and Civill Science,) to see a farre off the miseries that hang over them, and cannot without such payments [taxes] by avoyded'.

49 The same effect is illustrated on the Athenian side when Athens embarks on the disastrous Sicilian Expedition, which shows, again, the value of the correct calculation of expected utility.

> You are the only men, as it seemeth to us, by this consultation, that think future things more certain than things seen, and behold things doubtful, through desire to have them true, as if they were already come to pass.[50]

This is of course precisely the kind of miscalculation Hampton refers to. Melian shortsightedness, emboldened by irrational hope, presents, I think, a rather striking mirror-image of an extremely prominent exemplar of irrationality Hobbes discusses in the *Leviathan*, namely the 'Foole' in chapter 15, who 'hath sayd in his heart, there is no such thing as Justice'. I have no evidence that Hobbes modeled his foole on Thucydides's Melians, but the parallels are tantalizing and seem obvious enough. Hobbes's foole believes that in the case of promises given in the state of nature, when the other party has already performed it is against reason to perform. Hobbes argues, famously, that is not against reason to perform in that situation. His argument parallels the Athenian argument against the Melians – he reproaches the foole effectively for harboring irrational hopes. The foole, breaking his promise, may through 'some accident which he could not expect' get away with it; but the point is that the foole was not entitled to this hope, the same way the Melians are not entitled to rely on their irrational hopes of a favorable outcome. The fact that the foole might, by accident, get away with promise-breaking does not 'make it reasonably or wisely done'. The fact that his behavior went unnoticed and unsanctioned is itself due to errors on the part of those he is freeriding upon, and the foole is no more warranted to rely on such errors as the Melians are to rely on the gods, the Spartans, or improbable good luck. Such 'errours a man cannot reasonably reckon upon as the means of his security'. Because the foole (or the Melians) depend on wishful consequences they are not ex ante entitled to depend on – consequences they 'could not foresee, nor reckon upon' – such reliance is 'against the reason of [their] preservation'.[51]

5 Why Thucydides?

This ties in with the very foundations of the edifice of *Leviathan*. The natural laws presented there are laws, probably of a causal nature, that prescribe those actions that are necessary for self-preservation and peace. They are dictates of reason in precisely this sense, and to act against them simply is to act

50 Thuc. 5.113. There is a sense that had the Athenians been allowed to make their case before the people, the many might have acted more rationally than the few.

51 *Leviathan*, ch. 15, p. 224.

irrationally. The natural laws are of a causal, empirical nature in the sense that they concern how the world works. They are prudential norms of practical rationality, built on an a priori normative foundation – on the claim that self-preservation is the real good – and they derive their obligatory nature from this normative foundation, but they are themselves not purely a priori.[52] This would seem to go a long way in explaining why Hobbes found Thucydides so enormously important and useful. It is because Thucydides's account is true that Hobbes could glean from it the kind of insight that he would eventually formulate as laws of nature dictated by reason. Hobbes thought that the utility of his moral and political philosophy could be seen 'by the calamities we receive' from being ignorant of that philosophy. The cause of these calamities – war, especially civil war – is, Hobbes thinks, 'that men know not the causes neither of war nor peace'.[53] As Hampton puts it, Hobbes seems to think that 'one cannot be rational if one pursues a goal incorrectly in circumstances in which one could have gained access to the information one needed about how to achieve that goal'.[54] It is this kind of information that Hobbes himself seems to have found in Thucydides's history of the Peloponnesian War before he went on to distill it in the natural laws of *Leviathan*.

Hobbes, in his 'On the Life and History of Thucydides', defended Thucydides vigorously against the criticism of Dionysius of Halicarnassus. Dionysius had reproached Thucydides for not having written sufficiently edifying history, as

52 For a defense of such an account of Hobbes on obligation, see T. Nagel, 'Hobbes's Concept of Obligation', *Philosophical Review*, 68:1 (1959), pp. 68–83. For the view that 'Hobbes's argument in *Leviathan* is meant to demonstrate the truth of a certain critical piece of causal information', see Hampton, *Hobbes*, p. 47 and passim. To what extent self-preservation is defended by Hobbes as the real good, something that it is more rational to aspire to than other goods, cannot be discussed here. For a defense of Hobbes as holding a merely instrumentalist conception of rationality, see Hampton, *Hobbes*, pp. 34–42; but Hampton acknowledges that Hobbes's natural laws have objective, not merely conventional, status (pp. 42–51) and later argued that Hobbes implicitly falls back on a non-instrumental conception of rationality: Hampton, 'Hobbes and Ethical Naturalism', *Philosophical Perspectives*, 6 (1992), pp. 333–353. For the argument that Hobbes is making a normative claim when defending self-preservation as the real good, see, e.g., B. Gert, 'Introduction', in Thomas Hobbes, *Man and Citizen*, ed. B. Gert (Indianapolis: Hackett Publishing, 1991); A. Abizadeh, *Hobbes and the Two Faces of Ethics*, ch. 4. Pettit, *Made with Words*, pp. 87f., makes an interesting argument for Hobbes defending a non-instrumentalist conception of rationality: it would be (88) an 'absurdity', for Hobbes, 'to want to cease living, since living entails desiring' and it would be 'an absurdity to desire not to desire'. I find the normative interpretation more plausible.

53 Hobbes, *De Corpore*, in W. Molesworth (ed.), *The English Works of Thomas Hobbes*, vol. 1 (London: John Bohn, 1840), p. 8.

54 Hampton, *Hobbes*, pp. 36f.

opposed to Herodotus. Herodotus, Dionysius claimed, had chosen 'a noble argument', while Thucydides had taken 'an evil argument', writing about a war that was 'neither honourable nor fortunate'. Better, Dionysius wrote (in Hobbes's translation of his *Letter to Gnaeus Pompeius*), to write with Herodotus 'of the wonderful acts both of the barbarians and Grecians, than of the pitiful and horrible calamities of the Grecians; so much wiser is Herodotus in the choice of his argument than Thucydides'. Note Hobbes's choice of translation for *páthê*, 'calamities', in line with the view about the usefulness of his philosophy expressed in *De Corpore*. Hobbes goes on to defend Thucydides against Dionysius by pointing out the reliability of Thuydides's account. Unlike Herodotus, Thucydides 'was able certainly to inform himself'. By 'propounding' the 'miseries' that happened, Thucydides 'sheweth that it was a great war, and worthy to be known; and not to be concealed from posterity, for the calamities that then fell upon the Grecians; but the rather to be truly delivered unto them, for that men profit more by looking on adverse events, than on prosperity'.[55]

Dionysius next accuses Thucydides of a lack of patriotism, but Hobbes has no more patience for this line of argument. If, he writes, 'the injury, upon which the war arose, proceeded from the Athenians; then the writer, though an Athenian and honoured in his country, ought to declare the same'. This is because the historian has to write 'not as a lover of his country but of truth'.[56] Hobbes sides with Lucian instead and quotes from Lucian's treatise on history with approval: 'a writer of history ought, in his writings, to be a foreigner, without country, living under his own law only, subject to no king, nor caring what any man will like or dislike, but laying out the matter as it is'.[57]

Lastly, and entirely to the point of my chapter, Dionysius charged Thucydides with portraying the Athenians in the Melian Dialogue in a way that 'was contrary to the dignity of the state'. Hobbes answers this charge by pointing out that the Athenian people had very likely given their envoys at Melos discretionary powers:

> [I]f the Athenian people gave in charge to these their captains, to take in the island by all means whatsoever, without power to report back unto them first the equity of the islanders' cause; as is most likely to be true;

55 Hobbes, 'On the Life and History of Thucydides', in Thucydides, *The Peloponnesian War: The Complete Hobbes Translation*, with notes and a new introduction by David Grene (Chicago: University of Chicago Press, 1989), pp. 578f. For Hobbes's use of Thucydides, cf. also Evrigenis, *Images of Anarchy*, pp. 26–43.

56 Ibid., p. 580.

57 Ibid., p. 581.

> I see then no reason the generals [sic] had to enter into disputation with them, whether they should perform their charge or not, but only whether they should do it by fair or foul means; which is the point treated of in this dialogue.[58]

The Melian Dialogue was about whether or not Melos should be taken over by 'fair or foul means', and it seems that in Hobbes's view, the Melians themselves, not equipped with the kind of 'prospective glasses'[59] afforded by Thucydides's historiography or Hobbes's philosophy, brought it upon Melos that it was taken ultimately by foul means leading to the destruction not only of the Melian state, but of every individual adult male Melian as well. It seems that, according to Hobbes, fair means would have consisted in the Melians accepting Athenian sovereignty by acquisition and, thus, Melian self-preservation. While in this particular case Athenian expansion could be justified, the Athenians would soon themselves exhibit a similar lack of 'prospective glasses' and an excess of irrational hopes when embarking on their Sicilian adventure.

6 Conclusion

What results is a picture of the state of nature not characterized by Athenian and 'Hobbesian realism', nor by Machiavellian expansive aggression, but by the kind of far-sighted prudence and enlightened self-interest that is supplied by reason and the laws of nature. The state is but a means to individual self-preservation and 'commodious living', and the laws of nature provide the normative rules that will yield peace; no (natural) law, no peace. The laws of nature bind sovereigns in the state of nature and create rights and some duties, even to a limited extent *in foro externo*.[60] These normative rules are universal and hold

58 Ibid., pp. 583f.

59 *Leviathan*, ch. 18, p. 282.

60 *Leviathan*, ch. 15, p. 224: covenants in the state of nature are binding 'where one of the parties has performed already'. G. Kavka, *Hobbesian Moral and Political Theory* (Princeton: Princeton University Press, 1986), p. 351, draws out the implication: non-performers 'act unjustly if they do not' perform. For similar lines of argument, see D. Dyzenhaus, 'Hobbes on the International Rule of Law', *Ethics & International Affairs*, 28:1 (2014), pp. 53–64; E. Fox-Decent, 'Hobbes's Relational Theory: Beneath Power and Consent', in D. Dyzenhaus and T. Poole (eds.), *Hobbes and the Law* (Cambridge: Cambridge University Press, 2012), pp. 118–144. This interpretation of Hobbes's concept of obligation is in tension with the one recently defended by Arash Abizadeh in *Hobbes and the Two Faces of Ethics*, who postulates a far greater gap between Hobbes's laws of nature and his account of contractual obligations than I find convincing.

in the international realm as well, which is the reason why Hobbes's 'gladiators' ought to abide by them and, if skillful, will abide by them. This requires a certain optimism about the ability of the reason of sovereigns to recognize, and eventually to converge on, those rules of natural law – an optimism Thucydides is very unlikely to have shared, but one that Hobbes seems to have upheld.

One reason to think that Hobbes's optimism in this regard is warranted might be that states could conceivably have a better chance at avoiding shortsightedness. States, that is, might have better access to the rules of natural law by virtue of the kind of juridical order they have already created internally. Having achieved civil order along the lines conditioned by Hobbesian natural law states overall tend to be in a better epistemic position in the state of nature than individuals are, because to exist they must have already successfully implemented and institutionalized natural law internally. States may therefore simply *know* the laws of nature better than individuals do, and having the laws of nature as a guide further extends the state's relevant knowledge about what to do in the face of the uncertainty that is characteristic for the state of nature.[61] Uncertainty, which plays a large role in creating conflict in the state of nature, will as a result be far less pronounced for states in the state of nature than for individuals. This results in a picture where states, having better epistemic abilities than individuals, will encounter less uncertainty because they know reasonably well whether particular other states are modest or vainglorious and will, if their leaders are rational, assign not as much value to their survival qua states than to the survival of the individuals inhabiting these states.

Select Bibliography

Primary sources

Grene, David (ed.), *Thucydides, The Peloponnesian War: The Complete Hobbes Translation*, with notes and a new introduction (Chicago: University of Chicago Press, 1989).

Hobbes, Thomas, *Leviathan*, ed. by N. Malcolm, 3 vols. (Oxford: Clarendon Press, 2012).

61 For an interesting account of law as having the function of extending knowledge, see J. R. Lucas, *On Justice* (Oxford: Oxford University Press, 1980), pp. 111f. For uncertainty as one of the key drivers of conflict in the state of nature, see Chung, 'Hobbes's State of Nature'. For a convincing argument about the relevance of Hobbes's laws of nature for interstate relations, see P. Schröder, *Trust in Early Modern International Political Thought, 1598–1713* (Cambridge: Cambridge University Press, 2017), pp. 107–119.

Secondary sources

Abizadeh, Arash, *Hobbes and the Two Faces of Ethics* (Cambridge: Cambridge University Press, 2018).

Dyzenhaus, David, 'Hobbes on the International Rule of Law', *Ethics & International Affairs*, 28:1 (2014), pp. 53–64.

Evrigenis, Ioannis, *Images of Anarchy: The Rhetoric and Science in Hobbes's State of Nature* (Cambridge: Cambridge University Press, 2014).

Hoekstra, Kinch, 'Hobbes's Thucydides', in A. P. Martinich and K. Hoekstra (eds.), *The Oxford Handbook of Hobbes* (Oxford: Oxford University Press, 2016), ch. 24.

Iori, Luca, 'Thomas Hobbes Traduttore di Tucidide: Gli *Eight Bookes of the Peloponnesian Warre* e le prime tracce di un pensiero Hobbesiano sulla paura', *Quaderni di Storia* 75 (2012), pp. 149–193.

Hampton, Jean, 'Hobbes and Ethical Naturalism', *Philosophical Perspectives,* 6 (1992), pp. 333–353.

Malcolm, Noel, 'Hobbes's Theory of International Relations', in id., *Aspects of Hobbes* (Oxford: Oxford University Press, 2002), pp. 432–456.

Schröder, Peter, *Trust in Early Modern International Political Thought, 1598–1713* (Cambridge: Cambridge University Press, 2017).

CHAPTER 2

Missing Terms in English Geographical Thinking, 1550–1600

Mary C. Fuller

Abstract

This essay considers what the first few decades of English maritime expansion can tell us about perceptions of pre- or extra-civil conditions in regions beyond Europe, using as its main archive the document compilations of Richard Hakluyt, *Principal Navigations* (1589, 1598–1600). The first half of the essay examines evidence from theorists and patrons of exploration on the application of natural law principles to English actions in the Americas. The second half of the essay turns to observations by travelers. In the record preserved by Hakluyt, the lists of negatives that classically marked societies as uncivil – for instance, the lack of metallurgy, fermentation, and bread-making – appear most frequently in accounts of Arctic societies, across a band stretching from present-day Nunavut to Arctic Russia. The Arctic case makes evident the degree to which ideas of 'civility' were environmentally specific. At the same time, observations of indigenous technologies, the presence of real and imagined settler societies in the Arctic, and English aspirations in the North tested the possibility of thinking in different terms.

Keywords

Arctic – civility – cultivation – environment – travel – Hakluyt – natural law

 | DOI:10.1163/9789004499621_004

> At Oxford Mr. T[homas] H[obbes] tooke great delight there to goe to the booke-binders' shops, and lye gaping on mappes.
>
> JOHN AUBREY, *Brief Lives*

•••

> In the beginning, all the world was America.
>
> JOHN LOCKE, *Second Treatise*

1 Introduction

Behind late seventeenth century discourse on the state of nature lay observations of world geography, and especially of the regions and peoples newly contacted by Europeans in the late fifteenth and sixteenth centuries. Such observations already embed ideas about what was to be observed – in other words, while they may have served the theorists of the late 17th century as raw material for thinking about nature and natural law, the narratives of mariners, merchants, and would-be settlers who traveled beyond Europe were themselves shaped and organized by implied theories and requirements even while they registered the press of the real.[1] In the English record more broadly, theoretical reflection on law and rights in territories 'not possessed by any Christian prince,' or at least not possessed by recognizable sovereigns, was less visibly and elaborately articulated than in Spain; these primary sources on geography, a record more generally and frequently disseminated in print than was the case for comparable Spanish sources, thus assume a particular interest.

1 On the complexity of early modern travel literature, see Joan Pau Rubiés, 'New Worlds and Renaissance Ethnology,' *History and Anthropology* 6, no. 2 (1993), pp. 157–197, at 158. This is not the place to give a full account of other factors shaping such documents, among them genre, navigational practices, or the informational demands of corporate, state, or individual sponsors (see, *inter alia*, William H. Sherman, 'Distant Relations: Letters from America, 1492–1677,' *Huntington Library Quarterly* 66, no. 3/4 (2003), pp. 225–245.) In the context of a collection focused on international law, however, it may be pertinent to mention the influence of English legal culture on the form and even content of primary source documents (see Lauren A. Benton, *A Search for Sovereignty: Law and Geography in European Empires, 1400–1900* (Cambridge; New York: Cambridge University Press, 2010), pp. 25–28.) However, the English situation of privately organized and funded exploration did not produce the systematically organized demands for information observed in the Spanish context (for discussion of information gathering by the Council for the Indies, see *inter alia* María M. Portuondo, *Secret Science: Spanish Cosmography and the New World* (Chicago: University of Chicago Press, 2009), ch. 3, 6.)

Early English observations of the world beyond Europe acquired by far their most lasting and important dissemination as gathered together and published by the editor Richard Hakluyt (1552?-1616) in his massive compilation, *Principal Navigations of the English Nation* (1598–1600). The three geographical compilations published by Hakluyt between 1582 and 1600 provide a *summa* of English activities overseas along with a sampling of their supposed medieval precursors, of charters and letters patent, and a modest amount of theories and proposals.[2] In other words, more often than not readers accessed the heterogeneous materials produced by seafarers, colonists, soldiers and merchants in a single work shaped by Hakluyt's selection, sequencing, and categorizing of texts.

The figure of Richard Hakluyt bridges the practice of discovery and settlement, and reflection or projection about its principles, strategies and meanings.[3] A cleric and geographer who studied and taught at Oxford, Hakluyt was famously introduced to his avocation in his elder cousin's chambers at the Middle Temple. Later in life, Hakluyt knew key thinkers in the tradition of civil and international law either personally or through translating their work, and he was familiar with writings by many of the Spanish humanists and clerics whose works documented the conquest of territories in the Americas, and the kinds of nature and populations found there.[4] Hakluyt also knew the men who planned and participated in the English reach beyond Europe: navigators, merchants, promoters, soldiers. He consulted on, advised, promoted, facilitated and finally memorialized all the major discovery projects of his era, from searches for a northern route to Asia to trade with Malaysia and settlement in Jamestown.

The first half of the essay considers some of the explicit and implicit propositions about rights, possession, and civility made in Hakluyt's work. In the second

2 The three compilations are *Divers Voyages* (London, 1582); *Principall Navigations* (London, 1589), cited as *PN* 1589; and *Principal Navigations* (London, 1598–1600), in 3 volumes, cited as *PN* 1600. Citations will be to *PN* 1600 unless otherwise noted.

3 For background on Hakluyt, see Peter C. Mancall, *Hakluyt's Promise: An Elizabethan's Obsession for an English America* (New Haven: Yale University Press, 2007); Anthony Payne, *Richard Hakluyt: A Guide to His Books* (London: Quaritch, 2008); Daniel Carey and Claire Jowitt, eds., *Richard Hakluyt and Travel Writing in Early Modern Europe*, Hakluyt Society, Extra Series 47 (Farnham, Surrey, England; Burlington, VT: Ashgate, 2012). Still valuable older sources include E. G. R. Taylor, ed., *The Original Writings & Correspondence of the Two Richard Hakluyts*, 2 vols., Works Issued by the Hakluyt Society, 2nd Series 76–77 (London: Hakluyt Society, 1935); David B. Quinn (ed.), *The Hakluyt Handbook*, 2 vols., Works Issued by the Hakluyt Society, 2nd Series 144–45 (London: Hakluyt Society, 1974); George B. Parks, *Richard Hakluyt and the English Voyages* (New York: American Geographical Society, 1928).

4 For instance, Hakluyt produced a new edition of Peter Martyr's *De orbe novo … decades* in 1587; he also translated parts of José de Acosta's *Historia natural y moral* in the 1590s (see note 8 below). Translated excerpts from Spanish sources on the Americas are frequent in vol. 3 of *PN*.

half, I turn to some of the primary sources compiled by Hakluyt. How might we recognize moments when English authors believed they were observing people in something like a state of nature? Hobbes described the state of nature as a condition in which there was 'no place for Industry ... no culture of the Earth; no Navigation ... no commodious Building; no Instruments ... no Knowledge ... no account of Time; no Arts; no Letters; no Society.'[5] Such lists of missing terms have long roots in classical antiquity; they also recur across European accounts of the societies newly contacted by mariners from the late 15th century forward, and especially in the Americas.[6] Whether the claim is that people in a state of nature have no law, faith or king, or no use of corn, wine, and metal, the linked features of listing and negation function as one distinguishing marker of discourse about pre-civil conditions. In looking for ideas of a 'state of nature' in the primary sources, my approach will be to trace this formal marker.

The time boundaries of this study are the beginnings of sustained maritime exploration in England circa 1550, and the publication of Hakluyt's third and final compilation, the longer second edition of *Principal Navigations* (1600). That work organized the records of sixteenth century exploration projects (and their prehistory) into public, printed form just prior to the inception of the East India Company and the Virginia Company, entities whose activities would profoundly change the nature of English engagements with the larger world, and provide new motives and tasks for writers. It thus provides a snapshot of what and how Englishmen (sic) thought about regions beyond Europe on the eve of permanent settlement and the institutionalization of global trade.

2 Imagining Possession: Freedom of Travel and Natural Fellowship

Jamestown was founded in 1609. Following settlement and, especially, the native attack of 1622, writers associated with the company reflected explicitly on rights of possession in the new space of North America.[7] Andrew Fitzmaurice has shown that the promoters of the Virginia colony both knew

5 Hobbes, *Leviathan*, XIII: 62, cited in Ioannis D. Evrigenis, *Images of Anarchy: The Rhetoric and Science in Hobbes's State of Nature* (Cambridge: Cambridge University Press, 2014), 144. See ch. 8 in particular for consideration of America by Hobbes. See the essay by Tom Sparks in this volume for a view of Hobbes' privatives in relation to international environmental law in the present.

6 For antiquity see, for instance, the description of archaic Greek society in the first chapter of Thucydides, *History of the Peloponnesian War.* (My thanks to Benjamin Straumann for this reference).

7 A first-person account of the attack can be found in Edward Waterhouse, *A Declaration of the State of the Colony and Affaires in Virginia: With a Relation of the Barbarous Massacre ...* (London, 1622).

and drew upon considerations of rights in the Americas by Spanish writers, particularly Francisco de Vitoria and José de Acosta.[8] As he argues, the propositions made by this corpus of materials – sermons, pamphlets, longer printed books – were not necessarily coherent, even internally.[9] But certainly with continuous settlement, and continuous contact with indigenous Americans, the need emerged to engage in a more explicit and sustained way with the question of who had rights over American land and what was necessary in order to hold those rights; as they did so, English writers showed familiarity with the existing discourse. Such explicit reflection is harder to find in the England of the sixteenth century.[10] Samuel Purchas, the Jacobean editor and cleric who inherited Hakluyt's library – and his project of publishing geographical materials – made liberal use of Vitoria and Acosta's writings in arguments about the nature of indigenous Americans and the consequent legitimacy of seizing their land; their texts are repeatedly referenced in the margins of his work.[11] Symptomatically, while Purchas's work engaged extensively with Acosta's account of American cultures and its consequences, Hakluyt's printed works treated Acosta's *Historia natural y moral de las Indias* (1590) purely as a witness to the geography and hydrography of Amazonia.[12] When scholars on the historical and geographical side have compared Hakluyt to his successor, David Armitage complains that it is 'as if Hakluyt had no philosophy (and hence no place in intellectual history).'[13] Recent work exploring the more

---

8 On Vitoria, see also the essay by Daniel Allemann in this volume. My overview of writing associated with the Virginia Company summarizes the discussion by Andrew Fitzmaurice, *Sovereignty, Property and Empire, 1500–2000*, Ideas in Context 107 (Cambridge: Cambridge University Press, 2014), ch. 3. Acosta's *Historia natural y moral de las Indias* (Seville, 1590) was translated into English by Edward Grimstone (London, 1604). However, Hakluyt was familiar with Acosta's work earlier, providing Sir Robert Cecil with translations from Acosta sometime in the 1590s as background for Walter Raleigh's interest in Guiana (Joyce Lorimer, ed., *Sir Walter Ralegh's Discoverie of Guiana*, Works Issued by the Hakluyt Society, 3rd Series 15 (London: Hakluyt Society, 2006), lxxxvi. Lorimer references TNA, SP/12/235, no. 43).

9 Fitzmaurice, *Sovereignty*, p. 83; *Humanism and America: An Intellectual History of English Colonization, 1500–1625* (Cambridge: Cambridge University Press, 2003), ch. 5.

10 Christopher Tomlins, however, considers that the developments in colonial discourse attributed to the early seventeenth century by Fitzmaurice are 'well in evidence a quarter-century earlier,' that is, during the 1580s (*Freedom Bound: Law, Labor, and Civic Identity in Colonizing English America, 1580–1865* (Cambridge; New York: Cambridge University Press, 2010), 132 n. 41.) Chapters 3 and 4 of *Freedom Bound* examine the thought of this earlier period. My discussion of Sir George Peckham, below, takes modest issue with some details of Tomlin's argument for continuity.

11 See Fitzmaurice, *Sovereignty*, pp. 79–82.

12 Hakluyt, *PN 1600*, 3: 698.

13 David Armitage, *Ideological Origins of the British Empire* (Cambridge: Cambridge University Press, 2000), p. 82. As David Harris Sacks observes, however, 'Hakluyt has

abstract and tacit parts of the editor's intellectual universe encourages us now to weave these lines of scholarship together, and producc a more comprehensive account of this key figure.[14]

Hakluyt was not educated in the law, or indeed familiar with its technical vocabulary.[15] But he was at least in conversation, personally or intellectually, with the developing discourse about natural law and rights of possession, as well as with the common law tradition invoked in the letters patent that licensed English projects of colonization and discovery.[16] The younger Hakluyt worked closely with his older cousin of the same name, a barrister at the Middle Temple – an Inn of Court whose members were particularly engaged with 'western discoveries.'[17] At least one prominent civil jurist also figures in the younger Hakluyt's biography; at Oxford in the 1580s, where he professed geography, he was a close associate of Alberico Gentili, regius professor of civil law and a frequent advisor to the queen.[18] Gentili's *De Jure Belli* (London, 1589) considered a number of matters relevant to English interests in the New World.

---

not made it easy for us ... to discern the roots of his thought' ('Discourses of Western Planting: Richard Hakluyt and the Making of the Atlantic World,' in *The Atlantic World and Virginia, 1550–1624*, ed. Peter C. Mancall (Chapel Hill: Published for the Omohundro Institute of Early American History and Culture, Williamsburg, Virginia, by the University of North Carolina Press, 2007), p. 418).

14 See, for instance, the work of Perillo, Sacks, Armitage, Fitzmaurice, Tomlins and Macmillan cited in this essay.

15 See David Armitage, 'Introduction,' in *The Free Sea*, by Hugo Grotius (Indianapolis: Liberty Fund, 2004), xxiii.

16 For discussion of 16th-century letters patent, see MacMillan, *Sovereignty*, ch. 3.

17 On the interests of Middle Temple barristers, see Wilfrid R. Prest, *The Rise of the Barristers: A Social History of the English Bar, 1590–1640*, Oxford Studies in Social History (Oxford [Oxfordshire]: New York: Clarendon Press; Oxford University Press, 1986), p. 174. The geographical and colonial interests of Hakluyt the elder can be traced in Taylor, *Original Writings*; some documents by his hand are included in *PN*. Analysis of his thinking, as distinct from that of his younger cousin, is provided by Tomlins, *Freedom Bound*.

18 On Gentili, see also the essay by Francesca Iurlaro in this volume. In a letter to their mutual friend Jean Hotman, Hakluyt referred to Gentili in familiar terms (François Hotman and Jean Hotman, *Francisci et Joannis Hotomanorum Patris et Filii, et Clarorum Virorum Ad Eos Epistolae* (Amsterdam, 1700), p. 292). The letter appears to date to 1582. For a detailed consideration of Gentili's connection with Hakluyt, see Diego Pirillo, 'Balance of Power and Freedom of the Seas: Richard Hakluyt and Alberico Gentili,' in *Richard Hakluyt and Travel Writing in Early Modern Europe*, ed. Daniel Carey and Claire Jowitt, Hakluyt Society, Extra Series 47 (Farnham, Surrey, England; Burlington, VT: Ashgate, 2012), pp. 177–86. For Gentili's role as advisor, see MacMillan, *Sovereignty*, pp. 28, 45. For an examination of his thinking on 'vacant places,' see Tomlins, *Freedom Bound*, chaps. 3–4 passim.

After publishing the second edition of *PN*, Hakluyt would also produce an early translation into English of Hugo Grotius' *Mare Liberum* (Amsterdam, 1608), a key text at the origins of modern international law. The translation of *Mare Liberum* was never published, remaining in manuscript until David Armitage's modern edition; basic questions about its motivation and reception remain unanswered, and the larger context of Hakluyt's career will provide only a few points of orientation. Peter Mancall points out that *Mare Liberum* was an exception to Hakluyt's general preference for history over theoretical reflection.

> Unlike ... any of the other travel accounts that Hakluyt had typically spent his time translating or cajoling others to translate, Grotius's book did not provide new information about shipping routes or commodities to be found in exotic locations. Instead, the jurist intended to lay out a justification for freedom of commerce on the high seas.[19]

Mare Liberum also stands out as a translation *by* the editor, who facilitated the appearance in print of many translated works on geography, but infrequently did the work of translating himself.[20] We can suppose that Hakluyt's translation was prepared as a work of private counsel, perhaps for the East India Company for whom he consulted periodically from 1601 on. Yet Hakluyt's own view of Grotius' propositions can't be assumed with any certainty; all we can say is that either Hakluyt or his employers thought them important.[21] In the same way, though Hakluyt's letters referred to Gentili as 'Gentilis noster,' the civil lawyer's important work is never referenced explicitly by him in print or otherwise.

Hakluyt's clearest references to natural law and the conditions before, and between nations, like the later translation of Grotius, appeared in manuscript

19 Mancall, *Hakluyt's Promise*, p. 275.

20 See 'Books by, or associated with, Richard Hakluyt, 1580–1625,' in Payne, *Richard Hakluyt: A Guide to His Books*, pp. 83–115. The list given by Payne updates the still useful bibliography in Quinn, *The Hakluyt Handbook*.

21 On Grotius, see also the essay by Emile Simpson in this volume. Hakluyt's employment by the East India Company in the same years provides one plausible occasion, since Grotius's specific concern with rights to trade with the East Indies were as pertinent to that body as to Grotius's VOC patrons. Disputes with the Dutch over fishing rights in the North Sea offer another historical context, in this case weighting English interests away from the proposition of free seas; as we will see, Hakluyt was not unsympathetic to related arguments for a 'closed' sea.

rather than in his voluminous print collections.[22] In a memorandum conjecturally dated to the 1590s and dealing with a case not dissimilar to the one that would occasion Grotius' treatise, Hakluyt responded to complaints that Spanish sovereignty and possession in the West Indies had been violated by the voyages of Sir Francis Drake (1570–96). The memorandum invokes 'the law of nature' as guarantee of a general 'right of navigation in the sea and ... right of traffique.'[23] In the printed works, however, we can see evidence both of this view and of one quite opposed to it.

In the epistle dedicatory to the first edition of his compilation, *Principall Navigations* (1589), Hakluyt tells a famous story that sketches an expansive vision of global exchange as part of God's design for the world. On a visit to the chambers of his older cousin and guardian at the Middle Temple, the young Hakluyt was shown by him on

> a universall mappe ... all the knowen Seas ... with declaration also of their speciall commodities, & particular wants, which by the benefit of traffike, & entercourse of merchants, are plentifully supplied.[24]

Hakluyt's moment of instruction echoed a tradition of understandings about the natural need for trade and for the sociability it promotes, stretching from Aristotle forward through Erasmus, Jean Bodin, and Hugo Grotius.[25] Both editions of *Principal Navigations* provide ample evidence of English mariners exercising the right to sail wherever they chose, and to trade as they wished; accounts of voyages by Drake and John Hawkins are prominent examples of that right being exercised and, indeed, forcefully asserted. A survey of Hakluyt's printed works, however, troubles any cohesive account of his thinking on freedom of trade and freedom of the seas.

---

22 As William Sherman points out, in the English context 'political, social and economic debate' largely circulated in manuscript (William Sherman, *John Dee: The Politics of Reading and Writing in the English Renaissance*, Massachusetts Studies in Early Modern Culture (Amherst: University of Massachusetts Press, 1995), p. 116.)

23 'Notes ascribed to Richard Hakluyt, 1598,' in Taylor, *Original Writings*, 2: 424. Hakluyt's brief memorandum, whose language and concerns seem to echo more systematic exponents of political and legal theory like Grotius and Gentili, has been cited prominently by scholars in the tradition of political theory and legal history. See Armitage, *Ideological Origins*, pp. 107–8; Richard Tuck, *The Rights of War and Peace: Political Thought and the International Order from Grotius to Kant* (Oxford: Oxford University Press, 2001), p. 113.

24 Hakluyt, 'Epistle Dedicatorie,' *PN* 1589.

25 This tradition of a natural basis for communication and trade is traced in Sacks, 'Blessings of Exchange,' pp. 76–83.

The second edition of *Principal Navigations*, in particular, is clearly marked by the intellectual agenda of John Dee (1527–1609), the mathematician and geographical consultant who was, before John Selden, the most prominent English advocate of a closed sea and of English dominion over its maritime surroundings.[26] Dee was at the heart of planning and training for English enterprises through the early 1580s, and appears to have supplied a number of antiquarian and personal documents to Hakluyt's compilation. The second edition of *PN* includes numerous older documents originally identified in Dee's work as informing on the nature and extent of the Queen's title to northern lands and seas: the voyages of Madoc, Edgar, Nicholas of Lynn, King Arthur, and Ohthere all appear to come directly or indirectly from Dee's library.[27]

One example of Hakluyt's role in amplifying Dee's thinking can be found in a document he titled 'The navigation of King Edgar,' whose source was Dee's limited-circulation *Generall and rare memorials* (1577); *Memorials* was written to provide context and support for contemporaneous projects of northern exploration by Gilbert and Sir Martin Frobisher.[28] Hakluyt excerpted a panegyric in praise of King Edgar (r. 959–74), who embodied 'the selfe same Idaea' of naval power recommended to the Queen by Dee 'for the godly prosperitiee of this British Empire.'[29] Drawing on a variety of medieval sources, Dee described a monarch whose 'prosperous pastime' was the annual circumnavigation of the island of Britain with a numerous and powerful navy, a spectacular enactment of dominion that

26 See Sherman, *John Dee*, pp. 194–199.

27 For Dee's legal advice on English colonizing projects, see Ken MacMillan, ed., *John Dee: The Limits of the British Empire*, 1st edition (Westport, Conn: Praeger, 2004), pp. 13–19. For his familiarity with civil and common law, including Roman law, see MacMillan, *Sovereignty*, pp. 57–58. For related documents in *PN*, see Quinn and Quinn, 'Contents and Sources.' For Dee's books and how he used them, see R. Julian Roberts and Andrew G. Watson, ed., *John Dee's Library Catalogue* (London: Bibliographical Society, 1990); Sherman, *John Dee*.

28 Frobisher's three voyages in 1576–78 are thoroughly documented in both editions of *PN*. Gilbert's abortive voyage of 1578 is documented in David B. Quinn, *Voyages and Colonising Enterprises of Sir Humphrey Gilbert*, 2 vols., Works Issued by the Hakluyt Society, 2nd ser., nos. 83–84 (London: Hakluyt Society, 1940). Dee's *Memorials* had a press-run of only 100 copies; Hakluyt's familiarity with a text that can't have circulated widely adds another piece of evidence about, at least, the shared interests, relationships, and intellectual alignment of the two men. On Dee's connection with these projects, see MacMillan, *Limits*, pp. 10–14, 18–20, 25–26; Sherman, *John Dee*, pp. 164–65, 173–75. Gilbert's visit to Dee's house at Mortlake on November 6, 1577 is noted in Dee's diary. Hakluyt also printed several letters to and from Dee on assorted topics (Quinn and Quinn, 'Contents and Sources.')

29 Dee, 'The Navigation of King Edgar,' p. 7.

> made evident to the whole world, that as he wisely knew the ancient bounds and limits of this British Empirc, so that he could and would royally, justly, and triumphantly enjoy the same, spite of the devil, and maugre the force of any forreine potentate.[30]

Edgar exercised rights and powers that Dee urged the Queen and her advisors 'discreetly and valiantly [to] recover and enjoy.'[31] In particular, he wrote in a marginal comment, 'Note the Queen's Majesties royalty over the British Ocean sea, round about the British Empire.'[32]

In the volume preface, Hakluyt called attention to an additional source concerning the 'victorious Saxon prince king Edgar' and his 'huge fleet': 'the libel of English policie.'[33] *The Libell of English policie* was an anonymous fifteenth-century verse treatise advocating for an aggressive commercial and naval policy.[34] *Libell* recalled Edgar and his navy approvingly in the context of an argument that England should maintain control over both sides of the Channel, control the movement of goods to and from Flanders, and – at need – restrict supply of its own export goods. *Libell*'s policy recommendations sought to constrain rather than expand trade. Like Dee, the poem imagines the sea around England as ideally not a space of passage but a wall: 'As though England were likened to a citie,/ and the wall environ were the see.'[35] While the heterogeneous nature

30 Dee, pp. 7–8.

31 Dee, p. 7, 6.

32 Dee, 9. The gloss is Dee's rather than Hakluyt's. For the historical foundations of the legend as it was later elaborated, see N.A.M. Rodger, *Safeguard of the Seas: A Naval History of Britain 660–1649* (New York and London: Norton, 1998), p. 20. The celebration of Edgar's sea power had some basis in early sources such as the *Anglo-Saxon Chronicle*, which was known to Tudor antiquarians; but the accounts of Edgar's annual circumnavigation, as of a navy numbering some 3600–4800 sail, are what Rodger characterizes as 'late traditions,' and it is on these later sources (used selectively) that Dee relies.

33 Hakluyt, 'To the Reader' (*PN* 1600, Vol. 1), **1v.

34 Carol Meale describes two versions or editions of the poem, one composed 'sometime between the autumn of 1436 and the early part of 1438,' in response to the threats posed by the Franco-Burgundian alliance of 1435, and the second 'between 9 December 1437 and 6 June 1441' (Carol Meale, ' "The Libelle of Englyshe Polycye" and Mercantile Literary Culture in Late-Medieval London,' in *London and Europe in the Later Middle Ages*, ed. Julia Boffey and Pamela King, Westfield Publications in Medieval Studies 9 (University of London, 1995), pp. 206–207.) For editions see Sir George Warner, *The Libelle of English Polycye: A Poem on the Use of Sea-Power 1436.* (Oxford: Clarendon Press, 1926); Anthony Paul Bale and Sebastian I. Sobecki, *Medieval English Travel: A Critical Anthology* (Oxford: Oxford University Press, 2019). Sobecki revisits the question of authorship in *Last Words: The Public Self and the Social Author in Late Medieval England* (Oxford: Oxford University Press, 2019), ch. 3.

35 'Libell,' pp. 206–207.

of the compilation usually prevents us from associating the views of any particular component document with those of Hakluyt himself, *Libell* is an exception: in his preface to the volume, Hakluyt singles out the poem's 'true and sound policy.'[36]

These two documents, both complicating or limiting Hakluyt's apparent commitment to freedom of the seas and of trade as principles, belong to a group of older materials in the first volume of the compilation; these support Hakluyt's contention that English maritime activity had a long and continuous tradition, an argument aimed against perceptions that his compatriots were late or inactive in the kinds of maritime discoveries and trades famously enacted by Spanish, Portuguese and Italian navigators.[37] But this history also had a legal valence.

In a 1584 treatise written at the instance of Elizabeth's secretary of state, Sir Francis Walsingham, and presented to the Queen, Hakluyt considered the arguments by which European powers could legitimate claims to sovereignty over American territories.[38] 'Particuler Discourse,' a work of counsel associated with Sir Walter Raleigh's 1584 letters patent for discovery, focused on the advantages of settling North America and the dangers of not doing so; prominent in Hakluyt's exposition were concerns with the European balance of power, unsettled by Spanish possession of the Americas, and the need to provide lands and work for England's population.[39]

---

36 Hakluyt, 'To the Reader' (*PN* 1600, Vol. 1), *6v.

37 Giovanni Battista Ramusio's influential *Navigationi e Viaggi* (Venice, 1555–57), for instance, originally included no voyages attributed to the English; Sebastian Cabot's explorations on behalf of Henry VII, and the later Northeast Passage voyage of Stephen Borough (1557), were added only in 1583 (see George Bruner Parks, *The Contents and Sources of Ramusio's Navigationi* (New York: New York Public Library, 1955), p. 29.) Hakluyt made the 'argument' of *PN* explicit in the dedication to the first edition of 1589 (Hakluyt, 'Epistle Dedicatorie.')

38 For a survey of evidence about the sole extant manuscript, see Richard Hakluyt, *A Particuler Discourse Concerninge the Greate Necessitie and Manifolde Commodyties That Are like to Growe to This Realme of Englande by the Westerne Discoueries Lately Attempted, Written in the Yere 1584*, ed. David B. Quinn and Alison M. Quinn, Works Issued by the Hakluyt Society, Extra Series 45 (London: Hakluyt Society, 1993), pp. 204–209. 'Particuler Discourse,' also known as 'Discourse of Western Planting,' will be cited from the Quinns' edition as 'PD.'

39 Armitage suggests that 'PD' should be read alongside Hakluyt's digest of Aristotle's *Politics*, presented to the Queen in the same year, thus framing 'English overseas activity in the context of classical civil philosophy'(Armitage, *Ideological Origins*, pp. 72–76.) A recent study by Payne views such a connection between these two works as unlikely, however; see Payne, 'Hakluyt, Aristotle, and Oxford,' in Anthony Payne, ed., *Hakluyt & Oxford: Essays and Exhibitions Marking the Quartercentenary of the Death of Richard Hakluyt in 1616* (London: Hakluyt Society, 2017), pp. 10–13. The connections between 'PD' and the *Politics* are implicit from context rather than articulated at the surface of the

The *general* question of whether and how the English could lawfully take land for settlement in North America was not a prominent focus of 'Particular Discourse,' but it was also not absent. The issue of rights appears in the form of an argument about the respective 'title' of the Spanish and English crowns, confuting 'the unlawful title of the … Spaniards to all the West Indies' and maintaining

> the justness of her Majesty title and of her noble progenitors if not to all yet at least to that part of America which is from Florida beyond the circle Arctic.[40]

Hakluyt's argument for Elizabeth's title took a principally historical form, seeking to establish that England had prior claim to have discovered lands in the northern Americas. He argued that the Welsh Prince Madoc 'discovered and planted large Countries … south westward of Ireland' in the 12th century, as recorded in 'auncient and authenticall Chronicles'; that Christopher Columbus had intended to offer his discovery to Henry VII, who would have accepted it but for a series of accidents; and finally that while Columbus had discovered the islands of Hispaniola and Cuba, much of 'the continent as of the Islands' had been discovered for England in 1496 by Sebastian Cabot (c. 1481/2–1557), predating Columbus's first sight of the mainland in 1498. Hakluyt cites 'Fabian in his auncient chronicle' to show that Cabot 'did more than see the contrie': he

---

text; while 'PD' has been made available in a number of modern editions, the absence of a print edition of Hakluyt's digest have further obscured the connections put forward by Armitage. Only Hakluyt's dedication is printed in Taylor, *Original Writings*. It is not discussed in Quinn, *The Hakluyt Handbook*, or included in Quinn's documentary collection, *New American World: A Documentary History of North America to 1612*, 5 vols. (New York: Arno Press and Hector Bye, 1979). The two extant mss. of Hakluyt's digest are discussed in Lawrence V. Ryan, 'Richard Hakluyt's Voyage into Aristotle,' *Sixteenth Century Journal* 12, no. 3 (1981), pp. 73–84.

40 Hakluyt, *Particuler Discourse*, p. 88. The chapter of 'PD' that follows this discussion of the Queen's title attacks the Bull of Donation as a basis for Spanish dominion over the Americas; but it is actually in an earlier chapter that Hakluyt makes what could have been the most radical argument against Spanish title: citing a series of atrocities recorded by Las Casas, Hakluyt charges Spanish colonizers with having returned lands under their dominion to a less cultured and less civil conditions. "Our Spaniardes by their cruelties and cursed doings have dispeopled, and made desolate more then tenne Realmes greater then all Spaine … which Realmes as yet … remaine in a wildernes and utter desolation, having bene before time as well peopled as was possible (*PD* 55, ll. 1295–1301.)" However, Hakluyt doesn't make the argument that this conduct forfeits rights acquired by improving land, or that it violates the law of nature; only that indigenous Americans will be ready to ally with anyone who helps them throw off Spanish dominion.

had landed in various places to take possession of the country under his patent from the crown, and brought home three American captives.[41]

To a modern eye, Hakluyt was not able to ground his historical case on impressive documentary foundations. In *Particuler Discourse,* he relied on an anecdote recounted by the Italian editor Giovanni Battista Ramusio, one that Quinn notes was inconsistent with other information about Cabot in Ramusio's collection.[42] No evidence concerning the voyages was brought to bear from English archives or testimony, though Sebastian Cabot had died only in 1554, and would have been personally known to a number of Hakluyt's connections. The editor's information was also rife with factual errors (for some, Cabot's own claims may have been responsible). Sebastian's father John Cabot, not Sebastian himself, led the voyage of 1497 and another in 1498; Sebastian's voyage to the Arctic as captain probably took place 10 years later. On the evidence of maps, contemporaries of the Cabots knew of these or other early English voyages to the Americas, and viewed them as significant. Yet there is no clear indication of where either Cabot sailed or landed, and no documentary record of any act of possession.[43] Neither Sir Humphrey Gilbert's 1578 letters patent nor the account of his formal act of possession at St. John's, Newfoundland in 1583 make reference to a prior English discovery in the region.[44] Nonetheless, the intention is clearly to make the case – resembling one made at more length by Dee in the 1570s – that England had a claim to sovereignty in the North Atlantic based on a tradition of previous discoveries, and in a region where Spain could not claim either contact or knowledge.

Hakluyt's printed works echoed this thinking in a different mode, one characterized less by explicit statement than by the imprint of implicit argument on

41 Hakluyt, *Particuler Discourse*, pp. 91–92. Quinn's notes provide valuable background on the sourcing of Hakluyt's information in a passage from vol. 1 of Ramusio, *Navigationi et viaggi* (Venice, 1550). The chronicle history cited by Hakluyt was actually the 'Great Chronicle of London'; the relevant passage is printed by Quinn, *New American World,* 1: 102.

42 See his note to Hakluyt, *Particuler Discourse*, p. 179.

43 See, for instance, the world map of Juan de la Cosa (1500), at the Museo Naval, Madrid. On the confusion between Sebastian and John Cabot, see Peter Pope, *The Many Landfalls of John Cabot* (Toronto: University of Toronto Press, 1997). For a summary of recent research, see Evan T. Jones and Margaret M. Condon, *Cabot and Bristol's Age of Discovery* (Bristol: University of Bristol, 2016).

44 On Gilbert's act of possession, see Hayes, 'Report of the Voyage,' 3: 150–51. On the English tendency to 'forget' Newfoundland, at least officially, see Mary C. Fuller, *Remembering the Early Modern Voyage: English Narratives in the Age of European Expansion* (New York: Palgrave Macmillan, 2008), ch. 3.

the selection of materials. All three print compilations presented the elements of the claim made in *PD*, that the Cabot discoveries supported Elizabeth's title to North America. In *Divers Voyages* (1582), Henry VII's letters patent to the Cabots appeared both in Latin and English as evidence that lands in North America 'of equity and right appertain unto us.'[45] Following the letters, Hakluyt added an excerpt from Ramusio's *Navigationi e Viaggi*, again actually concerning Sebastian's voyage of northern exploration in 1508 rather than the voyage led by Sebastian's father, John Cabot, in 1497. The second edition of *PN* in 1600 provided a similar (and equally inconsistent) set of sources; the letters patent and license to travel granted to the Cabots by Henry VII were fleshed out with excerpts from Peter Martyr and Ramusio, improved only with a legend from Cabot's own world map.

Like Geoffrey of Monmouth's account of Arthur conquering the North Pole, or the vague account of a medieval discovery of America by Madoc – both prominent in *Principal Navigations* – the Cabot documents seem problematic as history; yet they formed part of an intellectually coherent effort to assert English claims to sovereignty over a region that could not convincingly be claimed by Spain either under the papal bull granting rights to lands undiscovered by Christian princes, or by prior knowledge and occupation. As a matter of national honor, Hakluyt sought to graft the exploration projects of his contemporaries onto an existing history, so that (for instance) 'no man should imagine that our forren trades of merchandise ... have not bene of any long continuance.'[46] His older materials also constituted a history of prior discovery that could be translated into actual possession if appropriate actions were taken to establish English presence in the region.[47]

The first attempts to solidify the potential of this presumed sovereignty over the northern Americas came late in the 1570s, and were extensively documented in both editions of *PN*.[48] In 1578, Sir Humphrey Gilbert (1537–83)

---

45 Richard Hakluyt, *Divers Voyages* (London, 1582), ¶r.

46 Hakluyt, 'To the Reader" (PN 1600),' 1: *5v.

47 MacMillan outlines the kinds of actions associated with actual possession visible in English colonizing projects from the late sixteenth century onwards. These included, in addition to settlement and occasional symbolic acts (like the ceremony undertaken by Gilbert at St. Johns, Newfoundland in 1583), fortification, mapping, and formal recognition by other states (*Sovereignty*, ch. 4–6; for Gilbert, see Hayes, 'A report of the voyage,' 3: 151.)

48 I focus principally on the projects associated with Humphrey Gilbert, since earlier voyages by Martin Frobisher were largely focused on the search for a passage (and subsequently on mining), with settlement as a late afterthought.

successfully petitioned the crown to license voyages of discovery aimed at planting a settlement in North America.[49] Gilbert's patent entitled the recipient to

> to discover, finde, search out, and view such remote, heathen and barbarous lands, countreys and territories not actually possessed of any Christian prince or people, as to him, his heires & assigne, … shall seeme good: and the same to have, hold, occupie and enjoy to him, his heires and assignes for ever, with all commodities, jurisdictions and royalties both by sea and land: and the sayd sir Humfrey and all such as from time to time by licence of us, our heires and successours, shall goe and travell thither, to inhabite or remaine there, to build and fortifie at the discretion of the sayde sir Humfrey, and of his heires and assignes.[50]

(As Tomlins points out, the letters acknowledge only Christian dominion over land; indigenous dominion is not considered).[51] Gilbert set out a voyage in the same year, one not documented by Hakluyt, which turned back without crossing the Atlantic. The project he eventually undertook in 1583, however, was extensively documented in *PN*.[52]

Although Gilbert had serious intellectual interests, his own writing did not engage with theoretical questions about the rights he was granted by the Queen.[53] His *Discourse of a discoverie* (London, 1578), drafted in the years when he was contemplating a discovery project, engaged with classical sources purely for questions of hydrography: what evidence supported the existence of a passage to Asia north of the American mainland, and might

---

49 Hakluyt printed the letters patent given to Gilbert, his half-brother Sir Walter Raleigh (1584), and brother Adrian Gilbert (1585), the three recipients of letters patent for discovery and settlement (as distinct from trade privileges and charters) granted in the sixteenth century by the English crown. (Other important voyages – for instance, the Northwest Passage voyages of the 1570s undertaken by Martin Frobisher – don't appear to have fallen under the same legal regime; the late patent for settlement Frobisher apparently received for his third voyage does not appear in *PN*).

50 'Letters Patents … to Sir Humfrey Gilbert.' The original patent is enrolled in The National Archives (TNA): PRO C 66/1178 Chancery and Supreme Court of Judicature: Patent Rolls, 21 Eliz. I, Part 4, mm. 8–9.

51 Tomlins, *Freedom Bound*, p. 21.

52 Ten items under Hakluyt's heading, 'Voyages made to Newfoundland …' relate to Gilbert's project (*PN* 1600, vol. 3). Additional documents have been printed by Quinn, *Voyages and Colonizing Enterprises*, and in *New American World* vol. 3.

53 Gilbert's proposal for a third university can be found in Humphrey Gilbert, *Queene Elizabethes Achademy*, ed. F. J. Furnivall, Extra 8 (Early English Text Society, 1869).

it be feasible for navigators?[54] Yet among Gilbert's grantees, one appears to have reflected deeply on the legal basis for taking lands in North America, the rights and nature of Amerindians, and the natural basis for trade with distant peoples.

The name of Sir George Peckham (?-1608) was on Gilbert's original petition for rights of discovery in 1574; he invested in Gilbert's exploratory voyage of 1583, aimed at locating possible sites for a settlement.[55] Peckham hoped to found a refuge for English Catholics somewhere in North America, and purchased from Gilbert rights to several million acres of land.[56] On hearing of the proposed colony, the Spanish ambassador had vigorously dissuaded English Catholics from engaging in such an enterprise because 'these lands belonged to [Philip II].'[57] A Catholic himself, Peckham had a particular reason to reflect on the legal basis for taking American land as part of 'her Majesties Dominion.' He appears to have consulted both Hakluyt and John Dee on the legality of a northern colony as well as its prospects.[58] Peckham's apology for settlement under the Gilbert patent, *True reporte, of the late discoveries* (London, 1583) was reprinted by Hakluyt alongside Gilbert's 'Discourse' and several first-hand accounts of the 1583 voyage (on which Peckham also drew). His title, however, belies the content of a text far more interested in history and theory than in observation or narrative.[59]

Peckham followed Hakluyt in offering a historical account of the Queen's title to North America, founded again on Sebastian Cabot's discovery; this argument dealt with competing claims by other European nations. But he placed questions about the *general* lawfulness of English actions first, and in greater prominence. Following a brief account of Gilbert's voyage, Peckham turned to this topic immediately:

---

54 Drafted circa 1566, the text was separately printed in 1578, and appeared in both editions of *Principal Navigations* as 'A Discourse … to Prove a Passage by the Northwest.'

55 James McDermott, 'Peckham, Sir George (d. 1608), Colonial Adventurer,' Oxford Dictionary of National Biography, https://doi.org/10.1093/ref:odnb/21743, accessed on 29 May 2019; Quinn, *Voyages and Colonising Enterprises*, 1: 29 n.1.

56 See Quinn, *New American World*, 3: pp. 215–26, 236–39.

57 Don Bernardino de Mendoza to Philip II, tr. Quinn, *Voyages and Colonising Enterprises*, 2: 279.

58 Sir Francis Walsingham wrote to Hakluyt that he had learned from Peckham of the 'great light' Hakluyt had provided regarding Western discoveries (*PN 1600*, 3: 181.) Peckham's consultation with Dee is recorded in Dee's diary for July 3, 1583. These documents also appear in Quinn, *Voyages and Colonising Enterprises*, 2: 280, 313, 346.

59 All citations are to the text printed in *PN*.

> for that the lawfulnesse to plant in those Countreyes in some mens judgements seemeth very doubtfull, I will beginne the proofe of the lawfulnesse of trade, traffique, and planting.[60]

Rights to trade and settle in America rested on the 'mutual societie and fellowship betweene man and man' prescribed 'by the Lawe of Nations.'[61]

> … for traffique, I say that the Christians may lawfully travell into those Countries and abide there: whom the Savages *may not* justly impugne and forbidde in respect of the mutuall societie and fellowshippe betweene man and man prescribed by the Law of Nations (italics mine).
>
> For from the first beginning of the creation of the world, and from the renewing of the same after Noes flood, all men have agreed, that … the Sea with his Havens should be common: … And that strangers should not bee driven away from the place or Countrey whereunto they doe come:
>
> If it were so then, I demaund in what age, and by what Law is the same forbidden or denied since …[62]

Peckham expected that, once present on the ground (as they were thus licensed to be), English settlers could confidently expect to be given title to land by the 'franke consents' of indigenous Americans. Such consent would be motivated by gentle and generous treatment and by help in 'continuall warres' with their neighbors, 'especially the Cannibals,' but would also reflect

> the great abundance that they have of Land, and how small account they make thereof, taking no other fruites thereby then such as the ground of it selfe doeth naturally yeelde.[63]

These ideas of consent and mutual benefit coexisted in Peckham's text with a readiness to use force, justified as enforcement of the natural rights of navigation, fellowship and trade that underwrote English presence.[64]

60 Peckham, 'True Reporte,' 3: 168.

61 For specifically English views on such rights, see Sacks, 'Blessings of Exchange.'

62 Peckham, 'True Reporte,' 3: 168.

63 Peckham, 3: 169.

64 Peckham writes: "But if after these good and fayre meanes used, the Savages neverthelesse will not bee herewithall satisfied, [margin: The seconde kinde of planting.] but barbarously will goe about to practise violence eyther in repelling the Christians from their Ports & safelandings, or in withstanding them afterwards to enjoy the rights for which both painfully and lawfully they have adventured themselves thither: Then in such a case

Peckham's imagined future of coexistence and exchange led into a second idea, hinted at by his characterization of indigenous societies as making only 'small account' of lands they did not exploit or transform: that 'God did create land, to the end that it should by culture and husbandry yeeld things necessary for mans life.'[65] Peckham anticipated that as the English would benefit from the generosity of indigenous Americans in granting use of their lands, so they would also confer benefit by teaching their neighbors the principles of use and 'improvement,' both agricultural and social, that formed part of the divine plan.

> And admit that they had (as they have not) the knowledge to put their land to some use: yet being brought from brutish ignorance to civilitie and knowledge, and made then to understand how the tenth part of their Land may be so manured and employed, as it may yeeld more commodities to the necessary use of mans life, then the whole now doeth: ... over and beside the knowledge how to till and dresse their grounds, they shal be reduced from unseemely customes to honest maners, from disordered riotous routs and companyes to a well governed common wealth, and withall, shalbe taught mechanicall occupations, arts, and liberall sciences.[66]

Such ideas figured prominently in the thinking of Spanish apologists for conquest, where they sometimes carried stronger implications: the perceived failure of indigenous Americans to cultivate land or create a 'well governed common wealth' were breaches of natural law that could constitute a rationale for dispossession and conquest, or indeed call into question the status of such people as fully human.[67] (Exploitation of nature as resource was thus not only

I holde it no breach of equitie for the Christians to defend themselves, to pursue revenge with force, and to doe whatsoever is necessarie for the atteining of their safetie (p. 170.)" Tomlins suggests that both Gentili and Grotius believed the natural rights of trade and fellowship could legitimately be defended by 'just war,' since denying them was 'against nature' (Tomlins, *Freedom Bound*, p. 24.) Related documents used 'conquest' to describe Peckham's project, and his text was unusually bullish on the honor and glory of Spanish conquests in the New World as something to emulate."

65 On the links between improving and possessing lands, see Fitzmaurice, *Humanism*, ch. 5, 'Natural law: *res nullius*, trade and friendship' and Patricia Seed, *Ceremonies of Possession in Europe's Conquest of the New World, 1492–1640* (Cambridge: Cambridge University Press, 1995), ch. 2.

66 Peckham, 'True Reporte,' p. 177.

67 See Anthony Pagden, *The Fall of Natural Man: The American Indian and the Origins of Comparative Ethnology*, Cambridge Iberian and Latin American Studies (Cambridge: Cambridge University Press, 1986), pp. 64, 119. Nicholas Canny argues that the English

a right associated with sovereignty, a conjunction explored in Tom Spark's analysis of state-of-nature thinking and international environmental law; it was a duty incumbent on human beings).[68] Peckham's assumptions that Americans had failed to understand or act on the principles of cultivation, however, were *not* deployed as a justification of possession, but rather served to support a wishful vision in which the needs and capacities of settlers and natives would, ideally, complement each other: albeit one that was again underwritten by the willingness to enact it by force.

Within the corpus assembled by Hakluyt, Peckham's articulation of natural law principles was uniquely clear and specific – although the extensive display of learning displayed in 'True Reporte' ignored texts by jurists in favor of scripture and ecclesiastical history. As a Catholic, Peckham was unusual among the generally Protestant cohort of Elizabethan voyagers and promoters of voyages. More importantly, he had at best distant and inaccurate information about the actual inhabitants of the Americas; as both Peckham's account and its source text by Edward Hayes make clear, Gilbert's brief stay in Newfoundland did not bring his company into contact with its indigenous inhabitants. Although Peckham did consult several travellers who had been to the Americas, including a ship from St. Malo that likely sailed into the St. Lawrence, his most extensive interview with David Ingram would not have provided high quality information.[69] In general, Peckham's text conflated information derived from a spectrum of contemporary sources without a sense of regional or cultural specificity. The settlement project did not proceed, and thus his ideas of how an encounter might play out were almost entirely theoretical, untainted by experience on the ground. In the remainder of the essay, I turn to a second set of texts, in which peoples beyond Europe were observed and described by first-person authors.

– including future colonial projectors such as Gilbert – applied similar thinking to the Gaelic Irish in the 1560s and 1570s. Nicholas P. Canny, 'Ideology of English Colonization: From Ireland to America,' *William & Mary Quarterly* 30 (1973): pp. 575–98.

68 See Sparks, 'The Place of the Enviroment in State of Nature Discourses: Reassessing Nature, Property and Sovereignty in the Anthropocene,' ch. 13 of the present volume.

69 Sources cited by Peckham include Peter Martyr's *Decades* and Francisco López de Gómara's *La historia general de las Indias*, both as translated into English. Peckham may have used Richard Eden's translation of Martyr, *Decades of the newe world* (1555) and an English edition of the *Historia general, The Pleasant Historie of the Conquest of the Weast India, Now Called New Spayne*, trans. Thomas Nicholls (London, 1578). Ingram, a seaman left ashore by Sir John Hawkins, claimed to have traversed the continent from the Gulf of Mexico to Cape Breton, although Quinn finds it 'very unlikely that he did so.' Peckham was present for his examination by Sir Francis Walsingham (Quinn, *Voyages and Colonising Enterprises*, 1: 64, 2: 283 n. 5) Ingram's relation was omitted from the second edition of *PN*, presumably because Hakluyt came to doubt its reliability.

3 Absences and Artifice in the Arctic

If a litany of negatives serves as a formal signature of the state of nature, one familiar example for Anglophone readers is Shakespeare's imagination of a society that had

> no kind of traffic .../ Letters should not be known .../ Bourn, bound of land, tilth, vineyard, none;/ No use of metal, corn, or wine, or oil;/ No occupation. ... / No sovereignty ...
>
> *Tempest* 2.1.129

Gonzalo's speech paraphrases Michel de Montaigne's account of the Brazilian Tupi, one of the societies deemed by Europeans to be in a state of nature having 'no Law, Faith, nor Ruler.'[70] It also itemizes the repertory of customs, technologies and institutions whose *presence*, in the eyes of early modern European thinkers, demonstrated civility and the ability to discern and follow natural law.[71] In records produced by English observers during the first decades of sustained exploration, such absences were not associated with the temperate regions – the Chesapeake, New England, even Quebec – where Englishmen hoped to plant colonies. The images of coastal North Carolina included in Theodor de Bry's edition of Thomas Hariot's *Briefe and True Reporte* (1590) represented an indigenous society possessing key signifiers of civility: walled towns, carefully cultivated fields, religious ceremony, deference to political authority, technologies that transformed nature. Only true religion and advanced technologies such as metallurgy were lacking.

Karen Kupperman comments on the watercolors that served as De Bry's source for the image of Pomeioc that 'the depicted village would have been reassuringly familiar to the English.'[72] Such images served to suggest a practical

---

70 Montaigne, 'Of the Cannibals,' was translated by John Florio in 1603. Purchas's characterization of the Tupi in *Purchas his Pilgrimage* (London, 1613) is cited by Fitzmaurice, *Sovereignty*, p. 81.

71 For references and examples, see Pagden, *Fall of Natural Man*, pp. 73–77, 90–91.

72 Karen Ordahl Kupperman, *Indians and English: Facing off in Early America* (Ithaca, N.Y.: Cornell University Press, 2000), p. 144. Joyce Chaplin notes that the 'props' included in De Bry's engraved depictions of indigenous people argued to viewers that they were 'capable of the kind of artifice that distinguished humans from animals and made them similar to the English'; she sees the volume's positive depiction of Roanoke and its possibilities as a response to the difficulties of motivating interest subsequent to the financial disaster of Frobisher's exploring voyages in the 1570s (Joyce E. Chaplin, 'Roanoke "Counterfeited According to the Truth,"' in *A New World: England's First View of America*, ed. Kim Sloan (Chapel Hill, N.C: The University of North Carolina Press, 2007), p. 56).

FIGURE 2.1 "The Tovvne of Pomeiooc." Plate XIX, Theodor de Bry, *A briefe and true report of the new found land of Virginia* (Frankfurt, 1590)
COURTESY OF THE JOHN CARTER BROWN LIBRARY

FIGURE 2.2 "The Tovvne of Secota." Plate XX, Theodor de Bry, *A briefe and true report of the new found land of Virginia* (Frankfurt, 1590)
COURTESY OF THE JOHN CARTER BROWN LIBRARY

counterpart to Peckham's imagination of a non-violent colonialism, based on beneficial exchange and the expectation of commensurate understanding; they would later be superseded by the requirements of actual settlement and the experience of actual indigenous resistance. In the sixteenth century, however, the hope of finding (and celebrating) an alternative to the violence attributed to Spanish conquest and settlement provided a motive to 'see' indigenous societies in the target region of the mid-Atlantic as both civil and welcoming.

In the Arctic and northern Atlantic, however, no colonies were intended beyond the garrisons envisioned by Sebastian Cabot (in the East) and Martin Frobisher (in the West) as a means to support ships in transit through the sea routes to Asia that explorers hoped to find.[73] The Arctic did not offer lands the English hoped to claim, or populations they expected to have as neighbors. Here, the formal signature of signifying absences repeatedly occurred in observers' accounts of societies that were, accordingly, characterized as defective and undeveloped. In the remainder of the essay, I'll examine some case studies of materials in *PN*, describing societies from Arctic Siberia in the east to Qikiqtaaluk/Baffin Island in the west.

In the late 9th century, a Norseman named Ohthere sailed from the neighborhood of modern-day Tromsø around the North Cape of Scandinavia and into the White Sea; he told the story of his voyage to a scribe at the court of King Alfred, who attached his text to an Anglo-Saxon translation of Orosius's *Historia adversos Paganos*. Rediscovered by Tudor antiquarians, Ohthere's 'Relation' circulated from the 1550s onward in circles interested in exploration, both in manuscript – copies were owned by the Muscovy Company advisor Robert Recorde and by John Dee – and in a modernized transcription done by the Anglo-Saxon scholar Lawrence Nowell in the 1560s. (Humphrey Gilbert cited Nowell's translation of the 'Relation' in 'Discourse of a discoverie.')[74] Hakluyt finally included the 'Relation' in the second edition of his compilation, as precedent for the Northeast Passage searches that he documented in great detail and presented as an achievement of particular national glory. In this context, Ohthere's relation to Alfred of the route he had discovered invites comparison with the discoveries of other, later navigators performed under the aegis of the Spanish, Portuguese, and English crowns. It also provides a

73 See Cabot, 'Ordinances … 1553'; Best, 'True Discourse.'

74 'I have for the better assurance of these proofs, set down some part of a discourse, written in the Saxon tongue, and translated into English by M. Nowel servant to Master Secretary Cecil, wherein there is described a navigation, which one Octher made' (Gilbert, 'A Discourse,' 3: 13.)

clear and early instance of the depiction of the Arctic as a space of absences, and one that was evidently of interest in Hakluyt's day.

> Ohthere dwelt on the coast of modern Norway at the northernmost edge of Norse settlement, beyond which the land is all desert and not inhabited, unlesse it be very few places, here and there, where certeine Finnes dwell upon the coast, who live by hunting all the Winter, and by fishing in Summer.[75]

Curious how far the land extended and 'whether there were any habitation of men North beyond the desert,' he sailed northwards for three days, beyond where 'the whale hunters use to travel,' and continued following the coast past the North Cape until it bent east and, eventually, south into the White Sea. Finally, he came to a river.

> At the entrie of which river he stayed his course, and in conclusion turned backe againe, for … the countrey was thorowly inhabited: which was the first peopled land that he had found since his departure from his owne dwelling: whereas continually throwout all his voyage he had evermore on his steereboord, a wildernesse and desert countrey, except that in some places, he saw a few fishers, fowlers, and hunters, which were all Fynnes …[76]

Onto the route he described, Ohthere mapped a taxonomy of human activity. First, his own home, at the northern limits of his own people; then, the region used by whale hunters; then, a wilderness that is desert except for other people, Finns (Samí) who hunt and fish; then, further to the south again, land that is 'thoroughly inhabited, the first peopled land he had seen.'[77]

Although these people living on the shores of the White Sea were unknown to Ohthere, he classed their relation to the land as 'inhabiting' and 'peopling,' while the presence of the Finns to the north did not really keep the land they populated from being 'desert.' We can make some guesses about what Ohthere identified as 'inhabiting,' because the Anglo-Saxon scribe who transcribed the relation included Ohthere's answers to questions about his own way of life. He was said to be very wealthy for a Norseman; he practiced husbandry and

75 'The Voyage of Octher,' 1: 4.
76 'The Voyage of Octher,' 1: 5.
77 See László Kontler's essay in this volume on eighteenth century efforts to locate the Samí on a developmental timeline of human cultures (that is, in stadial history).

agriculture near his settled dwelling, and commanded tribute from the migratory herders and hunters who live to the north of him. Yet just as the Samí were foreign to Ohthere, Ohthere's own way of life seems to have marked him as foreign to his Anglo-Saxon auditors. Although he owned a large herd of reindeer, his holding was poor in other domesticated animals: he had 'but 20. kine, and 20. Swine, and that little which he tilled, he tilled it all with horses.' Ohthere enjoyed wealth only conditionally, in 'such riches, wherein the wealth of that countrey doth consist': the Samí paid tribute to him 'in skinnes of wilde beasts, feathers of birds, whale bones, and cables, and tacklings for shippes made of Whales or Seales skinnes.' As the Samí delivered tribute to Ohthere, so he delivered his knowledge to Alfred, lord of a land where all that was scarce or absent among the Norse and Samí existed in abundance. Along the north-south axis, gradations of resources and lifeways mapped closely to power.

In 1556, the navigator Stephen Borough attempted to extend Ohthere's journey beyond the White Sea in search of a Northeast Passage to Cathay.[78] Borough's company sailed east roughly as far as Vaygach Island, to the south of Novaya Zemla, before being turned back by ice. Borough's direct experience of indigenous Northerners was almost entirely mediated by Russian interlocutors, who told one of his companions that when they sought to land at Vaygach, the Samoeds 'will kill them and eate them.'[79] (Borough sent men on shore at Vaygach 'to see if they might speake with any of the Samoeds, but could not.')[80] Nonetheless, the English navigator attentively recorded three kinds of contact with indigenous Siberians. First, he met a young man who gave him gifts of wildfowl.[81] Then, a Russian fisherman brought him onshore to a place where he could observe 'a heap of the Samoeds idols.' Finally, the fisherman gave Borough an account of the indigenous groups living eastward along the coast. Borough's transcription of the fisherman's account echoes not only the deficiencies marked in Ohthere's relation but the formal sequences of negation associated with classic accounts of the state of nature: 'they have no houses,' 'they have no other beasts to serve them, but deer only,' 'bread and

78 Borough (1525–84) was an early navigator for the Muscovy Company who studied mathematics with John Dee; Richard Eden praised Borough's expertise and dedication to advancing English knowledge of navigation in his preface to Cortés, *The Arte of Navigation* (1561). For the importance of Borough and his brother William in the development of English expertise in navigation, see Eric Ash, *Power, Knowledge, and Expertise in Elizabethan England* (Baltimore: The Johns Hopkins University Press, 2004), pp. 113–134.

79 Johnson, 'Certaine Notes ... 1556,' 1: 284.

80 Borough, 'Navigation ... toward the River of Ob ... 1556,' 1: 281. The citations that follow are to the same passage.

81 Borough, p. 279.

corn they have none,' 'they know no letter.' Borough's response to the site he actually observed was both intense and extensive (in the context of a generally laconic journal): the images he identified as idols were 'the worst and the most unartificiall worke that ever I saw,' 'very grossly wrought,' marked with blood that suggests sacrifice, heaped up amidst other 'broken' and 'spoyled' objects of daily life. Borough understood what he saw and was told about Arctic people in terms of what they failed to have or achieve: his description centers around negation and disorder.

English contacts with indigenous people in the Russian Arctic were infrequent or unrecorded on the few subsequent voyages that attempted to penetrate further east over the next half-century. Such contacts were both more frequent and more intensive on the series of searches for a Northwest Passage that took Elizabethan mariners to Qikiqtaaluk/Baffin Island, in the 1570s, and Western Greenland in the 1580s. In both cases, contacts were prolonged over days or weeks, and voyages returned repeatedly to the same places and communities over serveral years. For at least one of these mariners, understandings about the 'Samoed' in the Asian Arctic mapped onto thinking about Inuit people in the North American Arctic. George Best wrote that

> by late conference with a friend of mine (with whom I did sometime travell in the parts of Moscovy) who hath great experience of those Samoeds and people of the Northeast, I find that in all their maner of living, those people of the Northeast, and these of the Northwest are like.[82]

(Hakluyt's marginal note emphasizes the point: 'the people ... like unto Samoeds'). As in the Siberian Arctic, English observers readily understood the lifeways of Inuit people whom they actually encountered as indicating a failure to understand how one should live. Diet was one particular focus for description and judgment; Best and his colleague Dionyse Settle observed that the Inuit ate raw meat, without the use of salt or utensils, and speculated that these dietary practices indicated a 'ravenous' disposition extending to cannibalism.[83]

Yet English writers observed other things as well: Frobisher's men, like John Davis's in Greenland, were met with offers of gifts and trade. In particular, the Inuit sought to trade for iron, suggesting a keen perception of its value as well

82 Best, 'True Discourse,' 3: 93.

83 Best, 3: 68, 94; Settle, 'The Second Voyage of M. Martin Frobisher ... Anno 1577,' 3: 38. On diet as a marker of civility, see Pagden, *Fall of Natural Man*, pp. 87–89.

as a thorough understanding of how trade between disparate peoples might supply (in Hakluyt's phrase) 'particular wants.'

> They use to traffike and exchange their commodities with some other people, of whom they have such things as their miserable Countrey, and ignorance of Art to make, denieth them to have, as barres of yron, heads of yron for their darts, needles.[84]

Observers described the *use* of metal in the Arctic, and attributed the perceived failure of Inuit people to 'have' metal – in the sense of producing it – to extrinsic causes: 'their miserable Countrey.'[85] Yet, as Joyce Chaplin remarks, trade, technology and artifice – a variety of transformations of nature – were *observed* by Frobisher's men at Qikiqtaaluk/Baffin without deeply affecting English understandings that its inhabitants were not (and perhaps could not be) truly civil: unable to reorganize categories that depended in deep ways upon environment, 'the English had no way to order the phenomena they saw.'[86]

The Arctic also had settler societies, both real and imagined. What happened when ethnicity and 'heathen' beliefs were taken out of the picture? Two final texts in Hakluyt's compilation afford a different perspective on the entangled strands of civility, artifice, and environment found in observations of northern peoples. The first is Arngrímur Jónsson's *Brevis commentarius de Islandia* (Copenhagen, 1593), printed by Hakluyt in Latin and English as *A briefe commentarie of Island*. The *Commentarie* was written by an Icelander about Iceland, with very little attention to English activities. Hakluyt included it as a corrective to the errors about Iceland promulgated in learned texts, and because it demonstrated that learning was possible even in 'that Northren climate which most men would suppose could not affourd any one so learned a Patrone for it selfe.'[87] Perhaps the case of Iceland served as reassurance that a kind of civility *could* flourish in the kind of northern lands that Hakluyt argued had been 'reserved for the English nation to possesse.'[88]

---

84 Best, 'True Discourse,' 3: 94.

85 Archaelogists have documented extensive use, manufacture, and circulation of iron artifacts across the western Arctic, both through contact with early Norse settlements but also through exploitation of meteoric iron in northwestern Greenland. See, *inter alia*, McGhee, 'Contact between Native North Americans and the Medieval Norse.'

86 Chaplin, *Subject Matter*, p. 55. A valuable discussion of Inuit trade and technology, as observed and described by Best and other Englishman, can be found at pp. 51–59.

87 Hakluyt, 'To the Reader" (PN 1600).

88 Marginal comment, Hayes, 'Report of the Voyage,' 3: 144.

Hakluyt described Arngrímur Jónsson (1568–1648) as his country's learned *patron*, in the sense of its champion; as the description suggests, Arngrímur was (in his own words) a disputant rather than a historiographer or geographer.[89] An Icelander educated in Denmark, he set out to 'withstand the unjust violence of others' against his country by correcting errors of fact and judgment commonly and repeatedly made by cosmographers on the continent – bold-face names like Sebastian Munster, Olaus Magnus, Albert Krantz, Gemma Frisius, Abraham Ortelius – as well as in more slanderous terms by a German poem reprinted in several editions at Hamburg.[90] While some errors concerned Iceland's physical environment, the parts of the text I'll focus on discuss the manners of its people. Arngrímur sought to refute claims that practices adapted to Iceland's climate and environment indicated the failure of its people to develop a society capable of transforming nature in the proper way: in other words, absence of resources was readily translated by European geographers into the absence of civility.

One claim was that only the advent of English and Danish merchants had taught Icelanders the use of money and fermentation; until recently, they had lived in 'holy simplicitie, not seeking any more then nature doeth afforde.' Now, however,

> they have learned to brew their water with corne … Nowe they covet golde and silver like unto our men.[91]

This movement from nature to culture was only partial, however. Icelanders were said to share dwellings and food with their livestock, and to sell both young animals and their own children readily to strangers: no secure distinction separated the categories of human and animal. Continental writers also pointed to the defects of Icelanders' diet, which lacked bread, failed to use salt for preserving meat, fish, and milk, and relied on water in place of beer or wine. Rather than building in wood or stone, Icelanders were said to 'inhabite for the most part in caves,' and to build – when they did – 'with the bones of fishes, and Whales.'[92]

As David Koester observes in his astute discussion of Arngrímur's text, such empirical facts acquired the force of insult, because the

89 Jónsson, 'Briefe commentarie,' 1: 553.

90 The poem was Gories Peerse, 'Van Yslandt' (Hamburg, 1561). Ortelius is alluded to circuitously as 'a certaine Cosmographer in his Map of Island' (Jónsson, 1: 567.)

91 Jónsson, 1: 580.

92 Jónsson, 1: 578, 581, 584, 577.

ethnographic categories of diet, housing, and so on invoked by travel writers and cosmographers

> had European standards that, unmarked or praiseworthy, expressed Christianity and/or civilization: houses were expected to be built and made of sturdy, durable materials; food included bread, salt, and meat; sexual relations were ordered as monogamous marriage. For each category there were dishonorable variants that established the low status of the people described: houses that were caves or tents; food that was breadless, saltless, and meatless, or the other extreme, that included human flesh.[93]

Yet Arngrímur insisted that the absence of cultural markers like bread, wine, salt, or wooden buildings was not an absence of culture itself. Adapting to the conditions of their environment with ingenuity given by God, Icelanders had found other ways of nourishment and dwelling that supported both life and virtue – not out of inclination or ignorance of other possibilities, but because the practices of civility invoked by continental writers – brewing beer, using money, building wooden houses and churches – relied on resources that were present in Iceland only when imported from outside.

Arngrímur nonetheless complained. His prefatory address to Christian IV framed Iceland's poverty in particular resources as a petition, remarking that 'many ... things ... are wanting in our country': grain for bread, wood for building.[94] Shortfalls in practically and symbolically valuable commodities could be supplied by the crown, given the will to remedy intrinsic conditions of scarcity and absence. In a self-denigrating flourish, he promised that the prediction that Iceland's climate and culture would produce 'gross and barren' wits *could* be proved wrong if 'envious poverty' did not hold him back.[95]

The final text was a fantasy about the Arctic that found wide credence and circulation among continental as well as English geographers. The relation of the Zeno brothers, an apocryphal account of 15th century Arctic voyages by three Venetian brothers, figured prominently in Dee's geographical work, and provided a set of placenames – Estotiland, Drogio, Frisland – that persisted on maps of the Arctic long after the narrative's first publication in 1558, by a

93 Koester, 'Power of Insult,' p. 21.
94 Jónsson, 'Briefe commentarie,' 1: 569, 551.
95 Jónsson, 1: 588.

MAP 2.1 Abraham Ortelius, *Theatrum Orbis Terrarum*, Call #: STC 18855, plate 102

descendant and namesake of the eldest brother.[96] It is one of the few documents to appear in all three of Hakluyt's compilations. Generations of scholars have wrestled over whether the Zeno narrative – of an Arctic that juxtaposed civilization on a European model with familiar tropes of cannibalism and savagery – can be linked to actual topographies or travels. It has been most recently considered as a pastiche, an attractive approach that helps account for the traces of fact among its conspicuous fabrications.

96 Nicolò Zeno, *De i commentarii del viaggio in Persia di M. Caterino Zeno* (Venice, 1558); also printed in G. B. Ramusio, *Navigationi et viaggi*, 2 (1574), ff. 254v–37v and, in translation, by Hakluyt in *Divers voyages* (1582), *Principall Navigations* (1589), and *Principal Navigations* (1600). Citations are to the version in *PN* 1600. See Elizabeth Horodowich, *Venetian Discovery of America: Geographic Imagination in the Age of Encounters* (Cambridge: Cambridge University Press, 2018).

The non-existent monastery of St. Thomas, which can be observed on maps of Greenland in the atlases of Ortelius and Mercator, provides a representative example. Described as reliant on the kind of geothermal energy actually available in Iceland, the foundation is described as a Utopian outpost of abundance, agriculture, and artifice in the frozen North.

As the story goes, Nicolo Zeno sailed north until he arrived in 'Engroneland.' There he found a Dominican monastery and church dedicated to St. Thomas, next to a hot spring whose water the friars used to heat their buildings, 'dresse their meat,' bake bread, and maintain 'smal gardens' with 'flowers and fruites and herbes of sundry sorts.' The hot springs kept open a harbor, attracting 'infinite multitudes' of fish and sea fowl exploited by the monastery. But the availability of energy was channeled towards more than abundant and complex forms of diet and of household production; it provided the friars with a kind of political power, because

> the rude and savage people of those partes seeing these supernaturall effects, doe take those Fryers for Gods.

The bounty of the natural environment enabled a complex society, drawing in

> a great number of people round about, which they kepe in continuall worke, both in building and taking of foules and fish, and in a thousand other necessarie affaires and busines.

The existence of this service class freed the Friars to trim their gardens and plan 'faire and beautifull buildings, but especially handsome and commodious':

> neyther are they destitute of ingenious and paineful artificers for the purpose; for they give very large payment, and to them that bring them fruits and seedes they are very bountifull, and give they care not what.[97]

St. Thomas's monastery does more than defy the expectations of lack and disorder in the Arctic; it fulfils early modern criteria for an ideally developed society, not only Christian and Latinate but exhibiting artisanal and social complexity, elaborate buildings, and intensive cultivation. The conjunction of European presence and abundant geothermal energy was imagined as enabling the

97 Zeno, 'The Voyage of M. Nicolas Zeno,' 3: pp. 123–124. All citations are from these pages.

Arctic environment to be transformed in material ways: gardening, cooking, building.

Two markers of an actual Arctic setting nonetheless persist in this imagined scene. The first is the monastery's 'wealth' of fur and fish – no longer treated concessively, as in the 'Relation of Ohthere,' these wild goods have been trans-valued to make the monastery a hub of commerce, supporting a vigorous traffic that supplies wood, grain and cloth as well as fruits and seeds:

> ... in change of the two aforesaid commodities all the nations bordering round about them covet to trafficke with them, and so they without any travell or expences have that which they desire.

The second describes the boats that inhabitants of Engroneland use to take fish; described in great detail as examples of marvelous ingenuity, these are recognizably kayaks. (Hakluyt makes the connection in a marginal note: 'M. Frobisher brought these kinde of boats from these parts into England.')

> The fishers boates are made like unto a weavers shuttle: taking the skins of fishes, they fashion them with the bones of the same fishes, and sowing them together in many doubles they make them so sure and substanciall, that it is miraculous to see, howe in tempests they will shut themselves close within and let the sea and winde cary them they care not whether without any feare either of breaking or drowning.

In the neighborhood of heat, Christianity, and cultivation, the kayak could be perceived as 'miraculous' in its ingenuity, enabling fishermen to master their environment at its most unruly.

The discourses about rights that I've invoked in examining these sources begin from European understandings about the kinds of human activities and lifeways that 'counted' as civil and humane, and manifested both awareness of the laws of nature and the capacity to fulfil them. In the north, environment itself made the enactment of 'cultivation' in its various forms unlikely, if not materially impossible. How could one manure, till, or dress the Arctic? Smelt ore, forge iron tools? Could society be imagined or indeed recognized on such impossible grounds? Not without contestation, apparently: not only for indigenous peoples but also for settler societies in resource-poor areas. The narrative of the Zeno brothers mapped these European understandings of civility as enabled by environmentally specific conditions onto an almost entirely imagined Arctic, warmed to fruitfulness by Christian mastery of heat. In it, the 'weavers shuttle' of actual Arctic ingenuity – perceptible and even celebrated in this landscape of fiction – serves as a reminder of what first-person observers could see, and even describe, *without* seeing.

Select Bibliography

Primary sources

Bry, Theodor de, ed. *A Briefe and True Report of the New Found Land of Virginia: Of the Commodities and of the Nature and Manners of the Naturall Inhabitants*. America 1. (Frankfurt, 1590).

Hakluyt, Richard. *A Particuler Discourse Concerninge the Greate Necessitie and Manifolde Commodyties That Are like to Growe to This Realme of Englande by the Westerne Discoueries Lately Attempted, Written in the Yere 1584*. Edited by David B. Quinn and Alison M. Quinn. Works Issued by the Hakluyt Society, Extra Series 45. (London: Hakluyt Society, 1993).

Hakluyt, Richard. *Divers Voyages*. (London, 1582).

Hakluyt, Richard. *The Principall Navigations, Voiages, and Discoveries of the English Nation*. Edited by David B. Quinn and R. A. Skelton. 2 vols. Works Issued by the Hakluyt Society, Extra Series 39. (Cambridge: Published for the Hakluyt Society and the Peabody Museum of Salem at the University Press, 1965).

Hakluyt, Richard. *Principal Navigations*. 3 vols. (London, 1598–1600).

Secondary sources

Benton, Lauren A. *A Search for Sovereignty: Law and Geography in European Empires, 1400–1900*. (Cambridge: Cambridge University Press, 2010).

Chaplin, Joyce E. *Subject Matter: Technology, the Body, and Science on the Anglo-American Frontier, 1500–1676*. (Cambridge, Mass.: Harvard University Press, 2001).

Fitzmaurice, Andrew. *Sovereignty, Property and Empire, 1500–2000*. Ideas in Context; 107. (Cambridge: Cambridge University Press, 2014).

MacMillan, Ken. *Sovereignty and Possession in the English New World: The Legal Foundations of Empire, 1576–1640*. (Cambridge, New York: Cambridge University Press, 2006).

Tomlins, Christopher L. *Freedom Bound: Law, Labor, and Civic Identity in Colonizing English America, 1580–1865*. (Cambridge: Cambridge University Press, 2010).

CHAPTER 3

Do Shepherds Live in a State of Nature?

From Peculium *to Civilization*

Francesca Iurlaro

Abstract

This chapter traces an intellectual-historical narrative of the legal concept of *peculium*. Etymologically, the word *peculium* refers to 'what shepherds possess as flock', as showed by the Latin word for flock (*pecu*), which also originates the Latin word *pecunia* (money). *Peculium* is a Roman law concept, defined in the *Corpus Iuris Civilis* as 'everything that cannot be described as *dominium*', and is, thus, a prerogative of subaltern categories of society (enslaved people, shepherds, women, children).

In this chapter I will argue that *peculium* provides us with a unified legal framework to think about 'otherness in the state of nature', and to genealogically imagine how property rights can be originated. To do so, I will explore three different theorizations of the legal concept of *peculium*; Alberico Gentili's interpretation of Virgil's *Eclogues*, in which the question of whether shepherds are able to donate their *peculium* is addressed; Samuel Pufendorf's genealogical argument about the pastoral origins of society; and finally, I will look at Giambattista Vico's *La Scienza Nuova*, in which the Neapolitan philosopher reflects on the injustice of *peculium* and identifies it as the most fundamental drive behind the creation of the commonwealth, as the servants rebel against their masters to acquire full *dominium*.

Keywords

peculium – state of nature – stadial theories – *dominium* – legal subalternity – pastoralism

 | DOI:10.1163/9789004499621_005

> "Some day, son, all this will be yours!" Only, when my father made the offer, it was as if he were telling me I could have it as long as I was willing to push him off the roof to get it.
>
> LENNY BRUCE, *How to Talk Dirty and Influence People: An Autobiography* (New York: Fireside, 1992), p. 9

1 Introduction

Recent years have seen the explosion of a lively interest in pastoralism.[1] Due perhaps to an unprecedented environmental crisis, as well as to the massive consequences of centuries of fierce capitalism we are facing, we find ourselves longing for (a perhaps unattainable ideal of) a simpler, greener life. One in which human intervention in the world is not necessarily exploitative towards nature and animals, but in which man and his environment can live according to an ecological, rather than egological pattern of interaction. Unsurprisingly, ideals of pastoral life, as witnessed by the enormous success of the book *The Shepherd's Life: A Tale of the Lake District*, published in 2015 by James Rebanks, himself a sheep-farmer, seem to respond to the urgent need to find alternative ways to escape from or deal with the current challenges of the global world.

Pastoralism was often an invention of poets, as Rebanks wittingly says in his book, which is a descriptive and yet incredibly poetic account of his daily work as a shepherd. Poetic pastoralism mostly has nothing to do with the reality of the job – it often idealizes landscapes and places that are inhabited by real people who have been farming animals for generations, and dispossesses their culture while turning their environment into a perfect, idyllic shelter away from civilization.[2]

---

1 I would like to gratefully acknowledge Anne Peters and Mark Somos and all the contributors to this volume. Their feedbacks and suggestions were extremely inspiring, and so were their respective chapters. Thanks are also due to Nehal Bhuta, Paul J. du Plessis, Rián Derrig, Martti Koskenniemi, Edward Jones Corredera, Rebecca Mignot-Mahdavi, Emma Nyhan, Marie-Catherine Petersmann, Gabriella Silvestrini, Dimitri van Den Meerssche, Nico Weber, Julie Wetterslev, Tleuzhan Zhunussova, for providing valuable feedbacks to this paper.

2 James Rebanks, *The Shepherd's Life: A Tale of the Lake District* (Long Preston, North Yorkshire: Magna Large Print, 2015).

Whatever the reasons behind our unconscious fascination for pastoralism, the figure of shepherds is a *topos* of primitive and yet organized life but also, as research conducted on early modern pastoral genre has shown, a powerful allegory to convey political ideas.[3] Often, early modern debates concerning the birth of pastoral poetry as the 'first' ever invented poetic genre tie in with genealogical discourses concerning the beginning of social life. This circumstance is due to the particular ability of shepherds of being both poets and legislators of their fictional world: as the fathers of poetic invention, which was first born out of the imitation of birdsongs, as well as the first humans introducing some legal order in the world (famously, the word *nomos* means both 'pasture' and 'law').[4]

In this contribution, I will explore how narratives concerning the birth of pastoral poetry, as the first poetic genre arguably ever invented, are connected to the language of natural rights and political economy. I will do so by focusing on the Roman law concept of *peculium*. Etymologically, *peculium* refers to 'what shepherds possess as flock', as showed by the Latin word for flock (*pecu*), which also originates the Latin word *pecunia* (money). Additionally, *peculium* is also referred to, in *Corpus Iuris Civilis*, as 'everything that cannot be described as *dominium*'.[5] This second meaning of the term, while clearly indicating that *dominium* is a prerogative of free men, suggests that *peculium* is what subordinate legal categories possess by concession of a *dominus*.[6] Among

3 Katherine Little, *Transforming Work: Early Modern Pastoral and Late Medieval Poetry* (Notre Dame, IN: University of Notre Dame Press, 2013); Annabel Patterson, *Pastoral and Ideology: from Virgil to Valéry* (Oxford: Clarendon, 1987). Also, on Virgil's pastoral, see Michael J. Putnam, *Virgil's Pastoral Art: Studies in the Eclogues* (Princeton, NJ: Princeton University Press, 1970); David S. Wilson-Okamura, *Virgil in the Renaissance* (Cambridge: Cambridge University Press, 2010); Margaret Tudeau-Clayton, *Jonson, Shakespeare and Early Modern Virgil* (Cambridge: Cambridge University Press, 1998); Andrew Wallace, *Virgil's Schoolboys: The Poetics of Pedagogy in Renaissance England* (Oxford: Oxford University Press, 2011); Craig Kallendorf, *A Bibliography of the Early Printed Editions of Virgil*, 1469–1850 (New Castle: Oak Knoll Press, 2012); Craig Kallendorf, *The Protean Virgil: Material Form and the Reception of the Classics* (Oxford: Oxford University Press, 2015); I refer to these books for further bibliography concerning Virgil's reception.

4 As in Carl Schmitt's famous *The Nomos of the Earth* (New York: Telos Press, 2006). For a recent, although very esoteric, treatment of the subject, see Monica Ferrando, *Il regno errante: l'Arcadia come paradigma politico* (Vicenza: Neri Pozza, 2018).

5 Varro, *De re rustica*, 1, 17, 5; Dig. 33.8, tit. *de peculio legato*.

6 According to Mastrangelo, in the beginning of societies *peculium* referred to possession of the flock: only later on, with the commercial progress of societies, it started to indicate everything that was granted by a *paterfamilias*. The holder of *peculium*, had, however, a certain independence in managing it. See Luigi Mastrangelo, 'Il *peculium quasi castrense*. Privilegio dei palatini in età tardo antica', *Revue Internationale des Droits de l'Antiquité* 52 (2005), p. 272. See also Jean-Jacques Aubert, '*Dumtaxat de peculio*: What's in a *Peculium*, or Establishing the

these categories we find enslaved people, women, children, and, of course, shepherds. Interestingly enough, in the Italian legal system, *peculium* is, to this day, the amount of money that inmates possess when entering prison, or the remuneration they receive for prison labor (*peculio dei condannati*).[7]

In my view, the idea of *peculium* constitutes a powerful social motive behind the creation of society and property rights. In fact, it provides us with a unified legal framework to think about 'otherness in the state of nature', as a way to genealogically imagine how property rights can be originated. To this effect, this paper will explore the interrelations between *peculium* and 17th-18th century stadial theories of society, i.e. the so-called four-stages theories of civilization, composed of an age of hunters, an age of shepherds, the age of farmers and, finally, the age of commerce.[8] In other words, emphasis on *peculium* and the role of shepherds as the 'children of society' allows us to think of property as originating from a hereditary right rather than from an original act of occupation. As a matter of fact, indeed, *peculium* cannot be transferred to heirs, as it is a concession from a *dominus*: which means that either the *dominus* has to die, so that his children can acquire full *dominium*, or it has to be transformed into a proper *dominium* through social struggle and the emergence of new institutions.

To do so, I will explore three different theorizations of the legal concept of *peculium*; Alberico Gentili's interpretation of Virgil's *Eclogues*, in which the question of whether shepherds are able to donate their *peculium* is addressed; Samuel Pufendorf's genealogical argument about the pastoral origins of

---

Extent of the Principal's Liability', in Paul J. du Plessis (ed), *New Frontiers: Law and Society in the Roman World* (Edinburgh: Edinburgh University Press, 2013), pp. 192–206. I thank Paul J. du Plessis for this suggestion on the historical evolution *peculium*.

7 *Legge sull'ordinamento penitenziario*, L. 26 luglio 1975, Aggiornato al 17/02/2020, art. 25; D. P. R. 20 giugno 2000, *Regolamento Penitenziario*, art. 57.

8 On this see Norbert Elias, *The Civilizing Process: the History of Manners and State Formation and Civilization* (Oxford: Blackwell, 1997); Nathaniel Wolloch, 'The Civilizing Process, Nature and Stadial Theory', *Eighteenth Century Studies* 44:2 (2011), pp. 245–260; Pier Luigi Porta, Roberto Scazzieri and Andrew Skinner (eds), *Knowledge, Social Institutions, and the Division of Labour* (Cheltenham: Edward Elgar, 2001); Harro M. Höpfl, 'From Savage to Scotsman: Conjectural History in the Scottish Enlightenment', *Journal of British Studies* 17:2 (1978), pp. 19–40; Istvan Hont, *Jealousy of Trade: International Competition and the Nation State in Historical Perspective* (Cambridge, MA: Harvard University Press, 2010); Istvan Hont, 'The Language of Sociability and Commerce: Samuel Pufendorf and the Theoretical Foundations of the Four-Stages Theory', in Anthony Pagden (ed), *The Languages of Political Theory in Early-Modern Europe* (Cambridge: Cambridge University Press, 1981), pp. 253–276; David B. Schorr, 'Savagery, Civilization and Property', *Theoretical Inquiries in Law* 19:2 (2019), pp. 507–531.

society: after Adam's death and the gradual transformation of his children's *peculium* into property rights, shepherds play a fundamental role in guiding humanity from the state of nature to civil society. Finally, I will look at Giambattista Vico's *La Scienza Nuova*, in which the Neapolitan philosopher reflects on the injustice of *peculium* and identifies it as the most fundamental drive behind the creation of the commonwealth, as the servants rebel against their masters to acquire full *dominium*. From his perspective, the real *nomos* is not introduced by shepherds, but by agrarian law.

From this analysis, it can be argued that there is a constant strategy of conceptual negotiation between arguments about the role of shepherds in creating society and analogous ones drawn from poetic theory. In other words, where the role of shepherds as creators of society is acknowledged, so is their primacy as the first poets ever; vice versa, changes and evolutions in poetic canon and tastes (i.e. preference to other genres, such as heroic poems or Virgil's *Georgics* instead of pastoral poetry), also determine a difference in the way in which the origins of society are imagined.[9]

2 Gentili's Shepherds: The Poetic of *Peculium* in His *Lectionis variae virgilianae liber* (1603)

According to a well known *topos*, poets are the first legislators of the world. Poetry is then acknowledged as a legislative faculty – poetic *nomos* has the power to shape the world through the persuasiveness of its metrical structure.[10] This distinctively legislative capacity is acknowledged to poets because of their capability to imitate and invent poetic fiction, and by so doing, create whole worlds of meaning. But due to the semantic ambiguity of the

9 On this point, I follow recent insights from Joanna Craigwood, Christopher Warren and Timothy Hampton and their studies on the 'co-evolving', 'co-constitutive' relationship between literature on diplomacy in the early modern period. See Joanna Craigwood, 'The Place of the Literary in European Diplomacy: Origin Myths in Ambassadorial Handbooks', in Tracey A. Sowerby, Joanna Craigwood (eds), *Cultures of Diplomacy and Literary Writing in the Early Modern World* (Oxford: Oxford University Press, 2019), p. 28; C. N. Warren, *Literature and the Law of Nations, 1580–1680* (Oxford: Oxford University Press, 2015), p. 34; Timothy Hampton, *Fictions of Embassy: Literature and Diplomacy in Early Modern Europe* (Ithaca, NY: Cornell University Press, 2013).

10 In Ancient Greek musical culture, *nomoi* are also 'solo pieces (based on a specific narrative content, presumably related to the mythology of the god to whom they were addressed) that were sung to the accompaniment of either the kithara or the aulos, or were purely instrumental'. Eleonora Rocconi, 'The Music of the Laws and the Laws of Music: Nomoi in Music and Legislation', *Greek and Roman Musical Studies* 1 (2016), p. 72.

term *nomos*, shepherds are also endowed with a similar legislative capacity. Famously, Plato uses the analogy of shepherds to explain that the statesman rules over the world just like a shepherd herds his sheep; similarly, these structures of dominion are none but the reflection, from a wider perspective, of God's stewardship over the world – a concept will turn out to be particularly crucial for Christian ontology[11].

What is distinctive of pastoral genre is, however, the suggestive identification it creates between poets and shepherds. In pastoral poetry these two figures merge with interesting consequences – *why* precisely is the shepherd an inventor of poetry and society? Is there an ideal shepherd? What values are embodied in his lifestyle, and why are they relevant for the creation of human societies? The question then, to establish who are the first poets that ever existed – either chronologically, or genealogically, as Arthur Lovejoy would have claimed[12] – has important implications as far as structures and dynamics of modern political societies are concerned. This is a widely debated question already in antiquity, where alternative narratives can often be found: for example, according to Lucretius' *De Rerum Natura*, poetry was invented after the creation of society: "men lived already fenced in with strong towers, and a land split up and parceled out [...] and poets began to celebrate in verse the mighty deeds of old".[13]

Historical, pastoral poetry is a rather late invention, being the product of the Hellenistic cultural landscape. And yet one of its most recurring motives is that shepherds-poets are the first legislators of society, and inventors of poetry in toto. These questions are addressed in their legal implications by Alberico Gentili (1552–1608) in his *Lectionis Virgilianae Variae Liber ad Robertum filium*

11 In the words of Kathryn Gutzwiller, 'kingship itself exists only because human beings have learned to herd animals, the paradigm for all social organization'. See Kahtryn J. Gutzwiller, *Theocritus' Pastoral Analogies: The Formation of a Genre* (Madison, Wisconsin: University of Wisconsin Press, 1991) p. 73. On the wider resonance of the shepherd-flock analogy, see for example Bernard Aubert, *The Shepherd-Flock Motif in the Miletus Discourse (Act 20:17–38) Against its Historical Background* (New York: Peter Lang, 2009).

12 Arthur Lovejoy, *Primitivism and Related Ideas in Antiquity* (Baltimore: Johns Hopkins University Press, 1997). Lovejoy distinguishes primitivism into 'chronological' and 'cultural', but here I replaced 'cultural' with 'genealogical' because I think it better renders the general idea of ontological fixism typical of some a-historical, non-stadial reconstructions of the state of nature.

13 Lucretius, *On the nature of the universe*, v, vv. 1440–4 (Oxford, 1999). According to Craigwood, Gentili, in his *De legationibus* (1585) quotes this exact same passage to argue that poetry and diplomacy were born at the same time, as a reaction to the asperities of the state of nature described by Lucretius (Joanna, Craigwood, 'The Place of the Literary', p. 28).

(Hanau 1603, from hereafter: *LVVL*), a less known commentary to Virgil's *Eclogues*.[14] Written to his son Robert as a pedagogic commentary to Virgil's first poetic work, *LVVL* has, to date, received little scholarly attention, mostly because of its antiquarian and erudite character.[15] In spite of this, it provides us with one of the few examples of Gentili's activity as a literary criticist, as well as with some relevant information concerning the importance played by Virgilian poetry in his legal doctrine, a question of 'law and literature' that has generated a lively scholarly interest in the past few years.[16]

In his commentary, while following Julius Caesar Scaliger's and echoing Philip Sidney's accounts of poetry,[17] Gentili insists that only shepherds were in the appropriate conditions to create pastoral genre: unlike hunters or fisherman, pastoralism is the only pre-agricultural activity where singing is not detrimental to the activity itself, i.e the husbanding animals. Rather, it might even help flocks gathering together.[18] Famously, some decades before Gentili, the Neapolitan humanist Jacopo Sannazaro wrote his *Eclogae Piscatoriae*, an experimental idyllic poem where shepherds are replaced with fishermen. A choice widely contested by Scaliger and, subsequently, by Gentili, for its lack of verisimilitude: how can fishermen both sing *and* successfully fish at the same time, if fishes are famously scared of human voices[19]?

---

14 *Alberici Gentilis Lectionis Virgilanae ad Robertum filium*, apud Guilielmum Antonium, Hanau 1603. The dedicatory epistle of this book, dedicated to Alberico's father Matteo, was written by the young Robert himself at the age of 10. See Francesca Iurlaro (ed.), *Alberico Gentili: Libro di varie letture virgiliane al figlio Roberto* (Macerata: EUM, 2020).

15 According to Binns, it contains 'many glosses of a philological, etymological, grammatical, and antiquarian character, but it is principally concerned with commenting on the *Eclogues* from a legal point of view'. James W. Binns, *Intellectual Culture Elizabethan and Jacobean England* (Leeds: Francis Cairns, 1990), pp. 355–356.

16 James W. Binns, 'Diritto e Poesia nell'opera di Alberico Gentili', in *Alberico Gentili (San Ginesio 1552-Londra 1608). Atti dei convegni nel quarto centenario della morte*, Vol. II, (Milano, 2010), pp. 175–188; Maria Rosa Di Simone, 'Alberico Gentili e la controversia sul teatro nell'Inghilterra elisabettiana', in *Alberico Gentili (San Ginesio 1552-Londra 1608)*, Vol. II, pp. 377–410; Christopher Warren, 'Gentili, the Poets, and The Laws of War', in Benedict Kingsbury and Benjamin Straumann (eds), *The Roman Foundations of the Law of Nations: Alberico Gentili and the Justice of Empire* (Oxford: Oxford University Press, 2011); Christopher Warren, *Literature and the Law of Nations*, ch. 2.

17 Julius Caesar Scaliger, *Poetices libri septem ad Sylvium Filium*, Lyon 1561, I, 4; Sidney wrote an *Apology for Poetry* in 1579, but it was only published in 1595. Philip Sidney, *An Apology for Poetry (Or The Defense of Poetry)*, ed. by R. W. Malsen (Manchester: Manchester University Press, 2002).

18 *LVVL*, pp. 127–8.

19 Sannazaro published his *Eclogae Piscatoriae* in 1525. See Jacopo Sannazaro, *The Piscatory Eclogues*, ed. by W. P. Mustard (Baltimore: The John Hopkins Press, 1914); Nicholas Smith,

Additionally, it is worth mentioning that a rigid literary canon concerning the order of Virgilian poems corresponded to the *topos* of pastoral poetry as the first poetic genre ever produced. As famously stated by Marcus Honoratus Servius, one of the most influential of Virgil's commentator: 'Donatus says that Virgil, in writing his poetry, followed the natural order of things: in the beginning, there was pastoral life on the mountains, then love for agriculture. And, finally, concern for military activities' (*et dicit Donatus in scribendis carminibus naturalem ordinem secutum esse Vergilium: primo enim pastoralis fuit in montibus vita, post agriculturae amor, inde bellorum cura successit*').[20] In other words, what made Virgil's poems so accurate is that they were not only describing different aspects of human life, but also organizing them according to a chronological criterion: shepherds were the first poets (and pastoral is the first genre ever invented), precisely because, according to what Servius describes as a 'natural order of things', a society of shepherds was actually the first society that ever existed – a statement also echoed by Gentili who, in his *De iure belli libri tres* (1598), claims that the Roman empire itself was born from 'the huts of shepherds'.[21]

Secondly, another crucial characteristic that makes pastoral genre the original poetic form concerns the imitation of nature. In the *LVVL*, the capability of engaging into imitative practice is conceded precisely to shepherds: although apparently barbaric and rude in their behaviour, they are able to produce, by the simple imitation of bird-songs, both *a solo* poems as well as Amoebaean singing. The imitative nature of pastoral is further unravelled by the etymology of the word 'idyll': 'indeed, as they represented something through imitation, from the *species*, namely the image' [the Greek word εἰδύλλιον comes from εἶδος, 'image'].[22] They were, then, called with the diminutive 'idylls', 'for their modesty and brevity'.[23] Here Gentili connects the Greek etymological clarification with the Latin one provided by Festus' *De verborum significatione*: '*imago ab imitatione dicta*'.[24] The fact that the poetic 'image' derives from imitation

---

'The Genre and Critical Reception of Jacopo Sannazaro's *Eclogae Piscatoriae* (Naples 1526)', *Humanistica Lovaniensia* 50 (2001), p. 216.

20 *Ivi*. Servius' quotation is from *Servii Grammatici qui Feruntur in Vergilii Carmina Commentarii*, ed. by G. Thilo and H. Hagen, 3 vols (Hildesheim: G. Olms, 1961), III, 3–4.

21 Alberico Gentili, *De iure belli*, III, 4. See also Francesca Iurlaro, 'Pirati, barbari e pastori: Tre figure al limite dell'*humanitas* nel pensiero di Alberico Gentili (1552–1608)', *Historia et Ius*,10 (2016), paper 8.

22 *LVVL*, p. 120.

23 *Ivi*.

24 Sextus Pompeius Festus, *De verborum significatione quae supersunt cum Pauli epitome*, IX, ed. by K. G. Müller (Lepzig: Teubner, 1839).

also implies that there is a relationship of subordination between the image and the imitated object. Quite interestingly, in his *De iure belli* Gentili similarly suggests that imitation is a second nature for human beings, in the sense that from the imitation of other people's behaviours we are actually capable of changing ours.[25] This anthropological dynamism is particularly important for those human categories which are considered inferior: and Gentili vindicates for them the possibility to behave humanly, by simply imitating behaviour *secundum naturam* (according to nature).[26] Again, Lucretius' verses present a similar, and yet profoundly diverse, account. Shepherds lived a peaceful life, one that was not corrupted by greed, but imitation of songbirds did not coincide with the invention of poetry ('to imitate the liquid notes of birds with mouth and lips came long before men learnt to charm the ears by singing tuneful songs').[27] While Lucretius' historicized reading suggests a gradual learning of the art of singing, Gentili thinks of both moments as simultaneous.

These debates are not particularly innovative, as Gentili simply reproduces them from his most important source here, the already mentioned *Poetices libri septem* from Julius Caesar Scaliger. What is particularly interesting, instead, is how Gentili uses them to reflect on the legal status of shepherds. Are they endowed with *dominium*? What kind of humanity do they represent? Are they less human just because they are uncivilized? To tackle these issues, Gentili devotes a whole chapter of the *LVVL* to the discussion of the *peculium* of shepherds, by commenting on the famous Virgilian verse in which the shepherd Tityrus complains that, as long as he is being kept by Galatea, he has neither hope for freedom, nor concerns about his possessions (*nec spes libertatis erat, nec cura peculi*).[28] This verse seems to suggest that shepherds are in a state of subordination (i.e.: they do not own their flock, hence the word *peculium*) and that they do not have private property. However, Gentili warns that *peculium* not only comprised *pecora*, i.e. sheep, but also money (*pecunia*), as witnessed by Tityrus saying that although he had *peculium*, he never returned back from Rome with any money (*non umquam gravis aere domum mihi dextra redibat*).[29]

25 A. Gentili, *De iure belli*, I, 1.

26 *Ivi.*

27 V, 1379–80. Lucretius adds that wind taught these country men to play pipes 'then gradually they learnt the sweet laments the flute pours out pressed by a player's fingers, through pathless woods and glades and forests sounding, and shepherds' lonely haunts beneath the sky' (vv. 1386–9).

28 The verse is from Virgil, *Eclogues*, I, 32, in Virgil, *Eclogues. Georgics. Aeneid: Books 1–6*, trans. by H. Rushton Fairclough, rev. by G. P. Goold, Loeb Classical Library 63 (Cambridge, MA: Harvard University Press, 1916).

29 *LVVL*. p. 21 (Virgil, *Eclogues*, I, 35).

The coexistence of pastoralism and money hints at the fact that Gentili, through the eyes of Roman law categories, thinks of shepherds as part of society, rather than anticipators of it.

To this discussion of *peculium* a similar one follows on a case of *donatio mortis causa* that Gentili identifies in the second *Eclogue:* 'I have a pipe formed of seven uneven hemlock stalks, a gift Damoetas once gave me and said, as he lay a-dying: *Now it claims you as its second master'*.[30] These kinds of donations are made by a donor (*donatarius*) who, afraid of dying, decides to donate some of his belongings (in the case of shepherds, it must be some sort of *peculium*) to someone. Through his poetic verses, 'Virgil does not describe the legal instruments',[31] Gentili says. Rather, he only indicates with just few words the fact that the shepherd Damoeta is dying and, therefore, he is making use of one of the three types of *mortis causa* donation, the one in which actual transferral of possession of the object donated (the pipe) is deferred to the moment of the death of the *donatarius*. Damoetas says the pipe claims Corydon as a *second* master, meaning that the donation happens in the present, but the pipe will only be effectively transferred after Damoeta's death.[32] Interestingly, Gentili also refers to the entanglements between *peculium* and donation in *De iure belli*. He rejects the validity of Constantine's donation by equating that of the sovereign to the *potestas* of a paterfamilias, who, just like a father is not entitled to donate his son's *peculium*, could not have donated Rome to the spiritual power of the Church.[33]

Peculium, then, appears to be, in Gentili's legal analysis, a complex legal concept that, while applying to social categories that do not enjoy *patria potestas*, also leaves room for some freedom to be exercised. Accumulating a significant amount of savings as *peculium* can allow enslaved people, servants and shepherds to buy their freedom, through the legal institute of manumission (had Tityrus been more prudent with his savings, perhaps he would have been able to ask for *manumissio*); additionally, while still 'depending' on a concession of the *dominus* or the father, *peculium* progressively becomes an independent possession that can be freely disposed of by its owner, as witnessed by the fact that one might indeed donate *peculium*. At the same time, the dependence of *peculium* from *dominium*, while hinting at a social coexistence of the two categories, also reflects the profound vulnerability of shepherds, who are

30 *Est mihi disparibus septem compacta cicutis fistula, Damoetas dono mihi quam dedit olim et dixit moriens 'te nunc habet ista secundum'* (*Eclogues*, II, 36–8).

31 *LVVL*, p. 29.

32 *LVVL*, ch. III.

33 *De iure belli*, III.15.

doomed to be what society tells them to be – poets, outsiders, and everything but landowners.

While historicizing the figure of shepherds in the reality of Roman law and society, Gentili paradoxically manages to give an a-temporal account of their poetic enterprise. The *ratio* behind this interpretation is to be found in the following anthropological argument made by Gentili: one might be a slave, a shepherd, or a child, but Gentili still thinks they are endowed with human figure, despite all appearances. Just being endowed with human figure makes them capable of imitation. What makes the shepherds' appearance wild and savage is their brutal and rural conditions of life, and the fact that they are creators of wonderful poetry despite all appearances is further proof of the universality of human reason. This means, Gentili claims in a distinctively humanistic fashion, that everybody can achieve a higher state of civilization through education, precisely as Gentili's young son Robert.[34] Quite interestingly, often in his LVVL, Gentili refers to the book he is writing as his son's *peculium*,[35] again emphasizing the analogy between children and shepherds, as well as the humanist *topos* of the pedagogic importance of virtue in the evolution of mankind.

3 Historicizing Shepherds: Samuel Pufendorf against the Primacy of Agriculture

The famous natural law theorist Samuel Pufendorf (1632–1694) might have not read Gentili's LVVL, which only had a very limited reception,[36] but we

---

34 LVVL, p. 189.

35 LVVL, p. 18.

36 Quite interestingly, it is possible to suggest a reception of LVVL within the context of eighteenth-century Italian academies, despite the fact that Gentili's *opera omnia* was added to the *Index librorum prohibitorum* in 1603. A copy of LVVL was possessed by the library of the *Accaademia dell'Arcadia*, founded in by Giovan Mario Crescimbeni and Gian Vincenzo Gravina in 1690. Crescimbeni was a fellow countryman of Gentili (he was also born in Macerata), and was a huge admirer of Scipio Gentili, Alberico's brother, author of a commentary to Tasso's Jerusalem Delivered. On Scipio Gentili, see: Anne Pallant, 'Scipio Gentili: A Sixteenth Century Jurist', *Kingston Law Review*, 14 (1984), pp. 97–125; Diego Pirillo, 'Tasso at the French Embassy: Epic, Diplomacy, and the Law of Nations', in Jason E. Powell and William T. Rossiter (eds.), *Authority and Diplomacy from Dante to Shakespeare*, (Farnham: Ashgate, 2013). Additionally, several years later, a first attempt to re-edit the works of both Alberico and Scipio Gentili was led by the *Accademia Georgica di Treia*, a learned society focusing on the development of agriculture in Gentili's origin birthplace, the Marche region. After a first attempt to re-publish Gentili's works failed

also find an interesting reference to *peculium* in his *De iure naturae ac gentium libri octo* (1672) in the context of his discussion of the origin of property.[37] Interestingly enough, unlike Gentili's legal-doctrinal account of *peculium*, Pufendorf uses the very same concept (as well as the *topos* of shepherds) to construct an evolutionary account of human civilization. Scholars have rightly attributed to Pufendorf a pivotal role in introducing the so called four-stages theory of society, and have insisted on the political-economical relevance of such introduction.[38]

In the attempt to explain how property originated, and to reject Grotius' account of the original communion of things, Pufendorf claims that God gave Adam full *dominium*, and hence his children were only left with *peculium*. However, Pufendorf is aware that his model creates a problem: Adam's children could only acquire full *dominium* once Adam died, but even then, before the social convent, only had a general permissive right to use natural resources.[39] Pufendorf refers to this as a 'negative communion',[40] a state

because of the death of the Neapolitan editor Jean Gravier (who only managed to publish *De armis Romanis* and *De iure belli* in 1770), Luigi Ernesto Riccomanni, one of the founders of the Accademia, sent a letter to a new editor in Neaples to ask for a new edition of all the works of both Gentili's brothers. In this letter, Riccomanni emphasizes that the less known literary and philological works of the two (hinting, perhaps, at *LVVL*) were particularly requested by scholars (*Promemoria pel sig. Vincenzio di Aloisio stampatore in Napoli*, fol. 269, B39bis fasc.5, cartae 2, Archivio dell'Accademia Georgica di Treia).

37 On this topic, see T. Behme, *Samuel von Pufendorf: Naturrecht und Staat. Eine Analyse und Interpretation seiner Theorie, ihrer Grundlagen und Probleme* (Göttingen: Vandenhoeck und Ruprecht, 1995); Horst Denzer, *Moralphilosophie und Naturrecht bei Samuel Pufendorf: Eine Geistes- und Wissenschaftsgeschichtliche Untersuchung* (Munchen: Beck, 1972); Vanda Fiorillo, *Tra egoismo e socialità. Il giusnaturalismo di Samuel Pufendorf* (Napoli: Jovene, 1992); Kari Saastamoinen, *The Morality of the Fallen Man. Samuel Pufendorf on Natural Law* (Helsinki: SHS 1995); Hans Medick, *Naturzustand und Naturgeschichte der bürgerlichen Gesellschaft: Die Ursprünge der bürgerlichen Sozialtheory als Geschichtsphilosophie und Sozialwissenschaft bei Samuel Pufendorf, John Locke und Adam Smith* (Göttingen: Vandenhoeck und Ruprecht, 2011); Knud Haakonssen, *Grotius, Pufendorf and Natural Law* (Aldershot: Ashgate, 1999); Ian Hunter and David Saunders, *Natural Law and Civil Sovereignty: Moral Right and State Authority in Early Modern Political Thought* (New York: Palgrave Macmillian, 2002); Stephen Buckle, *Natural Law and the Theory of Property: Grotius to Hume* (Oxford: Clarendon, 1991); James Penner and Michael Otsuka (eds), *Property Theory: Legal and Political Perspectives* (Cambridge: Cambridge University Press, 2018).

38 On this point, apart from the already quoted contributions from Istvan Hont, see Arild Sæther, *Natural Law and the Origin of Political Economy: Samuel Pufendorf and the History of Economics* (New York: Routledge, 2017).

39 Samuel Pufendorf, DJNG, IV.IV.11.

40 Samuel Pufendorf, *De iure naturae ac gentium libri octo* (DJNG), IV.IV.5. References are taken from the English edition *On the law of nature and nations: eight books*, trans. by Mr.

which men can only exit by settling and dividing property through covenant.[41] Pufendorf claims that this is the only way in which society could have been originated, since, if everything was held in common as Grotius claimed, no one could really be sure to be the rightful possessor of something which was designed as a common, instead of an individual, property.

Pufendorf seems to make no reference to pastoral poetry and to the original imaginative power of shepherds – not at this stage, at least. Rather, he seems to ground his argument on another, influential *topos*, drawn from Biblical hermeneutic, as a means to explain the origin of human society.[42] As a matter of fact, as he explains:

> many have thought fit to appeal to the authority of the Scripture in this point; whence they have supposed that it may be made evident, that there never was any such communion as we have asserted, in the world: they tell us, that the universal mass of things passed immediately to Adam, by virtue of the divine donation; so that he held it as his own proper and entire possession. The force of which propriety was such, that it not only excluded all others from the universal possession which he enjoyed, but likewise from the right of taking to themselves any one particular thing: insomuch that even his children could claim no property, so long as they continued in the family of their father, unless he conveyed somewhat to them in the manner of a *peculium*, or separate stock: that they became proprietors, first, by possessing that share which he assigned them, when dismissed from under his tuition; and afterwards, upon his death, by dividing his store amongst themselves.[43]

Had God given everything in common to all mankind, no act of possession could be legally justified. Instead, Pufendorf claims that, by marrying Eve, Adam was able to have children and, hence, to transfer his *dominium* to them. However, the path from *peculium* to full *dominium* was a long one: property did not originate out of the blue, right after Adam died. According to Pufendorf's famous historicizing argument, in the beginning it was sufficient

> to fix a property in these things, which either afford an immediate use, not capable of being divided among many; as cloaths, cottages and stores

Carew (London 1729). See also contributions from David Grewal and Simone Zurbuchen in this volume.

41 Samuel Pufendorf, DJNG, IV.IV.6.

42 Accordingly, Pufendorf often describes *peculium* as God's flock.

43 Samuel Pufendorf, DJNG, IV.IV.11.

> of provision already gathered by particular men; or which require industry and improvement to make them fit for service: as household goods, an instruments, cattle and fields. [...] Thus, pasturage continued a great while in its first and common state; till upon the abundant increase of cattle, quarrels arising, the Division of this likewise was made necessary to peace and concord.[44]

Having a flock of sheep did not amount, in this phase, to a proper *dominium*, which could only be achieved by social covenant. This argument is consistent with Pufendorf's puzzling account of natural law, which is deemed to be pre-existing to society, but that still needs to be originated by the command of a superior. Following up on this, Pufendorf asks whether agriculture should be considered the real beginning of society. Pufendorf says that this statement can only be accepted with caution. He quotes Servius' commentary on Virgil, again a crucial source for these debates, to argue against the *topos* of *Ceres legifera*, namely that it was Ceres, the Roman goddess personifying agriculture, that introduced laws to humanity. 'This account ought not to be admitted without some limitation. Indeed, a more pompous train of laws became needful after properties were fixed, men being ruled before by a small number of ordinances; yet communion considered in itself, does not render life altogether lawless and unsociable, but only more simple and unpolished'.[45] Shepherds might be simple and unpolished, but so is the world they live in: this does not mean that laws did not exist in pre-agricultural societies. Interestingly enough, although he neither quotes Virgil's *Eclogues*, nor any debate on pastoral poetry, Pufendorf's mild rejection of the agricultural model of society is still inscribed in a rhetorical use of Virgil as the main topical source on the issue. However, although metaphorical ideas of the shepherds a 'metaphor of every man at a certain stage of human existence'[46] were a *topos* (one of 'civilization vs. barbarity') way before him, only after Pufendorf they become the basis of a political economic model.

4 The End of the Canon: Giambattista Vico on Poets and Shepherds

An interesting role in this brief overview of the concept of *peculium* at the intersection between poetics and stadial theories of society, is played by the

44 DJNG, *ibid*, p. 374b.

45 *Ivi*.

46 Kathryn Gutzwiller, 'The Herdsmen in Greek Thought', in Marco Fantuzzi & Theódoros D. Papanghelis (eds), *Brill's Companion to Greek and Latin Pastoral* (Leiden: Brill, 2006), p. 7.

famous philosopher Giambattista Vico (1668–1744).[47] While re-reading the classics of Italian Cinquecento on poetic theory,[48] as well as the most influential contributions in the field of Protestant natural law (Grotius, Hobbes, and Pufendorf), Vico provides a radical account of human history based on a fundamental parallelism between ontogenesis and philogenesis.[49] According to such theorization, the development of human civilization is nothing but a projection, on a larger scale, of the development of the human individual. Precisely as individuals are born as children, and progressively grow into adults by going through different stages of maturity and ratiocination, so the history of nations begins with the power of imagination of what Vico identifies as 'poetic wisdom'. Still unable to form sophisticated philosophical concepts, earliest forms of human societies created poetic representations to have a grasp of their reality.[50]

For this reason, children and poetry are once again crucial in Vico's account. However, while accepting the importance of poetic expression in the early stages of humanity and that poets are, to some extent, the first legislators, Vico rejects the very naïve interpretation of pastoral poetry as the first poetic genre invented on two grounds. First, pastoral poetry is far more sophisticated than

---

47 There is an extensive literature on Vico, of which I only quote here some selected titles: Benedetto Croce, *La filosofia di Giambattista Vico* (Bari: Laterza, 1922); Isaiah Berlin, *Vico and Herder: Two Studies in the History of Ideas* (London: The Hogarth Press, 1992); Frederick Vaughan, *The Political Philosophy of Giambattista Vico* (The Hague: Nijhoff, 1972); David L. Marshall, *Vico and the Transformation of Rhetorics in Early Modern Europe* (New York: Cambridge University Press, 2014); Alberto Donati, *Giambattista Vico. Filosofo dell'illuminismo* (Roma: Aracne, 2016); Marcel Danesi, *Vico, Metaphor, and the Origin of Language* (Bloomington: Indiana University Press, 1993); Ernesto Grassi, *Vico and Humanism: Essays on Vico, Heidegger and Rhetoric* (New York: Peter Lang, 1990); John D. Schaffer, Sensus Communis: *Vico, Rhetoric, and the Limits of Relativism* (Durham: Duke University Press, 1990); Donald P. Verene, *Vico's Science of Imagination* (Ithaca: Cornell University Press, 1981); Giorgio Tagliacozzo, Donald P. Verene and Vanessa Rumble, *A Bibliography of Vico in English, 1884–1984* (Bowling Green, Ohio: Bowling Green State University, 1986); Giorgio Tagliacozzo, & Hayden White, *Giambattista Vico: An International Symposium* (Baltimore: John Hopking Press, 1969), pp. 615–19.

48 Vico quotes the same sources taken into account by Gentili: Scaliger's *Poetices*, as well as Girolamo Fracastoro's *Naugerius* (Girolamo Fracastoro, *Navagero. Della Poetica*, Firenze 2005). I have addressed the issue of Gentili's sources in Francesca Iurlaro, 'Il testo poetico della giustizia. Alberico e Scipione Gentili leggono la *Repubblica* di Platone', *Pegé* 2 (2017), URL: https://doi.org/10.20318/fons.2017.3858.

49 Max Horkheimer, 'Vico and Mythology', *New Vico Studies* 5 (1987), pp. 63–76.

50 On Vico and poetry, see Franco Lanza, *Saggi di poetica vichiana* (Varese: Magenta, 1961); Giovanni A. Bianca, *Il concetto di poesia in Giambattista Vico* (Florence: G. D'Anna, 1967); Stefano Velotti, *Sapienti e bestioni: saggio sull'ignoranza, il sapere e la poesia in Giambattista Vico* (Parma: Pratiche, 1995).

poets want us to believe, as demonstrated both by the stylistic elegance of such compositions, as well as by the fact that, historically, this genre only emerged in highly 'civilized' periods (see the contexts in which both Theocritus's *Idylls* and Virgil's *Eclogues* were respectively written). Second, Vico also rejects the ideal of the age of shepherds as the first age of human development,[51] by replacing it with a more elaborate theorization of the origins of the commonwealth and, thus, of property. Rather, his account is based on the division into age of gods, age of heroes, and age of men. The transition between these last two phases is crucial, as it represents the exit from the state of nature into society – a transition that, according to Vico, the classic egalitarian models of the state of nature (like those of Grotius, Hobbes and Pufendorf) failed to grasp.

Like Pufendorf, however, Vico vindicates the importance of marriage and the birth of children as the first drives behind the creation of society (both are described by philosophers as the foundation of economic society).[52] Only by getting married, giving birth to children and, eventually, dying, can the first men perpetuate their *dominium* over the world, instead of leaving their children with an almost unusable *peculium*. According to Vico, the existence of testaments is proof of what he describes as the empire of families, which constitute the origins of society.[53] To explain the origin of families and, thus, of the social commonwealth, Vico recurs to the famous theory of *famuli*, i.e. servants

51 As claimed by Vico in his *De Constantia iurisprudentis* (1721), agriculture preceded pastoralism among western civilizations, whereas it was the other way around in the East (cap. XXI).

52 Giambattista Vico, *De uno universi iuris principio et fine uno* (1720), translated into Italian as *Del principio unico e dell'unico fine del diritto universale,* ed. by Enrico Amante (Napoli: Jovene, 1841) p. 78. Also, further on in the same passage: 'e quindi ebbe nascimento l'autorità economica o famigliare, in forza della quale vedevansi i padri esser sovrani delle famiglie, la libertà de' figliuoli tutta nell'arbitrio di lor collocata, avere il diritto di vender essi figliuoli, i quali negli acquisti non erano, come sapientemente gli chiama Aristotile, che animati istrumenti de' padri; da cui pur si ebbe origine il diritto del peculio, e che i padri su' figlioli quella tutela esercitassero che aveano delle loro cose, perché potevangli legal al modo stesso e affidare ad altri in testamento. Quando poi l'autorità, di solitaria che ell'era, si allargò e si distese in potestà famigliare; ampliando similmente il suo di ognuno o il dominio delle cose a ciascuno appartenenti, addivenne pecunia o possedimento di bestiami, di cui prima noi facciam menzione, perché antichissima fra le arti fu certo la pastorizia pecuaria; da cui provenne pecunia che fu ancora detta rispetto al padre vivente patrimonio, ed eredità *ab hero* o dal defunto padrone. Al modo stesso dalle libertà di ciascuno nacque la famiglia, così chiamata da' famoli o clienti, che colla coltura de' campi l'utilità famigliare promovevano'.

53 Going back to Gentili's intertwined analysis of *peculium* and donation among shepherds, one could even argue that some form of hereditary transmission of possession is granted even when there is no private property.

that have rebelled against their masters. These servants 'gave a beginning to society in the proper sense, with a view principally to utility, and consequently base and servile'. In Vico's imaginative account, *famuli* were refugees that 'were received by the heroes under the just law of protection, by which they preserved their natural lives under the obligation of serving the heroes as day laborers. So from the fame (*fama*) of the heroes, [...] the refugees were called *famuli*, and it was principally from these *famuli* that families took their name'.[54]

It is interesting to see what these *famuli* were entitled to: *peculium* of the lands owned by their masters. As such lands could be used for flocks to graze, shepherds, originally deprived of their foundational role of social institutions, become guides of their master's flock, since they live in a state of servitude. As noted by Vico, the Latin verb *pasco* means both 'shepherding' and 'nurture', which hints at the merely passive attitude of servants as 'consumers' of their master's resources instead of proper economic actors. Again, Vico emphasizes the kinship between children and *famuli*,[55] both oppressed by their own fathers or masters, and with similar limitations as legal subjects. In order to leave this natural state of subjection, Vico suggests that only the social struggle between patricians (the masters) and plebeians (*famuli*) may have originated civil governments:

> and among all human possibilities, once we have seen that civil governments were not born either of fraud or of the violence of a single man [...], one cannot imagine any way but the one we have described by which civil power could emerge from family authority, or the eminent domain of civil states from the paternal natural domains.[56] Thus the first cities were made up solely of nobles, who were in command. But because they had need of others to serve them, by a common sense of utility the heroes were constrained to satisfy the multitude of their aroused clients; hence they sent to them the first embassies which by the law of nations

54 Giambattista Vico, *The New Science*, translated from the third edition (1733) by Thomas G. Bergin and Max H. Fisch (Ithaca: Cornell University Press, 1948), II.IV, p. 190.

55 "In these families before the time of the cities, the *famuli* lived in a state of slavery. [...] To distinguish the sons of the heroes from those of the famuli, the former were called liberi, free. But it was a distinction without a difference", as dominus still had a power of life and death over both his children and his servants. In fact, Vico argues, "the absolute power of fathers is proven by the existence until imperial times, of the sole *peculium profectitium*." But then when fathers died, they freed the sons of the families from this "private monarchical rule, each son took it up entire for himself. [...] the famuli on the other hand went on living in that servile state" (*ivi*).

56 Giambattista Vico, *The New Science*, p. 190.

> are sent by sovereigns. And they sent them with the first agrarian law in the world, under which, as the strong to, they conceded to the clients the least they could, which was bonitary ownership of the fields the heroes might choose to assign to them. Thus it may be true that Ceres discovered both grain and laws.[57]

It was of course a precarious kind of ownership, a problem which plebeians tried to solve with the right of *connubium*, i.e. getting married and having children to transfer their property to.[58] However, quite interestingly, Vico here quotes the *topos* of *Ceres legifera* and claims that, whenever there is *peculium*, there can be no proper *dominium*.

5 Conclusions

In his famous *Lectures on Jurisprudence*, Adam Smith identifies flocks and herds as the first objects of human occupation,[59] by reprising Pufendorf's four-stages theory. At the same time, in his *Lectures on Rhetorics and Belles Lettres*, he claims, much like Vico, that poets were the first historians[60] and that, while 'poetry is cultivated in the most Rude and Barbarous nations', it is only through the introduction of commerce that prose is introduced as the 'language of business'. Instead,

> [...] Poetry is of pleasure and amusement. Prose is the stile in which all the common affairs of life all business and agreements are made. No one ever made a Bargain in verse; pleasure is not what he there aims at. Poetry on the other hand is only adapted for pleasure and entertainment; the very nature of poetry, the numbers it is composed in (for there can be no poetry without numbers) declare the intention is to entertain. In the first ages of Society, when men have their necessities on their hands, they keep their business and their pleasure altogether distinct; they neither mix pleasure with their business, nor business with their pleasure; prose is not ornamented nor is verse applied to subjects of business. It

57 *Ibid.*, p. 195.

58 *Ibid.*, p. 190.

59 A. Smith, *Lectures on Jurisprudence*, ed. by Ronald L. Meek, (Oxford: Clarendon Press, 1978), p. 15.

60 A. Smith, *Lectures on Rhetoric and Belles Lettres*, ed. by J. C. Bryce (Oxford: Clarendon Press, 1983), lecture xix.

> is only when pleasure is the only thing sought after that prose comes to be studied. People who are rich and at their ease cannot give themselves the trouble of anything where they do not expect some pleasure. The common transactions of life, as Deliberation and Consultation on what they are to do, are of themselves too dry and unpleasant for them, without the ornaments of language and elegance of expression. This then Deliberative and Judicial eloquence are studied and every ornament is sought out for them.[61]

In Smith's reconstruction, the urgency of poetry as an original act of imagination, capable of producing legal order in the world, is degraded to the role of mere amusement for the *bourgeoisie.* From this perspective, at least two final considerations can be made to conclude this paper. First, whereas Gentili conceives of pastoral poetry as an imaginative source of law, later discourses on civilization seem more reluctant to acknowledge such creative role to it. Additionally, this does not always coincide with a rejection of the role of shepherds as the first age of development of humankind: while this is the case for Vico, it is not for Pufendorf and Smith. However, what our brief analysis of *peculium* has shown, 17th-18th century stadial theories also introduce a distinction between *peculium* and *pecunia*: whereas the two coexist in Gentili's society of shepherds, later natural law theorizations progressively separate the concepts and only introduce *pecunia* at a later stage of society.

More genealogies of the economic model of *peculium*, as a conceptual alternative to both narratives of original acquisition of *dominium* and collectivism, could cast new, imaginative light on these issues. The second question left unanswered by this paper is how desirable is to acquire full dominium, at the expenses of *peculium*, and how sustainable is the political model it envisages. It could be argued that whereas the first pastoral society proposes an economic model of subsistence, in which shepherds are strongly embedded in the environment

61 *Ibid.*, pp. 137–8. On Smith's use of the classics, see Gloria Vivenza, *Adam Smith and the Classics: The Classical Heritage in Adam Smith's Thought* (Oxford: Oxford University Press, 2004); on the importance played by Scottish pastoral poetry in his own times, see: Jeff Strabone, *Poetry and British Nationalisms in the Bardic Eighteenth Century: Imagined Antiquities* (Cham: Palgrave Macmillan, 2018), p. 104; Gloria Vivenza, 'The Division of Land and the Division of Labour: Analogies and Differences between Ancient and Modern Times in Adam Smith's Thought', in Pier Luigi Porta, Roberto Scazzieri and Andrew Skinner, *Knowledge, Social Institutions and the Division of Labour*, pp. 331–350; Kurt Heinzelmann, 'The Last Georgics: Wealth of Nations and the Scene of Writing', in Stephen Copley and Kahtryn Sutherland (eds.), *Adam Smith's Wealth of Nations: New Interdisciplinary Essays* (Manchester: Manchester University Press, 1995).

in which they work in, exercise of full human agency that comes with dominium seems to introduce a proper exploitative one. However, the naivety of this view was already challenged by none other than Plato – who in his *Republic* claims that shepherds, unlike political rulers, are only moved by their personal interests and have no problems in first feeding, then slaughtering the animals they herd.[62] On the other hand, the *topos* of the care devoted by shepherds to their flock (a recurrent theme in contemporary Christian environmentalism),[63] might be further analyzed as far as the emergence of capitalist society in the modern age is concerned, and shed further light on the relationship between property rights, access to food and natural resources, and environmentalism.[64]

What is interesting, however, is the use of a pastoral state of nature (either one originating poetic fiction, or another originating the laws of social interaction, i.e.: property) to the purpose of engaging into a re-definition of its boundaries through figures of 'otherness' – children, enslaved people, shepherds, women, poets. Further research on the concept of *peculium* might be helpful, thus, in illuminating our understanding of legal subalternity. *Peculium*, as a matter of fact, seems a powerful conceptual tool to deny full *dominium* to subaltern categories of societies. But it also contains in itself the germs of private property, if only such subaltern categories were ready to literally kill their fathers, masters, or husbands, to make space for themselves in the world. It is an undoubtedly revolutionary, violent act, but a necessary one, Vico would suggest. The emancipatory quality of *peculium*, however, is a contested one. Quite evocatively, in *Das Kapital*, while complaining of the state of servitude of wage workers, Karl Marx claims that no matter how much *peculium* they accumulate, they will still be slaves ('a rise in the price of labour, as a consequence of accumulation of capital, only means, in fact, that the length and weight of the golden chain the wager worker has already forged for himself, allow of a relaxation of the tension of it').[65] Has the capital's lack of poetic imagination

62 Plato, *Republic*, 342b1, in *Plato, Republic, Volume I: Books 1–5*, ed. and trans. by C. Emlyn-Jones, W. Preddy, Loeb Classical Library 237 (Cambridge, MA: Harvard University Press, 2013).

63 Willis Henkins, *Ecologies of Grace: Environmental Ethics and Christian Theology* (Oxford: Oxford University Press, 2013).

64 On this, see Shelly H. Marguerat, *Private Property Rights and the Environment: our Responsibilities to Global Natural Resources* (Cham: Palgrave Macmillan, 2019), which engages into a criticism of the classical narrative of property rights, like James Tully's reconstruction *A Discourse on Property: John Locke and His Adversaries* (Cambridge: Cambridge University Press, 1980).

65 K. Marx, *Capital: A Critique of Political Economy*, vol. 1. Section 1 (London: Penguin, 1992), p. 769.

made the marginalized legal categories in our society more miserable, more vulnerable and more enslaved than ever?

Select Bibliography

Primary sources

Alberico Gentili, *Lectionis Virgilanae ad Robertum filium*, apud Guilielmum Antonium (Hanau, 1603).

Samuel Pufendorf, *On the law of nature and nations: eight books*, trans. by Mr. Carew (London, 1729).

Adam Smith, *Lectures on Jurisprudence,* ed. by Ronald L. Meek, (Oxford: Clarendon Press, 1978).

Giambattista Vico, *The New Science*, translated from the third edition (1733) by Thomas G. Bergin and Max H. Fisch (Ithaca: Cornell University Press, 1948).

Virgil, *Eclogues. Georgics. Aeneid: Books 1–6*, trans by. H. Rushton Fairclough, revised by G. P. Goold (Cambridge MA: Harvard University Press, 1999).

Secondary sources

Jean-Jacques Aubert, '*Dumtaxat de peculio*: What's in a *Peculium*, or Establishing the Extent of the Principal's Liability', in Paul J. du Plessis (ed), *New Frontiers: Law and Society in the Roman World* (Edinburgh: Edinburgh University Press, 2013), pp. 192–206.

Norbert Elias, *The Civilizing Process: the History of Manners and State Formation and Civilization* (Oxford: Blackwell, 1997).

Kahtryn J. Gutzwiller, *Theocritus' Pastoral Analogies: The Formation of a Genre* (Madison, Wisconsin: University of Wisconsin Press, 1991).

Istvan Hont, 'The Language of Sociability and Commerce: Samuel Pufendorf and the Theoretical Foundations of the Four-Stages Theory', in Anthony Pagden (ed), *The Languages of Political Theory in Early-Modern Europe* (Cambridge: Cambridge University Press, 1981), pp. 253–276.

Annabel Patterson, *Pastoral and Ideology: from Virgil to Valéry,* (Oxford: Clarendon, 1987).

CHAPTER 4

After Vitoria

Natural Law and the Spanish Ideology of Empire

Daniel S. Allemann

Abstract

This chapter traces the lasting impact of Francisco de Vitoria's examination of the conquest of the New World on the early modern Spanish imperial discourse. If Vitoria did not deploy the concept of a 'state of nature,' he probed whether claims about the ostensibly natural condition of lands and peoples overseas, or arguments about the organic connectedness of humankind might justify Castile's imperial venture. The present chapter reconstructs how Spanish voices from the New World took a fresh approach to these issues in the later sixteenth and seventeenth centuries. In contrast to recent scholarship, it contends that thinkers like Alonso de la Vera Cruz, José de Acosta, and Juan de Solórzano y Pereira put forward novel visions of empire without jettisoning the Vitorian architecture of debate. These theorists not only revisited whether American lands, peoples, or oceanic space persisted in a pre-political state. But they also insisted on the centrality of a theologically grounded conception of justice and morality – even when defending Spain's right to rule the Indies against the emerging claims of rival European empires.

Keywords

Spanish conquest – natural slavery – occupation – intervention – free travel and trade – prescription – sovereignty over sea space

1 Introduction

In his letter to Luis Santángel of 1493, Christopher Columbus described the newly encountered lands in the New World as "most fertile to the utmost

 | DOI:10.1163/9789004499621_006

degree, and this to the extreme."[12] The sheer diversity of trees and forests, the profusion of rivers and birds, as well as the rich farmlands and fruits were to him a *maravilla*.[3] Similarly marvelous seemed the native inhabitants, who "all wander about naked" and "are so free of deceit and so generous with what they have that nobody would believe it, except he who sees it."[4] Indeed, Columbus emphasized, "I have not even understood whether they had personal goods; for it seemed to me that whatever somebody had was shared with everyone, especially regarding food."[5] This portrayal of the New World was in many ways that of a new Eden: a pristine place, where humans were still dwelling in a 'state of nature.'

Columbus's vision helped to buttress early Spanish claims for subjugating the ostensibly 'untamed' lands and peoples overseas, but it did not go unchallenged. For Spain's most influential and intellectually rigorous respondents to the colonial venture in America, the notion of the persistence of paradise and natural man was utterly inconceivable.[6] Francisco de Vitoria (ca. 1486–1546) and his followers at the University of Salamanca all emphasized the transformative impact of the watershed events of the Fall and the Flood. In the eyes of the Thomist theologians, these moments in sacred history had marked the end of the original state of humanity in Eden and rang in a novel, irreversible era of concrete political relations. While the things on earth had once been held collectively and peacefully by all, the postlapsarian world was marked by the existence of bounded kingdoms, private property, and wars. It is in this sense

1 I would like to thank Annabel Brett, Christiane Birr, David Grewal, Mark Somos, Benjamin Straumann, and Sarah Winter for their incisive comments on earlier versions of this chapter. I am also grateful to Anne Peters and Mark Somos for the invitation to participate in this stimulating project, and to all the contributors in these pages for fruitful discussions at our author workshop in Berlin in 2019.

2 All translations are my own unless otherwise indicated. Christopher Columbus, 'Carta de Cristoval Colon al escribano de racion Luis Sant' Angel,' ed. in *The Spanish Letters of Columbus, Written by Him on Feb. 15, 1493 to Announce the Discovery of America*, facsimile, transcription, and translation (London: Bernard Quartich, 1893), p. 2.

3 Ibid. On the language of marvel, see the classic study by Stephen Greenblatt, *Marvelous Possessions. The Wonder of the New World* (Oxford: Clarendon Press, 1991).

4 Columbus, "Carta de Cristoval Colon," p. 3.

5 Ibid, pp. 4–5.

6 On early Spanish responses to the conquest, see also José Luís Egío Garía, 'Matías De Paz and the Introduction of Thomism in the *Asuntos De Indias*. A Conceptual Revolution,' *Rechtsgeschichte – Legal History*, 26 (2018), pp. 236–62; and Christiane Birr, '*Dominium* in the Indies. Juan López de Palacios Rubios' *Libellus de insulis oceanis quas vulgus indias appelat* (1512–1516),' in *Rechtsgeschichte – Legal History*, 26 (2018), pp. 264–83.

that for the Spanish scholastics, the peoples of the Americas were not, and could not be, in a pre-political state of natural liberty.[7]

The historical vision of a move from Edenic freedom to the world of political communities was a salient feature in early modern natural law thinking. Other chapters in this volume show that Hugo Grotius (1583–1645) or Samuel Pufendorf (1632–94) similarly engaged with the distant past of biblical history.[8] But in the hands of Protestant thinkers of the seventeenth century, the state of nature also assumed a range of other meanings and functions. It could, for instance, account for the condition of people and peoples in the present.[9] It was deployed to conceptualize the state of sovereigns in the international arena.[10] Or, as Simone Zurbuchen writes in her contribution to this collection, it was imagined as a "hypothetical situation prior to the establishment of society" which served to explain why it was reasonable for humans to abandon their natural liberty, and to form commonwealths.[11] In early modern theories of politics, the state of nature was often a polyvalent concept: actual or imagined, past or present.

The same cannot be said of Vitoria and those who were writing in his vein. In fact, they did not use the locution 'state of nature' at all.[12] From Aristotle they inherited the conviction that the natural and the political were not mere opposites but closely intertwined, and they set themselves the task of

7 Annabel S. Brett, *Changes of State. Nature and the Limits of the City in Early Modern Natural Law* (Princeton: Princeton University Press, 2011), ch. 1; Anthony Pagden, *The Fall of Natural Man. The American Indian and the Origins of Comparative Ethnology*, 2nd rev. ed. (Cambridge: Cambridge University Press, 1986), ch. 4.

8 See the contributions by David Singh Grewal and Francesca Iurlaro in this volume.

9 In the present collection, Emile Simpson shows how Grotius conceptualized the state of nature in this way.

10 This theme is explored in these pages by Edward J. Kolla, 'Written in the Hearts of People? Natural and International Law during the Age of Enlightenment.'

11 Simone Zurbuchen, 'The State of Nature, the Family, and the State,' in this volume.

12 As Harro Höpfl has shown, the one scholastic who did use the locution *status naturae* as such was the Dutch Jesuit Martin Becanus, writing in the early seventeenth century. Yet Becanus's *status naturae* was not a pre-political 'state of nature.' For Becanus, the *status naturae* was the period in the biblical history of humanity after the Fall, when humans were solely governed by natural law. It was thus more properly a *status legis naturae*, a phrase that other scholastics used as well, as Höpfl rightly notes. This state, in Becanus's scheme, was followed by the legal regime of Mosaic law (*status legis Mosaïcae*) and eventually culminated in the lasting state of humanity after the arrival of Christ (*status gratiae*). See the excellent discussion in Harro Höpfl, *Jesuit Political Thought. The Society of Jesus and the State, c. 1540–1630* (Cambridge: Cambridge University Press, 2004), pp. 258–61; and the original passage in Martin Becanus, *De pontifice veteris testamenti*, in *Opusculorum theologicorum, tomus terius* (Lyon, 1621), preface, n. 1, p. 369.

negotiating the complex relationship between the two.[13] The debate about the Spanish conquest was one pivotal contribution to this broader venture. Vitoria famously pushed back against the view that the Amerindians were Aristotle's 'slaves by nature,' who could be justly dispossessed and dominated by the Spaniards. As he declared in his public lecture *De indis* of 1539, the notion that entire peoples were naturally unfit for the genuinely human, political life would have implied a failure of divine creation. Like all humans, Vitoria underlined, the peoples overseas too were made in the image of God. They were governed by reason, the natural law that God had implanted in the minds of men, and hence capable of governing their own actions, holding property, and exercising political rule.[14] Rather than being natural slaves, the American Indians had natural rights and "*possessed true dominion, both in public and private affairs*."[15]

This is noteworthy, not least because the New World was often envisioned as a space where states of nature had endured. "The savage people in many places of *America*," as Thomas Hobbes would later put it, "live at this day in that brutish manner."[16] Yet it is helpful to recall that Vitoria was writing in the immediate aftermath of the conquests of Mexico and Peru. The 'indios' he had in mind were quite unlike the half-naked manhunter-cannibals pictured in the frontispiece of Hobbes's *De cive*.[17] Vitoria was first and foremost writing about the descendants of the Aztecs and Incas, who had "properly organized cities, proper marriages, magistrates and overlords (*domini*), laws, industries, and commerce."[18] We might add that to describe these societies in terms of a 'state of nature' would not only be theoretically but also empirically flawed.

In the *De indis*, Vitoria's arguments from nature and natural law were not limited to the political status of the newly encountered human beings. His examination of the just and unjust foundations of the Spanish conquest also focused on the overseas territory. With recourse to Roman law, Vitoria maintained that it was just to take possession of all land that was 'unoccupied.' It was hence

---

13 On the relationship between nature and politics in early modern natural law, including the Protestant tradition, see Brett, *Changes of State*.

14 Brian Tierney, *The Idea of Natural Rights. Studies on Natural Rights, Natural Law, and Church Law, 1150–1625* (Atlanta: Scholars Press, 1997), pp. 269–70.

15 Vitoria, *De indis*, trans. Pagden and Lawrance, q. 1, concl., 251, original emphasis.

16 Thomas Hobbes, *Leviathan*, ed. Noel Malcolm, 3 vols (Oxford: Oxford University Press, 2012), II, ch. 13, p. 194, original emphasis.

17 On Hobbes's image of America and the state of nature, see Ioannis D. Evrigenis, *Images of Anarchy. Rhetoric and Science in Hobess's State of Nature* (Cambridge: Cambridge University Press, 2014), ch. 8.

18 Francisco de Vitoria, *De indis*, in *Vitoria. Political Writings*, trans. and ed. Anthony Pagden and Jeremy Lawrance (Cambridge: Cambridge University Press, 1991), q. 1, a. 6, p. 250.

possible that parts of the earth were not settled and – to phrase it in the terms of this volume – continued to exist in their 'state of nature.' But the New World did not qualify as such. As a consequence of indigenous political power, Vitoria made clear, these lands were under rightful jurisdiction and control.[19]

The Salamancan theologian also used arguments from natural law to sketch routes that might justify the conquest. If innocent individuals were sacrificed for cannibalism, for instance, the Spaniards could come to their aid and intervene, because "the barbarians are all our neighbours."[20] For Vitoria, and this is important, the original community of humans was not fully lost after the Fall. He placed great emphasis on the fact that all humans remained naturally connected to each other even in the post-paradisal world of separate commonwealths: Spaniards and Amerindians were part of one global society.[21] A further crucial consequence of this natural association was the *ius communicandi*, the right to travel and trade across borders. In theory, it was universal and reciprocal. But in the present context, it allowed Spaniards to permeate Amerindian polities so as to "export the gold, silver, or other things which [the natives] have in abundance."[22] Not surprisingly, this right has been dubbed as an early articulation of commercial imperialism.[23]

These brief examples show that questions of, and arguments from, nature loomed large in Vitoria's *De indis*. To be sure, his image of America was far from a state of nature beyond political society. Even arguments that lent support to the Spanish presence overseas recognized the legitimacy of indigenous commonwealths. And yet, to examine the justice of the conquest was, for Vitoria, to inquire into the very nature of human beings, their territory, and their relationships with each other. The contention of this chapter is that these issues had a lasting impact on subsequent Castilian theorists. Where scholars have questioned the persistence of Vitoria's conception of the conquest, I argue that his natural law thinking shaped Spanish visions of empire into the seventeenth century.

---

19 Ibid., q. 2, a. 3, pp. 264–5.

20 Ibid., q. 3, a. 5, p. 288.

21 See Brett, *Changes of State*, pp. 13–15.

22 Vitoria, *De indis*, trans. Pagden and Lawrance, q. 3, a. 1, p. 279. On the reciprocity of this right, see the discussion in Annabel S. Brett, 'Scholastic Political Thought and the Modern Concept of the State,' in *Rethinking the Foundations of Modern Political Thought*, ed. Annabel S. Brett and James Tully with Holly Hamilton-Bleakley (Cambridge: Cambridge University Press, 2006), pp. 130–48.

23 Martti Koskenniemi, 'Empire and International Law. The Real Spanish Contribution,' *University of Toronto Law Journal*, 61 (2011), pp. 1–36. See also Antony Anghie, *Imperialism, Sovereignty and the Making of International Law* (Cambridge: Cambridge University Press, 2004), ch. 1.

Francisco de Vitoria's engagement with the Spanish conquest left a deep imprint on the Western tradition of international political and legal thought. Historians have extensively examined his ideas of war and empire in relation to Protestant thinkers such as Alberico Gentili (1552–1608) and Hugo Grotius.[24] But it is only in recent years that scholars have also begun to trace the reception and impact of Vitorian arguments in the context of the unfolding ideology of the Spanish empire. In large part, this is due to an increasing interest in the work of the imperial jurist Juan de Solórzano y Pereira (1575–1655). Educated at the University of Salamanca, where he studied canon and civil law, Solórzano moved to the New World in 1609. He took up the prestigious post as judge (*oidor*) in the Audiencia of Lima, a high court with important governmental functions in colonial Peru.[25] But Solórzano, who had previously been on track for an academic career, did not abandon the writing of books when he left university.[26] In the two-volume *De Indiarum iure* (1629–39), he reflected on the rich first-hand experience he had gained as a colonial official in Peru.[27] He subsequently reworked the treatise into a vernacular version under the title *Política indiana* (1648), which made him one of the most widely read Spanish thinkers of his time.[28] In both works, Solórzano prominently revisited the question whether Spain's domination of the New World was licit.[29] And if

24 An early classic is James Brown Scott's *The Spanish Origins of International Law. Francisco de Vitoria and His Law of Nations* (Oxford: Clarendon Press, 1934), 3 and *passim*. For more recent studies, see e.g. Daragh Grant, 'Francisco de Vitoria and Alberico Gentili on the Juridical Status of Native American Polities,' *Renaissance Quarterly*, 72 (2019), pp. 910–52; and Noel Malcolm, *Useful Enemies. Islam and The Ottoman Empire in Western Political Thought, 1450–1750* (Oxford: Oxford University Press, 2019), ch. 11.

25 Biographical information on Solórzano is from Enrique García Hernán, *Consejero de ambos mundos. Vida y obra de Juan de Solórzano Pereira (1575–1655)* (Madrid: Fundación MAPFRE, 2007), chs. 2 and 4; and James Muldoon, *The Americas in the Spanish World Order. The Justification for Conquest in the Seventeenth Century* (Philadelphia: University of Pennsylvania Press, 1994), p. 8.

26 Solórzano held a chair in law at Salamanca from 1607 to 1609. And upon his arrival in Lima, he was offered the prime chair in law at the University of San Marcos, which he declined due to his commitments as oidor. See García Hernán, *Consejero de ambos mundos*, p. 90 and pp. 105–7.

27 Juan de Solórzano y Pereira, *De indiarum iure, sive de iusta indiarum occidentalium inquisitione, acquisitione, et retentione* (Madrid 1629); ibid., *Tomum alterum de indiarum iure, sive de iusta indiarum occidentalium gubernatione* (Madrid 1639).

28 Juan de Solórzano y Pereira, *Politica indiana* (Madrid 1648). I shall be quoting from the following edition: *Política indiana*, ed. and estudio preliminar Miguel Ángel Ochoa Brun, 5 vols (Madrid: Ediciones Atlas, 1972).

29 Solórzano, *Política indiana*, bk. I, chs. 9–12. In the earlier *De Indiarum iure*, this corresponds to Books II and III of the first volume. At the very outset of both the *Política* (chs. 1–8) and the *De Indiarum* (bk. I), Solórzano offered a description of the flora, fauna, and peoples that the Spaniards had encountered overseas.

we follow the verdict of recent scholarship, Solórzano's position vis-à-vis the Vitorian legacy is crystal clear: by the seventeenth century, the scholastic language of natural law had lost its purchase in the Spanish imperial discourse.

This chapter seeks to offer an alternative story. For one thing, this requires detailed attention to Solórzano's thought. But it also means that we must not treat the century after Vitoria as an intellectual void. In order to grasp the distinctiveness of Solórzano's interventions, it is vital to reconstruct key moves that other thinkers made in the second half of the sixteenth century. I will do so by turning to the writings of the theologians Alonso de la Vera Cruz (1507–85) and José de Acosta (1539–1600), which profoundly shaped the discourse of empire among early modern Spanish intellectuals. Like Solórzano, they were educated in Spain but spent large parts of their lives in the New World. Their concern with the realities and issues they encountered in the colonial context left a noticeable imprint on their intellectual production, and they were writing "for far wider and far more diffuse audiences"[30] than scholars based at universities in Iberia. But in what follows, I will argue that there was no sharp break between Vitorian ideas and the thought of later American-based theorists of empire.[31]

The first section takes its cue from Tamar Herzog's recent contention that Solórzano advanced a 'Lockean' conception of property *avant la lettre*. Her case is that Solórzano considered all land to remain in its communal state unless it was appropriated through labor – and thus "land would be the property not of those who had it 'first' but instead of those who used it 'better.'"[32] Spanish theorists of empire indeed questioned the notion that all the overseas territory was under indigenous authority. As we shall see, this had far-reaching implications. But I maintain that the upshot of Solórzano and others' disagreement with Vitoria was about historical facts rather than theoretical principles. It was possible to craft arguments in favor of taking American lands that had remained in a 'state of nature,' as it were, without challenging the conceptual

30 Pagden, *The Fall of Natural Man*, p. 200, makes this point in relation to Acosta.

31 On this point, see also Thomas Duve, 'Salamanca in Amerika,' *Zeitschrift der Savigny-Stiftung für Rechtsgeschichte. Germanistische Abteilung*, 132 (2015), pp. 116–51; Víctor Tau Anzoátegui, *El jurista en el Nuevo Mundo. Pensamiento. Doctrina. Mentalidad* (Frankfurt/Main: Max Planck Institute for European Legal History, 2016), pp. 8–12; and José Luís Egío García, 'La consolidación del estatuto teológico-político del pagano amerindio en los maestros 'salmantinos' y sus discípulos novohispanos (1512–1593),' *The School of Salamanca Working Paper Series*, 1 (2015), pp. 38–39.

32 Tamar Herzog, *Frontiers of Possession. Spain and Portugal in Europe and in the Americas* (Cambridge, MA: Harvard University Press, 2015), p. 124.

architecture of *De indis*. And a strikingly similar story can be told about the afterlife of natural slavery, the most notorious of Vitoria's titles of conquest.

Section Two probes the longevity of the idea of a universal, natural society of all humans. It begins by exploring the link between global fraternity (and sorority) and intervention in foreign commonwealths. But its principal aim is to uncover how Spanish theorists reconceptualized the notion of free travel and trade in the later sixteenth and seventeenth century. While nobody denied the right of communication *tout court*, some put forward critical caveats. The Jesuit José de Acosta, for instance, warned of the dangers that free migration posed to the political fabric of well-ordered cities. Imperfect commonwealths like those in the Americas, by contrast, were in need of politically savvy foreigners according to Acosta. This uneven configuration of global border-crossing gave the Spaniards a right to enter the Indies, while allowing them to block off migrants at home.

In Section Three, I will turn to the claim that the Spanish imperial discourse after Vitoria can be characterized in terms of a turn toward 'Machiavellian' power politics beyond any moral grounding.[33] Several scholars have made the point that the 'thick' account of justice, which had been so pivotal to Vitoria's analysis of the conquest, became increasingly irrelevant. In their view, the jurist Juan de Solórzano no longer cared whether Spain's belligerent ventures overseas had been legitimate or not. Instead, we are told, the author of the *Política indiana* invoked the legalistic notion of prescription.[34] "The time of conquest," as one scholar put it, "was over and the justice of Spanish presence could henceforth be received from long-term possession."[35] If we take a close look at Solórzano's writing, however, things look rather less straightforward. It is true that the idea of a merely retroactive vindication of the conquest was at odds with the scholastic conception of justice. But Spanish theorists writing

33 David A. Brading, *The First America. The Spanish Monarchy, Creole Patriots, and the Liberal State 1492–1867* (Cambridge: Cambridge University Press, 1991), p. 190. Brading makes this point in relation to Acosta, as we shall see in more detail below.

34 Most forcefully in Anthony Pagden, *Lords of all the World. Ideologies of Empire in Spain, Britain and France c.1500–c.1800* (New Haven: Yale University Press, 1995), pp. 89–90; and ibid. 'Conquest and the Just War. The 'School of Salamanca' and the "Affair of the Indies," ' in *Empire and Modern Political Thought*, ed. Sankar Muthu (Cambridge: Cambridge University Press, 2012), pp. 59–60. See also David A. Lupher, *Romans in a New World. Classical Models in Sixteenth-Century Spanish America* (Ann Arbor: University of Michigan Press, 2003), pp. 187–8.

35 Martti Koskenniemi, 'Colonial Laws. Sources, Strategies and Lessons', *Journal of the History of International Law*, 18 (2016), p. 254. Koskenniemi here follows the work of Anthony Pagden that is cited in the preceding footnote.

after Vitoria did not seek to legalize de facto possession at the expense of just titles. Rather, they sought to make prescription compatible with Vitorian natural law thinking.

As a coda to this chapter, the final section reconstructs the centrality of long-term possession in a different controversy that grew increasingly important in the seventeenth century. While the initial *taking* of the Indies remained a key theme in the Spanish imperial discourse, a neglected episode centered on the right to *keep* the overseas empire. It was by confronting this problem, I maintain, that Solórzano used prescription most powerfully and innovatively. In the face of competing colonial claims, he deployed the concept to carve out a new vision of littoral sovereignty that kept other European powers at bay. In so doing, Solórzano not only challenged Vitoria's vision of border-free communication across the globe. He also pushed back against those who claimed that the seas were exempt from political authority and remained in a perennial state of nature.

1.1 *State of Nature Redux?*

Let us begin by tracing the aftermath of the two Vitorian claims that are most closely related to the overarching theme of this book; that neither the inhabitants nor the lands of the New World were in a 'state of nature' when the Spaniards first set foot overseas. In his treatise on how to attend to the salvation of the Amerindians, the *De procuranda indorum salute* (1588), the Jesuit Acosta invoked Aristotle's theory of natural slavery in order to legitimate war against the "barbarians who roam around in the manner of wild beasts, without established settlements and laws."[36] Although Acosta did not wholly dehumanize these peoples, as Anthony Pagden showed, his tripartite categorization of 'barbarian' nations allowed Acosta to single out the most 'savage' ones.[37] Thus, the question remains whether claims about the ostensibly pre-political life of some Amerindians were turned into arguments for empire after Vitoria. A similar doubt arises in view of Solórzano's treatment of occupation: did he indeed insist that the unused lands of the Indigenous remained in their natural condition and, in John Locke's words, "so still lie in common"?[38]

36 I am quoting from the critical edition: José de Acosta, *De procuranda indorum salute. Pacificación y colonización*, ed. with parallel Spanish trans. Luciano Pereña et al. (Madrid: CSIC, 1984), bk. II, ch. 5, n. 1.

37 Pagden, *Fall of Natural Man*, pp. 162–165.

38 John Locke, *Two Treatises of Government*, ed. Peter Laslett (Cambridge, 1960; repr. 1988), II, ch. 5, §45.

1.2 *Revisiting Natural Slavery*

The first Spanish thinker who thought through the problem of natural slavery from the New World was Alonso de la Vera Cruz (1507–84).[39] After his studies in Salamanca, where he was one of Vitoria's disciples, Vera Cruz joined the Augustinian order and mission overseas. He permanently moved to New Spain and was appointed to the first chair in theology at the newly established University of Mexico in 1553. It was in this capacity that he revisited the by-then classic question of the just and unjust titles of the Spanish conquest. On the basis of his first lecture course, he prepared a treatise that he would later call *De dominio infidelium et iusto bello*.[40] This text restated many familiar claims that had originated in the Salamancan lecture halls. As David Lupher has put it, Vera Cruz essentially put forward "variations on themes sounded by his teacher Vitoria."[41]

With regard to natural slavery, this was indeed the case. The fact that some of the natives might qualify as natural slaves, who should "be directed and governed by others who are superior in foresight" was "no real objection" for Vera Cruz.[42] In every commonwealth, there were always some who "in their own way surpass all others."[43] But the natives obviously lived in political societies. Vera Cruz emphasized that they had magistrates, laws, and "orderly government."[44] Even if some of the Amerindians seemed savage, this did not therefore invalidate the political character of their communities at large.

A related point had already been put forward by Vitoria. In his *De indis*, he noted that even in Spain there were "many peasants who are little different from brute animals."[45] And nobody argued that the Spanish could therefore be conquered. But there was a deeper point that Vitoria implicitly conveyed

---

39 Biographical information on Vera Cruz is from Ernest J. Burrus, 'Introduction,' in *The Writings of Alonso de la Vera Cruz*, ed. Ernest J. Burrus, 5 vols (Rome: Jesuit Historical Institute, 1967–76), II (1968), pp. 9–15; Lupher, *Romans in a New World*, pp. 158–159; and the entry on Vera Cruz on Jacob Schmutz's excellent website *Scholasticon*, http://scholasticon.ish-lyon.cnrs.fr, accessed 24 May 2019.

40 The treatise circulated in manuscript form and was originally untitled, but Vera Cruz later referred to it as *De dominio infidelium et iusto bello* in the first edition of his *Speculum coniugorum* (Mexico City 1556). See Burrus, 'Introduction,' p. 53.

41 Lupher, *Romans in a New World*, pp. 164–165.

42 I am quoting from the translation by Ernest Burrus, but have occasionally modified it. Vera Cruz, *De dominio infidelium et iusto bello*, in *The Writings of Alonso de la Vera Cruz*, Latin ed. and English trans. Ernest J. Burrus, 5 vols (Rome: Jesuit Historical Institute, 1967–76), II (1968), Doubt 10, nn. 714–15.

43 Ibid., n. 716.

44 Ibid., n. 717.

45 Vitoria, *De indis*, trans. Pagden and Lawrance, q. 1, a. 6, p. 250.

in this passage, and which Vera Cruz later brought to the fore: "although the lowest of the commoners are farmers that seem wild and brutish, this is for the most part due to their not living in political society (*politia*)."[46] This portrayal of the peasant harks back to Thomas Aquinas's commentary on Aristotle's *Politics* from the later thirteenth century. Despite the inherently political nature of humans, and notwithstanding the central Aristotelian dictum that only beast and gods could live outside society, Aquinas had posited that there were people who did not dwell in political communities as a consequence of their "misfortune."[47] First and foremost, this applied to peasants "because poverty forces them to cultivate the fields or tend animals."[48]

By invoking the image of the unsocial peasant, Vera Cruz tapped into the received Thomist notion that not all political beings *lived* politically, and mapped it onto the New World. Importantly, this only concerned certain individuals within a larger whole. Vera Cruz was keen to stress that "at all times, there were among them some who were noble and of outstanding ability who could govern."[49] His distinctive achievement was thus to confront the problem that not all the natives appeared suited for civic life, while at the same time safeguarding the by-then transatlantic scholastic position that collectively speaking, the Amerindians had formed genuine commonwealths.

A rather different vision was later promoted by José de Acosta. The Jesuit is above all known for his vernacular *Natural and Moral History* (1590), which has earned him the reputation of a great Renaissance historian.[50] But while Acosta was a man of many hats, he was first and foremost a prolific theologian. He spent the better part of the 1570s and 80s in the Viceroyalty of Peru, where he was provincial of the Jesuit order, had a leading role in the Third Council of Lima (1582–3), and held the chair of theology at the University of San Marcos. And it was during this time that he also penned his groundbreaking *De procuranda indorum salute* that was first published in 1588.[51]

46 Vera Cruz, *De dominio infidelium*, trans. Burrus, Doubt 10, n. 719.

47 Thomas Aquinas, *Commentary on Aristotle's* Politics, trans. and ed. Richard J. Regan (Indianapolis: Hackett Publishing, 2007), ad. 1.1, 20, 16. I thank Anna Becker for pointing me to this passage some time ago, when pondering Vitoria's account of Spanish peasants for my master's thesis.

48 Ibid. The other kind of people who fell into this category were those banned from the commonwealth.

49 Vera Cruz, *De dominio infidelium*, trans. Burrus, Doubt 10, n. 719.

50 Anthony Grafton, 'José de Acosta. Renaissance Historiography and New World Humanity,' in *The Renaissance World*, ed. John Jeffries Martin (New York: Routledge, 2007), p. 170 and *passim*.

51 Biographical information on Acosta is from Pagden, *The Fall of Natural Man*, pp. 147–9; Brading, *The First America*, pp. 184–5; and from the entry on Acosta on *Scholasticon*.

The categories of 'barbarians' that Acosta defined in the preface of that work had vital ramifications for his treatment of natural slavery. He identified three classes of non-European societies in a way that bears resemblance to later stadial theories of the Scottish Enlightenment.[52] The first was reserved for those 'barbarians' who were both political and lettered – essentially the Chinese – while the Amerindians all fell into Acosta's second and third categories. He placed the Aztecs and Incas in the middle of his scheme, for they lacked systems of script but were nevertheless politically organized. On the lowest level were all those "who neither have a commonwealth of their own, nor magistrates, nor laws, but roam around in the manner of wild beasts, without established settlements and laws."[53]

Whereas Vera Cruz had integrated 'naturally slavish' individuals into a larger political whole, Acosta insisted that entire communities in the Americas were wholly unpolitical. As a corollary, the Spaniards could justly impose their authority with "a certain moderate force because they must, by all means, be persuaded to live like humans and not like beasts."[54] But what licensed this venture was not that these natives "had no *meum* and *tuum*, no mine and yours,"[55] as Andrew Fitzmaurice argues. It is important to note that Acosta was not making a point about the lack of indigenous property rights, but about the absence of political organization and authority.

Consider what Acosta said about those Indian societies that *did* have public power. Whoever posited that due to their nature

> it is licit to snatch away from the barbarians the sovereignty (*imperium*) that they already have, will by the same reason conclude that one can tear away, by force, rule from a woman or from an adolescent wherever they govern, and similarly from an unskilled king the kingdom, and from an unlearned pope his office.[56]

---

52 See John G. A. Pocock, *Barbarism and Religion. Volume 4. Barbarians, Savages and Empires* (Cambridge: Cambridge University Press, 2005), ch. 9, especially at pp. 164–167. On stadial theories and the state of nature, see also Francesca Iurlaro's chapter in this volume.

53 Acosta, *De procuranda*, bk. II, ch. 5, n. 1. Note that Vitoria's colleague Domingo de Soto had made a similar claim about individuals who were roaming around like beast in *Europe*. See Brett, *Changes of State*, p. 26.

54 Acosta, *De procuranda*, bk. II, ch. 5, n. 1.

55 Andrew Fitzmaurice, *Sovereignty, Property and Empire, 1500–2000* (Cambridge: Cambridge University Press, 2014), p. 77.

56 Acosta, *De procuranda*, bk. II, ch. 5, n. 1.

This passage illustrates that arguments about the comparatively inferior nature of the Amerindians could never serve to deprive them of their *imperium*. Just like female or adolescent rulers in Europe, they might not be ideally suited to govern but were nevertheless just holders of jurisdiction.

Why, then, was it just to wage wars of conquest against 'barbarians' of the lowest class? For Acosta, the decisive point was that they had failed to establish *imperium* in the first place. Political power was a consequence of man's natural dominion, but it did not naturally exist. It was something that had to be created.[57] Those who lacked laws, magistrates, and a commonwealth of their own – the Caribs, as well as the Chun'chu, the Guaraní, the Moxos, and the Iscaycingas in colonial Peru – clearly had not done so in Acosta's estimation.[58] As Juan de Solórzano later put it in his *Política indiana*, "in these barbarians of Acosta's third category one could verify, with full rigor, that which Aristotle says about the slavery of the ignorant."[59]

It is worth remembering that Vitoria, too, speculated that if American Indians were "so close to being mad, *that they are unsuited to setting up or administering a commonwealth*," then the Spaniards would have a right to subjugate and politicize them.[60] But this was something that Vitoria did "not dare either to affirm or condemn."[61] He was operating with a singular notion of the Amerindian, and to insist on the 'madness' of any given community came with the danger of asserting the pre-political state of the Indigenous *tout court*. With Acosta's ethnographically informed political theory, however, it became possible to vindicate natural slavery as a just, if partial, title of conquest. In his view, those communities who had failed to move beyond the naturally necessitated life of beasts could legitimately be governed into a state of civil society.

1.3 *Revisiting Occupation*

Turning now to the title of occupation, let us recall that for Vitoria, the lands of the Amerindians had been rightfully occupied when the Spaniards first arrived overseas. In constructing this argument, as Lauren Benton and Benjamin Straumann have shown, Vitoria applied the private law concept of occupation from Justinian's *Institutes* "to the acquisition of public ownership or

57 See ibid., n. 4. This argument was a congruent with Vitoria's theory of civil power, as discussed in Brett, *Liberty, Right and Nature*, ch. 4.

58 These were the groups that fell into Acosta's third category, as well as all the peoples of Florida and Brazil. See Acosta, *De procuranda*, prooemium.

59 Solórzano, *Política indiana*, bk. 1, ch. 9, n. 31.

60 Vitoria, *De indis*, trans. Pagden and Lawrance, q. 3, a. 8, p. 290, original emphasis.

61 Ibid.

sovereignty by way of analogy."[62] But this was only one side of the coin. Vitoria likewise invoked occupation in its originally Roman sense, and embedded it within his narrative of sacred history. The upshot of this second sense of occupation was that Spaniards had a right, as individuals, to export natural riches like gold or pearls that had been left communal after the Fall and thus became "the property of the first taker according to the law *Ferae bestiae* (*Institutions* II.1.12)."[63] Vitoria refuted arguments for appropriating native land but allowed the acquisition of things with reference to the idea of occupation.

Alonso de la Vera Cruz drew inspiration from the creative flexibility with which Vitoria had deployed the concept. In his own lecture on the dominion of the Amerindians, he introduced a small but important shift in focus in his account of the public dimension of occupation. In general terms, Vera Cruz argued, it was prohibited to occupy "uncultivated lands (*terras incultas*)" among the Indigenous.[64] This was so, he went on to explain, because any "land that is within the limits of a people belongs to the people itself, even if it remains uncultivated."[65] However, there was a crucial exception to this rule:

> those who have pastureland among the indios called Chichimecas, either because such lands were not held in possession or because they were left for derelict, since they neither have inhabitants nor peoples who have their distinct limits; I say those who have such lands licitly own them, especially since these roaming indios live in the manner of beasts and do not cultivate or inhabit the land (*terram non colerent*), for no injury is done to them if the Spaniards' herds of cattle, or beasts of burden, graze the pasture.[66]

This is a most remarkable passage. Vera Cruz's point here was not to suggest that the Chichimecas lived wholly unpolitically, and neither did he argue that they had failed to properly 'use' their land. What justified the occupation of their soil was that, in fact, it was not theirs at all. The Chichimecas, for Vera Cruz, did not define their community with reference to any distinct territory. And it was this complete absence of a link between the abstract space of their political community and a concrete, delimited place – an aporetic idea that

62 Lauren Benton and Benjamin Straumann, 'Acquiring Empire by Law. From Roman Doctrine to Early Modern European Practice,' *Law and History Review*, 28.1 (2010), p. 21.

63 Vitoria, *De indis*, trans. Pagden and Lawrance, q. 3, a. 1, p. 280.

64 Vera Cruz, *De dominio*, Doubt III, n. 125.

65 Ibid., n. 126.

66 Ibid., n. 148.

was, strictly speaking, inconceivable in early modern natural law[67] – that justified the occupation of the land.

The upshot of Vera Cruz's argument was that some lands in the New World were beyond the reach of indigenous jurisdiction and had remained, so to speak, in a 'state of nature.' Accordingly, these *terras incultas* could be legally occupied "either by princely authority or by one's own [...] in the same way that it was done in the beginning of time by the sons of Adam and later, after the Flood, by the sons of Noah."[68]

When the jurist Juan de Solórzano revisited the title of occupation in the seventeenth century, he tapped into precisely this vision. All the islands and lands, Solórzano argued, which

> had never been inhabited before, or, if they had, the natives then moved on to other lands and left them uncultivated (*incultas*); it cannot be negated that this means [...] that the natives gave this prize to the Spaniards' industry and wanted that the free thing cedes to those who first find and occupy it.[69]

In her analysis of this passage in *Frontiers of Possession*, Tamar Herzog maintains that in his emphasis on industry, Solórzano "linked (correct) use to rights" in the very same way that John Locke would later do.[70] However, I hope that we are now in a position to detect that this sounds rather more strikingly Vera Cruzian than Lockean. Solórzano restated the idea that derelict territories among nomadic natives could be justly occupied. And he added that this also applied to all the New World lands and islands that had never been peopled before. Solórzano's mention of the Spaniards' diligence was not about their supposedly superior use of the soil, but rather related to the pains they had taken in their search for vacant territory. The central point was that the lands that were up for grabs were *libres*, free things, because they were untouched and uninhabited.

Conceptually speaking, this was consistent with Vitoria's understanding of occupation. Indeed, Solórzano himself was keen to emphasize that he was using "the same terms" as Vitoria and others, arguing that "deserted and uncultivated places remained in their natural liberty and belong to the one who first occupies them as a prize for his industry."[71] But it was a sharp

67 See Brett, *Changes of State*, p. 1 and *passim*.

68 Vera Cruz, *De dominio infidelium*, trans. Burrus, Doubt III, n. 147.

69 Solórzano, *Política indiana*, bk. I, ch. 9, n. 13.

70 Herzog, *Frontiers of Possession*, p. 257.

71 Solórzano, *Política indiana*, bk. I, ch. 9, n. 18.

factual disagreement with the Salamancan master. For Vitoria, there was no *terra inculta* overseas, and hence the idea of discovery "provides no support for possession of these lands."[72] By contrast, Vera Cruz and Solórzano argued that some areas of the New World were abandoned and – to invoke the theme of these pages once more – in a 'state of nature.' In so doing, they unlocked a door to empire that Vitoria had previously closed.

2 Natural Society and Empire

We have seen that appeals to the title of occupation persisted in the century after Vitoria. Nobody claimed that it was a title of conquest *tout court*, or that it could have served to dispossess the Aztecs and Incas. But the idea that unowned property and land remained in its communal condition was an increasingly attractive lens through which to develop claims for Spanish ownership of things overseas and authority over parts of the New World.

For Vitoria, as well as those who were writing in his vein, occupation was embedded in a broader story of natural partnership and communication. This was a key premise for why the Spaniards had a right to penetrate Amerindian cities in the first place.[73] It was a relic of the original unity of humanity in Eden. Even though the natural state of innocence was lost, Vitoria noted, "it was never the intention of nations to prevent men's free mutual intercourse with one another."[74] Therefore, "*the Spaniards have the right to travel and dwell in those countries, so long as they do no harm to the barbarians, and cannot be prevented by them from doing so.*"[75] This prompts us to inquire whether Vera Cruz, Acosta, and Solórzano followed Vitoria on this point. Did they, too, deploy a mutual right of communication and thus perpetuate the Vitorian narrative of 'empire lite'? Or did they rather shy away from theorizing the kind of natural cosmopolitanism that was the root of Vitoria's idea of free travel and trade?

2.1 *Intervention and the Love of One's Neighbor*

Before we turn to these questions, let us first consider a related issue that equally homes in on the connectedness of human beings across political boundaries: the notion that it was right to defend the innocent "*from unjust*

72 Vitoria, *De indis*, trans. Pagden and Lawrance, q. 2, a. 3, p. 265.

73 On the ambiguities resulting from this merger, see Benton and Straumann, 'Acquiring Empire by Law,' pp. 21–22.

74 Vitoria, *De indis*, trans. Pagden and Lawrance, q. 3, a. 1, p. 278.

75 Ibid., original emphasis.

death" through human sacrifice, because "God gave commandment to each man concerning his neighbour (Ecclus. 17:14)."[76] For Vitoria, it was irrelevant whether the subjects of a tyrannical ruler opposed or "consent to these kinds of rites and sacrifices," or indeed if they "refuse to accept the Spaniards as their liberators in the matter."[77] If human beings were routinely and unjustly put to death in a foreign commonwealth, any prince could intervene by right of war and depose the tyrannical ruler.

Alonso de la Vera Cruz agreed with the opinion of his former teacher. He explained that no human being could justly wish to die. Homicide was unlawful, since the ownership of life resided exclusively with God. For this the reason, it was *always* just to defend the innocent.[78] At the same time, however, Vera Cruz was cautious when confronting the question if this was what had happened in the Indies.[79] He singled out the example of the Aztecs, who had previously governed the lands where Vera Cruz was now settled, and warned: "Perhaps what seems tyrannical to another nation was appropriate and beneficial for this barbarous people, so that it was better for them to be governed by their lords with fear and command (*imperium*) rather than with love."[80]

Yet Vera Cruz's attempt to redescribe the entrenched contemporary image of indigenous despotism did not have a lasting effect. The notion that the Spaniards had freed the natives from the shackles of tyranny became ever more central to the Castilian historical imagination.[81] By the time that Solórzano was writing, the formerly speculative title of conquest had become the received story. For him, there was no doubt that the peoples overseas had been "oppressed and subjected by their petty kings (*reyezuelos*) with infinite impieties and cruelties, without having anybody who could come to their aid."[82]

However, not all the Spanish theorists of empire were open to this view. José de Acosta put forward a sweeping deconstruction of the right of intervention in foreign cities. Against the opinion of the "illustrious theologians" at Salamanca, he stressed the detrimental consequences of this dictum.[83]

76 Vitoria, *De indis*, q. 3, a. 5, p. 288, original emphasis.

77 Ibid.

78 Vera Cruz, *De dominio infidelium*, Doubt XI, n. 827.

79 This is also acknowledged in Burrus, 'Introduction,' p. 49.

80 Vera Cruz, *De dominio infidelium*, Doubt XI, n. 820.

81 See especially Juan de Matienzo, *Gobierno del Perú, 1567*, ed. and étude préliminaire Guillermo Lohmann Villena (Paris: Institut français d'études andines, 1967), parte I, ch. 4.

82 Solórzano, *Política indiana*, bk. I, ch. 9, n. 35; and ibid., ch. 11, nn. 17–18.

83 Acosta, *De procuranda*, bk. II, ch. 6, n. 1.

In his estimation, the belligerent incursions of the Spaniards killed far more innocent people than the "barbarous tyranny" of the natives.[84] "Morally speaking," it was therefore "hardly or rather never at all possible to invoke the defense of the innocent as a just cause, after having waged war against the indios."[85]

This was a point that he also rehearsed in his short 'opinion' (*parecer*) against Spanish intervention in Macao. In the arena of global politics, one had to weigh up *derecho* and *hecho*, legal and factual considerations.[86] The problem was, Acosta elucidated, that

> the theologian presupposes the fact, but it is better and safer not to do so without a very elaborate account; because laymen – who lust for war by other ends resulting from their interests and pretensions – take literally the opinion of the theologians and jurists, and they will say that this is a matter that has already been approved by legal scholars.[87]

Acosta here launched a blunt attack on his own guild. He called for greater attention to the explosive real-world impact of the discussions that theologians and jurists were having in their books and lecture halls. In this sense, where Vitoria had emphasized 'thick' sociability, Acosta pushed back by giving prominence to a 'thick' morality that was grounded in the practice of politics.

2.2 *Natural Communication*

We can trace a similar clash of judgments regarding the idea of natural communication. On one side, there was Alonso de la Vera Cruz. He rehearsed all the arguments in favor that Vitoria had made earlier on. More than that, he went on to propound that traveling to foreign cities was at the very heart of what it meant to be human: "man is by nature a political animal," Vera Cruz argued, "but political society (*politia*) and communication are established

84 Ibid., n. 2.

85 Ibid.

86 José de Acosta, 'Parecer sobre la guerra de la China (1587),' in *Obras del P. José de Acosta de la Compañia de Jesús*, ed. and introduction Francisco Mateos (Madrid: Atlas, 1954), p. 331. A good exposition of the *Parecer* is avaliable in Víctor Zorrilla, 'Consideraciones sobre la doctrina del derecho de guerra de José de Acosta,' *in Normatividades e instituciones eclesiásticas en la Nueva España, siglos XVI–XIX*, ed. Otto Danwerth, Benedetta Albani, and Thomas Duve (Frankfurt: Max Planck Institute for European Legal History, 2018), pp. 39–42.

87 Acosta, 'Parecer sobre la guerra de la China,' p. 331.

through this kind of peregrination, just as much as through the residence in the city that comes first."[88] The idea of a world community was not new in itself and had previously featured in scholastic natural law.[89] But Vera Cruz put forward a most astounding and, to my knowledge, unique vision, in which the crossing of borders was not merely permitted but a *telos* and thus constitutive of the political end of humans.

On the other side, there was José de Acosta. In general terms, he agreed that inter-political travel was a remnant of the Edenic 'state of nature' and a universal right. It was God's will that the people on earth "should remain loyal to each other through a certain community."[90] But Acosta raised a crucial caveat. Drawing on Aristotle's *Politics*, he warned his readers that immigration posed a danger to the stability and order of polities, because "foreigners stir up riots."[91] All the cities that were "properly and perfectly established" could therefore justly stop others from entering.[92] Acosta's central point, however, was that

> for the barbarians the situation is very different, and indeed for this same reason they need foreigners, so that their commonwealths may be set up properly, yes indeed, so that they may have a commonwealth that is worthy of this name.[93]

By bringing his narrative of human political development to bear on the idea of natural communication, Acosta deconstructed the reciprocity of free travel that his predecessors had, at least in theory, endorsed. His 'experiential' understanding of politics once more trumped merely abstract principles. Only this time, it was not about safeguarding the New World natives from the perils of interventionist action. Having developed an original critique of empire, Acosta went on to forge a new, powerful link between communication, 'barbarism,' and the Spanish right to rule the New World.

---

88 Vera Cruz, *De dominio infidelium*, Doubt XI, n. 903.

89 See Vitoria, *De potestate civili I*, q. 3, a. 4, in *Vitoria. Political Writings*, trans. Pagden and Lawrance, p. 40. See Brett, *Changes of State*, pp. 13–14.

90 Acosta, *De procuranda*, bk. II, ch. 13, nn. 1–2.

91 Acosta, *De procuranda*, bk. II, ch. 13, n. 5. Acosta's quote corresponds to the Latin text in contemporary editions of the *Politics*, such as in *Aristotelis Stagiritae omniae quae extant opera ..., tertium volumen* (Venice 1574), *Politicorum*, bk. V, ch. 3, fol. 272 r. In modern editions, this corresponds to 1303a26–30.

92 Acosta, *De procuranda*, bk. II, ch. 13, n. 5.

93 Ibid.

3 Prescription and Natural Law

The preceding sections showed that arguments from the law of nature remained central to the Spanish imperial discourse. Even if Vitoria's titles of conquest were at times creatively modified and re-interpreted, they continued to provide the conceptual architecture of the debate. Recent scholarship, however, casts doubt on the notion that a preoccupation with just titles still offered the adequate means to confront the challenges that Spanish theorists of empire were facing in the later sixteenth and seventeenth centuries. If we follow Anthony Pagden, the decisive shift came with the concept of prescription: Solórzano invoked it to show that "it is not, in the end, the moment of founding that conferred legitimacy upon a society; it was its survival over time."[94] This raises the question whether Solórzano, as Pagden suggests, ultimately legalized an unjustly acquired empire with reference to factual long-term possession.[95] Had the time of natural law, and of morally 'thick' reasoning, passed after all?

3.1 *Prescription and the Conquistadors*

Vitoria had not touched upon prescription in any substantive way in *De indis*. But the concept, and this is important, was not a priori at odds with scholastic natural law thinking.[96] It had a long history in Roman law and medieval canon law, two bodies of sources that Vitoria and his followers extensively read and drew on. In the most general terms, prescription centered on the idea that long-term possession of land or movable property could turn into rightful ownership. It thus regulated the process from factual control to legitimate and full-blown title. For some early modern thinkers, this mode of acquisition included territory that had previously been in a communal, primeval state.[97] But first and foremost – and for the scholastics anyway – it homed in on cases where the prescribed thing was acquired by someone at the expense of another, previous owner.[98] In the present context, therefore, the question

94 Pagden, 'Conquest and the Just War,' p. 59.

95 Ibid., p. 60.

96 For an excellent recent overview, see Jan Hallebeek, 'Early Modern Scholasticism on Acquisitive and Extinctive Prescription,' in *Limitation and Prescription. A comparative Legal History*, ed. Harry Dondorp, David Ibbetson, and Eltjo J. H. Schrage (Berlin: Duncker & Humblot, 2019), pp. 229–62.

97 E.g. for the sixteenth-century Spanish jurist Fernando Vázquez de Menchaca. See the discussion in Brett, *Liberty, Right and Nature*, pp. 186–9; and Edward Cavanagh, 'Prescription and Empire from Justinian to Grotius,' *The Historical Journal*, 60.2 (2017), p. 285.

98 As noted in Hallebeek, 'Early Modern Scholasticism on Acquisitive and Extinctive Prescription,' pp. 233–4.

whether prescription might justify the Spanish empire in America constitutes a counterpoint to inquiries into supposed states of nature overseas.

While continued possession over a long interval of time was crucial, prescription was always also subject to further conditions. Most importantly, it required that the thing in question had to be held in good faith, a point that went back to the classical Roman origins of the notion.[99] Yet the precise role of *bona fides* was subject to debate.[100] According to Roman legal sources, good faith was required at the moment of the taking of a thing. If at some point during the period of prescription – which could extend over several decades for immovables – the possessor realized that she was not the rightful owner, this did not invalidate the process. The rationale for this, as one scholar put it, was that "good order in society depends on drawing a curtain on antiquated claims."[101] The medieval church, however, disagreed. At the Fourth Lateran Council in 1215, it was enacted that good faith was required not just initially but for the whole duration of the prescription. Doubts about the legitimacy of one's possession were an issue of conscience and therefore problematized prescription. This became the authoritative position of the *Liber extra* and, eventually, of the late scholastic theologians.[102]

Alonso de la Vera Cruz explained the matter in the following terms: "prescription confers dominion through a just law in penalty for the negligence of the true owner [...] with the supposition that the one who takes advantage of the prescription is acting in good faith."[103] And it was precisely on this basis that he set out to challenge its applicability in the colonial context. The Indigenous, he wrote, had been "the true and long-standing owners before the coming of the Spaniards."[104] Arguments of prescription, therefore, could never serve to legitimate acts of conquest. Indeed, to argue otherwise would be to endorse the idea that only Christians could hold legitimate property and political power – and that "the Spaniard, merely because he was born in Spain, brought up there, and sprung from Christian parents, has a just title to usurp and deprive of true ownership those who were infidels, idolaters, hateful of God, and accordingly were in unjust possession of the land [...]."[105]

99 See D.41.3.10 on *usucapio*, the Roman law precursor of prescription, and the helpful discussion in Benton and Straumann, 'Acquring Empire by Law,' pp. 16–17.

100 I thank Christiane Birr for alerting me to this crucial point.

101 Richard H. Helmholz, 'Canon Law and Roman Law,' in *The Cambridge Companion to Roman Law*, ed. David Johnston (Cambridge: Cambridge University Press, 2015), p. 401.

102 The key locus was X.2.26.20. See Hallebeek, 'Early Modern Scholasticism on Acquisitive and Extinctive Prescription,' pp. 244–5.

103 Vera Cruz, *De dominio infidelium*, trans. Burus, Doubt I, n. 41.

104 Ibid., n. 44.

105 Ibid., n. 42.

Vera Cruz was not here launching an attack on the imperial venture of the Catholic Monarchs as such. He was rather concerned with the wrongdoings of the most notorious agents of empire, the conquistadors, who had appropriated indigenous territories without a title.[106] But his handling of prescription illustrates that it could be, and was, used as a rhetorically powerful device to expose the absence of justice and morality overseas. The case of Vera Cruz cogently shows that Spanish theorists did not simply use the concept to legalize that which had originally been unjust.

3.2 *Prescription and the Conquest*

The Jesuit José de Acosta saw things rather differently. Considering the early wars of conquest, he suggested that "it is not necessary to dispute this matter amply, but rather, the slave of Christ should act in best faith, as if it had already been prescribed."[107] The specific mention not only of *bona* but of *optima fides*, best faith, is noteworthy. Acosta's point was that the Spaniards could in no way abandon the New World without a great detriment to the *Christian* faith. To do so would be to accept the relapse of the converted Amerindians back into a state of infidelity.[108]

Vitoria had made a similar point in the *De indis*, where he too insisted on the Spanish duty to remain overseas so as to secure the salvation of the neophytes, "once a large number of the barbarians have been converted."[109] Yet Acosta went a decisive step further. To underline the urgency of the claim that Spain must keep its American empire, he turned to Roman history in the pages of the Bible. Although Roman lordship was "for the most part introduced tyrannically,"[110] Paul and Peter nevertheless insisted on the obligation to obey rather than to resist the Caesars "for the sake of conscience."[111] Despite the unjust origins of empires, Acosta concluded, Scripture taught that subjects were always bound to defer to their rulers.[112]

According to the historian David Brading, Acosta's praise of violent imperialism was a "Machiavellian defence of *raison d'état*, so typical of the servants

106 See the overarching question to which Vera Cruz responded the first "Doubt" of his treatise: "whether those who hold natives without any title to them may justly receive tribute or whether they are bound to restore the tribute and free the natives" (ibid., n. 3).

107 Acosta, *De procuranda*, bk. II, ch. 11, n. 1.

108 Ibid., n. 2.

109 Vitoria, *De indis*, trans. Pagden and Lawrance, conclusion, p. 292.

110 Acosta, *De procuranda*, bk. II, ch. 11, n. 2.

111 Ibid. Acosta here quoted from Romans 13:5 and 1 Peter 2:18.

112 Ibid.

of absolute monarchy."[113] And it seems hard to draw a different conclusion. But a careful reading of the *De procuranda* nevertheless raises questions about this interpretation. For some chapters earlier on, Acosta had argued the exact opposite: the "tyrannical usurpations" of the Romans, and their enforcement of might rather than right, "have little to do with the present affair."[114] This condemnation of Rome's despotic politics of expansion sounded rather similar to the argument of the Salamancan theologian Domingo de Soto, who famously criticized the idea of a Roman title to the New World.[115] What, then, are we to make of Acosta's wavering take on Roman imperial violence?

Let us consider his final verdict on prescription:

> whether the reign of the Indies was usurped unjustly or if it was done with justice and order – which is what must be supposed and recommended more, inasmuch as it concerns the administration of the kings – it is in no way expedient to withdraw the government of the Indies, which is most profitable for its eternal salvation, from the Christian princes.[116]

Once again, Acosta's central message was that the Spanish empire had to persist in view of the overarching end of saving the natives. And once again, he did not offer a plain account of how prescription was situated within his vindication of the conquest. Most likely, he thought, the Spanish venture overseas had been licit and prescription was a hypothetical title of conquest, as it were, for the unlikely case that he and others had erred. But whatever way we look at it, the concept did not sit easily with the overarching story that Acosta was telling. It was an alien element, and his cautious treatment of it suggests that he realized this too.

In the next century, Juan de Solórzano set out to revisit the issue in more depth. It was clear that he took his cue from the "the learned and prudent José de Acosta," who had suggested that the Spaniards move on with their empire "with good faith" and treat it "like a prescribed thing."[117] But where Acosta had struggled to fit prescription into his conceptual scheme, Solórzano placed it right at the heart of the natural law discourse. Its application to the Indies

---

113 Brading, *The First America*, p. 190. For a similar argument, see also Zorrilla, 'Consideraciones sobre la doctrina del derecho de guerra de José de Acosta,' p. 46.

114 Acosta, *De procuranda*, bk. II, ch. 5, n. 2.

115 Lupher, *Romans in a New World*, pp. 65–8.

116 Acosta, *De procuranda*, bk. II, ch. 5, n. 2.

117 Solórzano, *Política indiana*, bk. I, ch. 11, n. 12.

> is compatible with what master Vitoria had taught before Acosta; namely that whoever consulted wise men to take possession of a doubtful thing, and then did so by following their judgment, remains safe in that which he acquired; and he retains the thing with this pretext, even if later on it becomes clear that they erred in their counsel.[118]

Solórzano forcefully sought to read the idea of prescription into the *De indis*. And much of what he claimed was congruent with Vitoria's position. At the outset of his lecture on the American Indians, Vitoria had explained that in cases of morally uncertain ownership, one was bound to consult the expert opinion of theologians. Once they approved the case, the possessor could keep the thing in good faith. Because she had done all that she could to resolve the doubt, she was safe in conscience even if in reality her possession was illegitimate.[119] So far, Solórzano had it right. Yet Vitoria, and this is key, never suggested that such ownership continued to be just when new doubts arose. Quite the contrary, at a later stage "an equally competent authority" could put forward "a conflicting opinion which reopens the case, or leads to a contrary verdict."[120] Indeed, the whole point of Vitoria's opening discourse had been to demonstrate why his own inquiry into the justice of the Spanish conquest was needed in the first place.

Solórzano sidestepped this issue. But he did go on to highlight that prescription was a contested concept, at least in the sense that Acosta had previously discussed it; as a retroactive legitimation that served to purge the tyrannous origins of empires.[121] Yet the affair of the Indies was a radically different matter for Solórzano. Any objections to the Spanish conquest were irrelevant, "for the acquisition, as we have said, was made with title and good faith, and such circumstances, which are *accompanied* with the long passage of time, make it irrevocable."[122] Solórzano pointed to the many just titles that the Spaniards had on their side, again emphasizing that the liberation of the Indigenous from their cruel rulers was especially obvious.[123] "Every cause in itself," he

---

118 Ibid., n. 13.

119 Vitoria, *De indis*, trans. Pagden and Lawrance, introduction, pp. 234–7.

120 Ibid., p. 237.

121 Solórzano made this point with regard to an early sixteenth-century polemic penned by Jean Feu, who had rejected prescription in a defense of the autonomy of France from imperial subjection. See Solórzano, *Política indiana*, bk. I, ch. 11, n. 15.

122 Solórzano, *Política indiana*, bk. I, ch. 11, n. 15, emphasis mine.

123 Ibid., nn. 17–18.

concluded, "and all of them together are certain by fact, as is clear from the histories of these conquests."[124]

And yet, Solórzano returned to prescription again. "In conclusion to the force of these titles," he asserted that

> even if kings come into the additional possession of a dominion that is less perfectly or legitimately acquired, these causes are sufficient to revalidate and purge it of its defects: especially if the possessed peoples do not contradict, and if a long course of time has intervened, with which even tyranny is converted into a perfect and legitimate monarchy, as it happened with the Romans.[125]

By restating a version of the argument that Acosta had made before him, Solórzano was ultimately left with the same fundamental tension. But importantly, he did not seek to invalidate his preceding line of argument regarding the original justice of Spain's imperial venture. It therefore seems strange to suggest that Solórzano turned his back on the language of natural law and instead examined the conquest through the prism of a purely 'legal' and 'objective' understanding of Spain's right to rule the New World.[126] Prescription was not the essence of Solórzano's defense of the Spanish empire in America. His fraught venture was to write prescription into a broader story of a conquest that had been just from the beginning. In the end, it was the safety pin of a "fragrant bouquet of different flowers" that Solórzano had put together by picking "the best just titles."[127]

4 Solórzano *contra* Free Communication

By way of a coda to this chapter, I now want to turn to a different question, in the context of which the real significance of Solórzano's appeal to prescription becomes readily apparent. If prescription was not requisite to warrant the conquest, it was vitally important for a parallel enterprise of his: the defense of Spain's right to the Indies against the emerging claims of rival European

124 Ibid., n. 19.

125 Ibid.

126 Pagden, *Lords of all the World*, p. 90; restated verbatim in ibid., 'Conquest and the Just War,' p. 60; and similarly argued in Lupher, *Romans in a New World*, p. 188.

127 Solórzano, *Política indiana*, bk. 1, ch. 9, n. 3.

powers. By tracing Solórzano's intervention in the inter-imperial arena, we shall also revisit the idea of the state of nature in a novel context.

It was the Dutch incursions into the Indies from the close of the sixteenth-century onward, in particular, that troubled residents of colonial Peru like Solórzano. The most memorable event during his own lifetime was a bloody sea battle on the shores of Lima in 1615, on the heels of which the Dutch West India Company almost succeeded in sacking the viceregal capital.[128] There were "so many heretics and writers who are ill-inclined to our nation," Solórzano lamented, and who challenged the legitimacy of Spanish claims to the New World out of pure "envy of our nation."[129] By the time that he was writing, it was no longer sufficient to vindicate the justice of Spanish rule overseas as such. What was required were rock-solid grounds for corroborating that Spain alone, and nobody else, held legitimate authority over its American empire. To confront this novel challenge, Solórzano made a fundamental move against one of the quintessential Vitorian principles of natural law: he deconstructed the idea of free communication to the (now) Spanish Indies.

4.1 The Papal Donation *Contra* Communication

On the one hand, this move of Solórzano's was predicated on the notion that the bulls by which pope Alexander VI had entrusted the New World to Ferdinand of Aragon and Isabel of Castile in 1493 gave them "free, full, and absolute power, authority, and jurisdiction" over "all the dominions of the said lands."[130] The notion of a special mission to evangelize the 'infidels' overseas had been central to Spanish engagements with the conquest all along. For Vitoria and his disciples at Salamanca, Christian preaching was conceptualized as a fundamental right that could be enforced if hindered, and in this sense paved the way for establishing empire overseas.[131] But Vitoria had rejected the idea that the pope could make a *direct* grant of political power over infidels who were not, and had never been, under his spiritual authority.[132]

Historians have suggested that in endorsing the papal donation, Solórzano revived a medieval vision of the papal plenitude of power.[133] Solórzano himself,

128 García Hernán, *Consejero de ambos mundos*, pp. 121–128.

129 Solórzano, *Política indiana*, bk. I, ch. 9, n. 2.

130 Ibid., *Polícita indiana*, bk. I, ch. 11, n. 4.

131 I have made this argument at greater length elsewhere. See Daniel S. Allemann, 'Empire and the Right to Preach the Gospel in the School of Salamanca, 1535–1560,' *The Historical Journal*, 62.1 (2019), pp. 35–55.

132 Vitoria, *De indis*, trans. Pagden and Lawrance, q. 2, a. 2, pp. 258–64.

133 Above all, Muldoon, *The Americas*, 11 and *passim*. See also Brading, *The First America*, p. 225; and Paulino Castañeda Delgado, 'El segoviano P. Diego de Avenaño. Un teocrata

however, was keen to insist that his argument was in line with Vitoria's thinking, even though it seemed incompatible with the opinion of the Salamancan professor. He found the solution to this conundrum in the thought of the Italian Jesuit Robert Bellarmine (1542–1621), who at the end of his career published a book in which he offered critical revisions to his understanding of ecclesiastical power.[134] In it, Bellarmine offered a new conception of the papal donation from a scholastic perspective:

> When I wrote that which concerns Alexander VI's bulls about the division of the newly discovered world, and the victory over the American Indians, I had not yet seen the bull. Therefore, I followed the doctrine of Cardinal Cajetan [...], Francisco de Vitoria [...], and Domingo de Soto [...]. Both because of their arguments, as well as because Cajetan lived during and survived the time of Alexander VI, and so he could have easily known what pope Alexander wanted to convey when dividing the recently discovered world.[135]

Solórzano placed great emphasis on the Bellarminian turn of heart.[136] But like Bellarmine before him, he failed to confront the fact that for Vitoria and his followers, the rejection of the temporal force of the papal bulls had been a fundamental point about the limited scope of papal *potestas*.[137] This was, of course, precisely the point that Solórzano sought to sidestep. All that he wanted was to rely on the papal donation and to write himself into the scholastic tradition at the same time. And the authoritative opinion of the late Bellarmine was perfectly suited for this purpose.

For Solórzano, the papal donation was key because it equipped the Spaniards with unique access to their lands overseas. The supreme pontiff,

moderado, ecléctico, y tardío,' in *Proyección y presencia de Segovia en América*, ed. Mariano Cuesta Domingo (Segovia: Ayuntamiento de Segovia, 1992), p. 380.

134 On the broader context of Bellarmine's changing conception of ecclesiastical power, see Stefania Tutino, *Empire of Souls. Robert Bellarmine and the Christian Commonwealth* (Oxford: Oxford University Press, 2010), especially ch. 3.

135 Robert Bellarmine, *Recognitio librorum omnium Roberti Bellarmini* (Ingolstadt, 1608), recognitio librorum *De Romano pontifice*, p. 22. For Bellarmine's earlier conception of the papal donation, see his *De romano pontifice*, bk. V, ch. 2, in ibid., *Disputationes de controversiis Christianae fidei huius temporis contra haereticos*, 3 vols (Lyon, 1590), I, p. 848.

136 Solórzano, *Política indiana*, bk. I, ch. 11, n. 5. See also the parallel discussion in the *De indiarum iure*, bk. II, ch. 24, n. 22, where Solórzano quoted the Bellarminian retraction in full length.

137 See Vitoria, *De potestate civili I*, trans. Pagden and Lawrance, q. 5, a. 9, p. 100.

he maintained, had rightly held the authority to "divide among the Christian princes the limits of their commerce and navigation with the express prohibition that some must not enter, nor interfere with the affairs of others."[138] For otherwise, it would be impossible to prevent the spread of the very same heresies, which had troubled Christianity in Europe since the advent of the Reformation, to the New World.[139]

4.2 Littoral Sovereignty *Contra* Free Communication

The problem was, however, that Spain's imperial competitors did not buy into this and put forward rival arguments. There were "many heretics," Solórzano expounded, who not only insisted that the conversion of the pagans "must be free to all nations" but who likewise demanded "a right to trade with each other, and to sail and navigate the seas for these and other effects."[140] The papal donation, Solórzano realized, was not enough to counter these claims.

The idea that oceans were "by natural law common to all" was originally from Roman law and prominently echoed in Vitoria's *De indis*.[141] For the latter, it was part and parcel of the broader story of human communication and connectedness after the Fall that we encountered above.[142] But as Solórzano pointed out, it was the work of another Spaniard that became the occasion of "*gran fiesta*," great celebration, among Spain's adversaries: that of the jurist Fernando Vázquez de Menchaca (1512–69).[143] Vázquez took the notion that the seas were held in common into a different direction than Vitoria. His point was that oceanic space could not be subject to prescription, because prescription required a clash between a de jure owner and a de facto possessor – and this was a priori impossible, given that the seas could never be owned in the first place.[144] It was this doctrine that was prominently revived by Solórzano's *bête noire*, the Dutchman Hugo Grotius, who in his *Mare liberum* (1609) insisted that the seas "had remained in a state of nature."[145]

---

138 Solórzano, *Política indiana*, bk. I, ch. 11, n. 30.

139 Solórzano, *Política indiana*, bk. I, ch. 11, n. 28.

140 Ibid., n. 29.

141 Inst. 2.1.1; restated in Vitoria, *De indis*, trans. Pagden and Lawrance, q. 3, a. 1, p. 279.

142 See Section 2 of this chapter.

143 Solórzano, *Política indiana*, ch. 11, n. 11. Solórzano here referred to Fernando Vázquez de Menchaca, *Controversiarum illustrium usque frequentium libri tres* (Venice 1564), bk. II, chs. 28 and 89.

144 See Cavanagh, 'Prescription and Empire,' pp. 286–7; and Brett, *Changes of State*, p. 204.

145 Benjamin Straumann, *Roman Law in the State of Nature. The Classical Foundations of Hugo Grotius' Natural Law*, trans. Belinda Cooper (Cambridge: Cambridge University Press, 2015), p. 41. See Solórzano, *Política indiana*, bk. I, ch. 11, n. 11, for the explicit reference to Grotius's *Mare liberum*.

In the face of the Grotian critique, the papal donation was insufficient to substantiate Spain's right to block off travel and trade to the Indies. Solórzano thus saw himself forced to probe alternative arguments, and to approach his contention from a new angle:

> even without a preceding [papal] concession, only through the long use of time, it is possible for kings and lords to acquire and prescribe a particular right in the seas that they have close to their states (*estados*) and dominions, with the prohibition of foreigners, the imposition of tolls and taxes, and with the exercise of high and low jurisdiction in these waters. This is a most received opinion by almost everybody in general, and it was practiced not only by the Venetians in the Adriatic Sea, but also by the Savoyans in their ocean, by the Genovese in the Ligurian, by the Romans in the Tyrrhenian, by the Greeks in the Ionian and Aegean, and by the French in the Sea of Narbonne.[146]

In the passage that followed right after, Solórzano pointed to John Selden's *Mare clausum* (1635). That treatise, as its title suggests, argued the exact opposite of what Grotius had previously maintained; that both sea and land *could* be owned and occupied since, in fact, there was no essential difference between territorial and oceanic space.[147] But Solórzano himself, and this is important, did not follow this forceful opinion. (In fact, it seems that he primarily pointed to Selden to show off that the Englishman had "in many parts cited our writings.")[148] The notion of a fully closed-off sea was well-beyond Solórzano's own position. He was keen to safeguard the (Vitorian) idea that oceans remained, in principle, the property of all. What Solórzano sought to advocate was sovereign control over coastal waters.

This is readily apparent from the long quote above, and it becomes even clearer in the corresponding discussion of this issue in the *De indiarum iure*.[149] In his more expansive Latin treatise, Solórzano expressly defended the freedom of the seas, as a space that was exempt from "usurpation and occupation," while simultaneously making a case for the exercise of "jurisdiction over the

146 Solórzano, *Política indiana*, bk. 1, ch. 11, n. 34.

147 John Selden, *Mare clausum, seu de de dominio maris libri duo* (London, 1635). See the discussion in David Armitage, *The Ideological Origins of the British Empire* (Cambridge: Cambridge University Press, 2004), pp. 113–24.

148 Solórzano, *Política indiana*, bk. 1, ch. 11, n. 35.

149 Solórzano himself referred the reader to his earlier treatise in the marginal notes to ibid., n. 34.

seas and coasts that were adjacent to the dominions of rulers."[150] These claims went back to the Italian jurists Bartolus of Sassoferrato (1313–57) and his student Baldus de Ubaldis (1327–1400).[151] From the latter, Solórzano borrowed the most fundamental point of all, namely that it was possible to project one's territorial sovereignty onto the surrounding seas of the city.[152]

Solórzano was not the only one to revive early Renaissance jurisprudence in order to vindicate the occupation of maritime space. As Lauren Benton has shown, the Italian jurist Alberico Gentili made a strikingly similar move, arguing that "the word territory was applied equally to land and to water," and a commonwealth's boundaries could therefore be pushed into the ocean for "one hundred miles, even though it be said that the sea is common."[153] But where Gentili placed this claim in a traditionally Mediterranean context, Solórzano was the first to apply it to the New World. In so doing, he ultimately offered a fresh rationale for Spain's control of the Atlantic and Pacific shores in the New World.[154] Based on the dual pillars of occupation and prescription, Solórzano put forward a new vision of littoral sovereignty that kept the Spaniards in, and all other Europeans out of 'his' America.

5 Conclusion

To sum up, we saw that Francisco de Vitoria's language of natural law left a deep imprint on the Spanish imperial discourse into the seventeenth century. The theologians and jurists writing from the New World creatively tapped into the account of the conquest presented in the *De indis*. Sometimes, they restated Vitorian arguments with a minor twist. Think of Juan de Solórzano's insistence that Spanish intervention in defense of the innocent was not only a hypothetical title but had happened thus. At other times, they framed factual disagreements as conceptually compatible with the position of the Salamancan master. Consider the case of Alonso de la Vera Cruz, who posited that some lands overseas were beyond the reach of indigenous jurisdiction and

---

150 Solórzano, *De indiarum iure*, bk. III, ch. 3, n. 35.

151 See Cavanagh, 'Prescription and Empire,' pp. 282–83.

152 Solórzano, *De indiarum iure*, bk. III, ch. 3, n. 35.

153 Though Gentili based his claim on Bartolus rather than Baldus: Alberico Gentili, *Hispanicae Adocationis Libri Duo*, trans. and ed. Frank Frost Abbott, 2 vols (New York: Oxford University Press, 1921), II, bk. I, ch. 8, p. 35. See the discussion in Lauren Benton, *A Search for Sovereignty. Law and Geography in European Empires, 1400–1900* (Cambridge: Cambridge University Press, 2010), pp. 125–31.

154 If we believe Solórzano's citations, he was unaware of Gentili's earlier argument.

could therefore be acquired with reference to the Vitorian understanding of occupation. And at other times still, Spanish voices from America openly disagreed with the argument of the *De indis*. Such was José de Acosta's point that the global community of humans did not give rise to a right of unconditional border-crossing, since immigration destabilized the fabric of well-ordered cities. In all those cases, Castilian theorists of empire navigated and responded to the Vitorian framework of just and unjust titles of the Spanish conquest.

If the focus of this essay has been on the connections and continuities from Vitoria to Solórzano, the final section also invites us to ponder the place of the *Política indiana* in the wider context of seventeenth-century international and imperial thought. Solórzano's vision of littoral sovereignty is a case in point. It was a rhetorically powerful move against Hugo Grotius's *Mare liberum* and thus allows us to explore the famous debate on the freedom of the seas from a new and unfamiliar angle.

But I would like to conclude on a slightly different note. In fact, the Grotian ocean was not wholly unsusceptible to human power and authority. For the ships of sovereigns could traverse it as 'islands' and 'vectors of law,' to use Lauren Benton's imaginative language, that carried jurisdiction with them onto the seas.[155] Solórzano and Grotius thus agreed that oceanic space was, in principle, exempt from political power and remained in a 'state of nature.' And at the same time, they both carved out arguments for exercising sovereignty at sea in ways that served their very different ends. In this sense, the comparison between Solórzano and Grotius is a powerful reminder that the languages of early modern political theory were as much about 'politics' as they were about 'theory.'

Select Bibliography

Primary sources

Acosta, José de. *De procuranda indorum salute. Pacificación y colonización*. Edited with parallel Spanish translation by Luciano Pereña et al. (Madrid: CSIC, 1984).

Gentili, Alberico. *Hispanicae Adocationis Libri Duo*. Translated and edited by Frank Frost Abbott. 2 vols. (New York: Oxford University Press, 1921).

Grotius, Hugo. *Mare liberum sive de iure quod Batavis competit ad indicana commercia dissertatio*. (Lyon 1609).

155 Benton, *A Search for Sovereignty*, pp. 112 and 135–6.

Solórzano y Pereira, Juan de. *Politica indiana*. Edited and estudio preliminar by Miguel Ángel Ochoa Brun. 5 vols. (Madrid: Ediciones Atlas, 1972).

Vera Cruz, Alonso de la. *De dominio infidelium et iusto bello*. In *The Defense of the Indians. Their Rights*. Vol. 2 of *The Writings of Alonso de la Vera Cruz*. Edited with parallel English translation by Ernest J. Burrus. Rome: Jesuit Historical Institute, 1968.

Vitoria, Francisco de. *Vitoria. Political Writings*. Translated and edited by Anthony Pagden and Jeremy Lawrance. Cambridge: Cambridge University Press, 1991.

Secondary sources

Benton, Lauren, and Benjamin Straumann. "Acquiring Empire by Law. From Roman Doctrine to Early Modern European Practice." *Law and History Review* 28, no. 1 (2010): 1–38.

Brett, Annabel S. *Changes of State. Nature and the Limits of the City in Early Modern Natural Law*. Princeton: Princeton University Press, 2011.

Herzog, Tamar. *Frontiers of Possession. Spain and Portugal in Europe and in the Americas*. Cambridge, MA: Harvard University Press, 2015.

Lupher, David A. *Romans in a New World. Classical Models in Sixteenth-Century Spanish America*. Ann Arbor: University of Michigan Press, 2003.

Muldoon, James. *The Americas in the Spanish World Order. The Justification for Conquest in the Seventeenth Century*. Philadelphia: University of Pennsylvania Press, 1994.

Pagden, Anthony. *Lords of all the World. Ideologies of Empire in Spain, Britain and France c.1500–c.1800*. New Haven: Yale University Press, 1995.

CHAPTER 5

Fleeing "*Polyphemus*'s Den"

Locke's State of Nature as Sanctuary

Ioannis D. Evrigenis

Abstract

Although he identified Filmer as his primary target and never named Hobbes in the *Two Treatises of Government*, John Locke nevertheless declared in necessary to "consider what State all Men are naturally in," in order to understand the nature and origin of political power. Locke thus adopted Hobbes's device of the state of nature, albeit with certain crucial amendments. Foremost among these were the concept of trust, which Locke used to describe the relationship between God and human beings, and which served as the foundation for the right relationship between a people and its government, and a natural right to property, which can never be surrendered. In Locke's framework, a human being's duty of self-preservation towards God and her natural right to property provide the juridical basis for an "appeal to Heaven," when an absolute and arbitrary ruler puts himself in a state of war with his erstwhile subjects. Hobbes had described the state of nature as a condition to be avoided at all costs. Even though Locke wavered between describing it as both desirable and dangerous, he nevertheless insisted that, for all its uncertainty, when compared to life under a tyrant, the state of nature could be seen as a sanctuary.

Keywords

John Locke – Thomas Hobbes – state of nature – law of nature – trust – liberty – equality – property – tyranny

Although he refused "to submit uncritically to the strong tradition which dictates that Locke should always be considered alongside of Hobbes," Peter Laslett[1] nevertheless acknowledged that "[n]o one who set out, as Locke did,

1 John Locke, *Two Treatises of Government*, ed. Peter Laslett (Cambridge: Cambridge University Press, 1960), II § 228, hereafter cited parenthetically by treatise and section numbers.

 | DOI:10.1163/9789004499621_007

to argue from consent to absolute authority, could have avoided arguing to some extent in parallel with the already infamous *Leviathan*," adding, "Hobbist notions were in the air: Locke must have absorbed them, more perhaps from the attacks on them than from direct acquaintance."[2] Locke's single reference to Hobbism in his *Essay concerning Human Understanding* (I.iii.5) is not conclusive evidence for or against Laslett's assertion, although it is hard to believe that someone with Locke's interests would not have read Hobbes's political works. In any case, following Laslett, it has become fashionable to dissociate the two as much as possible.[3] Earlier commentators, however, did not hesitate to identify obvious affinities and even "cribs" on Locke's part.[4] One clear instance of affinity is the basic structure of Locke's political theory, which makes use of all of the fundamental components of Hobbes's counterpart, such as natural law, natural right, punishment, property, and government by agreement, if only to reach dramatically different results. Within that framework, the most arresting point of agreement is Locke's claim in the opening to the *Second Treatise* that the right starting point of an inquiry such as his is the state of nature, a concept that owed its prominence to Hobbes.[5] Yet, whereas for Hobbes the state of nature represented a condition to be avoided at all costs, for Locke it also represented a sanctuary to which subjects could turn when their tyrannical ruler declared war on them through policies that revealed a "settled" design. As the pendulum of power swung from anarchy to despotism, Locke discovered a formula that was inspired by Hobbes and aimed at justifying rebellion when rulers reached too far and, thereby, breached the law of nature.[6] This formula was aided by a subtle, if not entirely clear, distinction that Locke drew

---

I would like to thank Julian Franklin, Victor Gourevitch, Emile Simpson, and Mark Somos for very helpful comments on an earlier version of this chapter.

2 Peter Laslett, Introduction to *Two Treatises of Government*, by John Locke, ed. Peter Laslett (Cambridge: Cambridge University Press, 1960), p. 21.

3 John Locke, *An Essay concerning Human Understanding*, ed. Peter H. Nidditch (Oxford: The Clarendon Press, 1975). For instance, apart from a single reference to the aforementioned passage from the *Essay*, Woolhouse does not mention Hobbes or Hobbism in his biography of Locke (Roger Woolhouse, *Locke: A Biography* [Cambridge: Cambridge University Press, 2007], p. 227).

4 Maurice Cranston, *John Locke: A Biography* [London: Longmans, Green, & Co., Ltd.: 1957], pp. 61–62. See also W. von Leyden, Introduction to *Essays on the Law of Nature* by John Locke [Oxford: The Clarendon Press, 1958], pp. 37–38.

5 See Ioannis D. Evrigenis, *Images of Anarchy: The Rhetoric and Science in Hobbes's State of Nature* (Cambridge: Cambridge University Press, 2014).

6 There are other important sources of inspiration for Locke, including Grotius, Lawson, and Pufendorf. I cannot address those connections here, but some are addressed by Emile Simpson and David Grewal in this volume.

between government and society, so that the dissolution of the former would not necessarily result in the dissolution of the latter. To achieve this, Locke followed the general structure of Hobbes's argument, which on its face appears to map the temporal transition from the state of nature to civil society. By changing the story of the former, Locke was able to introduce new possibilities for the latter. Another important part of that method is the impression that the argument begins from an absolutely basic foundation, and proceeds in logical steps, which eventually amount to an edifice whose integrity cannot be denied. As such, it is necessary to follow Locke's structure.

Locke does not mention Hobbes in his *Two Treatises of Government*, but Hobbes's presence in the background is unmistakable: at the outset of the *Second Treatise*, Locke proposes that if one wishes to understand political power and identify its origin, it is necessary to inquire into the "State all Men are naturally in" (II § 4).[7] As with Hobbes's, Locke's state of nature is one of liberty and equality, although in Locke's case these characteristics come with important caveats. Locke sees that natural state as one in which men are masters of their actions, possessions, and persons "as they think fit, within the bounds of the Law of Nature, without asking leave, or depending upon the Will of any other Man" (II § 4). Locke explains the significance of these boundaries in the following way: although man is free to "dispose of his Person or Possessions, yet he has no Liberty to destroy himself, or so much as any Creature in his Possession, but where some nobler use, than its bare Preservation calls for it". It is for this reason, then, that Locke cautions that "though this be a *State of Liberty*, yet it is *not a State of Licence*" (II § 6).[8] This distinction is based on a key move that shapes the rest of Locke's theory, namely the assertion that in their natural condition human beings are the property of God only. Thus, it becomes clear that in the state of nature no human being can have a claim on any other, since she would be claiming something to which she has no right. What is more, the freedom and power that characterize men in the state of nature are gifts from God to each individual, and hence, inalienable. It is for this reason that the state of nature is one of equality (II §§ 5–6). At the same time, as God's property, human beings have a duty towards Him to preserve themselves.

---

7 "*Political Power* then I take to be a *Right* of making Laws with Penalties of Death, and consequently all less Penalties, for the Regulating and Preserving of Property, and of employing the force of the Community, in the Execution of such Laws, and in the defence of the Commonwealth from Foreign Injury, and all this only for the Publick Good" (II § 3).

8 On the evolution of this position in Locke's thought see Tully, "Locke," p. 625.

From the fact that all men are the "Workmanship of one Omnipotent, and infinitely wise Maker" – His property, bound by His will – Locke infers the principles of the law of nature:

> Every one as he is *bound to preserve himself*, and not to quit his Station wilfully; so by the like reason when his own Preservation comes not in competition, ought he, as much as he can, *to preserve the rest of Mankind*, and may not unless it be to do Justice on an Offender, take away, or impair the life, or what tends to the Preservation of the Life, the Liberty, Health, Limb or Goods of another (II § 6).

Locke's emphasis on God's workmanship, property, and will here signifies that human beings have a dual capacity: they are trustees of their persons vis-à-vis their Creator and, effectively, owners of their persons in relation to other human beings. Given that the law of nature is meaningless if there is no way to enforce it, and that each human being has an obligation to God to preserve herself, the enforcement of this law falls into the hands of every individual, for lack of a higher authority with the power to do so.[9] This lack of a higher authority is not just an observation, on Locke's part, of the situation in the state of nature. Rather, it follows from the second characteristic of that state, namely equality: "For in that *State of perfect Equality*, where naturally there is no superiority or jurisdiction of one, over another, what any may do in Prosecution of that Law, every one must needs have a Right to do" (II § 7). The power that flows from one human being's right to prosecute the law of nature is in full accordance with the freedom and equality that characterize the state of nature. This means that it may be used only when someone has transgressed against another. In such a case, the offender has violated the dictates of the law of nature and has attempted to place herself in a position of advantage with respect to the sufferer. Furthermore, by doing so the transgressor has attempted to upset the principles of freedom and equality, since the aim of any attempt to subject someone to one's will is ultimately to put that person's freedom into question and to render her somehow lesser with respect to oneself. Under such circumstances, Locke argues that the sufferer not only has a right to, but is bound by the law of nature to take the situation into her own hands and punish the offender. Such, then, is the power that individuals

9 See II § 7: "the *Execution* of the Law of Nature is in that State, put into every Mans hands". In II § 19, Locke defines the state of nature in the following way: "Men living together according to reason, without a common Superior on Earth, with Authority to judge between them, is *properly the State of Nature*".

are endowed with in the state of nature, and Locke cautions that it is in no way absolute power, even when invoked with respect to an offender, but rather such power as is necessary "for *Reparation* and *Restraint*" (II § 8). With a view to these two principles, "one Man may lawfully do harm to another" and this is what Locke understands as "*punishment*" (II § 8). It is important to note that the first principle of the law of nature (one's duty to preserve oneself) is what allows someone to punish another who has tried to transgress against her. The second principle of the law of nature (one's duty to preserve mankind) allows each individual to punish any offender, even if the offence was not directed against her, since in such a case the punishing of the offender would fall under one's actions aimed at the preservation of mankind.[10]

Locke anticipates a serious problem that stems from the kind of situation that he sees as characteristic of the state of nature. On the one hand, self-love will lead human beings to be partial judges when it comes to themselves or their friends. On the other hand, passion and revenge will lead them to tend to extract greater reparation than the offence demands and to lose sight of restraint in punishing the offender (II § 13). Locke concedes that "the Inconveniences of the State of Nature [...] must certainly be Great" and that "God hath certainly appointed Government to restrain the partiality and violence of Men" (II § 13). However, he is quick to point out that absolute monarchs cannot possibly fall within this category of governments which serve as remedies for those inconveniences, since they too are but human beings and thus subject to all the limitations that are true of every other human being.[11] In fact, Locke argues that in situations where a multitude is submitted to the will of an absolute monarch (and thus to his pleasure, passions, mistakes, etc.), it is clear that "Much better it is in the State of Nature, wherein Men are not bound to submit to the unjust will of another: And if he that judges, judges amiss in his own, or any other Case, he is answerable for it to the rest of Mankind" (II § 13). It is clear, then, that government, broadly speaking, is only a qualified solution to the problems raised in the state of nature and that an absolute monarchy falls outside the scope of such solutions,

10 See II § 8. What distinguishes this case from the previous one is that the person who takes it upon himself to punish by himself or assist the offended individual to punish the offender has a right only to that part of punishment aimed at restraint, since the reparation extracted from the offender belongs always and only to the offended party (see II §§ 10–1).

11 See also II § 172: "This is a Power, which neither Nature gives, for it has made no such distinction between one Man and another; nor Compact can convey, for Man not having such an Arbitrary Power over his own Life, cannot give another Man such a Power over it."

since it remedies none of the problems that warranted its institution in the first place.

Like Hobbes before him, Locke had to face a set of basic questions regarding the state of nature: What is its status? Is it historical, actual, or a thought experiment? As with Hobbes, there are good reasons for answering both questions in the affirmative. One has but to look at the heads of states, Locke argues, in order to see that there are always some men who are in the state of nature with respect to others. Absent an overarching authority, it is clear that the conditions characteristic of the state of nature amongst individuals hold true of states too (II § 14).[12] Moreover, Locke cautions that it is not any covenant that takes its parties out of the state of nature (and into some kind of community), but only those compacts in which the parties agree "together mutually to enter into one Community, and make one Body Politick" (II § 14).[13] To those who might object that there is no instance in history of any men ever having been in such a state of nature, Locke answers that this comes as no surprise, since usually the foundation of a society predates the emergence of historiography. Thus, by the time men come to inquire after the origins of their society, "they have outlived the memory of it. For 'tis with *Common-wealths* as with particular Persons, they are commonly *ignorant of their own Births* and *Infancies*" (II § 101). For Locke, not only does this account for the actual foundation of societies,[14] but it is also consistent with the existence and pre-eminence of the law of nature.[15] Furthermore, one need only look at historical examples of situations in which there is no supreme authority with the ability to legislate and adjudicate, and with the means to enforce the law, in order to find examples of situations in which punishment is *de facto* put into the hands of individuals or small groups. For example, as Tully points out,

> Locke's account of the individual and self-governing origins of political power would have been seen as historically plausible by his audience,

---

12 Locke will return to this point and use it in order to support his claims against absolute monarchy (see, e.g., II §§ 90–1). Hobbes had raised this point before Locke. See Thomas Hobbes, *Leviathan*, ed. Noel Malcolm (Oxford: The Clarendon Press, 2012), XIII: 63. Hereafter cited as "*Leviathan*," followed by chapter and original edition (1651) page numbers.

13 See also II § 15: "all Men are naturally in that State, and remain so, till by their own Consents, they make themselves Members of some Politick Society".

14 Locke cites the cases of Rome and Venice (II § 102).

15 Locke sees the existence of such a law as beyond dispute: "And Reason, which is that Law, teaches all Mankind, who will but consult it, that being all equal and independent, no one ought to harm another in his Life, Health, Liberty, or Possessions" (II § 6).

> even though it was 'strange' and subversively populist. The reason is that it is a fairly accurate redescription of the *accusatory* system of justice by which the Europeans governed themselves until the legal revolution of the twelfth and thirteenth centuries.[16]

In this light, Locke's claims that "the World never was, nor ever will be without Numbers of Men in that State" and that "all Men are naturally in that State" (II §§ 14, 15) acquire further force. Regardless of whether or not the accusatory system of justice was what Locke had in mind specifically when he wrote of historical instantiations of the state of nature, Tully's example is a successful one in that it provides a clear historical illustration of what takes place in the absence of such an overarching authority. Historically, then, examples of the foundation of particular societies coupled with actual instances of absence of a supreme authority were intended to make Locke's argument regarding the state of nature credible.[17]

Having listed the two fundamental dictates of the law of nature, Locke proceeds to examine the implications of the first one regarding man's duty to preserve himself. This duty has two distinct implications, one positive and one negative. A human being's self-preservation requires the acquisition of those means that are necessary for her sustenance. It also requires protection against the designs of another who might seek to overpower her. Locke calls such a situation a "state of war" and defines it as "a State of Enmity and Destruction; And therefore declaring by Word or Action, not a passionate and hasty, but a sedate setled Design, upon another Mans Life, *puts him in a State of War* with him against whom he has declared such an Intention" (II § 16). In such a situation, Locke argues, there is no doubt that the offended party has a right to "destroy that which threatens [him] with Destruction" (II § 16). The justification for this response lies in the very logic of the structure of the state of nature. Locke has argued already that the law of nature is available to any reasonable human being "who will but consult it" (II § 6).[18] Thus, one can safely

16 Tully, "Locke," p. 623.

17 Grant argues that the state of nature is logically necessary for Locke: if government is an artifice, it must have been preceded by a condition from which it was absent (Ruth Grant, *John Locke's Liberalism* [Chicago: The University of Chicago Press, 1987], p. 66).

18 See also § 12: "for though it would be besides my present purpose, to enter here into the particulars of the Law of Nature, or its *measures of punishment*; yet, it is certain there is such a Law, and that too, as intelligible and plain to a rational Creature, and a Studier of that Law, as the positive Laws of Common-wealths, nay possibly plainer; As much as Reason is easier to be understood, then the Phansies and intricate Contrivances of Men, following contrary and hidden interests put into Words." Locke returns to this point in II § 124. See also II § 172, where he argues that one who tries to enforce his designs upon

assume that any human being who decides to act in ways that are threatening to one's liberty and/or equality must be either incapable of consulting the law of nature or violating it on purpose.[19] In either case, that person is a menace to the well-being of others in the state of nature, and the dictates of the law of nature provide sufficient justification for the elimination of the danger that she poses.[20] Locke thinks it safe to assume that one who attempts to impair my freedom and/or alter my status as equal to every other individual in the state of nature is thereby taking the first step towards hindering my ability to ensure my self-preservation. In so doing, she is endangering my life. Thus, it is possible to reach a state of war by starting from a wide variety of offences, as Locke makes it clear when he discusses the examples of one's encounter with thieves, highwaymen, and other criminals, where he declares that it is within one's rights to kill those offenders, since when transgressed against, I have "no reason to suppose, that he, who would *take away my Liberty*, would not when he had me in his Power, take away every thing else" (II § 18).[21] As a subsequent section makes clear, such a condition is tantamount to slavery (II §§ 22–23), and Locke's earlier reference to absolute monarchs (II § 13) serves as a reminder of who the aspiring masters might be.

In what is a only a very thinly-veiled allusion to Hobbes, Locke dismisses "some Men [who] have confounded" the state of nature with a state of war, arguing that they are "as far distant, as a State of Peace, Good Will, Mutual Assistance, and Preservation [state of nature], and a State of Enmity, Malice, Violence, Mutual Destruction [state of war] are from one another" (II § 19).[22] When there is no common superior and no evidence of a design against another, human beings are still in the state of nature. As soon as there is such

another acts in a way revealing his "having quitted Reason, which God hath given to be the Rule betwixt Man and Man, and the common bond whereby humane kind is united into one fellowship and societie."

19 See, for example, II § 11: "[…] a Criminal, who having renounced Reason, the common Rule and Measure, God hath given to Mankind […]."

20 Locke argues that "one may destroy a Man who makes War upon him, or had discovered an Enmity to his being, for the same Reason, that he may kill a *Wolf* or a *Lyon*; because such Men are not under the ties of the Common Law of Reason, have no other Rule, but that of Force and Violence, and so may be treated as Beasts of Prey, those dangerous and noxious Creatures, that will be sure to destroy him, whenever he falls into their Power" (II § 16).

21 See also II § 207.

22 The distinction between the two states is not only necessary for Locke's argument, but also, as Laslett points out (II § 19, footnote to lines 1–5), serves a political purpose, since it is a rejection of the Hobbesian contention that the state of nature is necessarily a state of war. For Hobbes's position see: *Leviathan*, Chapter XIII, pp. 60–63.

a design, however, it "*makes a State of War*, both where there is, and is not, a common Judge" (II § 19). This move is of crucial importance, since by dissociating the state of war from the state of nature Locke makes their coincidence *possible*, but not *necessary*. Thus, the state of nature will not always represent a situation to be avoided at all costs. Indeed, there may be certain conditions that make it seem like an appealing alternative. The building blocks that have led to this point once again suggest a likely scenario: a peaceful state of nature that will offer sanctuary to those faced with a state of war like the one that an absolute monarch might wage against her subjects.

In society, Locke argues, the state of war ceases when an appeal to the law can take over from where force left off. However, "where no such appeal is, as in the State of Nature, for want of positive Laws, and Judges with Authority to appeal to, *the State of War once begun, continues*" (II § 20). This sentence is yet another step in the direction of rebellion. Here, Locke likens such a state of society to the state of nature, since for all practical purposes they are equivalent. The want of positive laws and of judges with authority refers quite clearly to a situation similar to that giving rise to problems in the state of nature, where there is no uniform way of dealing with transgressions and thus human beings are subject to someone else's will (II § 13). In other words, the formal condition of having a common judge is met (because judges are in place and there is some kind of legal system), but the substantive condition for which men entered into this association is not satisfied, since the common judge does not remedy the ills for which power was entrusted to him by the contracting parties. Indeed, Locke says as much, when he explains that

> where an appeal to the Law, and constituted Judges lies open, but the remedy is deny'd by a manifest perverting of Justice, and a barefaced wrestling of the Laws, to protect or indemnifie the violence or injuries of some Men, or Party of Men, *there* it *is* hard to imagine any thing but a *State of War*. For wherever violence is used, and injury done, though by hands appointed to administer Justice, it is still violence and injury, however colour'd with the Name, Pretences, or Forms of Law, the end whereof being to protect and redress the innocent, by an unbiassed application of it, to all who are under it; wherever that is not *bona fide* done, *War is made* upon the Sufferers, who having no appeal on Earth to right them, they are left to the only remedy in such Cases, an appeal to Heaven (II § 20).

This section introduces a new element to Locke's theory: the "appeal to Heaven." That Locke is here referring to a trial by combat between the warring parties is largely beyond dispute.[23] In summing up his argument regarding the state of war, Locke reminds us that to "avoid this State of War [...] is one great *reason of Mens putting themselves into Society*, and quitting the State of Nature" (II § 21). Locke reminds us that when an authority is present that can provide the ultimate remedy (i.e. adjudicate and enforce judgments), then the appeal to that authority ends the state of war, "and the controversie is decided by that Power" (II § 21). When such a power is absent, then those who suffer can appeal only to God, who, through natural law, established the rules and entrusted human beings with their self-preservation.[24]

An altogether different issue at stake is who will judge whether "another man hath put himself in a State of War with me, and whether I may as *Jephtha* did, appeal to Heaven in it?" (II § 21).[25] Fully aware of the consequences of his conclusion, Locke claims that "Of that I my self can only be Judge in my own Conscience, as I will answer it at the great Day, to the Supream Judge of all Men" (II § 21). It is clear, then, that should each individual feel that a state of war has been initiated against her by someone else, then it is up to that individual to weigh the extent to which she is justified in feeling so, assess the situation, and react according to her conscience. Should she, however, abuse her right to appeal to heaven on the pretext that a state of war has been declared against her, then in that case too God is the only authority capable of determining that fact and punishing her for it.[26] Beyond the threat of the Day of Judgment, one can assume that reasonable human beings, like those who sought to leave the state of nature for fear of a state of war, have no interest in perceiving states of war where they do not exist.[27] Such behavior would defeat the purpose for which the society was established.[28] Pragmatically, then, there is little reason

23 On the "appeal to heaven" and trial by combat, see, e.g., Henry C. Lea, *Superstition and Force: Essays on the Wager of Law, the Wager of Battle, the Ordeal, Torture*, 3rd ed. (Philadelphia: Henry C. Lea, 1878), esp. pp. 93–216.

24 Locke sees this as self-evident: "And therefore, in such Controversies, where the question is put, *who shall be Judge?* It cannot be meant, who shall decide the Controversie; every one knows what *Jephtha* here tells us, that *the Lord the Judge*, shall judge" (II § 21).

25 Judges 11:27.

26 As Locke puts it towards the end of the *Second Treatise*, "he that *appeals to Heaven*, must be sure he has Right on his side; and a Right too that is worth the Trouble and Cost of the Appeal, as he will answer at a Tribunal, that cannot be deceived, and will be sure to retribute to every one according to the Mischiefs he hath created to his Fellow-Subjects; that is, any part of Mankind" (II § 176).

27 See II §§ 13, 21, 223–5. In II § 230, Locke asks "Who can help it, if they, who might avoid it, bring themselves into this suspicion [i.e. of the government's motives]? Are the people to be blamed, if they have the sence of rational Creatures, and can think of things no otherwise than as they find and feel them?"

28 See, e.g., II § 21.

to assume that reasonable human beings will put themselves in a state of war with their ruler for no sufficient reason. As will become evident subsequently, this is part of Locke's contention, and history appears to be on his side.[29]

In the published version of *De Cive*, Hobbes noted that desire for civil society and ability to join it and remain in it are two different things (I.2, note to "Born fit"). Nevertheless, his critics took him almost universally as having dismissed natural human sociability. In a remark intended to signal opposition to such a view, Locke declares that

> GOD having made Man such a Creature, that, in his own Judgment, it was not good for him to be alone, put him under strong Obligations of Necessity, Convenience, and Inclination to drive him into *Society*, as well as fitted him with Understanding and Language to continue to enjoy it (II § 77).

Thus, the Lockean man is a being predisposed towards society, one that engages in all kinds of interactions even prior to his flight from the state of nature (II § 77).[30] So long as one's property was secure, there was no need to consider an alternative. Once the need for protection arose, individuals had to surrender their natural right to punish to the society, thereby rendering it "political," and

> because no *Political Society* can be, nor subsist without having in it self the Power to preserve the Property, and in order thereunto punish the Offences of all those of that Society; there, and there only is *Political Society*, where every one of the Members hath quitted this natural Power, resign'd it up into the hands of the Community in all cases that exclude him not from appealing for Protection to the Law established by it (II § 87).[31]

Thus, the community becomes the "Umpire, by settled standing Rules, indifferent, and the same to all Parties" (II § 87). The individual members' natural right is transferred by the community as a whole to certain individuals who are thereby charged with the task of maintaining peace. This transfer also marks the transformation of offenses from interpersonal to communal matters: The community identifies "Offences, which any Member hath committed *against*

29 Locke develops this point further in II §§ 223–5, 230.

30 See also II § 83: "For all the ends of *Marriage* being to be obtained under Politick Government, as well as in the state of Nature [...]."

31 Cf. Grotius, *De Jure Belli ac Pacis*, II.iii-iv.

the Society, with such Penalties as the Law has established" (II § 87, emphasis added). These characteristics, Locke claims, make it an easy matter to determine "who are, and who are not, in *Political Society together*" (II § 87, emphasis added):[32]

> Those who are united into one Body, and have a common estabish'd Law and Judicature to appeal to, with Authority to decide Controversies between them, and punish Offenders, *are in Civil Society*[33] one with another: but those who have no such common Appeal, I mean on Earth, are still in the state of Nature, each being, where there is no other, Judge for himself, and Executioner; which is, as I have before shew'd it, the perfect *state of Nature* (II § 87).[34]

Locke explains that in entering society, each individual gives up her power to interpret the law of nature and to punish offenders according to the dictates of that law. The transferal of that power to a collective authority recognized as supreme by all the individual members of the society gives rise to the legislature and the magistrate. These actions, Locke points out, still have their origin in the individuals who compose the society, since they originate either from them directly, or from their representatives (II § 88).

Thus far, Locke's comments regarding the unsuitability of absolute monarchy as a remedy for the ills that human beings face in the state of nature have been relatively mild and largely oblique.[35] At this stage of his argument, Locke makes the matter more explicit. Having explained in detail the ways in which society comes into being, he is now able to return to and substantiate his claim regarding absolute monarchs. Locke claims that absolute monarchy "is indeed *inconsistent with Civil Society*, and so can be no Form of Civil Government at all" (II § 90). He argues that since the aim of the exodus from the state of nature is to avoid situations in which one is judge in his own case, it makes no sense that the purported solution to the problem would in put one back into such a state, as in the case of absolute monarchs and their subjects. Should

---

32 That is, there is the possibility that someone (e.g. the ruler) might exclude himself from society.

33 From the title of Chapter VII as well as from II §§ 87, 89, it is clear that Locke uses the terms 'Community', 'Society', 'Political Society', 'Civil Society', and 'Common-wealth' interchangeably. Locke explains his usage of the term 'Common-wealth' in II § 133, where he indicates that it is not meant to imply any particular form of government.

34 Locke repeats this definition in § 89.

35 See, II § 13 on absolute monarchy, and Locke, II §§ 17, 20, 23 on absolute power (a clear, if covert, reference to his ultimate target).

any controversy arise between the absolute monarch and one or more of his subjects, the latter will have no authority standing above the warring parties to which to resort for the adjudication of the competing claims. Just as two parties without a common judge are in the state of nature, "so is every *Absolute Prince* in respect of those who are under his *Dominion*" (II § 90). An individual who claims both legislative and executive power to himself, no matter whether his title is "*Czar*, or *Grand Signior*, or how you please, is as much *in the state of Nature*, with all under his Dominion, as he is with the rest of Mankind" (II § 91).[36] Locke adds that in such a controversy (i.e. between an absolute sovereign and one or more of his subjects), "*there* they are still *in the state of Nature*" (II § 91, emphasis added).[37] This state of nature, however, is worse than the original, because in it individuals have not only been deprived of the power to punish, but they have also been denied the ability to judge whether or not they have been transgressed against. Thus, whereas in the original state of nature one had only attacks from others like her to fear, under an absolute monarch, that fear is multiplied, since the party that gives rise to it (i.e. the monarch) is not just "in the unrestrained state of Nature," but is also "corrupted with Flattery, and armed with Power" (II § 91). To fortify his argument here, Locke provides a dramatic sketch of the effects of absolute monarchy and cites the example of Ceylon.[38] The conclusion is a simple one: there is such a thing as a state of nature between the absolute monarch and his subjects, and if anything, it is much worse than the original one.[39] This move opens up the possibility that a return to that original might sometimes be preferable.

36 The last part of the sentence is a reference to § 14.

37 See also II § 231. Ashcraft points out that "Locke's argument [...] is framed in terms of the condition of individuals living in the state of nature where the ties of government have been dissolved [... because they thereby] confront the possibility of a state of war brought on by the 'designs' of a ruler who is attempting to claim absolute power and to identify the law with the exercise of his arbitrary will" (*Revolutionary Politics & Locke's Two Treatises of Government* [Princeton: Princeton University Press, 1986], p. 319).

38 According to Laslett, Locke is referring to Robert Knox's *An Historical Relation of the Island of Ceylon*, 1680, which Locke owned (II § 92, footnote to line 12, 327).

39 In II § 137, Locke explains that "Whereas by supposing [Men] have given up themselves to the *absolute Arbitrary Power* and will of a Legislator, they have disarmed themselves, and armed him, to make a prey of them when he pleases. He being in a much worse condition who is exposed to the arbitrary power of one Man, who has the Command of 100000. than he that is expos'd to the Arbitrary Power of 100000. single Men: no Body being secure, that his Will, who has such a Command, is better, than that of other Men, though his Force be 100000. times stronger. And therefore, whatever Form the Commonwealth is under, the Ruling Power ought to govern by *declared* and *received Laws*, and not by extemporary Dictates and undetermined Resolutions."

Locke argues that what semblance of a rule of law exists in such regimes between the subjects is there not because of the ruler's love for them, but "Love of himself, and the Profit they bring him" (II § 93). The real question, Locke proposes, is "*what Fence* is there in such a State, *against the Violence and Oppression of this Absolute Ruler?*" (II § 93). This question, however, is considered "presently the Voice of Faction and Rebellion" (II § 93). Yet, it would make no sense for everyone except one person – the ruler – to agree to be bound by rules made by that one. In Locke's colorful metaphor, it would be tantamount to seeking security from polecats and foxes by entering a lion's den (II § 93).

Under such circumstances, men are bound to feel that they are threatened, no matter what the situation is depicted as.[40] History affords some examples of gifted rulers who combined such absolute power with benevolence, but these are exceptions and cannot serve as the foundations of any regime over an extended period of time. Thus, Locke argues, even though some human beings have been entrusted with power "without any other caution" (II § 94), these cases cannot serve as the rule for government, because there is nothing to protect the subjects from what time and fortune will bring.[41]

In political society, no one can "avoid the force of the Law", and if someone does then he is "perfectly still in the State of Nature *and so can be* ***no part or Member of that Civil Society***: unless any one will say, the State of Nature and Civil Society are one and the same thing, which I have never yet found any one so great a Patron of Anarchy as to affirm" (II § 94, emphasis added). In declaring what by his subjects will be perceived as a design upon their freedom, an absolute sovereign puts himself in the state of nature vis-à-vis those subjects. A monarch behaving thus cannot be a part of that civil society, without

40 Here Locke is returning to a point that he made in II §§ 13, 21 and will return to in II §§ 168, 224–5: individuals are generally reasonable enough to feel when there is cause for alarm and they are also reasonable enough as to know what kinds of countermeasures a particular cause for alarm warrants. Thus, they will generally not perceive a state of war where one does not exist, and they will not rebel without due cause. On this see also II §§ 208–10.

41 It is interesting that one of the examples that Locke cites of situations in which things can go awry is when time "had brought in Successors of another Stamp" (II § 94). This is not only a good illustration of a lack of fixed measures guaranteeing the smooth operation of the civil society, it is also an apt characterization of the particular political situation that Locke's society was faced with. Hume's description is revealing: James, the Duke of York, upon the death of his wife, "openly declared his conversion to the church of Rome. Unaccountable terrors of popery, ever since the accession of the house of Stuart, had prevailed throughout the nation [...] Popery, which had hitherto been only a hideous spectre, was now become a real ground of terror; being openly and zealously embraced by the heir to the crown, a prince of industry and enterprize (*The History of England*, 6: 251)."

necessarily threatening the society. This seems to imply that the society can continue to exist even though the monarch has, by his actions, excluded himself from it.

Given that human beings are by nature free and equal, it is only their consent that allows the "*bonds of Civil Society*" to be placed upon them legitimately (II § 95). The individual decision of any one human being to subject herself thus does not affect anyone else, which is why any number of individuals who get together and decide to institute such a "*Community* or Government, [...] are thereby presently incorporated, and make *one Body Politick*" (II § 95). This passage reveals some of the conditions necessary for the institution of a civil society, but it also raises an important difficulty: why does Locke refer to the institution of a community *or* a government? We have seen that he uses the terms 'Community', 'Society', 'Political Society', 'Civil Society', and 'Commonwealth' interchangeably (II §§ 87, 89).[42] But what about 'government'? Although the way in which the passage is phrased does make the two terms seem as though they are interchangeable, it appears that such a reading would amount to a conflation of two quite distinct moments in the formation of the society. In coming together, individuals are forming a community, the aim of which is to establish a government.[43]

That there is a distinction is apparent in the fact that each individual enters the society of her own accord, which means that the decision is unanimous. Subsequent decisions are left to the majority, "unless they expressly agreed in any number greater than the majority" (II § 99). This agreement – "*all the Compact that is*" – marks the foundation of a commonwealth or society, the only thing that "did, or could *give* ***beginning*** to any *lawful Government* in the World" (II § 99, emphasis added). Locke finds the logic of this argument so compelling,[44] that he dismisses any objections as to its historicity or feasibility (II §§ 101–2).[45] To the mightier objection that in the earliest accounts of history government usually lay with a single man, Locke replies that this is so because in most cases government originated in small groups, such as families, with the father (II § 105), and that even the acceptance of this single individual

42 See also II § 133.

43 Locke is vague as to the nature of the act by which the government comes into being, but his description of the relative standing of the parties in question makes it sound less like a second contract (as in Pufendorf) and more like a conditional assignment, of the kind that Rousseau would posit later, in *Of the Social Contract*.

44 "Reason being plain on our side" (II § 104).

45 See also the relevant discussion of the same problem with regard to the state of nature, above, and in II § 14.

on the part of his subjects required the consent of those under his rule (II §§ 105–6).[46] This does not mean that monarchical government is in any way natural, but rather, that it was consented to in some cases because of the qualities present in the individual to whom obedience was given (II § 107).[47]

Following a series of historical examples in support of his version of the rise of commonwealths and a discussion of their evolution (II §§ 108–12), Locke attempts to explain how human beings born under government are still free to express their consent to that government. He distinguishes between express and tacit consent[48] and declares that he who has joined a commonwealth through express consent

> is perpetually and indispensably obliged to be and remain unalterably a Subject to it, and can never be again in the liberty of the state of Nature; unless by any Calamity, the Government, he was under, comes to be dissolved; or else by some publick Act cuts him off from being any longer a Member of it (II § 121).

In other words, he who has consented to the institution of a society and then of a government cannot, through his own actions, put himself back in the state of nature. If he attempts to transgress against another, then the magistrate will take over and perform his duty. Thus, any action that places the sovereign and one or more of his subjects in the state of nature with respect to each other, must come from the sovereign. Crucially, in Locke's view it is impossible for the subjects to initiate this process.[49]

---

46 This is one of the central issues of the *First Treatise*. In Chapter IX of *De Cive*, Hobbes makes a detailed case as to why the relationship between parents and children is not very different from that between conquerors and conquered. These "natural commonwealths" are effectively indistinguishable from commonwealths by institution in generating obligation.

47 Locke has provided a sketch of this argument in II § 94.

48 An example of express consent is the joining of a commonwealth (II § 120). An instance of tacit consent is the inheritance of land which is under the jurisdiction of the commonwealth (II § 121).

49 Locke argues that one whose obligation stems from his dwelling in and enjoyment of a piece of land over which the government has direct jurisdiction can leave or sell that land, and join other commonwealths or form his own, where there is unclaimed land (II § 121). One who has given express consent, however, "is perpetually and indispensably obliged to be and remain unalterably a Subject to [the commonwealth], and can never be again in the liberty of the state of Nature; unless by any Calamity, the Government, he was under, comes to be dissolved; or else by some publick Act cuts him off from being any longer a Member of it" (II §121).

To the extent that Locke's account of the potential perils of government has succeeded in persuading the reader, it has also given rise to a problem: if the state of nature is as good as Locke had claimed near the opening of the *Second Treatise* (e.g., II § 19), why would anyone leave it? In what at first glance might seem like a striking reversal, Locke corrects that impression by noting that the enjoyment of that state is "very uncertain, and constantly exposed to the Invasion of others" and that the state itself is "very unsafe, very unsecure" (II § 123). But why? Locke lists three things missing from the state of nature. First, there is no established law that may serve as a "Standard of Right and Wrong" (II § 124). The law of nature does not suffice for this purpose, since its dictates are obscured by men's interests. Second, there is no "*known and indifferent Judge,*" since each human being has the right to decide whether or not she has been wronged, as well as the right to punish the party that has transgressed against her (II § 125). Third, there is no such power as will ensure the enforcement even of those punishments that are just and according to the dictates of the law of nature (II § 126). The lack of these conditions leads human beings to exit the state of nature as soon as they can, and seek a situation in which all the missing elements are provided. Upon entering society, one gives up the unrestricted power to pursue the preservation both of herself and of others according to the law of nature (II § 129), as well as the power to punish those who have transgressed against her (II § 130). Locke notes, however, that the surrendering of these powers takes place only so that these individuals may better their situation. Thus, the actions of the society (to whom all these individual powers have been transferred) must be aimed at the common good.[50] Given this assumption, Locke is justified in concluding that "whoever has the Legislative or Supream Power of any Common-wealth, is bound to govern by establish'd *standing Laws*, promulgated and known to the People, and not by Extemporary Decrees" (II § 131).[51]

Locke points out that, in addition to their other disadvantages, absolute monarchies suffer from the increased likelihood that the monarch will tend to dissociate his interests from those of the community, since his position will not depend on the renewal of a mandate (II § 138). At this point, Locke makes it clear that he is not opposed to all instances of absolute power, since that may prove necessary under certain circumstances.[52] He does insist, however,

50 "the power of the Society, or Legislative [...], can never be suppos'd to extend farther than the common good" (II § 131).

51 Locke insists on this point and raises it again in II §§ 136–7.

52 As M. Seliger argues, Locke does not object so much to absolute power, but to *arbitrary* absolute power (*The Liberal Politics of John Locke* [New York: Frederick A. Praeger, 1969], p. 254f.).

that even in those cases the ultimate aim of the association – the common good – must not be lost sight of (II § 139). This aim yields certain principles, which, although general in nature, are clearly aimed at the rule of Charles II. Governments must adhere to the "trust that is put in them by the Society, and the Law of God and Nature" (II § 142). They must therefore: i) govern by established laws that hold for every member of the society; ii) tailor their laws to the pursuit of the good of the people; iii) not invade the property of the people, nor raise taxes without the people's consent; and iv) adhere to the rule that the legislative power cannot be transferred to any body other than the one designated by the people for that task (II § 142).

Although Locke's discussion of the three powers of a commonwealth is largely technical, it deserves our attention for the sake of a remarkable passage that is often overlooked. After introducing some of the fundamental elements of the legislative power, Locke turns briefly to the consideration of a different kind of power: the "*natural*" power. This power, Locke claims, "answers to the Power every Man naturally had before he entred into Society" (II § 145). He then draws attention to the distinction between the members of a commonwealth as individuals, in their internal relations vis-à-vis one another, and as one collective body, in the commonwealth's relations with other entities, *be they states or individuals*. This leads to the conclusion that

> the Controversies that happen between any Man of the Society with those that are out of it, are managed by the publick; and an injury done to a Member of their Body, engages the whole in the reparation of it. So that under this Consideration, *the whole Community is one Body in the State of Nature, in respect of all other States or Persons out of its Community* (II § 145, emphasis added).

Even though it is Locke's prelude to the consideration of the federative power of the government,[53] this passage makes it clear that there can be a situation in which the community is in the state of nature with another entity (not just one or more communities, but also individuals) without losing its status *qua* community.

In examining the relative status of the powers of the commonwealth, Locke notes that the legislative is supreme (II §§ 149–51), since the law of nature lurks always in the background (II § 142). The transition from the state of nature

53 That is, the management of the commonwealth's external affairs (see II § 146). On the issue of the status of princes vis-à-vis other entities in the international arena, see II §§ 14, 91.

into civil society does not remove human beings from the reaches of the law of nature, which still reigns supreme.[54] Since society is formed in order to provide a remedy for the fact that not all individuals are capable of interpreting the dictates of the law of nature in a workable and meaningful sense and then applying them to the particular cases that they are called to adjudicate in the state of nature. The legislative body in the state of society is thus called upon to provide a solution to this problem by interpreting the law of nature and deducing a set of codes from those fundamental dictates, such as can be applied to the particular disputes of individuals, thereby cultivating a predictable environment and paving the way for impartial judgments.

To the extent that the legislative body obeys the holder of the executive power, it does so only "*according to Law*" (II § 151). Thus, in a sense, when it does so, it is merely acting within the bounds of rules that it itself has set. Locke argues that customarily, the power of convening the legislative body is placed in the hands of the holder of the executive power (II § 154), but that this in no way means that the latter may use the force of the commonwealth that has been entrusted to her in order to "hinder the *meeting* and *acting of the Legislative*" (II § 155). If she attempts to do so she acts in violation of the people's trust and her action initiates "a state of War with the People, who have a right to *reinstate* their *Legislative in the Exercise* of their Power" (II § 155). Locke makes it clear that such a situation calls for desperate measures and that "In all States and Conditions the true remedy of *Force* without Authority, is to oppose *Force* to it" (II § 155). What is more, as the initiator of this state of war, the ruler who acts thus becomes the aggressor and thereby opens herself to the treatment that those of her kind deserve.[55]

As Locke had indicated earlier (II § 139), and any observer of politics can attest to, government is an unpredictable business. For this reason, it is necessary that the executive be granted a certain amount of discretionary power so that she may act in emergencies, such as the London fire of 1666, to which Locke may be alluding (II § 159). As in all other cases, this discretionary power must be guided by a view of the common good (II § 164). This provision is

54 See also II § 59. In II § 195, Locke points out that princes "owe subjection to the Laws of God and Nature. No Body, no Power can exempt them from the Obligations of that External Law."

55 In II § 172, Locke points out that arbitrary power "is *the effect only of Forfeiture*, which the Aggressor makes of his own life, when he puts himself into the state of War with another." What is more, "shaking off a Power, which Force, and not Right hath set over any one, though it hath the Name of *Rebellion*, yet is no Offence before God" (II § 196).

essential to the success of a good government, but it also invites bad government. What happens when this power is abused? Locke argues that

> Between an Executive Power in being, with such a Prerogative, and a Legislature that depends upon his will for their convening, there can be no *Judge on Earth*: As there can be none, between the Legislative, and the People, should either the Executive, or the Legislative, when they have got the Power in their hands, design, or go about to enslave, or destroy them. The People have no other remedy in this, as in all other cases where they have no Judge on Earth, but to *appeal to Heaven* (II § 168).

In fact, this time the argument for an appeal to heaven is taken somewhat further. The people have no right to give it up, since it stems from the law of nature, and is thus "antecedent and paramount to all positive Laws" (II § 168). That is, it flows from their obligation to God to preserve themselves. But will this lead to chaos? Locke returns to his earlier view that the inconvenience has to be extraordinary in order to lead to rebellion.

This examination of the development of Locke's argument brings us to the most contentious, but also the most important part of the *Second Treatise of Government*. From the outset, Locke warns that "He that will with any clearness speak of the *Dissolution of Government*, ought, in the first place to distinguish between the *Dissolution of the Society*, and the *Dissolution of the Government*" (II § 211). The agreement that brings men out of the state of nature, Locke argues, gives rise to "*one Politick Society*," by forming one body politic out of all the distinct individuals that unite. Locke points out that "[t]he usual and almost only way whereby *this Union is dissolved*, is the Inroad of Foreign Force making a conquest upon them" (II § 211). This much seems to be clear and straightforward: when conquered, the society can no longer exist as "*one intire* and *independent Body*" (II § 211), in which case the union is dissolved and every individual finds himself in the state of nature.[56] Also logical is the claim that when the society is dissolved, then so is the government of that society. The existence of the society is a prerequisite for that of the government,[57] and Locke finds that there are enough examples of this in history to require no further elaboration.

---

56 Here Locke appears to be departing from Grotius's view. See Emile Simpson's chapter in this volume.

57 Locke likens the impossibility of government without a society to the continuing existence of the frame of a house when its materials have been scattered (II § 211).

Conquest, then, explains the dissolution of government through external means. From the inside, Locke identifies any alteration of the legislative[58] as the principal cause behind the dissolution of government. In instituting the legislative body, the society gives rise to a means of expressing its will, namely the preservation of all according to the dictates of the law of nature. Locke sees this institution as the "first and fundamental Act of Society, whereby provision is made for the *Continuation of their Union*" (II § 212). When any man or group of men take it upon themselves to make what rules or laws they please (such as extemporary decrees), they thereby attempt to usurp the power invested by the people in the legislative body. Such an act violates the people's trust and immediately allows the people to "constitute to themselves a *new Legislative*, as they think best, being in full liberty to resist the force of those, who without Authority would impose anything upon them" (II § 212). At such a time, each individual is "at the disposure of his own Will," since the common authority that was put in place of the collective will has been annulled (II § 212).[59] In this formulation Locke sounds as though he is describing the dissolution of society, but I think that it is important to bear in mind the earlier statement, according to which the establishment of the legislature is the first and fundamental act of society, which in turn implies the existence of a society that acts.

Furthermore, the most obvious way in which a legislative may be altered, as we have seen, is through the issuance of extemporary decrees, or, of an element of arbitrariness in a system that to function properly must be fixed. Such arbitrary commands may have a massive effect on the society, as in the case of the raising of taxes without the consent of the parliament on the part of the king, but in any case, even the broadest ones do not affect *every* member of the society. More probably, the first signs of such arbitrariness will come in the form of particular decisions about particular matters. Thus, for instance, in the case of a monarch sympathetic to the Tories, who, upon accession to the throne, removes a Whig from office in order to transfer it to one of his political allies, the offended party may be but one, but the meaning of the action is clear. In other words, what Locke seems to be saying in the section above is that it is up to each individual, especially where those who are not immediately affected by a particular action are concerned, to make up his mind about

58 Locke has hinted at this in II § 142.

59 In comparing this passage with Locke's description of the state of individuals after the dissolution of society due to foreign conquest ("[...] every one return to the state he was in before, with a liberty to shift for himself, and provide for his own Safety as he thinks fit in some other Society") in the immediately preceding one (II § 211) it becomes clear that the two situations are hardly the same.

whether the king's behavior towards another constitutes an attempt to alter the legislative, and thus, to "joyn with him that is injur'd, and assist him in recovering from the Offender, so much as may make satisfaction for the harm he has suffer'd."[60] Consequently, even though certain individuals might not suffer directly from an arbitrary decision to raise taxes, they still might reasonably take that decision to be a sign of future ills; yet, whether they are right or not, only God can judge.[61]

Under a single hereditary monarch Locke sees five ways in which the legislative can be altered: i) when the monarch tries to replace the laws with expressions of his will (e.g. extemporary decrees) (II § 214); ii) when he hinders the legislative from assembling and acting freely (II § 215); iii) when he changes the electors or ways of election without the consent and contrary to the interest of the people (II § 216); iv) when either he or the legislative deliver the people "into the subjection of a Foreign Power" (II § 217);[62] and v) when the laws made by the legislative body with the public good in mind are never put into effect (II § 219). In this last case, in particular, it becomes clear that when "there is no longer the administration of Justice, for the securing of Mens Rights, nor any remaining Power within the Community to direct the Force, or provide for the Necessities of the publick, there is certainly *no Government left*" (II § 219). When the rule of law ceases by any of these means, then "the People become a confused Multitude, without Order or Connexion" (II § 219). But does this mean that the society has been dissolved? Locke seems to imply

60 II § 10. At II § 172 Locke argues that the offender "renders himself liable to be destroied by the injur'd person and the rest of mankind, that will joyn with him in the execution of Justice, as any other wild beast, or noxious brute [...] with whom Mankind can have neither Society nor Security."

61 See, for example, II §§ 21, 176, 240. In II § 209, Locke claims that in some cases the fact that the "Precedent, and Consequences" of the government's actions "seem to threaten all," even if they are addressed only to a small number of individuals. This Locke sees as an inextricable difficulty associated with government, but he goes on to explain that the overall behavior of the government will make it clear to the people whether the common good is its guiding principle or not. As Dunn puts it, "where the ruler has established in the minds of his subjects by even a small number of such actions an acute anxiety about the malignity of his future intentions, they are entitled to go to the aid of his previous victims and resist his abusive actions" (Dunn, *The Political Theory of John Locke*, p. 179).

62 An example of this is Charles II's secret alliance with France despite the fact that it was against the will of the representatives of his people (see Hume, *The History of England*, VI: 308–9). Also, as Ashcraft points out, Catholic kings were perceived as falling under this category, since their ultimate allegiance lay with the Pope. Ashcraft cites Thomas Hunt, who in his *Great and Weighty Considerations relating to the Duke of York*, claims that "a papist is looked upon as a person that has a Sovereign somewhere else than in England" (Ashcraft, *Revolutionary Politics*, p. 192, footnote 39).

that there is a point at which that may indeed come to be the case. However, he quickly adds that

> *the **Society** can never, by the fault of another, lose the Native and Original Right it has to preserve it self,* which can only be done by a settled Legislative, and a fair and impartial execution of the Laws made by it. But the state of Mankind is not so miserable that they are not capable of using this Remedy [i.e. to provide for themselves, by erecting a new Legislative], till it be too late to look for any. To tell *People* they *may provide for themselves*, by erecting a new Legislative, when by Oppression, Artifice, or being delivered over to a Foreign Power, their old one is gone, is only to tell them they may expect Relief, when it is too late, and the evil is past Cure (II § 220, emphasis added).

Thus, Locke finds that there are practical considerations that permit, and may even make it necessary, that the people take matters into their own hands before it is too late. If, then, action is taken as soon as the plans of the sovereign become apparent, then it is possible that a new legislative body may be put in place in time to avert more serious consequences.[63] Absolute tyranny such as will lead to the complete breakdown of a society is hardly possible from one moment to the next. In the course of an attempt to impose such a tyranny, the ruler will commit enough transgressions against his subjects as will alert the latter to the impending danger. In this sense, and given the passages with which Locke supplements the descriptions of the attempted alteration of the legislative, I think that it is clear that he does not argue, as Grant interprets him, that these cases are necessarily followed by the dissolution of the society.[64]

63 Locke points to the same argument in the works of William Barclay, in II § 239. On Barclay see Laslett's notes to II §§ 232 and 239.

64 Grant claims that "[s]ociety dissolves when it can no longer function as a unit to preserve the group and its members, and it cannot do so without an established legislative acting as the will of the society and authorized to punish breaches of the peace" (*John Locke's Liberalism*, p. 150). The first part of her claim seems reasonable. The second, however, is extreme. It is clear that members of the society retain the same ability to associate solely for the purpose of punishing violators of the law of nature that they had in the state of nature (see especially II §§ 10–11). Grant seems to qualify her earlier claim somewhat, when she argues that "a *successful* [emphasis added] alteration of the legislative leaves each individual free and in the state of nature" (1987: 150), as well as when she points out that "[w]hen the legislative has been altered and government and society have been dissolved, the chance of mounting a successful resistance is slim indeed" (1987: p. 150). These qualifications seem closer to the spirit of the passages in the *Second Treatise*, but I think that it is important to note that Locke found it necessary to distinguish between the dissolution of society resulting from foreign conquest and the possible effects of the

In addition to the ways in which a government is dissolved through the specific actions of the sovereign, Locke offers a second category stemming from his earlier discussion of the rise of commonwealths: the violation of the people's trust by either the legislative body or the sovereign (II § 221).[65] This category is broader and indeed may include some of the conditions for dissolution listed above, but the focus is different. This time Locke is emphasizing the fact that the legislative and the government are appointed trustees of the people's power and that when the common good (for which the legislative and government were established) is lost sight of, then the very rationale and morality underlying the transition from the state of nature to the state of society are effectively wiped out. Those who act in such a way, Locke argues, "put themselves into a state of War with the People, who are thereupon absolved from any farther Obedience, and are left to the common Refuge, which God hath provided for all Men, against Force and Violence" (II § 222).[66] By granting people the right to preempt the designs of the sovereign, however, Locke could be accused of providing the justification for rebellion without sufficient cause. Locke anticipates this accusation and returns to a point he made earlier (II §§ 13, 21, 168, 176, 208–10), telling his readers that this will not happen without sufficient cause. Reason dictates as much, but if this is not enough, then a look at history will provide the additional weight necessary to dispel any fears (II §§ 223–5, 230).[67] In fact, if anyone is to be accused of rebellion, it is those who violate the people's trust and use force for the imposition of their designs upon the people (II §§ 226–7). Locke writes that such rebels, in "removing the Legislative establish'd by the Society (in whose decisions the People acquiesced and united, as to that of their own will) they unty the Knot, and *expose the People a-new to the state of War*" (II § 227). If Locke's argument

---

dissolution of government stemming from the altering of the legislative, which Grant here is conflating. Indeed, historical experience shows that there is a difference between these two situations and that even the worst of tyrannies does not have the same effects on a society as some foreign conquests have had. I think therefore that Locke's distinction is valid and should be taken seriously: alterations of the legislative do not, except in highly unlikely circumstances, lead to a dissolution of the corresponding society. Franklin correctly points to this error in Grant's argument in his review of her book (Franklin, Review of *John Locke's Liberalism* by Ruth Grant, *Political Theory* 17, no. 1 [Feb. 1989]: pp. 157–60, esp. 159–60).

65 Locke offers the example of attempted seizing of property, which is not only a situation likely to muster the sympathy of the majority of any audience, but also one likely to strike a familiar chord with the subjects of Charles I and Charles II both of whom resorted to such practices often (see Hume, *The History of England*, V-VI).

66 That is, to "appeal to heaven".

67 Locke elaborates here on the point raised earlier, in II §§ 13, 21.

is to be followed consistently, then the knot he writes of here can only be that between the government and the people.[68] In other words, by violating the people's trust, the government thereby absolves the people from any obligation towards its commands.

In essence, a monarch who violates the trust placed in him by his people is performing the opposite function of that for which he was put in power initially. That is, instead of eliminating the possibility of a state of war arising between any parties of the society, he is actually introducing one between himself and his subjects.[69] Thus, not only does he fail to provide the required remedy, but he also becomes the very cause of disorder (II § 227). This type of situation demonstrates one of the important differences between a contract and an act of entrustment. Betrayal by a trustee carries significant psychological consequences, not the least of which is a sense of uncertainty and eventually of mistrust, which are precisely the kinds of reasons that individuals left the state of nature for.[70]

To those who are still skeptical of the possibility or reasonableness of a state of war between the government and the people, Locke proposes a case that is all too familiar. No one objects to resisting similar attempts at encroachment from the outside: any foreigner or nation with similar designs against a state is treated with hostility and the use of force merits not a second thought. Why, Locke asks, should domestic encroachment be treated any differently? (II § 231).

---

68 See II § 11, where Locke claims that a criminal, by his actions, has "declared War against all Mankind, and therefore may be destroyed as a *Lyon* or a *Tyger*, one of those Savage Beasts, *with whom Men can have no Society nor Security*" (emphasis added). See also II § 172: "the Aggressor […] renders himself liable to be destroied by the injur'd person and the rest of mankind, that will joyn with him in the execution of Justice, as any other wild beast, or noxious brute *with whom Mankind can have neither Society nor Security*" (emphasis added).

69 In such a case there is no longer rule of law, but only the expression of the particular will of the sovereign, which may change at any time (§§ 199–200). When this takes place, then the subjects have a clear right to resort to the use of force (II § 204), as shown above (e.g. II § 155).

70 Dunn aptly calls this "the brutal ambivalence" that is inherent in the very structure of absolute power. He points out that "the trust which men instinctively feel towards the good ruler is so complete that the force which they consign to him (which is in its physical composition and its moral status their own force) comes to be overwhelming. The trust which they feel derives from the peace which he provides for them. The 'trust' with which he is 'entrusted' is the preservation of this peace. Law is the barricade which protects this peace and confers this assurance. Law, consequently, is the antithesis of force. It represents ease as against anxiety, liberty as against subjection. It is the guarantor of all the elements of a fully human life in the complex societies of Locke's day. If the guarantee is reneged on, the betrayal is total" (Dunn, *The Political Thought of John Locke*, pp. 167–8).

This analogy is illuminating, as it accords also with Locke's mention of a state of nature between states and princes, examined above. This passage in § 231 reveals that Locke does indeed conceive of the state of war between the sovereign and his people in terms at least analogous to those of the international arena.[71]

It being abundantly clear that a tyrant is in the state of nature with regard to his people,[72] and that a subsequent violation of the trust placed in him initially leads to the declaration of a state of war between these parties (e.g., II § 227), it is necessary to consider the implications of Locke's argument for the people themselves under such circumstances. As Locke has indicated before,[73] people who find themselves the subjects of a tyrant may, based on early signs of his offensive behavior, preempt such actions of the sovereign as will limit their liberty. In trusting the sovereign with the power of the community to execute according to the dictates of the law of nature, the people also retain the right to report that trustee (II § 240). In so doing, they remain true to their duties to God as prescribed by the law of nature.[74] Ultimately, however, this means that the final judgment rests with God (II § 176). The decision, then, about whether the behavior of the sovereign constitutes sufficient grounds for the ultimate appeal (i.e. to heaven) rests with the people, but it is only an intermediate decision, since the adjudication of the dispute (should it be decided by the people that a dispute exists) is put in the hands of God (II § 241; see also II § 21). This process allows also for an early exit from the conflict, since if a conflict arose between the people and the sovereign on something not covered by law, then the "Body of the People" (II § 242) has a right to judge the extent of the sovereign's power. If the sovereign yields to the people's judgment, then there is no need for conflict. However, if the sovereign refuses to recognize the boundaries of the people's trust, then the only appeal open to the latter is to heaven (II § 242). Locke's concluding paragraph is quite revealing. He states that "*the Legislative can never revert to the People* whilst th[e] Government lasts" (II § 243). If, however, the ruler by his actions forfeits the power entrusted to him by the people, then "it reverts to the Society, and the People have a Right to act as Supreme, and continue the Legislative in themselves, or erect a new Form,

71 As seen in II § 91, above, Locke argues explicitly that a tyrant is in the state of nature with regard to his subjects as much as he is with other sovereigns. See also II § 14.

72 See II § 91 in particular.

73 See especially II §§ 222–8.

74 By definition, the state of nature involves theological connections. On theology in Hobbes's state of nature, see Evrigenis, *Images of Anarchy*; on Grotius, see Emile Simpson's chapter in this volume.

or under the old form place it in new hands, as they think good" (II § 243, emphasis added).

Despite some ambiguities, Locke appears to hold that even in a state of war with the sovereign the people do not cease to exist as a society.[75] As with his claims regarding the likelihood of unwarranted rebellion, he seems in this case too to be relying at least in part on a commonsensical observation: the dissolution of a society is no easy matter and it usually takes more than the collapse of a government, indeed more than a bloody civil war. Once a society emerges, the innumerable social bonds that develop are sufficient to unite its members even in the face of considerable trials, such as the dissolution of their government. That is not to say that the difficulties associated with the dissolution of a government are negligible. However, they are insufficient to lead to the complete breakdown of all other forms of association. In most cases, the remaining associations provide a foundation for the re-establishment of government so that the society may recover, resume its course and establish a fully functional government.[76] As we have seen, the principal confusion arises in passages in which Locke does not distinguish explicitly between the society and its government (e.g. II § 89). In such references, the function of the government, which is the reason behind the formation of the society, is not explicitly separated from the workings of the society itself, thereby raising questions about the relationship of one to the other. However, I think that a step-by-step tracing of the development of the argument leaves little doubt as to the distinction between the two. Although it is certainly possible that the dissolution of a government lead to the dissolution of a society, it is not likely and certainly not necessary. Even violent civil wars do not destroy underlying civil societies completely.

Locke's construction is ingenious in that the failure of a government to provide the protection for which it was instituted is not to be attributed to the society that entrusted it with power. In other words, the people are not to blame. The failure of the government signifies for Locke nothing more than the failure of the society to foresee its trustee's inability to abide by the dictates of the law of nature; it goes no further than that. Such a failure, according to Locke, does not constitute grounds for the dissolution of the society. If action is taken before it is too late, then it is possible for the people to regain power

75 Most notably in II §§ 211, 220, 243.

76 In Franklin's words, "[t]he critical point for theory is that no new agreement is needed to keep the community in being" (Julian H. Franklin, "Locke on the Dissolution of Society," in Adriana E. Bakos, ed., *Politics, Ideology and the Law in Early Modern Europe: Essays in Honor of J.H.M. Salmon* [Rochester: The University of Rochester Press, 1994]: 175–84, p. 176).

and place it in the hands of a new trustee. Franklin argues that "the 'society,' 'community,' or 'people,' must [...] itself be liable to dissolution if it fails to perform its function [i.e. the protection of the individual]."[77] The protection of the individual may be the ultimate reason for which the society is formed, but in Locke's scheme the function of protecting the individual is the task of the government. Thus, any liability stemming from the government's failure to perform its appointed task cannot fall to the community, except insofar as the latter does not take what measures it can to remedy the situation.

There is little doubt that the political aim of Locke's account of the state of nature and civil society was to condemn Stuart rule in particular and arbitrary rule in general, and the reception of his argument shows that it was influential among those who sought to justify revolution against absolute and arbitrary rulers.[78] I noted at the outset that in order to advance this argument, Locke utilized tools bequeathed to him by earlier thinkers, often of very different persuasions. Attention to the structure and details of Locke's argument in the *Second Treatise* shows clearly that Locke borrowed from Grotius and Pufendorf,[79] but that his greatest debt in that work was to Hobbes. This view has been challenged on a number of levels, with critics beginning from the absence of explicit evidence in Locke's works and even pointing to his denial of any knowledge of Hobbes's ideas. As Parkin puts it, however,

> Locke was not only familiar with (and very concerned about) public understandings of Hobbism, he also owned *Leviathan* and critiques of it. He had been attacked for the supposed Hobbism of the *Essay*. In this context Locke's denials start to look like a distinctive strategy for preserving

---

77 "Locke on the Dissolution of Society," p. 176.

78 There has been some debate as to Locke's influence on the American founders. The dominant view for a long time was that Locke had exerted great influence on them. That view was challenged more recently, but it is very hard to deny the striking similarity between some of the key phrases of the Declaration of Independence to passages in the *Second Treatise*, among other things. On Locke in America see Bernard Bailyn, *The Ideological Origins of the American Revolution* (Enlarged ed.; Cambridge, MA: The Belknap Press of Harvard University Press, 1992) and Mark Somos, *American States of Nature: The Origins of Independence, 1761–1775* (Oxford: Oxford University Press, 2019). On Locke's influence in France see S.-J. Savonius, "Locke in French: The *Du Gouvernement Civil* of 1691 and Its Readers," *The Historical Journal* 47, no. 1 (2004): pp. 47–79.

79 Laslett makes the case for Pufendorf, and considers the latter's engagement with Hobbes the surest way to link Locke with Hobbes. See Emile Simpson and David Grewal's chapters in this volume.

> his reputation rather than a genuine claim not to have known what was in Hobbes's book.[80]

Indeed, the structure and content of the argument of the *Second Treatise* show significant similarities between Hobbes's political theory and Locke's. The most noteworthy of these is Locke's decision to structure his argument on the Hobbesian framework centered on the juxtaposition of the state of nature to civil society. Hobbes had used these concepts in a number of different ways, taking full advantage of the flexibility their history and mental associations afforded him. Locke appears to have understood the utility of having a framework that bears all the marks of a linear and temporal account of the origin of government, but which can also function like a thought experiment, as well as a formal category that can be substantiated by contemporary examples.[81]

Even so, and precisely because of his insight into the flexibility of Hobbes's framework, the conclusions of the *Second Treatise* place Locke opposite Hobbes. Whereas for Hobbes the state of nature is a condition to be avoided at all costs, for Locke there are times when it becomes a sanctuary from a condition that is even worse. Others had disputed Hobbes's depiction of the state of nature as one of enmity and conflict, but it was Locke who most succinctly and memorably argued that the state of nature is not coterminous with the state of war. Where Hobbes thinks that any government is better than none at all, Locke gives society the chance to regroup after a ruler has violated its trust, to appoint a new one. The space in which this process takes place is the state of nature, which may sometimes be unsafe but which can also be safer than keeping company with a lion. The key to unlocking this revolving door was Locke's disagreement with Hobbes on the origin and nature of property. Whereas Hobbes had denied that property in any meaningful sense of the term was possible in the state of nature, Locke provided a sophisticated account of its origin and of the attendant right that an individual has to her person and goods.

A right present in the state of nature and never surrendered to anyone during the transition into civil society becomes a check on potential violations of

---

80 Jon Parkin, *Taming the Leviathan: The Reception of the Political and Religious Ideas of Thomas Hobbes in England 1640–1700* (Cambridge: Cambridge University Press, 2007), p. 401.

81 Seliger's account is sensitive to these important distinctions (*The Liberal Politics of John Locke*, pp. 82–91). See also the insightful interpretation of A. John Simmons (*On the Edge of Anarchy: Locke, Consent, and the Limits of Society* [Princeton: Princeton University Press, 1993], pp. 13–39).

the trust placed in those charged with establishing a stable and open environment that is freer and more reliable than the state of nature. Although Locke does not spell out the details of how governments are formed, it is clear that his compact involves no renunciation of this right by its parties. Instead, the act that gives rise to the government seems to be a different version of the act by which God entrusts human beings with the preservation of their persons and the rest of His creation: as God trusts human beings, human beings trust a government. Given this origin and locus of property, it is apt that disputes over it can ultimately be appealed only to Heaven. Hobbes had recognized the danger inherent in deciding to launch such an appeal and had tried to circumscribe it as much as possible, by making it very personal and applicable only to circumstances in which one's life is in indisputable and immediate danger. That was understandable, given that Hobbes's primary goal was to chart a path from a place of radical insecurity towards peace. For Locke, however, the price of peace has limits. When a long train of abuses leaves little doubt that the holder of the executive power fancies himself a Polyphemus, his people are entitled to flee his den.[82]

Select Bibliography

Primary Sources

Thomas Hobbes, *Leviathan*, ed. Noel Malcolm (Oxford: The Clarendon Press, 2012).

John Locke, *An Essay concerning Human Understanding*, ed. Peter H. Nidditch (Oxford: The Clarendon Press, 1975).

John Locke, *Two Treatises of Government*, ed. Peter Laslett (Cambridge: Cambridge University Press, 1960).

Secondary Sources

Richard Ashcraft, *Revolutionary Politics & Locke's Two Treatises of Government* (Princeton: Princeton University Press, 1986).

John Dunn, *The Political Thought of John Locke: An Historical Account of the Argument of the 'Two Treatises of Government'* (Cambridge: Cambridge University Press, 1969).

Ioannis D. Evrigenis, *Images of Anarchy: The Rhetoric and Science in Hobbes's State of Nature* (Cambridge: Cambridge University Press, 2014).

82 II § 228. In invoking Polyphemus, Locke is once again following in Hobbes's footsteps (Evrigenis, *Images of Anarchy*, p. 154).

Julian H. Franklin, "Locke on the Dissolution of Society," in Adriana E. Bakos, ed., *Politics, Ideology and the Law in Early Modern Europe: Essays in Honor of J.H.M. Salmon* (Rochester: The University of Rochester Press, 1994): 175–84.

M. Seliger, *The Liberal Politics of John Locke* (New York: Frederick A. Praeger, 1969).

A. John Simmons, *On the Edge of Anarchy: Locke, Consent, and the Limits of Society* (Princeton: Princeton University Press, 1993).

CHAPTER 6

Invisible People

The State of Nature in Hugo Grotius' Account of Global Legal Order

Emile Simpson

Abstract

This chapter considers how Hugo Grotius' (1583–1645) account of the state of nature represented a move, in legal terms at least, to urbanise the extra-civil condition, as opposed to drawing a sharp divide between nature and the city. The model of urbanisation was that of the Roman city. Grotius' account of the state of nature is best understood as a state of natural liberty, but as one in which it was nonetheless possible to subject others to servitude, and even to slavery. Once subjected in the state of nature, a person, or a whole people, became legally invisible. In this way, the state of natural liberty remained, at least on its visible surface, an account of free people, and free peoples. This account of the state of natural liberty provided Grotius with a means to account for empire that would inform the later development of international law.

Keywords

Grotius – state of nature – state of natural liberty – slavery – liberty – the city – Roman law – international law – empire – natural law – voluntary law

1 Introduction

The state of nature is typically contrasted to the civic state: nature versus city. However, in Grotius' account of the state of nature, which is the focus of this chapter, I will argue that, in a legal sense at least, we find the urbanisation of nature on the model of the Roman city. Grotius' account forms part of the genealogy of the presentation of international law as *public* international law, which, as the label suggests, models the legal world beyond the state by analogy to the civic condition.

 | DOI:10.1163/9789004499621_008

However, the more humans actually lived in nature, the less they had a place in Grotius' global legal order, let alone a say in its content. Thus, hunter-gatherers – the extreme case of people who did not live in settled political communities – are presented by Grotius as not rational enough, indeed, not human enough, to participate in a system of natural law. Rather, when Grotius' legal order encountered such people, it saw them as objects of punishment and subjection: the former as a mode of exclusion, the latter as a mode of inclusion, but one which destroyed their previous identity. Grotius proposed that hunter-gatherers were naturally disposed to servility – that it was 'natural' for those who actually lived in nature to be subjugated by those who did not – which goes to show how his conception of nature was based on *human nature*, and specifically the human nature of man living in a proto-civic or civic state, as opposed to the human nature of those who actually lived in nature, or any idea of nature meant in a sense beyond human nature.

As regards those within, rather than without, Grotius' global legal order – like the Roman legal order on which it was modelled – provided both an account of equality, and of servility, and distinct legal regimes to regulate both: a regime of rights as regards relations between the former; and a regime of powers as regards relations between the former and the latter. Servile people were present, but silent, and invisible: silent to the extent that they had no say over the law's content or normative stance; and invisible in the sense that, as when Rome (or at least Republican Rome) is envisaged as a free society, one visualises its citizens, and not its slaves, who were under the power of their masters – not to mention the position of those who formally were free, but who were nonetheless under the power of others, as were most of Rome's female citizens.

Thus Grotius' account of global legal order looked backwards and forwards. In looking back to the Roman world, but then projecting that model as an account of global legal order forward from the first half of the seventeenth century when Grotius wrote, we can learn something about how the idea of 'international order' would come to be associated with an inter-state order of free and sovereign nations in which subject peoples were accounted for through the state that had imperial power over them, not in their own right – just as servile people in the Roman city were accounted for within the household of their masters. That it was only in the twentieth century that international law started to 'see' subject peoples, and concern itself with the phenomenon of colonisation from the perspective of the colonised, goes to show how enduring was Grotius' stratified model of global legal order, of free and servile peoples, the visible and the invisible.

Since at least the 1990s, the historiography of the state of nature in early modern European political thought has tended: (1) to regard the state of nature as synonymous with the extra-civil condition; (2) to take the rules of the state of nature to be the rules of natural law; and (3) on that basis, to compare different writers' accounts of the state of nature by reference to their accounts of natural law. That approach has yielded a lively debate over whether Grotius had a 'thick' or 'thin' account of natural law / the state of nature, with the main comparator normally taken as Hobbes. That debate was sparked by Richard Tuck, who analysed Grotius' account of natural law as a minimalist, proto-Hobbesian account that justified predatory mercantile activity by European trading companies in the East Indies.[1]

That debate has served *inter alia* to draw the analysis of Grotius' account of natural law (and the historiography of natural law more broadly) into the overseas imperial context. However, for two reasons, the historiographical framing of that debate is in my view too narrow: first, if the state of nature is merely taken as meaning the extra-civil condition, its own technical function as a concept in its own right is overlooked; and second, if the rules of the state of nature are elided with natural law, the role of voluntary obligations in the extra-civic condition are overlooked. The reason why it is important not to overlook the state of nature as a concept in its own right (which, as shall be seen, is better understood as a state of natural liberty) and the role of voluntary obligations in the extra-civil condition, is that both are key parts of the architecture by which Grotius' account of global legal order structured the urbanisation of nature on the Roman model.

This chapter proceeds in three parts. First, I consider Grotius' state of nature as a concept in itself, and argue that it should be understood in terms of a state of natural liberty. Second, I consider the legal regime that applied in the extra-civil condition, the key argument being that it was not a uniform legal regime (i.e. it was not "thick" or "thin" in an absolute sense, but textured), because rights based on volition, and voluntary law, could apply alongside natural rights, and the fixed rules of natural law. And third, I consider Grotius' account of liberty and servility in the extra-civil condition to show that individual people, and whole peoples, could in fact be subjugated, including at the extreme being enslaved, while purportedly still being in a state of natural liberty, insofar as that state described all those in the extra-civil condition.

1 See Richard Tuck, *The Rights of War and Peace: Political Thought and International Order from Grotius to Kant* (Oxford: Oxford University Press, 1999). For a survey of this debate, see Janne E. Nijman, 'Images of Grotius, or the International Rule of Law Beyond Historiographical Oscillation', *Journal of the History of International Law* 17, no. 1 (2015).

2 The State of Nature as a State of Natural Liberty

Grotius rarely used the term 'state of nature' (*status naturae*) in his works on global legal order. He used it four times in the *De Iure Belli ac Pacis* (*The Rights of War and Peace*, 1625, hereafter IBP), and not at all in his earlier work, the *De Jure Praedae Commentarius* (*Commentary on the Law of Prize and Booty* (1604), hereafter IPC).[2]

Nonetheless, the assertion that Grotius was a major theorist of the state of nature is today a commonplace, founded on an assumption that the concept refers to the extra-civil condition. Take for example Benedict Kingsbury and Benjamin Straumann's article on *The State of Nature and Commercial Sociability in Early Modern International Legal Thought* (2010), which, to compare Grotius', Hobbes', and Pufendorf's accounts of the state of nature, uses as a comparator the definition of the concept as being the condition 'where ex hypothesi there was no state'.[3]

In one sense, the state of nature as a state of natural liberty does correspond exactly to the extra-civil condition, because it is that state in which individuals vindicate their own rights, potentially by force. They do this when beyond civil jurisdiction. Thus, in both the IPC and the IBP, Grotius makes frequent reference to the state of natural liberty as being a state before, or beyond, the establishment of courts, which he takes as an indicator of the absence of civil jurisdiction. For example, in a discussion of the right to punish in the IBP, Grotius writes how 'the ancient liberty, which the law of nature at first gave us, remains still in force where there are no courts of justice, as upon the sea. [...]. The same will take place in deserts, or where men lived after the manner of the nomads'.[4] The reference to nomads points to the fact that some people in the present still lived in the state of natural liberty because they had not yet

2 Note that only a revised version of Chapter 12 was published in his lifetime, in 1609, as the *Mare Liberum* (*The Free Sea*). The four references are at: IBP 2.5.9.2, p. 520; 2.5.15.2, p. 543; 2.7.27.1, p. 623; 3.7.1.1, p. 1360. Note that at IBP 2.6.5, p. 570, where the English text reads 'state of nature', Grotius in fact used the term '*ius naturae*'. All references to the IBP hereafter are to Hugo Grotius, *The Rights of War and Peace* (Indianapolis: Liberty Fund, 2005), ed. Richard Tuck; all references to the IPC hereafter are to Hugo Grotius, *Commentary on the Law of Prize and Booty* (Indianapolis: Liberty Fund, 2006), ed. David Armitage.

3 Benedict Kingsbury and Benjamin Straumann, 'The State of Nature and Commercial Sociability in Early Modern International Legal Thought', *Grotiana* 31 (2010), pp. 22–43.

4 IBP 2.20.8.5, p. 970. Manet tamen vetus naturalis libertas, primum in locis ubi iudicia sunt nulla, ut in mari. See a similar list in IPC 12, fol. 38, p. 103.

instituted civil jurisdiction, as exemplified, Grotius tells us, by the case of the native American Indians.[5]

However, the absence of courts could also follow a breakdown in civil jurisdiction, as during a civil war.[6] So too could a breakdown in jurisdiction, of a sort, be of very short duration, such as when, in a case of self-defence 'the matter does not permit of the delay necessary for judicial procedure'.[7] Likewise, while 'we know that the civil laws do not allow any man to do himself justice [...] [to enforce a debt obligation by force is permitted] where there are no courts at all to appeal to, [for] it is there we must have recourse to the law of nature [...] though the exercise of justice should but for the present be interrupted'.[8] In all of these examples, the common feature of the state of natural liberty, as revealed by the idea that it obtains where there are no courts, is that it is a space in which people vindicate, or 'execute' their own rights, as opposed to the situation in the civil state, where that is done by courts. Note however, that it is not the case that the state of nature as the extra-civil condition is legally sealed-off from the civil condition. Hence an obligation that a person self-enforces in the state of nature, say a debt obligation, may have been accrued in the civil state.

There is an identical analysis in the *IPC*, in which a distinction is drawn between two situations in which there is a defect in the means for judicial settlement: a defect 'in law' when there is no jurisdiction as may exist in deserts, islands, on the ocean or in any region where people live without states (*sine republica vivitur*); or a defect 'in fact' when civil authority is disregarded or breaks down. In the case of such defects, 'the situation becomes very much what it was before states and courts of justice were established (*antequam respublica et judicia instituerentur*)', in which there obtained 'the principle that each individual was the executor of his own right'.[9]

---

5 *IBP* 2.2.2.1, p. 421. For a detailed consideration of the position of American Indians in Grotius' Scholastic sources, and the wider context of Spanish early modern legal thought, see Daniel Alleman's chapter in this volume.

6 On civil war, see *IPC* 8 fol. 41', pp. 108–109.

7 *IPC* 8, fol. 37, p.102. Momentaneus est cum salvo jure nostro res eam dilationem non patitur, quae ad judicium necessaria est.

8 *IBP* 2.7.2.2, p. 582. Legibus quidem civilibus scimus vetitum esse sibi ius dicere [...] adeo quidem ut vis dicatur, siquis quod sibi debitum est, manu reposcat, et multis in locis ius crediti amittat qui id fecerit. Imo etiamsi lex civilis hoc non directe prohiberet, ex ipsa tamen iudiciorum institutione sequeretur hoc esse illicitum. Locum ergo habebit quod diximus ubi iudicia continue cessant; quod quomodo contingat explicavimus supra: ubi vero momentanea est cessatio, licita quidem erit acceptio rei, puta si alioqui nunquam tuum recuperare possis, aufugiente forte debitore.

9 *IPC* 8, fol. 38, p. 103.

The idea of the state of nature, or the state of natural liberty, as the state that exists where there is no civil state, and no courts, is a negative definition that tells us what it is not. When taken in isolation, it can produce a very broad account of the state of nature. Thus, in the opening passage of *IBP* Book 1, Grotius states how he sets out to provide an account of 'All the differences of those who do not acknowledge one common civil right, whereby they may and ought to be decided'.[10] It follows that if the state of nature simply means the extra-civil condition, given how the entire *IBP* is an account of the extra-civil condition, virtually anything Grotius writes in the *IBP* can be attributed to his account of the state of nature. That is, it becomes a general category, deprived of real analytical utility, rather than a concept in its own right.

Let us then look at other ways in which Grotius used the term state of nature, and state of natural liberty, to understand the concept's positive content. Of the four express references to the *status naturae* in the *IBP*, two appear in a sequence on marriage in which the state of nature is contrasted with the introduction of divine law.[11] This was a scholastic usage, not typical of Grotius' own terminology.[12] We shall return to Grotius' theological analysis of the state of nature below.

Another reference is provided as an answer to the following question: 'who shall judge of the right of succession to a crown? Whether the prince then reigning, or the people, either by themselves, or by judges deputed for them'.[13] The answer is that disputes over the succession of who holds the sovereign right do not fall under sovereign right 'and therefore disputes on that head are to be decided as in the state of nature, in which there was no jurisdiction (*quo nulla erat jurisdictio*)'.[14] What Grotius means here is that because the civil law, which

---

10 *IBP* 1.1.1: Controversiae eorum quos nulla juris civilis tenet communio, quales sunt & qui in gentem nondum coierunt, & qui inter se diversarum sunt gentium, tum privati, tum reges ipsi, quique par regibus jus obtinent, sive illi optimates sunt, sive populi liberi, aut ad belli aut ad pacis tempora pertinent. Sed quia bellum pacis causa suscipitur, & nulla est controversia unde non bellum oriri possit, occasione bellici juris quaecunque tales incidere solent controversia recte tractabuntur: ipsum deinde nos bellum ad pacem ut finem suum deducet. I have modified the English text, which otherwise reads '[…] which only provides for the interest of nations […]', as there is no reference to 'interests' in the Latin text.

11 *IBP* 2.5.9.2, p. 520; and 2.5.15.2, p. 543.

12 Suarez for example refers in this way to 'man in pure nature' (*homo in pura natura*). *De Legibus*, 4.2.3. In *Selections from Three Works of Francisco Suárez, Sj*. Translated by Gwladys L. Williams (Oxford: Clarendon, 1944).

13 *IBP* 2.7.27.1, p. 622. Solet et hoc quaeri, an de successione regni iudicare possit, aut rex qui nunc regnat, aut populus per se, aut per iudices datos.

14 *IBP* 2.7.27.1, p. 623. Successio enim Imperii non est sub iure imperii, ac proinde mansit in statu naturali, quo nulla erat iurisdictio. The English translation reads: 'For the succession

flows from sovereign right, cannot itself determine questions of succession of sovereign right, disputes over the succession must be by reference to the anterior state of affairs. Thus, Grotius goes on to say that '[…] if any question rise of the original will of the people (*primaeva populi volunt*[*as*])' in a succession dispute – that is, the will of the people who first set up the sovereign right over themselves by social contract – then 'it would not be amiss to take the advice of the people now in being; for they may be judged to be the same as those who lived formerly, unless it does plainly appear that the people who lived formerly, and by virtue of whose will this right was obtained, were directly of another mind'.[15] Thus, the people do not literally access the state of nature when they consult rules of natural law to decide the question, but, rather, are able (subject to the 'another mind' exception) to understand how decisions in the state of nature would have been made by that particular people.[16]

The key point for our purposes is that it is the *decision* which is made by reference to the state of nature, and therefore by reference to the people presently in being. Even the decision is not literally taken somehow to revert to a state of nature, but rather, is made 'as in' the state of nature, which might better be translated 'as if' in the state of nature, in the sense that the people presently in being are clearly in the civil state – as indeed they must be, since otherwise, there would be no succession dispute to speak of. So the state of nature is a purely hypothetical device that performs a technical function to determine a legal issue that the civil law cannot, but no one involved in the succession dispute need be outside of civil jurisdiction (and even if they are – think of a contender for the throne living abroad – that is irrelevant to the meaning of the state of nature in this context). To step back from the detail of this case, the

---

to the crown is not under the power of the crown, and therefore disputes on that head are to be decided as in the state of nature, in which there was no jurisdiction'. However, I have used instead a literal translation.

15 *IBP* 2.7.27.2, pp. 623–624. Attamen si controversi iuris sit successio, recte et pie facient qui ius vindicant, si de arbitris inter se. Populus vero omnem a se iurisdictionem in regem, et regiam familiam transtulit, nec ea durante ullas eius habet reliquias. De vero regno loquor, non de principatu. Attamen si de primaeva populi voluntate quaestio incidat, non abs re erit populum qui nunc est, quique idem cum eo qui olim fuit censetur, suum super ea re sensum exprimere, qui sequendus erit nisi satis certo constet olim aliam fuisse populi voluntatem, et ex ea ius quaesitum. Note that I have modified the English translation, which renders *primaeva populi voluntate* as 'primary will of the people'.

16 See also *IBP* 2.6.4, p. 569. [the body of the people] being formed by compact and agreement only, and therefore the right that it has over its particular members, is to be determined by the intentions of those who originally framed it […]. Though he does not cite it, this passage supports Tuck's account of the people as the 'sleeping sovereign', Richard Tuck, *The Sleeping Sovereign* (Cambridge: Cambridge University Press, 2015), pp. 81–84.

point of principle is that Grotius at times effectively used the state of nature as a device that could be resorted to in a hypothetical sense *within* the civil condition, which illustrates why the idea of the state of nature as an extra-civil condition must be taken with care – yes, it is always, technically, an extra-civil condition, but it is one that can be used to determine legal issues by people living within the civil state too.

The fourth and final reference to the *status naturae* in the *IBP* comes in the assertion that: 'There is no man by nature slave to another, that is, in his primitive state (*primaevo naturae statu*) considered, *independently of any human fact*, as I have a said in another place [*IBP* Book 2, Chapter 2, §11] [emphasis added]'.[17] This is a foundational claim, which derives from Roman law, to which we shall return. For terminological purposes, however, the utility of the passage is in the cross-reference, which allows us to read in Book 2, Chapter 2, §11 the following definition of the state of nature as a state of natural liberty:

> Nor is the taking up [of] arms upon the account of liberty, justifiable in particular persons, or a whole community; as if to be in such a state, or a state of independence, was naturally, and at all times, everyone's right. For when men are said to be by nature in a state of freedom, by nature is to be understood the right of nature, as it is antecedent to all human acts to the contrary (*de iure naturae praecedente factum omne humanum*); and the freedom there meant, is an exemption from slavery, and not an absolute incompatibility with slavery, that is, no man naturally is a slave, but no man has a right never to become such, for in this sense nobody living is free. [...] And therefore it is every man's apparent duty, who is reduced to a state of servitude, either civil or personal, to be content with his own condition [...].[18]

17 *IBP* 3.7.1.1, p. 1360. Servi natura quidem, id est citra factum humanum aut primaevo naturae statu hominum nulli sunt.

18 *IBP* 2.22.11, pp. 1105–06. Sed nec libertas sive singulorum sive civitatum, id est αὐτοναμία, quasi naturaliter, et semper quibusvis competat, ius bello praestare potest. Nam libertas cum natura competere hominibus aut populis dicitur, id intelligendum est de iure naturae praecedente factum omne humanum, et de libertate κατὰ στέρησιν, non de ea quae est κατ' ἐναντιότητα, hoc est ut natura quis servus non sit, non ut ius habeat ne unquam serviat: nam hoc sensu nemo liber est. quo pertinet illud Albutii: Neminem natum liberum esse, neminem servum; haec postea nomina singulis imposuisse fortunam. Et Aristotelis illud: νόμῳ τὸν μὲν δοῦλον εἶναι, τὸν δ' ἐλεύθερον. e lege venisse ut alius esset liber, alius servus. Quare qui legitima causa in servitutem, sive personalem sive civilem devenerunt, contenti sua conditione esse debent, ut et Paulus Apostolus docet, δοῦλος ἐκλήθης, μή σοι μελέτω. Vocatus es ad servitutem, ne id te torqueat.

Two features of the state of natural liberty stand out here. First, when 'by nature' and 'state of freedom' are taken together, we have an account of natural liberty as that state before any human acts render a person subject to another (literal slavery is only at the extreme end of Grotius' account of servility). Second, both individuals and whole peoples could be in a state of natural freedom.[19]

Note, however, that Grotius in the *IBP* distinguishes between free and unfree, as regards both individual persons and whole peoples. As concerns whole peoples, an unfree people was one that had alienated the sovereign right to their king, as opposed to a free people, which continued to be the ultimate owners of the sovereign right, the king merely holding it by way of usufruct on their behalf.[20] Yet the above citation concerns only servile people, and servile peoples. Does that mean that free people, and peoples, remain in the state of natural liberty at all times? No. Grotius does not consider that anyone, free or servile, is in the state of natural liberty in the civil condition. Rather, as regards free persons, the civil condition renders persons therein subject to sovereign authority. However, the state of nature provides at least two important functions to free subjects *within* the civil condition, which again draws attention to how the state of nature at several points in the *IBP* focused on legal order within the civil state, even if it did so by reference to the extra-civil state.

The first of these functions is that free people (he writes 'all people', but read against the passage just cited, Grotius clearly means all *free* people) have a natural right to rebel against injuries done to them by their sovereign. As a general rule, this natural right cannot be vindicated in the civil condition, since 'civil society being instituted for the preservation of peace, there immediately arises a superior right in the state over us and ours, so far as is necessary for that end'.[21] Exceptionally, however, this natural right can be vindicated in the civil condition, since: 'if in the conferring of the crown [that is, in the terms upon which the people erected the sovereign right over themselves], it be expressly stipulated, that in some certain cases the king may be resisted; [...] some part of natural liberty is reserved to the people, and exempted from the power of the king'.[22]

---

19 See *IBP* 1.4.2, p. 338; and 2.4.14, p. 503; *IPC* 8, fol. 41, p.109; 13 fol. 130, p. 290.

20 On this distinction see Emile Simpson, 'States and Patrimonial Kingdoms: Hugo Grotius' Account of Sovereign Entities in The Rights of War and Peace', *Grotiana* 39 (2018), pp. 45–76. See also Daniel Lee, 'Popular Liberty, Princely Government, and the Roman Law in Hugo Grotius's *De Jure Belli Ac Pacis*', *Journal of the History of Ideas* 72, no. 3 (2011), pp. 371–392.

21 *IBP* 1.4.2, p. 338.

22 *IBP* 1.4.14, p. 377. [...] si in delatione imperii dictum sit, ut certo eventu resisti regi possit, etiamsi eo pacto pars imperii retenta censeri non possit, certe retenta est aliqua libertas

What the state of natural liberty does here is provide a language by which free people in a civil state can claim that sovereign jurisdiction over them – that is, the ambit of civil law – is bounded by reference to those liberties that were reserved by the people at the moment of social contract. It would not only be anachronistic, but incorrect, to say that this analysis prefigured the idea of fundamental rights, since these natural liberties are all alienable, and it may be that none have been reserved in a given case.

The second of these functions is that for the purposes of natural law, free persons in the civil state are the equal of the sovereign ruler acting in his personal capacity. Thus, when Grotius considers whether contracts a king makes with his subjects are binding, he concludes that 'full and absolute promises being accepted, do naturally transfer a right to another, which respects kings equally with private men'. Hence contracts are enforceable by a subject when made with the king in his personal capacity.[23] However, they are not enforceable when the king contracts in his sovereign capacity, since: '[…] that subjects should force him [the king], to whom they are subject, is not lawful, which equals may do against equals by the right of nature, and superiors against inferiors by the civil law'.[24] That is, free subjects may not deal with the sovereign as if an equal in the state of natural liberty, for they are not equals under the civil law, even if free subjects are for other purposes legally equal, even as against the king himself in his personal capacity.

In sum, while the state of nature, or the state of natural liberty, was always in a technical sense an extra-civil condition, Grotius also used the concepts to perform technical functions both without and within the civil state. What we have here is a unified account of global legal order, focused on the inter-relations of persons who inhabit civil states whether in their inter-relations outside the civic state, but potentially even within it.

3 The State of Natural Liberty and Natural Law

As is clear in Grotius' assertion that 'the ancient liberty' was first given to man by natural law, the positive content of the state of natural liberty can be adduced from an account of bare natural law. As we shall see, Grotius' bare natural order also comprised of natural virtues, and natural rights. More broadly,

naturalis, et exempta regio imperio. Potest autem qui ius suum alienat, id ius pactis imminuere.

23 *IBP* 2.14.4, p. 806.

24 *IBP* 2.14.6.2, p. 809.

however, Grotius' account of the extra-civil condition was only at base and in origin a bare natural order. It also allowed for obligations based on voluntary agreements and voluntary law, which varied in time and space, thus creating a textured rather than a uniform account of legal order in the state of nature – that is, it is inaccurate to say that his account of the state of nature was either thick or thin, as if a binary.

Grotius' account of natural order was founded on human nature, and comprehended rules derived: (a) from the first impressions of nature, such as the instinct for self-defence known to all from birth; and (b) from (i) reason, and (ii) man's *appetitus societatis*, that is: 'a certain inclination to live with those of his own kind, not in any manner whatever, but peaceably, and in a community regulated according to the best of his understanding'.[25] Category (b) was expressed by the following five rules of natural law: abstaining from that which is another's; the restitution of what we have of another's, or of the profit we have made by it; the obligation of fulfilling promises; the reparation of a damage done through our own default; and the merit of punishment among men.[26] In effect, the last four of these rules of natural law were secondary rules that protected the integrity of the first, primary rule: to abstain from that which is another's.

In this way, the rules of natural law provided a legal structure which defined the autonomous other (and by implication, the autonomous self), and articulated, in Annabel Brett's apposite expression, the human capacity to recognise alterity.[27] Thus, Grotius' account bounded the use of force by legal rights: 'Right reason [i.e. (i) above], and the nature of society [i.e (ii) above] [...] does not prohibit all manner of violence, but only that which is repugnant to society, that is, which invades another's right'.[28]

25 *IBP* Prolegomena 6, pp.79–81. Inter haec autem quae homini sunt propria, est appetitus societatis, id est communitatis, non qualiscunque, sed tranquillae, & pro sui intellectus modo ordinatae, cum his qui sui sunt generis: quam οἰκείωσις Stoici appellabant. Quod ergo dicitur natura quodque animal ad suas tantum utilitates ferri, ita universe sumtum concedi non debet. This scheme follows a Ciceronian account of the Stoic idea of natural human sociability (*oikeiosis*), as expressed in the *De Finibus*, 3.16–21 (see Cicero, Marcus Tullius, *On Ends* (Cambridge MA: Harvard University Press, 1914), transl. by H. Rackham). See *IBP* 1.2.1.1, p. 180. On the differences between Cicero's concept of *oikeiosis* and the original Stoic concept in this context, see Benjamin Straumann *Roman Law in the State of Nature* (Cambridge: Cambridge University Press, 2015), pp. 88–119.

26 *IBP* 2.1.2.1, p. 394.

27 Annabel Brett, 'Natural Right and Civil Community: The Civil Philosophy of Hugo Grotius', *The Historical Journal*, 45 (2002) 1, pp. 31–51, at 42.

28 *IBP*, 1.2.3, p.184. Recta autem ratio ac natura societatis, quae secundo ac potiore loco ad examen vocanda est, non omnem vim inhibet, sed eam demum quae societati repugnat, id est quae ius alienum tollit.

Beyond this closed category of rules of natural law, Grotius also set out an open-ended category of natural virtues, defined by that which was not repugnant to reasonable beings.[29] If the rules of natural law provided a structural foundation for commutative justice which bound in law, the virtues of natural justice provided the foundation of an account of distributive justice, which bound in conscience.[30] The rationale for this approach seems to have been to find real world purchase by protecting the objective quality of formal legal rules, owing to how subjective could be the interpretation of what distributive justice demanded, especially in a global context (as Peter Haggenmacher nicely puts it, Grotius' account of *temperamenta* – natural virtues that in conscience moderated the strict legal rules of war – amounted to a 'bouquet of adjectives').[31]

Finally, Grotius provided that every person by nature has the following natural rights: to self-defence, to the recovery of one's own, and to punish.[32] Each represented a potential just cause for war, by which an individual could vindicate their rights falling under that ground in the absence of courts. Recovery was by far the largest ground of actionable rights, which Grotius analysed by analogy to Roman civil actions to vindicate personal and property rights.[33]

Because this scheme of natural order was purportedly universal to all humanity, it founded a global account of legal order – though as already noted, it was not in fact universal (at least by today's standards), as it only applied to those deemed to be rational human beings, from which certain indigenous peoples were excluded. At one level, this universality was grounded on the features already noted: those instincts that were universal to all humans from birth, reason, and natural human sociability. However, the universality of Grotius' account of natural order was further underpinned by the theological comprehension of the state of nature.

Thus, Grotius held that while divine law was given to mankind at the creation, after the flood, and under the Gospel (and given specifically to the Jewish

29 *IBP* Prolegomena 9–10, pp. 87–88; see also 1.1.3, p. 136; 1.1.10.3–4, pp. 153–154; 2.2.1, p. 182. quod tali judicio plane repugnat, etiam contra jus naturae, humanae scilicet, esse intelligitur.

30 This is structured along Cicero's distinction between justice and charity. See Cicero, *De Officiis*, 1.20; see also 1.14. (see Cicero, Marcus Tullius, *On Duties* (Cambridge MA: Harvard University Press, 1913), transl. by Walter Miller).

31 Peter Haggenmacher, *Grotius Et La Doctrine De La Guerre Juste* (Geneva: Les Presses Universitaires de France, 1983), p. 573.

32 *IBP* Prolegomena 8, p. 86. In the *IPC* there are four, as recovery is split between personal and property rights.

33 *IBP* 2.1.2.1, p. 394.

people through Moses) it only obliged when it was sufficiently known: 'Gentiles, who have not the [divine] law, do by nature (that is by following in their manners [i.e. without instruction], the rules which flow from the primitive source [...])'.[34] That said, natural law was itself consistent with divine law, 'since nothing could be commanded by God, who can never be unjust, contrary to [divine] law';[35] and it was God who had given men natural law after the flood:

> As before the flood, in the times of the giants, murders were very frequent and common; that the same licentiousness might not become customary, after the restoration of mankind, God was pleased to restrain it by more rigorous and effectual means. Having then abolished the indulgence of former ages, he put men in possession of their natural right; he expressly permitted what nature dictated not to be unjust, and declared every person innocent that killed a murderer. When civil tribunals were erected, that permission, for very strong reasons, was transferred solely to the judges.[36]

Furthermore, in Grotius' analysis of post-lapsarian man, following Erasmian and Arminian theology (and contrary to the Calvinist position), reason, and free will, was inherent in human nature, regardless of grace. As Sarah Mortimer notes, in analysing the *IBP* in conjunction with Grotius' later work *De Veritate* (*On the Truth of the Christian Religion*, 1627): 'For Grotius, human beings are able to evaluate the various ethical and theological claims they encounter, be these Christian, Jewish, Muslim or Pagan, and they can accept or refuse such claims as they see fit. [...] Natural law, for Grotius, contained some principles of religion, and all men were obliged to accept the existence of a God who had some kind of providential care for the universe. But natural law said nothing about the Christian religion, nor about the ethical demands made by Christ on his followers. Moreover, it was not necessary to presume that men were fallen

34 *IBP* 1.1.16, pp. 164–173. Caeterum in aliis omnibus locum habebat Pauli illud, [Romans 2.14] Cum gentes quae legem non habent, natura suapte (id est moribus ex primaevo fonte manantibus: nisi quis malit illud natura referre ad praecedentia, ut opponantur Gentes Iudaeis quibus statim natis lex instillabatur) faciunt ea quae legis sunt; isti legem non habentes sibi sunt lex.

35 *IBP* 1.1.17.

36 *IBP* 2.2.5, pp. 192–193. At cum iam ante diluvium, gigantum aetate, promiscua invaluisset caedium licentia, instaurato post diluvium humano genere, ne mos idem invalesceret, severius occurrendum Deus censuit: et repressa prioris saeculi lenitate, quod natura non iniquum esse dictabat et ipse permisit, ut insons esset qui homicidam occidisset. quod postea institutis iudiciis summas ob causas ad iudices solos restrictum est.

or corrupt in order to examine or analyse the laws of nature; all human beings were perfectly capable of acknowledging the content and force of these laws without any revelation'. Thus: 'Christianity did not affect these [natural] laws, instead it supplemented them – and thus Grotius hoped to keep theology and confessional conflict out of international law'.[37]

In sum, Grotius articulated an account of the state of natural liberty as originally a state structured exclusively by the rules of his bare natural order, comprising natural law, natural virtues, and natural rights. In his ground-breaking work, *Roman Law in the State of Nature* (2015) Benjamin Straumann argues, rightly in my view, that Grotius' account of natural order is primarily modelled on Roman civil law, and is inspired by a Ciceronian interpretation of Stoic ethics. However, Grotius' account of legal order in the extra-civil condition provided that voluntary obligations, founded on law or agreement, could displace the operation of natural law. In my view, it is not only in Grotius' bare natural order that we find an account of order modelled on the civil condition, but also in his account of voluntary law, and primarily, the voluntary law of nations.

Take first voluntary law, and in particular, the voluntary law of nations. In the *IBP*, Grotius' definition of the term '*ius*' in its third sense as 'law' distinguished between natural law and voluntary law; voluntary law was then divided into divine and human branches.[38] While the paradigm form of human voluntary law was civil law, different varieties could obtain in less or more extensive models of human community, for example households, or, in the case of the law of nations, the community of nations (which meant only free nations), which he referred to as the society of nations (*mutuam gentium inter se societatem*).[39] Thus:

37 Sarah Mortimer, 'De Veritate, Christianity and Human Nature', *Grotiana* 35 (2014), pp. 75–94, at 88–89. On Christianity as additional to natural law, see for example *IBP* 2.20.48.1, p. 1041. On Grotius' theology and his account of liberty, see further: Janne Nijman 'Grotius' *Imago Dei* Anthropology Grounding Ius Naturae et Gentium' in *International Law and Religion*, eds. Martti Koskenniemi, Mónica García-Salmones Rovira, and Paolo Amorosa (Oxford: Oxford University Press, 2017), pp. 87–110; Hans Blom, 'Styles of Hetrodoxy and Religious Achievement: Grotius and Arminianism', in *The Intellectual Consequences of Religious Heterodoxy*, eds. Sarah Mortimer and John Robertson (Leiden: Brill, 2012), pp. 47–73.

38 *IBP* 1.1.9, pp. 147–48. On the law of nations as a form of human law, see also *IBP* 2.3.6, p. 459.

39 *IBP* 2.8.1, p. 635; *IBP* 2.5.17, p. 545. Note how in the *IPC*, Grotius clearly sees households as political communities in microcosm, writing that before the establishment of states: 'it is reasonable to assume that these household heads had external as well as internal jurisdiction for their own protection and that of their families'. *IPC* 12.40, p. 107.

> [...] [in contrast to the law of nature] the voluntary law of nations (*ius gentium voluntarium*), [...] only provides for nations (*gentes*), not of those who are either no nation, or but part of one.[40]

Grotius' base model for the voluntary law of nations is civil law, and so too is his model for the *making* of the voluntary law of nations law-making in a city of free people – that is, a republic – which provides the analogy for law-making in the society of nations by majoritarianism:

> Besides this most natural society [i.e. marriage, which Grotius defines earlier in this chapter, at 2.5.8.1, p.513, as the most natural association], there are several other, both public and private; and the public are either between a people and the assembly or person who governs them, or composed of several nations. But all of them have in common to them, that in matters for which each association was instituted, the whole body, or the major part in the name of the whole body, oblige all and every particular members of the society.[41]

It follows for Grotius that the law of nations 'derives its authority from the will of all, or at least of many, nations'.[42]

There is not space here to detail all the differences between the effects of the law of nations and the law of nature in the *IBP*, and indeed, there are so many that it is not seriously arguable that the extra-civil condition as it existed *in his own day* was for Grotius exclusively a regime of bare natural law (notwithstanding that it originally was). That said, it is true that the law of nations was bounded by natural law, in the sense that the law of nations could not contradict the law of nature, even if the law of nature did not itself positively authorise the rule in question.[43]

Briefly to illustrate the point, I will deal with perhaps the most obvious way by which the law of nations could displace the regime of bare natural law, which was in the law of war. Thus, for Grotius 'public war is that whose authors

---

40 *IBP* 3.3.12, p. 1268. [...] verum est, sed ex una dumtaxat parte, idque ex iure naturali non ex iure voluntario gentium, ut quod gentibus tantum prospicit, non his qui sine gente sunt, aut pars gentis.

41 *IBP* 2.5.17, p. 545. Habent autem omnes hoc commune, quod in iis rebus ob quas consociatio quaeque instituta est, universitas, & ejus pars major nomine universitatis obligant singulos qui sunt in societate.

42 *IBP* 1.1.14, pp. 162–63. Latius autem patens est ius gentium, id est quod gentium omnium aut multarum voluntate vim obligandi accepit.

43 See for example at *IBP* 3.2.2.2, p. 1234.

are those that have jurisdiction [i.e. sovereign entities]; private without [i.e. non-sovereign entities]; and mixed where one side is public, another private'.[44] Public war is further divided into a formal and a non-formal variety.[45] While Grotius wrote virtually nothing in the *IBP* on non-formal public war, formal public war (*bellum solemne*) was for Grotius a fundamentally important institution of the law of nations, the rules of which take up most of *IBP* Book 3.

It follows that when sovereign entities fought one another in *bellum solemne*, their legal relationship was not regulated only by natural law; indeed, the legal effects of *bellum solemne* flowing from the voluntary law of nations displaced natural law. Conversely, the bare rules of natural law would apply in a private war, or mixed war (assuming civil law did not apply), for example 'a war against robbers, or a war made by a prince against his own subjects'.[46] Hence when, for example, Straumann writes in his account of Grotius' state of nature that just war was for Grotius 'a natural law institution', it is important to note that *bellum solemne*, which is the focus of Grotius' treatment of war in the *IBP*, was not.[47]

The rules of *bellum solemne* transformed the legal relationship between belligerent parties from what they otherwise would have been under bare natural law. This is a major topic in the *IBP*, which is beyond the scope of this chapter, though we can note some key differences.

First, *bellum solemne* conferred on the belligerents symmetrical rights. That in turn left the original just cause (whether self-defence, recovery, or punishment) legally, though not morally, irrelevant. Conversely, in a mixed or private war, belligerent rights applied on one side only, flowing as they did from the just cause.[48]

Second, a *bellum solemne* was not a punitive war in the sense that a private or mixed war could be when based on the right to punish. For this kind of punitive war gave belligerent rights to one side only, as if in the mode of a law enforcement operation against a criminalised enemy.

Third, just war fought on the basis of the natural right to self-defence did not generate proprietary rights (which were only available on the basis of restitution or punishment).[49] But that made no difference in *bellum solemne*, which

44 *IBP* 1.3.1, p. 240. Publicum bellum est quod auctore eo geritur qui jurisdictionem habet; privatum, quod aliter; mixtum, quod una ed parte est publicum ex altera est privatum. Literally: 'public war is that whose authors are those that have jurisdiction; private without; and mixed where one side is public, another private'.

45 *IBP* 1.3.4, p. 248.

46 *IBP* 3.3.11, p. 1267.

47 Straumann, *Roman Law*, p. 145.

48 *IBP* 3.3.11, pp. 1267–1268; see also 1.4.1, p. 336.

49 *IBP* 3.1.2 pp. 1186–87.

itself conferred title to captured property, regardless of whether the just cause was self-defence.[50]

Again, this example shows how the state of nature was not uniformly textured, as the debate over whether Grotius' account of natural law was 'thick' or 'thin' risks suggesting. For war between two parties who did not share a common civil right could take place upon radically different rules depending on whether the rules of *bellum solemne* applied or not.

That debate can also overlook the key question of *who* was in the state of nature, given that the answer to this question could transform the rules that applied therein. An apposite example of a situation in which a person could be subject to bare rules of natural law in one legal relation, but not in another, is the factual situation of the *IPC* itself. Thus, Grotius' argued that the Dutch captain, Jacob van Heemskerck, gained title to the Portuguese carrack *Santa Catarina* that he had captured off the coast of Johore in 1603 on the basis that: either he was a private actor, who having a natural right to punish the Portuguese for crimes they had allegedly committed against the local peoples, acquired title through just war, which assumes him to be in the state of nature in the sense of subject to the bare rules of natural law (*IPC* Chapter 12); or he was an agent of the Dutch East India Company, and as such was a Dutch state actor, who had captured the *Santa Catarina* in a public war (the states of Holland being at war with Spain at the time, and Portugal being under Spanish crown) and was not in a state of nature in the sense of a domain of bare natural law, in that the rules of public war displaced the rules of natural law (*IPC* Chapter 13).[51] These are alternative arguments – a standard legal technique – which cannot simultaneously be correct.

The role of obligations based on voluntary agreement (as distinct from voluntary law) is more complex. Some voluntary agreements did not displace the operation of the law of nature. Other types of agreement, however, did exactly that. Thus, Grotius distinguishes between two types of agreements between sovereigns (which we can anachronistically understand as treaties, as opposed to contracts): some 'that require such things only, as are agreeable to the law of nature, or those that add something more to it'.[52] He gives as examples certain types of peace treaties, and certain forms of 'leagues which provide for the freedom of commerce and entertainment of strangers on both sides' which

50 *IBP* 2.8.1.1, p. 634.

51 *IPC* 12, fol. 187', p. 184; 13, fol. 141, p. 313.

52 *IBP* 2.15.5.1, p. 821. At nobis accuratius instituenda partitio est, ut primum dicamus federa alia idem constituere quod iuris est naturalis, alia aliquid ei adiicere.

'[do] not insist upon any confederacy, but only so good an understanding, as might secure each other's rights'.[53]

Conversely, those types of treaties that did add something to the law of nature were classified as equal or unequal. The former 'respect either commerce, or the joining of forces, and sharing the expense of the war, or some other matters. Treaties of commerce may be various [...]'.[54] In the latter case, the treaty could impair the sovereignty of the other; or potentially, in cases of conditional surrender, extinguish it altogether.[55]

4 Liberty and Servility in the State of Natural Liberty

Roman law was divided into the law of people, things, and actions.[56] Grotius' account of the state of natural liberty in the *IBP* is framed in these terms, with free persons having rights in relation to people and things, and actions available to vindicate those rights, if necessary through force. Grotius sets up this account in *IBP* Book 2 through a two-stage story of human development. I outline this story, then consider how it underpinned Grotius account of liberty, and of servility.

Recall Grotius' assertion that: 'There is no man by nature slave to another, that is, in his primitive state considered (*primaevo naturae statu*), independently of any human fact'.[57] However, the expression *primaevo naturae statu* does not describe the totality of man in the pre-civil condition. Rather, the 'primitive' or 'primeval' stage was the first stage, in which things were held in common, and all humans had a use-right to those things to satisfy their needs (fishing from the sea for example).[58] In the second stage, Grotius presented the first divisions of property, which were amongst nations (which in the story of Abraham and Lot in Genesis that Grotius tracks, are effectively large family groups), and

---

53 *IBP* 2.15.5.3, p. 823. Sub hoc genere comprehend et federa quibus cavetur, ut utrinque ius hospitii, ut ius commercii sit, quatenus ista sub iure naturali veniunt, qua de re egimus alibi. [...] ubi non de societate ait quaeri, sed de commercio praebendi repetendique iuris.

54 *IBP* 2.15.6.2, pp. 824–825. Aequalia societatis, aut ad commercial pertinent, aut ad belli communitatem, aut ad res alias. Aequales de commerciis pactiones variae esse possunt.

55 *IBP* 2.15.7.2, p. 826; see also 1.3.21, p. 320.

56 *Digest* 1.5.1. See Justinian, *The Digest of Justinian* (Philadelphia: UPP, 2011), edited by Alan Watson.

57 *IBP* 3.7.1.1, p. 1360. See above.

58 Grotius grounds his analysis on Cicero's account in *De Officiis* (at 1.51) that all things produced by nature for mankind's common use should be maintained, whom he cites at *IPC* 12, fol. 102, p. 237. On Grotius' reliance on Cicero here, see Straumann, *Roman Law*, p. 153.

then amongst individuals within nations, as a means to prevent conflict when family groups grew too large.[59] However, as was central to Grotius' argument in the *IPC* against the monopolistic claims of the Portuguese over maritime trade routes, to the present day, the sea itself remained in the first stage, in a state of common ownership.[60]

Beyond its biblical elements, this stadial story was rooted in the narratives of a primeval 'Golden Age' found in classical poetry and philosophy, which had typically presented subsequent development pessimistically.[61] In Virgil's *Georgics* and Ovid's *Metamorphoses*, for example, as Peter Garnsey elegantly puts it: 'the introduction of private property belongs to an inferior age, in which skills and technology were on the advance but morality and happiness on the retreat'.[62] Grotius' account of the transition from the first to second stage, however, has both negative and positive features. The negative element, illustrated for example by the story of Cain and Abel, and the Tower of Babel, presents human nature as riven by vice and ambition.[63] By contrast, the positive element tells a story of man 'no longer willing to dwell in caves' evolving a system of co-operative exchange 'to live in a more commodious and more agreeable manner'.[64] In sum, the institution of private property was developed both to avoid conflict stemming from the breakdown of primitive human society, and to allow for a more advanced economic system.

What is linguistically confusing is that at times Grotius uses the term 'natural liberty' to refer to the primeval stage, but at other times, in a general sense which is not expressly confined to either stage. For example, as we saw above, he refers to the native American Indians as still living in the primeval stage, in which things are held in common. In a different context, he writes that '[…] in

---

59 *IBP* 2.2.2, pp. 425–26. On the references to Genesis, see Stephen Buckle, *Natural Law and the Theory of Property: Grotius to Hume* (Oxford: Clarendon, 1991), p. 40.

60 *IPC* 12 fol.104, p. 242; *IBP* 2.2.3, p. 428; 2.3.9, p. 460.

61 On the Golden Age in the *IPC*, see for example 12, fol. 100', p. 233. See also Francesca Iurlaro's chapter in this volume.

62 Peter Garnsey, *Thinking About Property* (Cambridge: Cambridge University Press, 2007), p. 122. It is beyond the scope of this chapter to examine the historical origins of Grotius' stadial account of human development, which is well covered by Garnsey in Chapters 5 and 6.

63 *IBP* 2.2.2.3, p. 425.

64 *IBP* 2.2.2, p. 426. […] nimirum quod cum non contenti homines vesci sponte natis, antra habitare, corpore aut nudo agere aut corticibus arborum ferarumve pellibus vestito, vitae genus exquisitius delegissent, industria opus fuit, quam singuli rebus singulis adhiberent. This stadial account of a transition from a purportedly barter-based to an exchange-based economy prefigures the work of classical economists such as Adam Smith two centuries later.

a case of absolute necessity, that ancient right of using things, as if they still remained common, must revive, and be in full force [...] in such cases, one might enter again upon the rights of the primitive community'.[65] He means to refer to natural liberty here, since earlier on in the sequence, he uses the term 'natural liberty' in reference to a state in which property could be acquired over things that remained undivided after the first partition (i.e. after the creation of private property).[66]

On the other hand, Grotius must mean the post-primeval stage when asserting how the state of natural liberty is that state in which people vindicate their own rights in his own day: for it would be absurd to write about vindicating property rights in the state of natural liberty if there were no private property rights therein.

What this linguistic confusion reveals, however, is how Grotius generally relied on the concept for both his account of property, and of liberty. As regards property, it explains how things in the extra-civil condition that have no owner, can, or cannot be appropriated, and underpins his account of necessity. As regards liberty, it underpinned an account of natural equality whereby individuals could vindicate their own rights. These claims are related insofar as the mechanism of appropriation assumes a natural equality, in the sense that no one has got a better claim to another over that thing.

What unifies the concept of natural liberty is the idea that natural law can work in two dimensions. Thus, Grotius clarifies how, while the Roman lawyers often used the terms law of nature and law of nations interchangeably, with the exception of the acquisition of property through war, acquisition of property in the extra-civil condition is regulated by the law of nature. In this way, while the law of nature in the first stage underpinned a regime of common ownership 'which flows purely and simply from nature', natural law also supported a regime of private property 'which takes place in consequence of an established property, and before all civil law'.[67] Indeed, to emphasise the centrality of the difference between the law of nature in its pure form, and in the context of an established property regime, Grotius claims that the very term *dominium*

65 *IBP* 2.2.6.2, p. 434. Hinc primo sequitur in gravissima necessitate reviviscere ius illud pristinum rebus utendi tanquam si communes mansissent; quia in omnibus legibus humanis, ac proinde et in lege dominii, summa illa necessitas videtur excepta. On this theme more broadly, see Francesca Iurlaro and Daniel Allemann's chapters in this volume.

66 *IBP* 2.2.5, p. 433.

67 *IBP* 2.8.1.1, p. 635. sed aut referendos ad ius naturae, non quidem merum, sed quod sequatur introductum iam dominium, et legem omnem civilem antecedat [...].

(ownership) and *communio* (common property) had a different meaning in the primeval stage.[68]

The key point, for the purposes of our account of liberty, is that when Grotius used the term 'natural liberty' to describe the extra-civil condition in his own day, he referred to a state in which there existed private rights, notwithstanding that the sea was not amenable to private ownership, and some things, which were not yet owned, were nonetheless ownable. A central implication of that presentation is that the state of natural liberty, at least when understood as obtaining in the extra-civil condition in Grotius' own day, was one in which it was perfectly possible to subject others to servitude, and even to slavery. That is linguistically odd. But the contradiction is in my view reconciled by servile people being legally invisible, as they were in the Roman city, leaving the state of natural liberty, at least on its visible surface, as an account of free persons. Let us now unpack this account, taking in turn Grotius' account of the free and servile person.

Grotius' account of the free person was the product of a triangular relationship between equality, liberty, and will. As we saw above, Grotius' theology provided a strong account of man born as a free agent. As he put it in the *IPC*:

> God created man [...] 'free and *sui iuris*', so that the actions of each individual and the use of his possessions were made subject not to another's will but to his own. [...] For what is that well-known concept, 'natural liberty', other than the power of the individual to act in accordance with his own will? And liberty in regard to actions is equivalent to ownership (*dominium*) in regard to property.[69]

The theological analysis here is strongly framed in terms of Roman law. Thus, in a footnote to this citation, Grotius references the title in Justinian's *Institutes* (533 CE) on 'the law of persons', which reads: 'In the law of persons, then, the first division is into free men and slaves. (1) Freedom, from which men are called free, is a man's natural power (*naturalis facultas*) of doing what he

---

68 *IBC* 12, fol. 100', p. 233.

69 *IPC* 2, fol. 10, p.34. Citing Aristotle *Politics* 6.2 (see Aristotle, *Politics* (Cambridge: Cambridge University Press, 2015), ed. by Thornton Lockwood, and Thanassis Samaras); and *Institutes* 1.3.1 (see Justinian, *Institutes* (Oxford: Oxford University Press, 1911), transl. by J.B. Moyle). Fecit enim Deus hominem [...], liberum suique juris, ita ut actiones uniuscujusque et rerum suarum usus ipsius, non alieno arbitrio subjacerent, idemque gentium omnium consensu approbatur. Quid enim est aliud naturalis illa libertas, quam id quod cuique libitum est faciendi facultas. Et quod libertas in dominium actionibus idem est dominium in rebus.

pleases, so far as he is not prevented by force or law; (2) Slavery is an institution of the law of nations, against nature subjecting one man to the dominion of another'.[70] The term 'against nature' here is elucidated by a later title, which holds that: '[...] wars have arisen, and [by the law of nations] produced captivity and servitude, which are contrary to the law of nature; since, by the law of nature, all men were originally born free'.[71]

So too is the term *sui iuris* (literally 'of his / her own right') taken from Roman law. It identified free Romans who were not *alieni iuris*, that is, subject to another's power, such as other free persons under the head of the household, or slaves.[72] Only persons who were *sui iuris* had unrestricted legal capacity, and were capable of owning property in their own right.[73]

What rights did Grotius' free persons have? They had in common with slaves the natural right to self-defence, which Grotius recognised as intrinsic to all humans.[74] Thus slave-owners could not kill their slaves unless the slave had committed a crime, and slaves could run away from their masters in cases of extreme cruelty.[75]

However, in the opening chapter of the *IBP*, having defined *ius* in the first sense as 'that which is just', Grotius distinguished the application of this first sense of *ius* according to the following principle of equality (or inequality, depending on how one looks at it):

> But as in societies, some are equal, as those of brothers, citizens, friends (*amici*) and allies (*foederati*, literally 'treaty partner'). And others unequal, by pre-eminence, as Aristotle terms it; as that of parents and

70 *Institutes* 1.3. Summa itaque divisio de iure personarum haec est, quod omnes homines aut liberi sunt aut servi. (1) Et libertas quidem est, ex qua etiam liberi vocantur, naturalis facultas eius quod cuique facere libet, nisi si quid aut vi aut iure prohibetur. (2) Servitus autem est constitutio iuris gentium, qua quis dominio alieno contra naturam subicitur. Grotius also references Aristotle, *Politics*, 6.1317b: This then is one mark of liberty which all democrats set down as a principle of the constitution. And one is for a man to live as he likes; for they say that this is the function of liberty, inasmuch as to live not as one likes is the life of a man that is a slave.

71 Jus autem gentium omni humano generi commune est: nam usu exigente et humanis necessitatibus, gentes humanae jura quaedam sibi constituerunt. Bella etenim orta sunt, et captivitates secutae et servitutes, quae sunt naturali juri contrariae. Jure enim naturali omnes homines ab initio liberi nascebantur [*Institutes* 1.2.2].

72 *Digest* 1.6.

73 See Helge Dedek and Martin Schermaier entry on '*Sui iuris*' in *The Encyclopaedia of Ancient History* (Wiley Online Library, 2012).

74 *IBP* 1.2.1, p. 184; also 2.17.2, p. 885.

75 *IBP* 2.5.28, p. 558; 2.5.29, p. 561.

> children, masters and servants, king and subject, God and man: so that which is just takes place either among equals (*aequo inter se viventium*), or amongst people whereof some are governors and others governed, considered as such. The latter, in my opinion, may be called the right of superiority (*jus rectorium*), and the former the right of equality (*aequatorium recte*).[76]

Grotius makes the point here that being comprised of equal and unequal entities, societies require distinct forms of legal relationships to regulate horizontal relationships between equals and vertical relationships between unequals. Grotius differentiated these two forms of legal relationships as: property and personal rights, as between equals; and as powers a superior held over an inferior, as between unequals. Thus, immediately following the above passage, Grotius presented his second sense of *ius* as 'a moral quality annexed to the person', which he further divided into 'faculties' (*facultas*) and 'aptitudes' (*aptitudo*) (his third and final sense of *ius* was as 'law').[77]

Faculties were rights 'a man has to his own' (*nomine sui appellant*), which were rights 'properly and strictly' so called (*ius proprie*); whereas aptitudes were what a person deserved by merit, not strict right.[78] Faculties were then categorised as either powers, or rights between equals, as follows: (1) 'a power (*potestas*) over ourselves, which is termed liberty (*libertas*)'; (2) '[a power] over others, such as that of a father over his children, or a lord over his slave'; and (3) property (*dominium*); and the right to demand what is due (*creditum*) – i.e. property and personal rights respectively.[79]

The unequal relationship between superior and inferior was expressed in category (2), which was a right understood as a 'power' over inferior others. Conversely, precisely because equals, by definition, could have no such powers over one another, their inter-relationships had to be expressed in terms of a

76 *IBP* 1.1.3, pp. 136–137. Sicut autem societas alia est sine inaequalitate, ut inter fratres, cives, amicos, federatos: alia inaequalis, καθ᾽ὑπεροχὴν Aristoteli, ut inter patrem et liberos, dominum et servum, regem et subditos, Deum et homines: ita iustum aliud est ex aequo inter se viventium, aliud eius qui regit et qui regitur, qua tales sunt: quorum hoc ius Rectorium, illud aequatorium recte, ni fallor, vocabimus.

77 *IBP* 1.1.4, p. 138. It is beyond the scope of this paper, but I follow Donahue's view, against Michel Villey's account, that the Romans had subjective rights. Charles Donahue '*Ius* in the Subjective Sense in Roman Law: Reflections on Villey and Tierney', in Domenico Maffei, Italo Birocchi, Mario Caravale, Emanuele Conte, and Ugo Petronio (eds.), *A Ennio Cortese* (Rome: Il Cigno Edizioni, 2001), 1:506–35.

78 *IBP* 1.1.5, p. 138; 1.1.7, p. 138.

79 *IBP* 1.1.5, p. 138; 1.1.7, p. 138.

categorically different body of rights, namely, category (3), which comprised of property and personal rights. Category (1) was simply the implication of category (2), namely that the person who had power over themselves was logically not under the power of another, and so was free, and being free, could only engage with other free individuals through the rights in category (3). In other words, the free person was an equal amongst equals, but simultaneously, could be a superior vis-à-vis inferiors.

Crucially, Grotius applied his account of liberty not only to individuals, but also to whole peoples: '[...] there is a difference between civil liberty, and that which is personal: the liberty of a private person is one thing, and that of the whole body of the people another'.[80]

In sum, the liberty both of individuals and whole peoples demanded that they were *sui iuris*. The boundaries of their liberty – their freedom to act in accordance with their own will – were expressed through a scheme of rights against equals, and of powers over inferiors.

Let us now turn to servility. How did one become a servile person, subject to the power of a free person? One way was by subjection, another by crime (*ex delicto*). We will take each in turn.

Subjection was divided between voluntary and involuntary forms.[81] Voluntary subjection could be private or public. The private forms were 'as various as there are various sorts of authority or command'.[82] These could range from men voluntarily selling themselves into 'utter and perfect' slavery (as was allowed under Roman law) to several other 'imperfect forms of servitude' whereby a freeman placed himself in long-term subordination to another, for example in debt-bondage.[83] Thus, as Gustaaf van Nifterik points out, when Grotius uses the term *servitus* in the *IBP*, while he sometimes does literally refer to slavery, the term can comprehend a spectrum of 'conditions of un-freedom'.[84]

The public form of subjection was 'that of a whole nation, who put themselves under the power and jurisdiction, either of one person or of several, or even of another nation'.[85] One can imagine that this would typically be under

80 *IBP* 1.3.12, p. 285. At sicut alia est potestas dominica, alia regia; ita et alia est libertas personalis, alia civilis, alia singulorum, alia universorum.

81 *IBP* 2.5.32, p. 565.

82 *IBP* 2.5.26, p. 555.

83 *IBP* 1.3.8, pp. 260–61; 2.5.17.1, p. 556; 2.5.30, p. 561; 2.5.30, pp. 561–62. On Roman law, see *Digest* 1.5.5.

84 Gustaaf van Nifterik, 'Hugo Grotius on Slavery', *Grotiana* 22/23 (2001/2002), pp. 233–244.

85 *IBP* 2.5.31, p. 563. Publica subjection est qua se populus homini alicui, aut pluribus hominibus, aut etiam populo alteri in ditionem dat.

duress, for example, with a peace treaty made by the losing party to a war by a people who 'in order to prevent greater mischief, have submitted without conditions'.[86] As with private subjection, Grotius sets out the condition of servility as regards whole peoples ranging from 'perfect subjection' to that which is for the benefit of both parties, a situation which for Grotius is described by the analogy of the husband's power over his wife.[87]

Notably, Grotius only mentions the literal enslavement of a whole people in the context of punitive war (notwithstanding that later in the *IBP* he allows for the enslavement of individual prisoners in *bellum solemne*, whatever the basis of the just cause). As he puts it: 'There is also an involuntary subjection arising from some crime or other, and this happens when he who has deserved to lose his liberty, is forced to submit himself to him who has a right to punish him'.[88] In this context there was no agreement to explain the terms upon which subjection of a whole people was based. Rather, Grotius argues that the criminal liability of a whole people to slavery was perpetual, because crimes are personal, and so, in distinction to the criminal liability of an individual, which did not pass to their children, the subjection of the people as an artificial person was perpetual, given how changes in the composition of a people did not stop it from being a people.[89]

Finally, an individual could become a slave by being born to a slave mother. Grotius only allowed that this applied under the law of nations, as a result of the mother having been reduced to servility by right of war (which follows Roman law).[90] However, outside that context, Grotius squared his view that man was born free through the very dubious argument that children born to slave mothers were obliged to slavery unless they could pay back their master for support received since infancy.[91]

---

86 *IBP* 1.3.10, pp. 280–81. [...] maioris mali vitandi causa, ita se dedidit ut nihil exciperetur.

87 *IBP* 1.3.8, p. 273. Sed nec illud universaliter verum est, omne regimen eius qui regitur causa esse comparatum; nam quaedam regimina per se sunt regentis causa, ut dominicum: nam servi utilitas ibi extrinseca est & adventitia. [...] Sunt alia regimina mutuae utilitatis causa, ut maritale. Sic imperia quaedam esse possunt comparata ad regum utilitatem, ut quae victoria parta sunt, & non ideo tyrannica dicenda sunt. (The English translation has been modified here by replacing 'civil governments' with '*imperia*' as per the original, given how the phrase civil government is confusing, since while clearly meant to identify the sovereign right in this context, it introduces an ambiguity as to the difference between patrimonial kingdom and the *civitas* which is not in the Latin original).

88 *IBP* 2.5.32, p. 564.

89 *IBP* 2.5.32, p. 565.

90 *IBP* 2.5.29.1, p. 559; 3.7.3, p. 1362.

91 *IBP* 2.5.30, p. 561.

All subjected people were invisible in the sense that they were *alieni iuris*, so to the extent that they were under the power of another, could not act for themselves in a state of natural liberty. But not all subjected people were alike, since some were personally free, even if the whole people of whom they formed part were not free (though this was an uneasy distinction), while other people were personally unfree too. Thus, Grotius distinguishes between two types of 'empire over the conquered (*de imperio in victos*)'.[92] In one case if the people were not already subject to a patrimonial king, the people alienated the sovereign right to their conqueror, who then ruled in the mode of a patrimonial king, though noting that 'There are also some people [i.e. self-ruling people, living in a republic, as opposed to a kingdom] that have other people under them, who are no less subject to them than if they were under kings'.[93] Alternatively:

> [...] sovereignty may be more absolutely acquired, as that which before was a state may cease to be a state; which may be done, either by adding it to another state, as the Roman provinces were, or without any such incorporation, when a king making war at his own charge conquers the people, so as to govern them not for their profit, but chiefly his own interest, which is the character of despotic power in opposition to civil government.[94]

The key difference was that in Grotius' account, unlike where the body of the people is dissolved, and its individual persons personally reduced to servility, in the patrimonial kingdom, while the body of the people itself was servile, individual persons within it remained free (this is the uneasy distinction that Grotius attempts, as noted above). Thus: 'When a people is alienated, it is not the men themselves, but the perpetual right of governing them, as they are a people'.[95] However, Grotius was clear that the people as a whole in the patrimonial kingdom were not free: 'As then personal liberty excludes the dominion

92 This is the title of *IBP* Book 3, Chapter 8.

93 *IBP* 1.3.8, p. 266. Iam vero et populi quidam alios sub se populos habent, non minus addictos sibi quam si regibus parerent: unde illa interrogatio.

94 *IBP* 3.8.1.3–3.8.2.1, pp. 1375–1376. Potest et amplius fieri, nempe ut quae civitas fuit civitas esse desinat, sive [ita] ut accessio fiat alterius civitatis, ut Romanae provinciae, sive ut nulli civitati adhaereat, ut si Rex suo sumtu bellum gerens populum sibi ita subiiciat ut eum regi velit non ad populi sed ad regentis praecipue utilitatem, quod herilis est imperii non civilis.

95 *IBP* 1.3.8, p. 287. Proprie tamen cum populus alienatur, non ipsi homines alienantur, sed ius perpetuum eos regendi, qua populus sunt.

of a master, so does civil liberty exclude royalty, and all manner of sovereignty properly so called'.[96]

Furthermore, since on Grotius' own view, a patrimonial king could rule despotically, the theoretical distinction between the free and unfree people seems to be a tenuous one, even by his own standard. Indeed, he accepts the possibility of there being 'mixed sovereignty [...] between the despotic and the civil, namely, when slavery is mixed with a kind of personal liberty. Thus we read some people have their arms taken away, and that they should use no other instruments of iron, but what were necessary for husbandry: others forced to change their language and method of living'.[97]

In my view, Grotius' account of an unfree people brought under the power of another, whether its people personally remained free or not, provided a model for empire, in which the subjugated people were present, but legally invisible. And Grotius' account of the state of natural liberty entrenches this invisibility, because it is an account of liberty that attaches to rights, and not to powers: to be free is to be an equal amongst equals, and equals order their inter-relations by rights, not powers.

Where the subject nation was incorporated into another, as in the model of the Roman provinces, they: 'are no longer a state, as we now use the word, but the less considerable members of a great state (*magnae civitatis*), as slaves are the members of a family'.[98] However, as we have seen, there were a wide range of other modes of subjection, ranging from the permanent and literal enslavement of a whole people unincorporated into the conquering nation, to situations in which individuals remained free, the sovereign paternalistically ruling over them in their interests. It seems to me that, by this analysis, Grotius provided a language of subjection that could describe the entire range of imperial arrangements that occurred in reality.

Finally, we must note a more extreme form of invisibility that Grotius deals with in the context of punitive war, which, as we saw above, could result in the terrifying predicament of literal and permanent enslavement of a whole

96 *IBP* 1.3.12, p. 285. Sicut ergo libertas personalis dominum excludit, ita libertas civilis regnum atque aliam quamvis proprie dictam ditionem.

97 *IBP* 3.8.3, p. 1376. Atque hinc intelligi potest quale sit mixtum illud imperium quod dixi ex civili et herili, nempe ubi servitus miscetur cum aliqua personali libertate. Sic populis legimus arma ademta, imperatum ne ferri quid haberent extra quam ad agriculturam, alios coactos sermonem et vitae genus mutare.

98 *IBP* 1.3.7, p. 259. Excludimus ergo populos qui in alterius populi ditionem concesserunt, quales erant provinciae Romanorum: hi enim populi non per se civitas sunt, ut nunc quidem eam vocem sumimus, sed membra minus digna magnae civitatis, quomodo servi membra sunt familiae.

people. It is evident on Grotius' analysis that objects of punitive war would typically not be sovereign entities, but indigenous peoples. Thus, Grotius defined the crimes that could give rise to the just cause of punishment as 'grievous violations of the law of nature or nations'.[99] In this sense, unlike self-defence or recovery, the just cause of punishment did not serve to define either the core, or the boundaries, of the legal self. Rather, it elucidated the identity of human society as a whole: it 'consulted' the benefit of human society (*humanae societati per poenas consulendi*).[100] That is, if Grotius' account of global legal order was modelled on the Roman city, his account of punishment defended its walls.

In this idiom, punishment was more a means of exclusion than correction. Hence the vivid examples of punishment Grotius provided in the *IBP* were not in taken from the inter-sovereign context but assumed the punishment of barbarians for purportedly grave violations of natural law:

> War may be justly undertaken against those who are inhuman to their parents, [...] against those who eat human flesh [...] and against those who practise piracy. If a man, says Seneca, does not infest my country, but is only vexatious to his own; though he is at a distance from my nation, yet if he disturb his own; so great a depravity of mind has cut him off from human society, and makes him to me, and all the world, a foe. [...] For of such barbarians, and rather beasts than men, may be fitly said what Aristotle spoke out of prejudice concerning the Persians, who were indeed nothing worse than the Greeks; that war against such is natural; and as Isocrates said in his Panathenaic, the justest war is that which is undertaken against wild rapacious beasts, and next to it is that against men who are like beasts.[101]

99 *IBP* 2.20.40.1, p. 1021. Sciendum quoque est reges et qui par regibus ius obtinent ius habere poenas poscendi non tantum ob iniurias in se aut subditos suos commissas, sed et ob eas quae ipsos peculiariter non tangunt, sed in quibusvis personis ius naturae aut gentium immaniter violant.

100 *IBP* 2.20.40.1, p. 1021.

101 *IBP* 2.20.40.3, pp. 1022–24. Sic non dubitamus quin iusta sint bella in eos qui in parentes impii sunt [...] in eos qui humanam carnem epulantur [...] qui piraticam exercent: Seneca16: Si non patriam meam impugnat, sed suae gravis est, et sepositus a mea gente suam exagitat, abscidit nihilominus illum tanta pravitas animi. [...] De talibus enim barbaris, et feris magis quam hominibus, dici recte potest quod de Persis qui Graecis nihilo deteriores erant, perverse dixit Aristoteles, naturale in eos esse bellum, et quod Isocrates Panathenaico dixit, iustissimum esse bellum in belluas, proximum in homines belluis similes.

This fits with Grotius' claim earlier in the *IBP* that: 'As Aristotle said, some men are naturally slaves [...] And some nations also are of such a temper, that they know better how to obey than to command'.[102] In the context of the passage, what Grotius means is not that they are born slaves, since that would not fit his general position, but that they are culturally disposed to slavery.

In this argument, Grotius followed the distinction, well-known at the time, set out by the Spanish Jesuit missionary José Acosta (c.1539–1600) in his *Natural and Moral Histories of the Indies* (1590, *Historia natural y moral de las Indias*), who had divided non-European 'barbarians' into three categories based on his travels amongst the American Indians.[103] Some barbarians, such as the Aztecs for example, lived in cities and had their own laws and magistrates. In this case, it can be implied that Grotius did not see them as beyond the bounds of human society, and indeed recognised the legitimacy of their jurisdiction. However, it was the hunter-gatherer type indigenous peoples that Grotius implicitly saw as fit for servility.

Grotius linked this anthropology to his analysis of the law of nature, in that while rules of natural law were adduced from human nature: '[...] some people are savage and brutish, whose manners cannot, with truth and justice, be reckoned a reproach to human nature in general [...] To judge of what is natural, we must consider those subjects that are rightly disposed, according to their nature, and not those that are corrupted'.[104] That is, ironically, while such people, like the native American Indians, might still live in a state of natural liberty, to the extent that they were savages, the content of that law was not determined by their own practices. This seems to me to mark the most extreme form of legal invisibility in Grotius' scheme of global legal order – and again, we see how those who actually lived in nature had no say in his account of the rules that obtained in the state of nature, as is consistent with the idea that

---

102 *IBP* 1.3.8, p. 264. Adde quod sicut Aristoteles dixit quosdam homines natura esse servos, id est ad servitutem aptos; ita et populi quidam eo sunt ingenio, ut regi quam regere norint rectius.

103 José de Acosta, *Historia Natural Y Moral De Las Indias* (Seville: Juan de Leon, 1590). Note that in the *IBP* Grotius actually cited from his slightly earlier work cf. Josephus Acosta, 'De Promulgatione Evangelii Apud Barbaros Sive De Procuranda Indorum Salute Libri Sex', in *De Natura Novi Ordinis Libri Duo Et De Promulgatione* (Salamanca: 1589). On the use of Acosta in general, see Andrew Fitzmaurice, *Sovereignty, Property and Empire, 1500–2000* (Cambridge: Cambridge University Press, 2014). For a detailed analysis of Acosta's position, see Daniel Allemann's chapter in this volume.

104 *IBP* 1.1.12, pp. 161–162. [...] quaedam nationes efferatae sunt, et factae inhumanae, ex quibus non oportet ab aequis iudicibus aestimatione facta humanae naturae convitium fieri. [...] quid naturale sit spectandum in his quae bene secundum naturam se habent, non in depravatis.

Grotius' account in fact presents the urbanisation of nature on the model of the Roman city, or *civitas*.

5 Conclusion

As noted at the outset, Grotius himself very rarely used the term 'state of nature'. Rather, the characterisation of his account of the state of natural liberty as a state of nature reflects the influence of later writers with whom his account is contrasted. For example, in the Preface to the *Law of Nations* (1758), Vattel uses the term state of nature to define the subjects of the law of nations, and then compares the accounts of the law of nations in Grotius, Hobbes, Pufendorf, and Wolff using that baseline.[105] Yet this represents a significant difference in approach from Grotius, for whom, as we saw, the state of nature did not only apply in his own day as between states, and whose account of global legal order extended beyond the analysis of legal order between states. However, we clearly see Grotius' influence in Vattel's characterisation of the state of nature as state of natural equality, meaning formal legal equality, regardless of actual power relations, as is captured in this famous passage:

> Since men are naturally equal, and a perfect equality prevails in their rights and obligations, as equally proceeding from nature – nations composed of men, and considered as so many free persons living together in the state of nature, are naturally equal, and inherit from nature the same obligations and rights. Power or weakness does not in this respect produce any difference. A dwarf is as much a man as a giant; a small republic is no less a sovereign state than the most powerful kingdom.[106]

In this way, we see the future influence of Grotius' account of the state of natural liberty as a projection of the Roman *civitas* onto the extra-civil condition of his own day. The extent of this projection can be seen in the irony that the natural order that purportedly governed those who most literally lived in a state of nature, namely, indigenous peoples, was not an expression of their own practices, but those of urban, and specifically Roman, people. The notion of the

105 Emer de Vattel, *The Law of Nations* [Le Droit des Gens] (Indianapolis: Liberty Fund, 2008), Preface, p. 8.

106 Vattel, *The Law of Nations*, Preliminaries, 18, p. 75. See also Preliminaries 4, p. 68.

state of nature as a projection of the Roman city is even stronger as regards the society of nations, within which, as we saw, obtained an account of the voluntary law of nations whose customary rules were legitimated through the identification of the will of the majority, as it would have been in the Roman republican city. Indeed, the presentation of international law as 'public international law' can be traced into this genealogy. More broadly, although he did not use the term, we might see in Grotius' account the literal 'civilization' (or '*civitas*–ization') of global legal order, for better or worse.

The essential feature of Grotius' free person, modelled on the free and *sui iuris* Roman citizen (who, incidentally, would nearly always be male) was being an equal amongst equals, who shaped his own future by virtue of his own free will. Conversely, the servile person did not shape his own future, being under the power of another, and was legally accounted for in the political community as an inferior part of a free person. Just as a *civitas* could be described as an order of free persons, it was implicitly also comprised of servile people under their power.

Likewise, when Grotius referred to the society of nations, its visible constituents were sovereign entities, who made their own legal world, and had a say in the formation of the voluntary law of nations. Conversely, its silent constituents were those servile peoples ruled over by sovereign entities in the imperial sphere, whose future was made for them. This model would provide the foundations for the later development of international law as a law of states, whose empires were accounted for, but invisible.

Select Bibliography

Primary Sources

Grotius Hugo, *The Rights of War and Peace* (Indianapolis: Liberty Fund, 2005), edited by Richard Tuck.

Grotius, Hugo *Commentary on the Law of Prize and Booty* (Indianapolis: Liberty Fund, 2006), edited by David Armitage.

Grotius, Hugo, *De veritate religionis christianae* (Leiden: Brill, 2004), edited by J.P. Heering.

Secondary Sources

Garnsey, Peter, *Thinking About Property* (Cambridge: CUP; 2007).

Lee, Daniel, 'Popular Liberty, Princely Government, and the Roman Law in Hugo Grotius's *De Jure Belli Ac Pacis*', *Journal of the History of Ideas* 72, no. 3 (2011).

Mortimer, Sarah, 'De Veritate, Christianity and Human Nature', *Grotiana* 35 (2014), 75–94.
Straumann, Benjamin *Roman Law in the State of Nature* (Cambridge: CUP; 2015).
Richard, Tuck *The Rights of War and Peace: Political Thought and International Order from Grotius to Kant* (Oxford: OUP, 1999).

CHAPTER 7

From the State of Nature to the State of Economy

Pufendorf on Commerce and Natural Law

David Singh Grewal

Abstract

The theoretical foundations of classical political economy often seem obscure. This paper argues that political economy derived from the social contract tradition, specifically, from considerations of "man" in his natural state. The key figure in this connection was Samuel Pufendorf, whose reconceptualization of the "state of natural liberty" as a "state of economy" provided a bridge between seventeenth-century *iusnaturalism* and eighteenth-century political economy. The result was a new understanding of the "oeconomic," opposed to both the Aristotelian conception of the *oikos* – since that was founded on natural hierarchy and a quasi-objective account of the good – and Hobbes's effort to politicize all social relations. This newly conceived "oeconomic" was a domain of non-political "society" based on private property relations and sub-political voluntary associations of a primarily commercial variety, produced through individual consent and corresponding to the demands of (divinely ordained) social progress. Of particular note is Pufendorf's extensive use of Roman private law in describing the state of nature. Ultimately, what Pufendorf represented as the natural condition of mankind presupposed the property and contract laws of an advanced empire.

Keywords

Samuel Pufendorf – political economy – state of nature – social contract theory – natural law – commerce – sociability

1 Introduction

Political economy is often represented as a discourse that sprang fully grown from the mind of Adam Smith (with philosophical assistance from David Hume) to fit the facts of "commercial society" as it had developed in western

 | DOI:10.1163/9789004499621_009

Europe, and Britain in particular.[1] There are both deep and contingent reasons for this longstanding misinterpretation. One contingent reason is that Adam Smith published *The Wealth of Nations* in the same year that Anne Robert Jacques Turgot's Physiocratic ministry spectacularly failed, following too rapid deregulation and liberalization; accordingly, Smith needed to distance his *opus* from the *économistes* of France from whom he had taken so much.[2] A deeper reason is that the Physiocrats themselves had been unable to admit their roots in late seventeenth-century French discussions of the limits and power of the consolidating state, since the Jansenist political theology that had birthed early *laissez-faire* discourse was forced underground after the 1713 papal bull *Unigenitus*.[3]

As I have tried to suggest in other work, classical political economy was intimately bound up with the emergence of the modern state: dependent on it both practically and intellectually, but in a way that meant it could not fully acknowledge its dependence. It was a discourse of state management that both presupposed the state and purported to identify quasi-natural limits to *raison d'état*, which it accepted in principle but wished to qualify in practice.[4] This complex relationship can be seen in the extensive use that classical political economists made of seventeenth-century political theory, particularly the concept of the "state of nature." While the use of the "state of nature" in political, legal, constitutional, and other discourses is widely acknowledged, its role in shaping economic discourse has largely been overlooked.[5] By the time of David Hume, the ambition to develop a "new science of man" in the moral

1 For a seminal version of this narrative, see Dugald Stewart, 'Account of the Life and Writings of Adam Smith,' (delivered January 21, and March 18, 1793), published in *Transactions of the Royal Society of Edinburgh*, Vol. III (1794).

2 For a discussion of Smith's intellectual debts to Physiocracy, including Turgot, see David McNally, *Political Economy and the Rise of Capitalism* (Berkeley: University of California Press, 1988), pp. 234–250; and on the failure of Turgot's Physiocratic ministry, ibid, pp. 131–133.

3 On Jansenism as a theory of state power and its limits, see Michel Foucault, *Security, Territory, Population: Lectures at the Collège de France, 1977–1978* (London: Palgrave Macmillan, 2007), p. 348; see also the lecture of 5 April 1978 (2007), pp. 333–367. On Jansenism and early *laissez-faire* argument, see David Grewal, 'Political Theology of *Laissez-Faire*,' *Political Theology*, 17:5 (2016), pp. 417–433.

4 David Grewal, *Invention of the Economy* (Cambridge: Harvard University Press, forthcoming).

5 In addition to Istvan Hont's important work, 'The Language of Sociability and Commerce: Samuel Pufendorf and the Theoretical Foundations of the 'Four-Stages Theory,'' (in *The Languages of Political Theory in Early-Modern Europe*, ed. by Anthony Pagden (Cambridge: Cambridge University Press, 1987)) establishing Pufendorf's centrality to the history of political economy, two recent contributions are worth noting, Arild Saether, *Natural Law and the Origin of Political Economy: Samuel Pufendorf and the History of Economics* (London: Routledge, 2017) and Heikki Haara, *Pufendorf's Theory of Sociability: Passions,*

sciences was tied to a repudiation of the constructivism of post-Hobbesian political thought, which had the effect of obscuring the origins of economics in social contract theory.

Yet the work of Samuel Pufendorf (1632–1694) reveals that the very idea of an economy (or "society") outside or before organized politics – and susceptible to the kind of analysis that the eighteenth-century moral sciences proposed – was deeply tied to "state of nature" argumentation. Pufendorf theorized a commercialized "state of nature," an expanded domain of the "oeconomic" that had little in common with the ancient *oikos* beyond the etymological. Following the lead of Grotius (1583–1645) in emphasizing the natural sociability of mankind, he developed an influential theory of pre-political "society," which he sometimes called the *status oeconomicus* or "economic state." By imagining the state of nature as both more pacific and more commercial than Hobbes (1588–1679) would ever have allowed, Pufendorf adapted social contract theory to represent the relations of property and commerce as "natural" and then grounded the legitimacy of the civil order in its respect for these supposedly pre-political imperatives of natural law.[6] Hobbes's war-prone

Habits and Social Order (Springer, 2018), concerning Pufendorf's relation to eighteenth-century political economy and moral theory generally.

6 The aim to render Hobbes's state of nature more peaceable and thus to thicken the forms of social life imagined within it was shared by other post-Hobbesian theorists of modern natural law, including Richard Cumberland (1631–1718), John Locke (1632–1704), Francis Hutcheson (1694–1746) and Jean-Jacques Burlamaqui (1694–1748). See Cumberland, *De legibus naturae* (A Treatise of the Laws of Nature), ed. by Jon Parkin, trans. By John Maxwell (Indianapolis: Liberty Fund, [1672] 2005), pp. 621–634, criticizing Hobbes's theory and arguing the natural state would not be endless war; and pp. 665–681 opposing Hobbes's arguments concerning property and natural equality, and arguing instead that property is pre-political, governed by God's natural law. Locke's arguments concerning property are complex: compare his *Two Treatises of Government* (Cambridge: Cambridge University Press, 1988) §27–36, where he countenances individual appropriation in the state of nature according to his famous two provisos and §87–88, where it is explained that the aim of civil society is 'the preservation of the property of all the members of that society, as far as is possible' (§88), with §97–99, where a strict majoritarian decision-rule is set forth as the only foundation of legitimate government and §120 where he suggests that ownership rights ('possessions') would accordingly be revised after the formation of civil society. Some of this complexity comes because Locke calls all individual rights – rights concerning 'Lives, Liberties, and Estates' – by the general name 'property' (§123), and it is for the preservation of this expansive idea of property that society is instituted, not merely for the preservation of the pre-political distribution of 'possessions' (i.e., private property) (§120). Francis Hutcheson's moral theory opposed the Hobbesian in several respects, as he made clear in choosing the 'natural sociability of mankind' as the theme of his inaugural lecture upon taking up the Professorship of Moral Philosophy at Glasgow in 1730. Against 'certain writers' who denied natural sociability and instead depicted 'human nature in the worst and most disgraceful

"state of nature" was thus recast as a commercialized "state of natural liberty," laying the groundwork for the eighteenth-century division between state and "society" that would prove central to classical political economy and all later social theory.[7]

The modern concept of "the economy" was built on these theoretical foundations, though the terminology of natural or commercial "society" would remain the dominant way of expressing the concept for some time.[8] Unlike the ancient concept of *oikonomia*, which had been concerned with the management of the household or estate, "the economy" implied a social universe modeled on God's harmonious cosmic arrangement, *oikonomia tou theou*.[9] The reconfiguration of natural jurisprudence that stood behind this revision

---

light' (p. 195), he maintained that 'social life (in the state unrestrained by government) is natural to man for its own sake' (p. 215) and thus reevaluated the 'state of natural liberty' accordingly (*Logic, Metaphysics, and the Natural Sociability of Mankind*, ed. by James Moore and Michael Silverthorne (Indianapolis: Liberty Fund, 2006)). This general approach to a more sociable state of nature was reflected, too, in the popularizing works of Jean-Jacques Burlamaqui, *Principes du droit naturel* (Geneva: Barillot et fils, 1747), and *Principes du droit politique* (Amsterdam: Zacharie Chatelain, 1751), which drew on the famous editions of Pufendorf and Grotius by Jean Barbeyrac (1674–1744) (on which, see footnote 15 below). For useful secondary sources on the early modern history of natural rights theory, see Knud Haakonssen, *Natural Law and Moral Philosophy: From Grotius to the Scottish Enlightenment* (Cambridge: Cambridge University Press, 1996), T.J. Hochstrasser, *Natural Law Theories in the Early Enlightenment,* (Cambridge: Cambridge University Press, 2000), and Ian Hunter and David Saunders, *Natural Law and Civil Sovereignty: Moral Right and State Authority in Early Modern Political Thought* (New York: Palgrave Macmillan, 2002).

7 On the rise of the eighteenth-century category of 'society' and its relation to the emergent social sciences, see Björn Wittrock, Lars Magnusson, and Johan Heilbron, *The Rise of the Social Sciences and the Formation of Modernity: Conceptual Change in Context, 1750–1850* (Dordrecht: Kluwer, 1998). On the break between this way of thinking and seventeenth-century political theory, see John Dunn, 'From Applied Theology to Social Analysis: The Break between John Locke and the Scottish Enlightenment,' in *Wealth and Virtue: The Shaping of Political Economy in the Scottish Enlightenment*, ed. by Istvan Hont and Michael Ignatieff (Cambridge: Cambridge University Press, 1983); cf. Sheldon Wolin, 'Liberalism and the Decline of Political Philosophy,' ch. 9 in *Politics and Vision: Continuity and Innovation in Western Political Thought* (Princeton: Princeton University Press, 1960); Keith Michael Baker, 'Enlightenment and the Institution of Society: Notes for a Conceptual History,' in *Main Trends in Cultural History: Ten Essays*, ed. by Willem Melching and Wyger Velema (Amsterdam: Rodopi, 1994), pp. 95–120.

8 On the changing terminology of "economy," see Keith Tribe, *The Economy of the Word* (Oxford: Oxford Press, 2015), ch. 2, which discusses Hutcheson and other mid-eighteenth-century authors in light of the changing conceptions of *oikonomia*/economy, but not Pufendorf's usage, on which, see the section "The *Status Oeconomicus*" below.

9 See John Reumann, 'The Use of 'Oikonomia'[…]' (PhD diss., University of Pennsylvania, 1957), pp. 391–394; see also my discussion in Grewal, 'Political Theology of *Laissez-Faire*.'

of *oikonomia* emerged from a partial appropriation and partial rejection of Hobbes's radical account of politics, producing a commercial rendering of natural society and a new account of how conflicting individual wills might be systematically reconciled. The political economy of Hume, Smith, Turgot, and other key figures in the development of classical political economy built on this reconfiguration of natural jurisprudence. Perhaps even more significant, so, too, would a series of legal codification projects aimed at producing a coherent juridical order predicated on consolidated rights of private property and freedom of contract, which served as the basis for the revolutionary French Civil Code.[10]

2 Pufendorf and Modern Natural Law

The eighteenth-century discourse of classical political economy was predicated on a conception of commercial sociability in the "state of natural liberty" that borrowed from and reworked Hobbes's political theory. The result was a new understanding of the "oeconomic," which opposed the Aristotelian conception of the *oikos* – founded as it was on natural hierarchy and a quasi-objective account of the good – but which also denied Hobbes's effort to politicize it. Instead, the "oeconomic" was reconceived as a domain of non-political "society," based on private property relations and sub-political voluntary associations of a primarily commercial variety, produced through individual consent and corresponding to the demands of (divinely ordained) social progress.

The key figure associated with this strand of post-Hobbesian thought was Samuel Pufendorf, a professional academic born in Saxony, who taught at a variety of Swedish and German universities and held the first chair in "natural law" in the Protestant world.[11] Pufendorf's first book, the *Elementorum jurisprudentiae universalis*, published in 1660, contained the "first philosophically serious discussions of Hobbes's ideas."[12] The *Elementorum* was followed by

10 Jean Domat, *Les loix civiles dans leur ordre naturel* (Paris: La Veuve de Jean Baptiste Coignard, 1695–1702), Domat, *The Civil Law in its Natural Order*, trans. William Strahan (London: E. Bell et al., 1722). On the French Civil Code, see footnote 62 below.

11 Leonard Krieger, *The Politics of Discretion: Pufendorf and the Acceptance of Natural Law* (Chicago: University of Chicago Press, 1965).

12 Richard Tuck, *The Rights of War and Peace: Political Thought and the International Order from Grotius to Kant* (Oxford: Oxford University Press, 1999), p. 141. Citations of the *Elementorum* are to W. A. Oldfather's 1931 translation, ed. by Thomas Behme (Indianapolis: Liberty Fund, 2009).

Pufendorf's lengthy masterwork, *De jure naturae et gentium* of 1672,[13] which was then abridged into a summary version in 1673 as *De officio hominis et civis juxta legem naturalem*.[14] The two later political works appeared in several English and French translations in the late seventeenth and early eighteenth centuries, most famously in editions by the Swiss-French jurist, Jean Barbeyrac.[15] In addition, Pufendorf published major histories of the German Empire, the kingdoms of Europe, and the Catholic Church, and he responded, over several volumes, to controversies that his work had raised. He was perhaps the preeminent academic of the later seventeenth-century Protestant world, a theorist not only of its form of state, but of its commerce and religion, and its foreign relations in an era of French expansionism.[16]

Before examining the substance of his political theory in greater detail, it is worth observing that Pufendorf's tone and style reflected the increasingly commercial character of life in early modern Europe in a way that Hobbes's writing did not – even though his *Elementorum* was published only ten years after *Leviathan*. While Hobbes drew on the standard set of mainly classical references familiar to late Renaissance humanism, Pufendorf added examples from commerce and trade with a distinctively contemporary flavor: merchants transacting abroad, bankers loaning money to princes, and buyers determining for themselves the "true value" of commodities.[17] Despite the overlap in their lives – Hobbes was already forty-four years old when Pufendorf was born but would then live almost another five decades – Hobbes should be seen as a late sixteenth-century figure, given his overriding concern with state-building in the midst of confessional conflict. By contrast, Pufendorf was a bridge to that

13 Citations of *De officio hominis* are to Andrew Tooke's 1691 translation, ed. by Ian Hunter and David Saunders (Indianapolis: Liberty Fund 2002).

14 Citations of *De jure naturae* are to C. H and W. A. Oldfathers' translation of 1934 (Oxford: Clarendon Press).

15 Jean Barbeyrac, *Le Droit de la Nature et des Gens* (Amsterdam: Gerard Kuyper, 1706); *Les Devoirs de l'Homme et du Citoien* (Amsterdam: Henri Schelte, 1707).

16 Of Pufendorf's other political writings, his *Dissertatio de statu hominum naturali* of 1674 is perhaps the most important, and was republished with an excellent introduction by Michael J. Seidler, *De statu hominum naturali* (*Samuel Pufendorf's On the Natural State of Men: The 1678 Latin Edition and English Translation* (Lewiston: Edwin Mellen Press, 1990)); see also Seidler's study of several other academic 'dissertations' from Pufendorf's time teaching in Lund and Heidelberg, "'Monstrous' Pufendorf: Sovereignty and System in the Dissertations,' in *Monarchism and Absolutism in Early Modern Europe*, ed. by Cesare Cuttica and Glenn Burgess (London: Pickering & Chatto, 2012).

17 This feature is most obvious in Pufendorf's popular works, the *Elementorum* and *De officio*; by contrast, the massive *De jure naturae* comprises detailed analysis of the canonical texts of natural and Roman law.

preoccupation with commerce and manners that would dominate eighteenth-century social thought, and which so often seems to take a settled civil order for granted in a way that was impossible for earlier humanists. Notably, he wrote in the opening decades of the modern system of states, after the *ancien régime* nations of Europe had assumed the inner constitutions and outer boundaries they would mostly maintain through to the French Revolution.[18] His prompt was not so much the devastation of civil war as the dangers of French expansionism; and unlike the English, French, and Dutch authors whose political context was a modern (or modernizing) state, Pufendorf's was the loose confederacy of German principalities, which did not realize any kind of consolidated sovereignty until long after his death.[19]

Pufendorf nevertheless utilized the jurisprudential framework that these earlier authors had inaugurated, becoming, along with Grotius, the preeminent figure in the construction of what has been called "modern" natural law.[20] He acknowledged in his Preface to the *Elementorum* his debt to both Grotius and Hobbes, and claimed that he would follow the method of *De cive*.[21] He also stated that he would offer no further indication as to what he had taken from these two authors nor how he differed from them. For this reason, Pufendorf has often been grouped together with Hobbes in later criticisms of social contract theory, though we should understand his arguments as a selective reworking of Hobbesian premises aimed at rival conclusions.[22] Pufendorf's debts and differences become clearer, however, on a careful examination of his major work, *De jure naturae*, which featured detailed examinations of Grotian and

---

18 James Tully, introduction to *On the Duty of Man and Citizen according to Natural Law*, by Samuel Pufendorf (Cambridge: Cambridge University Press, 1991), pp. xviii–xxi; Seidler, *De statu hominum naturali*, pp. 3–31.

19 Tuck, *Rights of War and Peace*, pp. 150–151.

20 On "modern" natural law, see Tuck, 'The 'Modern' Theory of Natural Law,' in *The Languages of Political Theory in Early-Modern Europe*, ed. by Anthony Pagden (Cambridge: Cambridge University Press); *Philosophy and Government 1572–1651* (Cambridge: Cambridge University Press, 1993); Hochstrasser, *Natural Law Theories*.

21 *Elementorum jurisprudentiae universalis* (hereafter cited in notes as *EJU*), pp. 10–11.

22 The interpretation offered here is indebted to Tuck, 'Samuel Pufendorf,' ch. 5 in *Rights of War and Peace*; Richard Tuck, 'Grotius, Hobbes and Pufendorf,' ch. 2 in *The Sleeping Sovereign: The Invention of Modern Democracy* (Cambridge: Cambridge University Press, 2016); Istvan Hont, *Jealousy of Trade: International Competition and the Nation-State in Historical Perspective* (Cambridge: Harvard University Press, 2005); T. J. Hochstrasser, *Natural Law Theories*; Craig L. Carr and Michael J. Seidler, 'Pufendorf, Sociality and the Modern State,' *History of Political Thought* 17:3 (1996), pp. 354–78. For biographical and bibliographic information on Pufendorf and excellent overviews of Pufendorf's political theory, see Tully's introduction to his edition of *De officio hominis* (1991) and Seidler's to his translation of '*De statu hominum naturali*.'

Hobbesian arguments set within a study of the Roman lawyers and, to a lesser extent, Jean Bodin (1529/30–1596).

It is plausible to read Pufendorf as endeavoring to establish natural law on a footing that precluded Hobbes's more radical conclusions by adapting Grotian arguments about natural sociability to limit the reach of Hobbesian political theory.[23] More particularly, and with a view to his influence on later economic thought, Pufendorf differed from Hobbes in two related respects. The first was his highly commercial rendering of the "state of nature." The second was his more limited conception of political sovereignty, understood both in its formation and in the bounds imposed on it by natural law. These two features of Pufendorf's thought are of course related, but I will focus here mainly on the first, in keeping with the theme of this volume.[24]

3 The State of Natural Liberty

Pufendorf's account of the "state of natural liberty" depended on his particular conception of natural law. He distinguished divine natural law from divine positive law, and both in turn from civil law, which is positive but man-made.[25] Divine natural law is universal, shared by all humanity after the Fall, and obvious from the observation of nature.[26] By contrast, God's positive law was given as a command to those who accept him in particular. It was therefore deemed the proper province of theology and not natural law, a demarcation that was essential to Pufendorf's project of producing a *natural* jurisprudence.[27] The

23 See Tuck, *Rights of War and Peace*, pp. 148–152 and Hochstrasser, *Natural Law Theories*, pp. 60–65 for discussions of Pufendorf's criticisms of Hobbes. For an account that emphasizes Pufendorf as a 'disciple' of Hobbes, and connects his theory of *socialitas* not to Grotian or neo-Stoic sociability but to Hobbesian self-preservation, see Fiammetta Palladini, 'Pufendorf Disciple of Hobbes: The Nature of Man and the State of Nature: The Doctrine of Socialitas,' *History of European Ideas*, 34:1 (2008), pp. 49–59, who suggests that Pufendorf exaggerated his distance from Hobbes in order to distinguish himself from the charge of Hobbism. This seems plausible enough, and yet not incompatible with an account emphasizing consequential points of difference within a broadly shared commitment to social contract theory.

24 A more detailed account of the second theme will be found in Grewal, *Invention of the Economy*, ch. 6.

25 Samuel Pufendorf, *The Whole Duty of Man, According to the Law the Nature* (*De officio hominis et civis juxta legem naturalem*), I.2.16 (hereafter cited in notes as DOH), cf. Pufendorf, *De jure naturae et gentium*, p. 112 (hereafter cited in notes as DJN).

26 *DJN*, II.3; *DOH* I.3.

27 *DJN*, p. 40; *DOH*, pp. 7–13. This demarcation between theology and natural law was influential for later Protestant theorists, including Christian Thomasias, see Ian Hunter, *The*

state of nature, which Pufendorf called (following Hobbes and Bodin before him) a "state of natural liberty" was a state governed by natural law alone. Its "liberty" was a freedom from instituted civil authority, but not from divine commands with universal purview.[28]

Unlike Hobbes, and in a domesticating twist on Grotius, Pufendorf imagined a reasonably durable commercial life existing before or outside the institution of civil authority.[29] This commercial society was governed by natural law, and its basis was private property, which Pufendorf – following Grotius and in explicit opposition to Hobbes – assumed to be a pre-political institution founded in common agreement, possibly express but probably tacit.[30] While he argued that the state of nature was ultimately unstable (and thus needed to culminate in civil society), it was nevertheless *social*.[31] Even while recognizing a sociable state of nature, Pufendorf was nevertheless clear about the need for a state, for reasons that ranged from a Hobbesian concern about epistemic uncertainty and the dangerous quest for glory in interpersonal relations[32] through to a more straightforward Augustinian anxiety about the need to discipline fallen man and ensure the efficacious enforcement of natural rights.[33] It was for these reasons that God had commanded the institution of the civil state, which corresponded to the needs of social progress.[34]

Secularisation of the Confessional State: The Political Thought of Christian Thomasius (Cambridge: Cambridge University Press, 2007), pp. 5–7; Hunter, *De officio hominis*, pp. 198–202.

28 *DJN*, II.2.11, III.3.19–20.

29 On Pufendorf as a critic of Grotius, see Tuck, *Rights of War and Peace*, pp. 152–165.

30 Grotius's idea of tacit consent proved enormously influential to all subsequent theories of private property. While its foundations are in Roman law, it seems to have been his particular innovation. As Benjamin Straumann argues: 'Grotius's originality in *De iure belli ac pacis* consisted in combining the Roman-law doctrine of the natural acquisition of ownership [...] with the Roman-law concept of tacit agreement' *Roman Law in the State of Nature: The Classical Foundations of Hugo Grotius' Natural Law* (Cambridge: Cambridge University Press, 2015), p. 186, cf., pp. 185–187. Pufendorf followed Grotius's lead in assuming the origin of property in *tacit* consent, as in *DJN* IV.4, esp. pp. 540–541, cf. pp. 547, suggesting that the first *dominion* was accomplished through seizure, after which tacit pacts ensued to consolidate the pre-political system of private property. He thus explicitly opposed Hobbes's views on the political origin of property *DJN*, pp. 1135, 1276. See generally, Peter Garnsey, 'The State of Nature and the Origin of Private Property: Grotius to Hegel,' ch. 6 in *Thinking about Property: From Antiquity to the Age of Revolution* (Cambridge: Cambridge University Press, 2007).

31 *DJN* II.2.5; cf. *DOH*, pp. 55–60.

32 *DJN*, V.13.2; V.13.10; VII.1.2–4, 10.

33 *DJN*, VII.1.7–8, 11; cf. *DOH*, II.5.

34 *DJN*, VII.3.2; cf. *DOH*, II.9.

Crucially, however, Pufendorf theorized the formation of *civil* society as but the limit case of a more general process of societal consolidation achieved through the merging of individual wills that began with natural man considered in his liberty. Across all his political works, Pufendorf opposed the Hobbesian conception of the "state of nature," even while he partly reintroduced it to explain the need for civil government.[35] In the *Elementorum*, he argued that the state of nature was not one of universal war, which applied only to unsociable "wild beasts," because men are "bound by the law of nature to foster social relations with one another," and necessarily found in society.[36] Moreover, the state of nature as a war of all against all "has never existed, so no conclusion can be drawn from supposing it, contrary to what the actual facts show."[37] Extensive elaborations along these same lines can be found in *De jure naturae*, *De officio*, and in an important later composition, "*De statu hominum naturali*," in which Pufendorf responded to controversies raised by his use of social contract theory.[38] In *De jure naturae*, he repeated that the natural life of humankind is "utterly different from that of the beasts,"[39] and hence, "it is not proper to oppose a state of nature to a social life, since even those who live in a state of nature can, and should, and frequently do, lead a mutually social life."[40] In the state of natural liberty, we should expect only "particular" conflicts that "arouse individuals against individuals," not "a universal war of all men against all others."[41] A Hobbesian war of that kind is only "tolerable" as hypothesis,[42] or as he put it later in *De officio*, "represented to us *notionally* and by way of *Fiction*."[43] Useful only as a thought experiment, it was unrealistic to imagine "that all the mutual Ties, by which Mankind are one way or other united together, were now dissolv'd."[44] Thus, as he summarized in *De jure naturae*: "the term 'the natural liberty of man', should under all circumstances be understood as something conditioned by a certain restraint of sound reason and natural law."[45]

---

35 *Per contra*, Palladini, 'Pufendorf Disciple of Hobbes,' pp. 52–59 argues that Pufendorf conceived the state of nature on Hobbesian lines as a state of war, not a pre-political condition with tolerable social life.

36 *EJU*, p. 33, cf. p. 320.

37 *EJU*, p. 319.

38 DJN, p. 8; see also, Seidler, *De Statu hominum naturali*.

39 *DJN*, p. 8.

40 *DJN*, p. 166.

41 *DJN*, p. 171.

42 *DJN*, p. 168, cf. pp. 8–9.

43 *DOH*, p. 166.

44 *DOH*, p. 168.

45 *DJN*, p. 153.

As should be clear from his view of the state of nature, Pufendorf did not entirely subscribe to that skeptical anthropology characteristic of humanism in the late sixteenth and early seventeenth centuries.[46] His was a confident view – confident in the relative clarity of God's universal commands, in the reliability of divine punishment for transgressions of these laws of nature, and even in the possibility of communicating sufficiently one's intentions in the state of nature to permit commercial contracting backed by non-binding third-party arbitration.[47] At the same time, as we shall see, the broader structure of his argument reflected a conception of the self-interested individual and of the constructive possibility of willing that originated in post-skeptical moral and political theory rather than an earlier Aristotelian naturalism. He thus understood the construction of civil sovereignty in contractarian terms – as "artificial," as Hobbes had put it – but nevertheless hemmed by the natural laws of pre-political society, conceived as foundationally commercial.

The central role Pufendorf accorded natural society is apparent in the very structure of his political works. While the *Elementorum* was organized as a series of definitions leading to conclusions on natural jurisprudence, the later *De officio* was divided into two books: the first on humanity in its natural state (that is, governed only by natural law) and the second on "adventitious" or artificial states (comprising families and commonwealths both), which corresponded respectively to Books I–V and VI–VIII of his much lengthier *De jure naturae*. This organization followed the formal division of "Libertas" and "Imperium" in Hobbes's *De cive* (but without its final section on "Religio," owing to Pufendorf's strict separation of natural law from theology).[48]

---

46 See DOH, pp. 28–30 for Pufendorf's rejection of skeptical epistemology; note, however, the somewhat skeptical argument about the need to establish a *rule* for our actions as creating civil government in pp. 42–43.

47 See DJN, V.13 for the discussion of third-party arbitration. Pufendorf assumed that the mutual intelligibility of human beings was sufficient to understand the law of nature, which as we have seen commands sociability, thus largely precluding the problem of epistemic conflict. The law of nature, he explained, can be 'made out by that Natural Light which is engrafted in Mankind' (DOH), p. 56, and it is further apparent when we consider the fragile condition of human beings outside society. Although it is not instinctual, the meaning of the law of nature is 'plain and clear,' for it is 'written in the hearts of men' (DOH), p. 58, cf. pp. 57–59. See also DJN, I.4.4 (countering Hobbes and positing a general, pre-political agreement on the nature of the good).

48 This makes the organization of the *De jure naturae* parallel to that of Hobbes's *Elements of Law*, which only circulated privately in manuscript; Pufendorf cites to all of Hobbes's Latin works (as well as *Leviathan*) but does not seem to have known this earlier English composition.

There was, however, a crucial addition in *De jure naturae* not found in Hobbes's works: several hundred pages of detailed discussion of the principles of Roman private law. Significantly, these were placed in its early books on the "natural state of mankind" outside civil authority.[49] Pufendorf's explication of the laws of nature – which he argued were imparted to each person's conscience by divine command and constituted his or her sound reason[50] – thus began with elementary principles conducive to social life, but culminated in Roman contract and property law, rationalized as part of the natural law.[51]

The relations supposed among the *ius civile*, the *ius naturale*, and the *ius gentium* were debated in ancient Roman legal practice and thought and occupied a great deal of attention in the later Roman law tradition.[52] An identification of the Roman *ius civile* with the law of nature was well known from Cicero's *De legibus*, usually thought to reflect Stoic influences adapted by him to an *apologia* of Roman *imperium*. But the more authoritative legal materials of the *Corpus* consistently distinguished *ius civile* and *ius naturale* and *ius gentium*, though precisely how varied with the jurist and the Roman historical institutions in question. At a theoretical level, the relation among these forms of law became a major feature of reflection from the early medieval recovery of the *Corpus* on, often tied to a conception of the *ius naturale* as divine law (on either a rationalist or voluntarist conception).

In Pufendorf's particular rendering, the equation of natural law and Roman law was made in the context of post-Hobbesian social contract theory. Thus, beyond the conventional derivation of the law of nature from natural reason, Pufendorf's account further imagined a pre-political "state of nature" governed by laws of nature that reflected natural sociability of a modern, commercial kind, whose details were obviously drawn from the history of Rome. Indeed, the fourth and fifth books of his *De jure naturae* describing the "natural state of mankind" can read at times like a summary of the *Digest*: Pufendorf discussed in great detail the origin, acquisition, and modes of transferring *dominion* with constant reference to Roman law doctrines, on the assumption of elaborate (if imperfectly realized) property relations in natural society. This does not mean

49 *DJN*, III–V.

50 *DJN*, pp. 217–219.

51 *DJN*, II.3.

52 For an overview of Roman law, see Arthur Schiller, *Roman Law: Mechanisms of Development* (The Hague: Mouton Publishers, 1978), pp. 556–560; Cicero's identification is usually thought to have been influenced by Stoic arguments, which he adapted to an *apologia* of Roman *imperium*. On the Ciceronian tradition of Roman thought, see Benjamin Straumann, *Crisis and Constitutionalism* [...] (Oxford: Oxford University Press, 2016).

that he was not often very critical of the Roman lawyers, but that he interpreted Roman law as predicated on the law of nature or nations in distinction to the general drift of the jurists before Ulpian, at least.[53]

In attempting to develop a "system" or "science" of natural law, Pufendorf culled and refined what he took from the inherited Roman law sources – attempting, in effect, to wrest these away from Rome's particular history and to claim them for reason or nature more generally. Perhaps unsurprisingly, he evidently felt the need to justify this rather wholesale use of developed legal principles to describe an allegedly pre-political state. He repeatedly insisted that much of the civil law known from Roman historical sources must have once been simply natural law,[54] and he accordingly puzzled over the original (natural) status of several technical legal doctrines.[55] In the Preface to the Second Edition of *De jure naturae*, he admitted that he had treated Roman law not as the residue of a past civil society (and thus as Roman *positive* law), but as a rough approximation to natural law as such. He excused this assumption by arguing "everyone knows that most of the material in the books of the Roman Law concerns the subject of the Law of Nature and Nations, that is, the law which obligates all men and nations; but there is interspersed with it much that is positive, and of application to the special nature of the Roman state."[56]

More precisely, Pufendorf treated the law of nations as equivalent to the law of nature, and then assumed that a great deal of the Roman private law was general to all people (not only Roman citizens) as part of the *ius naturale* or *ius gentium*.[57] While this move allowed him to develop an independent system of natural law, it is worth observing that he was following out the implications of some of the Roman sources in making it. In the later Republic, and under the influence of the praetors, Roman law developed a conception of the *ius*

53 As Mark Somos has noted (pers. comm.), it is striking how often Pufendorf criticizes or ridicules the Roman lawyers (see, e.g., *DJN*, I.iii.x.31; II.iii.ii.118). On Ulpian, see Tony Honoré, *Ulpian: Pioneer of Human Rights* (Oxford: Oxford University Press, 1994).

54 See, e.g., *DJN*, p. 199 ('All civil laws, indeed, presuppose or incorporate the general principles at least of natural law'); p. 1132 ('if you would reclaim for natural law all that the interpreters of civil law have so far included in a general way, the civil law would be condensed into a fairly small compass').

55 Pufendorf struggled to naturalize the more sophisticated Roman legal doctrines, for example, questioning what in *usucapio* (or acquisition by prescription) is inherent in natural law (*DJN* pp. 652–655), and whether the right to make a will comes from natural or positive law (*DJN*), p. 615.

56 *DJN*, p. iii.

57 See *DJN*, pp. 226–227; see further discussion below in footnotes 116–118 and accompanying text.

gentium as something like a common commercial law for subjects of diverse citizenship, a universal juridical solvent for the expanding Roman empire.[58]

Nevertheless, acknowledging that he may have failed adequately to distinguish Roman and natural law, Pufendorf promised to produce later an index specifying what in Roman law is "Natural, or universal Law," as against "Roman Law properly so called, or that peculiar to the Roman state."[59] Lacking any further clarification, however – for the promised index never appeared – what is patent is that he naturalized a great deal of Roman law (perhaps following the lead of earlier Roman jurists in so doing), adapting it to his account of natural sociability. Like the rest of natural law – which he argued, too, included most of the Ten Commandments – the doctrines he took from the *Corpus* and ascribed to humanity were argued to be divinely willed, apparent to inner reason, and universal in scope.[60] If Hobbes's state of nature was a "state of war," Pufendorf's was the Roman law without the *res publica*, a legal ordering without politics.[61] Importantly, his innovation here would not remain a matter of natural jurisprudence alone, for he was followed in these essentials by other *iusnaturalists*, including the French Jansenist, Jean Domat, whose work selectively codifying civil law would prove enormously influential for all later French (and European) law codes.[62]

---

58 Elaborating the *ius gentium* in this way avoided the problem of either needing to enfranchise, in effect, foreign subject peoples (by granting them rights under the *ius civile*) or disenfranchising Roman citizens (subjecting them to foreign *iura*), in the event of a conflict between a Roman citizen and a foreigner subject to Rome's expanding *imperium*; moreover, it solved the problem of choice of law where *peregrini* of different nationalities came into conflict, whether within the city of Rome or elsewhere in the empire. For a more extensive discussion of this aspect of the *ius gentium* in antiquity, see Grewal, *Invention of the Economy*, ch. 2. On the role of the *praetors*, see the authoritative two volumes, Corey T. Brennan, *The Praetorship in the Roman Republic* (Oxford: Oxford University Press, 2001).

59 *DJN*, p. iii.

60 *DJN*, p. 1137.

61 As Straumann argues about Grotius, whom Pufendorf followed in his use of Roman law to elaborate the state of nature: 'Grotius's state of nature [...] comes to resemble the Roman Forum, a place governed by the rules and remedies of private Roman law,' *Roman Law in the State of Nature*, p. 19. It is perhaps ironic that Pufendorf argued (as in *De origine et progressu disciplinae juris naturalis* III) that the discipline of natural law must be developed independently of any existing religious or classical legal sources, given that his discussion so often reads as a summary of Roman law; on Pufendorf's ambitions for natural jurisprudence, see Hochstrasser, *Natural Law Theories*, p. 67.

62 Domat, *Les loix civiles dans leur ordre naturel* (1695–1702). On the French civil code, see Jean-Louis Halpérin, *L'impossible code civil* (Paris: Presses Universitaires de France, 1992); cf. James Gordley, 'Myths of the French Civil Code,' *The American Journal of Comparative Law*, 42:3 (1994).

4 Commercial Sociability

The argument that God has willed through the law of nature that humans should be "sociable" is perhaps the central feature of Pufendorf's theory.[63] In elaborating the law of nature, he borrowed the standard formulations from Roman law: "Injure no man" and "Give to each his due."[64] These injunctions were found in a variety of ancient ethical sources; as one would expect in a theory arguing for extensive social interaction of a pre- or sub-political kind, Pufendorf drew particularly on Stoic authors in describing natural men as rational and sociable.[65] He then used this conception of natural sociability, with debts to Grotius's *appetitus societatis*, to elaborate two "fundamental laws of nature" reformulating Hobbes's account of the fundamental right of nature, self-defense, and the fundamental law of nature, to seek peace.[66] In the earlier *Elementorum*, these were still articulated as two separate laws, namely, the right of each person to "protect his own life and limbs, as far as he can, and save himself and what is his own" and the duty not to "disturb human society" or "do anything whereby society among men may be less tranquil."[67] In the *De Jure Naturae*, however, they were folded into one "fundamental law of nature" covering both: "to cultivate and preserve towards others a sociable attitude."[68]

On Pufendorf's view, the reason that we enter into "society" is ultimately for our own advantage or "self-love."[69] This position has led observers from his own time to ours to class him – and often condemn him – as a follower of Hobbes.[70] Importantly, however, Pufendorf described the sociable attitude

---

63 See *EJU*, II. Obs 3; *DJN*, I.6.7, II.2–3.

64 *EJU*, p. 216. The formulation comes from Ulpian's *Rules* as cited in the opening book of the *Digest*, I.I.10.

65 *EJU*, pp. 205–206; cf., *DJN* II.3.14–15.

66 Hobbes, *De cive*, I.7, II.2.

67 *EJU*, p. 327.

68 *DJN*, p. 208.

69 *EJU*, p. 319; cf. *DJN*, II.4; VII.1.2.

70 Since his own era, Pufendorf has often been called 'Hobbesian,' owing both to his contractarian political theory and his conception of *socialitas* as based on individual self-love; for recent views of this kind, see Theodore Christov, 'Pufendorf's Anti-Hobbesian Camouflage,' ch. 5, *Before Anarchy: Hobbes and His Critics in Modern International Thought* (New York: Cambridge University Press, 2015), esp. pp. 148–152; Palladini, 'Pufendorf Disciple of Hobbes'; cf. Hont, *Jealousy of Trade*, pp. 173–176. Note, however, that on the Stoic conception from which Pufendorf borrowed, there was no ultimate opposition between self-love and sociability. Moreover, too close an assimilation of Hobbes and Pufendorf on the basis of an allegedly shared starting point such as individual self-love or utility as the basis of social integration risks overlooking the relevant contrasts between them on natural law, political sovereignty, and epistemology. This is true, too, of parallels

founded in self-love as coming to encompass a concern for others, as on the Stoic account of *oikeiosis*.[71] The natural society formed through the maturation of self-love was argued to consist in forms of partial association based on family relationships or commercial ties using the property that God allows us to claim, provided that such appropriation contributes to a "polished" or "cultivated" social life.[72]

Pufendorf thus understood commercial sociability as predicated on self-love but also as maturing through institutions of family, property, and contract in ways that transform its character. While many of his discussions of natural sociability relied on the standard Stoic examples of parental love for children or the affinities of kinship groups,[73] he was most interested in theorizing voluntary associations entered into for individual advantage. The commonwealth was such an association – here he followed Hobbes's reasoning – but the best examples in the state of nature were commercial entities.[74] In this category, he included sub-political, voluntary associations larger than the family but lacking civil authority, which he called "societies" (and which Bodin had earlier treated as "colleges" or associations).[75]

While a commercial conception of natural society saturates Pufendorf's political works, these sub-political "societies" or partial associations of a commercial variety were central to his version of contract theory. From the argument that the promises underlying commercial contracts were legitimate according to the law of nature, Pufendorf went on to justify the formation of

---

between Hobbes and eighteenth-century figures, whether Hume (as in Paul Russell, 'Hume's Treatise and Hobbes's the Elements of Law,' *Journal of the History of Ideas* 46:1 (1985), pp. 51–63 based on skeptical anti-clericalism) or Smith (as in Istvan Hont, *Politics in Commercial Society: Jean-Jacques Rousseau and Adam Smith* (Cambridge: Harvard University Press, 2015), pp. 16–24, based on a shared genealogy of *amour-propre* and legacy of the 'selfish system'), which focus on one proposed continuity while downplaying other differences, including especially in the analysis of the different mechanisms of social choice, which is perhaps the most enduring quarrel within the modern moral and political sciences.

71 On Pufendorf's account of self-love and sociability, and its connection to Stoic moral theory, see Carr and Seidler, 'Pufendorf, Sociality and the Modern State,' pp. 368–369. See also the extensive comments on *oikeiosis* and the Grotian *appetitus societatis* in Straumann, *Roman Law in the State of Nature*, pp. 92–119, passim; and the discussions in Hans W. Blom and Laurens C. Winkel (eds.), *Grotius and the Stoa* (Assen: Van Gorcum, 2004), especially Reinhard Brandt, 'Self-Consciousness and Self-Care [...],' pp. 73–92.

72 On this requirement, see Tuck, *The Rights of War and Peace*, pp. 155–156, 173.

73 See, e.g., *DJN* VI.2.4. For further discussion of families in the state of nature tradition, see Simone Zurbuchen in this volume.

74 See, e.g., *EJU*, pp. 193–194; pp. 348–350; *DJN*, pp. 13–15.

75 Bodin, *Rep.*, I.2, III.7.

voluntary associations as a partial (rather than universal) merging of the wills of different individuals to create a corporate persona.[76] He accordingly distinguished "public" societies (on the model of the *polis*, *civitas*, or *societas civilis*) from "private" ones: "*Private societies* are not merely families, but also what are called guilds of merchants, and of craftsmen, and the like."[77] Thus, as on Hobbes's earlier account, social order was argued to emerge through a form of reciprocal promising, but in this case it occurs without a collective renunciation of the individual "right to all things," and in smaller groupings than the political whole. The resultant "private societies" of the state of nature did not comprise relations of political sovereignty, even while they were sociable entities. Furthermore, Pufendorf argued, there can be many societies of this kind within any single state, and he did not follow Hobbes in suspecting such partial associations of undermining the basis of political order by persevering in an implicit state of war.[78] As he argued: "it is by no means necessary for all men to coalesce into one society in which all are equal to one another; but it is sufficient if the same persons get together in several and distinct groups, which are, nevertheless, by no means altogether mutually unsociable."[79]

It is striking to observe how many essential features of the eighteenth-century analysis of "commercial society" were established in Pufendorf's far-reaching theory of natural individuals contracting with one another without assumed political obligations or thick moral agreement. As we have seen, he predicated the commercial character of natural society on the assumption of private property existing outside or before politics. This dominion over things was analyzed as a moral relation among persons, a natural "imposition of men"[80] upon other men that arose from "agreement, whether tacit or express."[81] *Contra* Hobbes, it did not necessarily come into being with political community,[82] but could develop piecemeal across time as demanded by historical circumstances, such as through the intensification of interdependent productive activities.[83] Its foundation was "confirmed at least by a tacit pact, which contained at the same time a tacit renunciation on the part of the rest,"[84] though

76 *EJU*, p. 41; cf., *DJN*, pp. 13–15.

77 *EJU*, p. 42; cf. *DJN*, I.1.13. Note that, on this description, guilds cohere as a matter of individual consent in the state of natural liberty, not as the product of civil regulation.

78 See *De cive* V.10; *Lev.*, XXII.

79 *EJU*, p. 317.

80 *DJN*, p. 533.

81 *DJN*, p. 536.

82 See *DJN*, pp. 1135, 1276.

83 *DJN*, IV.IV.6.

84 *DJN*, p. 540.

Pufendorf admitted, following Grotius, that its very first origin may have been seizure, after which it spread via tacit agreement because "tacit renunciation" furthered social peace.[85] Commercial exchange emerged naturally with private property since a right to transfer property was deemed intrinsic to "the nature of full dominion."[86] In the state of natural liberty, before efforts by civil authorities to set prices via "legal decree," such commercial exchange would be based on the "natural" or "common" price given by individual subjective evaluation in bargains, later aided by the use of money as a means of facilitating transactions.[87] Society was accordingly understood as based on free labor and unforced exchange, while sovereignty was represented as a subsequent and essentially unproductive political hierarchy of "command" necessitated by security concerns.[88] The self-love that drives commercial exchange was seen as harmonized and softened through it, on an analogy with the mature individual's coming to acknowledge the needs of others as a concomitant of recognizing one's own. Setting aside Pufendorf's *iusnaturalist* foundations and his consequent elaboration of civil sovereignty in contractarian terms, this account of natural man in commercial society could be Hume's or Smith's.[89]

5 Value in the State of Nature

Drawing the parallel to Hume and Smith raises the related question of how Pufendorf understood the "value" of something exchanged in the "state of natural liberty," since classical political economy was very much a theory of society built on a particular theory of (exchange) value. As we have seen, Pufendorf assumed that rights of transfer and alienation were intrinsic to private property, which he assumed was both natural and divinely sanctioned. Accordingly, he revisited the canonical ancient examples of commercial exchange, including

85 *DJN*, p. 547; see also note 27 above on Grotius and the tacit compact generating property.

86 *DJN*, p. 606; Pufendorf allowed that civil limitations on the right of commerce may be made concerning foreign trade (*DJN*, p. 568) or to regulate illicit conduct (*DJN*, p. 109).

87 *DJN*, pp. 675–686, 689–690.

88 *DJN*, pp. 951–952.

89 Perhaps the most important figure intervening between Pufendorf and Smith other than Hume was Smith's own teacher, Francis Hutcheson, whose work, including his *System of Moral Philosophy* (1755), was deeply indebted to Pufendorf's *De jure naturae*. Nevertheless, Hutcheson's emphasis on natural benevolence was targeted against Pufendorf (and, of course, Hobbes) and his critique of social contract theory (alongside his retention of natural rights) was deeply influential for Smith's theory of commercial sociability. On Hutcheson's sociable state of nature theory, see footnote 6 above.

the story of the grain merchant discussed in Cicero's *De officiis*.[90] Cicero took a strong view against the morality of a grain dealer charging whatever the market would bear in a famine-struck city.[91] By contrast, Pufendorf, in spite of his Stoic-derived account of natural sociability, upheld the grain merchant's right to sell at whatever price he might wish, defending the "the validity of the contract" even "on the basis of the law of nature, because, as a matter of fact, at that particular moment at which the grain was sold, it was worth that amount."[92] On these grounds, Pufendorf went on to defend usury[93] and even to countenance gambling, which, because it occurs through "mutual consent," should only be prohibited if deleterious to "the interests of the Commonwealth."[94]

It is perhaps to be expected, given his anti-Aristotelianism and his focus on *individual* advantage in the state of nature that Pufendorf held the value of a good (its "worth" or "true value") to depend on the desires of the parties in a commercial transaction.[95] In all his political works, he devoted entire chapters to the question of "worth" in commerce, offering an analysis of "natural price" according to what we now call "subjective value."[96] Since he believed that natural law legitimated private commercial contracts, the value of the goods exchanged in such contracts must be left to individual determination unless prohibited by an explicit command of Scripture,[97] manifestly contrary to divinely ordained social progress, or (in a condition of civil society) opposed by positive law.[98] Admittedly, the determination of the good through commercial exchange was hemmed by an explicit recognition of divine and civil limits to commodification, barring, for example, prostitution, the sale of confessional or judicial services, and the like.[99] However, the clear consequence of his argument is that beyond expressly prohibited activities, it is "human bartering"

---

90 Cicero, *De officiis*, III.50–54.

91 Cicero, *De officiis*, III.52. The Stoic philosophical position that 'nature has joined all men in alliance' (Cicero, *De officiis*, III.53) prevented any independent valorization of exchange, since human sociability and the related laws of nature were thought to provide a higher moral ground for the regulation of commercial life than merely bilateral reckoning.

92 *EJU*, p. 194.

93 *DJN*, pp. 752–754, cf. p. 762 on limits to usury (allowing no collateral in the person); *EJU*, p. 197.

94 *EJU*, p. 201; cf. *DJN* V.9.5–7.

95 *EJU*, p. 196; *DJN*, p. 687.

96 See *EJU*, pp. 98–102 ('Worth'); *DJN* V.1 ('On Price'); *DOH*, I.XIV ('On the Price and Value of Things').

97 *EJU*, p. 207.

98 *EJU*, pp. 216–217.

99 *EJU*, p. 100, cf. *DJN*, p. 109.

that determines the value of things based on the "utility or delectation."[100] Pufendorf adopted an essentially legalistic conception of the good: "a good action is one which agrees with law; a bad action is one which disagrees with the same."[101] Thus, within the bounds set by divine positive law (Scripture) and the divine laws of nature (that man, as a sociable creature, should progress in "cultivation"), as well as any civil limits to commodification, individuals should enjoy a very extensive liberty of contract and association, determining for themselves the inherent "worth" of their activities.

Pufendorf thus supposed that the value of any exchange was internal to the exchange itself, rather than determined by broader moral regulation; the law of nature countenances exchange, but sets no further limits or conditions to it where it is not expressly prohibited. He was accordingly motivated to develop an account of the "natural or common" price of a commodity outside legal regulation, including offering an embryonic "cost of production" approach to price-formation alongside his main account, which focused on subjective demand, including distinguishing between what we now call real and nominal prices.[102] In doing so, he drew on the ancient discussions of *philia* by Aristotle and Seneca, but emphasized those parts of their arguments that concerned commerce rather than gift-exchange, extracting the lesson that the "natural price" would be based on what the bargain can bear (rather than some other normative desideratum).

Pufendorf seems to have been the first major figure to offer a general theory of the good as determined by individually self-assessed subjective utility in exchange. That this normative position led rather straightforwardly to an early analysis of price-formation through market competition has been generally overlooked, though it should perhaps come as unsurprising on reflection.[103] His account combined a skeptical understanding of the good as given by subjective self-assessment with a naturalizing account of commercial exchange as the institutional expression of individual willing in the pre-political state. It was obviously not the first modern theory that looked to "utility," which played a role in Hobbes's account as well as in the work of those Renaissance thinkers who advanced hedonic conceptions of the good in a revival of ancient

100 *DJN*, pp. 677–678; *DOH*, p. 141.

101 *EJU*, p. 235.

102 See *DJN*, p. 680 (on reasons why a price 'rises or falls'); p. 676 (on 'ordinary' and 'eminent' prices, the latter denominated in monetary value); pp. 687–8 (on the price set by the seller).

103 Two recent studies of Pufendorf's theory rightly note this feature of his argument; see Saether, *Natural Law*, and Haara, *Pufendorf's Theory of Sociability*.

Epicurean ethics.[104] But Pufendorf divorced the assessment of the utility of an action (particularly a commercial transaction) from the idea that such utility must be assessed in relation either to a thickly prescriptive idea of "nature," as in earlier forms of ethical hedonism, or through a collective political procedure, as on Hobbes's account. While Aristotle had famously noted the puzzle of the relation between the value of an object "in use" and "in exchange," Pufendorf provided a theory of value that justified the outcomes of commercial exchange with reference to nothing beyond exchange itself. He then made this form of self-assessed value a general feature of "society," rather than something limited to a quarantined domain of explicitly commercial dealing, as in the original Roman law categories or in earlier ancient and medieval accounts of commodity exchange. It was because Pufendorf understood individual choice as conferring value and finding its natural institutional expression in commerce that he was led to defend activities such as gambling and, more generally, to valorize luxury, which had been treated with great suspicion in all earlier analyses of "utility," excepting perhaps the ancient Cyrenaic position on pleasure (which had no enduring influence except in discrediting conflations with Epicureanism).[105]

In the mid-twentieth century, some economists of the "Austrian" school, following Hayek's lead, sought to discern the roots of subjective utility theory in the "School of Salamanca."[106] It is true that Dominican and Jesuit scholars in

104 The modern conception of utility emerged from one pole of the classical moral pairing of *utilitas* and *honestas*, familiar from Cicero's *De officiis* and many other ancient texts. Recall that a rational hedonism focused on *utilitas* was the basis of Utopian moral philosophy and discussed at length in Book II of *Utopia* (pp. 159–179 in Thomas More, *Utopia, Latin Text and English Translation*, ed. by George M. Logan, Robert M. Adams, Clarence H. Miller (Cambridge: Cambridge University Press, 1995)). A sort of Christianized Epicureanism was fairly widespread in the Renaissance (following the recovery of Epicurean philosophy in Lucretius's *De rerum natura* and, later, Epicurus's *Vita* in Diogenes Laertius's *Lives*), exemplars of which include De Valla's early *De voluptate* of 1433, and Erasmus's *De contemptu mundi* of 1521 (arguing that the true Christian should be an Epicurean) and his end-of-life dialogue on ethical hedonism, the *Epicureus* of 1533.

105 Early modern forms of ethical hedonism, like most ancient precedents, generally sought the satisfaction of simple (i.e., non-luxurious) pleasures, argued to be in conformity with nature and/or religious strictures; Cyrenaicism seems to have been an exception in celebrating luxurious pleasures. On Cyrenaic ethics, see the discussion in Sextus Empiricus, *Outlines of Pyrrhonism* 1.215, and on Cyrenaicism generally, see Voula Tsouna-McKirahan, *The Epistemology of the Cyrenaic School* (Cambridge: Cambridge University Press, 1998).

106 A student of Hayek, Marjorie Grice-Hutchinson's *The School of Salamanca* (Oxford: Clarendon Press, [1952] 2016), collected some of these writings. By contrast with Hayek, Joseph Schumpeter was characteristically more cautious, and did not assert any grand claims for the School; compare his *History of Economic Analysis* (Taylor & Francis, [1954] 2006), pp. 160–161.

sixteenth-century Castile advanced what might be thought an early form of monetarism, and explored the morality and efficacy of price controls in that context.[107] However, their arguments about price-determination in markets free from princely intervention cannot be considered in isolation from their broader commitment to an overall ethical conception that is far removed from modern subjective utility theory and based instead on a Thomistic (rather than post-Hobbesian) conception of "natural law." Moreover, they did not posit a constructed social totality, whether through politics, as on Hobbes's account, or commerce, as in Pufendorf's commercialized state of natural liberty, but considered only limited domains of exchange in which individual willing might determine the "natural" or market price hemmed by a broader commitment to natural law as the divine law. Indeed, on this more limited point, what the Austrians claim as an important innovation of the Salamancans – the recognition of the role of subjective self-assessment in commercial exchanges – long predates the sixteenth century; we find discussions of it not only among earlier scholastic figures but all the way back to antiquity.[108]

What we discover in Pufendorf, by contrast, is not just the idea of particular transactions being left to the discretion of buyers and sellers but the idea that the entire social order is commercial in character. This commercial society can be understood as the product of aggregated human willing and the value in any commercial exchange given by individual subjective assessment of the parties to the transaction. The key difference between Pufendorf and earlier writers on this point was his post-Hobbesian context: he followed Hobbes's skeptical anthropology and constructivist theory of individual will, but applied this orientation – as Hobbes himself patently did not – to an analysis and defense of modern commerce rather than the modern state. Thus, once it is accepted (as Pufendorf was at pains to argue against Hobbes) that the state of nature is one of durable commercial sociability, the idea of "nature" itself provides little

---

107 For more careful analyses of the 'School of Salamanca,' see Louis Baeck, 'Spanish Economic Thought: the School of Salamanca and the Arbitristas,' *History of Political Economy*, 20:3 (1988), pp. 381–408 and *The Mediterranean Tradition in Economic Thought* (London and New York: Routledge, 1994), pp. 178–187; Odd Langholm, 'Price and Market Manipulation,' ch. 5 of *The Legacy of Scholasticism in Economic Thought* [...] (Cambridge: Cambridge University Press, 1998), which situate Iberian monetarism in its longer moral tradition.

108 For example, Seneca supposed that the value of 'benefits' in gift exchange should be determined by subjective valuation, in contrast to cases of legally mediated commercial exchange, which require (in remedy, at least) a non-personal, objective valuation: 'a benefit is subject to no law [unlike a legal contract for debt], it makes me the judge (*arbitrio*)' (*De Beneficiis*., VI.6.1). Of course, Seneca did not identify the good as such with the value of these benefits received, but focused instead on the intention of the giver.

additional constraint on or guidance to individual activity. It leads to no normative conclusions beyond a very general injunction to "live in society" where society is thought to embrace the conveniences of commercial life according to the naturalized principles of Roman private law.

6 The *Status Oeconomicus*

Pufendorf's account of natural commercial sociability depended on this precise theoretical maneuver, which transformed the conventional understanding of the "oeconomic." In the first book of the *Elementorum*, he explained that, "those who live in states, especially Christian states, are divided commonly into three statuses, *ecclesiastical*, *political*, and *economic*."[109] The first two statuses, he held to be "public" and the last "private," depending not on any civil authority or conception of "the good of society as such" but only on "each individual's own free will," which tended "immediately and directly to the advantage of individuals as such."[110] Pufendorf's assimilation of commercial relations to a natural realm of the "private" altered the predominant conception of the "oeconomic" and began the process by which the ancient word denoting household management (*oikonomia*) could come to describe a system of self-interested commercial exchange ("the economy").[111] Notably, his conceptual innovations drew on an *oikeiic* vocabulary in describing the commercialized state of natural liberty as the *status oeconomicus.*

Pufendorf introduced here an important innovation on an older tradition of the "three statuses" or "three estates" (*Dreiständelehre*) central to Lutheran thought.[112] In that tradition, individuals were considered as members of three

109 *EJU*, p. 36. The original reads: 'Porro qui in civitatibus, potissimum Christianis degunt, in triplicem vulgo statum dispescuntur, *Ecclesiasticum*, *Politicum* & *Oeconomicum*.' *Elementorum jurisprudentiae universalis libris II* (Hague, 1660), p. 17.

110 *EJU*, p. 36.

111 The fuller argument about the post-Pufendorfian history of the transformation of political economy is forthcoming in Grewal, *Invention of the Economy*, ch. 7–8. For a helpful discussion of the changing lexicon of *oikonomia*/economy (which does not address Pufendorf, however), see Tribe, *Economy of the Word*, ch. 2.

112 On the *Dreiständelehre*, see Ian Hunter, *The Secularisation of the Confessional State*, pp. 130–136. This three-fold division of status and duty is thought to have helped secure the authority of the clergy alongside secular (Protestant) government, while denying special jurisdictional powers for the Church, as in the earlier medieval pairing of civil and canon law (John Witte, *Law and Protestantism: The Legal Teachings of the Lutheran Reformation* (Cambridge: Cambridge University Press, 2002): 7 ff). It may be thought that the innovation of *political* status comes only after the Fall: ecclesiastical and 'oeconomic'

statuses or estates (*Stände*): the family or household (*oikos*), the civil order (*polis*), and the church (*ekklesia*). In the original formulation, the "oeconomic" referred to the sphere of the family, especially the marital bond, such that the *Dreiständelehre* identified the domains of (and duties to) spouse, prince, and minister, respectively. Pufendorf altered the category of the "oeconomic" in the *Dreiständelehre* by emphasizing not strictly family relations but a "private" status based on individual will and aiming at personal advantage, which was productive of sub-political "private" societies. It was this *oeconomic* status or "economic state" that Pufendorf claimed was governed by natural law in particular. By contrast, the family was analyzed as the first of the "adventitious states," the foundation of the commonwealth but not itself one.[113] This reworking of the *Dreiständelehre* tradition recurred in *De jure naturae*, in discussions of the *status naturalis*, and in *De officio hominis*, where he specified the duties of mankind as arising from the "three springs" of nature, civil authority, and revelation. In his discussion of nature in the *De officio*, Pufendorf explained that "from the First of these proceed all those most common Duties of a Man; more particularly, those that constitute him a *sociable Creature* with the Rest of Mankind."[114] Thus the Lutheran *status oeconomicus* was interpreted via a conception of "nature" that commanded "the Preservation of Society amongst Men,"[115] where "society" included a range of voluntary partial associations along with more familiar examples of familial ties.

To understand the kind of liberty presupposed in the state of natural liberty, we must ask what kind of agent populates the enlarged "economic state" of Pufendorf's conception. Neither the political animals of Aristotelian theory nor the honorable men of Stoic moral philosophy nor the diffident creatures of Hobbes's state of nature would seem to fit a world of self-interested but sociable commerce outside politics. Pufendorf supposed instead a generic subject of natural law, a social animal ("man") without citizenship or religion, which he considered forms of particular membership with corresponding positive obligations (from civil sovereign and God respectively). This conception of the

statuses are original because in the Edenic condition, Adam could be identified as both God's subject and Eve's husband (see ibid: pp. 93–94). The relation of the three estates to the Lutheran conception of God's 'two kingdoms'– namely, of God and the world – is a complex matter; for a recent critical overview of previous interpretations, see William Wright, 'Interpretations of Luther's Idea [...]' ch. 1 in *Martin Luther's Understanding of God's Two Kingdoms* (Grand Rapids: Baker Academic, 2010).

113 *DJN*, p. 839, passim.

114 *DOH*, p. 16; cf. *DJN*, I.1.11–13 on the different statuses that an individual can have and the corresponding moral personae.

115 *DOH*, p. 17.

agent of natural society was later consolidated in the moral sciences of the eighteenth century, and remains so familiar today as to sometimes seem to have no history.

Yet it does have a history, as revealed in Pufendorf's heavy reliance on Roman legal and ethical authorities focused on tendencies alleged to be general to all humanity. These sources came mainly from the end of the Republic and early centuries of the Principate, at a time when Roman citizenship became increasingly disconnected from active political participation, even while Roman law was extended over a vast and growing empire. Pufendorf's focus on recovering the *ius gentium*, the law of nations or peoples, is especially telling in this respect. While it remains the subject of scholarly controversy, the Roman *ius gentium* seems to have been thought to encompass the "human race" in its entirety.[116] It was probably developed in particular for the *peregrini*, the free but non-citizen subjects of Rome, often foreigners or resident-aliens involved in trade, who comprised the majority of the Empire's residents before the Edict of Caracalla granted universal citizenship to all free subjects.[117]

In his discussion of the *ius gentium*, Pufendorf noted in particular this link to the *peregrini*: "for the Roman Jurisconsults the law of nations is the right to actions and business belonging to aliens in the Roman state, while the civil law is that of citizens only, excluding aliens."[118] On this division, while marriage (*ius conubium*) is regulated by civil law, because it pertains to citizenship, "contracts fall under the law of nations" since even non-citizens were allowed to execute them with each other and with citizens.[119] It was on these grounds that

---

116 See discussion above in footnote 57 and accompanying text. For an overview of *ius* in Roman legal theory, see Arthur Schiller, *Roman Law*, pp. 556–560; on the *ius gentium*, see Max Kaser, *Ius gentium* (Cologne: Böhlau, 1993). For a discussion of the reception of the *ius gentium* and its relation to natural law among earlier authors, see Annabel Brett, 'Natural Law,' ch. 3 in *Changes of State: Nature and the Limits of the City in Early Modern Natural Law* (Princeton: Princeton University Press, 2011).

117 On the *peregrini* and Roman law, see Ralph Mathisen, 'Peregrini, Barbari, and Cives Romani [...],' *American Historical Review*, 11:4 (2006), pp. 1011–1040; Clifford Ando, 'Aliens, Ambassadors, and the Integrity of the Empire,' *Law and History Review*, 26:3 (2008), pp. 491–519 and *Roman Social Imaginaries: Language and Thought in the Context of Empire* (Toronto: University of Toronto Press, 2015). On Caracalla's Edict or the 'Antonine Constitution,' see Clifford Ando, 'Sovereignty, Territoriality, and Universalism in the Aftermath of Caracalla' in *Citizenship and Empire in Europe 200–1900: The Antonine Constitution After 1800 Years*, ed. by Clifford Ando (Stuttgart: Franz Steiner Verlag, 2016), pp. 7–25.

118 *DJN*, p. 227.

119 *DJN*, p. 227. On Roman marriage, see Susan Treggiari, *Roman Marriage: Iusti Coniuges From the Time of Cicero to the Time of Ulpian* (Oxford: Clarendon Press, 1991); and on *conubium* and the complex array of citizenship classifications (including the Latin

Pufendorf incorporated the body of Roman private law – "ways of acquiring things, contracts, and the like" – into the "law of nations," even while following Hobbes in denying that there was a law of nations distinct from the general commands of the "law of nature."[120] Through these equations, the Roman private law thus became Pufendorf's law of nature, governing a social state that did not depend on political citizenship. The non-citizen subject of this naturalized Roman law – the *peregrinus* or, in earlier Greek terminology, the *metic* – provided a model for natural man outside particular civic obligation. Like these aliens of the Roman Empire, the agents in the *oeconomic* state of nature are free (i.e., self-owned) but lack the political powers of active citizenship, regulated instead by laws that come from above (from God or emperor) enjoining them to peaceable commerce. In the early nineteenth-century, freedom of this kind would be presented as the realization of a specifically *modern* liberty, but it is worth observing that its roots were in a natural jurisprudence that drew on ancient sources concerned with those denizens of the Roman Empire who were neither slaves nor citizens, but enjoyed rights of self-ownership and contractual liberty even while excluded from political power.[121]

Pufendorf's commercialization of the *status oeconomicus* proved enormously influential for later authors from Cumberland, Locke, and Burlamaqui through Hutcheson and Smith – who followed him in imagining the "state of nature" as a "state of natural liberty" organized through pre-political property relations and the sociability of commerce.[122] But Pufendorf did not simply elaborate the content of natural law using commercial examples; rather, the very category of "society" (as distinct from "civil society") appeared in his work as a consequence of this theoretical reorientation.[123] Further, Pufendorf analyzed commercial society as evolving in an historical progression based on changing modes of production, which provided the foundations of the "four stages" theory so prevalent in French and Scottish political economy of the mid-eighteenth century.[124] Finally, it is worth observing that Pufendorf's conception of the "state of natural liberty" presented in embryonic form the ideal

---

peregrini) in Rome, Saskia Roselaar 'The Concept of Conubium in the Roman Republic' in *New Frontiers: Law and Society in the Roman World*, ed. by Paul J. du Plessis (Edinburgh: Edinburgh University Press, 2013).

120 *DJN*, p. 226.

121 On the conception and instantiation of a Roman "ontology of the social" see Ando, *Roman Social Imaginaries*.

122 For discussions of Cumberland, Locke, Burlamaqui, and Hutcheson, see footnote 6 above.

123 On the later development of the concept of "society," see footnote 7 above.

124 See discussion in footnote 167 below.

of "modern liberty," which became a political and constitutional touchstone in the early nineteenth century in the aftermath of the French Revolution.

Pufendorf thus laid the foundations for the eighteenth-century account of commercial society, as scholars such as Hont and others have noted, though it is worth observing further that he did so partly by deploying a renovated vocabulary of the *oeconomic* that drew on but transformed earlier terminology. His conception of the *status oeconomicus* or "economic state" served as a bridge between seventeenth-century social contract theory and eighteenth-century political economy. His work was drawn on by all the major British authors of political economy, from Locke to Hume to Smith, and he was important (if less frequently cited, perhaps owing to religious difference) to the varied and prolific French discourses on commercial society that emerged in the later seventeenth century and continued with increasing vigor up to and through the Revolution. In effect, he described and justified a new social ontology, something very much like the circulation of commodities according to the division of labor that theorists would spell out more directly in the generation immediately following him, delineating the boundary between state and "society" in a manner that contemporary scholars often call liberal (or at least "proto-liberal") despite the possible anachronism.

Pufendorf's conceptual innovations and his adaptation of the ancient vocabulary of *oikonomia* to describe the "economic state" complicate efforts to offer a late date for the emergence of modern economic discourse. For example, several scholars have suggested that the term "the economy," employing the definite article and conceiving the economy as "an autonomous social system,"[125] only emerged in the twentieth century, a by-product of new techniques of economic policymaking and statistical analysis. After a study of five major Anglophone periodicals, Mike Emmison concluded that "[i]t is not until the mid-1930s that the category 'the economy' in its modern sense is coined [...] closely tied to developments in theoretical economic discourse, most obviously the writings of Keynes."[126] Citing him, Adam Tooze has argued that,

---

125 Adam Tooze, *Statistics and the German State, 1900–1945: The Making of Modern Economic Knowledge* (Cambridge: Cambridge University Press, 2001), p. 9.

126 Mike Emmison, 'The Economy: Its Emergence in Media Discourse,' in *Language, Image, Media*, ed. by Paul Walton and Howard Davis (Oxford: Blackwell, 1983), p. 147. Emmison's initial study concerned the appearance of the term "the economy" in five major English-language newspapers or magazines (the *Times* of London, the *New Statesman*, the *New York Times*, *Time* magazine, and the *Economist*). He noted the use of cognate phrases such as "the economic system" as early as the 1920s, but linked the emergence of the term "the economy" to new forms of Keynesian management, which posited a discrete and autonomous social system capable of administrative steering (1983: 148–149); for further commentary, see also Emmison and Alec McHoul 'Drawing on the Economy: Cartoon

in England, " 'the economy' as a term with which to refer to the entire system of production and exchange did not come into common use until the 1930s."[127] Likewise, Timothy Mitchell has suggested that before the 1930s, the meaning of "economy" was restricted to its ancient or early modern usage, continuous with *oikonomia*: "no economist before the 1930s referred to an object called the economy."[128] The difficulty with these claims is that a media study may prove useful as a barometer of popular understanding, perhaps particularly of new techniques of macroeconomic management, but risks missing earlier and arguably deeper currents of thought that utilized a different vocabulary in describing a comparable ontology.[129]

Most scholars have claimed an earlier, usually eighteenth-century transformation in conceptualization, including in associated vocabulary, concerning the economy. For example, in the opening pages of *The Ancient Economy*, Moses Finley pointed to Francis Hutcheson as an example of an author who persisted in using "oeconomics" in the ancient sense of household-management into the middle of the eighteenth century.[130] Finley then presented it as a puzzle that Adam Smith's commercialized idea of the "oeconomic" emerged only a few decades after, and from one of Hutcheson's own students: "There was no road from the 'oeconomics' of Francis Hutcheson to the *Wealth of Nations* [...] twenty-four years later."[131]

Without entering fully into this controversy, it is worth emphasizing that the expansion of the ancient term *oikonomia* to cover the conditions of modern commerce began with Pufendorf's innovations, a generation before Hutcheson. He deviated both conceptually and terminologically from Hobbes's

---

Discourse and the Production of a Category,' *Cultural Studies* 1:1 (1987), pp. 93–111 and Emmison, 'Visualizing the Economy: Fetishism and the Legitimation of Economic Life.' *Theory, Culture & Society* 3.2 (1986), pp. 81–97.

127 Tooze, *Statistics and the German State*, p. 9.

128 Timothy Mitchell 'Rethinking Economy,' *Geoforum*, 39:3 (2008), p. 1117; see more generally, Timothy Mitchell, 'The Work of Economics: How a Discipline Makes its World', *European Journal of Sociology*, 46:2 (2005).

129 Citing to Emmison's study, Tooze's and Mitchell's work links the emergence of the term "the economy" in popular discourse to new techniques of statistical measurement (Tooze, *Statistics and the German State*, p. 9 ff) and new "socio-technical practice" (Mitchell, 'Rethinking Economy,' p. 1116 ff). While not widely followed in the history of economic thought, for reasons I suggest here, Emmison's work has been widely cited in media studies, including in studies of how popular visualizations – including in cartoons (on which, see Emmison, 'Drawing on the Economy') – depict "the economy."

130 Moses Finley, *Ancient Economy* (Berkeley: University of California Press, 1973), p. 17; see pp. 17–20 on Hutcheson's use of 'oeconomics.'

131 Finley, *Ancient Economy*, p. 20.

slightly earlier account, which was extremely skeptical about the durability of natural "society," and viewed pre-political associations as a temporary and fragile concord of wills.[132] Indeed, only at the end of a discussion of "other" laws of nature, did Hobbes mention commerce, declaring it "a law of nature, *That men allow commerce and traffic indifferently to one another*."[133] Notably, the example he used was the dispute over trade that sparked the Peloponnesian War, and the reason he counseled freedom of commerce was to avoid showing favor in a way that might engender enmity among different polities (not because he saw trade as particularly valuable in itself).

Terminologically, Hobbes used "oeconomy" in several established senses. When he discussed the "oeconomy of the commonwealth" in *Leviathan*, he meant it in the sense of *he politike oikonomia*, familiar from ancient studies of public administration as the ordering of productive affairs through political command.[134] Hobbes also used the term in an accepted though somewhat less common way when he described the organization of bandits living by plunder in the "mere state of nature" as a "kind of trade" [*quasi oeconomia quaedam erat*] while making the point that natural law is "silent" under these conditions.[135] It is worth noting that *oeconomy* was frequently used to denote an organization of parts into wholes – as in studies of animal *oeconomy* (i.e.,

132 Hobbes, *Elements*, I.19.4, I.19.6.

133 Hobbes, *Elements*, I.16.12.

134 Hobbes, *Leviathan: Revised Student Edition* (Cambridge University Press, 1996), p. 167. Hobbes conceived what we now call the economy as an outgrowth of the state, as in *Leviathan*, Ch. XIV: 'Of the Nutrition, and Procreation of a Common-Wealth.' On the ancient usage of *politike oikonomia*, see Carlo Natali, 'Oikonomia in Hellenistic political thought,' in *Justice and Generosity* [...], ed. by Andre Laks (Cambridge: Cambridge University Press, 1995), p. 98.

135 See *De cive*, V.2. The original reads: 'Ideoque priscis temporibus vitae institutum, & quasi oeconomia quaedam erat, quam vocabant ληστρικην, Rapto Vivere.' Hobbes, *De cive* (Amsterdam: Apud Ludovicum Elzevirium, 1647), p. 79. Note that in Silverthorne's translation, which I followed above, the word *oeconomia* is translated as 'a kind of trade' relating to a 'way of life.' Compare the Samuel Sorbière translation of 1647 into French: 'on a vu jadis en cette forme de vie, qui n'était que piraterie et brigandage, quelque espèce d'économie qui y était observée' (Sorbière, ed., *Le citoyen, ou les fondements de la politique* (Paris: Garnier-Flammario)), p. 140. Note that in antiquity, *oikonomia* was sometimes used to describe the 'distribution of spoils,' as after a military campaign (Reumann, 'The Use of 'Oikonomia,' p. 490). The idea of primitive people 'living by plunder' (*Rapto Vivere*) was common in classical representations; Virgil used the phrase in a line from the *Aeneid* (vii.748), describing the pre-Roman Italians as plowing while armed (which was picked up later by Montaigne in his essay 'Of Vanity,' where it is cited in the midst of laments about the civil wars oppressing France). Mark Somos has helpfully pointed out to me that Hobbes is likely sparring with Augustine at this point (concerning the famous passage on piracy and sovereignty from *De civitate dei*, IV.4).

anatomy) – and that such an idea of an *oeconomy* of the commonwealth was implied by the organizing metaphor in *Leviathan* of the body politic as a *body*.

These usages of *oeconomy* were carried forward, after Hobbes, in ways that developed into the modern conception of the economy. Most immediately, Pufendorf explicitly opposed Hobbes's claim that the "economy" in the state of nature would consist in anarchic banditry or brigandage.[136] The Pufendorfian *status oeconomicus* allowed for adequately peaceable commercial relations, as we have seen he argued. Moreover, while Pufendorf did not employ the term extensively, the idea of an "oeconomy of the commonwealth" was frequently used by later authors, who drew on Hobbes's metaphor of the commonwealth as a body (with circulation among its parts) so vividly depicted in the opening pages of *Leviathan* and continuing in the state-centered conception of commodity circulation in its neglected twenty-fourth chapter.[137] The use of *oeconomy* to describe an internal organization or system of parts, which was well established in antiquity, was employed by other early modern authors to present commerce as conforming to a providential arrangement. Writing at roughly the same time as Pufendorf, Richard Cumberland drew a parallel to "animal *oeconomy*" in his analysis of the "common good," which he argued was based on a division of God's creation into private property – a division claimed to be in the "Interest of all" and enabling us to "learn the *Limits* of a laudable *Self-love*."[138] Similarly, and looking forward, the third Earl of Shaftesbury (whose grandfather put Locke in charge of his early education) frequently used "oeconomy" in the familiar Stoic manner to describe a cosmic ordering or administration, calling the prime mover of the universe a "wise Oeconomist" and drawing a parallel between an "animal-order, or Oeconomy" and the general system regulating all Creation.[139] However, in the conclusion to his *Inquiry Concerning*

---

136 See *DJN*, pp. 173; Pufendorf's discussion here followed on his analysis of Hobbes's *De cive* V.2 on natural law being 'silent' in the state of nature. While he did not cite to Hobbes at this point, he referenced the same passage from the *Aeneid* that Hobbes had used, where *vivere rapto* ('living by plunder') described the state of primitive life; on which, see footnote 135 above.

137 *Lev.* XIV.

138 See Richard Cumberland, *De legibus*, pp. 663, 665, 675, and 679 respectively (italics original). His argument was explicitly directed against Hobbes with respect to the assumption of equality in the state of nature and to property's political origins, which Cumberland not inappropriately drew together to suggest a radical Hobbesian egalitarianism (that he wished to counter); see ibid, pp. 680–681.

139 See Anthony Ashley Cooper Shaftesbury, *Characteristicks, Men, Manners, Opinions, Times*, Vol II, (Indianapolis, Liberty Fund [1737] 2001), p. 7 (discussing the 'OEconomy or Government of the Universe'); p. 11 ('there is a System of all Animals; an Animal-Order or OEconomy, according to which the animal Affairs are regulated and dispos'd'); pp. 12,

Virtue or Merit, he went further, and made "our *Balance* and *OEconomy*" the basis of an extraordinary anti-skeptical argument concerning the benefits of virtue, cached out in terms of a "*Sum* or general Account of Happiness," which he called a "Moral Arithmetick."[140]

Likewise, while Finley was correct to note that Francis Hutcheson had used the word "oeconomy" in the ancient sense in his *Short Introduction to Moral Philosophy*, Hutcheson nevertheless followed Shaftesbury's innovating usage in his more important work, *The Nature and Conduct of the Passions*.[141] Here, he even repeated Shaftesbury's wording, linking "balance" and "oeconomy" to a view of summed moral goodness. Human life has "a superiority of Goodness and Happiness" over disorder, Hutcheson argued, with a "just Ballance and Oeconomy which constitute the most happy State of each Person, and promote the greatest Good in the whole."[142] *Pace* Finley, it is not hard to see how this conception of the "oeconomic" could migrate from Hutcheson to his student Smith in a single generation. Francis Hutcheson used the term both ways, sometimes employing an antique usage of "oeconomy," as Finley emphasized, but also describing a system of beneficial commerce using the same term. For the latter usage, as we have seen, the decisive transformation in the meaning of *oikonomia* began a generation earlier: when Pufendorf adapted the Hobbesian theory of constructive individual willing to justify commercial "society" within the *status oeconomicus* of the Lutheran *Dreiständelehre*, now represented as a state of nature. Following Pufendorf's innovation, this new meaning of "oeconomy" would become increasingly prevalent in educated circles in Western Europe, borrowing from the ancient account of *oikonomia* considered not as household-management but as an ordering of parts, now applied to a providential pattern allegedly visible in commercial society.

7 Making Sovereignty Sociable

Despite his confidence in natural law, Pufendorf was clear throughout and across his political works that commerce ultimately required the coercive

53–54, 77, 80, 99 as a synonym for system or constitution, especially pp. 53–54 on 'oeconomy of the passions;' and p. 208 ('O wise OEconomist, and powerful Chief, whom all the Elements and Powers of Nature serve!').

140 Shaftesbury, *Characteristicks*, Vol II, p. 99.

141 Francis Hutcheson, *An Essay on the Nature and Conduct of the Passions and Affections, with Illustrations on the Moral Sense* (Indianapolis: Liberty Fund, [1742] 2002), e.g. pp. 47, 79, 107, often following nearly identical usages in Shaftesbury.

142 Hutcheson, *Nature and Conduct of the Passions*, p. 47.

power of the state to enforce the promises that constitute it.[143] As we have seen, he hedged on whether civil society was required to overcome epistemic confusion or simply to support the law of nature with an additional level of coercion. But the state usually appeared in Pufendorf's work as a disciplinary mechanism brought in to enforce the *social* rather than *political* construction that humans accomplish "naturally," according to their inclinations and in keeping with the laws of nature.[144] Civil society did not have, as on Hobbes's view, an essentially constructive task since its justice and morality were argued to be determined largely by natural law. Positive legislation could only complement, not override God's universally binding commands. Civil authority was not in itself productive beyond its enforcement of natural law and as the articulation in a particular socio-historical context of God's dictate that we be sociable to one another.

The willed "private societies" of Pufendorf's expanded *oeconomic* status prove compatible with the equally willed institution of organized civil society only given a particular account of the formation and limits to political sovereignty. Writing in a post-Hobbesian vein, Pufendorf did not depict the state as natural, as on a teleological account, but artificial; moreover, it emerged owing to fear, not from need, since needs could be satisfied through sociable commerce.[145] His organizing conception was thus of a vertical structure of political command layered atop and securing the horizontal contractual exchanges constituting natural society.[146] The overall aim of individuals in forming this hierarchy of command was "security for their property, and especially for their lives"[147] through the creation of an apparatus of centralized enforcement, including for the protection of the rights of the few against the many.[148] Natural law was thought to impose broad restrictions on the legitimate scope of civil authority since it held chronological, conceptual, and

143 *DJN*, VII.1, VII.3.2.

144 For example, compare *DOH* I.2 on the 'confusions' (p. 42) and *DOH* II.1 on the 'inconveniences' (p. 170) of the natural state – both fairly 'Hobbesian' accounts emphasizing conflicts of individual judgment – with *EJU* II.V (especially pp. 383–384), which introduces sovereignty as a means of securing the law of nature among otherwise self-sufficing family groups, which makes epistemic conflict a secondary concern justifying a 'second pact' by which the united society decides a government (*EJU*, pp. 368–370). Both views may be found in the main chapter of *De Jure Naturae* on the motive for establishing a state; compare *DJN* VII.1.8 with VII.1.10.

145 *DJN*, VII.1.5–7.

146 *DJN*, p. 951.

147 *DJN*, p. 1148.

148 *DJN*, pp. 959, 986–987, 1016.

normative priority. Thus, before the formation of their political union, the citizens-to-be would already have extensive juridical commitments as natural individuals, which could be buttressed and complemented, but not repudiated by later civil legislation.[149]

The priority of natural society was at the root of Pufendorf's account of the formation of sovereignty, which countered Hobbes's social contract theory with what has been termed a "double-contract theory," likely indebted to earlier Calvinist versions,[150] and self-consciously so to Grotius's analysis of the *summa potestas* in a state.[151] In place of the Hobbesian social contract, by which a disorganized multitude becomes a sovereign "people," self-constituted as a political decision-making body, Pufendorf argued that civil sovereignty was founded through "two pacts and a decree."[152] As he explained, civil sovereignty emerged from a first pact (however tacit) establishing "society" as a pre-political entity, followed by a decree on what kind of rule will be established in that society, and then finally a second pact uniting rulers and ruled on the express basis of that decree. Importantly, the first "pact" forming the people could be tacit, following Pufendorf's general account of the association of private wills under conditions of natural liberty.[153] Recognizing the advantages of civil government, this already-formed but pre-political "people" would then consent to a decree concerning what kind of regime they would support, according to a vague but perhaps majoritarian decision rule (which does not, however implausibly, yet constitute them as

149 *DJN*, pp. 1015–1016, 1055, 1133.

150 For discussions of the 'double contract' theory in Pufendorf, see Jean-Fabien Spitz, 'La théorie du double contrat chez Grotius et chez Pufendorf,' *Cahiers de philosophie politique et juridique* 11 (1987); Ross Harrison, *Hobbes, Locke, and Confusion's Masterpiece* [...] (Cambridge: Cambridge University Press, 2003), pp. 153–154; Helena Rosenblatt, *Rousseau and Geneva: From the First Discourse to The Social Contract, 1749–1762* (Cambridge: Cambridge University Press, 2007), pp. 99–101. Double contract theories were common in Calvinist political thought, interpreting God's covenant as an original pact, with princely obligation occurring through a subsequent agreement. Johannes Althusius's was perhaps the most familiar version of this kind of theory; see his *Politica* IX; XIX–XX; and Thomas Hueglin, *Early Modern Concepts for a Late Modern World: Althusius on Community and Federalism* (Waterloo, Ontario: Wilfrid Laurier University Press, 1999), pp. 99–108. Note that Pufendorf did not cite to Althusius, though he did to earlier double-contract theorists, such as the Calvinist *monarchomach*, François Hotman (*DJN*, p. 1071). However, unlike theirs, Pufendorf's theory did not equate the original pact with God's covenant (which would generate, on his account, divine *positive* law not natural law).

151 *DJN* VII.3.1–2; cf. VII.4.14.

152 *DJN*, p. 976.

153 Pufendorf several times noted that the initial formation of a people could be 'tacit': see *DJN*, pp. 976, 977.

a collective decision-making body).[154] The future citizens of this regime are then imagined as pledging either absolute or conditional support to the proposed regime.[155]

Following the decree, a second pact – the pact that creates civil sovereignty – is finally made between a single ruler or set of rulers and the subjects who have accepted him or them, producing a "finished state."[156] Pufendorf offered the history of the Roman *civitas* as an example of this process: "a multitude of men came together to found a new home, between whom there intervened a kind of tacit pact;" afterward, they deliberated about the form of government, while still "held together only by the first pact," before taking the "next step [...] sovereignty is then tendered to Romulus," thus creating the Roman state.[157] In its essentials, he thus imagined a contract between two entities: the "people" who are constituted initially through pre-political agreement, which may be merely tacit (i.e., expressed through historic descent or commercial bonds) and their rulers, chosen on the basis of a previously determined decree. The result of this contract was the institution of civil sovereignty, the source of positive law.

The "two pacts and a decree" framework allowed Pufendorf not only to distinguish civil sovereignty from familial and despotic relationships, but also to analyze many different forms of state, including "irregular" ones that Hobbes had criticized.[158] It also provided the rudiments of later resistance theory, since the second pact establishing the state could be made conditional on the ruler's compliance with both natural law and any preconditions to popular assent, such as respect for private property or religious toleration: "subjects by the submission of their wills do not destroy their natural liberty of will."[159] While Pufendorf argued it would be better for an aggrieved citizen to flee an unhappy political situation, he believed resistance could nevertheless be justified in extreme circumstances, as when a ruler disobeyed the terms of the second pact.[160]

As Tuck has observed, Pufendorf's double-contract theory formalized and clarified Grotius's earlier account along these same lines, which supposed an historically coherent but essentially non-legislating "people" contracting with

---

154 See the discussion in Tuck, 'Grotius, Hobbes and Pufendorf.'

155 *DJN*, p. 974.

156 *DJN*, VII.2.8.

157 *DJN*, pp. 976–977.

158 See *DJN* VI.3.1; VII.5.2.

159 *DJN*, pp. 972–973.

160 *DJN*, p. 980, VII.8; *EJU*, p. 210. For less extreme cases, Pufendorf suggested emigration when 'the administration is of little value to some man's private interests [...] or can be looked after better somewhere else' (*DJN*, p. 1349).

a sovereign, who then held both the *summa potestas* and the ordinary administrative functions that Bodin and Hobbes had distinguished as "government."[161] Grotius's analysis of sovereignty rather obviously rationalized the history of the modern Dutch republic – much as his theory of natural right served as an apology for Dutch privateering[162] – but it left the dynamics of the initial formation of the people unclear, as did Pufendorf's account of the first pact. However, what this theory of sovereignty emphasized was the limitation imposed on any form of state, however "absolute," by preexisting natural law (as well as other requirements of respecting the pre-political identity of an historically given "people").[163] For his part, Pufendorf constantly added the protection of "property" alongside life as the reason for exiting the state of natural liberty, criticizing Hobbes for allegedly missing this point, and insisting that because "pacts intervened in the formation of states," civil authority arrived already bound by natural laws concerning property and commerce.[164] Thus, his somewhat awkward double-contract theory served to make explicit that the *socialitas* of natural law, concretized in the first pact forming natural society, necessarily underlay the foundation of the future civil state.

The effect of this framework was to render sovereignty *sociable*: to make it conform to the dictates of natural law, where the content of natural law was given by Pufendorf's theory of commercial sociability. It thus blurred any sharp distinction between civil society and the "state of nature," for the civil state was preceded and conditioned by the *status oeconomicus*, which was at the same time a *status naturalis*. Relatedly, the double-contract theory avoided the Hobbesian theory of primitive democracy, the idea (laid out clearly in *De cive*) that the original civil society was necessarily democratic.[165] Pufendorf accepted the historical but not the conceptual or normative priority of democracy among types of civil state.[166] However, the initial formation of the people in the first pact was not democratic – as Grotius had seemed, vaguely, to suggest – but merely

161 Tuck 'Grotius, Hobbes and Pufendorf.'

162 Grotius, *De indis* (1604/5); cf. *Mare liberum* (1609).

163 *DJN*, p. 1064.

164 *DJN*, VIII.1.3; VIII.5.2.

165 *DJN*, VII.2.12; cf. I.6.2 for a discussion of ancient democracy as a procedural agreement constituting the law-making assembly. As Tuck suggests, Hobbes's argument on this point may have been meant to correct Grotius; see Tuck, *The Sleeping Sovereign*, pp. 111–112. That Pufendorf would later criticize Hobbes for this view explicitly (as in *DJN* VII.3.8) shows the essential continuity between the Grotian and Pufendorfian view as against the Hobbesian.

166 *DJN* VII.5.4 (on democracy as the first historical form of state); cf. VII.3.8 (*contra* Hobbes on the priority of democracy).

sociable.[167] To institute a democracy would require a decree announcing that form of political decision-making and an express second pact accepting it, as with the selection of any other form of regime. Pufendorf noted that requiring a second pact to create democracy might seem odd – since the people must then be understood to contract with itself somehow – but he insisted that civil sovereignty of any kind could only come about through this route.[168] Indeed, democracy recurred as an awkward form of regime in Pufendorf's analysis because civil sovereignty was only instituted, on his theory, through a contract between a pre-existing people and its rulers, with those rulers then possessing the sovereignty.[169] By contrast, on Hobbes's account, democracy was necessarily foundational because majoritarianism was how a people constituted itself politically out of a natural multitude, with monarchical or aristocratic regimes then resulting from a later transfer of sovereignty by the people away from itself.

Accordingly, a further effect of Pufendorf's double-contract theory was to blur the distinction between "sovereignty" and "government" that Hobbes had taken from Bodin, and which posited two distinct levels of legislation, with the sovereign responsible for fundamental rather than routine lawmaking.[170] The people – the original sovereign in Hobbes's account – are rendered a sociable multitude in Pufendorf's. They do not legislate for one another but nevertheless form contractual associations, including, ultimately, the state, which is then the source of all positive legislation (whether fundamental or quotidian). In choosing a government via the "second pact," they thus simultaneously choose a civil "sovereign" who must legislate in conformity with pre-existing natural law and any pre-political conditions put on its formation. Thus Pufendorf, like Grotius before him, denied the Bodinian distinction between sovereign and government, at least if viewed in terms of mundane legislation. However, it may be possible to identify sovereignty at another level in Pufendorf's theory: possessed by the divine author of natural law, the universal legislator whose fundamental commands hem all positive enactments by subordinate civil authority.

---

167 On Grotius's vague majoritarianism in the formation of the people, see Tuck, *The Sleeping Sovereign*, pp. 72–74. Note that Pufendorf's alternative, a tacit agreement forming the people, was probably adapted from Grotius's justification of property. On Grotius's tacit consent theory of property, see Straumann, *Roman Law in the State of Nature*, pp. 185–187, discussed in footnote 27 above.

168 *DJN*, VII.2.8.

169 *DJN*, VII.5.6–7; VII.2.8; cf. *EJU*, pp. 146–148.

170 See Tuck, *The Sleeping Sovereign*, pp. 109–119 on Pufendorf's response to Hobbes's distinction between sovereignty and government.

Pufendorf's theory of sociable sovereignty would prove enormously influential to the eighteenth-century German social contract theory of Thomasius, Wolff, Vattel and others – which Kant later opposed and rearticulated on much more Hobbesian lines.[171] It was also important for John Locke, whose social contract theory seems to vacillate between Hobbesian and Pufendorfian conceptions of the people.[172] Later interpreters tended to drop or deemphasize the first pact, seeing tacit coordination rather than express (but somehow non-political) agreement in the initial constitution of the people, and then jettisoning the decree in favor of more straightforward historical arguments.[173] The result was a simpler idea of a single contract (in fact, Pufendorf's second pact) between the people (or "society"), constituted through socio-historical development, and their governors ("the state" or sovereign), which offered a familiar and popular form of social contract theory in the early eighteenth century.

David Hume would later denounce this sort of vulgar social contract theory as "delirious," and offered his theory of coordination via social convention as an alternative to the fiction of a decisive moment of political agreement.[174] Yet while Pufendorf's account of civil authority would help generate the social contract theory that Hume criticized, his conception of the state of nature – with its suggestion of the possibility of tacit coordination in natural society – proved essential to Hume's own idea of social convention. Unburdened of its juridico-theological language of right and promise, the Grotian idea of property as originating in *tacit* consent, in which Pufendorf persevered, was at the core of Hume's influential analysis of commercial society.[175] Tacit consent theory would be stripped of its *iusnaturalist* scaffolding, lifted from the specific justification of property in the state of nature to provide a more general analysis and defense

171 On the relation of Hobbes and Kant in this respect, see Christopher Meckstroth, *The Struggle for Democracy: Paradoxes of Progress and the Politics of Change* (Oxford: Oxford University Press, 2015), pp. 118–121; Tuck, *The Rights of War and Peace*, pp. 204–219; on German contract theory, see also Ian Hunter, *Rival Enlightenments: Civil and Metaphysical Philosophy in Early Modern Germany* (Cambridge: Cambridge University Press, 2001).

172 Tuck, *The Sleeping Sovereign*, pp. 117–120.

173 For a brief overview, see Melvin Dalgarno, 'Taking Upon Oneself a Character: Reid on Political Obligation' in *The Philosophy of Thomas Reid*, ed. by Melvin Dalgarno and Eric Matthews (Dordrecht: Springer Netherlands, 1989), pp. 369–388, at 369–371.

174 David Hume, 'Of the Original Contract,' in *Essays Moral, Political, Literary*, ed. Eugene F. Miller, (Indianapolis: Liberty Fund, 1987), p. 470. For his discussion of convention as an alternative to the express promise of the social contract, see Hume, *Enquiry Concerning the Principles of Morals* (London: A. Miller, 1751); see also David Grewal, *Network Power: The Social Dynamics of Globalization* (New Haven: Yale University Press, 2008), pp. 59–61.

175 On the Grotian theory of property, see footnote 30 above.

of social conventions (including private property).[176] Imagined as a temporal succession, the pacts of the *status oeconomicus* establishing a commercial order could be conceived as conventional responses to changing material conditions (most famously, the increase of population). On this basis, it would be possible to produce a natural history of commercial society, as was formalized in eighteenth-century political economy in the theory of four successive stages of production.[177]

Yet for this natural history of society to be fully formulated, the private orderings of the *status oeconomicus* would need to be rendered more durable than Pufendorf had allowed, so that his ultimately contractarian political conclusions could be deemphasized or abandoned. In other words, even Pufendorf's "economic state" required still a theory of the market mechanism as an instrument specially fitted to a world of selfish passions. *Pace* Weber, that theory first emerged not with Pufendorf or other Protestant contract theorists, but in a religious dispute in the heart of Catholic France concerning the divine management of sin, which delivered the idea of "private vices" turning to "public benefit" through the operation of the market.[178] In Pufendorf's natural law theory, by contrast, the role of the state remained foundational – and thus, the underlying identification of the "economic state" with the pre-political state of nature is all the plainer and more potent for us to observe today.

Select Bibliography

Primary Sources

Hobbes, Thomas. *Elementa philosophica de cive*. (Amsterdam: Apud Ludovicum Elzevirium, 1647).

Grotius, Hugo. *De Jure belli ac pacis.* Paris: Nicolas Buon, 1625.

176 This would include the tacit consent that Hume admitted as the initial foundation of government in savage society, which is maintained by its utility not its legitimacy; see Hume, 'Of the Original Contract,' pp. 478, 481. Of eighteenth-century analyses of commercial society, Hume's was the most radical in reconceiving the foundations of social order in terms of utility and convention; the Physiocrats, by contrast, tended to persevere in a modified language of natural right and natural law (while coming to many of the same conclusions as Hume).

177 For an account of Pufendorf as innovator of the four-stages theory, see Hont, 'Natural Liberty and Global Competition,' ch. 1 in *Jealousy of Trade*; for a criticism, see Peter Stein, 'The Four Stage Theory of the Development of Societies,' in *The Character and Influence of the Roman Civil Law: Historical Essays* (London: Hambledon Press, 1988: 395–409), who finds only a three-stages theory (familiar since antiquity) in Pufendorf, and identifies a clear instance of the latter only in Lord Kames and successors.

178 Grewal, 'Political Theology of *Laissez-Faire*.'

Pufendorf, Samuel. *Elementa jurisprudentiae universalis*. The Hague: Adriaen Vlacq, 1660.

Pufendorf, Samuel. *De jure naturae et gentium libri octo*. Lund: Adam Junghans, 1672.

Pufendorf, Samuel. *De officio hominis et civis juxta legem naturalem libri duo*. Lund: Adam Junghans, 1673.

Secondary Sources

Haakonssen, Knud. *Natural Law and Moral Philosophy: From Grotius to the Scottish Enlightenment*. Cambridge: Cambridge University Press, 1996.

Hochstrasser, T. J. *Natural Law Theories in the Early Enlightenment*. Cambridge: Cambridge University Press, 2000.

Hont, Istvan. "The Language of Sociability and Commerce: Samuel Pufendorf and the Theoretical Foundations of the 'Four-Stages Theory.'" In *The Languages of Political Theory in Early-Modern Europe*, edited by Anthony Pagden, 253–76. Cambridge: Cambridge University Press, 1987.

McNally, David. *Political Economy and the Rise of Capitalism: A Reinterpretation*. University of California Press, 2018.

Tuck, Richard. *The Sleeping Sovereign: The Invention of Modern Democracy*. Cambridge: Cambridge University Press, 2016.

CHAPTER 8

The State of Nature, the Family and the State

Simone Zurbuchen

Abstract

This chapter explores the theories of the family in the social contract theories of Thomas Hobbes, Samuel Pufendorf and John Locke. It takes up the missing half of the social contract theories which Carole Pateman brought to the fore in her pioneering study on the "sexual contract", albeit from a more historical and contextual point of view. Based on Pufendorf's distinction between a fictitious and a realist account of the state of nature, the chapter first shows how Pufendorf and Locke justified the exercise of power in the private realm of the family – a complex society in which the subordinated societies between husband and wife, parents and children, and master and servant, or slave, are united under the domestic rule of the *paterfamilias*. This reconstruction relies on the fictitious state of nature in which all human beings (women no less than men) are free and equal. The chapter then turns to the realist conception of the state of nature in order to assess how the social contract theorists conceived of the family as origin of the state. In this context, it proves useful to include the theory of the family Hobbes developed in his account of the commonwealth by acquisition. The comparison with Hobbes's theory brings to the fore that Pufendorf and Locke struck a difficult balance when they attempted to reconcile the hypothetical contractual with the conjectural-historical origin of the state.

Keywords

State of nature – family – marriage – paternal power – master-slave relationship – *paterfamilias* – pact – social contract – sovereignty – state – patrimonial kingdom

1 Introduction

Early modern political philosophers such as Hobbes, Locke, and Rousseau are best known for their social contract theories and often discussed together with new versions of social contract theory developed in the twentieth century by

 | DOI:10.1163/9789004499621_010

John Rawls or David Gauthier. From this perspective, the state of nature is understood as a hypothetical situation prior to the establishment of society, i.e., a situation in which men are free and equal. Combined with a theory of human nature and motivation, the state of nature serves as a methodological device for demonstrating why men ought to submit to political authority and how the latter has to be conceived in order to be legitimate. In contemporary reconstructions of social contract theory, the phrase 'man' is usually taken as a generic term and thus regarded as substitutable with 'human being', or 'individual'. Before feminist histories of political philosophy were developed in the second half of the twentieth century, differences of sex, or gender, and the status of women in social contract theories were generally neglected.[1] This is all the more surprising if we consider that in political theory from Antiquity up to the sixteenth century and Bodin's *Six Books of the Commonwealth* (1576) the family, and the role of the wife and mother within it, has been considered as a precursor and constituent of the political order.[2] This leads quite naturally to questions such as: what is the place of the family in early modern social contract theories? How was the latter conceived as social institution? Is it natural or artificial? What is the difference, if there is any, between patriarchal and political power?

This chapter aims to explore how early modern social contract theorists accounted for the family and what place they accorded to the latter in regard to the state of nature and to the civil society, or state. I will mainly focus on Samuel Pufendorf and John Locke, who dealt extensively with the family, but also draw on comparisons with Hobbes' and Rousseau's more cursory remarks on the subject. One plausible way for assessing the place of the family in social contract theories relies on the ambiguity of the very concept of the state of nature, which could be conceived – albeit more or less explicitly – as a theoretical construct or as description of a situation that existed in reality before states were founded. In his *De officio hominis et civis*, Pufendorf explained this distinction in the following way:

1 See Gordon Schochet, 'Models of Politics and the Place of Women in Locke's Political Thought,' in *Feminist Interpretations of John Locke*, ed. Nancy J. Hirschmann and Kirstie M. McClure (University Park, PA: The Pennsylvania State University, 2007), pp. 131–53, here pp. 132–3. A pioneering study bringing this to the fore is Carole Pateman, *The Sexual Contract* (Stanford University Press, 1988).

2 See *ibid.*, and Nancy J. Hirschmann, 'Hobbes on the Family,' in *The Oxford Handbook of Hobbes*, ed. A. P. Martinich and Kinch Hoechstra (Oxford: Oxford University Press, 2016), pp. 242–63, here p. 243.

> It would be a fiction if we supposed that in the beginning there existed a multitude of men without any dependence on each other, as in the myth of the brothers of Cadmus, or if we imagined that the whole human race was so widely scattered that every man governed himself separately, and the only bond between them was likeness of nature. But the natural state which actually exists shows each man joined with a number of other men in a particular association, though having nothing in common with all the rest except the quality of being human and having no duty to them on any other ground. This is the condition [...] that now exists between different states [...] and between citizens of different countries [...], and which formerly obtained between heads of separate families.[3]

What Pufendorf affirms here, and what early modern contract theorists presuppose (explicitly or tacitly) is that before states were founded, the state of nature obtained between heads of different families. As we well see below, the family is a complex social unit which comprises the society between husband and wife, or matrimony, the society between father (or parents) and children, or paternal society, and the society between master and servant, or slave, the *societas herilis*.[4] These three societies are united under the will of the *paterfamilias*, or head of the family, who in his various roles as husband, father, and master exercises power over his wife, his children, and his servants or slaves. This raises the question how social contract theorists justify authority within the family, since they also maintain that conceived as a fiction or theoretical construction, the state of nature is a state of freedom and equality, where no one is subjected to the authority of any other, and that for this reason authority of one over the other needs to be justified. This question will be examined in the first part of this chapter.

The second part of the chapter will deal with yet another question regarding the relationship between the fictitious and the realist conception of the state of nature: if in reality the state of nature obtains between the heads of independent families, this implies that only the latter participate in the social contract by which the state is founded.[5] Since the social contract serves as a

3 I quote from the English translation: Samuel Pufendorf, *On the Duty of Man and Citizen According to Natural Law*, ed. James Tully, transl. Michael Silverthorne (Cambridge: Cambridge University Press, 1991), (book) II, (chapter) 1, (§) 6, p. 116.

4 The expression 'societas herilis' figures in the original Latin version of Pufendorf's *De jure naturae et gentium* (1672), VI, 3, 4.

5 Pufendorf explicitly acknowledges this in a chapter where he criticizes Hobbes for making 'subject' and 'citizen' equivalent terms. He argues instead that only the fathers of families, by whose pacts a state was first formed, are 'citizens', while the wills of women, boys, and slaves

hypothetical construction for showing how political power can be justified, one has to ask how states were, or might have been founded in reality. The dichotomy between the fictitious and the real foundation of the state has been theorized by Hobbes, who draws a clear distinction between the commonwealth by institution, founded by a contract of every one with every one, and the commonwealth by acquisition, or natural commonwealth, which rests on force or physical strength. In this latter case, sovereign power is acquired either by generation (i.e., by extension of the power of the *paterfamilias* to his adult sons and their own families) or by conquest.[6] This dichotomy is also at work, albeit less clearly visible, in Pufendorf's and Locke's account of the transition from the family to the state.

The guiding question of this study is how the fictitious and the realist conceptions of the state of nature are intertwined with each other in early modern accounts of the family and the state. Although important in itself and also a worthy object of research, I will rather leave to one side the question of sociability. This question is closely linked with the realist or empirical conception of the state of nature. From this point of view, the family is s kind of small society which precedes the state and is constitutive of it, and it can as such function as a test case for examining whether humans are by nature sociable beings. If we recall that in Aristotle's political theory the social nature of man unfolds gradually, from the family to the village and to the city, one could ask how the social contact theorists deal with the bonds of affection between spouses as well as parents and children, how they distinguish the ties between family members from those between citizens in a state, and how they position themselves in regard to Aristotle's hypothesis that man is a social animal. It is well known that Hobbes radically rejects this hypothesis,[7] while Pufendorf develops, for example, a much more nuanced position when he argues that he presumes in men a love of society, but that this does by no means imply that they are led by nature to civil society.[8] The focus on the empirical or realist conception of

are included in the will of the father. Samuel Pufendorf, *De jure naturae et gentium*, vol. 2, The Translation of the Edition of 1688 by C. H. Oldfather and W. A. Oldfather (Oxford: Clarendon Press, 1934), VII, 2, 20, p. 995.

6 Thomas Hobbes, *On the Citizen*, ed. and transl. Richard Tuck and Michael Silverthorne (Cambridge: Cambridge University Press, 1998), VIII, 1, pp. 102–3. Here and in what follows, I will mainly refer to this work, where Hobbes brings out most clearly the difference between these two kinds of commonwealth. On sovereignty by acquisition in the *Leviathan*, see Benjamin Straumann's chapter in this volume.

7 See for instance ibid., V, 4–5, pp. 70–2; see also Thomas Hobbes, *Leviathan*, part 2, XVII, pp. 117–21.

8 Pufendorf, *De jure*, VII, 1, 1–5, pp. 949–58, here p. 952.

the state of nature would also allow to inquire about the continuities between early modern social contract theories and conjectural histories developed by Scottish philosophers later in the eighteenth century. These philosophers reject the idea of a social contract and therefore account for the origin and the legitimacy of the state in a new manner, which is however reminiscent of the empirical study of the origin of the state in social contract theories.[9] In the present study, I will leave these interrogations to one side and focus instead on the question how a selected number of social contact theorists accounted for the legitimacy of the exercise of power within the family and how they thought this power differs from the sovereign power of the state.

2 The State of Nature and the Family

As we will see below, Hobbes deals with the family in the context of the commonwealth by acquisition. He develops a rather rudimentary theory of the family, which clearly serves, and is subordinated to his overall political argument according to which the sovereign power in the commonwealth is absolute and unlimited, whether the latter is instituted or acquired.[10] In contradistinction, Pufendorf developed the first full-blown theory of the family, which was partly

9 These questions are investigated in Justine Roulin's doctoral dissertation *Autorité, sociabilité et passions: La philosophie de la famille de Thomas Hobbes à John Millar* (Diss. Lausanne, 2019). I wish to express my gratitude to Justine Roulin. The continuing discussions we had on the theories of the family from Hobbes to the Scottish enlightenment were of great help for making up my own mind on the questions I deal with in this chapter. A pioneering study on natural law and eighteenth-century British philosophy with a chapter on the family and the question of polygamy is Colin Heydt, *Moral Philosophy in Eighteenth-Century Britain: God, Self, and Other* (Cambridge: Cambridge University Press, 2018). The continuities between the empirical conception of the state of nature and modern social thought has been explored in regard to Locke by Barry Hindess, 'Locke's State of Nature,' *History of the Human Sciences* 20/3 (2007), pp. 1–20. The critical response to Hobbes by Shaftesbury, Mandeville, and Hutcheson is discussed by Paul Sagar, *The Opinion of Mankind: Sociability and the Theory of the State from Hobbes to Smith* (Princeton: Princeton University Press, 2018). For the state of nature and sociability in Pufendorf, see David Singh Grewal's chapter in this book.

10 Hobbes' conception of the family has found more attention than the theories of Pufendorf, Locke, or Rousseau. See Hirschman, 'Hobbes on the Family'; Paul Sagar, 'Of Mushrooms and Method: History and the Family in Hobbes's Science of Politics,' *European Journal of Political Theory* 14/1 (2015), pp. 98–117; idem, *The Opinion of Mankind*, pp. 67–81; Theodore Christov, *Before Anarchy: Hobbes and His Critics in Modern International Thought* (Cambridge: Cambridge University Press, 2015). On the place of women see Nancy J. Hirschmann, Joane H. Wright (eds.), *Feminist Interpretations of Thomas Hobbes* (University Park, PA: The Pennsylvania State University, 2012).

resumed by Locke, albeit with a special emphasis on paternal authority in the context of his critique of Filmer's patriarchal political theory. This explains why I will begin by accounting for Pufendorf's and Locke's theory of the family before I will get to Hobbes in section 3 below.

Social contract theories famously rely on the idea that in the state of nature human beings are free and equal, and are therefore in their own right and power, and not subject to the authority of any other person.[11] In contradistinction to Hobbes, Pufendorf and Locke maintain that men are free to order their actions according to their own judgment and discretion only within the limits of natural law, which is given to them by God. As Locke famously put it, the state of liberty is not a state of license.[12] Both authors argue that men are obliged by natural law to preserve themselves. Regarding their relationship to others, Pufendorf holds that the law of nature imposes on men three kinds of duties, i.e., the duty not to harm others, the duty to treat each other as equals, and the duty to promote the well-being of others.[13] Locke places special emphasis on the duty not 'to harm another in his Life, Health, Liberty, or Possessions'.[14]

As a state of liberty and equality, the state of nature is however rather a theoretical construction or a fiction than a state existing in reality. As we have seen above, Pufendorf explains that in reality the state of nature first subsists between heads of separate families. Once states have been founded, it designates the condition between different states, and between citizens of different states. This description of the state of nature as a reality has important consequences in regard to the function Pufendorf assigns to the fiction of a natural state of liberty and equality: he refers to this latter condition not only to justify the institution of the civil society (*via* a sequence of pacts and an intermediary decree), but also of the family. He conceives of the latter as an 'association' (*collegium*) composed of three simple 'societies' (*societas*), which are united under the rule of the *paterfamilias*.[15] Referring to the theoretical

11 Pufendorf, *On the Duty of Man and Citizen*, II, 1, 8, p. 117. John Locke, *Two Treatises of Government*, ed. Peter Laslett (Cambridge: Cambridge University Press, 1988), II, 2, 4, p. 269.

12 Ibid., II, 2, 6, p. 270.

13 Pufendorf, *De jure*, III, 3, pp. 346–78. See also Simone Zurbuchen, 'Dignity and Equality in Pufendorf's Natural Law Theory,' in *Philosophy, Rights and Natural Law: Essays in Honour of Knud Haakonssen*, ed. Ian Hunter and Richard Whatmore (Edinburgh University Press, 2019), pp. 147–168, here pp. 149–51.

14 Locke, *Two Treatises*, II, 2, 7, p. 271.

15 Pufendorf, *De jure*, VI, 1, 1, pp. 839–40 (definition of the family); VI, 2, 6, pp. 917–919 (head of family).

state of nature, Pufendorf thus examines on what condition authority in the domestic sphere of the family is legitimate.

In contradistinction to Pufendorf, Locke limits himself to illustrate the state of nature as a reality by pointing to the condition of governors of independent communities. He also mentions the case of promises and bargains between two men, for example 'between a *Swiss* and an *Indian*, in the Woods of *America*'.[16] It would thus seem that while Pufendorf opposes the theoretical state of nature first to the condition of men in the family, and then in the civil society, Locke limits himself to opposing it to the latter. On the other hand, he considers the family – just like Pufendorf – as a kind of society in which the subordinated societies between husband and wife, parents and children, and master and servant, or slave, are 'united under the Domestick rule' of the *paterfamilias*, or 'master of a family'.[17] And Locke leaves no doubt that the *paterfamilias* in his various functions as husband, father, and master, has power over the different members of the family, which are thus not free and equal in relation to him. How does Locke then justify the power the master exercises in the domestic sphere of the family if he does that at all? Does he consider the family as conventional or as natural society? This question seems all the more salient if we recall that Rousseau, whose theory of the family is heavily indebted to Locke, claims at the outset of the *Social contract* that the family is the only natural society.[18]

2.1 *The Society between Husband and Wife, or Matrimony*

Pufendorf introduces matrimony as 'the first example of social life and at the same time the seed-bed of the human race'.[19] For constituting this first society,

---

16 Locke, *Two Treatises*, II, 2, 14–5, pp. 276–8. For a more complete analysis of Locke's account of the state of nature see Hindess, 'Locke's State of Nature', and A. John Simmons, 'Locke's State of Nature,' *Political Theory* 17/3 (1989), pp. 449–70.

17 Locke, *Two Treatises*, II, 7, 86, p. 323.

18 Jean-Jacques Rousseau, *The Social Contract*, I, 2. See also Simone Zurbuchen, 'La famille, une société naturelle?', *Rousseau Studies* (2018), pp. 129–53. For a broader account of Rousseau's theory of the family see Friederike Kuster, *Rousseau – die Konstitution des Privaten* (Berlin: Akademie Verlag, 2005).

19 Pufendorf, *On the Duty of Man and Citizen*, II, 2, 1, p. 120. On the conception of marriage in natural law theories see Sabine Doyé, 'Das Eherecht der deutschen Frühaufklärung im Spiegel des neuzeitlichen Naturrechts: Hugo Grotius, Samuel Pufendorf, Christian Thomasius, Christian Wolff,' in *Geschlechterordnung und Staat: Legitimationsfiguren der politischen Theorie (1600–1850)*, ed. Marion Heinz, Sabine Doyé (Berlin: Akademie Verlag, 2012), pp. 57–117; Ursula Vogel, 'Private Contract and Public Institution. The Peculiar Case of Marriage', in *Public and Private. Legal, political and philosophical perspectives*, ed. Maurizio Passerin d'Entrèves, Ursula Vogel (London and New York: Routledge, 2000), p. 177–99; John Witte, Jr., 'The Nature of the Family, the Family of Nature: The Surprising

the partners commit themselves by agreement, without however being at liberty to choose the end of matrimony. Indeed, the latter is defined by God, who by creating the human race would have aimed at preserving human life and assuring procreation. To this end, he endowed both sexes 'with a burning attraction to each other', not for the procuration of idle pleasure, but for rendering the commerce between the married persons sweet and agreeable and to make them easily accept the natural functions of which depends the perpetuation of the human race (the incommodities of pregnancy and the troubles of education).[20] Marriage having be arranged by God in this way, the duties incumbent on the partners derive from its end.

When dealing with the partners' commitment to marriage according to natural law, Pufendorf first recalls 'that by nature all individuals have equal rights, and no one enjoys authority over another, unless it has been secured by an act of himself or of the other'. This would imply that although ordinarily 'the male surpasses the female in strength of body and mind', this superiority alone does not confer any authority to the former over the latter. Consequently, if a man has any right over his woman, the latter depends on her consent.[21] Marriage thus has to be founded by a contract, and it can be either simple and irregular, or perfect and regular. In the former case, which Pufendorf considers to be legitimate according to natural law, the partners agree 'to give each other the service of their bodies' for a certain time, without securing a right of one over the other, and without committing themselves to cohabitate. The time for conceiving having passed, marriage ends, and the children born from this union will be under the power of the mother, 'if the pact set forth that she is seeking offspring for herself and not for her husband'. The marriage he calls 'irregular' allows Pufendorf to take into account, for example, the mode of living of the Amazons.[22]

Pufendorf is however mainly interested in regular marriage. In this case, the agreement consists of a number of articles which testify to an asymmetry between the sexes and serve to legitimate the submission of the women to the man, albeit exclusively concerning the affairs of marriage and the family. The first article stipulates that the woman 'should solemnly promise to the man

Liberal Defense of the Traditional Family in the Enlightenment,' *Emory Law Journal* 64/3 (2015), pp. 596–676; Alfred Dufour, *Le mariage dans l'Ecole allemande du droit naturel moderne au XVIIIe siècle* (Paris: Librairie générale de Droit et de Jurisprudence, 1972).

20 Ibid., II, 2, 2, p. 120.

21 Pufendorf, *De jure*, VI, 1, 9, pp. 853–4. I omit here the possibility that the right of a man over his woman might also be founded on a just war.

22 *Ibid.*, VI, 1, 9, pp. 854–5.

that she will not grant the use of her body to anyone except him'. Normally, the man would then promise the same to her. Pufendorf justifies this temporal sequence and thus the asymmetry between the sexes by arguing that it 'is most appropriate to the character of both sexes that the contract should be initiated by the man', and since the latter is interested in having children of his own, the woman has to promise fidelity first.[23]

The second article consists in the promise of the wife to live with her husband without interruption 'and to make the closest association of their lives together and to form one family'.[24] In order to justify this further promise, Pufendorf points to the great joy for couples to live together and also to the interest of the husband to be sure of his wife's fidelity. The third article transforms the initial asymmetry between the sexes into the subordination of the wife to the husband. Pufendorf argues that the woman 'should be liable to the direction of her husband', since 'it is particularly in keeping with the natural condition of both sexes not only that the man's position should be superior but also that the husband should be the head of the family which he has established'.[25] Pufendorf thus refers to the natural condition of the sexes in order to justify the authority of the husband to decide where they live. As a consequence, the wife is not allowed to travel or the spend the night outside their home without her husband's agreement.[26] Pufendorf also stresses, however, that the authority of the husband is limited: it includes neither the right of life and death, nor the right to severe punishment, or 'the full power of any or all of the wife's property', except when this is established by agreement or, once the state has been founded, by the civil laws.[27]

Locke's conception of marriage is in many regards akin to Pufendorf's. Like his predecessor, he considers marriage as the first society, which is founded 'by Compact between man and woman', and ordered by the law of nature in regard to its ends, i.e., procreation and mutual support and assistance.[28] Since Locke also acknowledges that men and women are by nature free and equal, the authority of the husband over his wife he aims to establish requires justification. He observes that husband and wife have different understandings and

23 Pufendorf, *On the Duty of Man and Citizen*, II, 2, 4, p. 121; *De jure*, VI, 1, 10, pp. 855–6. On Pufendorf's conception of male superiority in marriage see Susanne Sreedhar, 'Pufendorf on Patriarchy,' *History of Philosophy Quarterly* 31/3 (2014), pp. 209–27.

24 Pufendorf, *On the Duty of Man and Citizen*, II, 2, 4, p. 121.

25 Ibid.; *De jure*, VI, 1, 11, p. 860.

26 Pufendorf, *De jure* ; VI, 1, 10, p. 856.

27 Pufendorf, *On the Duty of Man and Citizen*, II, 2, 4, pp. 121–2; *De jure*, VI, 1, 11, pp. 860–1.

28 Locke, *Two Treatises*, II, 7, 78, p. 319 and II, 7, 83, pp. 321–2.

wills, and since he deems it necessary that the last determination of the will has to be attributed to the one or the other, he concludes that the determination, or rule, 'naturally falls to the Man's share, as the abler and the stronger'.[29] In a manner reminiscent of Pufendorf, Locke immediately adds that the power of the husband only concerns the couples' common interest and property, and leaves the wife 'in the full and free possession of what by Contract is her peculiar Right', and if the latter allows it, she can even have the liberty to divorce, on condition however that the children are out of dependency for support on the parents' help.[30] Given that Locke has nothing to say about the home and the oath of fidelity, his conception of marriage looks slightly more egalitarian than Pufendorf's.

2.2 *The Society between Parents and Children, or the Paternal Society*

Pufendorf and Locke both acknowledge that mother and father alike contribute to the generation of their children, and that they share in the duty to care about and educate them. Nevertheless, they use the expression 'paternal power' for designating the authority of the parents over their children. This is consistent with their account of the superiority of the father over the mother. Thus, Pufendorf maintains that the authority of the father over the children 'normally' surpasses the authority of the mother. He concedes however that when a child was conceived outside marriage, 'it will belong primarily to the mother', and that a couple who lives in the natural state may agree 'that it is the mother's right, not the father's, that prevails'. In states which 'have certainly been formed by men, not women', the father's right would however prevail.[31] In regard to the justification of paternal power, it is interesting to observe that Pufendorf also refers, in this context, to the consent of the dominated. While acknowledging that in practice the parents' authority is established when the latter acknowledge the child, feed and educate it, he argues that tacit consent of the child is also required. This consent is hypothetical, since an infant is not yet able to express his rational agreement:

> One may rightly assume that if the infant had had the use of reason at the time of birth, and had been able to perceive that he could not survive without his parents' care and the government implied by that care, he would gladly have agreed to it, and stipulated in return that they give him a good upbringing.[32]

---

29 Ibid., II, 7, 82, p. 321.
30 Ibid., II, 7, 80, p. 320.
31 Pufendorf, *On the Duty of Man and Citizen*, II, 3, 3, pp. 124–5.
32 Ibid., II, 3, 2, p. 124.

The tacit consent of the child is important, since it allows Pufendorf to define the limits of the parents' authority over the child and to show that despite their natural superiority and the 'most tender affection for them', which is implanted in them by nature, the parents can wrong the child when they do not acknowledge that the latter 'shares the same human condition' as they themselves.[33] Hence, Pufendorf points out that the parents do not have the right to abort the child in the mother's womb or to abandon and kill the new-born; nor do they have the right of life and death for wrongdoing.[34] The parents' authority over the children is thus limited, but suffices for allowing them to fulfill the duty imposed on them by natural law to care for their children and to bring them up properly 'so that they may turn out to be good members of human society'.[35]

As is well known, Locke deals extensively with the nature of paternal power in the context of his critique of Filmer's theory of patriarchy.[36] I only highlight one aspect of this critique here, namely Locke's interest in proving that acknowledging the authority parents have over their children does not challenge the basic assumption according to which men are by nature free and equal. Faithful to his definition of liberty in the state of nature, which is distinct from license, he maintains that liberty has to be conceived within the bounds of the law of nature, which is imposed on men by God, their creator. Because children are unable to know the law of nature, they need to be directed by their parents, who are obligated by the law of nature 'to preserve, nourish, and educate' their children. The power of the parents over their children originates in this obligation.[37] When he stresses that beginning from Adam and Eve, all the parents were obligated to care for their children 'not as their own Workmanship, but the Workmanship of their own Maker, the Almighty, to whom they were to be accountable for them',[38] Locke leaves no doubt that generation is not at the basis of the moral relationship (of direction and obedience) between parents and children.

33 Ibid.; *De jure* VI, 2, 4, pp. 914–5.

34 Pufendorf, *De jure*, I, 1, 7, pp. 7–8.

35 Pufendorf, *On the Duty of Man and Citizen*, II, 3, 2, p. 124; II, 3, 4, p. 125.

36 See Gordon Schochet, *Patriarchalism in Political Thought: The Authoritarian Family and Political Speculation and Attitudes Especially in Seventeenth-Century England* (Oxford: Blackwell, 1975); Melissa A. Butler, 'Early Liberal Roots of Feminism: John Locke's Attack on Patriarchy,' in *Feminist Interpretations of John Locke*, 91–130; Kristin A. Kelly, 'Private Family, Private Individual: John Locke's Distinction Between Paternal and Political Power,' *Social Theory and Practice* 28/3 (2002), pp. 361–80.

37 Locke, *Two Treatises*, II, 6, 56–58, pp. 305–6.

38 Ibid., II, 6, 56, p. 305.

By deriving the obligation of the parents to preserve and educate their children from the law of nature, Locke is in line with Pufendorf, who also maintains that this duty is imposed on them by natural law.[39] However, whereas Pufendorf founds paternal power *also* on the tacit consent of the child, Locke derives this power *exclusively* from the obligation imposed on the parents by God. Indeed, it seems that Locke considers the origin of paternal authority to be natural rather than conventional when he points to the helplessness and the defects of the imperfect state of the child, which the parents have to supply.[40] He also mentions the tenderness and affection for their offspring God would have implanted in man's nature, and he considers this affection as a 'strong byass of Nature', preventing thereby that the parents abuse their power and that they exercise it only for the best of the children.[41] The impression that Locke considers paternal power to be natural rather than conventional is further strengthened by the sharp contrast he draws between the parents' authority over the children under age, and the power the father may continue to exercise over his adult sons. As we will see in more detail in section 3 below, the latter needs to be established by contract in order to be legitimate. Likewise, Locke argues that while a child 'is under his Fathers Tuition and Authority, till he come to Age of Discretion', he is not born a subject of a country or government. Indeed, in relation to the government his father is a subject to, the son is in the state of nature and has to be considered as free until he, once he is an adult man, consents to subject himself to a government.[42] In contradistinction, Pufendorf argued that women, boys and slaves are indirectly subjected to the state by being included in the head of the family's will.[43]

Locke's account of paternal power proved to be especially influential, since Rousseau referred to it in his writings in order to establish, as he contended in the *Social contract*, that the family (which he reduces there to the society between father and child) is the only natural society, and justified as such.[44]

2.3 *The Society between Master and Servant, or slave*

In keeping with their basic assumption that in the fictitious state of nature human beings are free and equal, early modern social contracts theorists

39 Pufendorf, *De jure*, VI, 2, 4, p. 914.
40 Locke, *Two Tratises*, II, 6, 56, p. 305.
41 Ibid., II, 6, 67, p. 312.
42 Ibid., II, 8, 116–118, p. 345–7.
43 See note 5 above.
44 Rousseau, *The Social Contract*, I, 2. See Zurbuchen, 'La famille, une société naturelle?,' pp. 134–6.

criticized Aristotle's doctrine of natural slavery. This does not imply, however, that they rejected slavery altogether. Quite to the contrary, they developed new arguments for justifying the power of the master over the slave (*servus*), and thereby also introduced new conceptual distinctions allowing them to discriminate between 'servitude', which rests on mutual agreement, and 'slavery', which rests on force.[45]

In a manner reminiscent of Grotius, Pufendorf accounts for two kinds of slavery, which he assigns to different historical periods. He thereby conflates the fictional and the realist conception of the state of nature with one another, by showing at the same time how slavery may have been instituted in history and on what condition it appears legitimate. Since he does not refer to slavery in the New World, it is difficult to tell to what kind of social reality he refers in his own time, except in regard to the domestic servant or wage-earner hired for a limited period of time. The first kind of slavery he mentions is founded on a voluntary pact. Pufendorf points to the first ages of humanity and surmises that persons lacking intelligence and being unable to preserve themselves 'probably offered themselves of their own free will' to serve as slaves in order to escape poverty.[46] They committed themselves to serve their master in perpetuity in exchange of food and necessities of life.[47] While observing that this kind of slavery has been abolished by many peoples in his own time, and that the latter would have their household tasks accomplished by temporary wage-earners, Pufendorf still deals with perpetual slavery in order to show that even in this case natural law imposes limits on the power of the master, who must

45 The distinction between 'slave' and 'servant', which both translate the Latin 'servus', is a complicated question, since one needs to refer to various modern translations of Grotius and Pufendorf. See on that issue Zurbuchen, 'Dignity and Equality', pp. 155–6. On theories of slavery see Bernd Franke, *Sklaverei und Unfreiheit im Naturrecht des 17. Jahrhunderts* (Hildesheim: Olms, 2009); on slavery in Grotius, John W. Cairns, 'Stoicism, Slavery, and Law,' *Grotiana* 22/23 (2001/2002), pp. 197–231; idem, 'The Definition of Slavery in Eighteenth-Century Thinking: Not the True Roman Slavery,' in *The Legal Understanding of Slavery: From the Historical to the Contemporary*, ed. Jean Allain (Oxford University Press, 2012), pp. 61–84. On Locke and slavery (and mainly the question whether Locke justified slavery in the new world, a question I leave to one side here), James Tully, 'Rediscovering America: the 'Two Treatises' and aboriginal rights,' in idem, *An Approach to Political Philosophy: Locke in Contexts* (Cambridge: Cambridge University Press, 1993), pp. 137–76; James Farr, 'Locke, Natural Law, and New World Slavery,' *Political Theory* 36/4 (2008), pp. 495–522; William Uzgalis, 'Racism, Slavery, and Indian Lands,' in *The Oxford Handbook on Philosophy and Race*, ed. Naomi Zack (New York: Oxford University Press, 2017), pp. 21–30.

46 Pufendorf, *On the Duty of Man and Citizen*, II, 4, 1, p. 129.

47 Ibid., see also II, 4, 3, pp. 129–30.

life and is then called 'servant'. It needs to be added however, that Pufendorf agrees with Hobbes that 'not every captive in war whose life is spared is understood to have entered into a pact with the victor' and that it is quite possible that the death is but postponed, and the captives are held in prisons, workhouses, or chains. In this case, the master reserves for himself the 'license of war' and can therefore 'take his life, whenever he pleases, on the plea of a state of war'.[57] In like manner, Locke argues that the state of war between the victor and the vanquished may continue to exist, and he explicitly acknowledges that not only 'servants' but also 'slaves', who are 'by the Right of Nature subjected to the Absolute Dominion and Arbitrary Power of their Masters' may be part of the family and as such be under the domestic rule of the *paterfamilias*. Since the slaves have forfeited their liberties and their estates together with their lives, they would neither be capable of any property nor become part of civil society.[58]

Locke acknowledges yet another origin of slavery, namely just punishment, which is closely linked with the 'strange doctrine'[59] that in the state of nature everyone has the executive power of the law of nature:

> Indeed having, by his fault, forfeited his own Life, by some Act that deserves Death; he, to whom he has forfeited it, may (when he has him in his Power) delay to take it, and make use of him to his own Service, and he does him no injury by it. For, whenever he finds the hardship of his Slavery out-weigh the value of his Life, 'tis in his Power, by resisting the Will of his Master, to draw on himself the Death he desires.[60]

It is clear that this kind of slavery can only obtain while independent families exist in the state of nature. For by founding states, the heads of families renounce the right to punish those who transgress the law of nature.[61] In Locke's view, capital punishment and enslavement are justified in the state of nature if a man puts himself in a state of war against another one, by attempting to take him away his freedom and to subject him to his absolute power.[62] Moreover, a thief who intends to take away one's money or whatever he pleases likewise puts himself in a state of war against the victim, simply by the use of

57 Pufendorf, *De jure*, VI, III, 6, p. 938.
58 Locke, *Two Treatises*, II, 7, 85, pp. 322–3.
59 Ibid., II, 2, 13, p. 275.
60 Ibid., II, 4, 23, p. 284.
61 Ibid., II, 9, 128, p. 352.
62 Ibid., II, 3, 17, p. 279.

force without right, which makes the latter suppose that the thief might take him away everything else, if he were in his power.[63]

In the literature on Locke's theory of slavery, much attention has been paid to the question whether Locke intended this theory to justify slavery in the New World, or whether it could at least be used to this effect.[64] This question is of course very important, but not our concern here. To conclude this overview, I rather wish to stress that despite the ambiguities that characterize Pufendorf's and Locke's justifications of servitude, and slavery, their references to the fictitious natural state of freedom and equality also contained the potential for challenging the most extreme form of power within the family. As we have already seen, Pufendorf exploited Hobbes' distinction between the slave and the servant with the intention to point to the limits of the master's authority over the servant. Locke went further and contested that any kind of perpetual slavery could be founded by contract. Rousseau presented a more subtle and polemical version of the same critique at the beginning of the *Social Contract*, and he also developed a powerful argument for criticizing slavery founded on the law of war.[65] Quite paradoxically, Rousseau refrained however from deploying the emancipatory potential of the contractual argument in regard to the authority of the husband over his wife. Indeed, by declaring the latter to be natural, as opposed to conventional, he confirmed the legitimacy of the subordination of women to men in the private domain of the family.[66]

3 From the Family to the State

As we have seen above, Pufendorf and Locke both consider the family as a complex unit that consists of three different societies where the man exercises power as a husband over his wife, as father over his children, and as master over the slave. In addition, they also deal with the power the *paterfamilias*, or head of the family, exercises as such, over the household.

Neither Pufendorf nor Locke deal with this power in a separate chapter, they rather consider it when they point to the limitations of the power a father has over his children, or the master over the servant. They also account for the power of the *paterfamilias* when they turn to the realist conception of the state of nature and ask themselves how states were founded, or may have

63 Ibid., II, 3, 18, pp. 279–80.

64 See note 45 above.

65 Rousseau, *The Social Contract*, I, 1, 4.

66 See Zurbuchen, 'La famille, une société naturelle?'

been founded, in history.[67] In this context, the crucial question they address is whether and to what extent the family in the state of nature is, or resembles, a state.

What is at stake here can best be evidenced when we first look at Hobbes' account of the power within the domestic sphere of the family, which he subordinates to the question of the origin of the state, or commonwealth.[68] Thus, in the *De cive* he first deals with the commonwealth *by institution*,[69] which is founded in a reciprocal agreement of every one with every one, and then proceeds to examine the commonwealth by *acquisition*, or *natural* commonwealth, in which the right of dominion (*dominium*) is acquired 'by natural force or strength'.[70] In this context, Hobbes famously asserts that dominion over the person of another in the family is the same as in the commonwealth:

> The most important things to know here are the ways by which the right of *Dominion* (*Dominium*) is acquired over men's *persons*. Where such a right has been acquired, there is a kind of *little kingdom*. For to be a *King* is simply to have *Dominion* over many *persons*, and thus a *kingdom* is a *large family*, and a *family* is a *little kingdom*.[71]

Hobbes then distinguishes between two ways of acquiring (as opposed to instituting) the right to dominion. The first way 'is, on being captured or defeated in war or losing hope in one's own strength, one makes (to avoid death) a promise to the victor or the stronger party, to *serve* him, i.e. to do all he shall command'. In virtue of the promise, the vanquished owes the victor service and obedience 'simply and without restriction', and he is then called 'slave' (*servus*), and the one to whom he is bound a 'master' (*dominus*).[72] Hobbes then introduces the distinction between the 'servant' and the 'slave' we have already dealt with above: the vanquished who agrees to serve the master in exchange for his life, is bound by his promise and owes the latter obedience. In contradistinction to the 'slave' held in chains or in the workhouse, he is called 'servant'. Hobbes

---

67 Locke (*Two Treatises*, II, 8, 101, p. 334) explicitly acknowledges that history gives us but little account of how men actually lived in the state of nature.

68 In what follows, I only refer to the *De cive*, because in this work Hobbes brings out most clearly the difference between the commonwealth by institution and by acquisition. For a more complete account of this theme see Sagar, 'Of Mushrooms and Method'; Christov, *Before Anarchy*, ch. 3, pp. 67–103.

69 *Civitas institutiva*, translated as 'commonwealth by design' in the translation I refer to.

70 Hobbes, *On the Citizen*, 8, 1, p. 102.

71 Ibid.

72 Ibid., pp. 102–3.

insists however that dominion over the 'servant' does in no way differ from dominion over the 'slave': the master owns him 'like any other thing, animate and inanimate', and may sell the dominion at his own will.[73]

The important point here is that in the chapter on the acquisition of the right of dominion by war, Hobbes explicitly identifies the right of dominion in the family with the same right in the commonwealth. His demonstration that dominion of the master over the servant is unlimited, and that therefore the master cannot do him wrong, clearly aims at showing that the sovereign power in a commonwealth by acquisition is unrestricted and that the sovereign can do no wrong to his subjects because 'whatever he does, is done with their consent'.[74]

The second way of acquiring dominion Hobbes examines relies on a comparison between the dominion of the father over his children and the sovereign power in the commonwealth. In this context, he first discusses at some length the foundation of the dominion over children, which in his view originally belongs to the mother and then passes from the mother to the father in various ways, for example by contract when the mother agrees that the children ought to belong to the father,[75] or when the mother is captured in war.[76] Hobbes' surprisingly egalitarian account of the rights of the woman and the mother in the state of nature is very interesting. It has found much attention in the feminist literature and is still subject to controversies.[77] I do not deal with these rights here, but turn directly to Hobbes' comparison between paternal power in the family and sovereign power in what he calls a 'patrimonial Kingdom'. The first thing to note is that Hobbes likens dominion over children to the dominion of the master over his slaves, for instance when he observes that 'in the state of nature every woman who gives birth becomes both a *mother* and a *Mistress* (*Domina*)'.[78] At the end of the paragraphs on the relationship between mother and father as well as husband and wife he confirms that originally the mother is the mistress of the children, and the father is their master by derivative right from her, and he concludes from this that '*children* are no less subject to those who look after them and bring them up than *slaves* are to masters, or *subjects* to the holder of *sovereign power* in the commonwealth'.[79] This implies that a

73 Ibid., 8, 2–4, pp. 103–4.

74 Ibid., 8, 7, p. 104.

75 Ibid., 9, 6–7, pp. 109–10.

76 Ibid., 9, 5, p. 109.

77 See Hirschmann, Wright (eds.), *Feminist Interpretations of Thomas Hobbes*; Hirschmann, 'Hobbes on the Family'.

78 Hobbes, *On the Citizen*, 9, 3, p. 108.

79 Ibid., 9, 7, p. 110.

parent cannot wrong a child as long as it is under his authority. The only thing children in the family have more than the slaves 'is that they perform more honourable services [...], and enjoy more luxuries'.[80] In consequence, Hobbes also argues that children are released from subjection in the same ways as subjects and slaves; emancipation is the same thing as manumission and disowning is the same as banishment.[81]

Although Hobbes insists that in the state of nature the children belong to the mother, even when she makes with a man a contract to live together, he leaves aside the possibility that any commonwealth, which arises from the family 'by generation',[82] and is called a patrimonial kingdom, might be established by the mothers of the family.[83] This must be the reason why he defines the family without even mentioning the wife or the mother: '*The father of the family, the children and the slaves*, united in one civil person by virtue of paternal power is called a FAMILY.'[84] The difference between the family and the commonwealth is one of degree only. When the former grows so big that it has a good chance of defending itself against an aggressor, it is called a 'patrimonial kingdom',[85] which in contradistinction to a commonwealth by institution is acquired by force but has exactly the same right of government as the latter. Therefore Hobbes can claim that the kingdom is a large family, and the family a little kingdom.

It is useful to keep in mind Hobbes' theory of the commonwealth by acquisition when we now turn to the way in which Pufendorf and Locke account for the transition from the family to the state. Their comparisons between the family and the state rely on the power they assign to the head of the family in the state of nature, which clearly differs from the power the latter exercises as father over the children. Indeed, when dealing with paternal power in *De officio*, Pufendorf emphasizes the distinction 'between the authority the father has as such and the authority and the power he has as the head of his household (*caput familiae*)'[86] – a power he exercises either in the state of nature or once he has submitted to the state. In the former case, Pufendorf argues, the heads of households 'had exercised in their homes a kind of princely authority' and the children who remained in their household had 'a duty to regard their

80 Ibid., 9, 9, p. 111.
81 Ibid., 9, 8, p. 110.
82 Ibid., 8, 1, p. 103.
83 Ibid., 9, 6, p. 110.
84 Ibid., 9, 10, p. 112.
85 Ibid.
86 Pufendorf, *On the Duty of Man and Citizen*, II, 3, 4, p. 125.

father's authority as supreme'.[87] He thus assumes that in the state of nature fathers, as heads of the family, had the power of life and death over their adult children, to be exercised in cases of wrongdoing. In order not to confound paternal power with the power of the *paterfamilias*, it needs to be stressed that the latter has the power of life and death only over the sons who, once they are adult, remain a part of the father's household, and this requires their tacit consent.[88] In the *De iure*, Pufendorf presents a more nuanced account of the analogy between family and state than in the *De officio*. He asserts in the former work that 'distinct families have somewhat of the form of states' and that 'their heads bear some analogy to royal sovereignty'. It would however be wrong, he argues, to call families states, like Hobbes, because the ends of families and states are different, and 'many parts of royal sovereignty do not fall upon families'. In addition to the right of life and death, to be exercised in the case of crimes, the heads of families would also have 'the right of arms and of concluding treaties'.[89]

While Pufendorf admits that in the state of nature the power of the *paterfamilias* bears some analogy to princely sovereignty, Locke seems to suggest otherwise in the paragraphs he devotes to the family. When he considers the 'Master of a Family' with all his subordinated relations 'united under the Domestick Rule of a Family', he affirms that despite its resemblance 'with a little Common-wealth', the family differs from the state in its constitution, power, and end. In comparison with the power of a monarch, the power of the *paterfamilias* would be very distinct, and 'differently limited [...], both as to time and extent', for excepting the slave (who is no necessary part of a family as such), he 'has no Legislative Power over Life and Death' over any of the family members.[90] While Locke stresses here that the family differs from a political society, which originates in a voluntary union of free men,[91] he admits in another context, where he deals with the historical origin of government, that the family, when it was numerous enough to subsist by itself, was indeed in

87 Ibid., II, 3, 7, p. 126.

88 Pufendorf, *De jure*, VI, 2, 10, p. 923.

89 Ibid., pp. 922–3. In his contribution to this volume David Singh Grewal points out that family relationships no less than commercial ties rest on man's natural sociability, formed through the maturation of self-love, and differ in this regard from the state. On self-love and sociability in Pufendorf's natural law theory see also Heikki Haara, *Pufendorf's Theory of Sociability: Passions, Habits and Social Order* (Cham, Springer Nature, 2018), pp. 80–85.

90 Locke, *Two Treatises*, II, 7, 86, p. 323.

91 Ibid., II, 8, 102, p. 335.

many places the first political society, or commonwealth, with a monarchical government.[92]

These are the well-known paragraphs in the *Second Treatise*, where Locke makes extended concessions to patriarchalism,[93] without giving up, however, his opposition to Filmer. Like Pufendorf, Locke likens the power of the head of the family to political power by considering the relationship between the former and his children 'when they were Men, and out of their Pupilage'. This required that the adult sons consented to remain in their father's family, to submit to his punishment and to give him the power to execute his sentence against any transgressor of the law of nature, 'and so in effect make him the Law-maker, and Governour over all, that remained in Conjunction with his family'.[94] In Locke's view, the father was the fittest to be trusted, since he already secured the property and interest of his children while they were under age, and the custom of obeying him made it easy for them to submit to his power. Yet another possible origin of the commonwealth Locke mentions in the same context is that several families may have met and set up the ablest to rule over them.[95] He further insists that at a time when people lacked instruction about the forms of government and were not yet experienced with the inconveniences of absolute power, such a frame of government was most obvious and simple, and well suited to the way of living 'in the beginning of things', where the adult sons were 'more in need of defence against foreign Invasions and Injuries, than of a multiplicity of Laws'.[96] For proving this, he points to the kings of the Indians in America as well as to the first kings of Israel, who were 'little more than *Generals of their Armies*' and had 'but a very moderate Sovereignty' in time of peace.[97]

While Locke seems not to exclude that in some instances – he mentions the examples of Venice and Rome[98] – the heads of independent families united into a political society by a compact of every one with every one and by giving up their power to the majority of the community,[99] his major hypothetical narrative relies on the monarchy as first form of government. He illustrates this origin of the government by pointing to the peoples of America, who were out

---

92 Ibid., II, 8, 105–6, pp. 336–8.
93 Ibid., II, 8, 105, p. 336, Laslett's note.
94 Ibid., II, 8, 105–6, pp. 336–7.
95 Ibid., II, 8, 105, p. 337; see also II, 8, 110, pp. 341–2.
96 Ibid., II, 8, 107, pp. 338–9.
97 Ibid., II, 8, 108, p. 339.
98 Ibid., II, 8, 102, p. 335.
99 Ibid., II, 8, 99, p. 333.

of reach of the Empires of Peru and Mexico and thus owned their own natural freedom.[100] He thereby strikes a difficult balance between two arguments he wishes to reject. On one hand, he insists against Filmer that the power even of the first kings rested on consent, and that they did not rule over the extended family in virtue of their paternal authority. This would become evident when considering the reason people had for continuing this form of government:

> Yet it is plain, that the reason, that continued the Form of *Government in a single Person*, was not any Regard, or Respect to Paternal Authority; since all petty Monarchies, that is, almost all *Monarchies*, near their Original, have been commonly, at least upon occasion, Elective.[101]

On the other hand, Locke also aims at demonstrating that the power of the first rulers was not arbitrary, even though it was put into one man's hand 'without any express Limitation or Restraint'.[102] Quite to the contrary, no one was entrusted with the rule 'but for the publick Good and Safety, and to those Ends in the Infancies of Commonwealths those who had it, commonly used it'. Locke continues this argument by asserting that 'without such nursing Fathers tender and carefull of the publick weale', all governments would have perished.[103] By this move, he likens the authority of the first princes to the authority of the father, while he attempted to distinguish these kinds of authority as neatly as possible in the context of the argument against Filmer. By way of conclusion, Locke points to the end of the Golden Age and the corruption of men's minds, which made it necessary for them to find out ways for preventing the abuses of power,[104] and this conclusion builds a bridge to his normative account of political society and government, and the well-known theory of the social contract.

In his commentary to the paragraph where Locke turns to the origin of the commonwealth, Peter Laslett observes that his argument is close to Tyrrell 'and perhaps even closer to Pufendorf'.[105] If we recall how Pufendorf accounts for the power the *paterfamilias* exercises over his adult sons, who remain in their father's family by their own consent, this remark seems indeed to be well warranted. It is however interesting to observe that Pufendorf's conjectures about the origin of states differ remarkably from those of Locke. More often

100 Ibid., II, 8, 105, p. 337; see also II, 8, 108, pp. 339–40.
101 Ibid., II, 8, 106, p. 338.
102 Ibid., II, 8, 110, p. 342; see also 107, p. 338.
103 Ibid., II, 8, 110, p. 342.
104 Ibid., II, 8, 111, p. 343.
105 Ibid., II, 8, 105, p. 336, note.

than Locke – who also frequently mentions, as we have seen, the peoples in America – Pufendorf refers to the Bible when discussing the origin of the human race and of the first states.[106] This is for example the case in the chapter on the motives leading men to the establishment of states, where he rejects Jonhann Friedrich Hornius' argument that the state 'is a work of nature which is produced by natural order and consequence'.[107] It is wrong to imagine, Pufendorf maintains, that the state is a kind of increased family, which emerged by extension form the first pair, which was 'bound in conjugal love', and to which their children were united 'in the same most tender affection'. On the other hand, he also regards it as 'fabulous' that 'a great number of men were congregated at the beginning, then scattered in woods and desert places, and finally collected into states'.[108] In his view, it is indeed more plausible to assume, and in line with the Holy Scriptures, that several sons of one father, when they were able to entertain a family, went out to establish their own homes, especially in the early periods when 'living was gotten almost entirely from agriculture and grazing alone'.[109] It was only when the wiser heads of families recognized that the disadvantages affecting separate families could be removed, that the latter 'gathered into the same group and formed a state' by deciding 'to combine their families by a pact and sovereignty'.[110] Pufendorf then goes on to show at great length that the motive for forming states was not want, but fear, and that the principal reason of men to leave their natural liberty was to defend themselves 'against the evils which threaten man from his fellow man'.[111]

In order to find out how Pufendorf conceived of the form of the first states, one needs to turn to his scattered remarks on this topic in the chapter on the forms of the commonwealth (*respublica*), which he calls 'regular' instead of 'simple', as this was traditionally the case, and where sovereignty 'without division and opposition, is exercised by one will in all parts of a state'.[112] Having confirmed that there are only three forms of regular state, namely democracy, aristocracy, and monarchy, Pufendorf first deals with democracy, not because it would surpass the other forms 'but because that was certainly the oldest form among nations'.[113] He does not provide historical evidence for this argument,

106 On this issue see Francesca Iurlaro's chapter in this volume.
107 Pufendorf, *De jure*, VII, 1, 5, p. 956.
108 Ibid., p. 957.
109 Ibid.
110 Ibid., p. 958.
111 Ibid., VII, 1, 6, p. 959.
112 Ibid., VI, 5, 2–3, p. 1024.
113 Ibid., VI, 5, 4, p. 1025.

he rather refers to reason and to the hypothetical situation of a free family father who voluntarily gathered with others like him into a state. In his view, it is not to be presumed that such a father 'could in a moment, as it were, so forget his former status, in which he used to dispose at his own pleasure all matters touching his safety, as to be willing to submit himself all at once to the judgment of one man on common affairs, with which also his own safety was involved'. This is the main reason why Pufendorf holds Aristotle's opinion about the antiquity of kingship to be wrong.[114] While he admits that ancient history often mentions kings, he contends that the latter would equally show that the majority of them 'enjoyed more the authority of persuasion than the power of command'. He concludes from this that 'in general, nations lived under a popular regimen and in liberty, until little by little that enormous mass of petty states was reduced, usually by force and warfare, into a few large ones'.[115]

It is interesting to observe that Pufendorf also examines the hypothesis (which he ascribes to anonymous authors) that the most ancient kind of sovereignty among men might have been a 'paternal kind', which was mild at the outset and then developed into the right of life and death, and was transmitted to the eldest son by a right of primogeniture, so that 'the heads of families gradually developed into petty kings'. Pufendorf rejects this hypothesis and thereby confirms the argument we have already encountered above: the eldest son could not have had regal sovereignty over his brothers without their consent, and 'those oldest men who passed under the name of kings were usually but the principal and eminent magistrates in democratic groups'.[116]

Unlike Locke, who deals at some length with the origin of commonwealths and is also concerned about the historical evidence for his conjectures, Pufendorf proves to be mainly interested in showing that various hypotheses about the oldest form of government cannot be used for invalidating his theory of the contractual origin of the state. This becomes clear when we recall that in his view the pact by which citizens subject themselves to the sovereign presupposes a pact by which individual men (or in reality heads of independent families) unite into one body, and then decide by majority vote to whom the supreme sovereignty will be entrusted, or about the form of the commonwealth.[117] According to Pufendorf, any commonwealth Hobbes calls 'commonwealth by institution', and which can be a democracy, an aristocracy, or a monarchy, thus passes, as it were, through an early democratic stage. This

114 Ibid., p. 1026.

115 Ibid.

116 Ibid.

117 Pufendorf, *On the Duty of Man and Citizen*, II, 6, pp. 135–8.

is the reason, I suggest, why he aims at showing that democracy was the oldest form of the commonwealth among nations. And this hypothetical account of the origin of the state is of course consistent with the fictitious or theoretical conception of the state of nature, in which men are free and equal and not subject to the authority of any other.[118]

It is beyond the scope of this chapter to further investigate why Pufendorf held monarchy (in the sense of a 'regular' state) to be the best form of government. To conclude, let me however point out a major difference between Hobbes' and Pufendorf's comparisons between the power of the *paterfamilias* and sovereignty in the state. As we have seen above, Hobbes claims that the paternal power of the father in the family and the sovereign power in the commonwealth are of like nature, in order to justify the 'patrimonial kingdom', which – like any kind of commonwealth by acquisition – rests on natural force or strength and not on consent. Since Pufendorf holds that the enlarged family – where the adult sons remain subjected to the power of the *paterfamilias*, which may then be transmitted to the oldest of the sons by right of primogeniture – is necessarily founded on consent, and therefore limited, it would seem impossible for him to justify a 'patrimonial kingdom'. It thus comes as a surprise that he still deals with this kind of commonwealth. He explains that a monarchy is called the patrimony of a king, when the latter 'possesses in plenary dominion' what he holds, 'no matter how he obtained it'.[119] Originally, patrimony of a father would have been understood to have to do with things the owner could use and misuse at his pleasure, but at later times slaves (but not wives and children) were included in the patrimony since they were classed as things (Pufendorf refers here to the *Digest*). Pufendorf adopts however a critical stance against the very concept of a patrimonial kingdom when he observes that 'later the ambition of rulers began to list among their chief possessions sovereignty over men' and deplores that many of them got accustomed 'to misusing the property of their subjects to the satisfaction of their lusts'.[120]

Pufendorf returns to the question of patrimony when he deals with the power of the sovereign over the property of his citizens. He admits that when the holder of supreme sovereignty was the first to acquire dominion over things embraced in the bounds of his state, the latter would hold over all property in the state the same power 'as every father of a family possesses over his own patrimony', and in this case 'citizens will hold their property by no other right than that by which slaves in ancient Rome held their trifling possessions, and

118 On the latter see David Singh Grewal's chapter in this volume.

119 Ibid., VII, 6, 16, p. 1080.

120 Ibid., p. 1081.

so their possession is merely precarious, revocable at the pleasure of the king whenever he so pleases'.[121] Pufendorf stresses however that these last remarks only apply to subjects of a state he just described, and not to citizens of a state where the holder of sovereignty 'is summoned to sovereignty by the free will of men who already had possession of all their property',[122] and he explicitly criticizes Hobbes, who falsely maintained in *De cive* that just like sons had propriety of goods granted them by their fathers, citizens had no propriety in which the ruler had no right. Again, Pufendorf expresses his disregard for the patrimonial kingdom when he points to examples such as the Pharaohs in Egypt, or the kingdom of Congo, and points to the observations Bernier made on the realm of the Great Mogul,

> to the effect that this absolute dominion of princes in that realm and in other oriental empires is the reason why those lands, otherwise so favoured, are daily sinking lower in ignorance, barbarity and poverty, or at least do not enjoy the prosperity seen in most kingdoms of Europe, where the princes encroach more sparingly upon the dominion of citizens, and where the latter can have something which they call their own even in opposition to the prince'.[123]

4 Conclusion

This chapter aimed at exploring how the family was conceived in early modern social contract theories, first in regard to the state of nature, and then in regard to the civil society, or state. Despite the fact that feminist historians of political thought devoted an important number of studies to the place of women in these theories and that theories of slavery and servitude have found much attention, especially in connection with slavery in the New World, the family has rarely been studied in its own right, i.e., as a complex society that comprises the society between husband and wife, parents and children, and master and servant, or slave. Quite paradoxically, Hobbes' theory of the family, which is less elaborate than that of many of his successors, has recently found the most attention.[124] In section 2 above, I have presented an overview

121 Ibid., VIII, 5, 1, p. 1274.

122 Ibid.

123 Ibid., p. 1275. This is a reference to François Bernier, *Histoire de la dernière révolution des Estats du grand Mogol* (Paris: Claude Barbin, 1671).

124 See note 10 above.

of Pufendorf's and Locke's theories of the family, with a specific interest in the question how they conceived and justified the power of the husband over his wife, of the parents over their children, and of the master over his servant, or slave. There would be much more to say about each of these small societies, especially regarding marriage. Indeed, like other social contract theorists, Pufendorf and Locke deal in this context at some length with questions related to divorce, polygamy, and incest, for example.[125] For reasons of coherence and of space, these topics have been left to one side, and I also refrained from raising the question of the origins of these theories of the family, because this would require a study in its own right. May it suffice to say here that Aristotle's theory of the family, who played a major role up to Bodin, remained certainly important. His concept of the *oikos* does however not appear in the social contract theories we have studied here,[126] most likely because Hobbes, Pufendorf and Locke refer to the Roman law figure of the *paterfamilias*, under whose rule the three simple societies are united.

As we have seen in section 3, the power of the head of the family, which differs from the authority he has as husband, father, and master, plays a key role in regard to the analogy between the family and the state. Except for Hobbes, who clearly puts his theory of power in the domestic realm of the family in the service of his overall argument about sovereignty in the state, our authors strike a difficult balance between an account of the origin of the commonwealth apt at confirming their normative theory of the state, and a conjectural narrative coherent with the sources they refer to (the Bible, reports about people in America, etc.). As we have seen, these narratives are remarkably different in Pufendorf and Locke, although they both argue, the first in opposition mainly to Hobbes, the second in opposition to Filmer, that the power of the paterfamilias is not the same as sovereignty in the state, and that despite some resemblances, the family is not a little kingdom.

Bay way of conclusion, let me come back to the various notions of the state of nature I have highlighted in this paper. There is first the well-known theoretical-conceptual notion, according to which men are by nature free and equal and not subject to any other. The social contract theorists' account of the family clearly shows that in this context 'man' is indeed a generic term and substitutable with expressions like 'human being' or 'individual'. As I suggested at the very beginning of this chapter, the state of nature as a 'fiction' needs to be carefully distinguished form the state of nature as a 'reality' in order to

125 On polygamy see Heydt, *Moral Philosophy in Eighteenth-Century Britain*, ch. 9, pp. 203–27.
126 Rousseau refers to the *oikos* in the *Discourse on Political Economy*.

understand how our authors hold the basic assumption of men's freedom and equality to be compatible with the existence of independent families before states were founded. In the last section of the chapter we have finally seen that the 'realist' notion of the state of nature needs further to be divided into a conjectural and a historical account of the origin of commonwealths. As Locke asserts very clearly, the historical record needs to be completed by hypothetical reasoning to the extent that 'Government is every where antecedent to Records, and Letters seldome come in amongst a People, till a long continuation of Civil Society has, by other more necessary Arts provided for their Safety, Ease, and Plenty'.[127] If we acknowledge the duality of the realist notion of the state of nature, the social contract theorists' account of the family and of the origin of commonwealths can as well be considered as a kind of blueprint of the conjectural histories that were later developed in the eighteenth century, on one hand by Rousseau in the *Second Discourse*, and on the other by the Scottish philosophers, who partly responded to the latter.

Select Bibliography

Primary Sources

Hobbes, Thomas. *Leviathan*, edited by Richard Tuck. (Cambridge University Press, 1996).

Hobbes, Thomas. *On the Citizen*, edited and translated by Richard Tuck and Michael Silverthorne. (Cambridge University Press, 1998).

Locke, John. *Two Treatises of Government*, ed. by Peter Laslett. (Cambridge University Press, 1988).

Pufendorf, Samuel. *De jure naturae et gentium*, vol. 2: The Translation of the Edition of 1688 by C. H. Oldfather and W. A. Oldfather. (Oxford: Clarendon Press, 1934).

Pufendorf, Samuel. *The Duty of Man and Citizen*, edited by James Tully, translated by Michael Silverthorne. (Cambridge University Press, 1995).

Secondary Sources

Hirschmann, Nancy J. "Hobbes on the Family." In *The Oxford Handbook of Hobbes*, edited by A. P. Martinich and Kinch Hoechstra, 242–63. (Oxford University Press, 2016).

Pateman, Carole. *The Sexual Contract*. (Stanford University Press, 1988).

Sagar, Paul. "Of Mushrooms and Method: History and the Family in Hobbes's Science of Politics." *European Journal of Political Theory* 14/1 (2015), 98–117.

127 Locke, *Two Treatises*, II, 8, 101, p. 334.

Simmons, A. John. "Locke's State of Nature." *Political Theory* 17/3 (1989), 449–70.

Sreedhar, Susanne. "Pufendorf on Patriarchy." *History of Philosophy Quarterly* 31/3 (2014), 209–27.

Vogel, Ursula. "Private contract and public institution: The peculiar case of marriage." In *Publicand Private: Legal, political and philosophical perspectives*, edited by Maurizio Passerin d'Entrèves and Ursula Vogel, 177–99. (London and New York: Routledge).

CHAPTER 9

Written in the Hearts of People?

Natural and International Law During the Age of Enlightenment

Edward J. Kolla

Abstract

During the Age of Enlightenment, two different and in some ways contradictory visions of natural law were common in contemporary discourse. One variant derived from Hugo Grotius' theories predicated on the virtue of self-preservation in a theoretical state of nature. "Grotian" natural law reflected norms in the contemporary states system – in which treaty obligations and custom, freely undertaken by sovereigns, were the sources of international law. The second version emphasized changes to society predicated on Enlightenment values. Enlightenment natural law was premised on reason, in theory, with commentators often claiming it to be written in peoples' hearts. It was Enlightenment natural law that became the target of derision by positivists, starting with Jeremy Bentham's attack on it as "nonsense on stilts." Meanwhile, nineteenth-century positivism can, in fact, be seen as a legacy of Grotian natural law. Both traditions continue to this day, with the attendant tension in international law.

Keywords

international law – natural law – international relations – Enlightenment – French Revolution – Westphalian system

1 Introduction

Utilitarian philosopher Jeremy Bentham (1748–1832) is famous, amongst other things, for calling natural law 'nonsense on stilts.'* In the same year as the outbreak of the French Revolution, he also coined the neologism 'international

* I would like to thank Anne Peters and Mark Somos for the invitation to participate in this volume, and for their feedback; Tom Sparks for his close reading and suggestions on this piece in draft, and Dan Edelstein on a much earlier one; and all the participants in the book

 | DOI:10.1163/9789004499621_011

law.'[1] At that point, natural law had long been intertwined with international law, since at least the lifetime of Hugo Grotius (1583–1645), whose epithet as the father of the discipline is reinforced today by an inscription in the library of the Peace Palace, site also of the International Court of Justice, in The Hague. At the turn from the eighteenth to the nineteenth century, however, Bentham committed an act of intellectual patricide in the history of international law. A new positivism based on clearly discernible sources began to triumph over the 'Law of Nature' Bentham so reviled, which he rejected as merely the 'sentiments' of a 'great multitude of people … about what is right and what is wrong.'[2]

Or, so most scholars believe.[3]

Grotius was the first in a series of theorists who launched an innovation in understandings of the law of nature, in response to the European Wars of Religion of the sixteen and seventeenth centuries. To eschew the confessional discord of that era, in which religious and moral claims proved enormously contestable, this new understanding was predicated on an uncontroversial proposition – the human desire for self-preservation in the state of nature. Grotius posited that humans, in this theoretical state, possessed a minimal set of natural rights and were bound by an equally minimalist natural law deriving from self-preservation. By making the moral analogy between people in the state of nature and states in the international system, these same rights and this same law applied in international relations.[4] Specialists often term this set

---

workshop in Berlin in summer 2019. All translations from the French are my own, unless otherwise noted.

1 Jeremy Bentham, *The Collected Works of Jeremy Bentham: An Introduction to the Principles of Morals and Legislation*, J. H. Burns and H. L. A. Hart, eds. (1789; repr., Oxford: Clarendon Press, 2005), p. xxxv, xlv. The former line is from 'Anarchical Fallacies, being an examination of the Declaration of Rights issued during the French Revolution,' 1843. In spite of this position, Bentham was 'a Francophile' who supported the Revolution 'while consistently opposing natural rights doctrines and Declarations of Rights,' according to Emmanuelle de Champs, *Enlightenment and Utility: Bentham in French, Bentham in France* (Cambridge: Cambridge University Press, 2015), 1, 11. Stephen Neff notes that Richard Zouche, the English judge and member of parliament, first dubbed the term 'international law' but did so in Latin, as *ius inter gentes*. See Stephen Neff, *Justice Among Nations: A History of International Law* (Cambridge, Mass.: Harvard University Press, 2014), p. 171.

2 Bentham, p. 27.

3 David Armitage, to cite one representative voice, has written how the late eighteenth and early nineteenth centuries are 'seen as crucial in a shift away from naturalism and to positivism in the realm of international law.' See his 'The Declaration of Independence and International Law,' *William and Mary Quarterly* 59, no. 1 (2002): 39, pp. 42–43. See also Peter and Nicholas Onuf, *Federal Union, Modern World: The Law of Nations in an Age of Revolutions, 1776–1814* (Madison: Madison House, 1993), p. 2.

4 See the works of Richard Tuck, especially chapter three of *The Rights of War and Peace: Political Thought and the International Order from Grotius to Kant* (Oxford: Oxford University Press,

of beliefs 'modern natural law,' but I dub it Grotian natural law to avoid confusion with variants that came subsequently.[5]

Because distinct forms of natural law did, indeed, arise.[6] One important alternative was Enlightenment natural law. In the whirl of the Enlightenment and especially in France, natural law was put forward as whatever any thinker, grand *philosophe* or 'Grub Street' hack, could persuasively claim via reason or rationality it ought to be.[7] In keeping with contemporary theories about the perfectibility of society and people, natural law during the Enlightenment assumed the mantra of a justification for making changes that seemed moral or laudable for ameliorating humanity. Although Grotian and Enlightenment natural law coexisted in the eighteenth century, it was the latter that Bentham found abhorrent, and that historians have singled out as being eclipsed by nineteenth century positivism. Few scholars have recognized this distinction.

It is necessary to clarify this historical record and disambiguate Grotian and Enlightenment natural law – to clearly demarcate and better understand exactly what Bentham attacked, why, and with what consequences. Bentham sought to develop an 'objective' approach to the law by emphasizing formal sources as opposed to moral criteria.[8] His first and greatest disciple, John Austin (1790–1859), reinforced this point by arguing that 'The *existence* of a law is one thing: its *merits* or *demerits* are another thing. Whether a law *be*, is one inquiry ... whether it agree with a given or assumed test, is another and a distinct inquiry.'[9] Sir Frederick Pollock (1845–1937), a British jurist and long-time

1999). For an alternative interpretation, which emphasizes freedom against servility in Grotius' state of nature, see chapter six in this volume by Emile Simpson.

5 I am not the first to use this moniker. See Hedley Bull, 'The Grotian Conception of International Society,' in *Diplomatic Investigations: Essays in the Theory of International Politics*, Herbert Butterfield and Martin Wight, eds. (Cambridge, Mass.: Harvard University Press, 1966), p. 51. See also Hersch Lauterpacht, 'The Grotian Tradition in International Law,' *British Yearbook of International Law* 23, no. 1 (1946): pp. 1–53.

6 As Michael Stolleis has written, 'there is no such things as 'the' natural law; instead, in the course of some one hundred and fifty years (1680–1830), the success of natural law was based on a variety of religious, theoretical and political approaches and motifs.' See his 'The Legitimation of Law through God, Tradition, Will, Nature and Constitution,' in *Natural Law and Laws of Nature in Early Modern Europe: Jurisprudence, Theology, Moral and Natural Philosophy*, Lorraine Daston and Michael Stolleis, eds. (Ashgate: Farnham, 2008), p. 51.

7 The term 'Grub Street' refers to the underbelly of the Enlightenment print production and is from Robert Darnton, *The Literary Underground of the Old Regime* (Cambridge, Mass.: Harvard University Press. 1982).

8 Jeffrey L. Dunoff, Steven R. Ratner, and David Wippman, *International Law: Norms, Actors and Process: A Problem-Oriented Approach* (New York: Aspen, 2002), p. 970.

9 John Austin, *The Province of Jurisprudence Determined* (London: John Murray, 1832), p. 278. Emphasis in the original.

correspondent with United States Supreme Court Justice Oliver Wendell Holmes, Jr. (1841–1935), wrote that Bentham and his followers believed 'quite honestly that the Law of Nature meant nothing but individual fancy.'[10] Bentham and Austin may have had critics of their own, over the years.[11] Nonetheless, the charge of 'nonsense' has stuck.

Bentham's attachment to positivism and its eventual triumph over Enlightenment natural law has distracted from the reality that Grotian natural law and what came on to be known as positivism, in fact, share a number of important characteristics. For example, Grotian natural law emphasized sources – in international law, treaties and custom – insofar as an international system predicated on the theoretical state of nature renders individual state sovereignty paramount. No higher-order law is deemed valid, and states are constrained only by the obligations they undertake of their own volition. As a result, between the Grotian and Enlightenment variants of natural law, the former was much more important to diplomatic practice in the eighteenth century – just as 'positivism' would be in the nineteenth and beyond. Grotian natural law, therefore, emphasized the real over the ideal because it was based on moral minimalism derived from the state of nature. Enlightenment natural law, meanwhile, could be used as a broad justification for all sorts of activities because it was simply, or even (supposedly) self-evidently, written in peoples' hearts. The tension between these two variants of natural law, for diplomatic activity, became clear during the French Revolution and continues to exist in international law to this day.

2 Some Natural Laws, from Antiquity to the Peace of Westphalia

Natural law had a long and varied existence before it was ever applied to or deemed important for international affairs. As Lorraine Daston and Michael Stolleis have noted, natural law is found in 'Aristotle in the *Nicomachean Ethics*, Cicero in *De legibus*, Romans 2:13–15 in the New Testament, Gratia in the *Decretum*, Aquinas in the *Summa theologiae*.'[12] According to Aristotle (385–323 BCE), the principles governing human relations are not based on agreements, conventions, or commands – but rather on universal justice that has

---

10 Sir Frederick Pollock, *Essays in the Law* (London: Macmillan and Co., 1922), p. 62.

11 One major salvo against Bentham and Austin came from H. L. A. Hart, who argued law existed not because of legitimate sources, but when people think it does. See his *The Concept of Law*, 2nd ed. (Oxford: Clarendon Press, 1994).

12 Daston and Stolleis, *Natural Law*, p. 2.

'everywhere the same force.'[13] Romans wedded the Stoic faith in natural reason with a belief in the possibility of one law for all of humanity – what Cicero (106–43 BCE) called 'a single joint community of gods and men.'[14] Cicero even went so far as to equate reason directly with law: 'However we may define people, a single definition will apply to all … For those creatures who have received the gift of reason from Nature, have also received right reason, and therefore they have also received the gift of law.'[15]

The link between natural law and reason continued into the Middle Ages. The greatest natural law theorist of that time, Thomas Aquinas (1225–1274), believed natural law to be the 'participation of the rational creature in eternal law.'[16] The Renaissance Jesuit and scholastic thinker, Luis de Molina (1535–1600), similarly believed that natural law was 'nothing other than a capacity to reason itself.'[17] Thomist natural law was the basis on which the jurists and theologians of the School of Salamanca, named for the great Iberian university where they taught, debated the rights of both Spaniards and Native Americans in the aftermath of Christopher Columbus' arrival in the western hemisphere in 1492.[18] Francisco Suarez (1548–1617), another Jesuit and member of the School, believed that natural law was a combination of right reason and submission to God's will, thus 'inherent in the human mind.'[19] Suarez, however, broke with the past. According to Stephen Neff, Suarez was the first truly to perceive international law as a law *between* states, and he characterized *ius gentium* as positive law because it is 'devised and established proximately by

13 Aristotle, *Nicomachean Ethics*, V, ch. 7, 1134b. Seneca (4 BCE-65 CE) believed humans were endowed with reason as a lex naturalis. Both cited in Alfred Verdoss and Heribert Franz Koeck, 'Natural Law: The Tradition of Universal Reason and Authority,' in *The Structure and Process of International Law: Essays in Legal Philosophy, Doctrine, and Theory*, R. St.J. Macdonald and Douglas M. Johnston, eds. (Dordrecht: Martinus Nijhoff, 1986), pp. 18–19. They argue that Aristotle therefore viewed law as 'binding by natural necessity, in order to secure a peaceful and well-ordered community.'

14 J. G. A. Pocock, 'Some Europes in their history,' in *The Idea of Europe: From antiquity to the European Union*, Anthony Pagden, ed. (Cambridge: Cambridge University Press, 2002), p. 42.

15 Cicero, *On the Laws*, 1.10.28–30, 43.

16 St. Thomas Aquinas, *Summa Theologiae*, II, 1, quaest. 91, art 2, on 1.

17 Luis de Molina, 1614, tom 6, disp 47, para 3, col 1701.

18 See for example Anthony Pagden, 'Dispossessing the Barbarian,' in *The Languages of Political Theory in Early-Modern Europe*, Anthony Pagden, ed. (Cambridge: Cambridge University Press, 1987), 79–98. For some, Francisco de Vitoria (1483–1546), the leader of the Salamanca school, and not Grotius is truly the father of international law. In this volume, in chapter four, Daniel Allemann explores how 'naturalness' impacted Vitoria's understating of the Spanish conquest of the Americas.

19 Francisco Suarez, 1612, lib 1, ch. 3, &10, p. 9.

men.'[20] Inscribed on a prominent bronze tablet at the Palais des Nations in Geneva, original home to the League of Nations, is a famous passage from Suarez's most important work, *De legibus* (1612): 'the human race, however many various peoples and kingdoms into which it may be divided, always preserves *a certain unity*, not only as a species, but also, as it were, as *a moral and political unity*.' Although Suarez maintained continuity with his predecessors in emphasizing that this law must be based on 'natural reason,' nonetheless, 'it is not provided in sufficient measure and in a direct manner' and therefore 'it was possible for certain special rules of law to be introduced through the practice of these same nations.'[21]

A systemic crisis – religious, intellectual, and political – helped spur further innovation in thinking about natural law. The Reformation and subsequent religious conflict, especially the Thirty Years' War (1618–1648) that caused the death of roughly a third of the population of Central Europe, undermined the notion of legal and moral unity that harkened back to the Roman Empire and was carried through into the medieval conception of Christendom. Furthermore, the internecine confessional struggle of the sixteenth century discredited the concept of absolute values, in general, which led a group of philosophers to elaborate a new law of nature with profound implications for international law.

The first was Grotius. He did not depart from the proposition that reason was central to natural law; he merely winnowed that which reason translated into law. He started with an idea that was eminently reasonable; went back to the Stoics, Epicureans, and Peripatetics of classical Antiquity; but had gained new urgency in the bloodbath of his own time – the virtue of self-preservation.[22] According to Richard Tuck, Grotius built on the moral implication of the psychological belief of sceptics – the yearn to survive – to make the post-sceptical claim of 'self-preservation as the fundamental natural right ... and the bare obligation not to harm other people *unnecessarily*' as 'a minimalist natural 'law'.'[23] First in *De Indis*, Grotius laid out this belief that it is always lawful to protect one's life, and the additional corollaries of avoiding what is

---

20 Quoted in Neff, *Justice*, p. 154. Although he credits Suarez with this innovation, Neff does recognize that the idea can be traced all the way back to the Church Father Isidore of Seville (c. 560–636), pp. 560–636.

21 Suarez, *De legibus*, II, ch. XIX, 3.

22 Richard Tuck, 'The 'modern' theory of natural law' in *Languages of Political Theory*, p. 111.

23 Richard Tuck, *Philosophy and Government 1572–1651* (Cambridge: Cambridge University Press, 1993), p. xvi. Emphasis in the original. While Tuck's interpretation presented here is not universally accepted, my purpose is less a detailed analysis of Grotius' thought than a reflection on its implications, in broad strokes, for international law.

detrimental to and acquiring what is necessary for life. These rights and this law were premised on a theoretical state of nature in which humans lived prior to the establishment of society, thus avoiding the competing truth claims that derived from social and cultural differences. As such, the force of his logic 'would have a degree of validity even if,' Grotius controversially claimed, 'there is no God.'[24]

Although Grotius made the critical innovation of basing natural law theory on minimal morality, Thomas Hobbes (1588–1679) is perhaps more famous for his depiction of the state of nature from which it was derived. Life in Hobbes' state of nature, 'solitary, poor, nasty, brutish, and short,' was of a crueller sort than in that of Grotius, because the latter believed that humans were naturally sociable and generally recognized the obligation not to harm one another.[25] In this, Hobbes found Grotius insufficiently sceptical. If all humans were naturally free to judge threats to their self-preservation, radical uncertainty would prevail, and the only true way to assure for one's safety would be, in fact, to eliminate all dangers – thus leading to Hobbes' other famed epithet, *bellum omnium contra omnes*, the 'war of all against all.'[26] This war is what drove people in the state of nature to seek the protection of the Leviathan, who provided the safety and order of society in return for people renouncing their natural freedoms.

By positing the appearance of the Leviathan, Hobbes accentuated the anarchy of interstate relations because of the lack of any such international overlord. Wilhelm Grewe, in his survey of the history of international law, describes Hobbes as the progenitor of the idea that 'a legal order in the true sense could not exist between States. There was no effective command mechanism which guaranteed the enforcement of legal rules against States.'[27] Grewe is certainly not alone among international law scholars in this belief.[28] Anachronistically, he analogizes Hobbes' position with the command theory of the nineteenth

---

24 Hugo Grotius, *De iure belli ac pacis libri tres*, Prolegomena, p. 11.

25 Thomas Hobbes, *Leviathan*, ch. xiii. Benjamin Staumann has an innovative analysis of Hobbes and the Melian Dialogue, with implications for the state of nature, in chapter one of this work.

26 Ibid.

27 Wilhelm G. Grewe, *The Epochs of International Law*, Michael Byers, trans. (Berlin: Walter de Gruyter, 2000), p. 350.

28 Rather than recognize the way Hobbes' thought is indebted to Grotius, Grewe believes William of Occam (1285–1347) to be the inspiration, p. 349. Tuck, meanwhile, describes how Friedrich Meinecke and Leo Strauss believed Niccolò Machiavelli (1469–1527) was the true father of this tradition, with the latter seeing Hobbes as having 'transplanted natural law on the plane of Machiavelli' in *Rights of War and Peace*, pp. 3–4.

century arch-positivist, Austin. However, again, it was Grotius who had been the true innovator in the history of international law, and first conceived of the moral equivalency of people in a state of nature and states in the international system, from which Hobbes concluded perpetual war in both realms.[29]

The genealogy of natural law theory after Grotius was rich. Publications on the subject grew through the mid-seventeenth century and peaked in the eighteenth, before dwindling in the early-nineteenth.[30] Although France was an outlier in this regard, most universities had chairs in 'the law of nature and nations,' the first such being at the University of Heidelberg and held by Samuel Pufendorf (1632–1694), starting in 1661.[31] Pufendorf developed a vision of international law predicated on the idea that treaties must be respected, even if they are not a formal source of law, and on custom, which rests 'only upon a tacit agreement.'[32] This was the practical outcome of Grotius' belief that the same, minimal law pertaining to self-preservation that bound people in nature, also applied to states.

This period also coincided with the birth and initial growth of the so-called Westphalian system. Although now discredited or seriously nuanced by most scholars, such as Pärtel Piirimäe, the idea that 'the Thirty Years' War ended up establishing a new international order has for a long time enjoyed the status of textbook knowledge.'[33] Many have interpreted Grotius' new vision of natural law as helping to underpin the Westphalian system, in which states, as autonomous and independent polities, were bound to no higher authority than themselves and the rules to which they freely subscribed.[34] It is common to characterize the nineteenth century international system, when positivism supposedly first reigned, as analogous with the Hobbesean state of nature. In

29 Grotius made this observation in *De Indis* and reiterated it in *De iure belli ac pacis libri tres*.

30 Stolleis, p. 50.

31 Ibid.; Stephen C. Neff, 'A Short History of International Law,' in *International Law*, Malcolm D. Evans, ed., 3rd ed. (Oxford: Oxford University Press, 2010), p. 9.

32 Cited in Verdoss and Koeck, p. 31, from Pufendorf's *De jure naturae et gentium libri octo*. For more on Pufendorf, see chapters seven and eight in this volume, by David Grewal and Simone Zurbuchen, respectively.

33 Pärtel Piirimäe, 'The Westphalian myth and the idea of external sovereignty,' in *Sovereignty in Fragments: The Past, Present and Future of a Contested Concept*, Hent Kalmo and Quentin Skinner, eds. (Cambridge: Cambridge University Press, 2010), p. 64.

34 See for example Hedley Bull, 'The Importance of Grotius in the Study of International Relations,' in *Hugo Grotius and International Relations*, Hedley Bull, Benedict Kingsbury, and Adam Roberts, eds. (Oxford: Oxford University Press, 1992): 'The idea of international society which Grotius propounded was given concrete expression in the Peace of Westphalia, and Grotius may be considered the intellectual father of this first general peace settlement of modern times.'

reality, international relations have never been as anarchic as Hobbes' vision requires. Moreover, there is no need to displace Hobbes from his own historical moment. The moral and legal minimalism of Grotian natural law, of which Hobbes was a notable offshoot, reflected the international system of the seventeenth and eighteenth centuries well. That system emphasized the idea of princes and their states as sovereign, with no overlord, and beholden only to the covenants or customs they willingly undertook in a perilous and uncertain, but not unremittingly hostile, environment.[35]

3 International Law during the Long Eighteenth Century

The term most commonly employed in the eighteenth century to describe what Bentham later called international law was the law of nation – or, in French, *le droit des gens*, a close translation of the Latin *ius gentium*.[36] To quote an anonymous pamphlet from 1748, *gens* 'is a synonym for the words 'people' or 'nation' … *Le droit des gens* is therefore the law respecting nations, or the law that governs them.'[37] Genevan legal and political theorist Jean-Jacques Burlamaqui (1694–1748) went further and used language presaging the nineteenth century French thinker, Auguste Comte (1798–1857), progenitor of 'positive philosophy,' by which 'Comte meant something like 'scientific' or 'objective' or 'empirical,' in contrast to speculative or religious modes of thought,' according to Neff.[38] Burlamaqui called *le droit des gens* 'the science of law that exists between nations or states.'[39] Jean Dumont (1667–1727), a French writer on international affairs, reiterated the division between natural and human-made law, going back to Suarez: '*Le Droit des Gens,* I believe, can and should be defined as the law relating to peoples, between one another and also among themselves and this is either *natural* or *contracted*.'[40]

35 See Lauterpacht, pp. 28–29: 'In stressing the practical analogy of states and individuals Grotius derived substantial assistance from the fact that in the century in which he wrote the emerging territorial state was a creature of personal rule … The rules of conduct binding upon states were … rules of law and morality governing the conduct of individual human beings.'

36 In many languages, the term came from a literal translation of the Latin *ius gentium*. See Verdoss and Koeck, p. 20.

37 *Observations sur les devoirs des hommes, relativement au droit naturel et au droit des gens* (Paris: Moureau, 1784), pp. 135–36.

38 Neff, 'A Short History,' p. 14.

39 J. J. Burlamaqui, *Principes du droit de la nature et des gens*, 7 vols. (Yverdon, 1746), 1:xxv.

40 J. Dumont, *Corps universel diplomatique de Droit des gens ; contenant un recueil des traitez* … 7 vols. (Amsterdam: P. Brunel, 1726), 1:i. Emphasis in the original.

Of central importance to eighteenth century international law was precisely this 'contracted' law, treaty law. Although the period between the Peace of Westphalia and the French Revolution witnessed a series of dynastic struggles and territorial transfers, they were always legitimized in the strictly legalistic terms of successions disputes, antiquated familial claims, and the like. Among the proto-positivists of this period are often counted Cornelius van Bynkershoek (1673–1743), Johann Jakob Moser (1701–1785), Samuel Rachel (1628–1691), and Wolfgang Textor (1693–1771).[41] It is not surprising that German jurists should figure so prominently in this list, given the complex constitutional structure of the Holy Roman Empire.

The seventeenth and eighteenth centuries also witnessed the first flurry of publication of voluminous compendia of treaties, sometimes listing sources from as far back as Charlemagne. The belief was that these accords, along with the memoirs, negotiations, and other papers of official ministers, constituted a 'public law of Europe,' another common synonym for the law of nations.[42] Burlamaqui, Dumont, and Gabriel Bonnot de Mably (1709–1785), a French abbot, diplomat, and historian, assembled some of the most famous collections.[43] George Frederic von Martens (1756–1821), another German, made his own, great compilation. In 1789, that same fateful year when Bentham coined 'international law,' he characterized *le droit des gens* as 'the ensemble of all the rights and obligations introduced among all, or among most of the peoples of Europe, either by particular or uniform treaties, or by tacit conventions and customs, that makes up the general and positive or modern law of nations of Europe.'[44] It is striking how well Martens presaged current definitions. The 1946 'Statute of the International Court of Justice (ICJ),' which lawyers habitually use to identify the sources of international law today, similarly lists the first two sources of the law as 'a. international conventions, whether general or particular, establishing rules expressly recognized by the contesting states; [and] b. international custom, as evidence of a general practice accepted as law.'[45]

41 Grewe, pp. 355–57. See also Verdoss and Koeck, p. 39.

42 See for example Pierre Joseph Neyron, *Principes du droit des gens européen conventionnel et coutumier, ou bien Précis historique, politique & juridique des droits & obligations que les Etats de l'Europe se sont acquis & imposés par des conventions & des usages reçus, que l'intérêt commun a rendu nécessaires* (Brunswick: Librairie des Orphelins, 1783), pp. 29–31. See also George Frederic Martens, *Précis du droit des gens moderne de l'Europe, fondé sur les traités et l'usage*, 3 vols. (Göttingen: Jean Chret. Dieterich, 1789), 1:13–14.

43 For Burlamaqui and Dumont, see notes 39 and 40 above, respectively; Gabriel Bonnot de Mably, *Le droit public de l'Europe, fondé sur les traités*, 3 vols., 4th ed. (Geneva: La Compagnie des Librairies, 1768).

44 Martens, 1:5.

45 Article 38.

Beyond mere cataloguing, Mably theorized an intrinsic connection between a state's diplomatic practices and any voluntary obligations assumed, and what could be called an emerging, beneficent international law. In his view, states' foreign relations had the potential, in an absolutist political environment, to be based on the whims of the prince. However, by undertaking treaties and other elective commitments, a body of law was created that served to restrict, and pacify, diplomatic behaviour. Marc Belissa has shown how Mably was more interested in distilling from treaty negotiation and law a certain moral logic, rather than simply listing conventions and the rules contained therein. As Belissa writes, 'the existence of a corpus of treaties and conventions make possible the creation of a peaceful law of nations.'[46] Mably saw treaties as a positive means of sociability and called them 'public instruments of good faith' which created juridical bonds between states based on synallagmatic, or reciprocal, commitments.[47]

The idea that promises must be honoured is perhaps the most elemental norm not just of international law but also of all law. The brocard *pacta sunt servanda*, which translates roughly as 'agreements must be kept,' is an ancient principle but it too was the subject of theoretical innovation at this time.[48] Indeed, respect for reciprocal agreements was central to both Grotian natural and early modern international law. The great twentieth century international lawyer, Hersch Lauterpacht (1897–1960), argued that for Grotius, *pacta sunt servanda* was perhaps the main precept of natural law.[49] The obligation to respect and honour good-faith agreements, again, derived from the theoretical state of nature. Some analysts have argued that Grotius, taking the lead from Suarez, was instrumental in 'severing the *ius gentium* entirely from natural law and relegating natural law to what was sometimes called the 'court of conscience.''[50] What this interpretation of Grotius neglects, is that he did not so

46 Gabriel Bonnot de Mably, *Principes de négociations, pour servir d'introduction au droit public de l'Europe*, Marc Belissa, ed. (Paris: Kimé, 2001), p. 29.

47 See Marc Belissa, 'La Diplomatie et les traités dans la pensée des Lumières : « négociation universelle » ou « école du mensonge »,' in *Revue d'histoire diplomatique* 4 (1999): p. 309, 312.

48 In international law, pacta sunt servanda comes from the ancient belief that early treaties were sacred and divinely protected: Shirley V. Scott, *International Law in World Politics: An Introduction* (Boulder: Lynne Rienner, 2004), p. 6. Nowadays, respect for treaties is not only a principle of customary international law, but also (somewhat circularly) codified in a number of instruments, for example, the 'Vienna Convention on the Law of Treaties.'

49 Lauterpacht, p. 22.

50 Neff, *Justice*, p. 162. Though contested in the historiography, this is a powerful interpretation of Grotius; see also for example F. H. Hinsley, *Sovereignty*, 2nd ed. (Cambridge: Cambridge University Press, 1986), p. 189: 'Grotius was the first man to insist on the need for a body of positive international law, separate from the natural law and deriving from the will and practice of states.'

much sever natural from international law, but rather, showed them to be connected at the base. In positing natural law as so morally minimal, he showed that honouring promises was, absent any higher enforcement in the theoretical state of nature, the system's basic tenet. Hobbes, by going to an extreme, illustrated these truths even more dramatically. He argued that the fundamental duty was the performance of agreements – between the Leviathan and the people, and otherwise – and that once undertaken, these agreements were inviolable.[51] Antje von Ungern-Sternberg has argued that Hobbes 'based his system of law entirely on human consent and left only a marginal role (the final origin of all legal obligations) for natural law.'[52] Leaving aside the point that the idea originally came from Grotius, one should hardly characterize the 'final origin of all legal obligations' as 'marginal.'

The same origin of obligations applies to the promises states undertake in their international relations, because of the moral analogy between people in the state of nature and states in the international system. Although such agreements represent the *content* of human-made or positive law, the legitimizing principle that makes mutual respect for agreements sacrosanct comes therefore from Grotian natural law.[53] Cultural factors during the eighteenth century reinforced this theoretical perspective. Paul Schroeder, writing from the perspective of a diplomatic historian, argues that, at the time, '[t]he principle *pacta sunt servanda* ... though seldom acknowledged, governed most commitments.'[54] Aside from the forcible reprisals that could occur if rulers should break their word, respect for treaties was, moreover, undergirded by the courtly culture of the dynastic states that largely made up the European system. What Norbert Elias called 'the prestige fetish' in domestic life could be transmuted into international relations: although a strong emphasis on dynastic glory might contribute to war, simultaneously, values such as honour, dignity, and chivalry promoted respect for treaties and therefore contemporary international law.[55]

---

51 Hobbes, p. 93.

52 Antje von Ungern-Sternberg, 'Religion and Religious Intervention,' in *The Oxford Handbook of the History of International Law*, Bardo Fassbender and Anne Peters, eds. (Oxford: Oxford University Press, 2013), p. 298.

53 Neff, although he does not attribute this premise to Grotian natural law, does seem sympathetic to the idea in general, when he writes, 'this core principle (pacta sunt servanda), it may be argued, can only be a principle of natural law.' See *Justice*, p. 235.

54 Paul Schroeder, *The Transformation of European Politics, 1763–1848* (Oxford: Clarendon Press, 1994), pp. 7–8.

55 Norbert Elias, *The Court Society*, Edmund Jephcott, trans. (Oxford: Basil Blackwell, 1983), p. 85.

The idea of a common European international legal community was not limited to dynastic culture. In the place of a (theoretically) unified Christendom during the Middle Ages, in the early modern period, the idea of a *societas humana* developed – based, just like some definitions of natural law, on universal reason and other shared attributes.[56] According to Karlijn van Blom, Martens thought Europeans 'shared rules, customs, standards and values' and so compared them to 'a people' at the Hobbesian moment 'just before it has decided to make a constitution, which means it has no recognized sovereign power above it.'[57] References to the public law of Europe also reflect this new, secular conception of continental unity.[58] Mably, who already felt conventions could lead to public morality, saw the amalgam of rules emanating from treaty law and diplomatic practice as constituting a nascent European republic. Figures as diverse as Edmund Burke (1729–1797), Frederich von Gentz (1764–1832), Gottfried Wilhelm Leibniz (1646–1716), and Voltaire (1694–1778) all suggested some form of this idea. Guillaume-François Le Trosne (1728–1780), a French jurist, economist, and leading physiocrat, wrote, 'the conformity of religion, morals, and government' and 'the treaties, alliances, Justice, [and] immediate sovereignty of those who have no superior on Earth' all contributed 'to make one single Republic of Europe.'[59]

Other thinkers went even further. Although few endorsed the surrender of states' sovereign rights and independence to a Hobbesian Leviathan, so as to bestow order on the international system, some thinkers did elaborate proposals for a voluntary union to promote amity and stability. Such works include *Essay towards the Present and Future Peace of Europe* (1693) by William Penn (1644–1718) and the most famous such project, that of French writer Charles-Irénée Castel, *abbé* Saint-Pierre (1658–1743), of 1713.[60] Saint-Pierre, in close alignment with Hobbes, recognized the extent to which sovereign states must

56 Grewe, p. 287.

57 Karlijn van Blom, 'A Very Uncertain Perspective … The Revolutionary and Napoleonic Age and International Relations in Europe, in the Views of Georg Friedrich von Martens (1756–1821),' in *In the Embrace of France: The Law of Nations and Constitutional Law in the French Satellite States of the Revolutionary and Napoleonic Age (1789–1815)*, Beatrix Jacobs, Raymond Kubben, and Randall Lesaffer, eds. (Baden-Baden: Nomos, 2008), p. 133.

58 Grewe, pp. 292–93.

59 Guillaume-François Le Trosne, *Discours sur le droit des gens, et sur l'état politique de l'Europe* (Amsterdam, 1762), pp. 43–44.

60 Saint-Pierre himself has precursors in Maximilien de Béthune, Duke of Sully (1559–1641) and his 1638 *Economies royales*, John Bellers (1654–1725), John Amos Comenius (1592–1670), Émeric Crucé (1590–1648), and François Fénelon (1651–1715); see Jean-Pierre Bois, *De la paix des rois à l'ordre des empereurs, 1714–1815* (Paris: Hachette, 2003), p. 61.

always worry about the threat posed by their neighbours and therefore concluded, '[t]he methods practiced until now to maintain Peace are entirely ineffective.'[61] He therefore proposed an association that would hardly meddle in the internal administration of individual states, but still codify a renunciation of conquest and establish commercial relation that were fair and equal for all.

Clearly, none of this came to pass. The legacy of Grotian natural law was an emphasis on sovereign autonomy, which mirrored the freedom of people in the state of nature. Next to no law existed in interstate affairs, except that which derived from the minimal right to self-preservation and, in a testament to the independence of sovereigns, whatever commitments or obligations they voluntarily assumed. Some thinkers like Burlamaqui, Dumont, and Martens sought to catalogue these commitments, and thereby identify general patterns of law in the community of states; others, like Mably, Penn, and Saint-Pierre, extracted sociological lessons for peace or developed ambitious proposals for greater stability from their examination of contemporary diplomatic practice.

Practice here is key. Bynkershoek, a Dutch jurist who lived roughly a century later than his co-national Grotius, said he was not interested in 'the testimony of ancient poets and orators' and, instead, that practice is 'the origin of the law of nations.'[62] International law in the late seventeenth and eighteenth century was, indeed, not based on poetry. Rather, human diplomatic activity culminated in customary and treaty law.[63] Grotius' thought helped legitimize this law through his analogy of the person in a theoretical state of nature and the state in the international system, whose rights derived from self-preservation and whose minimal law included the imperative to honour agreements. Natural law, at least of the Grotian variety, should not therefore be the subject of scorn from the likes of Bentham or later positivists; it underpinned both the moral and international system, although not in a direct manner. Perhaps this fact helps account for why the true legacy of Grotian natural law, and its close relationship to treaty law, has been misunderstood or ignored by so many – and, instead, attention has been lavished on the originality of nineteenth century positivism. Perhaps another reason for this misunderstanding is that,

---

61 Charles Irénée Castel de Saint-Pierre, *Projet pour rendre la paix perpétuelle en Europe* (1713; repr., Paris, Fayard: 1986), p. 21.

62 Cornelius van Bynkershoek, *Jurisdiction over ambassadors*, p. 42; Questions, pp. 6–7.

63 To cite but one example, van Blom describes how Martens queried the existence of general, positive international law, given that all of Europe had not codified a general treaty. However, like Mably, Dumont, and others, Martens examined the treaties, tacit agreements, and customs – derived from European practice – and concluded, 'It is the aggregate of the rights and obligations established among the nations of Europe that forms a positive law of nations.' See van Blom, p. 134.

during the eighteenth century and contemporaneous with the Grotian variant, there existed a wholly different sort of natural law. This other form was much closer to what Bentham ultimately derided as 'nonsense.'

4 Enlightenment Natural Law

During the Enlightenment, human reason formed an important foundation for natural law. To be sure, this source had antecedents going back to Thomas Aquinas and antiquity, but it enjoyed a new vitality in the eighteenth century given the emphasis then placed on reason and rational thought as, to paraphrase Immanuel Kant (1724–1804), a counter to superstition and devotion to authority or tradition.[64] What is more, the link between reason, natural law, and international law was widespread at this time. Lawyer Antoine-Gaspard Boucher d'Argis (1708–1791) wrote the article on 'the law of nations' for the *Encyclopédie*, the Enlightenment intellectual juggernaut co-edited by Denis Diderot (1713–1784) and Jean le Rond d'Alembert (1717–1783).[65] Boucher d'Argis summarized, and conflated, as follows: 'Natural right is the same thing as the law of nations, both being founded on the natural powers of reason.'[66]

---

64 It is important not to present a reified description of the Enlightenment. Like many others, Peter Gay has identified the sheer diversity of ideas and values that made up 'the Enlightenment,' calling it 'a loose, informal, wholly unorganized coalition of cultural critics, religious skeptics, and political reformers' with a program of 'secularism, humanity, cosmopolitanism, and freedom, above all freedom from arbitrary power, freedom of speech, freedom of trade.' See *The Enlightenment: An Interpretation: The Rise of Modern Paganism* (New York: Knopf, 1967), p. 3. Nevertheless, it is uncanny the way many writers took reason as a starting point and used natural law to embrace and expound an unending list of hackneyed Enlightenment priorities. Gaspard de Réal described natural law as that 'which deals with the existence and knowledge of truth, love of God, love of self, love of neighbour, and the order and subordination of duties.' See *La science du gouvernement, Ouvrage de Morale, de Droit, et de Politique, qui contient les principes du commandement & de l'obéissance ; où l'on réduit toutes les matières de Gouvernement en un cops unique, entier dans chacun de ses parties ; & où l'on explique les droits & les devoirs des Souveraines, ceux des Sujets, ceux de tous les Hommes, en quelque situation qu'ils se trouvent*, 4 vols. (Aix-la-Chapelle and Paris, 1761–65). This quotation is from the title of the third volume of this work (Paris: Saint & Saillant 1761) on natural law.

65 *Encyclopédie, ou dictionnaire raisonné des sciences, des arts et des métiers* [in English *Encyclopaedia, or a Systematic Dictionary of the Sciences, Arts, and Crafts*], (Le Breton, etc., 1751–66).

66 Antoine-Gaspard Boucher d'Argis, 'Droit des gens' in *Encyclopédie*, V:127. He wrote over 4000 articles on law for the *Encyclopédie*.

He was hardly alone. Louis de Jaucourt (1704–1779), a prolific contributor to the *Encyclopédie*, wrote that humans discover natural law, in his article on that subject, 'through the enlightenment of their reason.'[67] According to Gaspard de Réal de Curban (1682–1752), a French nobleman and jurist, natural law 'can only be known through the enlightening power of reason.' It is a 'rule that right reason reveals to people to guide their actions and to show them what is just and equitable.' Also, '[n]atural law founded on reason is eternal and immutable like reason.'[68] The same Burlamaqui who assembled a compendium of treaties, also wrote this description of natural law: 'the rules that only reason prescribe to people, to lead them surely to the goal they must desire ... a veritable and complete happiness.'[69]

The unbridled power of nature was a common Enlightenment trope and many thinkers believed in the possibility for nature to provide a moral guide for humans, at their core.[70] 'The most perfect work that ever left the hands of nature' was the human being, according to an anonymous pamphlet, and people 'received from nature the faculty to perfect [their] morality and intelligence.'[71] The protestant writer Jean Georges Pillichody (1715–1783) put it simply: 'natural laws are carved into the hearts of all people.'[72] Reason was so intrinsic to the human experience, according to legal writer Charles-Philippe Pattyn (1687–1773), it rendered natural law a fundamental imprint on the human character: '[n]atural law is therefore this light of right reason, that allows us to know what we ought to do, and what we ought to avoid ... written in the heart of every person [natural law] is *eternal and immutable*.'[73] Réal also combined reason, nature, and law as basic hallmarks of humanity when he wrote: '[r]eason, all pure, structured the basics of this law, for the security of the human race, and nature itself is the author of these rules, which, in their origin, have no other book that the spirit and the heart.'[74] Overall, these were

67 Louis de Jaucourt, 'Loi naturelle (morale)' in *Encyclopédie*, IX:666a.

68 Réal, 1:8, 3:8, 3:9. See also Béat Philippe Vicat, *Traité du droit naturel, & de l'application de ses principes au droit civil et au droit des gens*, 4 vols. (Lausanne: La société typographique, 1777), 1:16.

69 Burlamaqui, 1:1–2.

70 See for example Mary Ashburn Miller, *A Natural History of Revolution: Violence and Nature in the French Revolutionary Imagination, 1789–1794* (Ithaca: Cornell University Press, 2011), especially the background in chapter one.

71 *Observations sur les devoirs*, p. 15, 17.

72 Jean Georges Pillichody, *Le Droit naturel, d'un père à son fils: avec des notions pour servir à l'Etude du Droit Civil & à celle du Droit des Gens*, 2 vols. (Yverdon, 1769), 1:5.

73 C. P. Pattyn, *Le Commerce maritime fondé sur le droit de la nature & des gens, sur l'autorité des loix civiles & des traitez de paix, & rétabli dans la liberté naturelle*, trans. D'Hermanville (Malines: Laurent Van der Elst, 1727), 4. Emphasis in the original.

74 Réal, 3:8.

pervasive and powerful declarations. In his article in the *Encyclopédie* on 'natural law,' the *chevalier* de Jaucourt summed up, 'the characteristics of virtue are written in the depths of our souls.'[75] However, to think in Benthamite (and, therefore, anachronistic) terms about these descriptions, the origin or source of natural law often suffered from circular reasoning.

In recognition of the ontological difficulty of these foundation claims, Diderot himself acknowledged that natural law was both 'one of the most important and most difficult' aspects of morality to determine.[76] One aspect of that difficulty related to Enlightenment figures, perhaps most famously Thomas Jefferson (1743–1826) in the 'Declaration of Independence,' claiming the self-evident character of natural law and rights. Lynn Hunt has noted the paradox of such assertions: 'belief in them rests on their self-evidence, which can only be proved by belief in them.'[77] Another source of confusion related to the empirical study of phenomena in the natural sciences, and the counterpoint this posed to determinations of natural law. Marie Jean Antoine Nicolas de Caritat, marquis de Condorcet (1743–1794), French philosopher and one-time revolutionary, asked why, if people could discern law in the natural sciences through constants, could we not do the same for our internal and moral faculties? His study, however, confusingly led him to conclude with 'the strongest reasons for believing that nature has set no limit to the realization of our hopes.'[78] Modern scholars like Luigi Delia, for example, have highlighted the contradiction that many Enlightenment thinkers believed in 'universal and immutable juridical norms, independent of historical fluctuations and superior to the vicissitudes of time' but also possessed a 'sensualist theory of knowledge' that emphasized the uniqueness of each individual's perception.[79] Similarly, Lorraine Daston has noted how, during the Enlightenment, many had a mutable view of both facts and natural laws, and she underlined the confusion that emanated from the concurrent tendency to view nature as supreme

75 Jaucourt, 'Loi naturelle (morale)' in *Encyclopédie*, IX:666a.

76 Denis Diderot, 'Droit naturel' in *Encyclopédie*, V:115b.

77 Lynn Hunt, 'The Paradoxical Origins of Human Rights,' in *Human Rights and Revolutions*, Jeffrey N. Wasserstrom, Lynn Hunt, and Marilyn B. Young, eds. (Lanham, Md.: Rowman & Littlefield, 2000), p. 9. On the connection between human rights and slavery, see Sarah Winter in chapter ten of this volume.

78 Antoine-Nicolas de Condorcet, *Sketch for a Historical Picture of the Progress of the Human Mind*, June Barraclough, trans. (1795; repr., London: Weidenfeld and Nicolson, 1955), pp. 173, 175.

79 Luigi Delia, *Droit et philosophie à la lumière de l'Encyclopédie* (Oxford: Voltaire Foundation, 2015), p. 46.

authority and patent reality.[80] This tracks with a propensity in natural law systems, in general, to oscillate between normative and descriptive statements.[81] Many Enlightenment scholars have noted that, notwithstanding these avowals to reason, sentiment was truly believed to be the source of knowledge at this time.[82]

The overall zeitgeist of Enlightenment natural law was, therefore, especially non-specific in regards to its source, other than an abstract appeal to reason, nature, and the human heart or soul. It was, furthermore, acutely vulnerable to the abuse of self-definition. As Dan Edelstein has argued: '[s]o detached were these concepts from actual legal practices ... their meaning and relations could be easily redefined.'[83] It is no surprise that Martti Koskenniemi has concluded that, during the period, '[n]either Montesquieu nor Rousseau came up with anything like a stable international law. They attacked the existing practices of diplomacy, warfare and treaty-making yet offered only half-hearted abstractions in their place.'[84]

Another explanation for Enlightenment thinkers' inclination to eschew the foundations of Grotian natural law in the theoretical state of nature, in favour of a generalized appeal to nature and reason, was the relative marginality of Grotius' thought in France at the time.[85] This may have been the result of religious conflict. In Holland and Britain, the post-sceptical philosophy of Grotius and Hobbes was a response to the breakdown of, and conflict over, moral and legal order because of the profusion of fanatical religious dogmatists.[86] In France, where the Wars of Religion were fought, for the most part, between Catholics and Calvinist Huguenots, the resolution came in the form of a policy of official toleration from the highest state authority, captured in Henry IV's apocryphal quip, 'Paris is worth a mass.'

---

80 Lorraine Daston, 'Enlightenment Fears, Fears of Enlightenment,' in *What's Left of Enlightenment? A Postmodern Question*, Keith Michael Baker and Peter Hanns Reill, eds. (Stanford: Stanford University Press, 2001), p. 127.

81 Stolleis, pp. 52–53.

82 See for example Lynn Hunt, *Inventing Human Rights: A History* (New York: Norton, 2007).

83 Dan Edelstein, *The Terror of Natural Right: Republicanism, the Cult of Nature, and the French Revolution* (Chicago: University of Chicago Press, 2009), p. 8.

84 Martti Koskenniemi, 'The Advantage of Treaties: International Law in the Enlightenment,' *Edinburgh Law Review* 13 (2009): 42.

85 Historians such as Ernest Nys have recognized 'the minimal part played by France in the sixteenth and seventeenth century in the development of international law.' See his 'La Science du droit international en France' in *Les Théories politiques et le droit international en France jusqu'au XVIIIe siècle* (Brussels, 1899; Geneva: Slatkine Reprints, 1970), p. 111. Grewe, among others, makes a similar point, p. 351.

86 Tuck, 'The 'Modern' Theory' in *Languages*, p. 118.

Many French writers implicitly or explicitly opposed the basic tenets of Grotian natural law.[87] Rather than freedom in the state of nature being the starting point for an elaboration of a minimal natural law, Béat Philippe Vicat (1715–1770), a Swiss jurist and theologian, argued for example that 'humans base their free actions on the ends of their faculties, or, if one likes, of their nature, or that which makes up their constitutions.'[88] Réal believed that natural law applied 'whether [people] live alone, or they are members of a body,' rejecting the importance of the theoretical state of nature.[89] He went further, and mocked Grotius' minimalist morality derived from rights in a pre-societal environment. Réal accused Grotius of equating humans to animals: '[Grotius' premise] is based on a weak glimmer of reason in [people], and he reported the testimony of a writer [Pliny] who filled his book with fables and attributed virtues and passions to beasts.'[90] Some of these critiques linked to Grotius' humanist style. No less a prose master than Voltaire mocked, 'to cite the thoughts of earlier authors who have argued for and against, is not to think' and, justifiably, accused the Dutchman of being 'a real pedant.'[91] Another Enlightenment titan, Jean-Jacques Rousseau (1712–1778), condemned Grotius' 'invariable mode of reasoning' and quoted René-Louis de Voyer de Paulmy, marquis d'Argenson (1694–1757), a friend of Voltaire's who served as French Minister of Foreign Affairs in the 1740s, that, 'learned researches in public law are often nothing but the history of ancient abuses: and to devote much labour to studying them is misplaced pertinacity.'[92]

Hostility among Enlightenment writers to Grotius more often derived not from his theoretical precepts, or his technique, but rather from the ends his

87 Part of this implicit opposition was perhaps born from ignorance: *De Indis*, which in the nineteenth century was called *De iure praedae commentarius*, was only re-discovered in 1864 so was unknown to Enlightenment audiences. See Tuck, *Rights of War and Peace*, p. 81.

88 Vicat, 1:23.

89 Réal, 3:8.

90 Ibid., 3:17. Or, writers reversed the philosophical stream of many, earlier Grotian arguments, robbing them of their analytic sense. For example, instead of using a person's liberty in the state of nature as the theoretical tenet from which natural and international law derived their power, they instead used a casually invoked law of nations as a way to protect a nation's or an individual's freedom. See for example Gabriel-Nicolas Maultrot and abbé Jacques Tailhé, *Questions sur la tolérance; où l'on examine si les maximes de la persécution ne sont pas contraires au droit des gens, à la Religion, à la Morale, à l'intérêt des Souverains & du Clergé* (Geneva: Henry-Albert Gosse, 1758).

91 Voltaire, *Oeuvres Complètes* (Paris, 1820–1826), 35:232–35.

92 Jean-Jacques Rousseau, *The Social Contract and the Discourse on the Origin of Inequality among Mankind* (1762; repr., New York, 1971), p. 9.

thinking was seen to serve. According to Keith Baker, natural law theories such Grotius' were 'deployed to justify monarchical power on the grounds that the latter best served the purposes of peace and tranquility for which society and government had been instituted.'[93] Baker quotes Mably, who argued, 'despotism, with its prisons, its gibbets, its pillage, its silent devastation, and its imbecile and cruel ineptitudes, is the inevitable result of the principles of our jurisconsults.'[94] Baker highlights the sharpest reproach coming, again, from the great sage of Geneva:

> Rousseau was no less critical of the absolutist arguments he found in Grotius, Pufendorf, and Barbeyrac, as of Burlamaqui's defense of oligarchic rule in Geneva. The version of the social contract that leads to the final, dismal denouement of the *Discours sur l'inégalité* is a caricature of a theory that validates egoism and legitimates despotism. Rousseau portrays it as the most brilliantly conceived plan ever contrived by the human species, the perfection of reason in the service of a depraved humanity. In effect, the *Second Discourse* turned the intellectual procedures of the school of modern natural law against the views they had been used to sustain: its negative version of the social contract was the centerpiece of an indictment of modern society.[95]

The consequences were not only domestic tyranny. Jaucourt, who wrote extensively about law, also penned the *Encyclopédie*'s article about 'conquest,' and accused Grotius and Hobbes of giving early modern rulers the right to kill individuals and destroy the societies they vanquished in war.[96] Jaucourt was undoubtedly referring to warfare in Europe, but Richard Tuck has argued that 'the modern idea of natural rights arose in a period in which the Europeans nations were engaged in their dramatic competition for the domination of the

93 Keith Michael Baker, 'Transformations of Classical Republicanism in Eighteenth-Century France' in *Journal of Modern History* 73, no. 1 (March 2001): 32. He goes on: 'It also gave priority to civil liberty, and the peaceful enjoyment of rights protected by law, over political participation. In immediate political terms, then, it frequently served to defend the status quo.'

94 Ibid. For all his interest in the way treaty law could promote a tendency towards peace, Mably opposed the writings of Grotius and his successors because, in a domestic setting, according to Baker, '[i]n placing law over liberty, [Mably] argued in *Des droits et des devoirs du citoyen*, the doctors of natural law [like Grotius] had forgotten that unjust laws could destroy the state.'

95 Ibid.

96 Jaucourt, 'Conquête' in *Encyclopédie*, III:900b.

world' and shown how the philosophy of Grotius served the ambitions of the Dutch United East India Company, and European empire more broadly.[97]

Emmerich de Vattel (1714–1767), the Swiss author of the bestselling treatise on international law during the Age of Enlightenment, also the first to be written in a modern language, is a contradictory figure.[98] In his work, he wrote voluminously about the state of nature, and generally maintained Grotius' analogy between people in it and states in the international system.[99] As Vattel once reformulated it: 'a sovereign prince, however low he may rank in the scale of power, is as completely sovereign and independent as the greatest monarch, in the same manner as a dwarf is a man equally with a giant.'[100] But he also, in the words of Reinhart Koselleck, concluded that 'to be law at all, the law of nations must of necessity be and remain morally imperfect' and therefore prefigured the propositions of Bentham and Austin that aimed to disambiguate the 'existence' from the 'merits' of law.[101] Vattel's most important theoretical departure from Grotius related to sociability. For Grotius, the social nature of people was 'the mother of the law of nature' because they could interact in a natural state.[102] Hobbes, of course, abandoned the idea of human amiability in the state of nature, for all-out war. Vattel landed somewhere in-between, by moderating Grotius' strict analogy between people and states. He understood states to be more self-sufficient in international affairs than pre-societal humans, who were naturally more affable.

Vattel also differentiated basic law not into the binary opposition of natural versus positive but, rather, also included necessary law. Positive law was further subdivided into conventional law (or, the law of treaties), customary law, and voluntary law. The first two elements of Vattel's positive law, conventions and customs, echo early modern emphases as well as prefigure the first two sources of current international law according to the Statute of the ICJ. Vattel's third, voluntary law, established the premise that sovereigns were free to do as they wished in the international system, with the only caveat that 'whatever may be done by any one nation may be done by any other.'[103]

---

97 Tuck, *Rights of War and Peace*, p. 14 and also 108, pp. 203–31.

98 Emmerich de Vattel, *The Law of Nations or the Principles of Natural Law Applied to the Conduct and to the Affairs of Nations and States* (1758; repr. Washington: Carnegie, 1916).

99 Tuck, *Rights of War and Peace*, p. 192.

100 See Vattel, 4.6.§78, and 'Preliminaries,' §18.

101 Reinhart Koselleck, *Critique and Crisis: Enlightenment and the Pathogenesis of Modern Society* (Cambridge, Mass.: MIT Press, 1988), p. 47.

102 Grotius, *De jure*, Prolegomena, 16/1. Aristotle and the Stoics had all previously affirmed natural sociability.

103 Vattel, 'Preliminaries,' § 21.

This assertion of full freedom might seem classically Hobbesian, except when one considers Vattel's natural and necessary law. Necessary law 'consists in the application of the law of nature to Nations' and generally seemed to keep Vattel in the Grotian natural law tradition.[104] However, because Vattel used extremely vague language, he recognized a norm of moral rectitude, ambiguous and unenforceable though it may be, that was more in keeping with Enlightenment natural law.[105] Vattel therefore encapsulates well the mid-eighteenth century muddle between Grotian and Enlightenment natural law.

Carl Becker has suggested that most French *philosophes* implicitly rejected David Hume's (1711–1776) premise that reason alone could never answer fundamental questions about law, God, or existence.[106] There was another implicit rejection, that of the bases of Grotian natural law in favour of an amorphous belief in nature having written reason and ergo natural law in the hearts of all people. Becker characterizes the Enlightenment faith in 'reason' as, in fact, a veneration of 'virtue,' an ever-changeable appeal to morality that would become a favourite of French revolutionaries, Maximilian Robespierre (1758–1794) most notably.[107] Similarly, Robert Darnton has argued that the radicalism of the *philosophes*, in a different context, lay in their faith in (Enlightenment) natural law.[108] His point applies to international relations, too. By emphasizing Enlightenment natural law in international affairs, the *philosophes* and the revolutionaries who shared their views, gambled, for the first time since the Peace of Westphalia, with the large-scale re-application of moral or value judgments to international relations and law.

---

104 Ibid., § 7.

105 Ibid., § 9; Koselleck, p. 48.

106 Carl L. Becker, *The Heavenly City of the Eighteenth-Century Philosophers* (New Haven: Yale University Press, 2003), pp. 82–83. Verdoss and Koeck agree, noting that Hume was among the radical positivists who believed 'it is logically impossible to deduce value judgments from statements of fact,' p. 17. To underline this difference across the Channel, Adam Ferguson's description in *An Essay on the History of Civil Society* (1767) is almost perfectly Grotian: "[t]he law of Nature, with respect to nations, is the same that it is with respect to individuals. It gives to the collective body a right to preserve themselves; to employ, undisturbed, the means of life; to retain the fruits of labour; to demand the observance of stipulations and contracts. In the case of violence, it condemns the aggressor, and establishes, on the part of the injured, the right of defence, and a claim to retribution. Its applications, however, admit of disputes, and give rise to variety in the apprehension, as well as the practice of mankind."

107 Ibid.

108 Robert Darnton, 'In Search of the Enlightenment: Recent Attempts to Create a Social History of Ideas' in *The Journal of Modern History* 43, no. 1 (March 1971): 119.

5 Consequences

The Age of Revolutions was hardly the Benthamite moment that much of the historiography portrays. First of all, people have erroneously ascribed too much novelty to the advent of nineteenth century positivism and its relationship to international law. Generally speaking, they have failed to recognize the earlier manifestation of Grotian natural law in the eighteenth century, in practice, in treaty law. International relations scholars, especially, tend to identify the theoretical state of nature of Grotius' intellectual progeny, Hobbes, and its unbridled war, with the nineteenth century.[109] In opposition to this view, Richard Tuck has shown in his 'seminal work' that theorists from Grotius through Hobbes to Vattel were humanists who 'embraced Tacitism and elements of the reason-of-state tradition' which justified 'warfare for self preservation and self-defense on very broad grounds, encompassing preventative self-defense,' and thereby helped establish a legal paradigm based on state autonomy and the paramountcy of volition in international law.[110] Grotius' contemporary, Suarez, recognized that the law needed to be based on 'the common usage of mankind,' and, furthermore, 'cannot be said to be written upon the hearts of people by the Author of Nature.'[111]

And yet, during the eighteenth century, another vision of natural law was widespread and based precisely on this premise. The idea had existed since antiquity that a sort of law 'is imprinted on our souls,' to quote Domingo de Soto (1494–1560), of the School of Salamanca.[112] Natural law has often 'proved

109 See for example the description by Neff of international law in the nineteen century, and compare to the works of Dumont, Martens, Mably, in 'Short History,' p. 15: "the sum total, or aggregation, of agreements which the States of the world happen to have arrived at, at any given time. In a phrase that became proverbial amongst positivists, international law must now be seen as a law between States and not as a law above States. International law, in other words, was now regarded as a corpus of rules arising from, as it were, the bottom up, as the conscious creation of the States themselves, rather than as a pre-existing, eternal, all-enveloping framework, in the manner of the old natural law." Elsewhere, Neff ignores or rejects the proposition that Grotian thought is behind '[t]he principle 'legislative' devices for this new law of nations' which of course were 'treaties and customary practice (or 'usage' in the standard terminology of the time). Its doctrines and methods were therefore derived not from broad principles of morality but rather from a coldly unsentimental analysis of human political life as it was actually lived' as opposed to the theoretical state of nature. See Neff's *War and the Law of Nations: A General History* (Cambridge: Cambridge University Press, 2005), p. 86.

110 Benedict Kingsbury and Benjamin Straumann, eds. *The Roman Foundations of the Law of Nations: Alberico Gentili and the Justice of Empire* (Oxford: Oxford University Press, 2010), p. 3.

111 Suarez, *Treatise on Laws*, pp. 326, 332.

112 Domingo de Soto, 1569: quaest 4, art 1, p. 10.

semantically irresistible,' according to Michael Stolleis, because of both its vagueness and its importance, and such was the case with Enlightenment natural law.[113] It coexisted confusingly with Grotian natural law, in spite of the differences and indeed contradictions between the two, in the minds of contemporaries and many subsequent historians, both of whom rarely differentiated them. Proponents of Enlightenment natural law staked its claim to validity on its self-evidence – not, like the Grotian variant, on theoretical suppositions derived from the state of nature. Moreover, the believers in Enlightenment natural law also underscored its merits, to use Austin's term – that is, they lauded its validity through their own vision of morality. This was precisely the 'nonsense' Bentham opposed.

When Bentham was writing, on the eve of the French Revolution and during its early years, the European international system still operated according to Grotian principles and what Suarez called 'usage' – treaties, custom, and diplomatic practice. In terms that recall Vattel's voluntary law, Emile Bourgeois describes it thus: 'the political world consisted of the sovereign states, which admitted no other law than their interest, and accepted all means to serve it, whether ruse or violence. It was a society, if one wants, but anarchic.'[114] At the same time, many people invoked Enlightenment natural law to condemn that system for its inherent immorality. After the Revolution broke out, some saw this as an opportunity not only to remake the French state, but also the international system. Charles-François Lebrun (1739–1824), who would later serve as a Consul with Napoleon Bonaparte (1769–1821), after the coup of 18 Brumaire (November 9, 1799), argued for the return of morality to international relations: '[p]olitics and justice are two ideas that have too long been separated, but that the Republic is strongly determined never to disentangle.'[115] Some revolutionaries rejected all prior international law: Edmond-Charles Genêt (1763–1834), a French envoy to the United States, is supposed to have said he 'would throw Vattel and Grotius into the sea when ever their principles interfere with my notion of the rights of nations.'[116] Not only were these works of theory anathema to revolutionaries; so too was Old Regime treaty law, which

113 Stolleis, p. 51.

114 Emile Bourgeois, *Manuel historique de politique étrangère, vol. 2, Les révolutions* (1789–1830), 11th ed. (Paris: Eugène Belin, 1933), p. 6.

115 Cited in Albert Sorel, *L'Europe et la Révolution française, vol. 3, La guerre aux rois, 1792–1793* (Paris, Librairie Plon, 1925), p. 164.

116 Quoted in Linda and Marsha Frey, 'We Will Dance Together the Carmagnole: French Revolutionaries and the Ideal of Fraternity,' in *In Reflections at the End of a Century*, Morris Slavin and Louis Patsouras eds. (Youngstown, Oh.: Youngstown State University, 2002), p. 106.

was the result of the legal paradigm Grotian thought had helped underpin. Whereas Genêt opted to consign the fathers of international law to the depths, the Jacobin journalist and politician Camille Desmoulins (1760–1794) believed, 'The public law of Europe ought to be treated as Luther treated the canon law: all of the books about it should be thrown into the fire.'[117]

Historians have tended to overemphasize this sort of vitriol, with its basis in Enlightenment natural law, and simultaneously understate the way revolutionary France continued, initially at least, to operate in the traditional states system of the eighteenth century. The appeals to Enlightenment natural law certainly provoked revolutionaries' adversaries and exacerbated tension in Europe. They also promoted federative projects not unlike those of Penn and Saint-Pierre, such as the one contained in the 1795 'Declaration of the Law of Nations' by the *abbé* Henri Grégoire (1750–1831). Martens, the German cataloguer of treaties who recognized shared values in European international society, felt however that Grégoire's proposal was too vague and unworkable as an expression of law, should France ever endeavour to impose it on others. More importantly, he recognized much of it as a reversion to natural law, of the Enlightenment variety, and worried it would jeopardize state sovereignty and destabilize international relations according to the Westphalian – and thereby Grotian – model.[118] Enlightenment and Grotian natural law were clearly at odds in this tumultuous period.

Another more famous proposal for the reformation of European international society also appeared in 1795 – Kant's 'Perpetual Peace: A Philosophical Sketch.'[119] Kant rejected Hobbesian all-out war and, although he inherited from the Grotian tradition uneasiness with moral or metaphysical absolutes, his answer was toleration.[120] The proposal appealed to many revolutionaries although it, too, was never to be realistically endeavoured.[121]

The true effects of Enlightenment natural law on the French Revolution and the European system at the time were therefore much subtler than these dramatic pronouncements and proposals, which ultimately came to little in practice. However, Enlightenment natural law's actual ramification were not insignificant. The idea of a sovereign people as opposed to monarch, which

117 Camille Desmoulins, *Révolutions de France et de Brabant*, cited in Pierre Gaxotte, *The French Revolution*, trans. Walter Alison Phillips (London, 1932), p. 188.

118 Blom, pp. 136–37.

119 Immanuel Kant, *Political Writings*, Hans Reiss, ed., H. B. Nisbet, trans., 2nd ed. (1795; repr., Cambridge: Cambridge University Press, 1991), pp. 93–115.

120 Tuck, *Rights of War and Peace*, p. 213.

121 Ibid., pp. 220–22.

developed from Rousseauian social contract theory, is a hallmark of the French Revolution.[122] The proposition that this sovereign people is legally empowered to take control of the state, reform it, and enunciate its new form in a written constitution was justifiable only through Enlightenment natural law – that is, through a belief in the self-evident merits or morality of this project rather than in any other source law, as opponents of the French Revolution from Burke to Bentham would challenge.[123] The usurpation of control from a traditional, monarchical sovereign by the people, based on the virtue of popular government, is another way to think about the legal transformation of this period, rather than transition from natural to positive law. Indeed, there are similarities between the two purported shifts. The Dutch legal theorist Hugo Krabbe (1857–1936) posited that before the French Revolution, 'authority' was the source of law. This respect for conventional power structures and the codification of public instruments and treaties was fully in keeping with Grotian natural law. According to Krabbe, starting in 1789, something he termed 'legal conscience' became the new source of law. In his view, this change was made possible by the instantiation of the principle of popular sovereignty and representative government.[124] The rise of mass, popular 'conscience' – written in people's hearts? – in place of formal sources of traditional 'authority' might be one of Enlightenment natural law's greatest legacies. It might not, also, be very different from what Bentham derisively called the 'sentiments' of the 'great multitude.'

The Grotian principle of the freedom and autonomy of states continued to be important in international law for centuries to come. It was encapsulated, for example, in the famous if now slightly antiquated judgment in the *Lotus* case:

> International law governs relations between independent States. The rules of law binding upon States therefore emanate from their own free will as expressed in conventions or by usages generally accepted as expressing principles of law and established in order to regulate the relations between these co-existing independent communities or with a view to the achievement of common aims. Restrictions upon the independence of States cannot therefore be presumed.[125]

---

122 See, again, Rousseau's 1762 *On the Social Contract.*

123 See Pamela Edwards, in his volume in chapter eleven, on Burke and especially the relationship between the state of nature and British political thought.

124 Hugo Krabbe, 'L'idée modern de l'état' in *Recueil de l'Académie de droit international* III (1926): 559.

125 'Lotus', Judgment No 9, 1927, PCIJ, Ser A, No 10.

Enlightenment natural law has also persisted – in spite of Bentham's great assault, and seeming victory – and not only in the form of representative democracy according to Krabbe's analysis. For example, modern discussions of universal precepts of justice, such as by the Non-Aligned Movement and Group of 77 states, recall Enlightenment natural law.[126] According to E. H. Carr of the 'English School' of international relations theorists, Hobbesian anarchy notwithstanding, 'The historical tendency of nineteenth century thought … gave [natural law] a new direction' and, indeed, in the twentieth century 'natural law has resumed its sway, and theories of international law have become more markedly utopian than at any previous time.'[127] Like some of the 'sensualist' critiques of the Enlightenment, Carr argues that law cannot be founded on some universal, timeless standard; it is derived from the ethics of its time.[128] Likewise, James Leslie Brierly, (1881–1955) the British jurist and renowned authority on international law, made a case for relativism: natural law 'is always, and above all in the sphere of human conduct, relative to conditions of time and place.'[129] Both Carr and Brierly quote the German legal philosopher Rudolf Stammler (1856–1938) and the proposition that a pervasive feature of the modern paradigm is 'natural law with a variable content' – all of which suggests the survival if not triumph of Enlightenment natural law.[130] The simultaneous existence of Grotian and Enlightenment natural law therefore continues to this day.

Select Bibliography

Primary Sources

Diderot, Denis and Jean le Rond d'Alembert, eds. *Encyclopédie, ou dictionnaire raisonné des sciences, des arts et des métiers*. Le Breton, etc., 1751–66.

Dumont, J. *Corps universel diplomatique de Droit des gens ; contenant un recueil des traitez …* 7 Vols. (Amsterdam: P. Brunel, 1726).

Grotius, Hugo. *De iure praedae commentarius*. (Oxford: Clarendon Press, 1950).

126 Bull, Kingsbury, and Roberts, *Hugo Grotius and International Relations*, p. 3.

127 Edward Hallett Carr, *The Twenty Years' Crisis, 1919–1939: An Introduction to the Study of International Relations* (London: Macmillan, 1962), p. 174.

128 Ibid., p. 175.

129 J. L. Brierly, *The Law of Nations: An Introduction to the International Law of Peace*, 6th ed. (Oxford: Oxford University Press, 1963), p. 21.

130 Carr, p. 174; Brierly, p. 22. The idea and terminology come from Stammler's *Lehre von dem richtigen Rechte* (The Theory of Justice), pp. 1902–7.

Krabbe, Hugo. 'L'idée modern de l'état.' *Recueil de l'Académie de droit international* III (1926): 509–583.

Vattel, Emmerich de. *The Law of Nations or the Principles of Natural Law Applied to the Conduct and to the Affairs of Nations and States.* (Washington: Carnegie, 1916).

Secondary Sources

Baker, Keith Michael and Peter Hanns Reill, eds. *What's Left of Enlightenment? A Postmodern Question.* (Stanford: Stanford University Press, 2001).

Bull, Hedley, Benedict Kingsbury, and Adam Roberts, eds. *Hugo Grotius and International Relations.* (Oxford: Oxford University Press, 1992).

Daston, Lorraine and Michael Stolleis, eds. *Natural law and laws of nature in early modern Europe: jurisprudence, theology, moral and natural philosophy.* (Ashgate: Farnham, 2008).

Koselleck, Reinhart. *Critique and Crisis: Enlightenment and the Pathogenesis of Modern Society.* (Cambridge, Mass.: MIT Press, 1988).

Tuck, Richard. *The Rights of War and Peace: Political Thought and the International Order from Grotius to Kant.* (Oxford: Oxford University Press, 1999).

CHAPTER 10

From Natural Equality to *Frankpledge*

The State of Nature, Ancient Constitutionalism, and the Rupture of the Social Contract in Eighteenth-Century Antislavery Writings

Sarah Winter

Abstract

Antislavery writers Anthony Benezet, Granville Sharp, Thomas Clarkson, Quobna Cugoano, and Olaudah Equiano employ theories of the state of nature to demonstrate how slavery ruptures the social contract in both African polities and the British colonies, thus undermining the legitimacy of the British imperial constitution. Describing African societies as civilized and self-governing, Benezet's approach launches abolitionism's appeals to humanitarian sentiments. Clarkson theorizes how enslavement situates Africans in a state of nature where they are 'perfectly free and equal' in relation to Europeans who attack them. Sharp offers legalistic reasons for abolition based in biblical sources, common law, ancient constitutionalism, and radical democratic thought. His proposed constitution for a 'free settlement' of emancipated Blacks at Sierra Leone reconstructs their rights through equal property shares and the Anglo-Saxon *frankpledge*, a system of collective government and self-defence. Former slaves Cugoano and Equiano describe their experiences of kidnapping from Africa, evoking a state of nature represented by the innocence of childhood – shattered when slave merchants raided their families' homes. These alternative state of nature approaches to abolitionism envision the regeneration of Britons' moral sentiments through collective political action and forge representative notions of 'human rights' as legal rights distinct from natural law. Equiano's and Cugoano's texts demonstrate a more sceptical, antiracist strand of reasoning that questions whether the economic interests underpinning Atlantic slavery are amenable to political or moral reform.

Keywords

eighteenth-century antislavery writing – ancient constitutionalism – Sierra Leone settlement – Granville Sharp – Thomas Clarkson – Anthony Benezet – Olaudah Equiano – Quobna Ottobah Cugoano

 DOI:10.1163/9789004499621_012

1 Introduction

Between the 1750s and 1780s, three early antislavery writers, Anthony Benezet (1713–1784), Granville Sharp (1735–1813), and Thomas Clarkson (1760–1846) published influential tracts arguing that enslavement violates Africans' natural liberty, as upheld by natural law.[1] Although they all assume that the natural state of mankind must be one of equality, freedom, and cooperation rather than a Hobbesian struggle of all against all, theories of the state of nature play differing, often implicit roles in their writings. Conceptions of the social contract, based in biblical and classical sources or derived from theories of natural law and English common law maxims, underpin their arguments that the slave trade and the unlawful regime of colonial slavery violate innocent Africans' natural rights and must be abolished. While explicit references to theorists such as Hugo Grotius (1583–1645), Samuel Pufendorf (1632–1694), Charles-Louis de Secondat, Baron de Montesquieu (1689–1755), Francis Hutcheson (1694–1746), and William Blackstone (1723–1780), appear in their texts, more frequently these writers rely on evidence grounded in actual practices of the slave trade and colonial plantation system to indict the coercion, and thus the absence of consent, that undermine any basis for a valid social contract in slaveholding regimes.

When examined in light of explicit or implicit state of nature theories, early antislavery arguments also reveal a common assumption that the slave trade ruptures the social contract both in African polities and in Britain and its colonies, thus undermining the legitimacy of the imperial constitution and requiring far-reaching legal, political, moral, and social reforms to restore it. In different ways, all of these reformist writers depict colonial slaveholding societies as perpetrating a regime of localized and domesticated petty tyranny that encourages slaveholders' impunity, leading them to violate promises and contracts and commit aggressive acts ranging from theft to sexual assault and murder. On the imperial level, this vacuum of political legitimacy extends through the slave trade's onslaught into a virtual state of war against African societies. While Benezet's writings focus on defending Africans from unjust attacks on their capacity for ordered government, Clarkson's publications deploy an explicit theory of human equality in the state of nature to prove that human liberty by definition can never be bought or sold, and that consent to such purchase is impossible. For Benezet and Clarkson, incursions by Europeans

1 My thanks to Benjamin Straumann for helpful responses to an initial draft of this chapter, and to Wayne Franklin for his suggestions concerning early American antislavery writers.

and their agents into African kingdoms to capture slaves provoke a return to the state of nature and natural equality, rendering Africans innocent victims of an assault on their natural rights. Sharp's writings are the most concerned with legal remedies for slavery of the three, and provide an alternative, constitutionalist framework for restoring the social contract in both Britain and its colonies. Sharp's early publications focus on overthrowing slavery by means of the common law and the English courts. He also seems to have considered the ancient Anglo-Saxon constitution as a resource for every sort of egalitarian political reform. For example, he recommended to Benjamin Franklin (1706–1790) that the newly independent United States institute *gavelkind*, by which inheritances would be shared equally among heirs, principally sons but potentially including daughters, thus promoting equal distribution of property by eliminating primogeniture.[2] Likewise, his detailed plan for a 'free settlement' (rather than a colony served by a chartered trading company) founded for liberated Africans in Sierra Leone was a paternalistic, ancient constitutionalist scheme through which he attempted to institute a social contract based in natural human equality that would abolish most distinctions of wealth, race, and rank. Sharp's key reform was the adoption of 'the ancient English *frank-pledge*', or a system of collective government and self-defence by means of militias, which he viewed as a 'glorious Patriarchal system', and 'the only effectual antidote to unlimited or illegal government of any kind'.[3]

In contrast, the antislavery writings of two Afro-British former slaves, Olaudah Equiano (b. 1745, Essaka, Benin, now Nigeria, d. 1797) and Quobna Ottobah Cugoano (b. circa 1757, Agimaque, Fantyn, now Ghana), reveal the complicity of the wider British public in the legally sanctioned violence of the slave trade and the plantation system. Their personal narratives describing their kidnapping and enslavement evoke a state of nature represented by the innocence of childhood – shattered when African agents of European slave merchants raided their homes. While they supported the abolitionist cause, both Cugoano's and Equiano's texts also indict British imperial governance by exposing the rampant property interests and transactional notions of freedom, based in commercial calculations, that pervaded colonial slaveholding societies.

2 Benjamin Franklin, letter to Granville Sharp, 5 July 1785, in Prince Hoare, *Memoirs of Granville Sharp, Esq. composed from his own manuscripts, and other authentic documents in the possession of his family and of the African Institution: with observations on Mr. Sharp's biblical criticisms* (London, 1820), p. 250.

3 Granville Sharp, letter to Dr. Lettsom, M. D., 13 October 1788, in Hoare, *Memoirs of Granville Sharp*, pp. 315–20. All emphases and capitalization in original unless otherwise noted.

Early British antislavery writings have been carefully analysed for their conceptual and propagandistic roles in a humanitarian political reform campaign, but it is also important to discern the political and legal philosophies incorporated into these works.[4] All five writers share a sense of Christian mission that infuses their political aims with personal and collective spiritual goals. But nuances among their religious perspectives are not the primary focus here. Instead, this chapter studies what Mark Somos has called the analytical dimensions of state of nature theories, that is, the way such theories enabled writers to pursue political, legal, and moral arguments without postulating that an actual state of nature had existed historically.[5] These early writers' evocations of the state of nature reveal three interwoven but distinct political reformist arguments that would come to characterize the Anglo-American abolitionist movement. Benezet's approach, developed by Clarkson, launches abolitionism's appeals to humanitarian sentiments, based in Scottish Enlightenment notions of an innate moral sense possessed by all human beings, often referred to as the conscience. Sharp's writings feature legalistic arguments for slave emancipation and abolition of the slave trade, based in English statutes and legal authorities, and radical democratic thought. Although he frequently warned both officials and the public of the divine retribution that Britain would face for the iniquity of slavery, Sharp did not rely on sentimental appeals to sway readers. These alternative approaches would provide for British abolitionism a twofold framework of argumentation featuring individually-based moral regeneration collectivized through political action, on the one hand, and representative notions of 'human rights' as legal and political rights distinct from natural law, on the other. Equiano and Cugoano each reinforced these potential solutions while adopting the practical idea, advocated by Benezet and Clarkson, that the slave trade should be replaced by a mutually beneficial commerce between British merchants and African states. But their writings also put forward a third strand of state of nature reasoning that is more sceptical, overtly antiracist, and potentially radical by calling into question whether the entrenched economic interests underpinning slavery are amenable to political or moral reform.

---

4 For an extended analysis of the political morality of British abolitionism, see Christopher Leslie Brown, *Moral Capital: Foundations of British Abolitionism* (Chapel Hill: University of North Carolina Press, 2006).

5 Mark Somos, *American States of Nature: The Origins of Independence, 1761–1775* (New York: Oxford University Press, 2019), p. 7.

2 Natural Rights, Common Law, and the Social Contract in Benezet, Sharp, and Clarkson

Antislavery activists in the mid-eighteenth century initiated the international abolitionist movement by accusing those who sold and purchased slaves of unnatural and barbarous crimes against humanity, such as mass murder and human trafficking. Accounts of wars among African polities fomented by Europeans, as well as kidnappings, torture, massacres, assaults, and violations of the natural and legal rights of Africans pervade two early, influential eighteenth-century Anglo-American antislavery tracts, Philadelphia Quaker Anthony Benezet's *A Short Account of that Part of Africa Inhabited by the Negroes* (1762) and Granville Sharp's *A Representation of the Injustice and Dangerous Tendency of Tolerating Slavery in England* (1769). For both writers, colonial slavery is an immoral and un-Christian regime of legalized violence that must be exposed in order to incite public outrage and provoke official accountability and action toward abolition. Benezet opens his tract by considering how the 'Weakness and Corruption' of human nature render the passions of 'Covetousness and Pride' into powerful counterforces against conscience, so that with the reinforcement of custom and the corrupting example of others, amplified by self-interest and the 'Love of Gain', Anglo-Americans 'reconcile ourselves' to slavery's cruelties.[6] Benezet reveals his source for this formulation when he later quotes Hutcheson's account in his *System of Moral Philosophy* (1755) of the unlawfulness of slavery because 'each man is the Possessor of his own Liberty'. Contrary to classical Greek and Roman conceptions of slavery, Hutcheson argues that sparing the life of someone captured in war gives no man title to 'make him a Slave and sell him as a Piece of Goods', or to keep a man's wife and children in perpetuity as slaves, an act that is 'most unjust and inhuman'. Hutcheson also highlights how the combined power of custom and the 'high Prospects of Gain so stupefy the Conscience of Men, and all Sense of natural Justice' that they can learn to accept enslaving others, even within Christian states that value individual liberty.[7] Benezet may have considered Hutcheson as a pivotal authority for rejecting the enslavement of defeated enemies as a right of conquest held by such natural law theorists as Grotius and Pufendorf and echoed by later proslavery theorists.[8]

6 Anthony Benezet, *A Short Account of that Part of Africa Inhabited by the Negroes*, 2nd edn. (Philadelphia, 1762), pp. 3–4.

7 Francis Hutcheson, *A System of Moral Philosophy*, vol. 2 (Glasgow, 1755), pp. 210–11, 85; qtd. in Benezet, *Short Account*, pp. 34–5.

8 See Wylie Sypher, 'Hutcheson and the "Classical" Theory of Slavery', *The Journal of Negro History*, 24, no. 3 (July 1939), pp. 263–80.

Benezet also provides evidence from European travellers' accounts testifying to Africans' industriousness, sociability, hospitality to strangers, and the peaceable mutual relations of their various kingdoms. To prove trafficked Africans' innocence in respect to the violence they suffer, Benezet quotes multiple 'Eye-witness' accounts by those involved in the African slave trade to document that 'the *Europeans* are the chief Instruments in inciting the *Negroes* to the perpetration of those unnatural Wars, by which they are kept in continual Alarms, their Country laid waste, and such great numbers carried into Captivity …'.[9] As a result of the 'Tyranny, Oppression, and Cruelty', with which this trade is prosecuted, 'all social Connection and Tender Ties of Nature being broken, Desolation and Bloodshed [are] continually fomented in those unhappy People's Country'.[10] Benezet's use of a state of nature framework to target the slave trade as a rupture of the social contract of African societies becomes evident in his endorsement of a passage quoted from a 1760 antislavery pamphlet defending the natural equality of black-skinned Africans with white-skinned Europeans in Christian terms as 'being all of the same Species', so that

> one Man in a State of Nature, as we are with Respect to the Inhabitants of *Guiney*, and they with Respect to us, is not superior to another man, nor has any Authority or Dominion over him, or any Right to lay his Commands upon him … .[11]

In such a natural law conception, the state of nature that establishes human equality persists as a moral framework supporting all human actions at all times, so that acts of violence leading to the enslavement of other human beings can be clearly seen as a violation of natural rights, regardless of any legal, commercial, or colonial imperatives that might seem to authorize them.

In an expanded version of his text first published in 1771, Benezet discloses the diverse ways of life in what many Anglo-Americans referred to generically as the 'country of Africa' or Guinea through an account of the specific regions and peoples subject to the depredations of the slave trade. He provides further detailed evidence for the civility and resilience of African peoples, such as the Jalofs, Fuli, and Mandingos, living near the major rivers Senegal and Gambia. 'On impartial inquiry', Benezet asserts, 'we shall find that there is scarce a

9 Benezet, *Short Account*, p. 7, 10.
10 Ibid., p. 4, 5.
11 J. Philmore, *Two Dialogues on the Man-Trade* (London, 1760), qtd. in Benezet, *Short Account*, p. 38. See also Somos, *American States of Nature*, p. 315.

country in the whole world, that is better calculated for affording the necessary comforts to its inhabitants, with less solicitude and toil, than Guinea … and that their oeconomy and government is, in many respects, commendable'.[12] For example, drawing on European travel narratives Benezet explains that the Jalof kingdom's judicial system consists of a tiered circuit of judges under a viceroy, or *Kondi*, who together with the chief justice visits the various village courts and examines the performance of the chief magistrates, or *Alkadi*, of each district.[13] Without alluding explicitly to a state of nature theory, Benezet presents African societies as highly civilized and organizationally complex, thus indirectly defending their sovereignty against European slave merchants' incursions.[14]

Sharp's antislavery argument has a much more legalistic basis than Benezet's, and focuses on constitutional questions. His first antislavery publication was written in the context of a lawsuit instigated in 1767 by a slaveowner in London against Sharp and his brother for their attempt to defend the freedom of a fugitive slave, Jonathan Strong. Sharp relies specifically on the protections afforded in the Habeas Corpus Act of 1679 against anyone's being seized and deported from England, asserting, that 'they who kidnap Negroes, are not less guilty in the eye of the law, than those who kidnap white men'.[15] Referring to Montesquieu's attacks in *De l'Esprit des Lois* (1748) upon slavery as not only unjust but unchristian, Sharpe also criticizes the inhumane prejudices of slaveowners, who consider slaves '*as much private property as a horse or a dog*'.[16] While he does not refer to the state of nature, in refuting the legality of slavery Sharp does briefly entertain an analogy between free Africans in their own country and *ferae bestiae*, or wild animals. He asks the reader to '(pardon, for the present, the absurdity of such an idea)', but goes on to consider that Africans before they are enslaved 'had as much right to their *natural liberty* as

12 Anthony Benezet, *Some historical account of Guinea, its situation, produce, and the general disposition of its inhabitants: with an inquiry into the rise and progress of the slave trade, its nature and lamentable effects*, New edn. (London, 1788), p. 2.

13 Ibid., p. 8.

14 On the early modern debates over the legitimacy of imperial conquest and occupation, see Andrew Fitzmaurice, *Sovereignty, Property and Empire 1500–2000* (Cambridge: Cambridge University Press, 2014). See Daniel S. Allemann's chapter in this volume for a discussion of Salamancan theologian Francisco de Vitoria's theory of legitimate conquest by Spain of "unoccupied" lands in the midst of indigenous commonwealths in the Americas.

15 Granville Sharp, *A Representation of the Injustice and Dangerous Tendency of Tolerating Slavery in England; or of Admitting the Least Claim of Private Property in the Persons of Men in England* (London, 1769), p. 27.

16 Ibid., pp. 15–16.

wild animals, with which their native country (Africa) abounds'.[17] Mark Somos has argued that Sharp's reference to *ferae bestiae* (or *ferae naturae*) was 'a weak argument', although it did imply that 'even if they were considered as wild animals, they would be free when not owned, since no one can claim absolute property in them …'.[18] Sharp quickly abandons this line of analysis, however, to dispute the applicability to anyone in England of colonial conceptions of property claimed by slaveholders, asserting that

> the comparing of a man to a beast, at any rate, is unnatural and unjust; as well as the seizing, and detaining him as such, is dangerous to the pretended proprietors. For they cannot be justified, unless they shall be able to prove, that a Negro Slave, is neither man, woman nor child: and if they are not able to do this, how can they presume to consider such a person as a mere *"chose in action"?* or *thing* to be demanded in [legal] action?
>
> The Negro must be divested of his humanity, and rendered incapable of the King's protection, before such an action can lawfully take place.
>
> But how is he to be divested of his *human nature*? or of his just right to the King's protection?[19]

If formerly enslaved Africans, such as Jonathan Strong, are the King's subjects like all others residing in England, and thus have a right to the protection of the law, including habeas corpus if they are unlawfully detained, their human nature becomes not only obvious in their human bodies but also legally certifiable by common law courts, and therefore they cannot be considered as property.[20] Sharp seems to allude once again to the theory of *ferae bestiae*, however, when refers to Pufendorf's stipulation in *Of the Law of Nature and of Nations* (*De jure naturae et gentium*, 1672) to the effect that if an enslaved person is '"thrown into irons or OTHERWISE DEPRIVED OF HIS CORPORAL

17 Ibid., p. 14. See Somos's discussion of this passage in Sharp's text, referencing the state of nature derivations of Blackstone's discussion in Book II of his *Commentaries on the Laws of England* (1766) of *ferae naturae* and other natural resources such as water, light, and air that do not admit of absolute property (*American States of Nature*, pp. 315–18).

18 Somos, *American States of Nature*, p. 317.

19 Sharp, *Representation*, pp. 15–16.

20 Ibid., pp. 26–7. For a detailed analysis of the early legal cases concerning fugitive slaves in England in which Sharp was involved, see Sarah Winter, 'From Procedural Law to the "Rights of Humanity": Habeas Corpus, *Ex parte Somerset* (1771–72), and the Movement toward Collective Representation in Early British Antislavery Cases', in *Empire and Legal Thought: Ideas and Institutions from Antiquity to Modernity*, ed. by Edward Cavanagh (Leiden and Boston: Brill, 2020), pp. 388–424.

LIBERTY" ' without cause by his master, his contract of servitude is dissolved, because ' "his master is supposed to take off his *moral bonds*, by thus imposing *natural*" '.[21] By construing this statement as an admission that slavery's imposition of corporal bondage unlawfully violates natural equality and liberty, Sharp seems to turn Grotian and Pufendorfian state of nature theories to the advantage of his argument, even as he rejects their views that enslavement by contract can be permitted.[22]

Sharp takes particular care to disprove the related notion that a bill of sale for a slave can function as valid labour contract, since

> "*the perpetual service*" of a slave cannot, with propriety, be compared to the temporary service of an apprentice, because the latter is due only in consequence of a *voluntary contract*, wherein both parties have a mutual advantage; but in the former case, there is no contract, neither can a contract be even IMPLIED; because *the free consent of both parties* cannot possibly be IMPLIED likewise; and, without this, every kind of contract (in the very nature and Idea of such an obligation), is absolutely *null and void*.[23]

Since Sharp derives these arguments concerning slavery's disqualification as a contractual obligation from common law sources by Matthew Hale (1609–1676) and Blackstone, we can note the absence of explicit references to the state of nature while discerning that consent and voluntary contract remain key concepts in Sharp's antislavery critique, underpinning his objections to colonial slave regimes.[24]

Sharp was likely drawing on Blackstone's theory of constitutional rights as deriving from natural rights in Book I of his *Commentaries on the Laws of England, Of the Rights of Persons* (1765), which he cites in various parts of his argument.[25] Although Blackstone does not endorse the literal truth of social

---

21 Sharp refers to Book VI, chapter iii, of Pufendorf's *Of the Law of Nature and of Nations*, in *Representation*, pp. 10–11.

22 Sharp, *Representation*, pp. 10–11. In this volume, Emile Simpson shows that Grotius's conception of natural liberty under extra-civil conditions applies only to free persons, and thus allows slavery and other forms of servitude. See also Simone Zurbuchen's chapter on Pufendorf's contractual justifications for slavery and the limitations he places on the master's dominance within this relation.

23 Ibid., pp. 163–64.

24 Ibid., pp. 163–65. Blackstone's revision to the second edition of his *Commentaries on the Laws of England, Book I Of the Rights of Persons* (1768), allowed that a slave, though free in England, might still owe service to a master – a point that Sharp disputed.

25 Sharp, *Representation*, p. 163.

contract theories postulating an 'actually existing unconnected state of nature' prior to all laws, he conceives of society as having a contractual basis: 'every man, when he enters into society, gives up a part of his natural liberty, as the price of so valuable a purchase' of that 'political ... or civil liberty' which is 'infinitely more desirable than that wild and savage liberty which is sacrificed to obtain it'.[26] Nevertheless, municipal or civil law must still safeguard the 'absolute *rights* of individuals', 'such as would belong to their persons merely in a state of nature, and which every man is intitled to enjoy whether out of society or in it'.[27] Expressing the 'natural liberty of mankind', these are absolute rights to 'personal security', or 'a person's legal and uninterrupted enjoyment of his life, his limbs, his body, his health, and his reputation'.[28] Such notions of natural rights as vested in the human body and forming the basis of common law and constitutional rights are implied throughout Sharp's tract, particularly in his repeated disqualifications of colonial slave laws that indemnify slaveholders for inflicting bodily harm, including murder, on their purported human property.

Sharp also provides an inventory and critique of such harsh colonial slave laws to prove that no slave would ever consent to enter into a contract prior to departure for England, or while residing there, requiring return to such a punitive regime.[29] In addition, Sharp demonstrated the obsolescence in England of villeinage and cited the abolition by Parliament of vassalage in Scotland in 1747, to rule out the validity of enslavement annexed to ownership of a particular parcel of land or territory.[30] Sharp shared his tract in draft with eminent lawyers and jurists, including Blackstone, and it became an influential text consulted by antislavery lawyers in the *Ex parte Somerset* decision of 1772.[31] In this famous trial, Chief Justice of King's Bench, William Murray, Lord Mansfield (1705–1793), determined on the basis of a habeas corpus action that English law did not allow a fugitive slave in England, James Somerset, to be deported back to the West Indies and re-enslaved after he was kidnapped and detained by his former master, Charles Stewart.

---

26 William Blackstone, *Commentaries on the Laws of England, Book I Of the Rights of Persons*, edited by David Lemmings, general editor Wilfrid Prest (Oxford: Oxford University Press, 2016), pp. 38, 85.

27 Ibid., p. 36, 84.

28 Ibid., p. 85, 88.

29 Sharp, *Representation*, pp. 42–106.

30 Ibid., pp. 4–5, 107–67.

31 On Blackstone's contacts with Sharp, see also Wilfrid Prest, *William Blackstone: Law and Letters in the Eighteenth Century* (Oxford and New York: Oxford University Press, 2008), pp. 250–53.

Thomas Clarkson used state of nature theories more extensively than Sharp or Benezet. Unlike their independently authored texts, Clarkson's early anti-slavery text originated in an academic setting. After completing his BA in 1783 at St John's, Cambridge, Clarkson decided to become a clergyman. While furthering his religious studies, he entered the Latin prize competition in 1785 in response to the set topic 'Anne liceat invitos in servitutem dare?' or 'Is it lawful to enslave the unconsenting?'. Clarkson's prize-winning essay focusing on the African slave trade was translated into English and published as *An Essay on the Slavery and Commerce of the Human Species, Particularly the African* in 1786. A second enlarged edition (studied here) followed in 1788 that answered doubts concerning the accuracy of his first edition by providing more detailed documentation of the Atlantic commerce in slaves carried out by British merchants, based in Clarkson's personal research, including inspecting slave ships and interviewing their crews and other participants in the trade.[32] Clarkson's treatise is explicitly focused on recuperating imperial governance by ending the slave trade. In the first part, Clarkson draws on many Greek and Latin sources to recount how the ancient slavery of the Greeks and Romans was introduced as a practice derived from commerce; buying and selling human beings as property, like cattle, led to considering the enslaved as inferior brutes or barbarians.[33] Referring to Aristotle's disparaging characterization of barbarians in the *Politics*, 'so low were their capacities, they were *defined* by nature to *obey*, and to live in a state of perpetual drudgery and subjugation', Clarkson criticizes this notion of the natural slave often endorsed by proslavery writers.[34] To show the mere 'vanity' of the Greeks' assertion of their '*natural* right to dominion' over barbarians, he offers examples of celebrated ancient writers who were born slaves, including Aesop, Alcman, Epectetus, and Terence.[35]

Clarkson applies state of nature theories to African societies under siege by slave traders in the second part of his treatise, which also surveys conditions of enslavement within African societies. Pointing to both biblical and classical sources, Clarkson asserts, 'It appears that mankind were originally free, and that they possessed an equal right to the soil and produce of the

32 Thomas Clarkson, *An Essay on the Slavery and Commerce of the Human Species, Particularly the African; Translated from a Latin Dissertation, which was Honoured with the First Prize in the University of Cambridge for the Year 1785; the Second Edition, Revised and Considerably Enlarged* (London: J. Phillips, 1788); in *Thomas Clarkson and Ottobah Cugoano: Essays on the Slavery and Commerce of the Human Species*, ed. by Mary-Antoinette Smith (Peterborough, Ontario, Canada: Broadview, 2010), pp. 68–9.

33 Ibid., pp. 85–86.

34 Ibid., p. 87.

35 Ibid., pp. 88–90.

earth'.[36] To explain 'the history of modern servitude' in the context of the rise of empires, he relies on a stadial conception of history from Roman historians such as Sallust and Tacitus to chart an exit from the state of nature. He draws an analogy between Franco-Germanic tribes during the Roman empire, whose way of life exhibited a state of settled 'subordinate society', and contemporary African nations, in order to make the case that a leader could only emerge by consent of the group because no individual could truly dominate all others by force alone:

> An *empire* then could never have been gained at first by *compulsion*, so it could only be gained by *consent*; and as men were then going to make an important sacrifice [of their original freedom and equality], for the sake of their *mutual* happiness, so he alone could have obtained it, (not whose *ambition* had greatly distinguished him from the rest) but in whose *wisdom, justice, prudence, and virtue*, the whole community could confide.[37]

Clarkson draws the conclusion that '*liberty* is a *natural*, and government an *adventitious* right, because all men were originally free', so that legitimate government must be based in a contract, 'subject to various restrictions', the central purpose of which is 'the *happiness* of the people'. Because all possess their own bodies as a natural right, 'no just man can be justly consigned to *slavery* without his own *consent*'.[38] A just empire is based in consent of the governed, so a ruler or agent of empire who deprives anyone of liberty without their consent has violated the contract underpinning imperial rule, rendering it illegitimate because incapable of guaranteeing general happiness.

At this point in his state of nature analysis, however, Clarkson shifts African peoples from their position within his stadial account, where they exist in a state of subordination in relation to expanding European empires, into a theoretical state of nature where their natural rights as individuals are violated by a commercial conquest that perpetrates an unjust and fabricated 'right of empire' upon them, by attempting to render them into property:

> But if kings then, to whom their own people have granted dominion and power, are unable to invade the liberties of their harmless subjects, without the highest *injustice*; how can those private persons [slave merchants] be justified, who treacherously lie in wait for their fellow-creatures, and

36 Ibid., p. 119.
37 Ibid., pp. 122–23.
38 Ibid., p. 124.

> sell them into slavery? What arguments can they possibly bring in their defence? What treaty of empire can they produce, by which their innocent victims ever resigned to them the least portion of their *liberty*? ... Impious and abandoned men! ye invade the liberties of those, who, (with respect to your impious selves) are in a state of *nature*, in a state of original *dissociation*, perfectly *independent*, perfectly *free*.[39]

The slave merchant, therefore, 'acts surely, as if the use of empire consisted in violence and oppression ...'.[40] As Benezet had argued, the slave traders' assaults on Africans in order to enslave them reconstitutes a state of nature in which Africans must be considered as 'perfectly free' and equal to their attackers, and therefore entitled to defend themselves. By placing the enslaved Africans theoretically outside any government, however, Clarkson also detaches slavery and the slave trade from imperial rule itself, making these adventitious commercial ventures an inhumane and unlawful aberration, and one that can and must be excised from British imperial governance. Clarkson's theoretical state of nature argument combined with his stadial, historical account demonstrate that an externally imposed property right over human beings is unnatural, and therefore unjust and politically illegitimate.

Clarkson's account of Africans' human equality and innocence of any wrong in a state of nature undermined common arguments among proslavery writers, such as the Jamaica planter, Edward Long (1734–1813), in his three-volume *History of Jamaica* (1774), that slaves obtained from Africa for the colonial plantations were not kidnapped, but instead were condemned criminals, captives in African wars, or enslaved persons resold by other Africans, or 'sold by their brutal parents, or husbands'.[41] Long, whose works Clarkson could have read though does not cite, alludes to the theory of the natural slave by arguing that 'as the Africans are naturally thieves and villains, though slavery is the certain punishment now on their conviction, the breaking up of the slave trade might indeed alter the punishment to that of death, but would not reform them'.[42] By dismissing the possibility of reforming condemned Africans morally, Long not only justifies the slave trade but also forecloses the antislavery argument that the violence of colonial slavery delegitimises the British empire and

39 Ibid., p. 127.

40 Ibid., pp. 126–27.

41 Edward Long, *The History of Jamaica. Or General Survey of the Antient and Modern State of that Island, with Reflections on its Situation, Settlements, Inhabitants, Climate, Produce, Commerce, Laws, and Government*, vol. 2 (London, 1775), p. 388.

42 Ibid., p. 391.

necessitates its reform. Long even claims that, despite the deaths due to disease and harsh discipline that regularly take place among Africans on slave ships, deportation to the colonial plantations still amounts to rescue from certain execution.[43] He also defends the use of shackles and other harsh measures on slave ships due to the danger of slave mutinies: 'this rigor [is] wholly chargeable on their bloody and malicious disposition, which calls for the same confinement as if they were wolves or wild boars'.[44] For the overtly racist Long, considering Africans as *ferae bestiae* justifies their harsh treatment as a kind of property.

Possibly alluding to proslavery arguments such as Long's, Clarkson also considers slave rebellions in a contractual light. He attacks the injustice of colonial slaveholders' characterizations of Africans as naturally criminal and rebellious:

> If then [these enslaved Africans] are your subjects, you violate laws of government, by making them unhappy. But if they are not your subjects, then, even though they should resist your proceedings, they are not *rebellious*.[45]

Pointing to the slaveholding system as a form of tyranny, Clarkson once again leaves a back door open for legitimate rule to re-emerge in colonial legal systems if slavery could be eliminated and formerly enslaved Africans could be treated as free subjects. In the background of this formulation, there is perhaps a notion of a right to rebellion against despotic rule, as theorized by John Locke (1632–1704) in Chapter 19 of his *Second Treatise on Government* (1689–90), despite Locke's somewhat restricted acceptance of the Grotian just war theory of slavery.[46] For slaves, then, such a right would more emphatically exist because they never consented to the unjust and abusive rule of colonial slaveholders, and before that, their existing social contracts in Africa had been disrupted by the slave trade. If any allusions to Lockean political theory are present in Clarkson's text, it may be that he does not mention Locke by name due to an awareness of his role in the drafting of the *Fundamental Constitutions*

---

43 Ibid., p. 399.

44 Ibid., p. 397.

45 Clarkson, *Essay on the Slavery and Commerce of the Human Species*, p. 176.

46 James Farr points out that Locke did not follow Grotius in giving the victor the power to enslave the wives and children of defeated aggressors, 'Locke, Natural Law, and New World Slavery', *Political Theory* 36, no. 4 (August 2008), pp. 502–4. Ioannis Evrigenis's analysis in this volume would support the idea that Clarkson's state of nature theorizing was influenced by Locke's *Second Treatise*. See also Simone Zurbuchen's chapter on Locke's denial that slavery could be contractual.

of Carolina (1669), in which the master's absolute authority over his slaves was upheld.[47]

In consequence of this reasoning, the reconstituted state of nature also exists on the plantations, entitling enslaved Africans to resist their bondage. Clarkson demands of colonial slaveholders, 'But who are you, that have this exclusive charter of trading in the liberties of mankind?' and again insists that slaves 'have a right to resist your proceedings':

> It is not your money, that can invest you with a right. Human liberty can neither be bought nor sold. Every lash that you give them is unjust. It is a lash against nature and religion, and will surely stand recorded against you since they are all, with respect to your *impious* selves, in a state of nature; in a state of original dissociation; perfectly free.[48]

A legal bill of sale is no substitute for the political legitimacy arising from a just social contract based in consent of the governed. Clarkson's state of nature theorizing thus seems to recognize the ways that colonial slave codes allowed for an excessive dominion of masters over their slaves that would not be acceptable under the common law of England, as Sharp had studied in more detail in his early publications. Clarkson's reference to slave ownership as an 'exclusive charter' alludes both to the exclusive royal charters granted to colonial companies through which the plantation system was organized in North America and the West Indies, and to the Royal African Company, founded in 1660 and rechartered in 1672 as a slave trading enterprise with military powers. Jonathan A. Bush has analysed the 'passive, almost stealthy process of legal accommodation' by which the practice of slavery in the West Indian and American colonies was legalized in the context of the common law's silence on slave status, so that the imperial constitution became, in effect, permissive by default.[49] Bush explains that because colonies were originally dominions governed under royal prerogative, and either 'annexed to the crown or granted to lords proprietary', and did not come under the authority of Parliament or the

---

47 On Locke's reputation in the eighteenth century as a supporter of slavery, see Farr, 'Locke, Natural Law, and New World Slavery', pp. 508–12. On Locke's evolving position concerning slavery, see Holly Brewer 'Slavery, Sovereignty, and "Inheritable Blood": Reconsidering John Locke and the Origins of American Slavery', *American Historical Review* 122, no. 4 (October 2017), pp. 1038–78.

48 Clarkson, *Essay on the Slavery and Commerce of the Human Species*, pp. 212–13.

49 Jonathan A. Bush, 'The British Constitution and the Creation of American Slavery', in *Slavery and the Law*, ed. by Paul Finkelman (Madison, Wisconsin: Madison House, 1997), p. 379.

English common law, colonial slaveholders were able to design local laws governing slavery that became constitutional law in the colonies, thus garnering 'full legal protection' for slavery.[50] For Clarkson, then, contending that enslaved Africans in the colonies have reverted to a state of nature postulated a blank slate, within which punitive colonial slave laws that were widely understood by abolitionists to violate English law could be rendered null and void, so that British constitutional norms could be reinserted into the colonies by the abolition of the slave trade. Invoking feelings of 'indignation', followed by 'tear[s] of sympathy' and 'sigh[s] of commiseration' in contemplating the vast scale of human suffering of the '*nine millions*' of Africans 'torn from their dearest connections, and sold into slavery', Clarkson amplified the impact of his state of nature theory by appealing to his readers' innate moral sentiments, considered equally as 'a genuine production of nature'.[51]

3 'Conveyed to a State of Horror and Slavery': Cugoano and Equiano

For the former slaves Cugoano and Equiano, Africa was a homeland from which they had been abducted and deported. Both of them advertise the authenticity of their narratives as 'written by an African'. Yet their accounts confirm in certain ways what Benezet's and Clarkson's uses of state of nature theory revealed about the slave trade's violation of the social contract in Africa. Cugoano and Equiano (who also used the name Gustavus Vassa that he had been given as a slave), were both members of the Sons of Africa, an abolitionist group of educated free Blacks residing in London and allied with the Society for Effecting the Abolition of the Slave Trade, which included both Clarkson and Sharp. Both abolitionist groups were established in 1787, with their separate organizations suggesting a segregation of members by colour and class, but also a distinctive development of Black British political activism.[52] Published in the immediate context of these organizational efforts, Cugoano's *Thoughts and Sentiments of the Evil and Wicked Traffic of the Slavery and Commerce of the Human Species, Humbly Submitted to The Inhabitants of Great Britain* (1787) opens with an expression of gratitude toward other antislavery writers; he refers to Benezet's, Clarkson's and Sharp's work, as well as to other contemporary antislavery

50 Ibid., p. 381.

51 Clarkson, *Essay on the Slavery and Commerce of the Human Species*, p. 143.

52 For further analysis of Black antislavery radicalism, see Ryan Hanley, *Beyond Slavery and Abolition: Black British Writing c. 1770–1830* (Cambridge: Cambridge University Press, 2019), ch. 7.

texts. But Cugoano distinguishes his contribution by implying that his personal experience of enslavement is reflected in his discourse. He claims that such laws as may exist among 'the robbers of men, the kidnappers, ensnarers and slave-holders' prove nothing more than 'that there may be some honesty among thieves', admitting that 'This may seem a harsh comparison, but the parallel is so coincident that, I must say, I can find no other way of expressing my Thoughts and Sentiments, without making use of some harsh words and comparisons against the carriers on of such abandoned wickedness'.[53] Cugoano ties his radical attack on slave traffickers directly to the violence they have committed against him.

Cugoano pursues his biting, Christian polemic by undermining European hypocrisy and the prejudicial ways that moral associations assigned symbolically in religious discourse to whiteness and blackness have been applied to skin colour.[54] In referring to the men who kidnapped him to sell him into slavery, he leaves their origins, whether African or European, ambiguous:

> [I]f such men can boast of greater degrees of knowledge, than any African is entitled to, I shall let them enjoy all the advantages of it unenvied, as I fear it consists only in a greater share of infidelity, and that of a blacker kind than only skin deep. And if their complexion be not what I may suppose, it is at least the nearest in resemblance to an infernal hue. A good man will neither speak nor do as a bad man will; but if a man is bad, it makes no difference whether he be a black or a white devil.
>
> By some of such complexion, as whether black or white it matters not, I was early snatched away from my native country, with about eighteen or twenty more boys and girls, as we were playing in a field.[55]

The scene of Cugoano's kidnapping, while presented as autobiographical and therefore factual, has been abstracted somewhat by the omission of certain details such as the identity of the kidnappers. In the context of the other

53 Ottobah Cugoano, *Thoughts and Sentiments of the Evil and Wicked Traffic of the Slavery and Commerce of the Human Species, Humbly Submitted to The Inhabitants of* Great Britain, *by Ottobah Cugoano, A Native of Africa* (London, 1787), in *Thomas Clarkson and Ottobah Cugoano: Essays on the Slavery and Commerce of the Human Species*, edited by Mary-Antoinette Smith, p. 229.

54 See also Roxann Wheeler, '"Betrayed by Some of My Own Complexion": Cugoano, Abolition, and the Contemporary Language of Racialism', in *Genius in Bondage: Literature of the Early Black Atlantic*, ed. by Vincent Carretta and Philip Gould (Lexington: University Press of Kentucky, 2001), pp. 17–38.

55 Cugoano, *Thoughts and Sentiments*, pp. 229–30.

abolitionists' state of nature theorizing, the passage seems biblically inspired, representing an emblematic setting of a peaceful, Edenic natural state, where African children's innocence and their natural rights are violated by devils in human form.

As Cugoano pursues his narrative, however, after mentioning his birth in the city of Agimaque, located on the coast of Fantyn, and his father's status as a companion to a Fantee chief, he reveals that his abductors were Africans, who separated the children into smaller groups, tricked them into compliance by promising to take them to a feast, and then transferred them to men 'whose language differed from ours'. As he continued to travel with these men, he was repeatedly promised that he would be returned to his family, but instead he was conveyed to a coastal 'castle' or slave factory, where he joined many other imprisoned captives, and he was ultimately transferred to a slave ship bound for Grenada. Declining to describe 'all the horrible scenes which we saw, and the base treatment which we met with in this dreadful captive situation', cruelties afflicting thousands of other enslaved Africans, Cugoano recurs to his initial depiction of the peaceful scene of his entrapment:

> Let it suffice to say, that I was thus lost to my dear indulgent parents and relations, and they to me. All my help was cries and tears, and these could not avail; nor suffered long, till one succeeding woe, and dread, swelled up another. Brought from a state of innocence and freedom, and, in a barbarous and cruel manner, conveyed to a state of horror and slavery: This abandoned situation may be easier conceived than described.[56]

Communicating the powerful grief of an abducted child and his bereft parents through the language of moral sentiments shared with Benezet and Clarkson, Cugoano strengthens the abolitionist argument that Africans are forced from a state of natural equality and freedom into a state of bondage. But he also adds an admission 'to the shame of my own countrymen, that I was first kidnapped and betrayed by some of my own complexion, who were the first cause of my exile and slavery', stipulating 'but if there were no buyers there would be no sellers'.[57] Like Benezet's accusation that Europeans have brought mass murder, human trafficking, and wars to Africa, Cugoano's bitter personal account, despite his gratitude for his conversion to Christianity, shows that no natural innocence beyond that of childhood can survive in the regions of Africa

56 Ibid., pp. 230–33.
57 Ibid., p. 234.

penetrated by the slave trade or in the colonial plantations supported by 'the great and opulent banditti of slaveholders in the western part of the world'.[58]

Cugoano vigorously defends the natural rights of enslaved Africans, and asserts that they 'are born as free, and are brought up with as great a predilection for their own country, freedom and liberty, as the sons and daughters of fair Britain'.[59] He alludes to the universality of a social contract in all countries, linking it with the biblical golden rule to argue that 'a free, voluntary, and sociable servitude, which is the very basis of human society, either civil or religious, … is in all things requisite and agreeable to all law and justice'.[60] Both the slave's resistance to being bought and sold 'without his own consent', and a punishment of the robber of freedom by enslaving him in turn are just retributions for slavery's violence, according to Cugoano.[61] But he also wonders more radically what sort of 'revolution' will finally defeat slavery, whether a voluntary dissolution followed by the slaveholders' making 'restitution for the injuries that they have already done', or a divine vengeance, resulting in the 'destruction and overthrow of the transgressors'.[62] In the context of his attack on the greed and profits driving the slave trade, Cugoano's notion of restitution envisions financial as well as legal compensation to those unlawfully trafficked and exploited. Pointing out that commercial relations and colonial settlements could have been established with other nations peacefully by treaty, he also condemns the 'barbarous inhuman Europeans' for their treatment of the 'various Indian nations', stating 'as a certain general fact, that all their foreign settlements and colonies were founded on murders and devastations, and that they have continued their depredations in cruel slavery and oppression to this day', thus rendering their empires illegitimate products of conquest.[63]

Cugoano escaped the rigors of slavery in Grenada due to his purchase by a West Indian planter, Alexander Campbell, who took him to England and enabled him to be educated. Baptized in London in 1773, Cugoano likely emancipated himself in the wake of the *Somerset* decision. In *The Interesting Narrative of the Life of Olaudah Equiano, or Gustavus Vassa, The African. Written By Himself* (1789), Equiano recounts how in 1766, at the age of twenty-one, he purchased his freedom from his master, a Quaker merchant from Philadelphia named Robert King, for forty pounds sterling with his earnings from engaging

58 Ibid., p. 237.
59 Ibid., p. 245.
60 Ibid., p. 267.
61 Ibid., pp. 267, 275.
62 Ibid., p. 277.
63 Ibid, pp. 277–78.

in trade on his own behalf during his enslavement.[64] While Cugoano's text can be viewed as a work of political theory and critique, Equiano shapes his contribution to the antislavery cause (it was dedicated to the members of the House of Commons) in the form of a spiritual autobiography, so that his observations on commerce, law, and slavery unfold as he narrates his experiences and conversion to Christianity. Equiano's account of his childhood as the son of an Eboe (Ibo) *Embrenché*, a chief and local judge, in the Kingdom of Benin is highly detailed and resembles Benezet's descriptions of African societies and customs in *Some historical account of Guinea*, which Equiano cites.[65] Equiano's biographer, Vincent Carretta, raises doubts about the authenticity of Equiano's claim to have been born in Africa, based on his baptismal and naval records stating his birthplace as South Carolina.[66] Equiano's descriptions of the Eboe culture could have been the product of research and discussions with other enslaved people, as well as his recollections of his childhood upbringing, which 'had been implanted in me with great care, and made an impression on my mind, … which all the adversity and variety of fortune I have since experienced served only to rivet and record …'.[67] Even if partially fictional, these recollections of his African childhood would be analogous to the hypothetical state of nature theories of other abolitionist writers, and also served the text's key purpose to support the abolitionist movement by contributing an enslaved African's testimony.

Although he refers to Clarkson's text and most likely also read Cugoano's, a depiction of Africa in a state of nature is only very subtly present in Equiano's narrative of his abduction. He recounts that when he was eleven years old, while his parents were absent, he was playing at home with his sister when slave raiders suddenly climbed over the walls of the family compound. He and his sister were seized and transported in large sacks, and gagged so that they could not cry for help. On the following day, the grief-stricken children were separated, and Equiano was carried into a distant country and sold to another African family whose language, however, he still understood. At one point he attempted to escape into the woods with plans to find his way back to

64 Olaudah Equiano, *The Interesting Narrative of the Life of Olaudah Equiano, or Gustavus Vassa, The African. Written By Himself*, ed. by Angelo Costanzo (Peterborough, Ontario, Canada: Broadview, 2001), pp. 154–57.

65 Ibid., pp. 46–7.

66 Vincent Carretta, *Equiano, the African: Biography of a Self-Made Man* (New York: Penguin, 2005), pp. 1–16. For a response, see James H. Sweet, 'Mistaken Identities? Olaudah Equiano, Domingos Álvarez, and the Methodological Challenges of Studying the African Diaspora', *American Historical Review* 114, no. 2 (April 2009), pp. 279–306.

67 Equiano, *Interesting Narrative*, p. 61.

his parents, but while hiding he heard the searchers discuss how far away his home was, and he lost all hope of return:

> I began to consider that, if possibly I could escape all other animals, I could not those of the human kind; and that, not knowing the way, I must perish in the woods. Thus was I like the hunted deer:
>
> Ev'ry leaf and ev'ry whisp'ring breath
> Conveyed a foe, and ev'ry foe a death.[68]

A similar deconstruction of a proslavery trope occurs here to Cugoano's disentanglement of skin colour from estimations of sin or moral worth: Equiano shows that human animals are more dangerous than *ferae bestiae*. Demonstrating his sophisticated literacy and self-culture, Equiano's critique of the common European rationale for empire as a civilizing project comes in a poetic form that also disproves slaveholders' racist disparagement of Africans as natural slaves.

In Equiano's account, the African social contract seems susceptible to exploitation by the Atlantic trade's commercial incentives. The Eboes' milder form of slavery, however, has been rendered more violent by the European slave trade. In the context of recounting his transportation to the coast, Equiano, like Cugoano, admits fellow Africans' involvement in procuring slaves for Europeans, but he adds that 'I must acknowledge, in honour of those sable destroyers of human rights, that I never met with any ill treatment, or saw any offered to their slaves, except tying them, when necessary, to keep them from running away'.[69] Many months later, he was delivered over to a European slave ship and inducted into the brutality of the Middle Passage, experiences which his narrative describes in detail.

Equiano's notion that Africans' 'human rights' are violated by slave traders emerges within a context indicating that African societies like the Eboes' have a government, and therefore are not in a state of nature. His account thus implies that such 'human rights' are not simply natural rights but also legal and political rights belonging to subjects of African states. Like Clarkson, Equiano attacks slaveholders' systematic violation of 'that first natural right of mankind, equality and independency', and their usurping of 'a dominion over his fellows which God could never intend!'.[70] But in more specific terms than the other

---

68 Equiano, *Interesting Narrative*, pp. 64–5. Equiano quotes lines from a poem by John Denham, *Cooper's Hill* (1642).

69 Ibid., p. 65.

70 Ibid., p. 127.

writers, Equiano depicts his personal experiences of slaveholders' exploitation of forced labour for profit, extending even to one master's confiscation of the fish that an elderly Creole slave would catch during his brief free time to supplement his meagre diet.[71] Equiano shows how slavery financially incentivizes cruelty when he attacks male slaveholders' common practice of sexual assault on female slaves, and even their lack of shame in populating their plantations with their own progeny.[72] Instead of imagining slave revolts or a reversion to a state of nature in which resistance would be justified, however, Equiano frequently makes claim to his right to the wages of his labour that were appropriated by his masters. Even his own ability to purchase his freedom is framed ironically as a good bargain for his master's investment in slave property, when a ship captain who had subcontracted Equiano's labour to assist him on his trading voyages (including slave cargoes) persuades King to follow through on his pledge to free Equiano when he hesitates to fulfil it: ' "[Y]ou have laid your money out very well; you have received good interest for it all this time, and here is now the principal at last" '.[73] The 'interest' received refers to Equiano's wages paid by the captain directly to King. Equiano must still discharge the forty pounds 'principal' given for his purchase by his master as if it had been a mortgage on his life, or a debt imposed on his natural birth right to freedom. In a subtle critique, Equiano puns on the replacement of the legitimate political and natural law 'principles' of justice, equality, freedom, and remuneration for one's labour by the financial 'principal' materialized in the illegitimate contract of sale for an enslaved human being.

Robert King was tempted to break his promise to allow Equiano to purchase his freedom because slaveholding had no basis in a contract with a slave that the master was bound to honour. Because such breaches of promise were condoned by colonial slave laws, and rights were based in property ownership and asserted by means of racial discrimination, Equiano's narrative presents the imperial commercial system as potentially impervious to the fundamental moral, social, and political reforms that antislavery writers advocated. Prefiguring the monetary compensation to slaveholders that would follow British parliamentary abolition of slavery in 1833–34, the text also exposes the injustice of the financial transaction required to regain one's 'human rights' and freedom lawfully within such a system. Equiano's invocation of Africans' violated 'human rights', combined with his frequent crises of conscience as a witness to the atrocities of the slave trade, also make his own story potentially

71 Ibid., pp. 126–7.

72 Ibid., pp. 120, 126.

73 Ibid., p. 155.

representative of the need for a supervening, universal jurisdiction of conscience that could adjudicate on behalf of enslaved Africans against imperial commercial interests.

4 Frankpledge *and the Vicissitudes of a 'Free Settlement'*

Sharp's ancient constitutionalist project for Sierra Leone, funded in part by the British Treasury, sought to reconstruct formerly enslaved Africans' natural freedom and rights by equalizing property relations through a highly contrived and tutelary social contract. A major abolitionist goal of the settlement was to show that sugar and other crops could be produced profitably by free Black labourers. No longer considered as human property, the 'Black Poor', as they were called, who emigrated to Sierra Leone were to become landowners in the new settlement. While Sharp does not refer to a state of nature in *A Short Sketch of Temporary Regulations (Until Better Shall Be Proposed) For the Intended Settlement on the Grain Coast of Africa, Near Sierra Leona* (1786), his project envisions a model of democratic governance that would seek to rectify the imperial social contract ruptured by the Atlantic trade, particularly the dependence on coerced labour of plantations founded under British colonial charters. Sharp stipulates that all British settlements, including at Sierra Leone, must be based in the common law and the '*Religious Establishment of England*', though freedom of conscience and private worship would be guaranteed to non-Anglicans.[74] The constitutional arrangements Sharp proposed for the 'free settlement' included: the lawful purchase of settlement land from the African inhabitants by the Crown, followed by *gratis* allocation of land for houses and cultivation, apportioned equally to male heads of households and single settlers; a significant percentage of plots of land allotted to the settlement collectively as commons; equal labour requirements toward public works shared by all settlers; a strict limit of the working day on public projects to eight hours, so that ample time would remain for cultivation of private plots; additional plots to be purchased by exchangeable shares of labour time, so that the poor could buy land using loans to be discharged in units of labour hours on public projects; the prohibition of slavery and automatic freedom extended to all fugitive slaves; a jury system and elected public Council to take all important decisions collectively, including to amend the constitution; and frankpledge, based in

74 Granville Sharp, *A Short Sketch of Temporary Regulations (Until Better Shall Be Proposed) For the Intended Settlement on the Grain Coast of Africa, Near Sierra Leona*, 3rd ed. (London, 1788), iv.

the organization of settlers into hundreds that would cooperatively enforce mutual sureties for debts and labour shares, and provide settler militias for collective self-defence. Although Sharp's ancient constitutionalism may seem to imply a revival of feudalism, he considered the Anglo-Saxon frankpledge as predating the Norman conquest and villeinage; therefore, when conjoined with proprietorship in land, frankpledge would guarantee self-government for the free Black settlers, since by this means they could avoid relying on military forces supplied directly by the British government or by a chartered trading company.[75] Sharp's plan required that in addition to equal shares for all, 'no land must be appropriated but by *common consent*' of the public Council.[76] He also ruled out any individual landowner's engrossment of extensive land holdings through a rule that plots of public land must be distributed adjacent to any large private allotments.[77] Additionally, to ensure that 'all possibility of *domestic slavery* or *private oppression* will be excluded', indentured laborers and fugitive slaves who joined the settlement would owe repayment of their indentures or manumission, if such were required, to the '*public Exchequer only*',[78] the currency of which would be labour shares.[79]

These intricate measures codified constitutional principles that Sharp had articulated in his support for the American colonists in their demand for legislative representation, a position he continued to pursue through his activities as a member of the Society for Constitutional Information, founded in 1780 to advocate for constitutional reform in Britain.[80] The Preface to Sharp's tract *A Declaration of the People's Natural Right to a Share in the Legislature* (1774) defines a legitimate social contract by expressing his objections to the 'learned Civilian' Pufendorf's voluntarist notion, derived from Hobbes, considering law

---

75 Frankpledge could also be associated with chartered companies: Philip J. Stern notes that the establishment of English common law at the East India Company's colony at Bombay in the early 1670s was also based in ancient constitutionalism, including frankpledge, *The Company-State: Corporate Sovereignty and the Early Modern Foundations of the British Empire in India* (Oxford and New York: Oxford University Press, 2011), pp. 27–28. On some of the intellectual foundations of Sharp's views, see also J.G.A. Pocock, *The Ancient Constitution and the Feudal Law: A Study of English Historical Thought in the Seventeenth Century*, Reissue Edition (Cambridge: Cambridge University Press, 1987).

76 Sharp, *A Short Sketch*, p. 29.

77 Ibid., p. 40.

78 Ibid., p. 28.

79 Ibid., pp. 27–28.

80 On Sharp's involvement in the Society for Constitutional Information, see George Bernard Owers, 'Common Law Jurisprudence and Ancient Constitutionalism in the Radical Thought of John Cartwright, Granville Sharp, and Capel Lofft', *The Historical Journal* 58, no. 1 (2015), pp. 598–601.

as the will of the sovereign: once accepted as the means of exiting the violence of the state of nature, sovereignty thereafter implies that all laws receive an implicit consent from the governed.[81] For Sharp, this notion of implicit or tacit consent is a screen for absolutism, and takes no account of the English common law's requirement for natural equity, which he defines according to the legal maxim, '*Law, to bind all, must be assented to by all*'.[82] Sharp also defended the American colonists' protests against taxation by the Crown without representation in Parliament on the basis of this equitable requirement that 'there can be no legal appearance of *Assent* without some degree of *Representation*'. Therefore it becomes absolutely necessary 'to constitute an *effectual Legislature* for any part of the *British Empire*'.[83] Transplanting this principle into Sierra Leone enabled Sharp to conduct a further political experiment that, unlike the American revolutionary one, would both re-establish the ancient English constitution and outlaw slavery.

Founded in 1787, the Sierra Leone settlement at St. George's Bay was populated primarily by poor Blacks from London as well as loyal Blacks from North America, who had been freed from slavery after fighting for the British side in the American revolutionary war, and who afterwards settled in Nova Scotia, under conditions of extreme poverty.[84] The 'free settlement' itself was to be situated, however, in a kind of quarantine within the larger confines of a slave trading region of Africa, and the even more extensive spheres of the competitive European systems of Atlantic slavery. Commenting on the decision of some of the prospective Black settlers to back out of the emigration scheme before the ships' departure from London for Sierra Leone, Cugoano implies that their second thoughts were warranted:

---

81 Granville Sharp, *A Declaration of the People's Natural Right to a Share in the Legislature* (London, 1774), v-xiii. Sharp principally discusses Pufendorf's *Of the Law of Nature and of Nations*. David Singh Grewal's analysis in this volume supports Sharp's linkage of Pufendorf's thought with that of Hobbes.

82 Ibid., v. Sharp takes this maxim from Thomas Branch's *Principia Legis et Aequitatis* (1753) (a collection of legal principles, rules, and maxims). Grewal's chapter in this volume notes that Pufendorf's notion of tacit consent was derived from Grotius.

83 Ibid., p. 4, 10. Sharp also defended the right of the Irish to legislative representation, pp. 21–25.

84 Deirdre Coleman has pointed out that the London committee of white philanthropists who fostered the Sierra Leone settlement scheme also evinced 'segregationist policies … generated by whites' increasing anxiety in both America and Britain about the "problem" of emancipated blacks viewed as potential competitors with poor white labourers, *Romantic Colonization and British Anti-Slavery* (Cambridge: Cambridge University Press, 2005), p. 109.

> [A]s the old saying is, A burnt child dreads the fire, some of these unfortunate sons and daughters of Africa have been severally unlawfully dragged away from their native abodes ... by the insidious treachery of others [...]. [They are] afraid of being ensnared again; for the European seafaring people in general, who trade to foreign parts, have such a prejudice against Black People, that they use them more like asses than men [...]. For can it be readily conceived that government would establish a free colony for them nearly on the spot, while it supports its forts and garrisons, to ensnare, merchandize, and to carry others into captivity and slavery.[85]

The Black settlers had shrewdly taken measures in regard to this precarious situation prior to their departure by insisting that they receive certificates bearing royal arms proving their free status as 'Loyal [British] Subjects'.[86] Equiano was appointed in London to serve as Commissary, overseeing the equipping of the ships with supplies. However, he was dismissed from this post after he had complained of mismanagement of government funds by suppliers. He had also been particularly vocal in representing the grievances of the remaining Black settlers, who had been confined on the ships prior to their departure and suffered from an outbreak of fever.[87]

Equiano's disillusionment with and Cugoano's suspicions of the scheme were preludes to the misfortunes of the first group of settlers, which began when many died from malaria due to their arrival at Sierra Leone during the rainy season. Despite the settlers' belief that they had purchased land by treaty, instead by local custom the arrangement amounted to a renewable lease from the local Koya Temne sub-chief based on payment by goods and a promise of future good behaviour. Despite some conscientious efforts by the settlers, Sharp's detailed governmental scheme, including frankpledge, was not implemented, and a series of other unfortunate events ensued. Crops could not be planted in the rainy season, so settlers were obliged to trade their goods for food. Slave traders operating near the settlement attempted to seize several Black settlers, and some settlers became involved in the trade themselves. Once finally established and resupplied through Sharp's initiative, Granville

---

85 Cugoano, *Thoughts and Sentiments*, p. 320.

86 Stephen J. Braidwood, *Black Poor and White Philanthropists: London's Blacks and the Foundation of the Sierra Leone Settlement 1786–1791* (Liverpool: Liverpool University Press, 1994), p. 103.

87 For Equiano's account of this incident, see *Interesting Narrative*, ch. 12, pp. 242–45, and Braidwood, *Black Poor and White Philanthropists*, pp. 149–58.

Town was burned down in 1790 on the orders of the local sub-chief in reprisal for ongoing hostilities with some of the settlers. After his intensive organizational efforts and spending £1400 of his own funds, Sharp could not raise more financial assistance; in order to rebuild the settlement, he was obliged to accept the collapse of his constitutional plan, and to support the settlement's incorporation under a chartered company, firmly shifting its identity into a colony and commercial enterprise governed by a board of white abolitionist directors, (to which Sharp was elected).[88]

Such an outcome overturned the egalitarian political goals of Sharp's project. As he wrote to an interested friend in 1791, the settlers had lost their proprietorship of the entire district, since the chartered Sierra Leone Company had now been granted the land. They no longer had the right to elect their own governor and officers, 'nor any other circumstances of *perfect freedom* proposed in the *Regulations:* all these privileges are now submitted to the appointment and controul [*sic*] of the Company, and no settler can trade independently of it'. He acknowledged that 'I could not prevent this humiliating change', but 'all slavery, and the oppression of involuntary labour, are absolutely prohibited, and the laws of England are to be established'.[89] Sharp's attempt to guarantee freedom and self-determination for Black settlers in Sierra Leone amidst a rampant slave trade thus appeared as a kind of allegory for Britain's own false position in claiming to uphold the rule of law and guarantee its subjects' political rights and personal freedom while carrying on slavery and the slave trade in its imperial dominions.

5 Conclusion

Collectively, the state of nature arguments of these antislavery texts bring to light how the transactional commercial nature of the imperial social relations enforced by slavery – experienced by enslaved Africans through their being 'merchandized', as Cugoano put it – rendered the violent inequalities imposed by the colonial plantation system highly flexible and resilient due to their economic basis, and therefore resistant to schemes for political reform. Contracts of sale and colonial charters leading to legalized regimes of slavery had effectively

88 The Sierra Leone Company was created by Act of Parliament, passed on 30 May 1791, despite organized opposition by the West India and slave merchants' lobbies. See Braidwood, *Black Poor and White Philanthropists*, pp. 181–249.

89 Granville Sharp, letter to Dr. Lettsom, 5 October 1791, qtd. in Hoare, *Memoirs of Granville Sharp*, p. 362.

replaced constitutional protections of the rights of subjects, so that natural law became a highly abstracted foundation for the common law in colonial and imperial settings, and the common law itself was revealed, to Sharp's dismay, as an optional and restricted component of imperial governance. While Benezet and Clarkson formulated the appeals to innate moral sentiments of 'humanity' that would predominate within the political rhetoric of the organized abolitionist movement, Sharp's constitutionalism was left in a stark confrontation with the jurisdictional limitations of the common law and the financial dependence of the colonial system on chartered trading companies.[90] On a more positive side for the antislavery cause, a theoretical assertion such as Clarkson's of Africans' 'perfect freedom' in the state of nature exposed the lack of a just social contract, based in consent of the governed, across British dominions where slavery was practiced and therefore rebounding into Britain itself. In retrospect, and despite the scheme's paternalism, Sharp's provisions for equal distribution of property in land and self-government were also distinctive for their potential to promote the citizenship of free Black settlers at Sierra Leone, particularly in comparison to the apprenticeship system implemented after the 1834 abolition of slavery in British dominions that was intended to constrain the emancipated Black peasantry within regimes of 'free labour' on existing plantations.[91]

Antislavery writers' resort both to claims concerning slaves' natural rights and state of nature theories reveal how the foundations of political rights in property ownership, under both the common law and colonial regimes, undermined early antislavery arguments based in legal and moral principles, perhaps causing their sentimental appeals to become more dominant as the abolitionist movement accelerated. Having been abused as human property, Equiano and Cugoano experienced this contradiction most acutely. Equiano's invocation of the collective 'human rights' of enslaved Africans nevertheless suggests that Sharp's legalistic and constitutional approach to outlawing slavery, combined with the personal narratives and testimony of former slaves, could form the bases of a representative political argument for the enslaved to move beyond natural rights and sentimental appeals by claiming the fundamental rights of British subjects and citizens, including property ownership. Implying that access to the rights of subjects would not adequately compensate enslaved Africans, however, Cugoano's demand for reparations presents the most radical expectation, arising in part from state of nature theorizing,

90 See Ian Baucom, *Specters of the Atlantic: Finance Capital, Slavery, and the Philosophy of History* (Durham, NC: Duke University Press, 2005).

91 See William A. Green, *British Slave Emancipation: The Sugar Colonies and the Great Experiment 1830–1865* (Oxford: Clarendon Press, 1976), pp. 129–61.

that victims of murders, kidnappings, and wars against Indigenous peoples in colonized regions might finally receive a comprehensive financial settlement from the national and corporate entities that benefitted from Atlantic slavery.

Select Bibliography

Primary Sources

Benezet, Anthony. *A Short Account of that Part of Africa Inhabited by the Negroes*. 2nd ed. Philadelphia, 1762.

Benezet, Anthony. *Some historical account of Guinea, its situation, produce, and the general disposition of its inhabitants: with an inquiry into the rise and progress of the slave trade, its nature and lamentable effects*. New edn. London, 1788.

Clarkson, Thomas. *An Essay on the Slavery and Commerce of the Human Species, Particularly the African; Translated from a Latin Dissertation, which was Honoured with the First Prize in the University of Cambridge for the Year 1785; the Second Edition, Revised and Considerably Enlarged.* London, 1788.

Cugoano, Ottobah. *Thoughts and Sentiments of the Evil and Wicked Traffic of the Slavery and Commerce of the Human Species, Humbly Submitted to The Inhabitants of* Great Britain, *by Ottobah Cugoano, A Native of Africa*. London, 1787.

Equiano, Olaudah. *The Interesting Narrative of the Life of Olaudah Equiano, or Gustavus Vassa, The African. Written By Himself.* London, 1789.

Sharp, Granville. *A Representation of the Injustice and Dangerous Tendency of Tolerating Slavery in England; or of Admitting the Least Claim of Private Property in the Persons of Men in England*. London, 1769.

Sharp, Granville. *A Short Sketch of Temporary Regulations (Until Better Shall Be Proposed) For the Intended Settlement on the Grain Coast of Africa, Near Sierra Leona*. 3rd ed. London, 1788.

Secondary Sources

Baucom, Ian. *Specters of the Atlantic: Finance Capital, Slavery, and the Philosophy of History*. Durham, NC: Duke University Press, 2005.

Braidwood, Stephen J. *Black Poor and White Philanthropists: London's Blacks and the Foundation of the Sierra Leone Settlement 1786–1791*. Liverpool: Liverpool University Press, 1994.

Brown, Christopher Leslie. *Moral Capital: Foundations of British Abolitionism*. Chapel Hill: University of North Carolina Press, 2006.

Coleman, Deirdre. *Romantic Colonization and British Anti-Slavery*. Cambridge: Cambridge University Press, 2005.

Hanley, Ryan. *Beyond Slavery and Abolition: Black British Writing c. 1770–1830*. Cambridge: Cambridge University Press, 2019.

CHAPTER 11

From the State of Nature to the Natural State

Transforming the Foundations of Science and Civil Progress in Eighteenth-Century British Political Thought

Pamela Edwards

Abstract

British political thought in the eighteenth century frequently built arguments on the foundations of 16th- and 17th-century accounts the State of Nature. Understood to be an original and pre-civil condition, this natural state was taken to be either a distant historical reality or an enduring allegory of peace and war. But whether hostile or benign, real or imagined, it established the operative principles for political and social argument and action in terms of a zero-sum game. It was also conceived of as a set of static conceptual binaries, which were held to undergird the scientific and rational nature of the world. But by the middle of the eighteenth century, the rise of a new and dynamic philosophy of action suggested, by extension, a new science of history. Increasingly biologized and progressive in nature, the rise of anthropogical history was bound to a new science of politics. In consequence, the question as it was formerly posed, as to whether the state of nature was some utopian ideal to be recaptured or a nightmare of conflict and instability to escape from, no longer held. Instead, the question was increasingly understood as a deep inquiry into the complexity of living systems, whether political, social or natural. The adaptive possibilities of this new political vitalism were both conceptually and rhetorically better suited to the comparative, developmental, and hybrid nature of commercial empire.

1 Reframing the Debate on Natural Society

It is a common place to associate seventeenth- and eighteenth-century narratives of government with the discourse of Nature. Less often considered are the ways in which the variety and complexity of that association shifted over the course of the 18th century. What, by the 1650's and 60's, had been crafted as an abstraction or allegorical device would, by the middle of the 18th century, be shaped as a scientific and empirically grounded account of power, process, and change in human society.

 | DOI:10.1163/9789004499621_013

Two principal narratives structured the seventeenth-century debate. Both defined the state of nature as an original and pre-political condition. For the optimists and the utopians, it was a world that placed human beings in an original condition of simplicity, purity, and innocence. It was a place of bounty where small familial bands lived lives of simple co-operation and filial affection. Considering this pre-political world as one of seemingly limitless resources where land was available to all, John Locke (1632–1704) could muse "In the beginning was all the World America". For others, and notably those of a pessimistic bent, the state of nature was a hostile and violent world of warfare and scarcity. In this savage and primitive state, the human condition was marked by animal cunning and ferocity, where the individual was driven by constant want and fear.[1] "Life" in this state of nature, as Thomas Hobbes (1588–1679) famously observed, was "nasty, brutish and short". Yet both Hobbesian and Lockean accounts of the pre-political state of nature rested on a binary model; a world divided into the political and the natural, where the balance of freedom and security was struck through contract or contest, man against man, or people against prince.[2]

By the middle of the eighteenth century those efforts, once made by common lawyers, to present the State of Nature as a legal fiction proved increasingly unsatisfactory. New enlightenment narratives of science and of history situated the discourse of human nature within the evolutionary development of civil society, offering an account of progress both as an expression and as

1 For discussion of the violent and chaotic characteristics of the state of nature – styled variously as primitivism, savagery, or barbarism – see Mary Fuller's account of absences and Laszlo Kontler's description of the agency of reception. Fuller has focused on the ways in which natural or pre-political societies were described by Hakluyt and others by the lack or absence of those markers which they identified with the rise of civilized societies. Kontler's account of stadial theory and its narrative uses, emphasizes its additions and accretions; of things folded in, combined and reassessed in ambivalent ways. Such 'creative adaptations' increasingly 'blurred the lines' between branches of knowledge, even as they solidified a narrative of progress 'from rudeness to refinement'.

2 A reappraisal of the conditions under which a people either escape from or evolve beyond a state of nature may be detected in both Ioannis Evrigenis and Benjamin Straumann's arguments regarding the process of establishing the sovereign power. Straumann emphasizes the deliberative negotiations between the Athenians and the Melians in Hobbes's *Thucydides*. Highlighting the reciprocity of contract over conquest he presents the 'capacity to promise' as the defining ground of political obligation. Evrigenis limits and complicates Locke's foundational right of Property. He presents it as a socially grounded condition of trust or stewardship where Man had 'no Liberty to destroy himself or any creature in his possession unless some nobler purpose require it'. While Hobbes and Locke drew different lines under the withdrawal of consent, some of the distance between them is bridged by their accounts of the limits of obligation and the bonds of Trust.

an extension of natural history. The stark comparative dichotomy of civil and natural society that had characterized the older allegories began to collapse. As the older distinction was overtaken by more complex and socio-biologically grounded accounts, a blended narrative emerged. These organic descriptions of civil and natural order increasingly framed juridical and constitutional understandings of the politics and law of the 18th century, not as expressions of providence, but as the natural refinement of a biological and sociological history. The once bright line between nature and artifice, and the elided discourses of virtue and corruption, decline and renewal, began to fade as the experimental and creative impulses of both social and scientific engineering found their way into the language of progress, advancement and improvement.

The question by the end of the eighteenth century was whether the new evolutionary accounts of progress, suggested a somatic or mechanical model of government. Was the political significance of the new science a more experimental approach to building the right constitutional machine? Or did the emergence of a social science of politics suggest political vitalism; a view of civil society as a critical extension of the theory of life? But whether the mechanical or organic model predominated, the new social scientific language of politics begged an older question: when and what was the state of nature? By the middle of the 18th century and Edmund Burke's (1729–1797) famous reframing of the argument, 'Natural Society' would eclipse 'State of Nature'; understood to be the constitutive substructure of an inherently dynamic, organic and vital system.[3]

This new iteration of the discourse of nature was for writers like Burke, deeply, indeed explicitly, political. It also suggested a new philosophy of history; a narrative not to be understood in terms of disjunctions and continuities, but rather as protean and transformative. Things did not break and end, nor did they remain unchanged. Rather, life evolved, metamorphosized, indeed regenerated, so that each iteration became something entirely new. Political thought – as a complex of ideas, as discourse, and as expressed in institutional design – also adapted. Accommodating this changing narrative, accounts of political power increasingly reflected the emergent and dynamic 'condition', rather than 'State', of nature. By the 1740's, the better question to pose concerned the nature of the state. Accordingly, accounts of government and civil

---

3 Pocock set the allegorical against literal understandings of what was effectively a biological continuity of trust and expectation. "We have made the state not only a family but as a Trust; not so much a biological entity, or the image of one, as an undying *persona ficta* which secures our liberties by vesting them in an immortal continuity." J.G.A. Pocock, 'Burke and the Ancient Constitution', *The Historical Journal*, Vol. 3 No. 2 (1960), pp. 125–143. at p.131.

society were increasingly crafted as systems of life, their regulation and health matters of growth and balance, as much as renewal and decay.

The 18th century shift from the allegorical accounts of the State of Nature towards a new social science of politics also modified earlier accounts of authority and power, reframing many of their scholastic and classical antecedents. Writers as varied in their opinions and interests as Bolingbroke (1678–1751), David Hume (1711–1776) and Burke would re-configure the works of Francis Bacon (1561–1626), Isaac Newton (1643–1727), and Ralph Cudworth (1617–1668), as well as those of Hobbes and Locke, to advance new and scientifically grounded philosophies of history. They did so, in part, by radically reimagining the philosophy of nature as a philosophy of action; an experimental and empirically grounded science of motion and life.

Power as action, power as force, power as freedom, and power as law, would all acquire new resonances as the Newtonian revolution reverberated through theological, philosophical, and political debate. The deists of the 1720's and 30's rejected the mysterious and inexplicable doctrines of providence, grace, and punishment; settling the balance of political and civil life on the axis of nature, now twice removed from God's imminence and super-intendency.[4] Ancient

4 Efforts were made in the 1680's, by latitudinarian bishops such as Samuel Tillotson, to expand Anglican accounts of Comprehension, harmonizing early 17th century strands of argument drawn from accounts of both 'natural' and 'revealed' religion. See for example Richard Ashcraft's political and structural account of these efforts in "Latitudinarianism and toleration: historical myth versus political history" in Kroll, R., ed., *Philosophy, Science and Religion 1640–1700* (Cambridge: Cambridge University Press, 1992), pp. 151–177. Ashcraft was dubious about the power of Enlightenment rationalism as a causative force in the Toleration debate. Nonetheless the shift towards a more complex Deism, if not secular view of reason and nature, is striking. More recently, following Mario Micheletti, scholars like Diego Lucci have drawn a distinction between the complex rationalism of the Cambridge Platonists and latitude men such as Benjamin Whichcote, whose philosophical inclinations were Baconian and whose religious sensibilities were deeply attached to personal conviction and liberty of conscience. His, was part of a wider and older strand of religious naturalism. Lucci links the contrasts between the older tradition and the newer and more secular strands of Deism, to the genesis of sociological history. Offering the example of Charles Blount's *Great is Diana of the Ephesians* (1680) as an early secular history of religion, he identifies the turn towards anthropological analysis. Diego Lucci, 'From Unitarianism to Deism: Mathew Tindal, John Toland, and the Trinitarian Controversy' in *The World of Seventeenth Century English Dissenters*, ed. Paula Barros, Anne Dunan-Page, and Laurence Lux-Sterritt, *Etudes Episteme*, no. 35, 2019. Naturalistic accounts of religion which, by the beginning of the 18th century, would increasingly set "Priests against Philosophers" are discussed by Fredrick Beiser who, offering a different line, associates them with the realignment of theological rationalism. Beiser described a new wave of Anglican rationalists, who employed reason as a weapon to criticize faith rather than as a tool to defend it. A shift, he argued, that polarized an earlier and more complex relationship between natural and revealed religion, presenting natural religion as an effective means to attack

authorities and sacred signs had once revealed, through miraculous occurrences, an established hierarchy; one it was held, that maintained the natural and political order of the world. But there were new portents to be read, both in the heavens and beneath the earth; celestial time receded as geological time advanced. Even as 18th century political discourse re-configured older understandings of social order – accommodating new priorities of political action – it advanced novel arguments for practice over prescription.

The dynastic crisis of succession and rebellion from 1715–1745 altered foundational assumptions about the state of nature; not only challenging the anchors of obedience and the measures of allegiance but questioning the natural bonds of blood and family. Writing in exile after the failed Jacobite rebellion of 1715, Henry St. John, Viscount Bolingbroke could reflect, not only on the perils of faction, but on the deeper and underlying philosophical questions of polarity and force. Borrowing Newton's laws of motion and force and applying them to the ordering of the moral and of the natural world, Bolingbroke reflected on the laws of attraction and repulsion as much as affiliation, arguing for the self-sufficiency of nature.[5] Divine intervention was not required in a world governed by a providence of second causes. By the 1740's Hume also joined this conversation, discounting the hand of providence while tracing the powers of perception, custom, and experience, the historical makers and markers of the natural and civilized worlds. Writing critically against the concept of miracles, he was accused of atheism. The intensity of this debate and its implications for the interests of religious and political order presented opportunity to the young Burke, who wrote a satire of Bolingbroke's philosophical system. Claiming to parody Bolingbroke's style while refuting his principles, Burke gave his first account of the follies of abstraction and the vanities of metaphysicians.[6] As he took aim against all the doctors of false philosophy, he

---

revealed religion. See Frederick C. Beiser, *The Sovereignty of Reason* (Princeton: Princeton University Press, 1996), p. 7.

5 Bolingbroke relied more heavily on Leibniz's system for his account of natural philosophy, yet still argued for the simultaneous simplicity and complexity of Newton's system; best understood through "these sure guides experiment and geometry". But Newton, he explained, who maintained "a learned humility", was "far from pretending to determine the efficient cause of his attraction, or what that force is which makes bodies and every particle of the body, mutually tend to one another, and thereby give us an idea of attracting, according to what has been taken notice of already." *The Philosophical Works of the late Right Honourable Henry St John, Lord Viscount Bolingbroke,* published by David Mallet in five volumes (London, 1754). vol I, p. 174.

6 Edmund Burke, *A Vindication of Natural Society or, A View of the Miseries and Evils Arising to Mankind from Every Species of Artificial Society* ed. Frank N Pagano (London, 1760, Indianapolis, 1982). Burke's anti-theoretical bent in his 'Vindication', his early suspicion of

paid considerable attention to the systems of Locke and, with a particular view, of Hobbes. But, as a Whig defender of Locke's principles in politics, Burke left some room for the case for Locke's system of nature.

2 Breaking the Binaries: Burke's Adaptation of Bolingbroke's Philosophical History

The Vindication of Natural Society is a brief but striking intervention, attacking the more politically subversive elements of Bolingbroke's deism, while fortifying and rehabilitating Locke's authority as a "pillar" of the Hanoverian establishment.[7] However, the underlying claims of Burke's '*Vindication*' suggest the furtherance of a more radical philosophical agenda. More than a broad denunciation of anti-trinitarian doctrine, either as a troubling new heterodoxy or a disruptive form of non-conformity that would destabilize the English church-state, Burke focused on Bolingbroke's very particular brand of deism; a doctrine of profound philosophical and political consequence, that was based on a misapplication (so Burke would argue) of Newtonian mechanics.[8] Most

---

the doctors of false philosophy, offers the first iteration of his late and famous attack on "sophists, economists, and calculators" in *Reflections on the Revolution in France* (1790).

7 Justin Champion argued that Locke's Socinianism was compatible with the Church establishment and its eccleisio-political orthodoxy. *The Pillars of Priestcraft Shaken: The Church of England and its Enemies, 1660–1730* (Cambridge: Cambridge University Press, 1992, 2014). See also Justin Champion, *Republican Learning: Toland and the Crisis of Christian Culture* (Manchester: Manchester University Press, 2003). Champion contrasted Locke's moderate position with John Toland's more theologically radical and, arguably, politically subversive opinions. Jonathan Clark points out the complex positioning of Locke's heterodoxy in the context of the revolution of 1688, a position that increasingly required distancing after the revolutionary settlement. See J.C.D.Clark, *English Society: Religion, Ideology and Politics During the Long Eighteenth Century* (Cambridge: Cambridge University Press, 2000), pp. 138–139. Jonathan Israel recently expanded his own thesis of a Radical Enlightenment, contending that the distance between Locke and Toland marks the divergence of moderate and radical strands of Enlightenment. He identifies that divergence as marking a shift in the conceptual dichotomy: "from the basic divergence between Reason based on Nature's Law as the sole criterion of truth and morality, and Locke's duality of truth (the dichotomy of empiricism and religious authority) the rift between radical and moderate enlightenment derives much of its relevance and force." See Jonathan Israel, 'Radical Enlightenment: A Game Changer' in *Reassessing the Radical Enlightenment,* ed. Steffen Ducheyne (Routledge, 2017), p. 37. For the counter-case on Locke, rational dissent, and its subtle interplay in Enlightenment discourses of science, religion and natural law see J.G.A. Pocock, *Barbarism and Religion,* vol. 5 (Cambridge: Cambridge University Press, 2011).

8 English Deism, described as "elusive" by scholars such as Robert Sullivan, was first associated with the works of Edward Herbert of Cherbury, notably *De veritate* (1624). An effort to trace its influence was offered by John Leland, who attempted to catalogue the varieties

critics have suggested that Burke's central purpose in attacking Bolingbroke's deism was the defense of revealed religion, ecclesiastical conformity, and with that the preservation of the sacramental foundations of political power.[9] But more striking dimensions of Burke's argument are to be found in his account of natural philosophy and his rejection of Bolingbroke's (purportedly) mechanical view of the world. Bolingbroke was drawn into the interpretive controversy that roiled around Newton's *Principia Mathematica* (1687) but he was also deeply interested in the system of nature that followed from Gottfried von Leibniz's (1646–1716) calculus, first published as *Nova Methodus pro Maximus et Minimus* (1684). While exiled in France, Bolingbroke closely followed the theological and metaphysical dimensions of the controversy between Samuel Clarke (1675–1729) and Leibniz, with particular focus on the essential question of the corporeal or bodily nature of God and Space. But it was the significance of these two systems for accounts of time and necessity that particularly intrigued Bolingbroke who by 1720 had read the unpublished draft of Newton's *Chronology of Ancient Kingdoms Amended* (1728) While much of the first volume of Bolingbroke's *Philosophical Works* involved a dismissive critique of Leibniz's *Monodology*, he was sympathetic to some aspects of Leibniz's reply to Samuel Clarke. Bolingbroke was dissatisfied with Newton's account of time, particularly in its implications for a philosophy of history. Bolingbroke thought that Leibniz's account offered more robust possibilities for a theory of historical agency and the active force of will than did Newton's.[10]

---

of English Deism in 1757. Leland wrote his catalogue the same year that Burke wrote the Preface to the *Vindication*. Tracing the influence of Herbert on naturalists and pantheists such as Charles Blunt, Leland also connected its branches and offshoots to the transcendentalism of Mathew Tindal, Thomas Chubb and Thomas Morgan who believed in the sufficiency of nature, as well as to the Necessitarians who followed the determinism of Anthony Collins.

9 See Ian Hampshire-Monk, 'Rousseau, Burke's Vindication of Natural Society and Revolutionary Ideology'. *European Journal of Political Thought*, vol. 9, issue 3 (July 2010), pp. 245–266.

10 For a discussion of Bolingbroke's reactions to reading Newton's *Chronology of Ancient Kingdoms Amended* (1728) see Jed Z. Buchwald and Mordechai Feingold, *Newton and the Origins of Civilization* (Princeton: Princeton University Press, 2013), p. 314. Citing an exchange with Brook Taylor (23 November 1721), they point to Bolingbroke's 'disillusionment' with ancient chronology, suggesting Bolingbroke's political and philosophical inclinations. The 'begged question' of Newton's *Chronology* suggested its inadequacy. Bolingbroke regarded the work as the foundation for a history without consequences. Returning to the question of efficient causes, both in history and in nature, Bolingbroke had largely taken the Newtonian position. Reading the exchange between Leibniz and Clarke, he had defended Newton and the English side of the argument which played out the consequences of Cartesian dualism for Physics and Theology. One of the begged

The Newtonian model of causation, adapted by Deists such as John Toland (1660–1722), and Anthony Collins (1676–1729) viewed history and the events of the world as a series of billiard balls colliding. Human freedom and agency are illusionary on this model, lacking the protean possibilities of spontaneity, creativity, and the independent force of imagination and will. Mirroring Arminian objections to Calvinist theology, the critics of Deist cosmology objected to its consequential implication; that the inevitability of events suggested by the mechanical model reduced all of nature to dead matter. Certainly, Bolingbroke argued for Nature's self-sufficiency or, as Newton conceived of it and Paley later described it, a ticking clock. But it was a chronometer of exquisite complexity, and no one individual could see all of its motions in every moment. That was the value of philosophical history.[11]

Burke's commentary on Bolingbroke's character is withering, and this is of course a central feature of the pamphlet's Preface; countering the force of an argument and shaping opinion through the creation or destruction of reputation. Bolingbroke had always been a favorite target of Whig invective. Lord Quicksilver, 'the man of mercury', having long been considered something of a walking metaphor for ambition, treachery, and ruthless self-promotion. As the principal architect of the country party's attack on the old lines of faction

questions, was whether Newton had sufficiently resolved this ancient dichotomy and its significance for the priority dispute. Leibniz's monism made no distinction between God's presence and extension, between mind and brain. The collapse of this distinction allowed Bolingbroke to formulate his own understanding of the self-sufficiency of Nature. In contrast, Newton had described space as God's sensorium. In doing so he set up a bifurcation of God and his nature, between God, and his organ of sense. A dualism, some would argue, that also confused Locke; in particular as it suggested a material, hence perishable, soul. Leibniz skeptically pointed to this conundrum as allowing a place for convenient intervention in a divinely ordered world. Referring to Newton and his followers, Leibniz argued in the first paper to Clarke (November 1715), "according to them" [the Newtonians] "God's watch – the universe – would stop working if he did not rewind it from time to time!" For Leibniz, if the universe was a clockwork, it was one of perpetual motion, and "the world always contained the same amount of force and energy, which changes only by passing from one material thing to another in accordance with the laws of nature and the beautiful order that God has pre-established." (Clarke I:26. xi. 1715).

11 Bolingbroke, *Letters on the Study and Use of History*, (1752) Letter II "Concerning the true use and advantages of the study of History", B writes of history as a reflection of human nature "The love of history seems inseparable from human nature, because it seems inseparable from self-love. The same principle in this instance carries us forward and backward, to future and past ages. ... The true and proper object of this application is a constant improvement in private and in public virtue. ... to make us better men and better citizens". *The Works of Lord Bolingbroke ... in four volumes*, ed. Henry G. Bonn (London, 1844), Vol. II p. 177.

and interest, the author of *The Spirit of Patriotism* (1736) and *The Idea of a Patriot King* (1738) had by his death in 1751 forever transformed the discourses of subject, state and sovereign. He had done so by adapting 17th century Whig arguments for the ancient constitution and, with the philosophical history and commentary of the Craftsman essays, advanced a new "British" national ideology of political virtue and propertied independence. But the anti-corruption political essays of Bolingbroke's great campaign against Walpole was not the legacy Burke chose to attack directly, though he would certainly attempt to rescue, restore or re-appropriate these arguments as a newly minted, modernized, and quintessentially Whig doctrine after 1760.

Burke's project in the *Vindication* is the annihilation of Bolingbroke's literary and philosophical legacy, or so the addition of a late 1760 preface would suggest. *The Philosophical Works* published posthumously, by David Mallet in 1754, three years after Bolingbroke's death, were intended to lift him into that great pantheon of English authors from Bacon to Locke, who had advanced a new philosophy of nature as the essential foundation for a new science of politics. Burke's anonymous *Vindication of Natural Society* followed in 1756. By 1760, Burke claimed to have borrowed Bolingbroke's style while condemning his principles. It may be fairer to suggest that Burke borrowed the principles by condemning the style.[12] But whether Burke's *Vindication* was in earnest, or caricature, or even a willful misunderstanding, he emphasized the stark rational antimonies of Bolingbroke's contrasts; between virtue and vice, mind and body, nature and artifice. And while Bolingbroke's arguments have more subtlety and complexity than Burke accords them, that is not the point Burke wanted to make. Nature, for Burke, was encountered through partial and progressive understanding; civilization and enlightenment shaped by experience and the refinement of custom. In this sense, the law was an extension of nature, and the Common Law the living manifestation of the Natural Law.[13]

12 See F.P. Lock's account in *Edmund Burke 1730–1784*, vol. I (Oxford: Oxford University Press, 2008), p. 83. There is argument about the composition of the preface and its usefulness as an interpretive compass for Burke's *Vindication*. While Lock holds that it was written as a satire, Murray Rothbart considered its late attachment to the 1760 edition which was published under Burke's name, an effort to distance himself from Bolingbroke's deism for political advantage. Rather, Rothbart argued, the anonymous and preface-less 1756 edition, which made no such demurrals, was the truer measure of Burke's sympathy with Bolingbroke's natural philosophy. This is complicated by the date for the composition of the preface in 1757; much closer to the original publication, it remains a post-script. Consequently, it is still the case that Burke did not feel the need to write the preface until a year after the first print.

13 Again, see Pocock's account of the Common Law as an 'immortal continuity' rather than as a re-imagined tradition. "He is not calling upon his contemporaries to return to the

While the question of parody and satire hangs over the core of Burke's *Vindication*, these observations are drawn from the apologetic preface to the 1760 edition which acknowledged Burke as the author. Opinion has been divided on whether the substantive elements of Burke's argument in his "Letter to Lord????" are to be read in quite the same way as the preface. Indeed, one critic argued that Burke was in earnest and that his project was to build on Bolingbroke's ideas; advancing an anarchist argument against "unnatural" government.[14] While Burke's central critique of government as an artificial and unnatural contrivance may have been sincere, the object of his commentary is not the abolition of government but the reform of government on natural grounds. But perhaps a more interesting aspect of the text is that the lines of the argument and the terms of the debate he described would have been clearly recognized by his readership. It is this intersection of the debate on nature, freedom, and historical agency with the crisis of empire that is particularly compelling.[15] Burke's questions suggest a view of enlightenment science and cosmology as inherently moral and political discourses, but also as a reflection on the Baconian project. What follows from the cataloguing of experience

17th century habit of mind, but assuming it is still alive and meaningful among them." "Burke and the Ancient Constitution", *The Historical Journal*, Vol. 3, No. 2 (1960), pp. 125–143, p. 129.

14 Murray Rothbart, "A Note on Burke's Vindication of Natural Society" *Journal of the History of Ideas*, Vol. 19, No. 1 (January 1958), pp. 114–118. An argument later supported and revived by Isaac Kramnick for its anticipation of William Godwin's arguments on nature and anarchy. See Isaac Kramnick, *The Rage of Edmund Burke* (New York NY: Basic Books, 1977).

15 See for example Richard Bourke, *Empire and Revolution: The Political Life of Edmund Burke* (Princeton: Princeton University Press, 2015) or for a careful and suggestive account of the formative role of natural philosophy in Burke's formation of a cosmopolitan humanistic politics see David Bromwich *The Intellectual Life of Edmund Burke from the Sublime and the Beautiful to American Independence* (Cambridge: Harvard University Press, 2014) . An earlier but compelling reflection on the exclusionary legacies of Burke's scientific naturalism and commercial cosmopolitanism for late 18th and 19th century policy, see Uday Singh Mehta, *Liberalism and Empire: A Study in Nineteenth-century British Liberal Thought.* (Chicago: University of Chicago Press, 1999) The crossroads of empire – either in its colonial or revolutionary contexts – with the new natural philosophy and sociological science of enlightenment have produced several excellent recent studies. Of particular note for the significance of anthropological history and colonialism is Silvia Sebastiani's *The Scottish Enlightenment: Race, Gender and the Limits of Progress* (Palgrave, 2013). For the formative uses of the 'State of Nature' trope, as well as the impact of the new naturalism of Buffon and the public science of Franklin and Rush, in the Atlantic crisis and suggesting the subsequent shaping of the American republic see Mark Somos, *American States of Nature: The Origins of Independence 1761–1775* (Oxford: Oxford University Press, 2019).

into distinct varieties of knowledge? Is it a more efficient delineation of social, moral, and natural science? Does it occasion the death of mystery and the end of magic? Is the obfuscation and sophistry of false science and false philosophy a new form of false religion? Suggesting an answer, Burke declared that "[t]he Professors of Artificial Law have always walked hand in hand with the Professors of Artificial Theology" (VNS p28).

Burke's key disagreements, or perhaps more tellingly, his 'disappointments' with Bolingbroke's efforts at writing a philosophy of history as a philosophy of nature reveal a great deal about his own positive inclinations toward Bacon's scientific and social project, particularly the implications of 'advancement and learning' for moral and political society. Defining his own Baconian project, Burke pointed out the errors of Bolingbroke's. He suggested that, though the ambition was great – and when with Bolingbroke was it not? – the execution was a huge disappointment. Referring to *The Philosophical Works* as a whole, Burke writes "Those who searched in them for new Discoveries in the Mysteries of Nature; those who expected something which might explain or direct the Operations of the Mind; those who hoped to see Morality illustrated and enforced; those who looked for new helps for Society and Government; those who desired to see the Characters and Passions of mankind delineated.... all these were certainly disappointed" (VNS p.5). This is a powerful set of elisions, as Burke essentially formulates the associative genesis of the social sciences. Or to run through it with an eye to the rise of the disciplines, that the empirical and Baconian project of discovery and the revelation of the life of nature, will explain faculty psychology, and with that the rational and emotional grounds of ethics and law, which will in turn provide a stable foundation for good government, prosperity, and a just and flourishing society. These are "such things" Burke tells us, "for all who consider such Things as Philosophy". They are the proper end of human inquiry, and "every philosophical Work" must "require some of them at least". (VNS p.5)

Not content with detailing the magnitude of Bolingbroke's philosophical and literary failure, Burke focused on the man himself. Giving an account of 'defective nature', Burke emphasized Bolingbroke's failure of character as much as the purported weakness of his substantive argument. He depicted Bolingbroke as a critic without conscience; a reckless wit and philosophical spoiler, conceptually tearing down the world without any consideration of the ruin and destructive mischief he might provoke. Bolingbroke would have been pleased, and no doubt regarded any such demolition as a proper Baconian clearing away of the old 'Idols', a necessary first phase of the Great Instauration. But Bacon was also Burke's favorite author, and he reveals much of his own understanding of the Baconian project through his account of Bolingbroke's purported vanities.[16]

Distaste for Bolingbroke's deism certainly carried weight for Burke's defense of the Whig establishment. But as its title suggests, *A Vindication of Natural Society* was staking deeper and more foundational claims. Lamenting that Bolingbroke's readers had experienced so many disappointments, Burke insisted they paled in comparison to the greatest disappointment. The singular failure of Bolingbroke's *Philosophical Works* was that they left "the Land-marks of Science precisely in their former Places" (VNS p. 5). This was "poor recompense", Burke contended, for suffering through the more destructive elements of Bolingbroke's system. Failing to move "the Land-marks of Science", Bolingbroke had done nothing but attack "every mode of religion" and "the Foundation of every Virtue and of all government". Moreover, he had done so in "a lively manner", striking at their roots as he "sapped [them]with great Art and much ingenuity". Despite the elegiac characteristics of Burke's later writings, he was in the tradition of his favorite author, an advocate of progress and by inclination a builder. The destructive, or rather skeptical, elements of Bolingbroke's system and commentary, Burke perceived as the most repulsive. He presented Bolingbroke's exclusively critical and materialist understanding of the world as an inherently perverse and corrupt one, in essence as an affront to nature.

While a Christian and classical condemnation of hubris may sit comfortably with Burke's prefatory satire of Bolingbroke, there are other notes on the economies of nature which may be more instructive. The question is posed directly by Burke as requiring two conditions, beauty and utility. Returning to his text "What advantage do we derive from such writings?" And modifying the question of utility, he offers Nature's "Mixed Cup" of pleasure and purpose: "What Delight can a man find in employing a capacity which might be usefully exerted for the Noblest of purposes, in a sort of sullen Labour, in which ... nothing could be more fatal to Mankind than his success?"(VNS p.5) It is tempting to hear an echo of Milton in Burke's depiction of Bolingbroke

16 Ian Hampshire-Monk has pointed to the Baconian assumptions underpinning Burke's understanding of truth and language. Burke had been particularly impressed by Bacon's account of rhetoric and its essential connection to reason in shaping and expanding right opinion. Bacon wrote "The end of Rhetoric is to fill the imagination to sacred reason and not to oppress it", quoting from *The Advancement of Learning* in *The Philosophical Works of Francis Bacon* (London, 1905), pp. 127–128. Ian Hampshire-Monk, 'Rhetoric and Opinion in the Politics of Edmund Burke', *History of Political Thought*, vol. 9, no. 3 (1988), p. 462.

as the Destroyer – the fallen Aristocrat like the fallen Archangel, blighted by perversity of will and squandered talent – but, once again, it is the retrograde mechanics of Bolingbroke's Deism that troubles Burke the most. The world as Bolingbroke described it was, for Burke, a world of automata and dead matter; "sapped" of life and toiling in "sullen labour". Burke's association of the relationship between freedom and animation is telling. Toiling joylessly, in 'sullen labour', was the lot of a beast or a slave. In neither case was it an account of action freely willed, or of power attached to the 'noblest purpose'.

Turning then to the core of Burke's *Vindication* in the "Letter to Lord????", the argument is to counter a series of false presumptions. The world is not a Manichean duality, not a simple binary model of force. It cannot be understood in terms of clean adversarial divisions such as virtue or corruption, nature or artifice, natural or civil society. While Burke employed these dichotomies in his account of government his purpose was to collapse them.[17] The efforts to draw principles out of these overly reduced categories had, according to Burke, always been a dangerous folly. The nature of man was the ultimate revelatory expression of the nature of nature, profound in its simultaneous complexity and simplicity. And here Burke wants to retain something of an older and, perhaps, alchemical magic but to consider it through a new and 'enlightened' lens.

Pointing both to the ends of government and the progress of human nature, Burke had much to say about abstract and utopian schemes for improvement. He confessed that "On considering political Societies, their Origins, their Constitutions, and their Effects, I have sometimes been in a good deal more than Doubt, whether the Creator did ever really intend man for a State of Happiness." The world is neither inherently corrupt, nor man essentially good. The project of trying to establish a fixed principle of nature, and then to design a perfect machine will always fail. It will fail because life is unexpected and always manifests its complexities through incalculable contingency. On the design of human nature, Burke observed, God "has mixed in his Cup a Number of natural Evils, (in spite of the boasts of Stoicism they are Evils) and every Endeavour which the Art and Policy of Mankind has used from the beginning of the World till this Day, in Order to alleviate, or cure them, only serve to introduce new Mischiefs, or to aggravate and inflame the old" (VNS p. 8).

17 David Womersley has underscored the shift away from dichotomous or binary narratives in the history writing of the eighteenth century with the advent of complex and sociological accounts from Bolingbroke and Hume to Gibbon. See for example *Gibbon and the "Watchmen of the Holy City": The Historian and his Reputation 1776–1815* (Oxford: Oxford University Press, 2002).

While Burke's account comports with the conventional soteriologies of his day, emphasizing the fallen nature of man and the insufficiency of a self-willed struggle to achieve either human perfection or a state of grace, it offers a cautionary diagnostic, addressing the question in somatic terms of inflammation, physic, and curative promise. He also referred to natural evils rather than sins. Burke's nod to the arguments of the old Stoics, and with them the Lucretian model of nature is interesting; as though a natural evil, or perhaps ill, was an imperfection or insufficiency, rather than a fatal flaw. He illustrated his point by emphasizing the active nature of mind, its generative possibility the highest expression of human nature. Perfection and completion are static principles, and on Burke's account, God made man restless. Whatever principle might be determined as formative for the 'origin' and 'effects' of 'political societies' and their 'constitutions', they will always be modified. They will be reversed, augmented, expanded, 'improved' or eroded, because these are living things and as such are principles of motion. He concluded, "Besides this, the Mind of Man is itself too active and restless a Principle ever to settle on the true point of quiet" (VNS p. 8). As all ideas are grounded in sense, and so all experience rooted in the body, Burke anchored his account of mind to appetite and passion. "It discovers every Day some craving Want in a Body, which really wants but little. It every day invents some new artificial Rule to guide that Nature which if left to itself were the best and surest Guide" (VNS p 8).

This new account of complexity, to be found in Hume but also in both Burke and Bolingbroke, had a different resonance to that of the older early modern accounts. Complexity, intricacy, and chance are no longer to be understood as forms of vicissitude and chaos. They are part of the fabric of nature. Machiavelli's project of virtu as prowess, as the capacity to stop fortune's wheel, was folly. And those who had read Bacon's *Novum Organum* (*1620*) as a blueprint to master nature had profoundly misunderstood its wisdom. Burke was convinced that efforts to manage these misunderstood or poorly realized accounts of nature only succeeded in introducing new and unexpected corruptions or mistakes. The persistence of this fallacy was a fatal consequence of the mechanical systems of Descartes and Newton; the result of severing the mind from the body, of universals or general laws from particulars, and of abstractions untethered from the concrete. Such abstractions and the mechanical model of nature they supported, could only produce artificial and inherently limited social and political arrangements.

Burke focused on superstition and false religion to illustrate what he took to be the political and moral problem of 'Artificial Society'; false principles derived from the bisection of human nature. For when the mind is restless and at odds with the world, "It finds out imaginary Beings prescribing imaginary

Laws; and then it raises imaginary Terrors to support a belief in the Beings, and an Obedience to the Laws" (VNS p 8). And turning his account to the hierarchy of the natural and 'speculative' imaginations, he ventured that "Many things have been said ... on the Subjection in which we should preserve our Bodies to the Government of our Understanding; but enough has not been said upon the Restraint which our bodily Necessities ought to lay on the extravagant Sublimities, and eccentric Rovings of our Minds" (VNS p 8). There is a fascinating account of the perils of absolutism buried in this passage. As Burke makes the analogy between subject and sovereign quite explicitly, his reader must have wondered if Princes would heed this advice. Would they practice judicious self-mastery, living within their means? and would they eschew foreign entanglements, avoid "eccentric rovings"? The Commons was the inferior branch as a matter of precedence, but it constituted the superior force; demographic power representing the heart of England. With that, Burke argued, it also represented the commercial power, the active power behind the national interest. At least, if the principles of government comport with Burke's account of the balance of nature. He makes his preference in substance and style quite clear: "The Body, or as some like to call it, our inferior Nature is wiser in its own plain Way and attends its own business more directly than the Mind with all its boasted Subtlety" (VNS p. 8).

A large part of the Letter to Lord???? involves a recounting of the history of human conflict.[18] Burke contended that the follies of artificial institutions and their flawed foundation in the Hobbesian account of the state of nature, are evident from the record of past societies. And it is this record rather than any direct knowledge of natural societies that has informed Hobbes' philosophy. A proper study of natural societies would, Burke argued, suggest a different view. Man, in his natural state, was not uniformly driven to conflict, and where conflict occurred it was on a small and largely ineffectual scale. Rather, it is the machinery of the state that creates the drive to war and the efficiency of warfare. Contra Hobbes, Burke argued "In a state of nature it had been impossible to find a number of men sufficient for such Slaughters; agreed in the same Bloody Purposes" (VNS p 16). As a matter of practice small bands not only lacked the scale, they lacked the will, and they had an ill-defined sense of common interest. There was no constant state of warfare, just as there was

18 Burke's account of conflict as an artificial economic and social development, rather than an inherently natural characteristic, was the core of Rothbart's arguments for the sincerity of Burke's voice in the VNS, and also of comparisons made by later scholarship, between Burke and Rousseau. Hampshire-Monk does not find the Rousseauvian interpretation of VNS to be persuasive.

no 'society' of all against all. And primitives, as Burke described them, lacked the 'Art' for war. He continued, as "the means that simple Nature has supplied them with, are by no means adequate to such an End; many scratches, many bruises ... but only a very few deaths" (VNS p 16). Summarizing his arguments on the true origins of social and civil violence, Burke made his purpose clear: "I now come to show that Political Society is quite justly chargeable with the greatest part of the destruction of the species" (VNS p. 15). Hobbes had been profoundly wrong. The political state, Burke argued, far from sheltering and securing man from the violence of natural society, was the chief architect and engine of war. But Burke's criticism of Political Society was not a Godwinian call for anarchy. It was, instead, an argument against the construction of artificial machines and with them the unnatural and abstract impositions of false principles grounded in a flawed and limited science.

3 Blending the Narratives: Progress, The Powers of Life, and the Nature of the State

In the decade that followed the accession of George III, the new sociological science of politics wrestled less with the division of natural versus civil society, and more with the consequence of the theory of nature as a theory of life. Burke had criticized depictions of the apparatus of government as a mechanical devise because such models were insufficient to the intricate complexities involved in 'constituting' a living system; effectively ordering and controlling a social, political and moral organism. The moral sense philosophy of Francis Hutchinson (1660–1739)[19] and the sociological and customary histories of David Hume are part of new efforts to confront the empirical challenge and understand not just the distinction between simple and complex ideas but, at the more profound level of Bacon's method, to explain their relationship. In attempting to do so, the new systems analysis of the 1760's and 70's, manifest in both social and biological science, increasingly blurred the lines between mechanical and organic arguments. Understanding the systems of nature, as systems of life, and in turn, developing and advancing vitalist accounts of natural system were, effectively, interleaved projects. The Baconian challenge of 'knowing nature' was increasingly understood in prospective terms; its object to invent or discover a taxonomy, classification, or some other principle

19 Hutchinson described the moral sense as a form of pleasure from God. Francis Hutchinson, *Inquiry into the Original of our Ideas of beauty and Virtue* (1725) ed. by Aaron Garrett (Indianapolis: Liberty Fund, 2003) I viii p. 83.

of organization that might achieve, not a prescriptive hierarchy, but a more nuanced method of observation. In finding better and more expansive explanations for descriptive variance, hoped the Optimists, more dynamic simulacra for enlightened practice might also be discovered.

Natural Philosophy provided the framework for Natural History, but increasingly the comparative and descriptive examples, and their developmental implications, dominated the texts. The philosophical quest for final causes increasingly gave way to the pursuit of depth of understanding in efficient causes. Natural Philosophy became a history of agency and origins; an empirically embedded description of man and society emerging amidst the rocks, the plants, and the animals, out of the ground of geological time. The new Natural History of the 18th century was also profoundly comparative and practical; as everything from law and language to anatomy, botany, animal husbandry, and archeology set to excavate, dissect, collect, catalogue, label and organize the past. But inevitably, this generated its own forms of revisionism, as things forgotten were found.

Certainly, an interesting parallel and expansion of the Burkean argument can be traced through the historical and juridical sensibilities of many of the Scot's literati, including Hutchinson and Hume. But the explicit effort to connect comparative anatomy, natural history, evolutionary linguistics with theories of social and political progress is notable amongst lawyers. The intellectual and professional contest between two Scots jurists is particularly suggestive of the shifting lines of the debate. Giving competitive accounts of society as a living organism rather than a fixed mechanism, both James Burnett, Lord Monboddo (1714–1799) and his rival Henry Home, Lord Kames (1696–1782) considered life as a "principle of organization".[20] Both responded to the interpretive controversy of Buffon and later Hunter over the Linnean classificatory

20 A contemporary of Monboddo and Kames, John Hunter had been credited as the principal architect of the vitalist debate by the early nineteenth century. Hunter, a renowned anatomist and surgeon wrote extensively on human anatomy, comparative anatomy, epigenesis, as well as gunshot wounds and Teeth. He defined Life as "the consequence of the principle of organization". His students at the Royal College debated whether that account was predicted on the operation of motion or matter, during the 'theory of life controversy' of 1819. This debate on the mechanical versus the vitalist account of life broke out in a series of lectures at the Royal College of Physicians and Surgeons, notably between the Englishman William Lawrence and the Scot John Abernathy. Both students of Hunter's, Lawrence argued the materialist position, not unlike LeMettre's, that man was machine. Abernathy took the view that life was something more; something, he maintained, central to Hunter's account of biomechanics. John Abernathy, *An Inquiry into the Probability and Rationality of Mr. Hunter's Theory of Life* (London: Longmans 1814).

analysis of Teeth. Kames emphasized the developmental significance of teeth as having to do with eating and consumption. Monboddo regarded the comparative development of teeth, mouth, and jaw as critical for the emergence of speech. Kames, like Monboddo, wrote an anthropological history of man, but he advanced a polygenic account of human origins. Monboddo was a monogenesist and, like the German anthropologist and naturalist Johnan von Blumenbach (1752–1840) argued for a single common line of development; one that later branched and diversified into ever more complex and advanced iterations.[21] One account of natural history can be read as a history of predation, the other suggested the rise of communication and social interaction through language. The materialist and nominalist tendencies of Kames' views would inform the rise of theological utilitarianism and have an impact on both William Paley and Thomas Malthus. Monboddo's evolutionist strand of British idealism would influence Erasmus Darwin and Samuel Coleridge, casting a longer shadow over the works of Charles Darwin and Herbert Spencer. But the dynamic and synthetic elements of Monboddo's works suggest the deeper and more comprehensive significance of his philosophical natural history. More than a new descriptive science of nature, it made explicit a new conception of power as motion and of motion as the animating force of all vital systems. Translating the natural philosophy of the seventeenth century into the natural history of the eighteenth, it made the conceptual line of descent from Cudworth and Newton to Bolingbroke and Burke, clear.

Monboddo wrote two philosophical histories: one focusing on the evolution of language and then, extending those speculations, another considering the metaphysical foundations of nature. He read law at Edinburgh and then studied the Dutch jurists on Roman Law at Groningen. Returning to Edinburgh he became an advocate and was subsequently appointed as a Judge to the Court of Sessions in 1767. Over the next six years he wrote his six-volume study of the *Origin and Progress of Language* (1773). Like Bolingbroke's *Philosophical Works,* it was heavily indebted to Ralph Cudworth's *True Intellectual System of the Universe* (1678). Reviving a pre-scholastic reading of Proclus and Plotinus, Monboddo developed his own accounts of a Platonic natural philosophy in *Antient Metaphysics or the Science of Universals* (1779–99).

In *Antient Metaphysics* Monboddo revealed his idealist inclinations toward history and life, as he pushed back against Hume's epistemology, and its Lucretian and materialist assumptions regarding human understanding. He

21 See for example Kames' discussion of distinct species, food and climate in *Sketches of the History of Man* in 4 volumes, 3rd ed. 1788, ed. James Harris (Indianapolis, Liberty Fund, 2007), Bk I p. 12.

also took issue with a particular reading of Newton, specifically with the reception of the mechanical model of motion and force that had been laid out in the *Principia Mathematica*. Suggesting a different interpretive framework for the *Principia* Monboddo, with Cudworth and later Bolingbroke, was drawn to the alchemical dimensions of Newton's Platonism. While Burke had criticized what he took to be the flawed Newtonianism of Bolingbroke's Natural Philosophy, Bolingbroke had praised Cudworth's *System*. And, it is Cudworth's work that Monboddo lauded as being comprehensively in accord with his own beliefs; the inspiration for his own preliminary natural history, his accounts of the evolution of man and society through language, and as possessing the fullest understanding of their foundations in a theory of life.

In Monboddo's account of the State of Nature many of Burke's objections to the mechanical system of Hobbes may be recalled. Describing the relationship between natural and civil society, he maintained that he "would not have it understood that man is naturally the enemy of man; and that the state of nature is a state of war of every man against every man". (OPL Bk II ch 2 p. 222) Monboddo rejected Hobbes' characterization of human nature as inherently violent and combative in a first and natural state. More significantly, he rejected the antimonies of this earlier view; denying that there was any clear line between the natural and artificial states. He argued that no such perfect and polarized conditions had ever existed; indeed, that a comparative view of species would consider such a condition to be profoundly unnatural. Hobbes, contended Monboddo, had described an absurdity; "such a state as neither does not exist nor never did exist in any species of animals". He pointed out that "Hobbes … however genius … [he] may have been … did not know what Man was by Nature, divested of all the habits and opinions he acquired in civil life" (OPL Bk II ch 2 p. 222). To know what man was by nature, required tracing "human nature up to its source" and "diligently" studying the manners of barbarous nations, instead of forming theories of men from what can be observed "among civilized nations" (OPL Bk I ch 10 p. 145). Amplifying Burke's objections to Hobbes' argument Monboddo explained his own position; defending the critical foundations of his method, "My system is founded, not upon hypothesis, but on the history of man, collected from facts, in the same manner as we collect the history of any other animal" (OPL Bk II ch 14 p. 444).

Monboddo's central assumption in *The Origin and Progress of Language* was also the underlying premise of his *Ancient Metaphysics*. That is, that ideas and with them the elements of life, evolve from simple to complex. He applied his principal Philology to the development of mind through language, but he also presented it as a foundation for all ideas of political and moral freedom. Monboddo regarded such ideas to be evolutionary concepts and tied them to the progress of civilization; a progress marked by the distance between man and the brute animals.

There was no reason, Monboddo thought, to consider man as distinct from other kinds of animals, at least not in so far as brute nature was concerned. However, he argued that the capacity to acquire new powers, understood as skills or refinements, was realized through language. In this sense language is the formative and protean power; it summons from the ether things created by the mind. For this reason, Monboddo advocated the study of the origins of language; effectively inventing a historical anthropology of comparative linguistics. The only effective laboratory for the study of man was to be found not in the civil or the natural states exclusively, but rather comparatively, in the various levels of advancement from barbarous living to civilized society. The more civilized the society, the more complex; the more refined and complex, the more rationally human and free. And this is the central developmental point of departure from the older and allegorical accounts of nature; man was not born free, not even (or perhaps especially) in the Garden. Primitive man had no innate understanding of freedom as an idea, much less experienced it as a state or condition. But, Monboddo suggested, if he could describe it he might in time acquire it.

Progress beyond 'simple nature' suggested the expanded augmentation of two interactive faculties. Monboddo described these two capacities as components of speech, comprising concepts and articulation. Through the association, exchange, and refinement of these powers Man was afforded not only the prospect of technical progress but, more significantly, the capacity to become more fully human. The connection between what can be said and what can be thought, is an intriguing part of Monboddo's argument here. He suggested that the reflection and refinement of an idea is a form of interactive cognitive advancement and is dependent on communication. It cannot, therefore, exist outside society. While man had the capacity for Language, much like the human inclination towards freedom, it was not in its first and original natural condition a fully realized capacity; it was not a gift of nature in a material sense, nor was it an innate idea.

Monboddo argued that Language, like Liberty, was acquired. He emphasized that the grunts and brutish noises of animals did not constitute a language and that he did not consider such "inarticulate Utterances" to be speech. Monboddo then went on to distinguish those natural, animal powers that we have from birth, from those which are developmental and the consequence of habit, comparative experience, and the expansion and refinement of skills. Language, he wrote, was "acquired by habit or art". "If it was [given] purely by nature, then it would be co-eval with nature" (OPL Bk I, ch i, p 10) and he contended that it was not. He delineated the various physical, natural powers that are given at birth, observing that men "do not speak from birth in the same manner as they perform the natural operations of breathing, or digesting, or the action of sucking by which an infant takes in the nourishment that is necessary to it" (OPL Bk I ch i, p 11). The distinction between the autonomic or instinctive power to answer the necessities of life, is offered by Monboddo as a contrast to the willed or chosen powers that are advanced though communication. And it is the significance of the social and communicative dimensions of Monboddo's description of the progress of language which is so telling. Making the larger point explicitly Monboddo wrote "the faculty of speech is not the gift of nature to men, but like many others is acquired by him" (OPL bk I ch i p12).

Monboddo's arguments for the advancement of language and the expansion of mind is a cornerstone of his account of the progress of civilization as an evolutionary process of both biological and epistemological significance. Indeed, Monboddo argued, that it was not initially men that made society, but rather society that made men. "[T]here must have been society before language was invented", he speculated. Moreover, "it must have subsisted for some considerable time" and "other arts have been invented before this most difficult one was found out". There is the very suggestive juxtaposition, in Monboddo's consideration of the process of the advancement of language and civilization, of two Baconian principles: invention and discovery. Indeed, without these principles, Monboddo marveled, how to give account of "so difficult an invention"; how to "account [for] how it could at all have been invented" (OPL Bk I ch I p.12). He was, nonetheless, determined to try.

Monboddo began his next chapter with an account of the powers and capacities that define human will and action. He suggested that to understand the biomechanics of human development and its cognitive implications, it was essential to consider the separate faculties distinctly. He enumerated four that need to be understood as essentially inter-related. Firstly, he described the 'energies' or the active operation of the faculties. He emphasized that they are first in the order of conceptions "being perceived by sense". He distinguishes these active impulses from the powers and faculties, which are "latent things" and so "object[s] of intellect and not of sense". He then goes on to consider the faculty that is anterior to the energies, their immediate cause, and "without which we cannot conceive them to be produced". The distinction would seem to be Monboddo's effort to bridge the connection between the perception of and the response to, the sensory faculties; to tie Locke's account of faculty psychology to some explanation of human agency and will. His third and fourth considerations are of Habit and the power of acquiring such habits. He identified Habit as a disposition arising from repeated experience. In this sense the faculty of acquiring a habit is similar to the action of a self-reinforcing loop; and all habits and dispositions may be said to originate in predispositions, which begin as faint inclinations and then become more vivid and more powerful through long repetition and adjustment. It is this connection, between habit and the process and power of acquiring the habit, that Monboddo identifies with learning and the developmental growth of mind. In its infancy it is only dimly self-aware. But as it expands, refines and grows, it gives way to the "dawn of consciousness" and with that "the rise of reason" (OPL Bk I ch ii p 24).

Again, Monboddo made a key and quite distinctive developmental point. Man was not born a fully rational, nor indeed a fully conscious being. Reason and consciousness are tied to some form of collective or communal understanding, and with them the possibility, in more advanced and civilized states, of the development of opinion which he presented as form of social intelligence. "The formation of opinion", contended Monboddo, "came late" and it is the last and most vital stage of this process. For it is only with the formation of opinion that any form of collective agreement or political will can be advanced. Law and government are ultimately dependent on recognition and the shared consensus or agreement of some form of community. Opinion is also the ground for advancing some sense of moral authority, an authority which Monboddo suggests is an artificial or acquired power.[22] He continued "But after we have formed opinions concerning what was good or ill, profitably or otherwise, in human life" we forsake "the guidance of nature and instinct" (OPL Bk I ch ii p 24).

Understanding the moral sense to be another one of Monboddo's acquired powers, and recalling his distinction between habits and powers, the argument follows that it is through the conscious awakening of this enlarged and higher rational habit that we have "resigned ourselves to the government of those opinions and become the artificial creatures we now are ..." Drawing out the significance of this transformative evolution from animal to human, Monboddo continued, "we lost those instincts by degrees, and nature yielded to artificial habit" (OPL Bk I ch ii p24). But he also makes an unusual and seemingly contradictory assertion. Having described nature as yielding to artifice he also suggested that it had been irrevocably altered; effectively becoming a new expression of nature. He described his "artificial creatures"

---

22 Monboddo's account of Moral Sense is strikingly different from Francis Hutchinson's account or indeed Hume's. Both of whom seemed to regard it as some kind of pre-cognitive intuition, spiritual in Hutchinson's account and physiological in Hume's.

and their altered powers, as being temporally conditioned; "these are the natural powers belonging to our species at present". But now, he contended, the altered human nature of modern man contemplates yet another and novel set of innovative powers. This newly self-conscious man would regard such powers as strange and separate. But, Monboddo contended, they are not. Instead, they are extensions or additions to our evolving natures; such that "we are next to speak of the acquired or advantageous powers which we have added to our nature by our own industry and sagacity" (OPE Bk I ch ii p 24).

Monboddo described the attributes and expertise of advanced civilization as constituting the "acquired or advantageous powers". He linked these ideas to his developmental thesis, suggesting an evolutionary gradualist, rather than stadial, account of progress and civilization. "Of this kind" he wrote "are all the sciences, all the arts liberal and mechanic, all the commodities and pleasures of life" (OPE Bk I ch ii p 24). All of these, he argued, are to be understood in terms of acquired advantage. "Even civil society itself, and almost everything belonging to it" were acquisitions that conferred adaptive advantage to this developing creature. Social evolution, much like biological human evolution, was for Monboddo, a story of adaptive hybridity. He presents the history of a dynamic organic system; at once both natural and artificial. And the things that belonged to civil society, the things of commerce and law, were equally extensions of this adaptive and synthetic nature.

Emphasizing the interplay between the natural and the acquired powers he observed, with an eye to man as he is 'presently' and actively constituted, "we shall find that our nature is chiefly constituted of acquired habits, and that we are much more creatures of custom and art than of nature" (OPL Bk I ch ii p 24). But again, suggesting the blended constitution of man, he continued "It is a common saying that Habit (meaning custom) is second nature. I add that it is more powerful than the first, and in great measure destroys and absorbs the original nature". Monboddo makes a point of considerable subtlety here. It is not the case that man has become wholly artificial. But the account of metamorphosis that he described, suggests that he viewed modern man as a qualitatively different creature from the animal he began as. It will take Monboddo some twelve chapters, and a long series of discussions regarding the fallacies of Locke, to work through this distinction. Although, he succinctly described his divergence from the broader impact of Locke's materialism and the inference that later authors would draw from it.

Pointing out the direction "Mr. Locke's philosophy naturally leads", Monboddo argued the consequence; that it "makes the mind so dependent on body as not to operate without it and knows nothing beyond sensation and its ideas as he calls them" (OPL Bk I ch vii p 86).[23] But the distinctive nature of Monboddo's emergent human being was to be found in its profound freedom from that dependence, and in its protean capacity for self-making. Returning to his discussion of habit, he wrote of the distinctive nature of human beings. Continuing his account of man's second nature, he observed "for it is the capital and distinguishing characteristic of our species that we can make ourselves, as it were, over again, so that the original nature in us can hardly be seen; and it is with the greatest difficulty that we can distinguish it from the acquired" (OPL Bk I ch ii p 25).

Locke's reductionism, as Monboddo presented it, had collapsed a theory of sense perception into a theory of ideas but with no theory of action; no account of the power or connection between them. Such a theory suggested limited and inadequate accounts of life and nature. He granted that Locke "did not mean to draw such consequences from his philosophy", but that "nonetheless such consequences have been drawn". Suggesting his own position in comparison, Monboddo explained "the philosophy that I have learned is of a very different kind; it teaches me that mind is the most ancient of things; and that it alone has activity, and the principle of motion in itself, is the efficient cause" (OPL Bk I ch vii p 88). While the suggestion here is that Locke's failure was to give an adequate account of innate ideas (even as he rejected them), the focus of Monboddo's critique is on the impact that Locke's materialism had on latter day empiricists and sceptics, or the 'mechanic philosophers'. For his own part, Monboddo sought to understand something, as he himself said, more ancient. His purpose was to develop a genealogy of mind, and to mark the progressive transformation of its powers of cognition as matters both of biological and conceptual significance. The description of this metamorphosis is striking, and it points to the immediate target of Monboddo's criticism, the historical empiricism of Hume.

When Monboddo alluded to the impact of Locke's *Essay Concerning Human Understanding* it was as a pointed barb for the author of *A Treatise of Human Nature*. With Hume in his sites, Monboddo gave his own developmental account of the emergent stages of man, writing "Thus man is formed, not however at once, but by degrees, and in succession: for he appears at first to be little more than a mere vegetable hardly deserving the name of zoophyte;

23 In this volume, Ioannis Evrigenis highlights the impediments and drives underpinning the politics of Locke's faculty psychology. In particular, he refers to Locke's depiction of Liberty as bounded by the law of nature, where even the social impulse was hard-wired. Man was materially conditioned to exit solitude as God had "put him under strong obligations of necessity, convenience, and inclination to drive him into society".

then he gets sense, but sense only, so he is but little better than muscle; then he becomes an animal of a more complete kind; then a rational creature; and finally a man of intellect and science, which is the summit and completion of our nature" (OPL Bk I ch xiv p 183). There are intriguing parallels both from comparative anatomy and from horticulture to Monboddo's embryology. But his is both a biological and cognitive account, where the development of consciousness is the consequence of an ever-increasing activity of mind. The early notion of planting seeds, and of simple things moving through more complex stages, first of muscle and raw nerves then with reflexive sense an animal of a more complete kind, gives way, through adolescence, to a more rational creature; becoming finally a man of reason, "where intellect and science complete our natures." It was the emphasis on the process of completion, of the translation of latent powers into action, that Monboddo regarded to have been absent in the philosophy of Locke. It was, he argued, equally absent in Hume's philosophy. But while Monboddo conceded that Locke may not have intended the adverse philosophical consequences of his *Essay*, he offered no such defense in Hume's case. In particular, and where it shaped Hume's account of History, it was an absence that revealed the more pernicious dimensions of his skepticism.

Much as Burke had railed against Bolingbroke's failure to shift the foundations of science, Monboddo's attack on Hume is suffused with more than mere critical disappointment. Hume's failure to ground his Philosophy of History in a proper 'scientific foundation', needed to be addressed through a deep consideration of its sources. Monboddo therefore applied his method to the philosophical roots of 'true science', or the *Ancient Metaphysics*. Building his case against Hume, Monboddo argued for an empirically grounded idealism, effectively giving an account of the relationship between what Kant described as the 'thing in itself' and our perception and understanding of it. In Book V of *Ancient Metaphysics* Monboddo explicitly defined his view of the 'first science', as he considered the fabric of the mind in its critical, but also, very situationally specific relationships with logic and language. Unequivocally stating that "The principles of all Arts and Sciences [are] to be found in Metaphysics" (AM BK V ch I p372), Monboddo linked the metaphysical to the epistemological question; maintaining that the integration of those two lines of inquiry provided the forensic bottom for all truth claims.

Contending that the principles of metaphysics are transcendental, and that they comprised the simplest of truths, Monboddo identified his central concern, declaring that the "Truth, of which I am to treat here" is of "Logical Truths". He chose to focus on these truths, he said, because most of the perceivable world is encountered through the experience and organization of sense.

But, he explained, these 'truths' are also perceived and ordered by the mind; "comparing together its own ideas or perceptions" (AM bk V ch I p 374). As Monboddo developed his account of the ancient philosophers, a fascinating inversion of his 'first principle' of science and nature occurred. Making the case for the bedrock of logical truth, he now rather counterintuitively "argued from art to nature, that is from the effect to the cause, {all art being derived from nature}, instead of arguing from nature to art, that is from the cause to the effect." Setting the elegant simplicity of the world alongside the complex fabric of the mind – his distinction between metaphysical truth and logical truth – Monboddo drew his account of the foundations of science into a larger consideration of the dynamic primacy of art and nature. In doing so, he also explained the epistemic link between the natural animals we once were and the artificial creatures we have become; such that the effect has now become the instrument and engine of change, absorbing and so replacing the anterior condition of nature, with its new iteration.

The relationship between mind and body had been philosophically severed by Descartes. A profound and fatal conceptional error which, according to Monboddo, had infected British ideas and contributed to Locke's misunderstanding of Aristotle. The view that Locke had been led astray by Descartes would persist, re-surfacing as late as 1818 in the writings of Samuel Taylor Coleridge (1772–1834). Coleridge was another admirer of Bacon, Cudworth and Newton, a staunch if complex defender of British Idealism, and the author of his own *Hints toward the Formation of a more Comprehensive Theory of Life.*[24] He wrote a series of philosophical letters on Locke, first to Josiah Wedgewood and later to Lord Liverpool.[25] In them he contended that the "mechano-corpuscular fallacy", or the crisis of materialism, first advanced by the works of the atomists Dalton and Lasage, was now manifesting in the new political economy of the Utilitarians. Increasingly seeping into policy circles, it exerted a pernicious influence on government. Making the political consequences of this 'fallacy' explicit, Coleridge described it as a form of modern Jacobinism; as a dangerous French Philosophy corrupting a morally vacuous British Politics.

24 Samuel Taylor Coleridge's, *Hints Toward the Foundation of a More Comprehensive Theory of Life* (1818) was composed for submission for the Hunterian prize. It was edited and published posthumously by Seth Watson M.D. (London: John Churchill, 1848). See Pamela Edwards, *The Statesman's Science: History, Nature and Law in the Political Thought of Samuel Taylor Coleridge* (Columbia University Press, 2004).

25 STC to Josiah Wedgwood of February 1801, in *Collected Letters* vol II p. 682. And to Lord Liverpool in *Unpublished Letters of S.T.Coleridge*, ed. by E.L.Griggs, vol. ii, p. 224.

While Monboddo did not make the case for the revolutionary significance of the new science as directly as Coleridge would later do, he was deeply troubled by the social and political implications of its skepticism. Considerable attention and focus in *Ancient Metaphysics* is devoted to countering the radical uses of Pyrrho made by the rational empirical philosophers of enlightenment.[26] Much as Burke had attacked Bolingbroke for the destructive critical dimensions of his *Philosophical Works*, Monboddo pointed to the ambitious and reckless uses of the Pyrrhonic thesis at the heart of Hume's skepticism. "The doubt concerning the existence of the material world was first started in modern times by Dr Berkeley, and greedily catched at by the author of the *Treatise upon Human Nature* and the *Essays*, as very favourable to his design of overturning all science and certainty, and evidence of every kind." Hume's critical project, as described by Monboddo, was to undermine the forensic ground of law and science. He continued his comparison of Pyrrho and Hume: "Pyrrho, who finding no other way to distinguish himself, and to get a name amongst the great philosophers, [was] … out of mere vanity … first to broach this extravagant paradox". Voicing his explicit objection, Monboddo summed up, "Mr Hume's purpose [is] of putting an end to all science" (AM BK V ch vi p 414). As a counter to Hume's method Monboddo proposed to preserve the experiential and forensic foundations of science and law by making his own arguments for induction.

The philosophical system that Monboddo defended in *Ancient Metaphysics*, may be regarded as a post-script to his developmental natural history of language. The fundamental arguments laid out in the first book of OPL are taken up critically in book two and then worked through as a historical anthropology of science and law in the final four volumes. Having rejected the dualism of Descartes, he suggested its fatal application in the materialist and mechanical philosophies that would follow. Addressing the political implications of this method in British ideas, Monboddo explained the errors of Hobbes, Locke, and now Hume. His commentary is intended once again to mirror his method, as he highlighted reductive error in reference to a more complex set of actions and impulses; as requiring a more active account of time and agency. Hobbes, Locke, even Hume, had not really understood the workings of history; more than a chronicle or mere catalogue of past events, it was the

26 While Monboddo paid considerable tribute to Cudworth, it was another Cambridge Platonist Henry More who acknowledged his own deep struggle with the Pyrrhonic thesis. More advanced a more complex and intuitive form of rationalism as a consequence of his deep encounter with the skeptism of Pyrrho.

evolutionary development of life and mind. Monboddo, by contrast had what Arthur Lovejoy once described as 'the genetic habit of mind'.[27]

Returning, in Book Two, to the errors of Hobbes, Monboddo took up the question of association and the uses of society. He did however concede one Hobbesian point; arguing that the origin and purpose of association was to "make the weaker more powerful than the stronger". But, he insisted, that did not validate the force of Hobbes's larger argument about the intrinsic violence of the state of nature; and that he did not "retract his view that Hobbes was wrong to declare the state of nature as a state of war". Instead Monboddo advanced the developmental point that had been made by Burke and a year earlier by Rousseau,[28] that "in the state of nature there were much fewer occasions for quarrel than in the state of society." There is another element of Burke's argument against Hobbes from the *Vindication* which is worth recalling. Monboddo offered a parallel critique to Burke's account of artifice and imagination as they shaped the needs of the body and wants of the mind. And as an older and wiser Burke would write in *An Appeal from the Old Whigs to the New*, "Art is the Nature of Man." However, much as this may suggest a Burkean echo in Monboddo, this too is an argument that will develop in a different direction.

Monboddo was no Mandevillian, but he was able to find a positive, and indeed progressive role for some of the more appetitive passions and to recognize the importance of ambition and reach. The language of honour, which Rousseau and Burke both cast in a positive, though ancient light, captures some of the substance of Monboddo's more modern rendering of "fame, power and pre-eminence". But it did not incorporate the evolutionary reach of Monboddo's account of pride, which far from being an occasion to Fall, is presented as the drive behind civilized advancement. But the key point Monboddo makes in his answer to Hobbes and Rousseau is that conflict is neither intrinsically from nature nor society, nor is it strictly a response to hierarchy or institutional inequality; it is from scarcity. In doing so, he shifted the grounds of the discussion to the political and economic question; how to justly or prudently distribute scarce commodities?

---

27 Arthur O Lovejoy, 'Monboddo and Rousseau', *Modern Philology*, vol. 30, no. 3 (Feb 1933), pp. 275–296.

28 Rousseau's *Discourse on Inequality* (1755) made parallel criticism. Ian Hampshire-Monk finds no direct link between *The Discourse* and *Vindication*. 'Rousseau, Burke's Vindication of Natural Society and Revolutionary Ideology', *European Journal of Political Theory*, vol. 3 (July 2010).

Monboddo considered the distinction between art and instinct as it pertained to acquired advantage, turning the epistemological question of imagination towards the uses and value of ambition. He continued "For in the natural state man can only quarrel about the necessaries of life and the gratification of natural appetite; whereas in the civil state man quarrels about fame, power, and pre-eminence, and all the numberless gratifications of vanity and luxury" (OPL Bk II ch X p 404). But having established the blended and progressive nature of man, ascending as he did from animal to human being, impelled by will and active reason to remake himself through acquired powers, Monboddo did not argue that ambition, and its "numberless" spurs, was necessarily a bad thing. And here his distance from Burke and Rousseau is evident. Dreaming beyond the 'necessaries', Monboddo would seem to suggest that progress is only bounded by imagination; translated into a shared purpose through a process of discursive deliberation.

4 Conclusion

By the second half of the eighteenth century, accounts of the State of Nature had increasingly been overtaken by considerations of the systems of nature and the social and economic nature of the state. The natural world may be viewed as a desert or a garden, and scarcity arises in primitive and advanced societies. The question that would eventually drive the political economists of the 19th century was whether the remedy to scarcity lay within the grasp of acquired powers? Developing accounts of the 'natural art' of such powers, historically minded critics such as Burke and Monboddo could imagine the second nature of the state. No longer suggesting the conceptual dichotomy of the old legal fiction, pitting civilization against a pure and primordial condition of savagery or innocence, the eighteenth century 'new histories' of enlightenment attempted to track the evolution of human societies as branches of natural and social science.

Advancing the terms of the debate on Nature, from the philosophical binaries and zero-sum economies of politics and war to a dynamic and vital social science of progress, Monboddo and Burke signal the enlightenment recovery of an empirically grounded Platonic natural philosophy. Focusing on the manifest power of human action, of advancement and self-making, it was a science of history as much as a philosophy of nature. The older and static accounts of the State of Nature which had justified dynastic authority and political order for Hobbes and for Locke were, increasingly after 1756, overtaken by this new science of history. It offered, by the 1770's, a blended narrative which could account for the adaptive hybridity and regulatory complexity of Empire, breaking the bonds of bloodlines and recrafting the measures of allegiance. Civil Society, as a second nature of the State, could now be understood as the self-sufficient and dynamic expression of a vibrant social ecology. No longer a debate about the state of nature, the new political vitalism of the eighteenth century reframed the question as a deep inquiry into the nature of the state.

Select Bibliography

Primary Sources

Bolingbroke, Henry St. John Viscount *The Philosophical Works of the Late Viscount Bolingbroke* ed. David Mallet in 5 volumes (London 1754).

Burke, Edmund, *A Vindication of Natural Society* ed. Frank N Pagano (Indianpolis: Liberty Fund, (Indianapolis: Liberty Fund, 1757, 1982).

Cudworth, Ralph, *The True Intellectual Nature of the Universe: wherein All the Reason and Philosophy of Atheism is Confuted* (London, 1678).

Kames, Henry Home, Lord *Historical Law Tracts* ed. James Harris (Indianapolis: Liberty Fund, 1758, 2019).

Monboddo, James Burnett, Lord, *Antient Metaphysics: or the Science of Universals*, 6 vol (Edinburgh 1779–99). *Of the Origin and Progress of Language* 6 vol (London: J. Balfour, 1774–92).

Secondary Sources

Bourke, Richard, *Empire and Revolution: The Political Life of Edmund Burke* (Princeton N.J.: Princeton University Press, 2015).

Bromwich, David, *The Intellectual Life of Edmund Burke from the Sublime and the Beautiful to American Independence* (Cambridge Mass.: Harvard University Press, 2014).

Buchwald Jed Z. and Mordechai Feingold, *Newton and the Origins of Civilization* (Princeton N.J.: Princeton University Press, 2013).

Clark, J.C.D.C, *English Society: Religion, Ideology and Politics During the Long Eighteenth Century* (Cambridge: Cambridge University Press, 2000)

Israel, Jonathan *Radical Enlightenment: Philosophy and the Making of Modernity 1650–1750* (Oxford: Oxford University Press, 2001)

Pocock, J.G.A. *Barbarism and Religion* vol 5 (Cambridge: Cambridge University Press, 2011).

Womersley, David, *Gibbon and the 'Watchmen of the Holy City': The Historian and his reputation 1776–1815* (Oxford: Oxford University Press, 2002).

Wootton, David, *The Invention of Science: A New History of the Scientific Revolution* (Penguin Random House UK, 2015).

Young, B.W. *Religion and Enlightenment in Eighteenth-century England: Theological Debate Between Locke and Burke* (Oxford: The Clarendon Press, 1998).

CHAPTER 12

Their Own State(s) of Nature

The Enlightenment Social Imaginary and the Invention of Hungarian Ethnic Origins

László Kontler

Abstract

The Jesuit scholar János Sajnovics's (1733–85) work on the 'sameness' of the Hungarian and Sámi language, first published in 1770, re-ignited discussion on the ethnic kinship and origin of the Hungarians, traditionally associated with the Turkic or 'Scythian' warrior peoples of the Eurasian steppe. Participants in this discussion relied extensively on international and domestic literature in ethnography and global geography, classifying these peoples according to the categories of stadial history as savage or barbarous. As Scythianism was entwined with discourses of social distinction and political privilege of the Hungarian elite, and the Kingdom of Hungary was both a multi-ethnic entity and part of the larger Habsburg composite polity whose enlightened reformist leaders were challenging these privileges, the subject had significant ideological implications. Representations of the Sámi even assumed dehumanising overtones. On a different level of abstraction, some of the contributors, like the par excellence Hungarian *philosophe* György Bessenyei (1746–1811), also dedicated important texts to larger questions of nature, human nature and culture. The paper examines the interferences among these different genres, and the ways in which assumptions about the nation's 'own' past and natural states, and their ambiguous confrontation with mainstream European intellectual developments, shaped emerging discourses of identity during the Hungarian national awakening, with long-standing consequences.

Keywords

Enlightenment in Hungary – stadial history – linguistic kinship – Sámi – Scythians – György Bessenyei

 | DOI:10.1163/9789004499621_014

> I believe that Atila is not needed for the augmentation of the glory of my noble nation: but I also believe that after Schlötzer [sic], who (at least to my mind) is one of the most nationally biased writers, *we are insulted* [emphasis added] by some of the newer and novelty seeking German authors when they want to call into question in one way or another that the Huns and the Hungarians derive from the same nation.[1]

•••

> What we know of our Asian ancestors is little, and for the most part uncertain. The newer history has even begun to *deprive us of the joy* [emphasis added] that we can regard ourselves as the offspring of Attila.[2]

∴

1 Introduction

This case study will attempt to highlight the peculiar ways in which stadial history as an interpretative framework central to the analysis of human society in the mainstream of Enlightenment thought fertilised, in ambivalent ways but with long-standing consequences, the self-understanding of Hungary's noble and educated elites in the late eighteenth and early nineteenth centuries.[3] Until recently, such processes of fertilisation between apparently more advanced and backward regions were usually studied from a perspective based on notions of belatedness, incompleteness and lack of originality. Such

---

1 Mihály Csokonai Vitéz to István Kultsár, 1802 [?], in Mihály Csokonai Vitéz, *Összes művei két kötetben*, ed. Cyrill Horváth (Budapest: Magyar Könyvkiadó Intézet, 1901), vol. 2, p. 907. – Unless indicated otherwise, translations from other languages into English are by the author.

2 Ferenc Kazinczy, *Tübingai pályaműve a magyar nyelvről* (1808), ed. Gusztáv Heinrich (Budapest: Régi Magyar Könyvtár, 1916), p. 148.

3 I thank Mary Fuller for her generous feedback on the first draft prepared for our project workshop, and the editors and all participants for further comments. An earlier version in Hungarian was published in Annamária Bíró and Emese Egyed (eds.), *Aranka György és a tudomány megújuló alakzatai* (Cluj: Erdélyi Múzeum-Egyesület, 2018), pp. 159–178. Some passages have been revised from Per Pippin Aspaas and László Kontler, *Maximilian Hell (1720–92) and the Ends of Jesuit Science in Enlightenment Europe* (Leiden and Boston: Brill, 2020), Chapters 6.3 and 8.2.

a perspective is indeed abundantly supported by evidence even of regional voices, like accounts of travellers from Eastern Europe lamenting the gap that separated their experiences in the progressive 'West' from their domestic realities. Yet, inquiries informed by this approach are analytically impoverished, and the outcome is uninteresting. Even if the intellectual history of 'peripheral' lands is meaningful to study largely as a history of receptions, it is reasonable to acknowledge the agency of the recipient side, including its intention and ability to produce not faint replicas of metropolitan ideas, but creative adaptations and original responses reflecting contingent and context-dependent agendas. Below, I hope to illustrate the merits of this assumption.

The Enlightenment whose social imaginary figures in the title was not a unitary project with a set of fixed propositions, but a series of debates about a largely shared range of questions, pursued with a shared spirit of critical inquiry (albeit with different approaches, methodologies and ideologies), in novel and specifically tailored cultural and institutional settings. At its heart were questions concerning 'humanity:' what it is to be human, and consequently, what 'mankind' is.[4] The analytical frameworks in which these questions were studied included the naturalisation of man (the exploration of human phenomena with the empirical approach of natural history), and the temporalisation of human difference (positing a single, unitary human species, ascribing differences to context in time and space). The chief endeavour was to understand the regularities or laws governing the functioning of human beings and societies, on the basis of data (accounts, descriptions, specimens, visual representations etc.) supplied by naturalists and philosophical travellers accompanying explorers, as well as laboratory work and observation on the domestic front, arranged into the intertwining disciplinary fields of the emerging science(s) of man: natural history (including physical anthropology and the allocation of man's place in systems of taxonomy), moral philosophy/psychology (as well as aesthetics), political economy, ethnology, geography, and stadial history.

The boundaries between these branches of inquiry were inevitably blurred. Stadial history embraced most of the others: it proposed to offer a narrative of progress in the mode of subsistence, cultural patterns, legal arrangements and institutions of government through stages from rudeness to refinement: a grand scale history of humans, self-regarding and suspicious by nature, but

---

4 For a brief statement, see Ann Thomson, '(Why) does the Enlightenment matter?', *Diciottesimo secolo*, 1 (2016), pp. 147–68. I discuss the early-modern "invention of humanity" in László Kontler, 'Inventing 'humanity': early-modern perspectives', in Heikki Haara, Mikko Immanen and Koen Stapelbroek (eds.), *Helsinki Yearbook of Intellectual History I: Passions, Politics and the Limits of Society* (Oldenbourg: De Gruyter, 2020), pp. 25–46.

applying their reason to the suppression of the violence of their passions and becoming sociable; a structural account of the refinement of manners (habits and standards of social interaction) thanks to the increasing sophistication of subsistence (through the stages of hunting-gathering, pasturing, agriculture, commerce) and leading to the establishment and consolidation of institutions of moderate government and rule of law, as well as to the development of the arts and sciences.[5] For the purposes of the present volume and this chapter, it is of crucial significance that eighteenth century stadial history owed a great deal of its theoretical approach and methodology to the proposition of the seventeenth century classics of natural law that the transition of human communities into the state of civil society and government was preceded and triggered by a considerable amount of socio-cultural progress in the state of nature.[6]

In many ways, this was a self-congratulatory vision of the purported rise of modern Western Europe to the top of the civilisational ladder, producing counter-images conceived in derogatory and orientalising terms, such as the

5 The literature on Enlightenment stadial history would fill a small library. Selectively, see Gladys Bryson, *Man and Society: The Scottish Inquiry of the Eighteenth Century* (Princeton: Princeton University Press, 1945); Michèle Duchet, *Anthropologie et histoire au siècle des lumières* (Paris: Albin Michel, 1971); Antonello Gerbi, *The Dispute of the New World: The History of a Polemic 1750–1900* (Pittsburgh: University of Pittsburgh Press, 1973); Ronald L. Meek, *Social Science and the Ignoble Savage* (Cambridge: Cambridge University Press, 1976); Peter J. Marshall and Glyndwr Williams, *The Great Map of Mankind: Perceptions of New Worlds in the Age of Enlightenment* (Cambridge, MA: Harvard University Press, 1982); Anthony Pagden, *The Fall of Natural Man: The American Indian and the Origins of Comparative Ethnology* (Cambridge: Cambridge University Press, 1986); Anthony Pagden, *European Encounters with the New World* (New Haven: Yale University Press, 1993); Roxann Wheeler, *The Complexion of Race: Categories of Difference in Eighteenth-Century British Culture* (Philadelphia: University of Pennsylvania Press, 2000); Hans Erich Bödeker, Philippe Büttgen, and Michel Espagne, eds., *Die Wissenschaft vom Menschen in Göttingen um 1800* (Göttingen: Vandenhoeck & Ruprecht, 2008); Silvia Sebastiani, *I limiti del progresso: Razza e genere nell'Illuminismo scozzese* (Bologna: Il Mulino, 2008), and the revised English edition, *The Scottish Enlightenment: Race, Gender, and the Limits of Progress* (Houndmills: Palgrave Macmillan, 2013). Cf. also the chapters by Francesca Iurlaro, David Grewal, Simone Zurbuchen and Pamela Edwards in the present volume. For Hungarian resonances, see Olga Penke, *Filozofikus világtörténetek és történetfilozófiák: A francia és a magyar felvilágosodás* (Budapest: Balassi Kiadó, 2000); Péter Balázs, *Biblia, história és bölcselet a felvilágosodás korában* (Budapest: L'Harmattan, 2013).

6 See e.g. Istvan Hont, 'The Language of Sociability and Commerce: Samuel Pufendorf and the Theoretical Foundations of the 'Four-Stages' Theory', in Anthony Pagden (ed.), *The Languages of Political Theory in Early Modern Europe* (Cambridge: Cambridge University Press, 1986), pp. 253–76; and the chapters by Ioannis Evrigenis and Emile Simpson in this volume.

'inventing of Eastern Europe.'[7] Compared to the extensive literature (see n. 4 and 5) on the applications of this pattern of interpretation in the mainstream Enlightenment, relatively little attention has been paid to its appropriations in the lands that were themselves 'orientalised' – as I shall attempt to show on the Hungarian example, with curious effects and strikingly long-standing repercussions.

2 Sámi Savages and Barbarous Scythians

The authors of the two quotations in the motto above – Hungary's greatest lyricist of the late eighteenth century, and the foremost broker of Hungarian literary life and the ultimate arbiter of taste, himself a writer of stature and a tireless champion of modernising Hungarian as a literary language – were enlightened patriots whose zeal for the fatherland and its virtues was of a measured, rational and critical sort. Several years later, Kazinczy even expressed his exasperation at the proliferation of epic works conceived in the 'Árpádiász' genre (adulating the ninth century chieftain who led the Magyar conquest of the Carpathian Basin and linking him with the legacy of Attila the Hun) and the concomitant 'rage of nationality', which he 'abhorred'.[8] Yet, the association of their nation with the epitome of the fearful warriors of the steppe was a source of 'joy' to them, and they could only conceive any questioning of it as 'insulting'.

The 'joy' and pride which the Hungarian elite took in its prestigious steppe kinship and its supposed derivation from the Huns was rooted in centuries-old, still compelling narratives of identity. It was incorporated in the *Gesta Hungarorum* (Deeds of the Hungarians) of the obscure twelfth-century royal notary Anonymus, whose account of the ninth-century 'reconquest' of the territory of the future Kingdom of Hungary by the Magyar descendants of the people of Attila became the basis of a fully-fledged social and political ideology of the Hungarian nobility in a work written in 1282–85 by Simon Kézai (Simon

---

7 For now classic discussions, see Larry Wolff, *Inventing Eastern Europe. The Map Civilization on the Mind of the Enlightenment* (Stanford: Stanford University Press, 1994); Maria Todorova, *Imagining the Balkans* (Oxford: Oxford University Press, 1997).

8 Csokonai once planned to write an 'Árpádiász' himself. Cf. Kazinczy to György Zádor, 16 December 1825. *Kazinczy Ferenc levelezése* (21 vols.), ed. János Váczy (Budapest: Magyar Tudományos Akadémia, 1890–1911), vol. 19. p. 485; Kazinczy to Sándor Kisfaludy, 1 May 1831. *Kazinczy Ferenc levelezése*, vol. 23, ed. Jenő Berlász, Margit Busa, Klára Cs. Gárdonyi, Géza Fülöp (Budapest: Akadémiai Kiadó, 1960), p. 403.

of Kéza), bearing the same title. Kézai made two fundamental propositions. The first one was that the nobility's social pre-eminence, privileges, and political rights derived from the military prowess demonstrated by their ancestors in the taking of the land. Second, Kézai claimed that a sort of *politia commixta*, mixed government existed already among the Huns of Attila, and was also preserved among their Hungarian offspring. In other words, this discourse of ethnic identity was at bottom an ideology of social distinction whose political aspect was a Hungarian version of ancient constitutionalism.[9] It was perpetuated by several later medieval and humanist chronicles, a significant literary tradition which even had a popular, orally transmitted branch, and the most frequently printed Hungarian book of all time: the 1517 *Tripartitum*, a collection of customary law by jurist and statesman István Werbőczy (1458–1541).[10] The works of Anonymus and Kézai were first printed in 1746 and 1781, respectively,[11] a period in which this theory still held considerable authority.

While Anonymus was edited by the Protestant scholar Mátyás (Matej) Bél (1684–1749) and his disciple Johann Georg Schwandtner (1716–91), and Kézai by the Piarist erudite Elek Horányi (1736–1809), it is noteworthy that historical interest among Hungary's Jesuits was also turning in this period from questions of chronology and dynastic issues to problems central to discourses of identity.[12] It was also the work of Jesuit scholars that was perceived as a major 'insult' by the adherents of the theory of Scythian origins because of affirming the 'affinity' or kinship of the Hungarian language with Finnish and Sámi or 'Lappish' (later identified as the Finno-Ugrian theory, and associated by Csokonai with the Göttingen scholar August Ludwig Schlözer [1735–1809]). The Sámi-Hungarian language kinship theory looked back to a century-old history, predominantly thanks to German scholars, when it was thrown into prominence by the appearance of Joannes (János) Sajnovics's (1733–85) *Demonstratio. Idioma Ungarorum et Lapponum idem esse* (first in Copenhagen [1770], and then in Trnava/Nagyszombat/Tyrnau [1771]). The treatise of Sajnovics, a mathematician and astronomer by training, was based on

9 See Jenő Szűcs, 'Theoretische Elemente in Meister Simon de Kézas *Gesta Hungarorum* (1282–1285): Beiträge zur Herausgestaltung der 'europäischen Synchronismus' der Ideenstrukturen,' in Szűcs, *Nation und Geschichte* (Cologne: Böhlau, 1981), pp. 263–328.

10 See several studies in Martyn Rady (ed), *Custom and Law in Central Europe* (Cambridge: Centre for European Legal Studies, 2003).

11 György Szabados, *A magyar történelem kezdeteiről: Az előidő-szemlélet hangsúlyváltásai a XV–XVIII. században* (Budapest: Balassi Kiadó, 2006), pp. 14, 19.

12 György Pray, *Annales veteres Hunnorum Avarum et Hungarorum* (Vienna: Schulz, 1761); György Pray, *Dissertationes historico-criticae in annales veteres Hunnorum, Avarum et Hungarorum* (Vienna: Bernard, 1774).

fieldwork among the Sámi during an expedition to northern Scandinavia for the observation of the 1769 transit of Venus, led by Maximilian Hell (1720–92), Sajnovics's boss at the university observatory in Vienna. Three decades later, Sajnovics's work received reinforcement from the *Affinitas linguae hungaricae cum linguis fennicae originis grammatice demonstrata* (1799) by Sámuel Gyarmathi (1751–1830).[13]

As we shall see, Sajnovics himself suffered a fair amount of abuse because of his embracing the derogatory affiliation with the supposedly inferior 'Lapps'. However, the singling out of Schlözer as a culprit by Csokonai and others was no pure accident either. Schlözer not only embraced, edited and published the work of earlier German scholars who had written on 'Finno-Ugrian' subjects, expressed his mind in agreement with them in his *Allgemeine Nordische Geschichte* (1771), appreciated the contribution of Sajnovics already in 1771, and enthusiastically encouraged the work of Gyarmathi. He was also well known as a political writer and a theorist of state sciences whose views were antithetical to a system of society and politics based on estates distinctions – views which were understood, for instance, to be contaminating the minds of those Hungarian supporters of Joseph II's (1740–90, r. 1780–90) enlightened absolutist reform policies who studied with him at the University of Göttingen. Inasmuch as he was 'anti-Hungarian' (or, as Csokonai put it, 'nationally biased'), this was largely due to his judgement on the attitudes of the bulk of the Hungarian political class.[14]

It is interesting to note here that in the Trnava edition of the *Demonstratio* Sajnovics (or presumably his superior Hell) made efforts to tacitly forge a link for the Sámi and the Hungarians with the Huns by tracing their languages back to a common origin in Chinese (supposedly the source of all Asian languages),[15]

---

13 For more details, see Per Pippin Aspaas and László Kontler, 'Before and After 1773: Central European Jesuits, the Politics of Language and Discourses of Identity in the Late Eighteenth Century Habsburg Monarchy', in Gábor Almási and Lav Šubarić (eds.), *Latin at the Crossroads of Identity. The Evolution of Linguistic Nationalism in the Kingdom of Hungary* (Leiden and Boston: Brill, 2015), pp. 95–118; on the expedition and its results, see Aspaas and Kontler, *Maximilian Hell*, Chapters 4–6.

14 On the central role of the University of Göttingen as a point of orientation and a source of inspiration for the rank-and-file of Hungarian Josephists', see Éva H. Balázs, *Berzeviczy Gergely, a reformpolitikus (1763–1795)* (Budapest: Akadémiai Kiadó, 1967), pp. 86–117. Some of the argument is worked into the same author's *Hungary and the Habsburgs 1765–1800. An Experiment in Enlightened Absolutism* (Budapest: Central European University Press, 1997).

15 Zsuzsa C. Vladár, 'Hell mint nyelvész: A Kar-jelia etimológia és a kínai hasonlítás példája,' in Tamás Forgács, Miklós Németh, and Balázs Sinkovics (eds), *A nyelvtörténeti kutatások újabb eredményei IX* (Szeged: SZTE, 2017), pp. 337–50, here pp. 338–40.

which may point to an awareness on their part that the theory put forward in the *Demonstratio* is likely to evoke resentment and needs attenuation. The same kind of attenuation was the purpose of the additions extolling the beauty and the richness of the Sámi language, as a repository for the improvement of Hungarian,[16] and even more of the references to the courage and valiance of the Sámi.[17]

There was indeed a great deal of anti-Sámi prejudice in contemporary literature to dispel if Sámi–Hungarian kinship was to be made appealing. The representation of Sámi in the standard international works – like *Lapponia* (1673) by Johannes Schefferus (1621–79) or the *Géographie historique, ecclésiastique et civile* (1755) by Maurist scholar Dom Jean-Joseph Vaissète (1685–1756) – was patently unflattering. In these accounts, the Sámi are described physically as of a small stature, and thin; their skin inclines to black because of the perpetual smoke in their tents; they have a large head and a protruding thorax, and small, cavernous, rheumy eyes; their nose is short and flat, their chin elongated, their mouth large and always open. They walk humped. With respect to customs and manners, 'for most of the year they have little society among themselves, as they live in the forest among the wild beasts; and each family is separated from the others by a vast stretch of land.' They are 'cowardly and timid, and abhor war, which they never wage'; they are 'cunning, and they sometimes cheat in trade.'[18] They are as close to the working hypothesis of natural man advanced in Rousseau's *Second Discourse*, published almost simultaneously with Vaissète's work, as they can be.

These stereotypes were faithfully reproduced in works of the same genre published in Hungary in the decades around the publication of the *Demonstratio*.[19] The Sámi are characterised in these in a vocabulary used in contemporary stadial history to describe 'savage' societies as yet resisting the influences of their more civilised neighbours. They invariably emphasize the bodily feebleness of the Sámi,[20] and the consequent lack of military prowess

16 Sajnovics, *Demonstratio. Idioma Ungarorum et Lapponum idem esse* (Trnava: Collegium Academicum Societatis Jesu, 1771), pp. 82–83, 107–10.

17 Sajnovics, *Demonstratio* (1771), pp. 119–29.

18 Dom [Jean-]Joseph Vaissète, *Geographie historique, ecclesiastique et civile, ou description de toutes les parties du globe Terrestre, enrichie de cartes géographiques* (Paris: Desaint & Saillant, Jean-Thomas Herissant, Jacques Barois, 1755), p. 101, following Scheffer. For other, earlier accounts of the Sámi ('Finns'), see Mary Fuller's chapter in this volume.

19 I am grateful to Ildikó Sz. Kristóf for having shared with me findings of her unpublished primary research, thanks to which I first became aware of the works mentioned in notes 20–29.

20 [Johann Hübner], *Geographica globi terraquei synopsis: A multis praesertim quod Hungariam attinet, erroribus, qui in Celeberrimo alias Geographo Hübnero,*

among them,[21] though one source claims that 'once upon a time, six hundred Lapps put twenty thousand Muscovites to flight.'[22] Occasionally, the portrayal of their physical features is conceived as a part of the general presentation of polar peoples. Thus, Sámi are linked with Fuegians (Patagonians), described as 'the most inferior variety of our human kind', whom 'it is impossible to behold without compassion and repugnance'; 'according to some writers, they form the link between humanity and the Troglodytes [i.e., apes].'[23] The continued adherence of the Sámi to 'pagan darkness'[24] and their primitive mode of subsistence and 'beastly existence'[25] is another persistent feature of their representation in these works. Some authors elaborate on this by emphasising the complete lack of agriculture and any other domestic animals than reindeer (which they utilise to full extent, including the drinking of their blood),[26] their simple domiciles, and the dominant role of fishing and hunting.[27] There are some important qualifications, too. One author asserts that while the Sámi are very ignorant and live among primitive conditions, 'they are not as miserable as some people think,' because they are 'nevertheless satisfied with their lot, and

aliisque circumferentur, expurgata, In qua omnium mundi Regionum, & locorum situs pro Mapparum Geographicarum usu exactissime describuntur (Trnava: Acad. Societ. Jesu, 1755), 160; [Pál Bertalanffi], *Világnak Két-rendbéli ismerete: Először A' mint Istentől teremtetett; Másodszor A' mint az Istennek, és a' természetnek Vezérléséből az emberektől külömbb-külömbbféle részekre, Országokra, Tartományokra, és kösségekre osztatott* [...] (Trnava: Academia, 1757), p. 648; [László Baranyi], *Rövid magyar geographia* (Pest: Trattner, 1796), p. 129.

21 [Hübner], *Geographica globi*, p. 214.

22 Bertalanffi, *Világnak Két-rendbéli ismerete*, p. 648.

23 [György Fejér], *Anthropologia vagy is az embe'r esmértetése* (Buda: Királyi Magyar Universitás, 1807), pp. 152–53. For a similar analysis, see [Mihály Katona], *Közönséges természeti Föld-leirás* (Pest: Trattner, 1824), p. 452.

24 István Vetsei P[ataki], *Magyar Geografiája: Az Az; Ez egész világ négy részeinek, ugymint Europának, Asiának, Afrikának és Amerikának;'s bennek levő sokféle országok nemzetségek; azok eredetek, természetek, 's nevezetesebb szokásainak, vallásainak, imperátorinak, királyinak, s több egyéb elmét vidámito hasznos dolgainak méltó és rövid le-irása* [...] (Carei: Károlyi Ferentz Typographiája, 1757), p. 225.

25 Bertalanffi, *Világnak Két-rendbéli ismerete*, p. 649.

26 [Georg Christian Raff], *Természethistoria a' gyermekeknek* (Veszprém: Számmer Mihály, 1799), pp. 537–38. On the reception of Raff's work in Hungary, see Ildikó Sz. Kristóf, 'The Uses of Natural History: Georg C. Raff's *Naturgeschichte für Kinder* (1778) in Its Multiple Translations and Multiple Receptions,' in Alison Adams, Philip Ford, and Stephen Rawles (eds), *Le livre demeure: Studies in Book History in Honour of Alison Saunders* (Geneva: Droz, 2011), pp. 309–33.

27 György Raff, *Geografiája a' gyengébbek elméjekhez alkalmaztatott, és magyarúl ki-adattatott* (Vác: Ambro Ferenc, 1791), p. 144.

live peacefully with one another.'[28] Elsewhere we learn that 'they are regarded ignorant, but an English traveller says: human love and affection is taught to polished nations; but in Lapponia, it is also exercised'[29] – resembling, though on somewhat different grounds, Linnaeus's judgment of the Sámi as noble savages who may have something to teach civilised nations.[30] In another perspective, Rousseau's image of humans in their natural state once again comes to mind: 'having among themselves no type of moral relations or acknowledged duties', and can be said to be neither vicious nor virtuous, they still cultivate pity and compassion as 'a natural sentiment, which, by moderating in each individual the activity of the love of oneself, contributes to the mutual preservation of the entire species. […] Pity is what, in the state of nature, takes the place of laws, mores, and virtue […].'[31]

As a matter of fact, the same works also include – sometimes very lengthy – accounts of the peoples of the steppe, or Scythia, 'an immensely large country occupying one-third of Asia,' from where the Magyars had also once departed in search of a better land and where 'even today, entire nations move around by the thousands because of the barrenness of the soil.'[32] They live mostly as nomadic shepherds – thus in a stage somewhat more advanced than the Sámi – and are also acknowledged to be bloodthirsty warriors. However, though the Greeks and Romans may have regarded them as barbarians,

> it is very true of the Scythians that they achieved more good by relying on nature than the Greeks by all the learned instruction of their philosophers […]. In addition, this people never bowed to a foreign nation, they even founded the Parthian and Bactrian empire, they defeated Cyrus and Darius, they put Alexander the Great to nothing, and the Romans never dared to attack them.

28 Raff, *Geografiája a' gyengébbek elméjekhez alkalmaztatott*, p. 144. It is noteworthy that Raff's work usually refrains from presenting lifestyles (the other two exceptions being the Muscovites and the Poles).

29 [János Ferenczy], *Közönséges geographia, mellyben a' Földnek mathematikai, természeti, és leg inkább politikai állapotja a' leg ujabb változások után elő adatik* (Pest: Eggenberger József, 1809), p. 153.

30 Lisbet Koerner, *Linnaeus: Nature and Nation* (Cambridge, MA, and London: Harvard University Press, 1999), pp. 56–81.

31 Jean-Jacques Rousseau, *Discourse on the Origin and Foundations of Inequality among Men*, in idem, *The Basic Political Writings*, trans. and ed. by Donald A. Cress (Indianapolis: Hackett, 1987), pp. 25–110, here pp. 52, 55.

32 Vetsei, *Magyar Geografiája*, pp. 355, 357.

Contradicting some earlier claims, it is stated that

> though they are pagans, like some other nations in this world, they never had any idol either cast or carved, they respected marital life, they cultivated the art of war, and many of them did not eschew the sciences either; they even had philosophers, studied the rules of justice, and many other laudable things were found among them, for which reason the Apostle Paul distinguishes them from the barbarians, Col. 3:11.[33]

Two observations are important to make here about these descriptions, in which the standard international knowledge on the subject was recycled for Hungarian audiences. First, one must notice the peculiar mingling of the dimensions of time and space, both central to the approach of stadial history, in the accounts about the Sámi and the Scythians. In the case of the latter, there exist both historical records transmitted from the deep past, and representations across vast geographic areas in the present. The combined effect is an image of pastoralists endowed with primitive virtues, but capable of both successful aggression and cultural achievement. By contrast, with hardly any evidence of properly historical nature available about the Sámi, their present may be understood as existence in a continuous past of hunters-gatherers who have failed to 'progress' or even to understand progression as a goal. Thus, second, while these savages and barbarians both have some potential to be recognized as 'noble,' with regard to the reception and uses of this scholarly knowledge, because of the ideological aspects mentioned earlier, there was a strong presumption in favour of accentuating this potential in the case of 'Scythians,' and against the same in the case of the 'Lapps' – even without the provocation of Sajnovics's *Demonstratio*.

3 The Politics of Stadial History

The repudiation of the Sámi kinship of the Hungarian language proposed by Hell and Sajnovics, framed in derogatory discussions of the Sámi, was especially prominent among the so-called bodyguard writers: men of letters of noble origin who gave voice to the sentiments of a sizeable elite group whose cultural and intellectual horizons, thanks to their education as members of

33 Vetsei, *Magyar Geografiája*, p. 360 (wrong pagination: properly p. 356).

Maria Theresa's (1717–80, r. 1740–80) famous Hungarian Guards in Vienna,[34] were broadly European, but whose vision of the future restoration of the erstwhile greatness of the Hungarian nation was predicated on galvanizing their own class to a new dynamism through modern letters and knowledge practices. This was a vision of improvement which, in their own view, depended on maintaining a discourse of identity built on the indissoluble union of a prestigious pedigree, social exclusiveness and political privilege. These pillars came under serious attack from the mid-1760s on by the Viennese court and government, towards which the attitudes of this group were therefore highly ambivalent. In this atmosphere, the implications of 'Lappianism' – understood by them as not only linguistic but also ethnic kinship – seemed highly disturbing.

Ábrahám Barcsay's (1742–1806) poetry abounds in rebuffs addressed to Sajnovics whose 'yoke' was perceived by him as a vital threat to ancient liberties, established on the cornerstone of the idea that Hungarians are 'the valiant grandsons of Scythians.'[35] Similarly, in Lőrinc Orczy's (1718–89) 'The Errors of Star-Watcher Sajnovits and Hell Being Refuted' (1773), the author points out the absurdity of the allegation that the progeny of Alexander the Great's brave opponents should be related to mere 'Lapps,' munching on dried fish. Orczy is profoundly ironic. Referring to the preface of the *Demonstratio*, he recalls that it was Hell who 'forced' the strange idea on Sajnovics – but 'I know you rejoiced in this kinship / with a noble nation like this / Lapps have always been so famous / just like eminent Tóts [Slovaks] among us.'[36] The reference to 'Tóts' is not accidental: Orczy concludes by recommending that 'the astronomer' return to *his* 'kind relatives,' an inaccurate hint at Sajnovics's Slavic (though in fact Croat) ethnic background.

---

34 On the Hungarian Guards, with references to the figures mentioned, see László Deme, "Maria Theresa's Noble Lifeguards and the Rise of the Hungarian Enlightenment and Nationalism", in Béla Király and Walter Scott Dillard (eds), *The East Central European Officer Corps, 1740–1920s: Social Origins, Selection, Education, and Training* (Boulder, Colorado: Columbia University Press, 1988), pp. 197–212. The Hungarian language literature isextensive. The standard monograph is Ferenc Bíró, *A felvilágosodás korának magyar irodalma* (Budapest: Balassi Kiadó, 1994), esp. pp. 69–92, 161–85.

35 *Barcsay Ábrahám költeményei*. ed. by László Vajthó (Budapest: Királyi Magyar Egyetemi Nyomda, 1933), pp. 50–51.

36 *Két nagyságos elmének költeményes szüleményei*, ed. by Miklós Révai (Bratislava: Antal Loewe, 1789); http://mek.oszk.hu/03300/03368/03368.htm#77 (accessed April 19, 2019). Cf. Piroska Balogh, '"Scytha vagyok, nem Lappon": Adalékok Csokonai *Halotti versek* című művének tudománytörténeti hátteréhez egy történész és egy poéta diskurzusából,' inidem, *Teória és medialitás: A latinitás a magyarországi tudásáramlásban 1800 körül* (Budapest: Argumentum Kiadó, 2015), pp. 180–203, here p. 182.

It is, however, not merely an ethnic hint. 'You could once be the lord of this people / leading it to the shore of the icy sea / raising it to glory / good Svatopluk having lost it shamefully.' Svatopluk (*c.*840–94, r.871–94) had been the Slav prince of Moravia ruling substantial parts of the western Carpathian Basin before the late ninth-century Magyar conquest. It was as a result of his demise that they ('Tóts') are now regarded, according to Orczy, as 'diligent serfs.' He gave Sajnovics a further piece of advice: 'You see, if servitude no longer pleases you / [...] / lordship may be your lot over there / as freedom does not accrue to serfs over here.'[37] While Sajnovics himself possessed a patent of nobility, his embracing – at Hell's instigation – the Sámi theory amounted to a disavowal of this status on his part, and a general assault on the entire system of social exclusiveness forming the basis of the ancient Hungarian polity. This leads us to the political context. Just a few years earlier, the diet of 1764–65 ended in bitter estrangement between the Hungarian nobility and the Viennese government. At this assembly, the Hungarian estates, jealous of their privileges, but also infuriated by a series of publications apparently commissioned by the government and directly challenging those privileges, refused the ruler's demand for increased war tax, a general overhaul of the entire system of taxation, and military reform at their own expense. In response, Maria Theresa's government decided to implement its plan by abandoning the dialogue with the estates and neglecting the diet in its future pursuit of the much-needed reforms.[38] This provoked the members of the nobility to a concentrated effort to entrench their ancient privileges, while some of them were to combine this reaction with a vernacular version of enlightened improvement.

During the debates of the diet and afterward, court propaganda in support of the proposed policies received a boost from a treatise by Ádám Ferenc (Adam František, Adam Franz) Kollár (1718–83), *De originibus et usu perpetuo potestatis legislatoriae circa sacra apostolicorum regum Ungariae* (1764). In this treatise, the commoner[39] and ethnic Slovak 'Hungarus'[40] Kollár called into

37 *Két nagyságos.*

38 The most comprehensive and up-to-date treatment of the Hungarian estates, the diet, and their relationship with the Viennese government is István M. Szijártó, *A Diéta: A magyar rendek és az országgyűlés 1708–1792* (Budapest: Osiris, 2005), shortened English version idem, *Estates and Constitution. The Parliament in Eighteenth-Century Hungary* (New York: Berghahn, 2020). Concisely, see R. J. W. Evans, 'Maria Theresa and Hungary,' in *Enlightened Absolutism: Reform and Reformers in Eighteenth-Century Europe*, ed. H. M. Scott (London: Macmillan, 1990), pp. 189–207.

39 Until his ennoblement in recognition of his services by Maria Theresa in 1776.

40 An educated denizen of the multi-ethnic and multi-confessional Kingdom of Hungary indebted to its Latinate cultural (and political) heritage. Of the extensive literature, see Moritz Csáky, 'Die Hungarus-Konzeption,' in ed. Anna Maria Drabek, Richard G. Plaschka

question many of the political and social privileges of the Hungarian ecclesiastical and secular elites, causing great consternation among the clergy and the nobility.[41] Characteristically, Kollár's anti-feudal polemics was readily associated by this constituency with anti-Hungarian sentiment, identified in his commentary on *Hungaria et Atila, sive de originibus gentis Hungariae*, a work by the sixteenth-century humanist Miklós Oláh (Nicolaus Olahus, 1493–1568), which Kollár edited and published in 1763.[42] These comments, which refer to the statistical minority of Hungarians in the multi-ethnic Kingdom of Hungary and predict the gradual demise of the language as well as the nation itself, became European currency through being quoted in Schlözer's *Allgemeine nordische Geschichte*, which in turn seems to have inspired Johann Gottfried Herder's (1744–1803) famous 'prophecy' to the same effect. The latter's prediction that the Hungarian nation, amid the 'ocean' of Slavic peoples, will inevitably perish, was underpinned by his theory (available in publication for the first time in the late 1760s and early 1770s) on the crucial role of language in the formation of human identities.[43]

For members of the Hungarian intellectual elite such developments sounded an alarm bell and would only add to Schlözer's notoriety as an anti-Hungarian. Kollár was cast in the same role in their eyes after 1764. A parliamentary committee assigned with the task of 'investigating' the *De originibus* found it to be 'the shame of living Hungarians' and achieved its inclusion in the Index of prohibited books; this, and a torrent of pamphlets and libels critical of Kollár, forced him to issue an *apologia*.[44] Despite the fact that Kollár was a distinguished scholar who as late as in 1763 drafted a plan of a Learned, or Hungarian Society (*societas litteraria* or *societas Hungarica*) for the promotion of the sciences in Hungary, and maintained intense correspondence about its establishment, he now lost credit even among a part of the learned

---

and Adam Wandruszka, *Ungarn und Österreich unter Maria Theresia und Joseph II* (Vienna: Verlag der Österreichischen Akademie der Wissenschaften, 1982), pp. 71–89; Ambrus Miskolczy, '"Hungarus Consciousness" in the Age of Early Nationalism,' in Almási and Šubarić (eds), *Latin at the Crossroads*, pp. 64–94.

41 Andor Csizmadia, 'Egy kétszáz év előtti országgyűlés évfordulójára: "Kollár contra Status et Ordines",' *Jogtudományi Közlöny* 19:4 (1964), pp. 214–27.

42 Cf. Dezső Dümmerth, 'Herder jóslata és forrásai,' *Filológiai Közlöny* 9:1–2 (1963), pp 181–83; Dümmerth, 'Kollár Ádám problémája,' *Filológiai Közlöny* 13:3–4 (1967), pp. 442–44.

43 Johann Gottfried Herder, *Treatise on the Origin of Language* [1772], in *Philosophical Writings*, trans. and ed. Michael N. Forster (Cambridge: Cambridge University Press, 2002), pp. 65–164, here pp. 131, 150. See also *Fragments on Recent German Literature* [1767–68], in Herder, *Philosophical Writings*, pp. 33–64, here p. 49.

44 Jan Tibenský, *A királynő könyvtárosa: Adam František Kollár élete és művei* (Budapest: Madách, 1985), pp. 60–1.

public.[45] Kollár later on welcomed the position advanced in the *Demonstratio* in his review of it,[46] which – had it not been anonymous – would have made him, if possible at all, even more suspect. Together with him, by championing the 'Lappish cause', for an influential segment of the contemporary Hungarian public scene Sajnovics and his mentor Hell seemed to be (ex-)Jesuit hirelings of a hostile court, employed in a plot that also involved willing collaborators from the camps of old and new national enemies, Germans and Slavs.

The ideological and political stakes of the available discourses of origin were thus formidable. It is small wonder that they also exercised the mind of the most outstanding of the bodyguard writers, the emblematic figure of the Hungarian Enlightenment and national awakening, György Bessenyei (1746–1811).[47] Among many other literary pursuits and genres, Bessenyei translated and adapted texts by Voltaire, Claude-Francois-Xavier Millot (1726–85), Louis-Sebastien Jacquet de Malzet (1715–1800), and Vaissète, and wrote original works devoted to the history of Hungarians in the period of settlement and state foundation in an European context, through a comparative analysis of manners, laws and institutions. Most of Bessenyei's contributions to philosophical history, the idiom for him to discuss the problem of linguistic kinship and ethnic origins, appeared in the 1770s. It is true that his direct engagement of the 'Lappish' theory – significantly enough, contained in a work entitled *Magyarországnak törvényes állása* (The legal status of Hungary [1802]) – derives from the time of his retirement to his estate, but the ideas advanced in it must have been generated by the debates several decades earlier.

45 Cf. Csizmadia, 'Egy kétszáz év előtti országgyűlés,' p. 224. For instance, Kollár suspected that the author of one of the attacks was the Jesuit historian István Kaprinai (1714–85). Kollár to Maria Theresa, May 22, 1765. *Kollár Ádám Ferenc levelezése*, ed. István Soós (Budapest: Universitas Kiadó, 2000), p. 179.

46 [Adam František Kollár], 'Joannis Sajnovics S.J. Ungari Tordasiensis & c. *Demonstratio idioma Ungarorum et Laponum idem esse,' Kaiserlich-königlich allergnädigst priviligirte Realzeitung der Wissenschaften, Künste und Kommerzien* (December 1770), pp. 18–23. Kollár is identified as the anonymous author of the review, and the whole of the text is included with commentaries in Zoltán Éder, 'Sajnovics Demonstratiójának első recenziója: "Viennensis Recensitor opusculi mei Hafniae editi",' *Magyar Nyelv* 110 (2014), pp. 85–94.

47 Given Kollár's situation vis-à-vis the court on the one hand and the Hungarian elite on the other, it is noteworthy that in the early 1770s, Kollár enthusiastically supported the young Bessenyei and recommended him for patronage to the empress. Theresia Grass to Kollár, December 4, 1772, April 16, and October 11, 1773, January 14, 1774; Kollár to Maria Theresa, April 16 and 18, 1773. *Kollár levelezése*, pp. 336, 341–46, 349–50. In 1779, Bessenyei became a custodian of the Imperial Library, of which Kollár was the director.

Bessenyei's criticism is developed in considerable detail, beginning with remarks on methodology. He recalls that 'a writer has voiced the opinion that the Hungarian nation derives from Lapponia, for the reason that their language contains words that mean the same as in Hungarian.' This is asserted to be flawed: 'But it is impossible to displace something of such a great consequence, on the basis of so little a circumstance [as language] and set it on a different footing. Instead of words, one should consider moral character and manners.'[48] Bessenyei was in fact by no means alone and not even the first in objecting to Sajnovics's (and Hell's) neglect of the tools fundamental to the approach of the eighteenth-century sciences of man. In commentaries to his own poem on the 'star-watchers,' Orczy also gibed:

> I cannot comprehend why your Reverend [...] makes no reference at all to the morals of the Lapps in order to underpin his opinion. [...] Morals are of their nature inscribed in us, and indelible marks of the customs inherited from our forefathers. [...] It is imperative to target the original source of morals. [...] The sounds of language follow history, they sometimes soften and sometimes harden according to the needs of the heart [...].[49]

It has been pointed out that Orczy wrote his poem in close collaboration with the learned Piarist history professor Károly Koppi (1744–1801) of Košice/Kassa/Kaschau (later Oradea/Nagyvárad, and finally Pest), who in his own comments also stressed that 'manners, mental disposition, domestic discipline, the pursuit of dominance and submission' take precedence in the study of national character over linguistic evidence based on word matches.[50] It is noteworthy that in these objections the standard contemporary argument from manners is turned upside down. In mainstream stadial history, the study of manners throws light on the dynamics of historical change in a society, whereas in the Hungarian writers' account they are indicative of a nation's permanent spirit – contrary to language, which is more malleable, and therefore not regarded by them as a reliable test of kinship. Nevertheless, there is a meta-level to their critique. In his exchanges with the historian György Pray (1723–1801) Hell somewhat arrogantly claimed the superiority of his method of deduction, based

48 György Bessenyei, *Összes művei: Prózai munkák, 1802–1804*, ed. György Kókay (Budapest: Akadémiai Kiadó, 1986), p. 232.

49 Extant only among Orczy's manuscripts, published in Balogh, '"Scytha vagyok, nem Lappon",' pp. 193–6.

50 Balogh, '"Scytha vagyok, nem Lappon",' pp. 185–6, 202. The full text of Koppi's commentary is published with Balogh's article, pp. 200–3.

on 'stringent formal logics and proof,' imported from the 'exact' sciences for application in the study of linguistic kinship.[51] The opposite happens here: the approach of Sajnovics and Hell is pointed out to be rigid and reductionist, lacking the sensitivity to incorporate a multiplicity of perspectives on the subject, and failing to consider contradictory evidence.

Returning to Bessenyei's argument, in the subsequent explicit comparison the lens of manners shows the 'Scythian' and the 'Lapp' to be separated by a yawning gap:

> The Lapp, when standing erect, is barely three elbows tall: he has a ghastly wide mouth, always kept open; his head is like a pigeon-house on his short body; his eyes are tiny and sunk deep in the head; his thorax is thick and swollen; his nose is short and flat; his long, protruding chin has no hair. Besides this ugliness of form, the Lapp is vile and fearful, it is such a subterranean mole nation, which loathes the fight; for the same reason, it never wages war. [...] If the writer was so familiar with the language that he formed a judgment about it, it is a pity that he forgot about these features of the nations, which could have placed the matter in a clearer light.[52]

It has been pointed out that Bessenyei closely follows Vaissète in his description of the Sámi.[53] But the vocabulary employed by him ('ghastly,' 'ugly,' 'subterranean mole') replaces passionate disparagement and repudiation for the attempted scholarly detachment of Enlightenment philosophical-scientific texts: the element of 'othering' one regularly finds in such texts about Sámi as a primitive nation (similarly to other 'savage' societies) becomes radicalized under the impact of the politically and ideologically inspired vantage point of the Hungarian nobleman.

This feature of Bessenyei's position is put into further relief by a consideration of the parallel characterization of Scythians:

> The people of Áttila [sic] is marked by triumph, valor, thirst for glory, and prudence required for domination, despite its paganism, ignorance, and ferocious nature. The only thing Attila wanted was conversion to Christianity, together with his foremost men, like Saint Stephen. Had he formed a kingdom and settled in his country in a Christian manner, no

51 Eötvös Loránd Tudományegyetem, Egyetemi Könyvtár (Budapest). Collectio Prayana 18:25.
52 Bessenyei, *Prózai munkák, 1802–1804*, p. 233.
53 Penke, *Filozofikus világtörténetek*, p. 65.

> court would have been superior to his in the prudent wisdom of government, in splendour, wealth, triumph, and glory.[54]

Soon enough, the 'moral strength and dignity' identified in the Huns by Bessenyei is asserted as the fundamental character of the Hungarians. While the potential of Sámi savages to be recognized as 'noble' is relentlessly suppressed by him, that of the steppe barbarians is developed and accentuated as a condition of a propensity to freedom:

> The Hungarian nation has always lived by prudence; it has always been governed under freedom and was full of princely men. For such were the captains. The fight, war, triumph have been its nourishment and domestic art since time immemorial. Its moral talent is not surpassed by any nation in the world. If it applies itself to science, art, or gallantry, it excels. And if it lags behind the English, the Germans and the French to a certain extent, this is not because of its feebleness, but because it does not possess the proper ways and means. It has already been established that until elevating its own language no nation in the world will be learned, nor any has ever been.[55]

In what appears an amazing flight of fancy, Bessenyei proceeds from an eulogy of Scythian–Hun–Hungarian military prowess through the supposedly concomitant adherence to the values of liberty and the resulting proneness to excel in learning as well, to urging the establishment of a Hungarian learned society, dedicated to the cultivation of the mother tongue as a tool of raising the nation to the status it deserves among modern European nations. However, in view of Bessenyei's overall intellectual project, and his program for social and cultural reform in Hungary, this is not at all surprising.[56]

In his *A magyar néző* (Hungarian spectator [1779]), Bessenyei surveyed the history of the world from a Hungarian perspective in a Voltairean framework. He proposed to give an account of the successive stages of the "mitigation" of rude manners, resulting from religion and learning, but also claimed that

54 György Bessenyei, *Magyarországnak törvényes állása*, in Bessenyei, *Prózai munkák, 1802–1804*, pp. 209–54, here p. 233.

55 Bessenyei, *Magyarországnak törvényes állása*, p. 234.

56 Cf. [György Bessenyei], *Egy magyar társaság iránt való jámbor szándék* (1781), excerpts in English as *A Benevolent Plan for a Hungarian Society*, in Réka Lengyel and Gábor Tüskés (eds), *Learned Societies, Freemasonry, Sciences and Literature in 18th-Century Hungary. A Collection of Documents and Sources* (Budapest: MTA, 2017), pp. 80–89.

military glory and polite letters, rather than being antagonistic, could mutually supplement one another.[57] This dovetailed with his overall conviction that *vera nobilitas* could derive from proficiency in letters as well as arms-bearing, a claim he made to urge a re-evaluation of the social roles of the nobility, which he still regarded as the chief repository of improvement – although it also depended on 'emulation between the great and the little.'[58]

Then, in *A magyar nemzetnek szokásairul, erköltseirül, uralkodásának modjairul, törvényeirül, és nevezetesb viselt dolgairul* (The customs, manners, modes of government, laws, and important deeds of the Hungarian nation [1778]), Bessenyei again provided a set of present-oriented historical reflections intended as an underpinning of his program. One of the theoretical cornerstones of his argument is the inequality of men by their natural condition:

> You claim that I am writing falsely; for nature has placed no-one above his fellow, and we are all equal; and our noble status is violence and injustice to the peasantry. But please listen to me; whence does it arise that one man is timid and weak by nature, and the other courageous and strong? […] it is nature's hand that induces men to fear and bravery, to strength and weakness. Do not believe, as some want to assert, that such differences among us are only nurtured by breeding.[59]

Bessenyei was an avid, though critical reader of Rousseau[60] who also claimed that inequality was a fact of nature in the original state of mankind, but it does not lead to hierarchy and subordination as long as the progress of needs does not make humans dependent on goods and services that they cannot provide for themselves. Bessenyei's analysis of the Sámi and the Scythians shows that

---

57 György Bessenyei, *Magyarság; A Magyar Néző*, Magyar irodalmi ritkaságok 16 (Budapest: Királyi Magyar Egyetemi Nyomda, 1932), p. 17.

58 György Bessenyei, *A Holmi*, ed. Ferenc Bíró, György Kókay, and Andor Tarnai (Budapest: Akadémiai Kiadó, 1983), p. 16.

59 György Bessenyei, *A magyar nemzetnek szokásairul* […], in Bessenyei, *Összes művei: Társadalombölcseleti írások 1771–1778*, ed. Péter Kulcsár (Budapest: Argumentum-Akadémiai Kiadó, 1992), pp. 89–154, here pp. 92–93.

60 Though Bessenyei's engagement with texts by the authors mentioned above (p. 342.) seems more direct (translation and adaptation), Rousseau is the most widely discussed French *philosophe* in the literature dedicated to French influences on him. Sándor Eckhardt, 'Bessenyei és a franczia gondolat', *Egyetemes Philologiai Közlöny* 43 (1919), pp. 193–220; Olga Penke, *Műfaji kísérletek Bessenyei György prózájában* (Debrecen: Kossuth Egyetemi Kiadó, 2008), especially the sections on social philosophy, pp. 214–30.

he regarded the former not to have reached this stage, but the latter already to have passed beyond it. His main point in this treatise, however, is that such natural inequalities may historically assert themselves in different ways. Achievements by the sword and by the pen are represented, in a somewhat laboured fashion, as two equally feasible paths to ennoblement – although Bessenyei held that among certain circumstances, such as in eleventh-century Hungary and Europe as a whole, the one took precedence over the other. His chief endeavour in this work is the demonstration of the parallel development of society in Hungary and Europe in the past, and the consequent chance to re-establish synchronicity for Hungary with European progress in the present – perhaps an echo of Montesquieu's notion that the shared deep structures of European societies and polities predestine them to progress toward a similar present and future. 'It seems as if the Hungarian nobility originated fully from warfare. It could not have been otherwise, for in old times it was impossible to rise to nobility by writing and the pen in a nation, which could neither write nor read, but only fought, triumphed, plundered and ruled.' But Bessenyei adds immediately that 'all nations in the world, which have since developed arts and sciences, began their nobilities in this way [...].'[61] An appendix entitled 'Egész Európa' formája a XI^{dik} Százban' (The form of the whole of Europe in the eleventh century – excerpted from Voltaire's *Essai sur les moeurs*, chapters 39–46) is intended to demonstrate that in those times Hungarians were no more barbarous than other European nations. 'If you observe only Hungary in the eleventh century, you will find that it dealt improperly with its kings; but was there anything other nations did not commit, although they had been Christians for a long time?'[62] The ubiquity of violent passions and ignorance was directly related to the overall rusticity of manners: 'The sum of customs and manners was excessive eating and drinking, pillage, recklessness in combat, and cruelty.'[63]

Thus far, this is more or less the standard Enlightenment narrative[64] of the feudal past, with the potential of the assessment of the present in equally standard terms of enlightened patriotism. Bessenyei hinted at the anachronistic

---

61 Bessenyei, *A magyar nemzetnek szokásairul*, p. 96.

62 György Bessenyei, 'Egész Európa' formája a XI^{dik} Százban', in Bessenyei, *Társadalombölcseleti írások*, pp. 155–66, here p. 164.

63 Bessenyei, 'Egész Európa' formája,' p. 163.

64 For this concept and its application to mainstream Western European material, see Karen O'Brien, *Narratives of Enlightenment: Cosmopolitan History from Voltaire to Gibbon* (Cambridge: Cambridge University Press, 1997); J.G.A. Pocock, *Barbarism and Religion*, esp. vol. 2, *Narratives of Civil Government* (Cambridge: Cambridge University Press, 1999).

distribution of social power and privilege in eighteenth-century Hungary. In the beginning,

> the plowman paid taxes to the bearer of arms in return for his own protection. So, in old times everything was based on services; but since servants became masters without bearing arms, the one part always obeys, and the other always commands. [...] This great nobility was once a standing army; now they lay idle in their homes [...].[65]

Bessenyei, however, nowhere arrived at the explicit conclusion that noble privileges, being no longer justified by military service, ought to be eliminated, although – as the commissioner of Hungarian Protestants in Vienna – he was more inclined to a compromise with the policies urged at court in social and national as well as confessional issues than most others. On the contrary: assigning an unassailable social pre-eminence to the nobility on account of its historical roles, what he sought was a new justification for these roles in superior learning, while he still regarded the gulf that separated the nobility from the peasantry as unbridgeable.

Bessenyei supported this by referring to Werbőczy in his *A' törvénynek útja* (Of the course of the law [1777]). His claim that the people raised 'captains' and masters above themselves through the voluntary consent of all echoes the relevant passages of the *Tripartitum* as well as Kézai's *Gesta* – although without explicit reference to the Huns and the presumed continuity with the Hungarians, in its political terminology recalling the staples of Scythianism.[66] The same applies to the justification of differences between the 'people' and the 'common folk': more generally, in terms of voluntary subordination of the cowardly to the brave warriors, and specifically by reference to forfeiture of right as a result of rebellion (almost a word-by-word quotation of Werbőczy's argument from the consequences of the 1514 peasant war).[67]

In this spirit, we find Bessenyei suggesting that '[u]ntil a different path is opened, you must accept that your nation has descended from Asia, or Tartar country. Those who occupied China (surmounting the five hundred mile wall) were presumably also of Scythian Hungarian blood.'[68] Once again, the freedom-loving nature of Hungarians is established on this ancestry, but now

---

65 Bessenyei, *A magyar nemzetnek szokásairul*, p. 153.

66 György Bessenyei, *A' törvénynek útja*, in Bessenyei, *Társadalombölcseleti írások*, pp. 167–90, here p. 175.

67 Bessenyei, *A' törvénynek útja*, p. 177.

68 Bessenyei, *Magyarországnak törvényes állása*, p. 234.

also combined with the assertion that, rather than just arising from 'pride', this love of freedom was compatible with respect for the law:

> There is no well-read and learned man in Europe who could point to a time in the memory of the world when the Scythian Hungarian nation would have served under a rule without lawful freedom. [...] If there is no moral uprightness in a nation, there is no merit, either. There is pride in the Hungarian nation in its lawful freedom, martial valour and wealth; but beside this, in other respects it has always been a noble and humane nation – *Generosus*. Under Attila, the gallant passion and triumph in it declined into cruelty, for it possessed neither knowledge nor religion, which could have uncovered in it the sober rules of humanity. Yet, wherever Áttila's [sic] clemency was sought, and people conceded and surrendered, clemency was given. But this was the way in which all pagan nations dealt with their enemies here in Europe before they were tamed and acquainted with human duty by learning and religion.[69]

Hailing the Hun-Scythian ancestry of Hungarians was thus intimately connected with standing up for a notion of national dignity understood in term of ancient constitutional liberties. As a result, the questioning of that ancestry with reference to the Hungarian-Lappish linguistic kinship almost inevitably invited passionate rejection – ironically, even from figures who, like Bessenyei, otherwise demonstrated an awareness of the largely bogus character of those liberties. Kinship with the 'fish-smelly Lappians' was from their perspective not merely methodologically problematic, but undignified and unwholesome, even treacherous and hostile. Many believed that such a denigration of the Magyar stock received intellectual ammunition from German academic circles, where ideas of enlightened bureaucratic centralization were also promoted, and encouragement from the Habsburg government, where such ideas were on the way of being implemented to the detriment of the ancient privileges of Hungary.

The fluctuation of the Habsburg–Hungarian relationship is a factor to consider in this regard. The retorts of Barcsay and Orczy date from a period in which the initial perplexity over Sajnovics's theory spilled over into consternation under the impact of the post-1765 disaffection with Vienna. True, there were more neutral voices already in the Josephian era, the 1780s, when relations were altogether also far from cordial, culminating in the conflation of Sámi,

69 Bessenyei, *Magyarországnak törvényes állása*, pp. 234–5.

Finns, Huns, Scythians, and Hungarians – locating them all in the 'empire of Karelia' – in the novels and plays of András Dugonics (1740–1818).[70] But it is noteworthy that Bessenyei's most relevant statement on the subject was conceived in a period when the 1794 Hungarian 'Jacobin conspiracy' had resulted in several executions and a wave of imprisonments (including Kazinczy and other leading figures of the Hungarian literary movement; Bessenyei himself was also suspect), and the new, unenlightened absolutism of Francis I (1768–1835, r. 1792–1835) understandably provoked retrenchment among Hungarian elite patriots.

Thus, we find the learned professor of the Calvinist college of Debrecen, Ézsaiás Budai (1766–1841) asserting in his three volume *Magyar Országnak históriája* (History of Hungary, 1805–12) that 'Sajnovits proposed the kinship of the Lapps and the Hungarians without sufficient ground, and confused many European scholars.'[71] The prolific Pauline teacher and man of letters Benedek Virág (1754–1830) expressed his sentiments on the matter even more poignantly in a letter to Kazinczy in 1803:

> Read, my dear Kazinczy, Sajnovics [...] I will have the occasion to speak of this man, and say blessing on his ashes, who found the traces of the Hetumoger [the seven Hungarian tribes] in that distant country. But I pray thee, read his lines [...] are you not abhorred? Do you not understand, what unhappy time it recalls, and what indolent Hungarians lived at that time?[72]

The 'Lappish' theory was represented as a disgrace only tolerable for 'indolent' Hungarians. Bessenyei's approach demonstrated a striking resilience and remained a standard feature of the discussion of topics relevant to Hungarian national identity; the imprint of the perspective of stadial history also remained strong.

---

70 On the complexity of the reception of the *Demonstratio*, see László Szörényi, 'Nyelvrokonság, őstörténet és epika a 18. századi magyarországi jezsuita latin irodalomban,' *Irodalomtörténeti Közlemények* 101:1–2 (1997), pp. 16–24; István Margócsy, 'A tiszta magyar: nemzetkarakterológia és nemzeti történelem összefüggései Bessenyei és kortársai nyelvrokonság-felfogásában,' in *A szétszórt rendszer Tanulmányok Bessenyei György életművéről*, ed. Csaba Csorba and Klára Margócsy (Nyíregyháza: Bessenyei Kiadó, 1998), pp. 131–40.

71 Ézsaiás Budai, *Magyar Országnak históriája a mohácsi veszedelemig* (Debrecen: Csáthy György, 1811), p. 49.

72 *Kazinczy levelezése*, vol. 3, p. 6.

In his *Magyar századok* (Hungarian Centuries, 1808) Virág reiterated that

> [t]he Hungarians [...] considered themselves to be Scythians [... a name] which belonged to all those nations which, while differing from one another in blood and language, possessed territories in the north of Europe and Asia. [...] [T]hus far no-one has been able to demonstrate that the Hungarians were not descending from Atila [... whose countries] were happily reconquered by the Hungarian people after the lapse of four-hundred and thirty-five years.[73]

Descent from the Huns is repeatedly emphasized, and the commonplaces of Scythian triumph over Darius, Cyrus and Alexander the Great are recalled as well.[74] But if these barbarian conquerors were brave warriors, they were by no means devoid of features one usually associates with higher stages of civilization. Prince Árpád

> [w]aged many wars which, at that time just as today, could not but cause severe harm to others. But this may perhaps be blamed more properly on the chief Christians, whether secular or ecclesiastical, than on Árpád and his Magyars. [...] According to the testimony of Anonymus, 'this people was wise and gentle [...] then, tired of ceaseless warfare, it grew so wild as to eat human flesh, and to drink blood.'[75]

Árpád is also described as a wise ruler who 'took up his princely office with great prudence and foresight,' and before long we are also told that in him the Hungarians were 'fortunate to have a valiant but moderate ruler' who treated the sons of many nations 'humanely.' Moving on to the first Christian king, Stephen I (Saint Stephen, c. 975–1038, r. 1000–38), Virág asserts that during this 'relatively quiet and blissful' reign, 'when patriotism was not subverted by foreignness, everything went well' – unlike during the subsequent fifty years, marked by external threat and internal feud, which the nation eventually surmounted thanks to the 'Scythian rigor which protected in it the natural sound reason against the stupor of Europe.'[76]

---

73 Benedek Virág, *Magyar Századok*, ed. Márta Mezei (Budapest: Neumann Kft., 2004), "Kilencedik század", http://mek.oszk.hu/04900/04919/html/, last accessed 4 June 2019.

74 Virág, *Magyar Századok*, 'Almus'.

75 Virág, *Magyar Századok*, 'Árpád'.

76 Virág, *Magyar Századok*, 'István'.

What is noteworthy about Virág's account is not its misrepresentation of the history of events (Stephen's reign was anything but 'quiet'), but the consistent ascription to the conquering Magyars of a moral character generally acknowledged to belong to a more civilized social condition (while the virtues of supposedly more advanced Christian nations in the period are equally consistently relativised). This was a feature already in some of the global geographies discussed earlier and resembles Bessenyei's strategy also in the sense that it is combined with reference to the Lapps as the dichotomous others of Huns/Hungarians. In this period of perceived national deprivation – the 1790s to the 1820s – there were even some who explicitly pointed to a conspiracy in the background of the Lappish theory. From the methodological point of view, the poet and cleric Endre Pázmándi Horvát (1778–1839) was one of very few to call attention to the fact in his essay 'A' Magyar Nemzet nem Finn származatú' (The Hungarian nation is not of Finnish origin, 1823) that linguistic and ethnic kinship are not necessarily the same:

> This resemblance, even some kinship between the two languages is not to be denied; but not of a measure and kind that national kinship, mutual descent, and ultima origo would follow from it. This resemblance was the spectre which deceived many, I do not doubt, well-meaning patriots who, because of the recognition they enjoyed thanks to their scholarly merits, managed to prevail on others to repeat the things they said; and foreigners echoed them many times [...][77]

Before long, however, Pázmándi contradicts his assumption about 'deceived' though 'well-meaning patriots', and expresses his suspicion as to the motivation of campaigning for kinship with (as he writes in his epic work on Árpád) 'greasy, ragged' Lapps: 'But I can see well what is behind the scenes. Namely, the desire to make us forget about our glorious, noble descent, and then ever more freely rejoice in our depreciation [...]'[78] The reasons why the association with Lapps is unflattering are expressed by Pázmándi in unambiguous terms:

> [...] Finns were never raised to the stage of civilization ... [i]t is easy to see that at the time of the putative separation [of Finns and Hungarians], the Finns were just as Tacitus (de. morib. Germ. 46.) describes them, 'extremely savage people, miserable, languishing in indigent poverty, and without arms,

77 Endre Pázmándi Horvát, 'A' Magyar Nemzet nem Finn származatú', *Tudományos Gyűjtemény*, 7:2 (1823), pp. 3–69, here p. 37.

78 Pázmándi Horvát, 'A' Magyar Nemzet', p. 55.

> horses, and shelter. Their nourishment consists of weeds, their clothes, of the skin of wild animals, their abode, the plain earth. [...] Which Hungarian writers would thus characterize the Magyars who came to Pannonia? These should be accorded priority of proof. In depicting the natural features of the nation, we have reason not to listen to the Ottos, the Keginos [sic] and the Dittmars.[79] For them, the vision of the ancient Hun world emerges at the sight of the Hungarian enemy; what else was to be expected than abhorrent descriptions? [...] Is it, then, conceivable at all that it was from the Finn-Lapps, this base, timid and unorganized, lazy and inert tribe, devoid of noble passion, unagitated by ambition, uninterested in the spirit of a higher character, that the glorious Hungarian nation arose?[80]

Ironically, Pázmándi clearly recognized and formulated the limitation of the applicability of a theory of linguistic kinship to the larger issues of ethnogenesis, which already Bessenyei defined as a matter of 'manners' – wider cultural and cognitive processes, encounters and transfers; and yet he regarded the Lappish theory (even as he was willing to concede some truth in it) to be established on dishonest intentions. The following years saw, first, perhaps the most absurd apotheosis of the quest for a glorious descent in István Horvát's *Rajzolatok a magyar nemzet legrégibb történetéből* (Sketches from the most ancient period of the history of the Hungarian nation, 1825) – according to the subtitle, 'a critical history of the Hungarian nation, beginning a few hundred years before Abraham, and continuing through the Holy Scriptures, the Greek and Roman classics, the Armenians, Syrian, Arabian and Persian writers, and the subsequent centuries, up to the time of Árpád;' and then, during the era of liberal reform, a relatively smooth coexistence, even a reconciliation of Scythian (Turkic) and Lappish (Finnish) explanations of ethno-linguistic kinship (sometimes, as in the case of the linguist and traveller Antal Reguly [1819–58], within one and the same oeuvre).[81]

---

79 Utto, bishop of Freising (?-907) and Dithmar (Theotmar, archbishop of Salzburg, 874–907) both fought against the Hungarians and died in the battle of Bratislava/Pozsony/Pressburg (907). They gave accounts of the Hungarians as murderous savages, as did Regino (c. 842–915), abbot of Prüm, in his chronicle.

80 Pázmándi Horvát, 'A' Magyar Nemzet', pp. 33–36.

81 Péter Dávidházi, *Egy nemzeti tudomány születése. Toldy Ferenc és a magyar irodalomtörténet* (Budapest: Akadémiai Kiadó, 2004), pp. 408–68; Gábor Klaniczay, 'The Myth of Scythian Origin and the Cult of Attila in the Nineteenth Century', in Gábor Klaniczay, Michael Werner and Ottó Gecser (eds), *Multiple Antiquities – Multiple Modernities. Ancient Histories in Nineteenth Century European Cultures* (Frankfurt and New York: Campus Verlag, 2011), pp. 183–210.

4 Aftermath

One might surmise that in consequence of the debates and achievements of the liberal Reform Era of the 1830s and 1840s, and its denouement in the Revolution of 1848, when social integration via cultural and economic improvement emerged as equal in importance with and a key to national emancipation, a discourse whose tendency was to reassert social exclusiveness and political privilege was rendered somewhat meaningless, even obsolete. What happened instead was the redirection of this vocabulary, and the conversion of an ideology of social distinction into one of national distinctiveness. Especially after the defeat of the revolution and the subsequent war of independence, in the atmosphere of the system of government known as neo-absolutism, the sense of national deprivation and suspicion re-emerged. Soon enough, two camps were up in arms for the 'Ugrian-Turkic war' whose major battles were fought – by linguists, ethnographers and historians whose positions on the main questions were far more shifting and ambivalent than the ferocity of the exchanges would have one believe – already after the 1867 compromise settlement between Austria and Hungary.

By that time, comparative linguistics had made great strides compared to its condition in the late eighteenth century, and the main contenders were prominent experts in the field. Yet, when the orientalist Ármin Vámbéry (1832–1913) took up the cause of demonstrating the Turkic-Tartar pedigree of Hungarians, he still referred to the 'national bias' of the foreign scholars with whom the Finno-Ugrian theory originated, and resorted to the examination of the manners and 'spirit' of peoples as the ultimate proof:

> There are ethnic and social reasons which not only support the Turkic-Tartar origin of Hungarians, but at the same time completely undermine the contrary opinion claiming Finno-Ugrian descent. [...] The sullen dweller of forests and mountains differs from the son of the plains no less in his intellectual character, that is, in political and social terms, than in his bodily constitution. [...] We cannot comprehend how it could escape one's sight that the political and martial spirit to which the Hungarians owed their successes, and which secured their survival among the surrounding foreign peoples, can only be the outcome of institutions, manners and customs rooted in an itinerant society of steppe dwellers and cattle breeders, not a society confined to patriarchal isolation within the boundaries of its rivers and forests, never venturing to any grand, heroic, world historic deed.[82]

82 Ármin Vámbéry, *A magyarok eredete. Ethnologiai tanulmány* (Budapest: Magyar Tudományos Akadémia, 1882), pp. 207–9.

This argument was simplified to the proposition that 'a man of Finno-Ugrian descent with his peculiar lifestyle could never have emerged as a warrior and a world conqueror' by Vámbéry's adversary Pál Hunfaly (1810–91), who added ironically: 'I eagerly await him to write the history of Hungarian world conquest, for I have nowhere seen it recorded as yet.'[83]

A fuller consideration of the 'Ugrian-Turkic war' itself is beyond the compass of the present paper. What I have attempted to show is that several decades earlier Enlightenment approaches and categories of "knowing" savagery and barbarism contributed significantly to developing the ideological dispositions, the conceptual apparatus and the practices of self-orientalisation which defined the terms of that debate. The patterns of thinking and expression forged by the social theorists of the Enlightenment, turned by Hungarian noble men of letters in the late eighteenth century to the rejuvenation of an ancient stock of ideas about social and political distinction, were sufficiently elastic to be re-instrumentalised several decades later for the purposes of framing the discussion about Hungarian national distinctiveness.

Select Bibliography

Primary Sources

Bessenyei, György, *Összes művei: Prózai munkák, 1802–1804*, ed. György Kókay (Budapest: Akadémiai Kiadó, 1986).

Bessenyei, György, *Összes művei: Társadalombölcseleti írások 1771–1778*, ed. Péter Kulcsár (Budapest: Argumentum-Akadémiai Kiadó, 1992).

Pázmándi Horvát, Endre, 'A' Magyar Nemzet nem Finn származatú', *Tudományos Gyűjtemény*, 7:2 (1823), pp. 3–69.

Rousseau, Jean-Jacques, *Discourse on the Origin and Foundations of Inequality among Men*, in idem, *The Basic Political Writings*, trans. and ed. by Donald A. Cress (Indianapolis: Hackett, 1987), pp. 25–110.

Vaissète, Dom [Jean-]Joseph, *Geographie historique, ecclesiastique et civile, ou description de toutes les parties du globe Terrestre, enrichie de cartes géographiques* (Paris: Desaint & Saillant, Jean-Thomas Herissant, Jacques Barois, 1755).

Secondary Sources

Aspaas, Per Pippin and Kontler, László, 'Before and After 1773: Central European Jesuits, the Politics of Language and Discourses of Identity in the Late Eighteenth

83 Pál Hunfalvy, *Ugor vagy török-tatár eredetű-e a magyar nemzet?* (Budapest: Magyar Tudományos Akadémia, 1883), p. 12.

Century Habsburg Monarchy', in Gábor Almási and Lav Šubarić (eds.), *Latin at the Crossroads of Identity. The Evolution of Linguistic Nationalism in the Kingdom of Hungary* (Leiden and Boston: Brill, 2015), pp. 95–118.
Balázs, Éva H., *Hungary and the Habsburgs 1765–1800. An Experiment in Enlightened Absolutism* (Budapest: Central European University Press, 1997).
Bíró, Ferenc, *A felvilágosodás korának magyar irodalma* (Budapest: Balassi Kiadó, 1994).
Hont, Istvan, 'The Language of Sociability and Commerce: Samuel Pufendorf and the Theoretical Foundations of the 'Four-Stages' Theory', in Anthony Pagden (ed.), *The Languages of Political Theory in Early Modern Europe* (Cambridge: Cambridge University Press, 1986), pp. 253–76.
Penke, Olga, *Filozofikus világtörténetek és történetfilozófiák: A francia és a magyar felvilágosodás* (Budapest: Balassi Kiadó, 2000).

CHAPTER 13

The Place of the Environment in State of Nature Discourses

Reassessing Nature, Property and Sovereignty in the Anthropocene

Tom Sparks

Abstract

International environmental law, and in particular climate change law, are topics of keen interest in modern international law. Yet even in their modern forms, they depend upon and are governed by principles which derive from much earlier periods of international law and political thought. This chapter identifies sovereignty, as it has been interpreted and applied, as a key obstacle to achieving substantive environmental protection through the means of law, and traces that concept back to its roots in State of Nature theory. It analyses three contrasting State of Nature theories, those of Thomas Hobbes, John Locke, and David Hume, in order to show that although their understandings of nature differ, each treats the natural world primarily as a resource. It then turns to modern international environmental law, taking as its case study the whaling regime, and argues that through the continued use of concepts drawn from the State of Nature tradition, an understanding of the environment as a resource to be maximally exploited is continuously re-entrenched. These conceptual foundations continue to restrain progress and development in modern environmental law.

Keywords

acquisition – Anthropocene – international environmental law – property – resource – sovereignty – state of nature – whaling

 | DOI:10.1163/9789004499621_015

> One day, when he was naughty, Mr Bunnsy looked over the hedge into Farmer Fred's field and it was full of fresh green lettuces. Mr Bunnsy, however, was not full of lettuces. This did not seem fair.
>
> TERRY PRATCHETT, *The Amazing Maurice and his Educated Rodents* (Doubleday 2001)

∵

1 Introduction

Though a close cognate, the environment has very little role to play in most accounts of the state of nature. Concerns of human-induced environmental degradation were unknown when its most notable versions were propounded by the philosophers and legal theorists of the seventeenth and eighteenth centuries, and their accounts offer little in the way of rules for the regulation of humanity's relationship with the natural world. Instead, "nature" – here understood broadly as the environment and its flora and fauna – is conceived as a resource. It appears in their discussions primarily as something to be *used* and, either as the means to enter into or following entry into the commonwealth, as something to be *owned*.[1] Though vitally present, its role is passive; a background to the human concerns which play out upon, within, and using it.

The reverse is not true, however. The state of nature plays an important – if often unacknowledged – role in shaping the ways in which "nature" or "the environment" is conceived, including at the level of international environmental law (IEL). This chapter will consider three state of nature theories – those of Thomas Hobbes, John Locke, and David Hume – chosen for the contrasting ways in which they use and understand nature.[2] Each will be examined (sections 3, 4, and 5, below) in order to ascertain what role nature and the natural environment play in human affairs both in the state of nature and in the transition to society, and to what extent each would be capable of supporting a

1 This conception of nature as resource is a common feature of state of nature discourses, and is highlighted in numerous of the contributions to this volume. See, in particular, Francesca Iurlaro, 'Do Shepherds Live in a State of Nature? From *Peculium* to Civilization'; and David Grewal, 'From the State of Nature to the State of the Economy: Pufendorf on Commerce and Natural Law' in this volume.

2 For further analysis of the state of nature theories of, respectively, Thomas Hobbes and John Locke, see the contributions of Benjamin Straumann and Ioannis Evrigenis in this volume.

logic of environmental protection. It will find that although Locke's theory of nature is more amenable to an environmental protection logic than those of Hobbes or Hume, even in Locke's case any environmental logic would be weak and minimal.

The countervailing factor in each case is sovereignty, which emerges in these theories as a derivative of or counterpart to individual property in land and in the resources of the land. In state of nature theories, sovereignty and an understanding of nature as a resource are co-constitutive. The Chapter will conclude, in section 6, by applying this logic to contemporary IEL. It will examine the whaling regime, and show that the conflict between pro- and anti-whaling States is expressive of a conflict between a logic of environmental protection and a view of nature as resource that is (at the least) highly reminiscent of Locke's state of nature theory. It will be shown that the structures of thought drawn from state of nature theories continue to present substantial obstacles to the use of international law to achieve effective and meaningful environmental protection.

2 Concepts in IEL

Key concepts used by international lawyers to construct and contest international environmental obligations have been significantly influenced by state of nature theorists. Sovereignty, a concept long identified by scholars as one of the most stubborn obstacles to environmental protection under international law, is perhaps the most notable example. With references usually to Thomas Hobbes or John Locke (and sometimes also to Christian Wolff, Samuel Pufendorf, or William Blackstone), sovereignty is identified as being maintained in fear of, and to an extent justified by, the wide-ranging chaos which would reign in its absence.[3] Whether conceived as a moment in history or a mere thought experiment, the state of nature is understood as inducing individuals to form societies for the protection of their persons and their property, in which process they cede a significant part of their freedom of action to The State in order to guarantee safety, order, and regularity. It thus, at the moment of inception and at a deep ideational level, binds together the State and its sovereignty; the State and its territory; and the State and its independence.

Since the end of the 19th century, the absolutism of sovereignty has been widely understood as eroding. The emergence of norms *ius cogens*,

3 For a discussion of Pufendorf elsewhere in this volume, see Grewal (n 1); and Simone Zurbuchen, 'The State of Nature, the Family, and the State' in this volume.

international human rights law, and international criminal law each qualify aspects of State sovereignty. These (and other) developments are significant, but as yet still limited, steps towards a subordination of sovereignty to international law.[4] But as the challenges besetting IEL clearly show, any claims that sovereignty is dead or dying still seem at the very least to exaggerate its diminution and decline:[5] Sovereignty dominates still.[6] From biodiversity to pollution control, climate change to river system management, and at every point in between, State sovereignty as currently understood bedevils international legal attempts to protect the environment.[7] Strikingly, many IEL

4 Anne Peters, *Beyond Human Rights: The Legal Status of the Individual in International Law*, trans. Jonathan Huston (Cambridge: Cambridge University Press, 2016), pp. 52–53 and passim; see also Anne Peters, 'Humanity as the A and Ω of Sovereignty', *European Journal of International Law* 20, no. 3 (2009), pp. 515–18 and passim; and further Bruno Simma, 'From Bilateralism to Community Interest in International Law', *Collected Courses of the Hague Academy of International Law* 250 (1994), p. 217; Antonio Cassese, 'States: Rise and Decline of the Primary Subjects of the International Community', in *The Oxford Handbook of the History of International Law*, ed. Anne Peters and Bardo Fassbender (Oxford: Oxford University Press, 2012). For an excellent overview and theorisation of the debate surrounding sovereignty see Martti Koskenniemi, *From Apology to Utopia*, Reissue with a New Epilogue (Cambridge: Cambridge University Press, 2005), p. 226 et seq.

5 MacCormick's predictions of the end of sovereignty now seem premature: Neil MacCormick, 'Beyond the Sovereign State', *Modern Law Review* 56, no. 1 (1993), 1; Neil MacCormick, *Questioning Sovereignty: Law, State and Nation in the European Commonwealth* (Oxford: Oxford University Press, 1999); see also Jarat Chopra and Thomas G Weiss, 'Sovereignty Is No Longer Sacrosanct: Codifying Humanitarian Intervention', *Ethics & International Affairs* 6 (1992), pp. 95–117.

6 See, e.g. Wouter G. Werner and Jaap H. de Wilde, 'The Endurance of Sovereignty', *European Journal of International Relations* 7 (2001), p. 283.

7 This will be a very familiar theme to environmental lawyers, and is almost unanimously agreed in the literature. Through a combination of exclusive territorial control, volunteerism, and the enervation of international dispute settlement, State sovereignty (as classically, and in many ways still currently, understood) frustrates general interest regulation by enabling individual States to prioritise their immediate national interests over longer term or common problems. Tarlock, for example, argues that classical sovereignty is, at best, suited to achieve 'a slightly less worse human condition' in the field of environmental protections: A. Dan Tarlock, 'Stewardship Sovereignty: The Next Step in Former Prime Minister Palmer's Logic', *Washington University Journal of Urban and Contemporary Law* 42 (1992), p. 22.

The purpose of this chapter is not to discuss or defend this contention, which it accepts as a starting point for the analysis here. For discussion see, among a very great many others, Susan H. Bragdon, 'National Sovereignty and Global Environmental Responsibility: Can the Tension Be Reconciled for the Conservation of Biological Diversity?', *Harvard International Law Journal* 33 (1992), pp. 381–92; Johan D. van der Vyver, 'State Sovereignty and the Environment in International Law', *South African Law Journal* 109 (1992), p. 472; Atsuko Kanehara, 'Some Considerations Regarding Methods of International Regulation in Global Issues: Sovereignty and Common Interests', *Studies in Transnational Legal Policy* 29 (1997), pp. 81–118; A. Dan Tarlock, 'Exclusive Sovereignty versus Sustainable Development of a Shared

scholars explicitly find the roots of the concept of sovereignty in the state of nature.[8]

Resource: The Dilemma of Latin American Rainforest Management', *Texas International Law Journal* 32 (1997), p. 37; Ivan Šimonvić, 'State Sovereignty and Globalization: Are Some States More Equal?', *Georgia Journal of International and Comparative Law* 28, no. 3 (2000), pp. 381–404; Duncan French, 'A Reappraisal of Sovereignty in the Light of Global Environmental Concerns', *Legal Studies* 21, no. 3 (2001), pp. 376–99; Thomas A Telesca, 'Sovereignty or the Precautionary Principle: Which Will Save Our Fish?', *Southeastern Environmental Law Journal* 12, no. 1 (2003), pp. 23–72; Thorsten Kiefer and Catherine Brölmann, 'Beyond State Sovereignty: The Human Right to Water', *Non-State Actors and International Law* 5, no. 2 (2005), pp. 183–208; Stephen Stec, 'Humanitarian Limits to Sovereignty: Common Concern and Common Heritage Approaches to Natural Resources and Environment', *International Community Law Review* 12, no. 3 (2010), pp. 361–89; Stephen C McCaffrey, 'Sustainability and Sovereignty in the 21st Century', *Denver Journal of International Law and Policy* 41, no. 4 (2013), pp. 507–14; Joseph A McMahon, 'Some Thoughts on the Future of Sovereignty in International Law Twenty Years from Now', *Irish Journal of European Law* 18, no. 1 (2015), pp. 48–63.

The specific challenges of regulating climate change in a polycentric system of States are highlighted by Daniel Bodansky, Jutta Brunnée and Lavanya Rajamani in their excellent *International Climate Change Law* (Oxford University Press 2017), pp. 2–4, and is highlighted in contexts going far beyond environmental law by Bruno Simma in his rightly fêted Hague Lecture: Simma, 'From Bilateralism to Community Interest in International Law'. Similarly, for a general statement of (one of the many) problems of regulating sovereign States see Ole Spiermann's comment that '[r]epeated invocations of the principle *pacta sunt servanda* and the notion of good faith [in the jurisprudence of the PCIJ and the ICJ] bear witness to the conception of the state as an international legal subject actually losing ground: systems secure in their normative character do not need to repeat themselves': Ole Spiermann, *International Legal Argument in the Permanent Court of International Justice: The Rise of the International Judiciary* (Cambridge: Cambridge University Press, 2005), p. 73. The point is also acknowledged by Martti Koskenniemi in 'What Use for Sovereignty Today?', *Asian Journal of International Law* 1, no. 1 (2011), pp. 61–70, who contributes a welcome broader perspective. As Koskenniemi rightly identifies, that sovereignty is a very real barrier to effective environmental protection (among other matters) is not a sufficient argument for its abolition or modification: it is necessary also to recognise its virtues and role in the international community as we know it. Its reformulation must therefore be approached with caution.

8 See, among a great many others: Ranee Khooshie Lal Panjabi, 'From Stockholm to Rio, A Comparison of Declaratory Principles of International Environmental Law', *Denver Journal of International Law and Policy* 21 (1993), p. 219; Michael M'Gonigle, 'Between Globalism and Territoriality: The Emergence of an International Constitution and the Challenge of Ecological Legitimacy', *Canadian Journal of Law and Jurisprudence* 15 (2002), p. 168; Usha Natarajan, 'TWAIL and the Environment: The State of Nature, the Nature of the State, and the Arab Spring', *Oregon Review of International Law* 14 (2012): passim, esp. p. 193; David Mence, 'The Cetacean Right to Life Revisited', *International Journal of Law in Context* 11 (2015): p. 32. Kingsbury and Straumann note the use of state of nature theories as foundational for international law more broadly: Benedict Kingsbury and Benjamin Straumann, 'State of Nature versus Commercial Sociability as the Basis of International Law: Reflections on the Roman Foundations and Current Interpretations of the International Political and Legal Thought of Grotius, Hobbes, and Pufendorf', in *The Philosophy of International Law*, ed. Samantha Besson and John Tasioulas (Oxford: Oxford University Press, 2010), p. 33.

Two aspects of sovereignty in particular are problematic in the IEL context: voluntarism and exclusive territorial control. These are corollaries of the concept defined and understood, in particular as it was during its nineteenth and (early) twentieth century heyday:[9] as exclusionary. On this view, the sovereign State alone has the competence to determine the legal norms in force within its boundaries, and to enforce them. The sovereign State is bound only by those norms of international law to which it consents so to be. And of all the actors present within its territory, the sovereign State alone is capable of bearing international responsibility for activities taking place there.[10] Intrusion into its domestic sphere of action, imposed from outside and absent its consent, is anathema.

But environments and environmental problems do not stop at borders. The Amazon basin spreads across five countries; the Nile basin, eleven.[11] Of the

9 Instrumental in the formation of this strong version of sovereignty was its "externalisation" by Emer de Vattel: Stéphane Beaulac, 'Emer de Vattel and the Externalization of Sovereignty', *Journal of the History of International Law* 5 (2003), p. 237; see also Emmanuelle Jouannet, *Emer de Vattel et l'émergence doctrinale du droit international classique* (Editions A. Pédone, 1998); Emmanuelle Jouannet, 'Emer de Vattel (1714–1767)', in *The History of International Law: The Oxford Handbook*, ed. Bardo Fassbender and Anne Peters (Oxford: Oxford University Press, 2012); Robert Schütze, 'The "Unsettled" Eighteenth-Century: Kant and His Predecessors', in *Governance & Globalisation: International Problems, European Solutions*, ed. Robert Schütze (Cambridge: Cambridge University Press, 2018), pp. 11–40.

10 'Sovereignty in the relations between States signifies independence. Independence in regard to a portion of the globe is the right to exercise therein, to the exclusion of any other State, the functions of a State.' *Island of Palmas Case (Netherlands and United States of America)*, Arbitral Award of 4 April 1928, Reports of International Arbitral Awards volume II, 829–871, 838. Lassa Oppenheim, similarly, defined sovereignty as '[S]upreme authority, an authority which is independent of any other earthy authority. Sovereignty in the strict and narrowest sense of the term includes, therefore, independence all round, within and without the borders of the country': Lassa Francis Lawrence Oppenheim, *International Law. A Treatise – Volume 1: Peace*, 2nd ed. (London: Longmans, Green and Co., 1912), p. 109; see also consonant definitions in Georg Friedrich Von Martens, *Summary of the Law of Nations, Founded on the Treaties and Customs of the Modern Nations of Europe* (Thomas Bradford, 1795), pp. 23–24; F. E. Smith, *International Law*, 4th Edn. (London: J. M. Dent & Sons Ltd., 1911); Georg Jellinek, *Allgemeine Staatslehre*, 3rd ed. (Berlin: Julius Springer, 1922), pp. 481–82; Henry Wheaton, *Elements of International Law* (Clarendon Press, 1936), p. 27; Travers Twiss, *The Law of Nations Considered as Independent Political Communities: On the Rights and Duties of Nations in Time of Peace* (Fred B. Rothman & Co., 1985), p. 9.

11 Günther Grill et al., 'An Index-Based Framework for Assessing Patterns and Trends in River Fragmentation and Flow Regulation by Global Dams at Multiple Scales', *Environmental Research Letters* 10, no. 1 (1 January 2015): 015001; Natasha Gilbert, 'World's Rivers "Awash with Dangerous Levels of Antibiotics"', *The Guardian*, 27 May

193 States members of the UN, 150 border the world's oceans.[12] Many habitats and ecosystems straddle international boundaries, which are routinely crossed by animals either as part of annual migrations, or the day-to-day search for food, water, and mates.[13] Environmental disasters cross boundaries, too: a 2002 report assessing the impact of the Chernobyl disaster found the accident had caused some level of radiological contamination of the ground in 'practically every country of the northern hemisphere'.[14] And at larger scales still, all States are affected by environmental harms affecting the atmosphere, of which the most prominent are ozone degradation and climatic change. Indeed, environmental harms regularly, and perhaps increasingly, affect States that had little role in their making.[15]

2019, available via <https://www.theguardian.com/society/2019/may/27/worlds-rivers-awash-with-dangerous-levels-of-antibiotics>, accessed 21.09.2021.

12 The degradation of the world's oceans is such that an increasing number of scientists are recommending a ban on high seas fisheries: Crow White and Christopher Costello, 'Close the High Seas to Fishing?', *PLoS Biology* 12, no. 3 (25 March 2014): e1001826; Manuel Dureuil et al., 'Elevated Trawling inside Protected Areas Undermines Conservation Outcomes in a Global Fishing Hot Spot', *Science* 362, no. 6421 (21 December 2018): pp. 1403–7; Daniel Pauly, A Global Ban on Fishing on the High Seas? The Time Is Now, interview by Richard Schiffman, 27 September 2018, available via <https://e360.yale.edu/features/a-global-ban-on-fishing-on-the-high-seas-the-time-is-now>, accessed 21.09.2021. Concern continues to rise, too, over the contamination of the oceans with plastic waste: Marcus Haward, 'Plastic Pollution of the World's Seas and Oceans as a Contemporary Challenge in Ocean Governance', *Nature Communications* 9, no. 1 (December 2018); Ana L. d. F. Lacerda et al., 'Plastics in Sea Surface Waters around the Antarctic Peninsula', *Scientific Reports* 9, no. 1 (December 2019); Michael F. Hochella et al., 'Natural, Incidental, and Engineered Nanomaterials and Their Impacts on the Earth System', *Science* 363, no. 6434 (29 March 2019).

13 The 2019 IPBES Global Assessment Report has revealed a near-disastrous decline in biodiversity in recent decades: Sandra Díaz et al., 'Summary for Policymakers of the Global Assessment Report on Biodiversity and Ecosystem Services', 4 May 2019, available via <https://doi.org/10.5281/zenodo.3553579>, accessed 21.09.2021.

14 Nuclear Energy Agency and Organisation for Economic Cooperation and Development, 'Chernobyl: Assessment of Radiological and Health Impacts' (OECD, 2002), p. 38.

15 Here too sovereignty serves a central function, although here one that is more useful to the cause of environmental protection. The territorial integrity of States, understood as an aspect of their sovereignty, grounds a rule against harm to the State's environment or people originating from the territory of another State: J.A. Beesley, 'Rights And Responsibilities of Arctic Coastal States: The Canadian View', *Journal of Maritime and Coastal Law* 3, no. 1 (1971), pp. 8, 10; see further *Corfu Channel* (*United Kingdom v Albania*) Merits, Judgment, (1949) ICJ Reports 4, 22; *Legality of the Threat or Use of Nuclear Weapons*, Advisory Opinion (1996) ICJ Reports 242, [29]; *Pulp Mills on the River Uruguay* (*Argentina v Uruguay*), Merits, Judgment (2010) ICJ Reports 14, [101]; *Certain Activities Carried Out by Nicaragua in the Border Area* (*Costa Rica v Nicaragua*) and *Construction of a Road in Costa Rica along the San Juan River* (*Nicaragua v Costa Rica*), Merits, Judgment

All of these factors should pose the question of whether the concepts IEL employs – seen in the context of the intellectual foundations they carry with them – are fit for its purposes. Indeed, IEL's uncritical acceptance of the conceptual and ideational foundations of the discipline means, according to Usha Natarajan and Kishan Khoday, that it has 'set itself up for failure'.[16] In this context, this chapter will look again at the state of nature, in order to consider to what extent it (and the co-evolution of sovereignty and resources it establishes) are obstacles to the international protection of the environment. It argues that the intellectual foundations of sovereignty in the state of nature mean that that concept, as classically understood, relies upon a conception of "nature-as-property" and "nature-as-resource" that entrenches unilateralism and volunteerism as regards environmental protection, and actively impedes the development of international law.[17] In order to avoid the perpetuation of these outdated attitudes in modern international environmental law, concepts such as sovereignty must be deeply interrogated, and reformulated in order to detach the modern incarnations of these concepts from the anchors of the past.[18]

(2015) ICJ Reports 665, [104]. In 2011 this principle was extended to apply to areas beyond the jurisdiction of any one State in *Responsibilities and Obligations of States Sponsoring Persons and Entities with Respect to Activities in the Area*, Advisory Opinion, 1 February 2011, ITLOS Reports 10, [148].

16 Usha Natarajan and Kishan Khoday, 'Locating Nature: Making and Unmaking International Law', *Leiden Journal of International Law* 27 (2014), p. 585; Weeramantry argues that a similar neglect of philosophy and conceptual history affects international law in general: Christopher Weeramantry, *Universalising International Law* (Leiden: Martinus Nijhoff, 2004), p. 87.

17 I here make the assumption, the discussion of which is beyond the scope of this short contribution, that concepts – to borrow from Giddens – act as structural elements which *enable and constrain* the discourses of which they are a part. See Anthony Giddens, *The Constitution of Society: Outline of the Theory of Structuration* (Polity Press, 1984), p. 25. To that extent, concepts act within discourses as Durkheimian "Things": Anthony Giddens, *Durkheim* (Fontana Press, 1978), p. 35; see further Emile Durkheim, 'Religion and Ritual', in *Emile Durkheim: Selected Writings*, ed. Anthony Giddens (Cambridge: Cambridge University Press, 1972). For a brief discussion of this aspect of concepts by the present author see Tom Sparks, 'The State', in *Concepts for International Law: Contributions to Disciplinary Thought*, ed. Jean d'Aspremont and Sahib Singh (Cheltenham: Edward Elgar Publishing, 2019), pp. 838–49.

18 We could describe this process, using (in a different context) Dowling's happy phrase, an 'Un-Locke-ing' of international environmental law: Anne C. Dowling, 'Un-Locke-Ing a Just Right Environmental Regime: Overcoming the Three Bears of International Environmentalism – Sovereignty, Locke, and Compensation', *William and Mary Environmental Law and Policy Review* 26, no. 3 (2002), pp. 891–960.

3 'Nasty, Brutish, and Short': The State of Nature of Thomas Hobbes[19]

Thomas Hobbes' *Leviathan* is, without question, one of the most important and enduring works of political and legal theory ever produced. In its account of the emergence of the commonwealth from the state of nature some have seen a description of the international system of States,[20] while others have found a dystopian nightmare which international law is designed to contain and control.[21] Whether as a positive or negative vision, it has echoed down the generations. In the preface to his own masterwork, *Le droit de gens*, for example, Emer de Vattel declares that despite what he describes as Hobbes' 'paradoxes and detestable maxims', in the pages of *Leviathan* one 'discover[s] the hand of a master'.[22]

In *Leviathan*, Hobbes describes the inception and founding of the commonwealth, and the source of sovereign power. He finds the roots of both in the covenant individuals form in order to escape "the state of nature", a chaotic condition of war 'every man against every man'[23] that arises from the combination of a lack of governing power, competition for resources, and the near equality of arms that means 'the weakest had strength enough to kill the strongest, either by secret machinations, or by confederacy with others, that

19 Thomas Hobbes, *Leviathan*, ed. C. B. MacPherson (first published 1651, this edition Penguin Books, 1985), p.186. All future references to *Leviathan* refer to the 1985 MacPherson edition.

20 Larry May argues that 'Hobbes's views can provide a solid grounding for the rules of war and international relations generally, contrary to the near universal belief that Hobbes is the *bête noire* of international law': Larry May, *Limiting Leviathan: Hobbes on Law and International Affairs* (Oxford: Oxford University Press, 2013), 1; see also Noel Malcolm, *Aspects of Hobbes* (Oxford: Oxford University Press, 2002), pp. 438–40.

21 Sellers argues, for example, that many of international law's subsequent great thinkers explicitly saw their task as refuting Hobbes and his vision of international order: M. N. S. Sellers, 'The Justice of International Law', *Transnational Legal Theory* 3, no. 3 (2012), p. 300; for a similar observation in philosophy in general see W G Pogson Smith, 'The Philosophy of Hobbes: An Essay', in *Hobbes's Leviathan: Reprinted from the Edition of 1651 with an Essay by the Late W.G. Pogson Smith* (Clarendon Press, 1909), ix, xvii. For examples of this view within international environmental law in particular see, Elli Louka, *International Environmental Law: Fairness, Effectiveness, and World Order* (Cambridge: Cambridge University Press, 2006), pp. 66–67.

22 Emer de Vattel, *The Law of Nations; or Principles of the Law of Nature Applied to the Conduct and Affairs of Nations and Sovereigns* (first published as *Le droit de gens* in 1758, this edition London: G. G. and J. Robinson, 1797), vii. For a discussion of Vattel, see Edward J. Kolla, 'Written in the Hearts of People? Natural and International Law during the Age of Enlightenment' in this volume.

23 *Leviathan*, p. 188.

are in the same danger as himselfe.'[24] That instability and condition of perpetual conflict places each individual in constant danger, and retards both individual and social development:

> In such condition, there is no place for Industry; because the fruit thereof is uncertain: and consequently no Culture of the Earth; [...] no Arts; no Letters; no Society; and which is worst of all, continuall feare, and danger of violent death; And the life of man, solitary, poore, nasty, brutish, and short.[25]

It is no surprise, therefore, that individuals seek to escape from the harsh privations and continuous violence of the state of nature. In order to do so, individuals conclude a covenant by which they all and in parallel surrender the major part of their natural freedom to the *Leviathan*, an imagined central "self" the personality of which is exercised through the sovereign of the commonwealth, to establish a system of laws and order, to mobilise the State's combined strengths to combat external threats, and to keep the internal peace.[26] Through the covenant, Hobbes thus establishes an absolute government possessed of the power of life and death over its subjects.[27]

The environment is ever-present in *Leviathan*, though generally as subtext rather than subject. It appears sometimes as a contrast to the condition of

---

24 *Leviathan*, p. 183.

25 *Leviathan*, 186. Hobbes was criticised for this highly unflattering portrayal of humans, and responded that the view did not stipulate that the majority or humans are evil or to be feared, but that their good intentions could not be presumed because a sufficient number would be so, and general suspicion is thus necessary because there is no way to distinguish the "wicked" from the "righteous": Noel Malcolm, 'Hobbes and Spinoza', in *The Cambridge History of Political Thought 1450–1700*, ed. J. H. Burns (Cambridge: Cambridge University Press, 1991), pp. 534–35.

26 *Leviathan*, pp. 223–227. Pufendorf's account of the state of nature, which followed *Leviathan* by twenty years and which references Hobbes, understands the escape from that condition to take place via two covenants, the first of which establishes a society among individuals, and the second a government which pertains to it: Samuel Pufendorf, *The Law of Nature and Nations in Eight Books*, trans. Basil Kennett (first published as *De jure naturæ et gentium libri otto* in 1672, this edition London: J. Walthoe and others, 1729), pp. 638–39. For a discussion of Hobbes' influence on Pufendorf see Grewal (n 1).

27 *Leviathan*, pp. 264–265; though see *contra* Richard Tuck, 'Introduction', in *Thomas Hobbes: Leviathan*, by Thomas Hobbes, ed. Richard Tuck (Cambridge: Cambridge University Press, 1991), xviii–xxv. Tuck introduces an important nuance, noting that 'it has often proved possible to read Hobbes as a surprisingly liberal author' (p. xviii). Zagorin, too, argues that there are important limits to the sovereign power: Perez Zagorin, *Hobbes and the Law of Nature* (Princeton: Princeton University Press, 2009), pp. 84–98.

humans, such as when Hobbes distinguishes the nature or temperament of humans from those of other animals;[28] and less frequently as a comparator, where a point of commonality is identified.[29] In general, however, references to the natural world view it as a passive space; a theatre within which human concerns are played out, and an implied condition of scarcity both causing and caused by the chaos of human affairs in the state of nature.[30] The environment, consisting of land and its flora and fauna, is conceived as a resource; in particular as a source of 'Nutriment, consisting in Animals, Vegetals, and Minerals, God hath freely layd them before us'.[31] Humanity's relationship with nature, according to Hobbes, is primarily that of use of a resource; its social expression: ownership.

Ownership and the ability safely and effectively to exploit the goods of nature is, in Hobbes' description, a product of the commonwealth. Although in the state of nature 'every man has a Right to every thing',[32] there can be no sole or longitudinal ownership:

> It is consequent also to the same condition, that there be no Propriety, no Dominion, no *Mine* and *Thine* distinct; but onley that to be every mans that he can get; and for so long, as he can keep it.[33]

It follows, Hobbes declares, there can be no meaningful exploitation of nature's resources,[34] and thus he arrives at the poverty of life in the state of nature,

---

28 *Leviathan*, p. 75, 100, 113, 124, 134, 197, 225–227.

29 *Leviathan*, p. 118. Pufendorf would later use the analogy with animals to great rhetorical effect (though the comparison was flattering to neither party) in describing humans in the state of nature as akin to animals: 'We should see nothing but a furious Multitude of Wolves, of Lions, of Dogs tearing and devouring one another. Every man would indeed be a Lion, a Wolf, a Dog, to his Neighbour, or rather a Monster, more pernicious and more spiteful than the fiercest of these Creatures; since Man, of all Living Things, is the most able to hurt Man, and, if left to his own furious Passions, the most willing.' Pufendorf, *The Law of Nature and Nations in Eight Books*, p. 100.

30 *Leviathan*, pp. 185–186, 294–296.

31 *Leviathan*, p. 295.

32 *Leviathan*, p. 189.

33 *Leviathan*, p. 188. In the state of nature the "laws of nature" (derived at *Leviathan*, pp. 189–192) exist, but are little more than a set of rational precepts which, if they could generally be followed, would enable peace. In the absence of enforcement, however, they remain laws improperly-so-called, and are secondary to self-preservation: Malcolm, 'Hobbes and Spinoza', pp. 535–38.

34 *Leviathan*, p. 186; see also p. 227. Hobbes later explicitly connects the availability of foodstuffs with industry: 'Plenty dependeth (next to Gods favour) meerly on the labour and industry of men'. *Leviathan*, p. 295.

'nasty, brutish, and short.'[35] It is for this reason that the first matter of the newly established commonwealth is the 'Division of the Land it selfe: wherein the Sovereign assigneth to every man a portion, according as he, and not according as any Subject, or any number of them, shall judge agreeable to Equity, and the Common Good.'[36]

It is here that a gap in Hobbes' description can be found: he does not explain the notion of *territorial* dominion,[37] as opposed to the *personal* dominion of the sovereign that results from the consent of individuals to the social contract.[38] How is it, in other words, that the commonwealth can be *spatially* defined? Though it can perhaps be speculated that the commonwealth's territorial scope is defined by that area controlled by its subjects, Hobbes nowhere addresses this point. He makes reference to territorial extent only in relation to banishment and exile, and the mechanism by which commonwealths acquire territory or define their territorial extents is thus left unclear.[39] Such a reliance on control would, however, not be fully satisfying as an explanation for the source of territorial extent. Hobbes is unequivocal that mere control cannot give rise to property of individuals; unlike in Locke's account (discussed below), the sovereign is entitled to apportion the territory of the newly-created commonwealth to its subjects in whatever shares 'he [...] shall judge agreeable to Equity, and the Common Good', and their pre-existing control of particular territories is not capable of generating rights for them.[40] Though it could be argued that territorial acquisition is distinct from property, and that the inability of control to give rise to *ownership* would thus not prevent its giving rise

35 *Leviathan*, p. 186.

36 *Leviathan*, p. 296. Here there is a parallel with Rousseau's theory which, though as with Locke acknowledges a property of individuals prior to the formation of societies, understands the social contract as vesting the sovereign with all the property of the contractors: Jean-Jacques Rousseau, *Du contrat social; ou principles du droit politique* (Amsterdam: Marc Michel Rey, 1762), I:ix.

37 This is perhaps surprising, given Hobbes' oft-observed concern with definitions. See, for example, Pogson Smith, 'The Philosophy of Hobbes', x; citing John Aubrey, *'Brief Lives,' Chiefly of Contemporaries, Set down by John Aubrey, between the Years 1669 & 1696*, ed. Andrew Clark, vol. 1 (Clarendon Press, 1898), p. 394.

38 As Schmitt observes, Hobbes' imagery of the leviathan, the State, and the Commonwealth is always that of a '"huge man," [or] a "huge machine,"' – i.e., it is personified rather than mapped: Carl Schmitt, *The Leviathan in the State Theory of Thomas Hobbes: Meaning and Failure of a Political Symbol*, trans. George Schwab and Erna Hilfstein (Westport: Greenwood Press, 1996), pp. 97–100.

39 Hobbes refers to banishment at p. 273 and 359, and comments also that 'whosoever enterth into anothers dominion, is Subject to all the Lawes thereof': *Leviathan*, p. 273.

40 *Leviathan*, p. 296.

to *dominion*, Hobbes' sovereign finds the source of its power in those rights and entitlements which individuals cede to it in the formation of the original covenant. It seems unlikely, therefore, that they could cede to it a right greater than that which they themselves possess.[41]

It may be that a means to square this circle can be found in the state of nature that persists between commonwealths.[42] Though the formation of the covenant and creation of the sovereign power within a commonwealth gives rise to a system of laws and regulations which govern the conduct of the individuals within its dominion, Hobbes notes on a number of occasions that an individual not party to the covenant remains in relation to the covenanters 'in the condition of warre he was in before; wherein he might without injustice be destroyed by any man whatsoever.'[43] Nor is there any restriction, internal or external, on the right of the sovereign to wage war against other commonwealths, save only that of prudence.[44] Such a state of affairs could, perhaps, be argued to apply also to the land itself. Under such a supposition the commonwealth would be able to acquire land not otherwise occupied – where the need for the consent of its inhabitants complicates matters – by dint of the right which 'every man has [...] to every thing'.[45] Thus the ephemeral condition of ownership by individuals in the state of nature must be taken also to apply to ownership by commonwealths: 'that to be every [commonwealth's] that [it] can get; and for so long, as [it] can keep it.'[46]

That insight implies that nature always remains outside of the commonwealth. Though individuals *within* the commonwealth may have a right *vis-à-vis its other citizens* to land, animal or plant; the *commonwealth's* dominion over land is occupation, not ownership. Its use of plants and subjugation of animals is opportunity, not entitlement.[47] And though Hobbes declares the

41 Though c.f. Malcolm, who wonders whether Hobbes 'needed to use a concept of contract at all': Malcolm, 'Hobbes and Spinoza', pp. 539–40.

42 Though May is among the more optimistic readers of Hobbes (in relation to international law), he nevertheless has no hesitation in agreeing with the majority of interpretations that '[t]he international realm is indeed a state of nature, and like all states of nature it is also a state of war': May, *Limiting Leviathan*, p. 193.

43 *Leviathan*, p. 232. Indications of this may be seen, too, in Hobbes' remarks on the status of foreigners (p. 273), and rebels (pp. 360–361).

44 *Leviathan*, pp. 234–235.

45 *Leviathan*, p. 189.

46 *Leviathan*, p. 188.

47 Blackstone would later re-characterise "rights" in the state of nature as "liberties", a distinction of which it seems likely Hobbes would have approved: William Blackstone, *Commentaries on the Laws of England: Book the First* (first published 1765, this edition The Legal Classics Library, 1983), p. 123; see also discussion in Mark Somos, 'Boston in the State of Nature, 1761–1765', *Jus Gentium* 3, no. 1 (2018), p. 63.

goods of the earth 'God hath freely layd [...] before us',[48] it seems likely (*pace* Sætra) that he would have largely accepted this characterisation.[49] In relation to nature, all rights are natural.

Such a conclusion is twice unhelpful to modern IEL. It is so, first, because the transposition of these ideas into modern legal forms would exclude a duty of preservation of nature of which the recipient would be nature itself.[50] Nature, being outwith the covenant which establishes the commonwealth is at best a resource to be exploited by it, and at worst an external "other" in relation to which the sovereign is constrained only by prudence and an assessment of the commonwealth's best interests.[51] The environment's value is entirely

---

48 *Leviathan*, p. 295.

49 Henrik Sætra, 'The State of No Nature – Thomas Hobbes and the Natural World', *Journal of International Scientific Publications: Ecology and Safety* 8 (2014), pp. 177–93.

50 For a similar observation see, e.g. Robert Garner, *The Political Theory of Animal Rights* (Manchester University Press, 2005), pp. 13, 48.

51 Note, however, Malcolm's conclusion that a part of that assessment of best interests must include 'the circumstances of each decision to see whether or not the dictates of natural law are applicable' (p. 440). Malcolm argues that Hobbes' laws of nature apply to the international arena and should constrain the actions of the sovereign (pp. 438–443, et *seq.*). Malcolm acknowledges too, however, that the laws of nature remain primarily obligations of conscience and self-interest (to the extent that they further self-preservation) until, through the establishment of a common sovereignty, they 'transition from the moral level to the jural' (pp. 437, 444). He thus establishes a weak, self-interested duty of good faith in international relations (pp. 446–449). See generally, Malcolm, *Aspects of Hobbes*, pp. 432–56.

A similar argument is made by May, who argues on the basis of a reading both of *Leviathan* (at p. 210 *et seq.*) and *De Cive* (the relevant passage is at pp. 142–143 of the 1991 Gert version) that Hobbes' natural law is a stronger bar to action in the prosecution of war than is conventionally supposed. In particular, May refers to Hobbes' prohibition of cruelty – defined as 'to hurt without reason' – as an absolute requirement of the law of nature which operates even prior to the institution of the commonwealth: May, *Limiting Leviathan*, p. 200; Thomas Hobbes, *Man and Citizen: De Homine and De Cive*, ed. Bernard Gert, trans. Charles T. Wood, T.S.K Scott-Craig, and Bernard Gert (Indianapolis: Hackett Publishing, 1991). Though May introduces this argument in the context of a minimum content for a *ius in bello* (i.e. as cruelty towards individuals or communities), if the argument holds good it could conceivably apply also to wanton and reasonless damage more broadly, including to environments and natural systems.

Ultimately, however, this argument is not convincing: Hobbes is emphatic that these laws of nature, until formalised by and made subject to the enforcement mechanisms of the commonwealth, are merely 'call[ed] by the name of Lawes; but improperly: for they are but Conclusions, or Theoremes concerning what conduceth to the conservation and defence of themselves': *Leviathan*, pp. 216–217. Even less do they bind *vis-à-vis* a non-intentional actor ("nature") than against an adversary in war: there is no risk to cruelty when it cannot inspire revenge (*Leviathan*, p. 210).

instrumental – in its ability to continue to provide goods for the commonwealth – and not intrinsic.[52] In other words: the State's sovereignty over a territory entails an illimitable freedom to exploit the resources within its area of control, without regard to the welfare of those environments or of any others, except insofar as its self-interest demands.

Perhaps of still greater concern, secondly, it speaks against any inherent obligation of the commonwealth to safeguard the environments of its neighbours, either indirectly (through the degradation of its own dominions), or through direct transboundary harms. In so doing it threatens to strip from sovereignty its single environmental virtue; that it gives rise to a right on the part of each sovereignty not to suffer harms to its territory arising from another sovereignty.[53] Hobbes' persisting state of war all against all does not, importantly, deny the possibility of the instigation of such a right between sovereigns by agreement.[54] Nevertheless, if his theory were understood to be a valid description of the ground state of the international legal order it would necessarily preclude the *pre*-existence of any right to be free of transboundary harms as

52 For a similar observation see Saskia Vermeylen, 'Materiality and the Ontological Turn in the Anthropocene: Establishing a Dialogue between Law, Anthropology and Eco-Philosophy', in *Environmental Law and Governance for the Anthropocene*, ed. Louis J. Kotzé (Hart Publishing, 2017), p. 158.

53 Phillipe Sands and Jacqueline Peel, *Principles of International Environmental Law*, 4th ed. (Cambridge: Cambridge University Press, 2018), pp. 201, 206–11; see also Louka, *International Environmental Law*, pp. 50–51; Günther Handl, 'Transboundary Impacts', in *The Oxford Handbook on International Environmental Law*, ed. Daniel Bodansky, Jutta Brunnée, and Ellen Hey, 1st ed. (Oxford: Oxford University Press, 2007), p. 531; Patricia Birnie, Alan Boyle, and Catherine Redgewell, *International Law and the Environment*, 3rd ed. (Oxford: Oxford University Press, 2009), pp. 137–64; Ulrich Beyerlin and Thilo Marahun, *International Environmental Law* (Hart Publishing, 2011), pp. 39–46; Pierre-Marie Dupuy and Jorge E. Viñales, *International Environmental Law* (Cambridge: Cambridge University Press, 2015), pp. 55–58; Daniel Bodansky, Jutta Brunnée, and Lavanya Rajamani, *International Climate Change Law* (Oxford: Oxford University Press, 2017), pp. 40–44; *Trail Smelter Case (United States, Canada)* Awards of 16 April 1938 and 11 March 1941, III RIAA 1905, 1965; *Corfu Channel* (n 15), p. 22; *Threat or Use of Nuclear Weapons* (n 15) [29]; *Pulp Mills* (n 15), [101]; *Certain Activities* (n 15), [104]. For this principle in Hobbes see David Peter Gauthier, *The Logic of Leviathan: The Moral and Political Theory of Thomas Hobbes* (Oxford: Clarendon Press, 1969), pp. 207–12.

54 Malcolm, *Aspects of Hobbes*, pp. 437–39. As Tuck observes, however, these must be regarded as somewhat short of a firm foundation for international collective action. Though such agreements can be made, '[n]o conventions or covenants are *secure* in the state of nature, since at any time they may be trumped by the force of the right of self-preservation and private judgment; but in the absence of such disruption they can maintain a weak existence': Richard Tuck, *The Rights of War and Peace: Political Thought and International Order from Grotius to Kant* (Oxford: Oxford University Press, 1999), p. 133.

a function of sovereignty. Contrary to the position in modern IEL, the right to be free from transboundary harms would need to be construed as a *limitation* on sovereignty instigated by agreement, rather than understood as an *aspect of* sovereignty that would itself require agreement to modify or suspend. The amelioration of the condition of nature is, therefore, unlikely to be assisted by a Hobbesian account of the state of nature.

4 The *Two Treatises*: The State of Nature in the Theory of John Locke[55]

Though his theory of the state of nature tends towards different ends than that of his near contemporary Thomas Hobbes, John Locke's contribution to the social and political thought of the seventeenth century has earned him an equally exalted position in the philosophical cannon. In the second of his *Two Treatises of Government*, originally published anonymously in 1690, Locke expounds a vision of the state of nature which differs in important ways from that of Hobbes: Locke's state of nature is less overtly bleak, more overtly religious,[56] and leads Locke to deny, rather than to affirm, the legitimacy of absolute monarchy. Like *Leviathan*, Locke's *Treatises* have had, and continue to exert, a pull on the development of political thought. The *Treatises* were an important influence on many other seminal thinkers (including Jean-Jacques Rousseau), and afterwards have been credited with

55 John Locke, *Two Treatises of Government and A Letter Concerning Toleration*, ed. Ian Shapiro (first published 1690, this edition, New Haven: Yale University Press, 2003). All references to *Treatises* refer to the 2003 Shapiro edition.

56 This aspect, though not taken up here, is vital to the proper interpretation of Locke's *Treatises*. For a fascinating discussion see Eldon Eisenach, 'Religion and Locke's Two Treatises of Government', in *John Locke's Two Treatises of Government*, ed. Edward J. Harpham (Lawrence, Kansas: University of Kansas Press, 1992), pp. 50–81, p. 50 et seq. Dunn argues that there is a limited extent to which Hobbes and Locke can even be compared for this reason. He argues that Locke 'never faced' Hobbes' central problem when writing the *Two Treatises*: 'the construction of a political society from an ethical vacuum. Locke['s …] central premise is precisely the absence of such a vacuum': John Dunn, *The Political Thought of John Locke: An Historical Account of the 'Two Treatises of Government'* (Cambridge: Cambridge University Press, 1969), p. 79. See also David Resnick, 'Rationality and the Two Treatises' in Edward J Harpham (ed.), *John Locke's Two Treatises of Government* (University of Kansas Press, 1992) pp. 82–117, pp. 82, 115 and generally; for a contrasting view see, *contra*, Wolfgang von Leyden, *Hobbes and Locke: The Politics of Freedom and Obligation* (St Martin's Press 1982), pp. 175–176 and generally.

providing an important intellectual background for the development of theories of human rights.[57]

The first of Locke's *Two Treatises* is a forensic and highly rhetorical denunciation of Sir Robert Filmer's *Patriarcha*;[58] the second – the focus of this discussion – Locke's own thought on the state of nature and the origins of political authority. Here Locke describes a state of nature largely free of the bleakness and poverty of the Hobbsian conception,[59] yet far from idyllic. For Locke, the state of nature is a state of insecurity that can easily deteriorate into something much more reminiscent of Hobbes: a state of war.[60] It is the lack of a judicial power that threatens such a slide into war because,[61] Locke argues, the absence of such a common authority turns every transgression into a potential conflagration.[62] It is the desire to avoid this state of war that is 'one great reason of men's putting themselves into society, and quitting the state of nature'.[63]

57 John Maurice Kelly, *A Short History of Western Legal Theory* (Oxford: Clarendon Press, 1992), p. 215; von Leyden, *Hobbes and Locke*, p. 100.

58 *Treatises*, I:§7–99.

59 Indeed, Locke describes the state of nature as 'a state of peace, good-will, mutual assistance and preservation': *Treatises*, II:§19. See in this volume, Evrigenis' characterisation of Locke's state of nature as a 'sanctuary': Evrigenis, 'Fleeing *"Polyphemus's Den"*'.

60 *Treatises*, II:§16–20. Despite Pufendorf's dim opinion of men in their natural state (see above note 29), his description of the state of nature has much more in common with Locke's than with Hobbes': Pufendorf, *The Law of Nature and Nations in Eight Books*, pp. 109–17.

61 *Treatises*, II:§20. A similar position is reached, though by a different route and with different consequences, by Immanuel Kant: 'Zwar durfte sein natürlicher Zustand nicht eben darum ein Zustand der *Ungerechtigkeit* (iniustus) sein, einander nur nach dem bloßen Maße seiner Gewalt zu begegnen; aber es war doch ein Zustand der *Rechtlosigkeit* (status iustita vacuus), wo, wenn das Recht *streitig* (ius controversum) war, sich kein kompetenter *Richter* fand, rechtskräftig den Anspruch zu tun, aus welchem nun in einen rechtlichen zu treten ein jeder den anderen mit Gewalt antreiben darf; weil, obgleich nach jedes seinen *Rechtsbegriffen* etwas Äußers durch Bemächtigung oder Vertrag erworben werden kann, diese Erwerbung doch nur *provisorisch* ist, so lange sie noch nicht die Sanktion eines öffentlichen Gesetzes für sich hat, weil sie durch keine öffentliche (distributive) Gerechtigkeit bestimmt, und durch keine dies Recht ausübende Gewalt gesichert ist': Immanuel Kant, *Die metaphysik der Sitten*, ed. Wilhelm Weischedel (first published 1797, this edition Frankfurt am Main: Suhrkamp Verlag, 1968), §44. [Original emphasis]. This point has been seen as central in other contexts, too. Somos notes that the closure of the Courts in pre-revolutionary America was seen by that period's major thinkers as highly significant in creating a state of nature in the colonies: Somos, 'Boston in the State of Nature, 1761–1765', pp. 104–10, esp. p. 107.

62 Evrigenis, 'Fleeing *"Polyphemus's Den"*'. For an alternative reading of the relationship between these states in Locke's theory see Richard A. Cox, *Locke on War and Peace* (Oxford: Clarendon Press, 1960), pp. 73–81.

63 *Treatises*, II:§21.

Importantly, though, he does not see this reason as sufficient as an explanation of the formation of societies. To it he must add an element apparently absent from Hobbes' atomistic and 'solitary' view of humans:[64] natural sociability.[65] In the 'strong obligations of necessity, convenience, and inclination, [that] drive him into society' Locke locates the impulse towards communal living that, in turn, gives rise to friction between individuals. On this double foundation, fear and sociability, Locke builds civil society.

He begins with property.[66] Unlike Hobbes who, as discussed above, premises all property on the social contract, Locke finds the origins of ownership in the state of nature.[67] Though like all rights before the institution of the contract he regards the natural right to property as tenuous, nevertheless his is a right to property properly-so-called, and it is in his discussion of acquisition that much of his thought on the relationship between humankind and the natural world is to be found.

Locke's theory of acquisition remains one of the best-known aspects of his philosophy,[68] and its basic premise is very simply stated:

> Though the earth, and all inferior creatures, be common to all men, yet every man has a property in his own person: this nobody has any right to but himself. The labour of his body, and the work of his hands, we may say, are properly his. Whatsoever then he removes out of the state that nature hath provided, and left it in, he hath mixed his labour with, and joined to it something that is his own, and thereby makes it his property. It being by him removed from the common state Nature hath placed it in, it hath by this labour something annexed to it that excludes the common right of other men. For this labour being the unquestionable property of the labourer, no man but he can have a right to what that is once joined to[.][69]

64 *Leviathan*, p. 186.

65 *Treatises*, II:§77.

66 David C. Snyder, 'Locke on Natural Law and Property Rights', *Canadian Journal of Philosophy* 16 (1986), pp. 723–24; Karen Iversen Vaughn, 'The Economic Background to Locke's Two Treatises of Government', in *John Locke's Two Treatises of Government*, ed. Edward J. Harpham (Lawrence, Kansas: University of Kansas Press, 1992), pp. 118–147, pp. 118–19.

67 J. W. Gough, *John Locke's Political Philosophy* (Oxford: Clarendon Press, 1950), pp. 73–74.

68 It was, for example, famously discussed (and one might say unfairly parodied) by Robert Nozick in his *Anarchy, State and Utopia* (Oxford: Basil Blackwell, 1974), pp. 174–82, esp. 174–75.

69 *Treatises*, II:§27. For an excellent discussion see von Leyden, *Hobbes and Locke*, pp. 103–9. Of this, too, there is an echo in Kant's theory, when he asserts that original

Through the improvement of a thing by their labour, individuals gain an exclusive right of use over what was previously a common resource.[70] Locke is conventionally read as having introduced two important caveats, however.[71] The first concludes the passage cited above, with Locke noting that this power of acquisition cannot eliminate the commons, or deprive others of their opportunity to gain property in it: the individual has a right to that which they have laboured on only insofar as 'there is enough, and as good, left in common for others'.[72] For a similar reason, it seems, Locke argued that it is not acceptable for any individual to amass to themselves a quantity of resources larger than could be used prior to their despoliation.[73] Importantly, this is not a rule against hoarding or the acquisition of wealth *per se*, but rather concerns wastage.[74] The telos of this rule is to restrain the enclosure or acquisition of more than any one person can use, because of the detriment that this represents to other individuals. Though natural right gives rise to property, that property is

possession (which, he argues, was first in land) is through an act of control ('nur durch Bemächtigung' – §14); that is to say physical possession combined with an act of will ('empirischen Bedingungen der Besitznehmung [...] verbunden mit dem Willen, den äußeren Gegenstand als den seinen zu haben' – §17). This, he insists, is a true possession ('eine wahre Erwerbung' – §15), but is only provisional until confirmed under a civil constitution. Kant, *Die metaphysik der Sitten*, §14–17; compare Georg W. F. Hegel, *Philosophy of Right*, trans. S.W. Dyde (first published as *Grundlinen der Philosophie des Rechts* 1812, this edition New York: Prometheus Books, 1996), §41–47 and following.

70 *Treatises*: II:§31. Snyder argues that acquisition through labouring on a thing is the *means* only of acquisition, which derives from Locke's conviction of the necessity that there be some form of acquisition: Snyder, 'Locke on Natural Law and Property Rights', pp. 734–36. Here the view is preferred that acquisition of property is the necessary extension of Locke's conviction of self-ownership (and thus ownership of labour).

71 A number of scholars have challenged this conventional view, and have argued that only the second – the spoilage condition – should be seen as a true caveat. See, for example, Jeremy Waldron, 'Enough and as Good Left for Others' (1979), *The Philosophical Quarterly* 29, pp. 319–328, *passim*, esp. p. 321; see also A. John Simmons, *The Lockean Theory of Rights* (Princeton: Princeton University Press 1992) pp. 282–83; Gorpal Sreenivasan, *The Limits of Lockean Rights in Property* (Oxford: Oxford University Press 1995), pp. 37–40, 48–50, *et seq.*

72 *Treatises*, II:§27.

73 *Treatises*, II:§37. Sreenivasan argues that the "spoilage condition" demonstrates that Locke's is not, contrary to a widely-held belief, a liberal theory of property: Sreenivasan, *The Limits of Lockean Rights in Property*, p. 101. Though note von Leyden's caveat, that 'it is doubtful whether there are conclusive criteria for determining this issue': von Leyden, *Hobbes and Locke*, p. 104.

74 *Treatises*, II:§46; see further Dunn, *The Political Thought of John Locke*, p. 107; Iversen Vaughn, 'The Economic Background to Locke's Two Treatises of Government', p. 135.

not absolute: it remains subject to certain communitarian rules.[75] No individual can take to themselves more land than can be worked or more fruits than can be eaten, because to do so would deprive others of the benefit of nature. It is no great step to argue, then, that in *using* their property, individuals must equally refrain from depriving others of the benefits of nature. In the state of nature each individual should (and once formalised in civil society would be obliged to) use their property in ways which maintain the health of the environment, because of the benefit this represents for others.

That Locke's process of original acquisition takes place in the state of nature – that is to say, outwith the contract which establishes civil society – means that he avoids, too, that lacuna of territorial scope discussed in relation to Hobbes. For Locke, the territorial scope of a society is defined by the possessions of its members; because property properly-so-called can exist in the state of nature, he need not resort to questions of control.[76] In this way, sovereignty and control of resources emerge as co-constitutive. Territorial sovereignty is the extrapolation of individual rights of use over land and the resources of the land.

Here too, though, some uncertainty persists. In the state of nature, it is clear that necessarily not all of the land within the compass of a particular political community will be owned; only that part which can be acquired without falling foul of the requirement that 'enough, and as good, [be] left in common for others.'[77] It is not clear whether, and if so how, these remaining commons come to be within the territory of any given society.[78] It could be speculated that the society has a liberty to acquire any remaining common spaces that derives from a source other than the individual accreted rights of the individuals who compose it, but such a solution does not seem promising. Such a conclusion would necessarily mean that the process of society creation results in some agglomeration of rights and capacities that is greater than the sum of the rights of the individuals who compose it, and thus would seem to contradict one of the core tenets of social contract theory. Perhaps more troubling still, that conclusion would directly contradict the natural rule that 'enough and as good'

75 Gough, *John Locke's Political Philosophy*, pp. 78–79. See also Snyder, who rephrases the Locekan proviso to read that 'the earth is given to man to enjoy but not to spoil or destroy': Snyder, 'Locke on Natural Law and Property Rights', p. 739.

76 *Treatises*, II:§120.

77 *Treatises*, II:§27.

78 Later readers often seem to skip over this question, subsuming it beneath the ways in which common land *within* the commonwealth may be apportioned: see, for example, Cox, *Locke on War and Peace*, p. 130.

in the form of unacquired common spaces should remain available to others; a rule which applies equally in state of nature and following the formation of societies. Alternatively, it could be that a Lockean international order (unlike that we see today – unless the high seas suffice) would necessarily require the persistence of an international commons, unclaimed by any society.

For present purposes it is not necessary to clarify that point here. Of greater concern is the question of what regime a Lockean conception of territory implies both for the international commons, and between the territories of sovereigns. Importantly, for Locke (as for Hobbes) the state of nature is not exhausted by the formation of the compacts which give rise to societies, but only displaced.[79] And yet it bears repeating that Locke's state of nature is neither ungoverned nor lacking in legal content: the law of nature exists as a true law, if one the enforcement of which is somewhat tenuous.[80] It therefore follows that if the argument in favour of a minimum duty to protect the environmental (for the good of others) sketched above holds at the individual level, it would apply also to the agglomerated territories of sovereign States. To the extent that a State's activities within its territory result in international, regional, or even local despoliation, it offends against its fellows and against the laws of nature. It is not only transboundary harms which fall under this heading: if a State's misuse of its own territory and resources result even in a purely territorial damage to the environment, '[it] offended against the common law of nature, and was liable to be punished; [it] invaded [its] neighbour's share, for [it] had no right [to the goods of nature], farther than [its] use called for any of them, and they might serve to afford [it] conveniences of life.'[81]

That conclusion remains, as noted, centred on interpersonal rights. The telos of environmental protection, in the guise of avoiding needless wastage, is the securing of others' rights of access. Nevertheless, even such a modest view of the relationship between human society and the environment is considerably more helpful to contemporary IEL's end of securing its international protection than that which derives from a Hobbsian reading of the state of nature. As the discussion of the whaling regime shows, however (below, section 6), its transposition into modern legal regimes can create an irreconcilable tension between the modern value of conservation and the Lockean focus on resource maximisation, that threatens to destabilise those regimes.

79 *Treatises*, II:§14; see also Cox, *Locke on War and Peace*, p. 136 *et seq*.

80 *Treatises*, II:§31.

81 *Treatises*, II:§37.

5 The State of Nature in the Scottish Enlightenment: David Hume[82]

Edinburgh-born philosopher David Hume was one of the key figures of the Scottish Enlightenment, and is recognised as one of the most important thinkers to have written in the English language. In the extraordinary influence his works have had directly, and in the reaction and contestation they drew from others including Immanuel Kant,[83] Hume has become a towering figure in moral philosophy and beyond. Though he is not primarily remembered as a theorist of the state of nature,[84] he nevertheless made a number of significant observations on (what he saw as) the co-emergence of property and civil society, which offer a useful contrast to the views of Hobbes and Locke discussed thus far. Hume completes the trilogy: While Hobbes found the origin of property only after the social contract, and while Locke regarded property properly-so-called as existing prior to any society; for Hume the concept of property crystallises from a position of non-emergent potential *at* the creation of society, with which it is co-constitutive.

To speak of "emergence" or "creation" in Hume, though, is to speak of these as constructions of thought, and not as historical events.[85] Unlike (certainly) Locke and (probably) Hobbes,[86] Hume did not believe that the state of nature was at any time a real and existing condition in which humans found themselves. It is rather, he argued 'a mere fiction, not unlike that of the *golden age*,

82 References to *Human Nature* in this chapter refer to the 1896 Selby-Bigge edition of Hume's *A Treatise of Human Nature*, ed. L.A. Selby-Bigge (first published 1739 (books I and II), 1740 (book III), this edition Oxford: Clarendon Press, 1896). All emphasis, unless otherwise indicated, is original.

83 Kant credited Hume with awakening him from his 'dogmatic slumber': 'Ich gestehe frei: die Erinnerung des David Hume war eben dasjenige, was mir vor vielen Jahren zuerst den dogmatischen Schlummer unterbrach, und meinen Untersuchungen im Felde der speculativen [*sic.*] Philosophie eine ganz andere Richtung gab.' Immanuel Kant, *Prolegomena zu einer jeden Künftigen Metaphysik: die als Wissenschaft wird auftreten können*, ed. Benno Erdmann (first published 1783, this edition Leipzig: Verlag von Leopold Voss, 1878), p. 8. Kelly cites Hume also as a significant influence on another giant of legal philosophy from the Germanophone world, Hans Kelsen: Kelly, *A Short History of Western Legal Theory*, p. 356.

84 For a discussion of the influence of Pufendorf on Hume see Grewal, 'From the State of Nature to the State of the Economy' in this volume.

85 Knud Haakonssen, 'Introduction', in *Hume: Political Essays*, by David Hume, ed. Knud Haakonssen (Cambridge: Cambridge University Press, 1994), pp. xi-xxx, p. xxvii; Charles Edwin Vaughan, *Studies in the History of Political Philosophy Before and After Rousseau*, ed. A. G. Little, vol. 1 (Manchester: Manchester University Press, 1925), pp. 321–22.

86 Tuck, *The Rights of War and Peace*, pp. 135–38; Straumann in this volume.

which poets have invented'.[87] Nevertheless, he regarded both fictions (and in particular their contrast) as useful tools for understanding the nature of social and interpersonal relations, and from them derived a theory of scarcity as a necessary condition for the idea of justice.[88] He argued that '[e]ncrease to a sufficient degree the benevolence of men, or the bounty of nature, and you render justice useless'.[89] Ownership, too, would be unnecessary in the absence of scarcity.[90]

Unlike later theorists (most notably, perhaps, Rawls) who used the foundation of scarcity to build a theory of justice as equality,[91] Hume pursues it to a different end. His first step results in the conclusion that some form of property rules must be brought into being. Scarcity combined with selfishness will induce individuals to seek to hold and retain at least as much of the necessities of life as they need, and this will bring them into conflict. In order to tread the narrow way between the golden age (closed to them by natural scarcity) and the state of nature (which they will avoid for sake of self-preservation), they will need to 'distinguish betwixt their own goods and those of others', and thus arrive at the concepts of '*mine* and *thine*'.[92] Moreover, these concepts must be 'stable, and must be fix'd by general rules', or the fragile order of this nascent society will collapse.[93] To this he adds the principles that property is

87 *Human Nature*, p. 493; see further Frederick Watkins, 'Editor's Introduction', in *Hume: Theory of Politics*, ed. Frederick Watkins (Austin: University of Texas Press, 1953), pp. vii-xxvii, p. xii.

88 *Human Nature*, p. 494. Though compare his later remarks on the subject in 'Of the Original Contract', in *Hume: Political Essays*, ed. Knud Haakonssen (first published 1748, this edition Cambridge: Cambridge University Press, 1994), pp. 186–201, pp. 186–90.

89 *Human Nature*, pp. 494–5; see further Martha C. Nussbaum, *Frontiers of Justice: Disability, Nationality, Species Membership* (Cambridge: Harvard University Press, 2006), pp. 46–47; George E. Panichas, 'Hume's Theory of Property', *Archive for Philosophy of Law and Social Philosophy* 69 (1983), pp. 391–93.

90 *Human Nature*, p. 495.

91 John Rawls, *A Theory of Justice* (First published 1971, this edition Oxford: Oxford University Press, 1973).

92 *Human Nature*, p. 494–5. This is strongly reminiscent of Grotius's idea of *dominium quoddam*: Hugo Grotius, *Commentary on the Law of Prize and Booty*, ed. Martine Julia van Ittersum (first published as *De jure praedae* in 1868 (of which one chapter, *Mare Liberum*: 1609), this edition Indianapolis: Liberty Fund, 2006), pp. 315–19; Richard Tuck, 'Grotius and Selden', in *The Cambridge History of Political Thought 1450–1700*, ed. J. H. Burns (Cambridge: Cambridge University Press, 1991), pp. 499–529, pp. 506–9. Buckle notes Hume's direct and acknowledged reliance on Grotius: Stephen Buckle, *Natural Law and the Theory of Property: Grotius to Hume* (Oxford: Clarendon Press, 1991), pp. 1–4.

93 *Human Nature*, pp. 497–8, 503; see also David Hume, 'Of the Origin of Government', in *Hume: Political Essays*, ed. Knud Haakonssen (first published 1777, this edition Cambridge: Cambridge University Press, 1994), pp. 20–23, pp. 20–21. As discussed above

transferred only by consent and that promises are to be performed, and thus arrives at his three 'fundamental laws of nature';[94] by which he means the bare minimum content of law that would naturally occur to the minds of individuals seeking to establish a society as necessary for that society to function.[95] To disregard them would threaten a state of nature; to comply with them is *justice*.[96]

He does not, however, take the subsequent step of Rawls and other theorists of justice, and conclude that it is possible from these premises to arrive at a substantively "just" distribution of property: his definition of justice would not support one.[97] Though he acknowledges that it would be preferable, 'no doubt, that every one were possess'd of what is most suitable to him, and proper for his use',[98] for Hume justice remains an entirely pragmatic concept.[99] It derives

---

(see note 69), this confirmation of provisional ownership is also a hallmark of Kant's theory of original acquisition.

94 As Kelly notes, this attempt to place the law of nature on a "scientific" (today "sociological" might be preferred) footing meant that Hume was understood in his own time as a critic of natural law theory, notwithstanding that Hume continued to use that vocabulary: Kelly, *A Short History of Western Legal Theory*, p. 271. Watkins explains this seeming paradox by noting that Hume eventually found it 'necessary to reconstruct the theory of natural law': Watkins, 'Editor's Introduction', p. xiii.

95 *Human Nature*, p. 526; see further Hume, 'Of the Original Contract', p. 196; John B. Stewart, *The Moral and Political Philosophy of David Hume* (New York: Columbia University Press, 1963), pp. 109–10. As McArthur notes, unlike for Hobbes, Hume regards the obligation to perform our promises not as the *substance* of the social contract, but as one of the necessary rules which emerge *within* it: Neil McArthur, *David Hume's Political Theory: Law, Commerce, and the Constitution of Government* (Toronto: University of Toronto Press, 2007), p. 39.

96 *Human Nature*, p. 527. Importantly, as Buckle points out, the fact that these principles are grounded in social practice means that 'it is not individual acts but the whole system of such acts that has value': Buckle, *Natural Law and the Theory of Property*, p. 257. For this reason, as Vaughan notes, it is not merely a negative fear of the state of nature which compels obedience to them; they exert also a positive draw as being in the interests of society as a whole: Vaughan, *Studies in the History of Political Philosophy Before and After Rousseau*, 1: pp. 319–20.

97 Stewart, *The Moral and Political Philosophy of David Hume*, p. 117. McArthur argues that this statement holds good only insofar as we are concerned with a *necessarily* just distribution. In his other works, Hume goes beyond discussing merely 'legitimate' systems of government in the search for an 'optimal' one: McArthur, *David Hume's Political Theory*, p. 40.

98 *Human Nature*, p. 502.

99 'Whenever we need to ask whether an act was right or wrong, *irrespective of its goodness or badness*, we implicitly refer to something beyond the attitudes or virtues of the individuals involved, namely to some kind of rule': Haakonssen, 'Introduction', p. xxvi. [Original emphasis].

from the steps and forms undertaken to ward off chaos, rather than being a governing influence in the choice of means thereto. He therefore concludes that individuals, in seeking a distribution which will provoke the least conflict, will light on the expediency that 'every one continue to enjoy what he is at present master of, and that property or constant possession be conjoin'd to the immediate possession',[100] giving as his justification that '[w]hat has long lain under our eye [...] *that* we are always the most unwilling to part with; but we can easily live without possessions, which we never have enjoy'd'.[101] In this way, albeit by a different route, Hume like Locke and Hobbes links the territorial scope of a society and its law-making power to the resource-ownership of individuals. Through the formation of a social body to regulate personal possession (and thus to enable conflict-free and efficient use of resources), sovereignty again is effused from the apportionment of nature.

In this way, a society is formed among the individuals who recognise the need for stable rules to determine ownership, conditions of transfer, and the performance of promises. Humans, Hume says, 'cannot change their natures. All they can do is to change their situation, and render the observance of justice the immediate interest of some particular persons, and its violation their more remote.'[102] In this pursuit they can, and likely will, establish some forms of police power, judiciary, and executive; as well as a legislature to assist them in specifying further rules likely to smooth their communal life.[103] And thus:

> [B]ridges are built; harbours open'd; ramparts raise'd; canals form'd; fleets equip'd; and armies disciplin'd; every where, by the care of government, which, tho' composed of men subject to all human infirmities, becomes, [...] in some measure, exempted from all these infirmities.[104]

---

100 Watkins notes that, like much enlightenment philosophy, this view of property from the propertied classes gave Hume's political theory 'a strongly aristocratic basis': Watkins, 'Editor's Introduction', pp. xvi–xvii.

101 *Human Nature*, p. 503. This has not, everywhere and at all times, been acknowledged as the overwhelmingly likely decision. Waldron provides an excellent discussion of a number of objections and challenges: Jeremy Waldron, 'The Advantages and Difficulties of the Humean Theory of Property', *Social Philosophy and Policy* (1994), pp. 85–123. In assessing this debate it is important to recall that Hume himself did not regard this as an historical description, but as a thought experiment.

102 *Human Nature*, p. 537.

103 *Human Nature*, pp. 537–539.

104 *Human Nature*, p. 539.

What role, in all of this industry, for the environment? Hume begins from a premise of resource scarcity, and it is therefore the apportionment of natural resources that is his primary concern. Beyond this original act of distribution, his theory has little to say on the rules applicable to property, whether property in nature or in other goods. Indeed, though he acknowledges that more extensive rules concerning the conduct of property owners may be made within the bounds of political society,[105] he implies that no such use condition is necessarily annexed to the minimum law of property which emerges from the state of nature. He holds that 'property, and right, and obligation, admit not of degrees'.[106] Perhaps, however, to conclude from that statement that *no* criteria exist for valid use of property would be an unfairly stark reading. A minimal requirement could emerge from the bare principle that property relations be stable – with the intention that each be enabled to continue to use that which they hold – that one's actions in using one's own property should not so extensively damage the property of others as effectively to deprive the latter of their enjoyment of it.

If such a duty may indeed be derived from Hume's first law of nature,[107] it is clear that it would apply equally powerfully to the international plane. Hume is emphatic that although the 'laws of nations' are 'super-added to the laws of nature, the former do not entirely abolish the latter; and one may safely affirm, that the three fundamental rules of justice, the stability of possessions, its transference by consent, and the performance of promises, are the duties of princes, as well as of subjects.'[108] Hume's laws of nature would thus dictate, perhaps, a middle course for international environmental protection; lying between Hobbes' denial of all extraterritorial responsibility

105 Vaughan, *Studies in the History of Political Philosophy Before and After Rousseau*, 1: pp. 323.

106 *Human Nature*, p. 530. [Emphasis omitted]. See also McArthur, *David Hume's Political Theory*, p. 39.

107 There is a disagreement to be found in the literature concerning how to characterise the right to property, which in turn would indicate to what extent we can derive limits therefrom. Stewart, for example, describes the rationale of Hume's property as being that 'everybody is to be left undisturbed in the enjoyment of his proper possessions': Stewart, *The Moral and Political Philosophy of David Hume*, p. 111. That individuals be "left undisturbed" could justify a strong requirement that individuals' properties suffer no harm as a result of the activities of others. See, *contra*, Panichas, who argues that Hume's is a system in which 'individual rights of ownership are supreme and virtually unconditional', which would seem to justify only (and if that) a narrow and weak duty: Panichas, 'Hume's Theory of Property', p. 398. Similarly, Buckle observes that Hume explicitly rejects a characterisation of justice that translates as the rightness of "avoiding harm to others". Buckle, *Natural Law and the Theory of Property*, pp. 284–86.

108 *Human Nature*, p. 567.

for environmental harm, and the more extensive obligation that arises from Locke's theory. A Humean system of IEL, while being fully open to the development of further environmental rules by agreement, would insist only on the condition of non-vitiation: that the actions of one sovereignty do not have an effect upon another equivalent to depriving the latter of its property rights.

6 Beyond Resource?

From the foregoing it will be clear that the state of nature as a philosophical device, even in the small sample assembled here, does not have the effect of inculcating a logic of environmental protection into the societies it envisages. On the contrary: it is at best neutral as regards nature. From Hobbes' land of stark privation, to Hume's premise of scarcity, to Lockean abundance, there is no agreement even on its role as a starting condition. In outcomes, too, these theories justify virtually the full range of extremes. The Hobbesian denial of any pre-social condition of ownership or right of enjoyment seems liable to deny even a minimal rule against harms between neighbours; and although it has been argued that Locke's state of nature gives rise to a much more extensive scheme of duties centred around a tentative and anthropocentric environmental ethic, Hume's account of the emergence of property would seem, at most, to admit of a weak rule against very significant transboundary harms. The environment is conceived as a resource, and it is governed primarily by rules relating to its exploitation. The strength of any duty of protection is determined by the force which attaches to resource ownership and, by analogy to property in land, to sovereignty over territory and the resources to be found there. Indeed, as was found in the theories examined, sovereignty over territory emerges largely as a result of or to enable the exploitation of nature's resources, and these ideas are co-constitutive.

That the late twentieth and twenty-first century concern with conservation is not to be found in these seventeenth and eighteenth century theories of sovereignty is, of course, neither surprising nor troubling. It becomes a matter of concern only if the influence of those theories on international law in the modern day impedes the reception into the system of more modern attitudes towards nature and the environment. In this sense, this paper is not, to use Orford's phrase, 'concerned with the past as history but with the past as law.'[109] In light of the foregoing conclusions, it is salutary to ask

109 Anne Orford, 'On International Legal Method', *London Review of International Law* 1, no. 1 (2013), p. 177. [References omitted].

whether similar structures of thought can be found in contemporary IEL. In other words: does contemporary IEL understand the environment as an object of conservation (i.e., as a good in itself), or as a resource for exploitation? Historically, the latter has largely been predominant. Although there are notable exceptions – the 1933 London Convention is worthy of mention, as is the Convention on Nature Protection in the Western Hemisphere of 1940[110] – the majority of the agreements which made up IEL in its early years have one of the two logics identified in state of nature theories: protection of sovereignty[111] and sustainable maximisation of resources.[112] It is not until the last decades of the twentieth century that a focus on conservation properly-so-called is routinely evidenced in the agreements concluded in the broad field of IEL, a move perhaps most notably demonstrated by the 1973 Convention on International Trade in Endangered Species of Wild Fauna and Flora,[113] and the conclusion of the Convention on Biological Diversity[114] and United Nations Framework Convention on Climate Change, both in 1992.[115] Although the logic of these conventions remains anthropocentric – the purpose of the climate regime, it is almost unnecessary to say, is the maintenance of a biosphere capable of supporting the continuation of human civilization in the

110 Convention relative to the Preservation of Fauna and Flora in their Natural State, (London Convention), signed 8 November 1933, in force 14 January 1936, United Kingdom Treaty Depository; Convention on Nature Protection and Wild Life Preservation in the Western Hemisphere, signed 10 December 1940, in force 5 January 1942, OAS Treaty Series no. 31. The preamble of both conventions seems to justify the preservation of nature as a good in itself, and not as an instrumental virtue.

111 This applies, for example, to conventions which seek to prevent or limit transboundary harms. Examples include the Treaty Banning Nuclear Weapons Tests in the Atmosphere, in Outer Space and Under Water signed 5 August 1963, in force 101 October 1963; Convention on Long-Range Transboundary Air Pollution, signed 13 November 1979, in force 16 March 1983, 1302 UNTS 217; Basel Convention on the Control of Transboundary Movements of Hazardous Wastes and their Disposal, signed 22 March 1989, in force 5 May 1992, 1673 UNTS 57.

112 See, for example, International Convention for the Regulation of Whaling (ICRW), signed 2 December 1946, in force 10 November 1948, United States Treaty Depository; Convention of Fishing and Conservation of the Living Resources of the High Seas, signed 29 April 1958, in force 20 March 1966, 559 UNTS 285; Convention for the Conservation of Antarctic Seals, signed 1 June 1972, in force 11 March 1978, United Kingdom Treaty Depository.

113 Convention on International Trade in Endangered Species of Wild Fauna and Flora (CITES), signed 3 March 1973, in force 1 July 1975, Switzerland Treaty Depository.

114 Convention on Biological Diversity (CBD), signed 5 June 1992, in force 29 December 1993, 1760 UNTS 79.

115 United Nations Framework Convention on Climate Change (UNFCCC), signed 9 May 1992, in force 21 March 1994, 1771 UNTS 107.

forms in which it currently exists[116] – they can also be seen as a shift away from a conception of nature-as-resource or nature-as-property, and towards an understanding of *environment* as having broader ramifications for human societies.

That shift, however, remains contested. The whaling regime offers a particularly striking example. The International Convention for the Regulation of Whaling (ICRW) was concluded in 1946, and was explicitly conceptualised as a resource-management agreement. The preamble recognises 'the great natural resource represented by whale stocks', and notes that 'increases in the size of whale stocks will permit increases in the number of whales which may be captured without endangering these natural resources'.[117] Conservation is mentioned only in the context of 'the effective conservation and development of whale stocks', which it declares is to take place on the basis of the principles articulated in the predecessor agreement to the ICRW, the International Agreement for the Regulation of Whaling of 1937.[118] In turn, the 1937 Agreement gives as the purpose of the governments concluding it their 'desir[e] to secure the prosperity of the whaling industry and, for that purpose, to maintain the stock of whales'.[119] The stated object and purpose of the ICRW is in no sense the preservation of whales for their own sake, or that of the wider marine environment: this is a fisheries agreement.[120]

Nevertheless, and against the strident objections of several of its members, the International Whaling Commission (IWC – the treaty body of the ICRW) in 1982 adopted a complete moratorium on commercial whaling to take effect from 1986.[121] Although this is framed as a "catch limit" (i.e., a catch limit of

116 See, for example the disastrous likely impacts of warming of just 1.5°C highlighted by the IPCC: IPCC, *Global Warming of 1.5°C: Special Report*, ed. Valérie Masson-Delmotte et al. (Geneva: IPCC, 2018).

117 ICRW (n 112), preamble.

118 International Agreement for the Regulation of Whaling, signed 8 June 1937, in force 7 May 1938.

119 *ibid*, preamble.

120 Ray Gambell, 'I Am Here, Where Should I Be?', in *The Future of Cetaceans in a Changing World*, ed. William C. G. Burns and Alexander Gillespie (Ardsley, New York: Transnational Publishers, 2003), p. 85; Patricia Birnie, 'The Framework for Conservation of Whales and Other Cetaceans as Components of Marine Biodiversity', in *The Future of Cetaceans in a Changing World*, ed. William C. G. Burns and Alexander Gillespie (Ardsley, New York: Transnational Publishers, 2003), p. 103; Jon L. Jacobson, 'Whales, The IWC, and the Rule of Law', in *Toward a Sustainable Whaling Regime*, ed. Robert L. Friedheim (Seattle: University of Washington Press, 2001), pp. 81–83.

121 'Verbatim Record of the Thirty Fourth Annual Meeting of the International Whaling Commission' (Brighton, United Kingdom, 19–24 July 1982), pp. 72–86; for discussion see Gambell, 'I Am Here, Where Should I Be?', pp. 69–70.

zero) and thus is situated as being within the core competence of the IWC, it was clear from the debate leading up to its adoption (and subsequently) that a number of the States advocating the moratorium were motivated by a fundamental opposition to whaling,[122] and that the science supporting a zero-catch limit was disputed. Japan, for example, commented that:

> We have discussed in the past meetings whether there is any scientific justification for this moratorium and the Scientific Committee has ruled many times in the past that there is not scientific justification or the biological need for a total or blanket moratorium [...] The question of the moratorium has been viewed by scientists as a political issue.[123]

For this reason, the Japanese Commissioner concluded, 'this proposal is clearly in violation of the present Convention'.[124] The Norwegian Commissioner, similarly, labelled the proposal for a moratorium 'deplorable', and stated that it was 'incompatible with the International Whaling Convention'.[125] Iceland denounced the 'adoption of a moratorium on all commercial whaling based on strength of votes but not on scientific findings' as 'most certainly contrary to the fundamental objectives and purpose of the Commission.'[126]

The conflict between the pro- and anti-whaling forces has continued in the IWC and elsewhere, including in the International Court of Justice (ICJ). In 2014 it issued its judgment in the *Case Concerning Whaling in the Antarctic*, in which Australia (with New Zealand intervening) challenged Japan's use of scientific whaling permits under its JARPA II programme as being intended to subvert the commercial whaling moratorium.[127] The question before the Court was whether the Japanese whaling programme could properly be said to fall within the scientific research exemption in Article VIII of the ICRW, and the

122 See, for example the comments of Antigua and Barbuda in 'Verbatim Record', p. 78.

123 'Verbatim Record', pp. 76–77.

124 'Verbatim Record', p. 77; see further Yasuo Iino and Dan Goodman, 'Japan's Position in the International Whaling Commission', in *The Future of Cetaceans in a Changing World*, ed. William C. G. Burns and Alexander Gillespie (Ardsley, New York: Transnational Publishers, 2003), pp. 3, 14.

125 'Verbatim Record', p. 79.

126 'Verbatim Record', p. 79; see also William T Burke, 'A New Whaling Agreement and International Law', in *Toward a Sustainable Whaling Regime*, ed. Robert L. Friedheim (Seattle: University of Washington Press, 2001), pp. 59–60; Christopher D. Stone, 'Summing up: Whaling and Its Critics', in *Toward a Sustainable Whaling Regime*, ed. Robert L. Friedheim (Seattle: University of Washington Press, 2001), pp. 271–72.

127 *Whaling in the Antarctic (Australia v Japan; New Zealand intervening)*, Merits, Judgment of 31 March 2014, (2014) ICJ Reports 226.

Court was therefore not called upon to assess the propriety of the moratorium as such, nor its accordance with the object and purpose of the Convention. The Court concluded that although JARPA II had valid scientific objectives, that the methods used in that programme (including the use of lethal sampling) had not been sufficiently justified in relation to those objectives, and that in consequence that Japan's scientific whaling permits 'are not "for the purposes of scientific research" pursuant to [...] the Convention'.[128] The Court also addressed directly the argument that the telos of the whaling regime had changed as a result of the adoption of the moratorium. It gave the idea very short shrift.

> Amendments to the Schedule and other recommendations by the IWC may put an emphasis on one or other objective pursued by the Convention, but cannot alter its purpose.[129]

The most recent act in this saga took place at the sixty-seventh meeting of the IWC in 2018, where Japan introduced a proposal (the "Way Forward" package) that would have reintroduced positive catch limits for some whale stocks, albeit under strict scientific supervision. The proposal fell by a margin of 27 States in favour to 41 against (with two abstentions), prompting Japan to promise 'a fundamental reassessment of its position in the IWC'.[130] Japan conducted that review, and decided to withdraw from the Convention, threatening the collapse of the entire regime. On the 30th June 2019, Japan's denunciation of the ICRW took effect.[131]

On one level, that Japan was pushed to the point of withdrawal (and that Norway and Iceland continue legally to take whales as objectors to the moratorium) speaks of the failure of the regime to achieve the most fundamental of its purposes: to mould the behaviour of States. Geoffrey Palmer, New Zealand's long-time Commissioner to the IWC, lamented even prior to Japan's withdrawal from the ICRW that 'while the [ICJ] case was won, the war was lost',[132]

128 *ibid* [227].

129 *ibid*, [56]; see also discussion in Joji Morishita, 'IWC and the ICJ Judgment', in *Whaling in the Antarctic: Significance and Implications of the ICJ Judgment*, ed. Malgosia Fitzmaurice and Dai Tamada (Leiden: Brill/Nijhoff, 2016), pp. 247–48.

130 Earth Negotiations Bulletin, 'Summary of the 67th Meeting of the International Whaling Commission' (Florianópolis, Brazil, 10–14 September 2018), pp. 7–8.

131 Status of the International Convention for the Regulation of Whaling, United States Treaty Depository.

132 Geoffrey Palmer, 'Whales and Humans: How Whaling Went from Being a Major Industry to a Leading Environmental Issue Then Landed Japan in the International Court of Justice for the First Time', *New Zealand Yearbook of International Law* 13 (2015), p. 126.

and that the fundamental conflict at the heart of the regime means '[t]he IWC is a dysfunctional embarrassment as an international organisation. Its future must be regarded as bleak.'[133] Even if one were to reject this gloomy outlook, it is undeniable that the evolution of the regime away from the management of a fisheries resource in order to maximise the sustainable yield, and towards a conservation framework represents a very significant shift in its telos, and not one that finds any support in the regime's founding treaty. Yet the regime (along with or prompting changes in public attitudes) has seen a very significant decline in the demand for whale meat and other products worldwide, a trend to be observed even in those States which continue to take whales.[134] In parallel, some whale populations are in the early stages of recovering (such as Southern Hemisphere blue whales and humpback whales), while for most others (including bowhead whales, and right whales) the moratorium seems at least to have halted these species' rapid decline.[135] If seen through the lens of a conservation regime, therefore, the ICRW seems to have been at least partly successful both in achieving concrete conservation goals, and in reorienting the conversation away from nature-as-resource and towards environmental protection.[136] That "success", though, has been hard-won, and may turn out to have been something of a pyrrhic victory.

The whaling regime is, in many ways, very Lockean in outline. Here resources in common – in the fauna of the oceans – are made property by an original act of labour-mixing. As Payne describes, the original understanding of the system was 'that ocean life belonged to no-one and could be made one's own property by capture.'[137] Indeed, it might be possible to see the formation of the regime itself as an instantiation of the "as much and as good" principle, aiming as it did to 'safeguard[] for future generations the great natural resource of whale

133 Palmer, 127; Peter J. Stoett, *The International Politics of Whaling* (Vancouver: UBC Press, 1997), pp. 147–48; see also Robert L. Friedheim, 'Introduction: The IWC as a Contested Regime', in *Toward a Sustainable Whaling Regime*, ed. Robert L. Friedheim (Seattle: University of Washington Press, 2001), p. 3.

134 Palmer notes, for example, that much of the whale meat produced by the Japanese industry is 'stored in huge frozen stockpiles' because of the decline in demand: Palmer, 'Whales and Humans', p. 127.

135 See IWC, 'Status of Whales', via <https://iwc.int/index.php?cID=status>, accessed 21.09.2021.

136 Stoett, *The International Politics of Whaling*, vii. Stoett calls it 'one of the more remarkable international regime transformations in ecopolitical history', though note, as Friedheim does, that 'preservation, as a new norm has not been internalized by key states to whom it is intended to apply': Friedheim, 'Introduction', 10.

137 Cymie R. Payne, 'ICJ Halts Antarctic Whaling – Japan Starts Again', *Transnational Environmental Law* 4, no. 1 (2015), p. 192.

stocks', and to 'permit increases in the number of whales which may be captured without endangering these natural resources'.[138] Perhaps most strikingly, the regime even appears to contain a despoliation provision. The International Agreement for the Regulation of Whaling – the predecessor to the ICRW, the principles of which the ICRW explicitly incorporates[139] – demands

> '[t]he fullest possible use [...] of all whales taken. Except in the case of whales or parts of whales intended for human food or for feeding animals, the oil shall be extracted by boiling or otherwise from all blubber, meat (except the meat of sperm whales) and bones other than the internal organs, whale bone and flippers, of all whales delivered to the factory ship or land station.[140]

It then goes on to prohibit the

> [T]ak[ing] for delivery to any factory ship or land station a greater number of whales than can be treated efficiently [in the manner described above] by the plant and the personnel therein within a period of thirty-six hours from the time of the killing of each whale.[141]

The Schedule to the ICRW includes very similar provisions which appear to tend to the same ends of fullest possible use and avoidance of wastage.[142] To that extent, the whaling regime offers an uncomfortable demonstration of how deeply unhelpful the Lockean logic – the most friendly of the three examined above – can be to the cause of environmental protection.

The irreconcilable schism at the heart of the whaling regime is an extreme example of a wider conflict within IEL. Tension between maximisation of resources and protection of environments results in many environmental regimes being pulled in two different directions; from whaling and other fisheries agreements,[143] to regimes to safeguard shared river

138 ICRW (n 112), preamble.

139 *ibid*, preamble.

140 International Agreement for the Regulation of Whaling (n 118), Article 11.

141 *ibid*, Article 12.

142 Schedule to the International Convention for the Regulation of Whaling, as amended by the Commission at the 67th Meeting, Florianópolis, Brazil, September 2018, Articles 19–20.

143 Award between the United States and the United Kingdom relating to the Rights of Jurisdiction of United States in the Bering's Sea and the Preservation of Fur Seals, Award of 15 August 1893, RIAA volume XXVIII, 263–276; Convention on Fishing and Conservation of the Living Resources of the High Seas, signed 29 April 1958, in force 20 March 1966,

systems,[144] to the as-yet somewhat plaintive calls for "sustainable development" in the UNFCCC and its Kyoto and Paris protocols.[145] A recent example can be found in the CITES regime, noted above as one of those most expressive of the "modern" spirit of conservation. The CITES Convention begins by hailing 'wild fauna and flora in their many beautiful forms [as] an irreplaceable part of the natural systems of the earth which must be protected', and notes the value of species conservation from 'aesthetic, scientific, cultural, [and] recreational' points of view, as well as having 'economic' value.[146] In its 2019 session, however, the Conference of the Parties considered and rejected two fundamentally opposing proposals from Parties to change the listing of African elephant populations in Botswana, Namibia and Zimbabwe. A proposal by those States to liberalise trade in elephant ivory stood directly contradictory to an alternative proposal by a group of ten States (none of which were directly affected) to 'transfer the populations of Botswana, Namibia, South Africa and Zimbabwe from Appendix II to Appendix I', a move that would have resulted in a far stricter trade regime for elephants and elephant products across the board.[147] In parallel, Botswana has lifted its internal ban on elephant hunting, including trophy hunting.[148] The African elephant remains

---

559 UNTS 285; Convention for the Strengthening of the Inter-American Tropical Tuna Commission ("Antigua Convention"), signed 14 November 2003, in force 27 August 2010.

144 Colleen P. Graffy, 'Water, Water, Everywhere, Nor Any Drop to Drink: The Urgency of Transnational Solutions to International Riparian Disputes', *The Georgetown International Environmental Law Review* 10 (1998), p. 399; see also Jonathan Chenoweth, 'International River Basin Management: Data and Information Exchange under International Law and the Case of the Mekong River Basin', *Energy and Natural Resources* 18 (2000), pp. 144–48.

145 UNFCCC, (n 115); Kyoto Protocol to the United Nations Framework Convention on Climate Change, agreed 11 December 1997, in force 16 February 2005, 2303 UNTS 162; Paris Agreement, agreed 12 December 2015, in force 4 November 2016, UN Doc. no. C.N.63.2016.TREATIES-XXVII.7.d; A Dan Tarlock, 'Exclusive Sovereignty versus Sustainable Development of a Shared Resource: The Dilemma of Latin American Rainforest Management' (1997) 32 *Texas International Law Journal* 37, *passim*, esp. pp. 43–45.

146 CITES (n 113) preamble.

147 See Proposals for amendment of Appendices I and II, available via <https://cites.org/eng/cop/18/prop/index.php>, accessed 21.09.2021; Nyasha Chingono, 'Raw Ivory Sales: Zimbabwe, Botswana and Namibia Call for End to Ban', *The Guardian*, 21 May 2019, https://www.theguardian.com/global-development/2019/may/21/raw-ivory-sales-zimbabwe-botswana-and-namibia-call-for-end-to-ban>, accessed 21.09.2021; CoP18 Prop.10–12, *Summary of the 18th Meeting of the CITES Conference of the Parties, 17–28 August 2019*, Earth Negotiations Bulletin volume 21, number 101, <http://enb.iisd.org/download/pdf/enb21101e.pdf> accessed 21.09.2021.

148 Jason Burke, 'Botswana Condemned for Lifting Ban on Hunting Elephants', *The Guardian*, 23 May 2019, <https://www.theguardian.com/world/2019/may/23/botswana-lifts-ban-on-hunting-elephants>, accesed 21.09.2021.

on the International Union for the Conservation of Nature's *Red List* as a 'vulnerable' species.[149]

This is the latest move in a longstanding dispute within CITES over the proper conservation status to be given to the African elephant,[150] and certainly has aspects reminiscent of the whaling conflict. Both instances challenge the character of the regimes within which these arguments take place, speaking of a sharp rift between the resource maximisation and environmental protection ends of IEL. In the treatment of nature as a resource, IEL appears to incorporate a view of nature appropriate to – if not drawn from – the state of nature theories of the seventeenth and eighteenth centuries, which are dominated by the instrumental, scene-setting, but otherwise anonymous role they give to the natural world. Nor can this be detached from the problem of sovereignty discussed above. As that analysis shows, sovereignty and the understanding of nature as resource are ideationally co-constitutive in the state of nature tradition. Sovereignty means, primarily, sovereignty over natural resources. The challenge by Natarajan and Khoday that IEL's failure to interrogate its foundations means that it has 'set itself up for failure' seems apposite indeed.[151]

The conclusions drawn here highlight the hidden assumptions and structures of thought that concepts drawn from the state of nature carry with them – sometimes directly, more often by implication – and that are incorporated into the writings of international environmental lawyers, and into the practice of international environmental law, through their use. The concepts often derived from the state of nature – sovereignty chief among these, and extending to the construction of nature itself – are often conceived there in ways which present significant obstacles. Indeed, the most influential state of nature theory, that of Hobbes, seems to treat relations between humans and nature as akin to a state of war; though the Lockean structure of the deeply troubled whaling regime gives pause even in relation to this apparently more amenable theory. Foundations matter. In the concepts routinely drawn from them, the ghosts of the state of nature's theorists haunt us still. Those concepts

149 J Blanc, 'Loxodonta Africana, The IUCN Red List of Threatened Species 2008'. Note that in the most recent (2021) version of the list, the African Elephant has been subdivided into two subspiecies: Loxodonta Africana Cyclotis (African Savana Elephant) and Loxodonta Africana Africana (African Forest Elephant): see K.S. Gobush, *et al*, 'Loxodonta africana (amended version of 2021 assessment). The IUCN Red List of Threatened Species 2021', available via <https://dx.doi.org/10.2305/IUCN.UK.2021-2.RLTS.T181008073A204401095.en>, accessed 21.09.2021.

150 Charis Thompson, 'Co-Producing CITES and the African Elephant', in *States of Knowledge: The Co-Production of Science and Social Order*, ed. Sheila Jasanoff (Abingdon: Routledge, 2004), pp. 67–86.

151 Natarajan and Khoday, 'Locating Nature', p. 585.

must be interrogated deeply and used advisedly, in the hope of an escape from the state of nature.

Select Bibliography

Primary Sources

Thomas Hobbes, *Leviathan* (1651).

Pufendorf *De jure naturæ et gentium libri otto* (1672).

John Locke, *Two Treatises of Government and a Letter Concerning Toleration* (1690).

David Hume, *A Treatise of Human Nature* (books I and II: 1739; book III: 1740).

Emer de Vattel, *Le droit de gens* (1758).

Immanuel Kant, *Die metaphysik der Sitten* (1797).

Secondary Sources

Jeremy Waldron, 'Enough and as Good Left for Others' (1979) 29 *The Philosophical Quarterly* pp. 319–328.

A. Dan Tarlock, 'Stewardship Sovereignty: The Next Step in Former Prime Minister Palmer's Logic', *Washington University Journal of Urban and Contemporary Law* 42 (1992): pp. 21–28.

Anne C. Dowling, 'Un-Locke-Ing a Just Right Environmental Regime: Overcoming the Three Bears of International Environmentalism – Sovereignty, Locke, and Compensation', *William and Mary Environmental Law and Policy Review* 26, no. 3 (2002): pp. 891–960.

Usha Natarajan, 'TWAIL and the Environment: The State of Nature, the Nature of the State, and the Arab Spring', *Oregon Review of International Law* 14 (2012): pp.177–201.

Usha Natarajan and Kishan Khoday, 'Locating Nature: Making and Unmaking International Law', *Leiden Journal of International Law* 27 (2014): pp. 573–593.

Saskia Vermeylen, 'Materiality and the Ontological Turn in the Anthropocene: Establishing a Dialogue between Law, Anthropology and Eco-Philosophy', in *Environmental Law and Governance for the Anthropocene*, ed. Louis J. Kotzé (Hart Publishing, 2017), pp. 137–162.

CHAPTER 14

The State of Nature, Prehistory, and Mythmaking

Karl Widerquist and Grant S. McCall

Abstract

This chapter provide an overview of two books, in which we name, define, and debunk the following false claims that still play important roles in contemporary political theories although they are not always defined and defended explicitly:
1. *The Hobbesian hypothesis*: sovereign states and/or the liberal private property rights system benefits everyone (or at least harms no one) relative to how well they could reasonably expect to live in the state of nature – i.e. a society lacking one or both of these institutions.
2. *The appropriation hypothesis*: private property in the form of liberal ownership rights develops naturally while collective, communal, common, or government-held property rights systems do not.
3. *The natural inequality hypothesis*: inequality is natural and inevitable, i.e. economic, social, and/or political equality cannot exist and/or cannot be created without a significant loss in negative freedom.
4. *The market-freedom hypothesis*: a market economy (and/or capitalism) is more consistent with negative freedom than any other economic system.
The third and fourth of these claims are not obviously claims about prehistoric or small-scale societies, but they are universal claims about all societies and so they include claims about even the most remote and distant societies from contemporary thinking.

Keywords

Hobbes – Locke – Lockean proviso – state of nature – social contract – Hobbesian hypothesis – mutual advantage

1 Introduction

When the state of nature is conceived as the absence of the state and/or of a liberal property regime, it refers to a real situation. Many peoples have lived

 DOI:10.1163/9789004499621_016

outside of sovereign states and/or without liberal ownership rights that state-of-nature stories about property rights are usually used to justify.[1]

Yet, philosophers often treat these versions of the state of nature as if they were hypotheticals. They make hypothetical claims, use those claims as premises in their arguments, and support those claims (if at all) with a priori reasoning or cursory empirical observations. Nothing is wrong with hypothetical stories if they illustrate a greater truth, but something is wrong if they illustrate a greater lie and give it the air of plausibility while freeing the storyteller from the responsibility to provide supporting evidence. That's destructive mythmaking.

Not all mythmaking is destructive. For example, one could use the Garden of Eden story to illustrate how people are born not knowing right from wrong, but when they learn the difference, they eventually choose to do wrong. That myth illustrates a truth people can verify in everyday experience. But one could also use a Garden of Eden story to illustrate the belief that women are temptresses with bad judgment and men should always make decision for them. That is a destructive myth, illustrating false empirical claims used to justify oppression.

This chapter highlights the link between the two books in our larger research project[2] and argues that Hobbesian and Lockean state-of-nature stories are destructive myths that illustrate the following four false empirical claims that are used heavily but seldom defined explicitly in contemporary philosophy.

1. *The Hobbesian hypothesis* (or the mutual-advantage hypothesis): sovereign states and/or the liberal private property rights system benefit everyone (or harms no one) relative to how well they could reasonably expect to live in a state of nature lacking one or both of these institutions.
2. *The appropriation hypothesis*: only private liberal ownership systems develop naturally; collective, communal, common, or government-held property rights systems do not.
3. *The natural-inequality hypothesis*: either economic, social, and/or political equality cannot exist at all, or, if these forms of equality can exist, they are incompatible with negative freedom.
4. *The market-freedom hypothesis*: capitalism is more consistent with negative freedom than any other economic system.

These false claims persist because they play into conventional prejudices; because centuries of repetition give them plausibility; and because state-of-nature theorists are seldom clear about what empirical truths (if any) their

1 Karl Widerquist and Grant S. McCall, *Prehistoric Myths in Modern Political Philosophy* (Edinburgh: Edinburgh University Press, 2017), pp. 16–21.

2 Widerquist and McCall, *Prehistoric Myths*; Karl Widerquist and Grant S. McCall, *The Prehistory of Private Property* (Edinburgh: Edinburgh University Press, 2021).

stories illustrate. Obscurity has actually helped perpetuate these beliefs. Philosophers go back and forth between the implications that the empirical content of the story is purely illustrative or necessary but obviously true. The illustrative implication protects them from the need to provide evidence. The implication of obviousness protects them from specifying how a purely illustrative story can support their conclusions. And so, neither version gets questioned or defended at a deep level. The claims we accept without thinking get far less scrutiny than the ones we self-consciously choose to accept. Significant argumentation and evidence are required to show that these claims are (1) *empirical*, (2) *about prehistoric or stateless peoples*, (3) *premises in prominent arguments*, and (4) *false*.[3] We hope that this article provides enough evidence to demonstrate all of this. If not, our books provide additional evidence and argument.[4]

Hobbes's critics have questioned these claims. Their credibility-from-repetition comes more from ignoring critics than from unanimity of belief. But our research project is the most extensive effort we know of to refute these four claims with empirical evidence from fields as diverse as anthropology, archaeology, and history. We hope it contributes to the wealth of new literature debunking false beliefs about prehistoric and small-scale societies.[5]

Some of our critics are likely to resurrect John Crawfurd's allegation that any positive depiction of indigenous people amounts to romanticizing the "golden age" of the "noble savage." Crawfurd originated this allegation in the 1850s because he believed that Victorian anthropology was not racist enough. The term is an intentional oxymoron ("nobles" have the highest qualities of "civilization;" "savages" lack any such qualities). It creates a false dichotomy: either one affirms the miserable, warlike nature of indigenous peoples, or one romanticizes the noble savage. Crawfurd's main target was Jean-Jacques Rousseau, who didn't use the term "noble savage" and held largely negative views of indigenous peoples. Crawford's allegation has outlived his overtly racist school of enthnograpy. It continues to give people studying indigenous societies reason to err on the side of negativity.[6]

3 Widerquist and McCall, *Prehistoric Myths*; Widerquist and McCall, *Prehistory of Private Property*.

4 Widerquist and McCall, *Prehistoric Myths*; Widerquist and McCall, *Prehistory of Private Property*.

5 Such as, James C. Scott, *The Art of Not Being Governed* (New Haven: Yale University Press, 2009); David Graeber, *Debt: The First 5,000 Years* (Brooklyn, NY: Melville House, 2011); Marlene Zuk, *Paleofantasy* (New York: ww Norton & Company, 2013); Ter Ellingson, *The Myth of the Noble Savage* (Berkeley, CA: University of California Press, 2001).

6 Ter Ellingson, *Noble Savage*.

Our project is not the result of a philosopher who read some controversial anthropology book and took it at face-value. It's a jointly authored project by a philosopher and an anthropologist, and it involves an extensive review of both fields. The empirical findings below reflect consensus opinions in contemporary anthropology. The consensus of empirical researchers is not pure truth, but it's likely to be closer to the truth than speculative extrapolations from the reports of racist settlers.

More powerful challenges to our empirical findings require arguing either that we inaccurately characterize the empirical literature or that the existing literature is wrong. The first strategy requires a literature review at least as thorough as ours; the second requires conducting better anthropological studies than currently exist.

2 The Hobbesian Hypothesis

The claim that contemporary states achieve mutual advantage became central to the mainstream justification of the state when Thomas Hobbes's (1588–1679) used it as the central premise of his social contract theory.[7] A few decades later, John Locke (1632–1704) used the claim that the property rights system achieves mutual advantage in what has become the mainstream justification of private property.[8] Both of these theories rely on an ethical premise that David Gauthier identifies as "the Lockean proviso," although he uses this premise more widely than most previous authors. As we interpret it, the proviso is a principle of mutual advantage: an institution can be imposed on people providing that everyone is at least as well off under its authority than they could reasonably expect to be outside its authority.[9] It is a first-order, fact-independent ethical principle, not subject to empirical verification or refutation.[10]

Hobbes justifies the state by unanimous consent and argues that consent is obtained because mutual advantage is achieved relative to the state of nature.[11] Contemporary contractarians usually retain mutual advantage but drop literal consent in favour of the imagined agreement of rational, reasonable, and fully informed.[12]

7 Thomas Hobbes, *Leviathan* (Cambridge: Cambridge University Press, 1996 [1651]).

8 John Locke, *Two Treatises of Government: Second Treatise* (Cambridge: Cambridge University Press, 1960 [1689]), ch. 5.

9 David P Gauthier, *Morals by Agreement* (Oxford: Clarendon Press, 1986), p. 205, 208.

10 Widerquist and McCall, *Prehistoric Myths*, pp. 2–3.

11 Widerquist and McCall, *Prehistoric Myths*, pp. 24–33.

12 Widerquist and McCall, *Prehistoric Myths*, pp. 40–43.

Locke applies a similar proviso to the property rights system: private property is justified if everyone is at least as well off as they could reasonably expect to be in a society without such private property – that is in a common property regime, in which land and other resources are available for nonexclusive use by everyone or at least by every member of a political community.[13]

It is uncontroversial to say that these theories rely on an ethical claim of mutual-advantage, but it is surprisingly controversial to say that these theories therefore require an empirical claim that any institution being justified actually achieves mutual advantage relative to the absence of that institution. Although our books spend a great deal of time considering and rejecting possible ways around the need for an empirical premise, it is a logical entailment of proviso-based theorizing: if someone wants to justify an institution on the principle of mutual advantage, they must show that the institution achieves mutual advantage as a matter of empirical fact. It's not enough to illustrate mutual advantage in a "thought experiment" unrelated to empirical reality.

This empirical premise that the Lockean proviso is fulfilled is what we call "the Hobbesian hypothesis." It is simply the claim of mutual advantage.

In social contract theory, the Hobbesian hypothesis is that everyone in state society is at least as well off in the relevant sense as everyone in stateless society. In property rights theory, the hypothesis is that everyone in a private property regime is at least as well off as everyone in societies with common property regimes. Societies with neither of these institutions do exist, and the relative wellbeing of people in such societies is therefore relevant to proviso-based justifications of the state and the private property system.[14]

Yet, in the 350 years since Hobbes and Locke, the role of the Hobbesian hypothesis has been largely ignored. Few theorists discuss its role and meaning. Fewer theorists state clearly that their conclusions rest on this empirical premise. Those who clearly assert this hypothesis rarely cite more than the most cursory evidence to support it.[15]

Hobbes asserts the premise as an empirical hypothesis writing, "Out of civil states, there is always war of every one against every one" – not *sometimes*; *always*. He supports this claim with a psychological argument that natural human inclinations inevitably lead to conflict whenever "men live without a common power to keep them in awe" and with empirical observations about

13 Widerquist and McCall, *Prehistoric Myths*, pp.70–73; Tom Sparks, "The Place of the Environment in State of Nature Discourses: Reassessing Nature, Property and Sovereignty in the Anthropocene" in this volume.

14 Widerquist and McCall, *Prehistoric Myths*, pp. 54–56.

15 Widerquist and McCall, *Prehistoric Myths*, pp. 24–111.

civil war, and with claims about stateless peoples. Hobbes writes, "[T]he savage people in many places of America … have no government at all; and live at this day in that brutish manner."[16]

Locke makes similar observations, "Americans … who are rich in land … have not one hundredth part of the conveniencies we enjoy: and a king of a large and fruitful territory there, feeds, lodges, and is clad worse than a day-labourer in England … in the beginning all the world was America."[17] The day-labourer comment supports his claim that propertyless people benefit from the property system. Hence, he claims the proviso is fulfilled; property rights are justified in part by the supposed truth of the Hobbesian hypothesis.

Hobbes and Locke were empirically correct that some Native American peoples lived in stateless societies with common property regimes, but they were empirically wrong to claim that they were more miserable than lower-class English people.

If Hobbes's or Locke's argument can be formulated to make their empirical claims irrelevant, neither of them spell it out, nor does it seem possible. Attempts to create a fact-independent version of the proviso or to reduce its level to make comparisons irrelevant either involve other dubious premises or amount to discarding mutual advantage altogether.[18]

Many contractarians equivocate between an incoherent a priori version of the argument (the Hobbesian hypothesis doesn't matter) and one based on a false premise (the hypothesis matters, but it's obviously true). The truth-value of the Hobbesian hypothesis cannot be obvious. It compares the welfare of two groups of people whose lives are very remote to privileged people in Western society: the least advantaged people in capitalist states and people in stateless societies. Few academics have significant first-hand experience with either group; fewer still have experience with both; and those who do are almost certainly specialists who study at least one of these groups.

This claim might have seemed obvious to Hobbes and Locke, who lived in a place and time where nearly everyone shared the prejudice that the lowliest "civilized man" was far superior to any "naked savage."[19] That prejudice should have been discarded long ago, but the idea continues to be repeated as it has been for thousands of years by people as diverse as the first emperor of China, Samuel Pufendorf (1632–1694), David Hume (1711–1776), Immanuel Kant (1724–1804), Robert Nozick (1938–2002), Murray Rothbard (1926–1995),

16 Hobbes, *Leviathan*, pp. 100–101.

17 Locke, *Second Treatise*, §41.

18 Widerquist and McCall, *Prehistoric Myths*, pp. 54–64, 81–85, 99–105.

19 Widerquist and McCall, *Prehistoric Myths*, pp. 37–38, 75–77.

Jean Hampton (1954–1996), David Gauthier, Gregory S. Kavka, Ian Hampsher-Monk, Christopher Heath Wellman, George Klosko, and others.[20]

Not all contractarians rely on this faulty premise. John Rawls's theory is invulnerable because his discussion of disadvantaged people is aspirational, calling on society to improve their wellbeing not just relative to statelessness but relative to any other social arrangement.[21]

Critics of the Hobbesian hypothesis include Lord Shaftesbury (1671–1713), Baron de Montesquieu (1689–1755), Thomas Paine (1737–1809), Henry David Thoreau (1817–1862), Herbert Spencer (1820–1903), Henry George (1839–1897), Karl Marx (1818–1883), Friedrich Engels (1820–1895), Henry Sumner Maine (1822–1888), John Robert Seeley (1834–1895), Henry Sidgwick (1838–1900), Carole Pateman, Alan Ryan, Charles Mills, Alasdair Macintyre, Thomas Pogge, and Peter Lindsay.[22]

In 1902, Peter Kropotkin (1842–1921) published the most extensive empirical investigation into this issue that we know of prior to ours[23] but assertions of the Hobbesian hypothesis continued with little regard to his findings. Part of the reason might be that critics, including Kropotkin, rejected the normative and empirical claims in these theories, allowing philosophers to continue focusing on normative aspects of the discussion. Our project is not about the norms, just the facts.

We examine Hobbes's claim that stateless societies are always violent. Evidence is limited, but it is enough to contradict Hobbes's claim that violence levels are usually or always intolerable in stateless societies. Homicide rates in observed stateless societies vary enormously from more than 1,000/100,000 to less than 1/100,000 – less than any in known state societies. The average is lower in contemporary state societies, but state societies also have enormous variation so that many stateless societies have lower levels of violence than the average state, and some stateless societies have levels comparable to the safest states.[24] Few if any stateless societies have homicide levels beyond a threshold

20 Widerquist and McCall, *Prehistoric Myths*, pp. 79–111.

21 John Rawls, *A Theory of Justice, Revised Edition* (Cambridge, MA: Harvard University Press, 1999).

22 Widerquist and McCall, *Prehistoric Myths*, pp. 79–111.

23 Petr Kropotkin, *Mutual Aid: A Factor of Evolution* (Project Gutenberg, 2011).

24 Robert L Kelly, *The Foraging Spectrum* (Washington DC: Smithsonian Institution Press, 1995), p. 203; Rafael et al Lozano, "Global and Regional Mortality from 235 Causes of Death for 20 Age Groups in 1990 and 2010: A Systematic Analysis for the Global Burden of Disease Study 2010," *the Lancet* 380, no. 9859 (2012), p. 2109; Widerquist and McCall, *Prehistoric Myths*, pp. 140–147.

of intolerability as Hobbesian theory requires to make the state universally preferable. None have the refugee crises that state societies often do.

Life expectancy in stateless societies is short relative to state societies today, but it is about the same as it was in state societies in Europe at the time Hobbes made is claim, and it is not short for the reason Hobbes supposed. The longer life expectancy in state society is explained by better healthcare and lower infant mortality rather than differences in violence levels. Longer life expectancy did not spread to the lower classes in Europe and North America until perhaps the middle of the nineteenth century. It did not spread to the poorest countries until the last decades of the twentieth century, and it has still not reached the poorest populations in the poorest countries or, for that matter, the poorest populations in the United States.

Stateless peoples are in many ways healthier during their lifetimes than people in state societies. Stateless societies have eliminated many of the things that kill stateless peoples, but stateless peoples are virtually invulnerable to many of the things that kill people in stateless societies, such as cancer, epidemics, and diseases connected to toxins in our environment or diets.[25]

State societies today produce far more luxuries than stateless societies, but their ability to meet the basic needs of the least advantaged is very often lower. Our high-luxury environments are often socially isolating and dedicated largely to the production of positional goods rather than goods that make everyone better off. State societies have no particular advantage in leisure or work effort for the average person. The least advantaged people in state societies work far more than people in any observed stateless society. Stateless peoples never have to obey the orders of a boss, and they are free from the alienation so common in the modern industrial workforce.[26]

Disadvantaged people in state society tend to be less free than their stateless counter-parts in terms of political freedom, negative freedom, status freedom, sexual freedom, and freedom from group-based oppression. Expressed preferences and observed choices of people who are familiar with both state and stateless societies do not show any solid trend in favour of state society. For most of human history, state societies tended to have stateless communities on their peripheries made up of people who intentionally tried to avoid incorporation into the state. Most of these peripheries are gone today not because their residents realized the benefits of state societies and liberal property rights systems, but because governments forcibly incorporated that territory.[27]

25 Widerquist and McCall, *Prehistoric Myths*, pp. 191–197.
26 Widerquist and McCall, *Prehistoric Myths*, pp. 180–191.
27 Scott, *The Art of Not Being Governed.*

The verdict is overwhelming: the Hobbesian hypothesis is false. Neither the state nor the property rights system achieves mutual advantage. Dozens of leading anthropologists have debunked Hobbes's description of life outside of the state in whole or in part.[28] Ernest Gellner sums up the anthropological consensus best, writing, "Hobbes [was] wrong: the life of pre-state man is not solitary, poor, nasty, brutish and short. Rather, it is gregarious and cohesive, relatively well-off, human and participatory, and with about as good a chance of longevity as that of his centrally governed contemporary."[29]

To deny that everyone is better off in state society is *not* to say that *everyone* is better off in stateless society, nor is it even to say that the *average* person is better off. The falsity of the Hobbesian hypothesis says only that as difficult as stateless life is, states today make life worse for a significant number of people. The tragedy of capitalist states today is that for all their wealth, they have consistently failed to surpass the very low bar they have set for self-justification. For proviso-based theories to justify the state and/or the property rights system in their own terms, state societies have to treat disadvantaged people better. Until then, the proviso remains unfulfilled. Mutual advantage remains unachieved.

3 The Appropriation Hypothesis

Literature on the "propertarian" (natural rights-based) justification of the liberal property rights system focuses almost exclusively on the ethical principles of the theory. But we argue that the justification of the property system also requires an empirical claim we call the "appropriation hypothesis," which is contradicted by evidence.

In Robert Nozick's characterization, propertarian theory involves the moral principles of appropriation, voluntary transfer, and rectification of past wrongs. The appropriation principle allows individuals to transform unowned external objects into private property. The transfer principle means that it remains theirs until they voluntarily transfer it to others. The rectification principle is some method by which wrongful transfers can be rectified.[30] Although propertarians differ substantially on many issues, these principles are at the heart of most rights-based justifications of private property.

28 See list, Widerquist and McCall, *Prehistoric Myths*, pp. 215–216.

29 Ernest Gellner, *Anthropology and Politics* (Oxford: Blackwell, 1995), p. 209.

30 Robert Nozick, *Anarchy, State, and Utopia* (New York: Basic Books, 1974), pp. 150–153.

What is the connection between these principles and a specifically *private* property rights system rather than communal, collective, or government property? Propertarians almost invariably employ one of two strategies to make that connection: treat it as obvious or tell a version of John Locke's appropriation story, in which, during the state of nature before any government comes into existence, individuals appropriate virgin wilderness.[31] In these stories, appropriators invariably set themselves up as private holders, and subsequently transfer their property to other private entities. Propertarians usually ignore the possibilities that groups might appropriate collective landholders or that individuals might set themselves up as monarchs of their land. In the story, collectives and governments simply don't appropriate. They come along later, and their powers are limited by pre-existing rights of private property.[32]

This fictional story supposedly explains why property rights must be private, but the work is being done more by the mindset the story encourages than by the principles it supposedly illustrates. Private individuals appropriate and trade; collectives do not. Propertarians do not claim that contemporary property holders have a direct connection with original appropriation, but they portray appropriation is something only private entities do.[33]

That is an empirical proposition that we call "the appropriation hypothesis." We argue that it is essential to the natural rights justification for private property and that it is false. Propertarians would like to believe their normative argument rules out collective or government ownership of property and all (plausible) circumstances. We, however, go through a great deal of propertarian literature showing that no such argument is available. Propertarian normative principles – without an empirical claim about what kinds of rights appropriators choose to establish – have no direct connection to exclusively *private* property.[34]

Most propertarians seem to believe either that the appropriation hypothesis is obviously true or unnecessary. Critics seldom challenge them on the empirical issue. The few propertarians who do cite evidence don't cite very much of it.[35] If a more thorough historical-empirical investigation supporting

31 Locke, *Second Treatise*, § 24–51.

32 Karl Widerquist, "A Dilemma for Libertarianism," *Politics, Philosophy, and Economics* 8, no. 1 (2009).

33 Karl Widerquist, "Dilemma."

34 Widerquist and McCall, *Prehistory of Private Property*, pp. 258–268.

35 F. A. Hayek, *Law, Legislation, and Liberty* (Chicago: University of Chicago Press, 1973), p. 108; Bruce L. Benson, "Enforcement of Private Property Rights in Primitive Societies: Law without Government," *The Journal of Libertarian Studies* IX, no. 1 (1989), p. 8; John Hasnas, "Toward a Theory of Empirical Natural Rights," *Social Philosophy and Policy* 22, no. 1 (2005); Jeffrey Evans Stake, "The Property 'Instinct'," *Philosophical Transactions of the Royal Society*

the appropriation hypothesis exists, it has escaped the notice of the prominent propertarian theorists cited throughout our book. In many cases, the anthropological sources propertarians cite undercut rather than support the appropriation hypothesis, showing that flexible, exception-laden, overlapping, and partly collectivist property rights regimes are far more common than the institutional structure propertarians present as natural.

We review the relevant anthropological and historical information to conduct a more thorough investigation than we are able to find in propertarian literature. It demonstrates not only that the appropriation hypothesis is unproven, but also that it is clearly false and that nearly the opposite is true. Property rights were not originally private, and in the absence of aggressive interference, they have not tended to become or remain fully private. Complex, flexible, overlapping, common, and at least partly collective resource rights have tended to develop and remain in place in the absence of significant violations of the appropriation and transfer principles.[36]

Nomadic hunter-gatherers – who meet many of the stated criteria for first appropriators – populated the vast majority of the world's habitable territory long before anyone using other economic strategies. If the social and political organizations of early, small-scale, nomadic hunter-gatherers most likely met propertarian requirements to be considered voluntary associations, all of their rules qualify as contractual (voluntarily accepted) obligations. All observed societies living in similar circumstances treat land as a commons – open for the shared use of all but the property of none. Ownership rights in tools and food were never fully private but generally had to be shared whenever there was enough to go around. That is, property systems of the original inhabitants on most of the world's land had little resemblance to those propertarians portray as "natural."[37]

B: Biological Sciences 359, no. 1451 (2004); David Schmidtz, "The Institution of Property," *Social Philosophy & Policy* 11 (1994).

36 Widerquist and McCall, *Prehistory of Private Property*, pp. 194–268.

37 Richard Borshay Lee and Richard Daly, "Foragers and Others," in *The Cambridge Encyclopedia of Hunters and Gatherers*, ed. Richard Borshay Lee and Richard Daly (Cambridge: Cambridge University Press, 1999), 4; Nurit Bird-David, "The Giving Environment: Another Perspective on the Economic System of Gatherer-Hunters," *Current Anthropology* 31, no. 2 (1990), pp. 190–192; Tim Ingold, *The Appropriation of Nature: Essays on Human Ecology and Social Relations* (Manchester: Manchester University Press, 1986), pp. 148–150; Allen Johnson and Timothy Earle, *The Evolution of Human Societies: From Foraging Group to Agrarian State*, Second Edition ed. (Stanford: Stanford University Press, 2000), p. 63; Elizabeth Cashdan, "Hunters and Gatherers: Economic Behavior in Bands," in *Economic Anthropology*, ed. Stuart Platter (Stanford: Stanford University Press, 1989), pp. 40–42.

Long before states appeared, many peoples settled into agricultural villages of usually less than 600 people, with diets usually supported by hunting in commons surrounding the village. Many such societies have been observed living at this scale, and their property institutions are nearly as communal as nomadic foragers. Agricultural land is treated as a commons. Everyone has a right to some space where they can farm, but not necessarily on the same plot every year.[38] Crops tend to be private but need can override the farmer's claim. No landless people work for wages. Many villages pick up and move every few years to avoid depleting the land, and individuals could easily leave the village at that time, but no known individual appropriators in indigenous societies at this scale set out on their own to set up private Lockean homesteads.[39] If the original farmers are taken to be the original appropriators, and if autonomous villages all over the world today can give any indication of how people practicing similar techniques lived thousands of years ago, the original appropriators exercised their free will to create common or communal property systems.

The earliest states probably dispossessed earlier landholders, but they seldom if ever dispossessed people holding private, individualistic property rights, as propertarians suppose. We use extensive historical investigation to argue that the now-global private property system was established almost everywhere, not by appropriation and voluntary transfer, but by aggressive and violent private and government force – disappropriating people practicing much more collectivist property institutions.[40]

Early states and chiefdoms have sometimes established more centralized property systems, such as large-scale irrigation agriculture. Institutions resembling private property rights developed earlier in cities, usually by privileged people carving out private rights over things that had been centrally controlled by government or communally held by villages.[41]

But partially communal villages (with chief- or state-sanctioned lords with varying levels of actual control at the head) persisted in rural areas throughout the world until the Enclosure Movement in Europe and the colonial movement

38 Martin J. Bailey, "Approximate Optimality of Aboriginal Property Rights," *Journal of Law and Economics* 35 (1992).

39 Matthew S. Bandy, "Fissioning, Scalar Stress, and Social Evolution in Early Village Societies," *American Anthropologist* 106, no. 2 (2004).; Christopher Boehm, *Hierarchy in the Forest: The Evolution of Egalitarian Behavior* (Cambridge, MA: Harvard University Press, 2001), p. 93.

40 Widerquist and McCall, *Prehistory of Private Property*, pp. 227–257.

41 Hudson, Michael, and Baruch A. Levine, eds. *Privatization in the Ancient near East and Classical World.* (Cambridge, MA: Harvard, 1996).

elsewhere forced the adoption of private land rights – usually by converting government-appointed lords into "private landlords."[42]

Every step in the process of separating people from their common access to land involved force to benefit privileged people at the expense of people with a much better claim to be the heirs of original appropriation.

This evidence raises doubts about the propertarian accounts of who owns property and what *kind* of property rights structure is justifiable. Most propertarians are open to the possibility that at least some non-titleholders have a legitimate claim to redistribution and rectification for past rights violations. But they assume any such redistribution will be private titles to private titles.[43] Without the appropriation hypothesis, the private nature of property no longer has sole claim to legitimacy or perhaps any claim to legitimacy.

The propertarian story in which private ownership develops naturally via appropriation and collective ownership through violent interference is exactly backwords. The original appropriators established common rights. The original private property holders got their "rights" by violent interference and disappropriation. Therefore, propertarian principles applied to our world's actual history provide little or no support for the supposedly natural individualistic, liberal property rights structure and little or no reason to rule out governments, ethnic groups, or other collective entities as potentially justifiable landholders. Governments – if genuinely owned by the people – might have as much or more right to tax their land as landlords have to charge rent for theirs. To the extent that private holders have any rights to land, it is derivative from and dependent on the legitimacy of government-held property rights in land.

4 The Natural Inequality Hypothesis

The natural inequality hypothesis (that inequality is natural and inevitable, or that equality is naturally in conflict with freedom) is also used to justify highly unequal property rights. This claim is not obviously about prehistory but it is a universal claim that must hold at all times to be true. We argue that it is widely

42 J. M. Neeson, *Commoners: Common Right, Enclosure and Social Change in England, 1700–1820* (Cambridge: Cambridge University Press, 1993), pp. 11–14, 319–330; James Alfred Yelling, *Common Field and Enclosure in England, 1450–1850* (Hamden, CT: Archon Books, 1977), p. 232; Carson, Kevin. *Communal Property: A Libertarian Analysis* (The Center for a Stateless Society, 2011); for further review of the literature, see, Widerquist and McCall, *Prehistory of Private Property*, pp. 240–257.

43 Widerquist and McCall, *Prehistory of Private Property*, pp. 258–268.

believed only because its adherents make such a narrow search for evidence. A look at small-scale stateless societies shows that this claim is unsustainable. Inequality is neither natural nor inevitable nor is equality inevitably in conflict with freedom.

Many indigenous communities known to anthropology have maintained high political, social, and economic equality, probably for thousands, perhaps tens or hundreds of thousands of years. If this evidence is correct, many policies dismissed as reducing freedom to promote equality, opportunity, or welfare, might in fact promote freedom by compensating people who are the least free under the prevailing system of unequal property rights. Additionally, contemporary egalitarian theory can benefit from the experience of small-scale egalitarian societies.[44]

Thousands of years of attempts to justify hierarchy with one or another version of the claim that inequality is natural and inevitable reveals strong disagreement about how, why, and in what ways people will inevitably be unequal. Dominant ideologies tend to assert that the level and type of inequality in society is close to that which is natural and inevitable. These arguments for the naturalness of inequality are usually used in arguments justifying a coercive power structure to enforce rules to maintain the level of inequality that is supposed to be inevitable.[45]

The two central testable claims from this discussion are: (1) equality is impossible to obtain (efforts to create it either entirely fail or replace one kind of inequality with another); and (2) equality is inevitably in conflict with freedom (efforts to create it also reduce freedom usually understood as negative liberty). The question is not whether we will find complete equality or complete inequality (both of which seem to be unachievable extremes) but whether we can find greater inequality than proponents of the thesis of inevitable inequality use it to defend and whether that equality can be shown to conflict with relevant conceptions of freedom.

Most states known to recorded history are hierarchical, as are the social groups of our closest primate relatives.[46] To go from this evidence to a claim of inevitability would be a hasty generalization based solely on the most readily available evidence. Nordic welfare states in the late twentieth and early twenty-first centuries have achieved greater economic equality than proponents of

44 Widerquist and McCall, *Prehistory of Private Property*, pp. 55–77.

45 Widerquist and McCall, *Prehistory of Private Property*, pp. 15–41.

46 Herbert Gintis, Carel van Schaik, and Christopher Boehm, "Zoon Politikon: The Evolutionary Origins of Human Political Systems," *Current Anthropology* 56, no. 3 (2015), p. 337.

natural inequality usually admit are achievable. There is some evidence of the existence for substantial equality in early historic or late prehistoric state societies. And state societies are not the only form of socio-political organization.

"Hunter-gatherer bands" (nomadic foraging groups of less than 60 people who do not store food) have been the most common form of human social organization since humans appeared on this planet. Their subsistence model usually involves people leaving camp alone or in small groups to hunt and gather, and returning later to share what they have found. Camps are mobile, moving whenever hunting and gathering resources decline in an area. Individuals come and go temporarily or permanently at will.[47]

All observed band societies are leaderless and have tremendous social, political, and economic equality. In an environment where people need to split up to forage, it's virtually impossible for one person to dominate others, who would simply walk away. No one could accumulate much in the way of goods, because they are limited to what they can carry from camp to camp. Band members consume the same varieties of food, live in the same types of shelters, use the same types of tools, and have the same types of ornaments or consumption goods.[48] Food is shared to the point that no one in the band goes hungry unless everyone is going hungry. People are also obliged to share tools or any other goods if they have more than they need at any given time.[49] Leaders exist only in the sense that some people have greater influence over group decisions than others.

The example of band societies clearly proves that social, economic, and political equality are possible, falsifying the claim that inequality is natural or inevitable. If, as Section 5 (below) argues, band societies also have high negative freedom, their example also falsifies the claim that equality is inevitably in conflict with freedom.

Although the circumstances of band societies are favourable to egalitarianism, it doesn't just happen. Sharing is clearly an obligation for everyone who camps with the band whether they prefer to or not,[50] as is the obligation to avoid obvious displays of superior wealth or ability. Bands maintain a

---

47 Johnson and Earle, *Evolution of Human Societies*, pp. 32–33, 58, 62, 80, 112.

48 Boehm, *Hierarchy in the Forest*, pp. 72–87.

49 Richard Borshay Lee, "Reflections on Primitive Communism," in *Hunters and Gatherers 1: History, Evolution and Social Change*, ed. Tim Ingold, David Riches, and James Woodburn (Oxford: Berg Publishing, 1988), p. 267; Alan Barnard and James Woodburn, "Property, Power, and Ideology in Hunter-Gathering Societies: An Introduction," in *Hunters and Gatherers 2: Property, Power and Ideology*, ed. Tim Ingold, David Riches, and James Woodburn (Oxford: Berg Publishing, 1988), p. 16.

50 Kelly, *The Foraging Spectrum*, p. 21, 164–166, 172.

reverse-dominance hierarchy with "leveling mechanisms." These include sanctions, such as ridicule, criticism, disobedience, expulsion, desertion (noncooperation), and in the most extreme cases execution. Leveling mechanisms other than sanctions include demand sharing, tolerated theft, and appeals to religious beliefs that ascribe equal status to all living people.[51]

Slightly larger-scale societies, called "autonomous villages," maintain significant levels of equality in settled communities of up to about 600 people. Many autonomous villages practice swidden agriculture, which involves moving every few years to avoid soil depletion and virtually no trade or specialization. Autonomous villages tend to have a nominal head or a group of "big men" with greater recognition and respect but without higher living standards or much if any power of command. All people, including headmen and religious leaders, produce their immediate family's consumption. There are usually no fixed property rights in land; all members of the village are entitled to access to land for farming but not necessarily to a particular plot. As in band societies, no one in the village starves unless everyone is starving.[52] No one has to get a job taking orders from a boss to earn the right to gain access to natural resources that can be transformed into consumption goods.

Leveling mechanisms exist in autonomous villages as in bands, but some of them, such as the ability to leave the group, are a little harder to exercise. A forager can pick up and go at a moment's notice. A farmer might have to wait until just before spring planting, although they do commonly split.[53]

Larger-scale societies, sometimes called "chiefdoms," can have anywhere from a few thousand to tens of thousands of people. In some circumstances, chiefs can become despotic rulers. But some chiefdoms, such as the Iroquois Confederation, were observed to be significantly egalitarian.[54]

51 Boehm, *Hierarchy in the Forest*, p. 84; Bird-David, "The Giving Environment"; Barnard and Woodburn, "Property, Power, and Ideology," p. 12, 21; Elizabeth Cashdan, "Egalitarianism among Hunters and Gatherers," *American Anthropologist* 82, no. 1 (1980), pp. 117, 120; Kelly, *The Foraging Spectrum*, pp. 21–22, 164–166; Nicolas Peterson, "Demand Sharing: Reciprocity and the Pressure for Generosity among Foragers," American Anthropologist 95, no. 4 (1993), pp. 860–874; Kent V. Flannery and Joyce Marcus, *The Creation of Inequality* (Cambridge, MA: Harvard University Press, 2012), pp. 59–60.

52 Colin Renfrew, *Prehistory: The Making of the Human Mind* (London: Phoenix, 2007), p. 142; Boehm, *Hierarchy in the Forest*,p. 3–4; Richard Borshay Lee, "Primitive Communism and the Origin of Social Inequality," in *The Evolution of Political Systems: Sociopolitics in Small-Scale Sedentary Societies*, ed. S. Upham (Cambridge: Cambridge University Press, 1990).

53 Bandy, "Fissioning," pp. 322–333.

54 Peter Bellwood, *The Polynesians*, Revised ed. (London: Thames and Hudson, 1987), 31–33; Lee, "Primitive Communism;" Boehm, *Hierarchy in the Forest*, p. 98.

During the Pleistocene, many, if not most, people lived in societies comparable to modern bands in scale and strategy: small, nomadic foraging groups that often hunted cooperatively, brought food to a central location, consumed it that day, and so on. If they also had similar socio-political organization, we can speculate that egalitarian societies have existed as long as humans have existed and perhaps into our evolutionary past. Similarity in scale and subsistence strategy is not proof of other similarities; the evidence is inconclusive and some anthropologists are leery about drawing any analogies between present and past foragers; but the available evidence suggests human foragers in the deep past were egalitarian.[55] We doubt that foragers of the distant past had any less desire to overthrow or abandon potential dominators than modern foragers have and we know that their foraging strategy would have given them similar ability.

The claim that inequality is natural and inevitable is clearly false. Inequality is produced by social institutions.

Adherents of the natural-inequality hypothesis might be tempted to change their claim to inequality is inevitable *within the context of a state society*. This change would diminish a genuinely universal claim to a context specific idea: inequality is inevitable if and when social institutions make it inevitable. Social institutions are subject to change. Even if inequality were an inevitable product of all state societies, the comedown would be problematic given that, as argued above, state societies are so unequal that they are harmful to their least advantaged members.

It is by no means proven that inequality is inevitable in the context of state society. To falsify this hypothesis by observation, one would have to conduct a large study of various historically recorded state societies and evaluate the extent of their equality or inequality. Although we're unlikely to see state societies practicing egalitarianism as strong as that practiced in band and autonomous village societies, many states have maintained greater socioeconomic equality than adherents of the natural-inequality hypothesis usually like to see.

Just as bands have leveling mechanisms, state societies have many coercive stratification-enforcing mechanisms. We do not yet know how much we could change the level of inequality within the context of state society. The leveling mechanisms of band societies – chief among them the amount of power they concede to the least advantaged members discussed in Section 5 – might provide a guide for what to try.

---

55 Boehm, *Hierarchy in the Forest*, p. 31.

5 The Market Freedom Hypothesis

Probably the most common and forceful justification for the market economy is what we call the market freedom hypothesis: the belief that capitalism is the "condition of men in which coercion of some by others is reduced as much as possible in society".[56] Most rights-based attempts to justify liberal private property rights use it in one way or another.[57]

Freedom from coercion and interference is not the only meaningful conception of freedom, but it is a coherent ethical concern for reasonable people. The empirical question of what socio-political arrangements reduce coercion as much as possible cannot be established definitively by a priori reasoning.

Freedom is inherently hard to measure because protecting people from one form of coercion often involves imposing another form. However, we argue below that an empirical comparison of levels of freedom is possible in relevant circumstances.

The negative freedom argument usually involves the claim that the freest imaginable socio-economic system is idealized propertarian capitalism in which everything is privately owned; the government, if any, does nothing but protect private property rights; and there are few if any taxes. Any deviation from that ideal supposedly involves a loss of negative freedom that must be justified against either the impossibility of fully realizing that ideal or by appeal to some value other than freedom. Propertarians usually use idealized propertarian capitalism as a starting point and argue that the introduction of taxation or regulation imposes new restrictions. This method ignores the coercive measures involved in establishing capitalism to begin with. Section 2 (above) briefly discusses the violent history that created the private property system.[58] In recent decades, many critics of propertarianism have argued that the imposition and maintenance of the private property rights system involves a great deal of coercion with the propertyless.[59]

---

56 F. A. Hayek, *The Constitution of Liberty* (Chicago: University of Chicago Press, 1960), p. 11.

57 For review of that literature, see, Widerquist and McCall, *Prehistory of Private Property*, pp. 79–99.

58 See also, Widerquist and McCall, *Prehistory of Private Property*, pp. 79–99.

59 Daniel Attas, *Liberty, Property and Markets* (Aldershot: Ashgate, 2005), p. 7; Cohen, *History, Labour, and Freedom: Themes from Marx*, pp. 301–302; Michael Otsuka, *Libertarianism without Inequality* (Oxford: Oxford University Press, 2003), p. 19; Jeremy Waldron, *Liberal Rights* (Cambridge: Cambridge University Press, 1993), pp. 20–21, 309–338; Karl Widerquist *Independence, Propertylessness, and Basic Income: A Theory of Freedom as the Power to Say No* (New York: Palgrave Macmillan, 2013).

Propertarians could concede this point theoretically and maintain the market freedom hypothesis empirically by conceding that the coercions propertarian capitalism requires delivers greater overall negative freedom for everyone. If true, everyone – even those who are coerced into accepting that the entire planet is the property of other people – actually wind up freer overall than in any other system. Everyone would be coerced less often or in less important ways: they would be less constrained over all, less likely to have labour extracted from them unwillingly, less often subject to non-contractual obligations, less often sacrificed to achieve the ends of others, and so on.

We make a pairwise comparison between the market economy and the hunter-gatherer band economy. This comparison is sufficient to show that propertarian capitalism is not particularly consistent with liberty.

Nomadic foragers might provide a low bar for *welfare* comparisons, but they provide an extremely high bar for *freedom* comparisons. Bands hardly subject their members to any coercion at all. This statement is well-documented and widely accepted by anthropologists,[60] and, importantly, by propertarians as well. Thomas Mayor, for example, calls them "The Original Libertarians."[61]

The anthropologist, Marvin Harris (1927–2001), writes,

> [T]he average human being enjoyed economic and political freedoms which only a privileged minority enjoy today. Men decided for themselves how long they would work on a particular day, what they would work at – or if they would work at all. ... Every man and woman held title to an equal share of nature. Neither rent, taxes, nor tribute kept people from doing what they wanted to do.[62]

Like all societies, bands have norms that restrain behaviour, but these restraints are voluntary in the idiosyncratic sense relevant to propertarian theory. All norms, folkways, and social conventions in band society are "contractual obligations" in propertarian terms because they come with the tacitly understood qualifier, *if you want to camp with us*. Individual or groups are free to go do things their own way if they don't like the band's way. Therefore, even the

60 For example, Marvin Harris, *Cannibals and Kings: The Origins of Culture* (New York: Random House, 1977), p. 69; James Woodburn, "An Introduction to Hadza Ecology," in *Man the Hunter*, ed. Richard Borshay Lee and Irven DeVore (New York: Aldine, 1968), p. 52; for longer list see Widerquist and McCall, *Prehistory of Private Property*, pp. 101–105.

61 Thomas Mayor, "Hunter-Gatherers: The Original Libertarians," *The Independent Review* 16, no. 4 (2012).

62 Harris, *Cannibals and Kings*, p. 69.

limited extent to which band members have explicit duties to each other is the result of an informal agreement that can be dissolved at a moment's notice by breaking camp, making band members free from almost all "noncontractual obligations." This freedom is secured by common access to the land, which they can use without interference.

The power of non-cooperation and the ability to pick up and go is perhaps the most striking institutional difference between hunter-gatherer band society and industrial capitalist, socialist, or welfare capitalist societies. Individuals in contemporary states might have a legal right to quit their job or exit a nation, but only the wealthy have the legal right to live by their own efforts without satisfying a boss or a client who has the money to pay them. The market economy's property rights system is a noncontractual obligation forcing nonowners to respect the holdings of owners. As Section 2 mentions, that obligation owes its existence to a long series of government aggressions and it is maintained by continued government coercion.

Propertylessness does not exist in band society. Because band economies don't impose the duty to respect landownership on anyone, everyone has access to land *without interference*.

Perhaps a more important loss of freedom follows from that central obligation of propertarian capitalism. Power over the resources other people need to survive entails power over people. Most people who aren't independently wealthy are coerced into a position where they must find a boss or a client and follow their orders. While people in band society can go for years or even a lifetime without hearing an order,[63] most people in propertarian capitalism have little choice but to take orders most days of the week, most weeks of the year, until they are too old to work.

Would-be non-cooperators in market economies are left with very few and very unattractive options, such as foraging in garbage cans. Homelessness, which does not exist in band society, makes people unfree to do some of their most basic human functions. Homeless people are unfree – in the most negative sense of the term – to urinate or have sex in a private place, unfree to sleep unmolested, unfree to sleep or urinate in any place they can legally be, and so on.[64]

The ownership of property does secure liberties that are unavailable when land is a commons. But it confers those freedoms only to the owners of property, not to nonowners. Robert Nozick admits that the establishment of a

63 Fried, Morton H. *The Evolution of Political Society* (New York: Random House, 1967), p. 8.

64 Waldron, *Liberal Rights*, pp. 309–38.

property rights system involves interference, but attempts to make up for it by changing the focus from freedom to opportunity, writing, "the things I do with the grain of sand I appropriate might improve the position of others, counterbalancing their loss of the liberty to use that grain."[65] Section 1 has argued that those opportunities have not made the least advantaged better off than they could be living under a common property regime. But even if it were true, "an opportunity to become free is not freedom. ... So long as the opportunity remains unconsummated, the person ... remains in a negative sense unfree."[66]

For capitalist society to be more consistent with negative freedom than band society, it would have to *relieve* everyone from forms of coercion that exist in band society. This is difficult to achieve because band societies have so few noncontractual obligations. For all but the independently wealthy, even if the market economy provides opportunities, it provides them only by establishing obligations, not by relieving coercion.

Although freedom is difficult to measure, this comparison can be made definitively because the freedom of the least free people in band societies *dominates* the freedom of the least free people in capitalist societies. That is, people in band societies have all the liberties that the least free people in capitalist societies do and more. They are free from many or more important forms of coercion that people in capitalist societies are subject to and not subject to any forms of coercion that people in capitalist society are free from.

If freedom is an overriding value, as some propertarians assert, everyone must become a nomadic hunter-gatherer. This finding obviously implies that the justification of any other system must rely at least partially on some other value, such as opportunity or welfare. Less obviously but perhaps more importantly, this finding implies that deviations from the propertarian ideal cannot be condemned as freedom-reducing because they create opportunity for the propertyless by interfering with the property owners. Redistributive policies can be structured to counteract freedom-reducing aspects of the market economy, creating greater equal freedom overall.[67]

6 Conclusion

This chapter has briefly argued four points: 1. The Lockean proviso is unfulfilled: neither the state nor the property rights system achieves mutual

65 Nozick, *Anarchy*, p. 175.

66 Jeromy Waldron, *The Right to Private Property* (Oxford: Clarendon Press, 1988), p. 411.

67 See also Karl Widerquist, *Independence*.

advantage. The least well-off people in contemporary capitalist states are worse off than they could reasonably expect to be in a stateless society with a common property rights regime. 2. The natural rights argument does not support a liberal property rights structure as usually supposed. The principles of original appropriation and voluntary transfer applied to actual history lead to complex and partly collectivist structure. The liberal property regime now ubiquitous around the world was established by a long series of government-led coercion and seems unlikely to develop without coercion. 3. The belief that political, social, or economic inequality is inevitable and/or that equality is inevitably in conflict with freedom is false. For most of human prehistory – most of the time humans have existed – they have lived in communities that were both very free and very equal. 4. The negative freedom argument for the market economy does not hold. Given the restrictions the property rights system imposes on propertyless people, the hunter-gatherer band economy is more consistent with negative freedom than capitalism.

This chapter has summarized the findings of our two books and shown the parallels between them. It has argued that (1) these four claims are empirical; (2) they are claims about prehistoric or stateless peoples; (3) they are used as premises in influential contemporary theories; and (4) they are false. This chapter's arguments are brief but, we hope, convincing. If not, our books offer more evidence and argumentation.[68]

The central implication of the falsity of these four claims is simple: our societies need to treat less advantaged people better. Perhaps the most tragic aspect of the mistreatment of the disadvantaged is that it is so unnecessary. Contemporary societies have tremendous wealth. They don't need to create a class of people so poorly off, so unfree, with so many reasons to feel disinherited, with so few reasons to feel they truly benefit from our political and social arrangements. A nation that benefits some at the expense of others is a parasitic society. Mutual advantage is within our reach, but myths we tell ourselves about the state of nature make it easier for is to ignore our failure to secure mutual advantage, equality before the law, and freedom for all.

Select Bibliography

Primary Sources

Tim Ingold, David Riches and James Woodburn (eds.), *Hunters and Gatherers volumes 1 and 2* (Oxford: Berg Publishing, 1988).

68 Widerquist and McCall, *Prehistoric Myths*; *Prehistory of Private Property*.

Hobbes, Thomas. *Leviathan.* (Cambridge: Cambridge University Press, 1996 [1651]).

Hudson, Michael, and Baruch A. Levine, eds. *Privatization in the Ancient near East and Classical World.* (Cambridge, MA: Harvard, 1996).

Johnson, Allen, and Timothy Earle. *The Evolution of Human Societies: From Foraging Group to Agrarian State.* Second Edition. (Stanford: Stanford University Press, 2000).

Kelly, Robert L. *The Foraging Spectrum: Diversity in Hunter-Gatherer Lifeways.* (Washington DC: Smithsonian Institution Press, 1995).

Kropotkin, Petr Alekseevich. *Mutual Aid: A Factor of Evolution.* (Project Gutenberg, 2011. 1902).

Locke, John. *Two Treatises of Government, Second Treatise.* (Cambridge: Cambridge University Press, 1960 [1689]).

Secondary Sources

Boehm, Christopher. *Hierarchy in the Forest: The Evolution of Egalitarian Behavior.* (Cambridge, MA: Harvard University Press, 2001).

Flannery, Kent V., and Joyce Marcus. *The Creation of Inequality.* (Cambridge, MA: Harvard University Press, 2012).

Graeber, David. *Debt: The First 5,000 Years.* (Brooklyn, NY: Melville House, 2011).

Ingold, Tim. *The Appropriation of Nature: Essays on Human Ecology and Social Relations.* (Manchester: Manchester University Press, 1986).

Scott, James C. *The Art of Not Being Governed: An Anarchist History of Upland Southeast Asia.* (New Haven: Yale University Press, 2009).

Index

www.ingramcontent.com/pod-product-compliance
Ingram Content Group UK Ltd.
Pitfield, Milton Keynes, MK11 3LW, UK
UKHW021421091026
15624UKWH00010B/352

9 789004 395176